# The Art *of* Leadership

## Managing Early Childhood Organizations

Edited by Bonnie and Roger Neugebauer

Exchange
PO Box 3249 • Redmond, WA 98073-3249 • (800) 221-2864
www.ChildCareExchange.com

# The Art *of* Leadership

# Managing

# Early Childhood Organizations

These articles were originally published in *Exchange, The Early Childhood Leaders' Magazine Since 1978*. Every attempt has been made to update information on authors and other contributors to these articles. We apologize for any biographical information that is not current.

*Exchange,* previously known as *Child Care Information Exchange,* is a bimonthly management magazine for directors and owners of early childhood programs. For more information about *Exchange* and other Exchange publications for directors and teachers, contact:

Exchange
PO Box 3249
Redmond, WA 98073-3249
(800) 221-2864
www.ChildCareExchange.com

ISBN 978-0-942702-24-8

Printed in the United States of America



**Acknowledgements**

**Consultant:**
Kay Albrecht

**Production Editors**
Carole White
Carol Weber

**Cover Photograph**
Bonnie Neugebauer

# The Art *of* Leadership

## Managing Early Childhood Organizations

## Table of Contents

# CONTRIBUTING AUTHORS

**ALBRECHT, KAY, PH.D.**, senior partner in Innovations in Early Childhood Programs, specializes in curriculum, staff and program development. She created HeartsHome Early Learning Center, a nationally accredited early childhood program in Houston, Texas and serves as executive director. HeartsHome is a training site for two universities, three community colleges, and one graduate school and provides international internship experiences for students from the European Community and Australia. Known as an advocate for optimal growth and development opportunities for young children, Kay is an author and frequent speaker.

**ALLEN, JOE**, is the owner and director of the Fawn Valley Human Resource Center for Children in Dallas, Texas.

**ANTONSEN, JOAN DUNN**, was executive director of the Fruit and Flower Child Care Center in Portland, Oregon.

**ARONSON, SUSAN, MD, FAAP**, is clinical professor of pediatrics at the University of Pennsylvania and a pediatrician in Philadelphia, Pennsylvania.

**BERL, PATRICIA**, is a division vice president of mid-Atlantic operations for Bright Horizons Family Solutions. She is known nationally as a conference presenter and author of articles in child care center management and supervision. She has been a regular contributor to *Exchange* since 1978. In addition to her lovely family, Patricia has a passion for orchids, Springer Spaniels, and travel.

**BESS, GARY, MSW**, holds a Ph.D. in social work from the University of Southern California and has an extensive background in nonprofit management and working with boards of directors for nonprofit agencies.

**BOSWELL, CRAIG, PH.D.**, has been active in child care and early childhood education for the past 20 years. He is currently an associate professor at the University of Central Oklahoma.

**BROWER, MARY R.**, has been providing financial services to child care centers for more than 15 years. Mary spent 11 years as the accounting director with a community based non-profit child care agency, and is currently working directly with child care programs providing financial management consulting and bookkeeping services. Mary operates a non-profit agency, Child Care Business & Education Resources with Theresa M. Sull. They can be reached at ccber@nc.rr.com.

**CALDWELL, BETTYE**, Donaghey Distinguished Professor of Education Emerita, University of Arkansas at Little Rock, and Professor Emerita, Department of Pediatrics, University of Arkansas for Medical Sciences, and past-president of NAEYC.

**CARTER, MARGIE**, is on the adjunct faculty of Shoreline Community College and Pacific Oaks College NW. She is a regular contributor to *Exchange* and travels widely to speak and consult. Margie is the producer of seven staff training videos and co-author with Deb Curtis of six books, one specifically for directors, *The Visionary Director: A Handbook for Dreaming, Organizing and Improvising in Your Program* (Redleaf Press, 1998). Her book, *Designs for Living and Learning: Transforming Early Childhood Environments* with 300 color photographs from around the country was released June 1, 2003.

**COHEN, ABBY J., JD**, is a consumer of child care and a child care law and policy consultant in Oakland, California. Formerly the managing attorney of the Child Care Law Center, she currently works for the National Child Care Information Center as a regional technical assistance specialist for Region IX. Additionally, she provides consultation services to child care providers, child care support organizations, foundations, and public officials. Her primary objective in working with child care programs is to make the law more understandable so as to avoid legal problems.

**CROMPTON, DWAYNE A.**, has served as executive director of KCMC Child Development Corporation, the Head Start grantee in Kansas City, for 28 years. He writes and speaks frequently on leadership development in early care and education, managing for quality child care, collaboration, and advocacy.

**CUNNINGHAM, BRUCE**, has worked in early childhood settings as an assistant, a teacher, a director, and an educator. He is currently an education coordinator with the Early Childhood Education and Assistance Program (ECEAP) through the Puget Sound Educational Service District in Seattle, Washington.

**DONOHUE, CHIP, PH.D.**, is the director of Early Childhood Professional Development Programs in the School of Continuing Education at the University of Wisconsin-Milwaukee where he teaches Administrator Credential courses in face-to-face and online formats, and provides faculty training on teaching and learning at a distance. He is recognized as a leader in the innovative use of technology and distance learning methods to bring training, continuing education, and professional development opportunities to child care administrators and teachers, and to promote "best practices" in early care and education.

**EISENBERG, EILEEN,** is an assistant professor and training coordinator for the Center for Early Childhood Leadership at National-Louis University. She oversees the recruitment and selection of participants for training and serves as a liaison to participating centers working with field supervisors and mentors in monitoring program quality improvements. She is also the editor of the *Director's Link*. Prior to joining the faculty of NLU, Eileen was a director of an NAEYC accredited non-profit early childhood center in Chicago. She regularly conducts workshops on accreditation and serves as a national NAEYC validator.

**FRANKLIN, WILLIAM H.,** is a consultant to entrepreneurs of small- to mid-sized companies. He speaks frequently to associations of owners of privately held companies, and he is the author of books and articles that address small business management issues. He is on the faculty of Georgia State University in Atlanta, where he specializes in entrepreneurship and small business development.

**GONZALEZ-MENA, JANET,** has been a preschool teacher, child care director, and a teacher educator. She also writes books and articles about early childhood education. One of her books is *Multicultural Issues in Child Care*. Another is *Dragon Mom*, which grew out of the Exchange article "Mrs. Godzilla Takes on the Child Development Experts."

**GREENMAN, JIM,** is senior vice president of CorporateFamily Solutions. He is the co-author with Anne Stonehouse of *Prime Times — A Handbook for Excellence in Infant and Toddler Programs* (Redleaf Press, 1996) and author of *Caring Spaces, Learning Places* (Exchange Press, 2005).

**HAYSLIP, WHIT, MA,** is coordinator of Infant and Preschool Special Education Programs for the Los Angeles Unified School District and a staff development consultant for a variety of agencies including the California Department of Education and the U.S. Department of Defense Dependents Schools. Over the last 30 years he has worked as a teacher, curriculum specialist, and administrator in inclusive early childhood programs.

**HENG, ANNETTE CANNATA,** has been in the early childhood field since 1979. She began her career with Children's World Learning Centers in 1984 as a center director. Currently, as executive vice president, she is responsible for 300 centers in the Eastern region. Annette's expertise is leadership management with an emphasis on retention of valuable people. She has been the recipient of both "Leadership in Excellence" and "Service Excellence" awards. Annette earned her Master of Arts in Education from the Erikson Institute in the study of Human Development with an emphasis on Early Childhood Education. She is deeply committed to excellence in child care.

**HEWES, DOROTHY,** has been a director and consultant of early childhood programs since the 1940s. She is Professor Emeritus at San Diego State University in the Department of Child and Family Development and has written extensively on management of preschool centers.

**JOHNSTON, JOHN M.,** is professor of early childhood teacher education at the University of Memphis, where he has collaborated with area directors and community college early childhood educators to develop a bachelors degree program in Preschool and Child Care Administration.

**JONES, ELIZABETH,** is a member of the Faculty in Human Development and co-director of Distance Learning at Pacific Oaks College in Pasadena, California. Her books include *Growing Teachers, The Play's the Thing, Master Players, Teaching Adults, Emergent Curriculum,* and *The Lively Kindergarten*.

**KATZ, LILIAN,** is co-director of the ERIC Clearinghouse on Elementary & Early Childhood Education and Professor Emerita of early childhood education at the University of Illinois at Urbana-Champaign. She is a past president of NAEYC.

**KLUGMAN, EDGAR,** is the co-founder of Playing for Keeps as well as Professor Emeritus of Early Childhood Education and Care at Wheelock College in Boston, Massachusetts. He is also a charter member of the Play, Policy, and Practice Interest Forum within the National Association for the Education of Young Children (NAEYC). Among his publications are *Play, Policy and Practice* (Redleaf Press), and *Children's Play and Learning: Perspectives and Policy Implications* (edited with Smilansky; Teachers College Press). He currently serves on the board of New England AEYC. And, he continues to play!

**KOSTELNIK, MARJORIE, PH.D.,** is Dean of the College of Human Resources and Family Sciences, University of Nebraska. A former child care/Head Start teacher and early childhood administrator, Marjorie has been actively involved in helping early childhood programs explore the implications of Developmentally Appropriate Practices. She is co-author of *Guiding Children's Social Development* (Delmar, 2002), *Children with Special Needs: Lessons for Early Childhood Professionals* (Teachers College Press, 2002), and *Developmentally Appropriate Curriculum: Best Practices in Early Childhood Education* (Prentice-Hall, 2004).

**KOULOURAS, KATHERINE,** is the former co-owner and educational director of Perry-Kay Nursery School and Kindergarten in Southfield, Michigan.

**LEVBARG, MARK,** admitted to practice before the Texas and U.S. Supreme Courts, is a member of the State Bar of Texas, the American Bar Association, the Texas Trial Lawyers Association, and the Association of Trial Lawyers of America.

**LUKASZEWSKI, THOMAS E., CPA,** heads an accounting firm in the Chicago-land area which focuses on business issues facing the child care industry as well as other non profit organizations.

**McCREA, NADINE L., PH.D.,** associate professor of early childhood education and was the foundational program director of early childhood education at the University of New England (1998-2001). Visit the university site at: www.une.edu.au. Nadine is currently associate dean (Teaching and Learning) for the Faculty of Education, Health, and Professional Studies at UNE. She has taught and written widely about the socialness of food, leadership, and professionalism in early childhood. Contact her at nmccrea@metz.une.edu.au.

**MITCHELL, ANNE,** is the president of Early Childhood Policy Research, an independent consulting firm specializing in evaluation research, policy analysis, and planning on child care/early education issues for government, foundations, and national non profit organizations. She is co-author of both the 1997 and 2001 editions of *Financing Child Care in the United States: An Illustrative Catalog of Current Strategies*, available at www.earlychildhoodfinance.org.

**MOORE, THOMAS,** is an early childhood consultant based in Charlotte, North Carolina. He is a nationally recognized keynote speaker and workshop leader and author of *Where is Thumbkin?*, a resource book for teachers. A well-known children's recording artist, his recordings include "I Am Special Just Because I'm Me," "Singing, Moving, & Learning," and "Songs for the Whole Day." Thomas can be contacted at www.drthomasmoore.com.

**MORGAN, HENRY M.,** spent his time as a member of various boards of directors after a long career in higher education and business. Throughout his career, he left a trail of industry-related child care, starting with the establishment of the KLH Child Development Center, a voucher program at Polaroid, and an on-site center at Ben & Jerry's. He taught with his wife, Gwen, in programs run by Wheelock College.

**NEUGEBAUER, BONNIE,** is editor of *Exchange* magazine and Exchange Press Books. She is program coordinator of the World Forum on Early Care and Education and content editor of www.ChildCareExchange.com.

**NEUGEBAUER, ROGER,** is publisher of *Exchange*.

**NYMAN, SESSY I.,** is the director of the Public Policy and Advocacy Program of the Day Care Action Council of Illinois. Before becoming director in 2001, Sessy worked as the government relations (lobbyist) and field organizer for the Program. By combining both positions, Sessy has been able to learn first hand the barriers to quality early childhood education around the state, and then bring these issues to the Illinois General Assembly in the form of legislative and administrative advocacy campaigns. Since 1999, Sessy has been involved in growing Illinois' child care program to be one of the best in the nation — so stated by *Working Mother* magazine. Included in her accomplishments are passing the Great START legislation, supporting funding to serve over 200,000 children per month, developing a statewide forum for parents and providers (called the Public Policy Caucus), as well as spearheading other policies and legislative efforts affecting low-income working families and their children. Ms. Nyman has her BA in Government and International Relations from The University of South Carolina and her MS in Cultural Geography from The University of Massachusetts-Amherst. While a graduate student, Sessy focused on methods and strategies of grassroots organizing, with a concentration in community participation and project sustainability. She conducted her research among highland agriculturists in the north-central region of Guatemala. As director, Sessy divides her time between the legislature in Springfield, visiting parents and providers around the state, and her office in Chicago.

**OLIVER, SUSAN,** is executive director of the national non profit organization Playing for Keeps, devoting her time to promoting and protecting the role of play in our culture. Prior to her association with Playing for Keeps, Ms. Oliver served in various positions at the National Lekotek Center, a national non profit organization dedicated to making play accessible to children with disabilities and the Family Resource Coalition of America, a national non profit organization committed to building community-based support and resources for children and families.

**PERREAULT, JOE,** is Family Child Care Program manager for the U.S. Army Community and Family Support Center in Alexandria, Virginia.

**PHIPPS, PATRICIA A., ED.D.,** is the executive director of the California Association for the Education of Young Children. Previously, she served as a faculty member in the Graduate School of Education at George Mason University in Fairfax, Virginia and prior to that in the College of Education at the University of Houston. She has also managed her own consulting firm — The Institute for Child Care Professionals. She is the author of numerous publications, including *Multiple Intelligences in the Early Childhood Classroom* and most recently, *The Complete Daily Curriculum* (co-authored with Pam Schiller).

**PORTER, MARY LYNN,** is the former director of Auburn Day Care Centers in Auburn, Alabama.

**RANCK, EDNA RUNNELS, ED.D.,** has worked for the State of New Jersey since 1986 and is currently Child Care Coordinator in the Department of Human Services. She directed a preschool child care program for eight years and a child care resource and referral agency for over four years.

**RATEKIN, CINDY, PH.D.**, is a professor of child development at California State University, Chico.

**RIEPE, LINDA**, has over 30 years' experience in the field of early education. She presents workshops and writes articles on various child care topics. She retired in July of 2002 from her full time position as Early Childhood Education program coordinator at Lane Community College in Eugene, Oregon. Currently, she is enjoying her free time and continues to do some writing and consulting in the field.

**SCHILLER, PAM, PH.D.**, is senior national early childhood consultant for SRA / McGraw-Hill, and a past president of the Southern Early Childhood Association. She was the administrator of a child care center for several years and has also taught in the public schools as a kindergarten teacher. She is senior author of *The DLM Early Childhood Program*, a full curriculum for preschool children, *The DLM Express*, a full curriculum for four year olds, and *Early Impressions: Start Smart Edition*, a full curriculum for infants and toddlers. Pam is also the author of several childrens books and more than 30 teacher and parent resource books.

**SCHON, BRUCE**, is director of marketing for *Exchange*.

**SEIDERMAN, ETHEL**, is nationally recognized for her innovative approaches to child care and family services. In 1973, she founded the Fairfax San Anselmo Children's Center which has served as a model for other programs throughout the nation. Ethel is the director of the Parent Services Project Inc., a family support model founded in 1980. She is the recipient of numerous awards and honors including the Senator Barbara Boxer sponsored "Women Making History" award and the Marin County Women's Hall of Fame" award. Ethel is married and the mother of two grown children and grandmother to two boys. She lives with her husband, Stan, in San Anselmo, California. She is co-author of *Serving Families*, available from the San Francisco Study Center.

**SENTER, SHERI A., ED.D.**, chief executive officer of NPSS Inc., a child care consulting and management company in California, noted author, and presenter.

**SILVERMAN, JAN**, was director of Lucky Lane Early Childhood Association in St. Louis, Missouri.

**SMITH, CONNIE JO**, is an Early Childhood Education Specialist at Training and Technical Assistance Services at Western Kentucky University. In this role she provides training and technical assistance to Head Start programs throughout the southeast. She has been a teacher of young children, a director of a Head Start center, and an adult educator. She is a co-author of *Growing, Growing Strong: A Whole Health Curriculum for Young Children*, published by Redleaf Press.

**STALEY, CARL**, is the former executive director of United Day Care Services in Greensboro, North Carolina.

**STEPHENS, KAREN, MS** in Education, became director of Illinois State University Child Care Center and instructor in child development for ISU Family and Consumer Sciences Department in 1980 after five and a half cherished years as an early childhood teacher. She has published two books and is author of *Parenting Exchange*, parent advice columns available on CD from www.ChildCareExchange.com.

**STEPHENS, KEITH, CPA**, is the former president of Palo Alto Preschools, once the country's largest privately owned child care chains, and past president of the National Association for Child Care Management.

**STRICKLAND, JIM**, is president of Human Services Risk Management (HSRM) and chairperson of both the National Day Care Liability Task Force and the Central Texas Risk and Insurance Management Society. In addition, he is a consultant to insurance companies and brokers.

**SULL, THERESA M., PH.D**, is an author, presenter, and early childhood educator. During her 25 year career, she has taught young children both with and without special needs, consulted to their families, taught college students and teachers, published articles, and coordinated public school, university, and non profit programs. Theresa co-founded a non profit agency, Child Care Business & Education Resources with Mary R. Brower. They can be reached at ccber@nc.rr.com.

**TALLEY, KAREN L.**, is an early childhood quality consutant, writer, lecturer, and a past president of the Massachusetts Association for the Education of Young Children.

**THAXTON, STEVEN M., M.ED.**, is an early childhood administrator with the Stanislaus County Office of Education, Modesto, California, and a part time instructor in early childhood.

**VINCENT, LISBETH, PH.D.**, an early childhood special educator who worked for the past 25 years with preschool programs that included children with disabilities. She is past president of the Division of Early Childhood of the Council for Exceptional Children and has retired from her professorship at the University of Montana. She is currently traveling throughout the U.S.

**WASSOM, JULIE**, is president of The Julian Group, Inc., a training and consulting firm with a specialty in child care marketing and enrollment building. She is the author of *The Enrollment Building Success Library* of learning programs and the weekly e-zine, *Wassom's Child Care Marketing Wisdom*. Julie can be reached at (303) 693-2306, juliewm@ix.netcom.com, or www.juliewassom.com.

**WEINSTEIN, MARLENE**, is the director of Child Care Matters: A Quality Child Care Initiative of Southeastern Pennsylvania, located in Philadelphia, and is a co-author of *Day Care: How to Plan, Develop, and Operate a Day Care Center* (Boston: Beacon Press, 1971) and *Changing Systems, Changing Lives* (Philadelphia: United Way of Southeastern Pennsylvania, 2000).

**WORK, PAULINE**, was director of Child Care Services for the YWCA of Metropolitan Chicago, in Chicago, Illinois.

**ZEECE, PAULINE DAVEY**, is a professor in the Department of Family and Consumer Sciences at the University of Nebraska-Lincoln where she served as the director of the Ruth Staples Child Development Laboratory for ten years.

# FOREWORD

Long ago, we created a brochure to market our magazine, *Child Care Information Exchange* (now called *Exchange, The Early Childhood Leaders' Magazine Since 1978)*, that asked the question: What has 14 hands? Twenty years later, we realize that the better question is: What has 7 heads, 14 hands, and a giant heart? For to be the leader of an early childhood organization requires much more than hands, the director must have a head full of information and expertise on a wide variety of topics. The director must be well-schooled in best practices in business, well-grounded in an understanding of child development, well-versed in family issues, well-connected in the community, and just plain well — filled with vigor and enthusiasm and creativity. But it isn't enough for this super director to have heads filled with knowledge and ideas, she or he must have the skills to act on understandings, hands to make things happen. And, of course, working all of this out in the arena of children and families requires a loving, nurturing spirit.

We have dedicated ourselves to helping directors achieve success at this monumental endeavor because we believe that to care well for young children is the most important service anyone can do. We visit centers, research across fields, ask questions, and listen, listen, listen. It is directors who have given us the information we share through our magazine and books about how to make quality happen. What we can offer is real because we have learned it from the experts.

This textbook, inspired by an inquiry from Sue Russell and Lauren Trine from Day Care Services Association in North Carolina, represents the best thinking from the first 25 years of *Exchange*. At Sue and Lauren's request we reviewed the many hundreds of articles for center directors that we have published and selected those that appeared in the first edition of *The Art of Leadership — Managing Early Childhood Organizations*. Since that first printing we have collected the ideas and experiences of a wide variety of trainers who have used this text, as well as the directors themselves. We have used their suggestions to update, replace, and select new articles in this entirely revamped edition. Not only have we chosen the very best articles for you, we have also updated each one to make the information as current as possible.

And so, we share with you, this textbook filled with the experiences of people like yourself, as well as the ideas and insights of experts in other domains, in order to help you be the best that you can be. *The Art of Leadership* is a unique and valuable tool for training directors because of the range and breadth of topics covered.

We ask that you, as leaders, make this your mission:

- to take very good care of our precious young children, recognizing what is appropriate for all children and learning what is particular for each child;
- to respect the needs and concerns of families, fostering a partnership with parents in the care of their children;
- to take staff where they are and help them grow in knowledge and skills, always challenging them to become stronger and wiser;
- to make your community aware of your program's potential as a source of support and hope;
- to be a voice for children across the globe, for just as all children are important, more so is each child;
- and finally, to take care of yourself — grow, connect, learn, risk, and play — so that you will have strength for your mission for all of your days.

Bonnie Neugebauer
May, 2003

# The Art of Leadership

## Managing Early Childhood Organizations

# Leadership

# Leading an Organization

## Chapter 1

# Are You an Effective Leader?

**by Roger Neugebauer**

*In centers where directors displayed warm and flexible leadership, the teachers were observed to be high in encouragement sensitivity, and creativity, and low in restriction. (Prescott)*

*Centers in which directors encouraged staff participation in decisionmaking exhibited significantly higher levels of staff motivation, mutual support and trust, communication, and clarity of objectives than did centers with authoritarian directors. (Neugebauer)*

You may not feel like a leader. Given the crisis management way in which you often spend most of your time, you may feel more like a paramedic, a plumber, an accountant, a fundraiser, a bureaucrat appeaser, a lawyer, or a supply clerk. If your child care center is to survive, you must perform well in all of these roles. Yet, when it comes to the quality of care children receive in your center, it is your performance as a leader that really matters.

But how can you know if you are being effective as a leader? To begin with, if the children in your program are clearly thriving or suffering, it is probably safe to assume that these extreme conditions are directly related to your strength or weakness as a leader. More specifically, the "Leadership Assessment Guide" on page 9 can help you evaluate the nature of your leadership.

Before reading any further, it might be helpful for you to take 15 minutes and rate yourself (on a separate piece of paper) using this Guide. Then read the remainder of this article to interpret this rating and to see if you can improve your leadership effectiveness.

## Four Types of Leaders

Four types of leaders can be identified in child care. What differentiates these types is the varying degrees of emphasis they place on achieving results and on promoting staff relations.

Emphasis on results is measured by the extent to which directors try and succeed in directing the efforts of the staff into accomplishing the objectives of the program. Emphasis on relations is determined by the degree of concern a director has for the personal and professional needs of her teachers as well as by the level of confidence she has in their ability and responsibility.

These four types can briefly be described as follows:

**The Task Master** places heavy emphasis on results and little emphasis on relations.

- Always works very hard herself but believes teachers are likely to slack off if tight supervision is not enforced from above.
- Seeks to control teachers' behavior through rules, notices, threats, and disciplinary action.
- Establishes clear goals for the program, designs a curriculum which can accomplish these goals, closely supervises teachers' implementation of this curriculum, and continually evaluates to see how the curriculum is working.
- Fosters only downward communication in the form of orders and instructions to teachers.
- Addresses center problems decisively and swiftly, but seeks little advice from teachers in dealing with these problems, and delegates little responsibility to them.
- Provides feedback through criticism of teachers' classroom behavior and rule breaking.
- Fosters a tense, impersonal environment, where creativity and risk taking are discouraged.

**The Comrade** places little emphasis on results and heavy emphasis on relations.

## Traits of Leaders

The traits for leadership success are humility, deep understanding of the nature of the business, deep respect for those on the firing line and those who can enjoy making the organization work, a demonstrated record of guts, industry, loyalty downward, judgment, fairness, and honesty under pressure.

— *Robert Townsend*

- Is not inclined to work overly hard and believes teachers work best when they are happy and friendly.
- Shies away from overt forms of control, seeks to encourage proper behavior through friendly persuasion.
- Allows each teacher to establish her own goals, to implement her own curriculum approach, and to evaluate her curriculum.
- Strives to keep everyone communicating with everyone on a personal as well as a professional level.
- Discusses center problems with teachers and actively seeks their advice, but fails to follow through and act decisively.
- Provides feedback through frequent praise of teachers' performance and ability.
- Fosters a warm, friendly environment in which teachers are encouraged to do their own thing.

**The Motivator** places heavy emphasis on both results and relations.

- Works very hard herself and believes teachers are naturally inclined to work hard if they are committed to their work.
- Encourages staff to exercise self-control over their own performance.
- Develops with teachers a set of goals they all believe in, works with teachers in designing and implementing a curriculum to achieve these goals and to implement an evaluation process to monitor their progress.
- Facilitates an open two-way communication flow.
- Addresses center problems promptly and decisively, and utilizes the knowledge and skills of all staff members in solving these problems.
- Encourages the frequent sharing of nonjudgmental feedback among all staff members.
- Fosters a warm, friendly environment which actively encourages creativity and risk taking.

**The Unleader** places little emphasis on either results or relations.

- Is not inclined to work very hard and believes her teachers, likewise, are inclined to avoid hard work.
- Seeks to maintain control through rules and procedures but is lax and inconsistent in enforcing them.
- Makes no effort to clarify the program's goals, to provide a sense of direction to the curriculum, or to evaluate what is happening.
- Is ineffective in promoting communications of any type.
- Complains about center problems a great deal around staff members, but takes no steps to deal with them.
- Provides little, if any, feedback to teachers.
- Fosters a tense, chaotic environment in which little effective activity, creative or otherwise, occurs.

## What Type of Leader is Best?

It is at this point in articles on leadership where this stock phrase is inserted: "No one type of leadership is always best — it depends upon the situation." Fortunately, in child care we need not be quite so noncommittal. Studies of administration in child care centers have yielded the following insights:

- A director's leadership style has been found to be strongly related to the style of teaching in the center. In centers where directors displayed warm and flexible leadership, the teachers were observed to be high in encouragement, sensitivity, and creativity, and low in restriction. Where directors' leadership was arbitrary and lacking in warmth, teachers' performance was rated low in encouragement and high in restriction and in lessons on rules for socializing, formal skills, and control and restraint. (Prescott)

## Demands on Leaders

The head of an organization unwittingly assumes the responsibility of being all things to all men who are related to the organization. He must revere the past, predict and succeed in the future, make a profit, carry the burdens of people and operations no longer efficient, and enjoy himself besides. His whim becomes magnified into other people's law. . . . His law is often treated as if it were whim. . . . If he demands that people produce, he is exploitative. If he treats them with beneficence, he is paternalistic. If he is unconcerned about their worries, he is rejecting. If he opposes what he believes to be irrational, he is hostile. If he gives in, he is weak.

— *Harry Levinson*

- A director's decisionmaking style has been found to be strongly related to the tone of interpersonal relations in the center. Centers in which directors encouraged staff participation in decisionmaking exhibited significantly higher levels of staff motivation, mutual support and trust, communication, and clarity of objectives, than did centers with authoritarian directors. (Neugebauer)

- Teachers have been found to prefer leadership which is high on results and relations. Teachers were motivated to work hard, not by praise from their director nor by friendly relations with the director and other teachers, but rather by satisfaction from doing meaningful work well. The majority of teachers preferred to have all staff members involved in major decisionmaking. (Neugebauer)

From these findings, it is clear that the Motivator is the best type of leader in a child care setting. The Motivator is able to combine a high emphasis on results with a high emphasis on relations. The key to her success is her confidence in the ability of her teachers to exercise self-control over their own performance. Rather than devoting her time to checking up on the teachers to be sure they are performing well, she concentrates on working with the staff in establishing goals and a curriculum to which they all are personally committed. The teachers, therefore, have a strong personal interest in helping the organization achieve results because it is their own objectives which they are seeking to accomplish.

The director in this setting plays a supportive role. She secures the resources which the teachers need, she provides frequent and objective feedback to teachers which they can use to improve their own performance, she keeps teachers informed of major issues affecting the center, and she works hard to secure their input in dealing with center problems.

In short, the Motivator does not lead from out front by issuing commands or giving pep talks. She works more from within the staff to maintain a close fit between the objectives of the individual teachers and the objectives of the organization. While she does not relinquish final responsibility for the overall direction of the program, she does succeed in having teachers accept responsibility for directing their own performance. The result is best summarized by Lao-tzu: "When the best leader's work is done, the people say, 'We did it ourselves!'"

### Responsibilities of Leaders

The vision of a manager should always be upwards — towards the enterprise as a whole. But his responsibility runs downward as well — to the people on his team. He has to make sure that they know and understand what is demanded of them. He has to help them set their own objectives. Then he has to help them reach these objectives. He is responsible for getting the tools, the staff, the information they need. He has to help them with advice and counsel, and, if need be, to teach them how to do better. Seeing his relationship towards them as duty towards them and as responsibility for making them perform and achieve rather than as *supervision* is a central requirement for organizing the manager's unit effectively.

*— Peter F. Drucker*

**The Task Master** can also be an effective leader in child care. The Task Master is more inclined to establish the goals for the program herself and simply issue instructions to the teachers on how to implement a curriculum to accomplish these goals. If the teachers respect the competence of this director and if they have no objections to her curriculum approach, they would probably suppress their personal feelings and work hard to make the program successful.

However, such cooperation would not result if teachers had serious reservations about the director's ability to develop a sound curriculum. Their objections to not being treated as responsible professionals would probably come to the fore. Frustration and hostility would erode their willingness to work hard.

Centers directed by Comrades or Unleaders, on the other hand, can only be successful in spite of their leaders rather than because of them. What would be needed in either setting would be for an effective, yet unofficial, leader to arise from among the teachers to direct teachers' efforts toward positive results. In this instance, the director would function more as a figurehead, an administrative aide, or a cheerleader.

## How Do You Rate?

If you assessed your leadership with the Leadership Assessment Guide, you ended up with a rating for *results* and one for *relations*. To find out what type of leader you are, compare your ratings with those below for the four types of leaders. For example, if your results rating is 23 and your relations rating is 46, you would be considered a *Comrade*.

| | | |
|---|---|---|
| **Task Master** | Results | 32-63 |
| | Relations | 0-31 |
| **Comrade** | Results | 0-31 |
| | Relations | 32-63 |
| **Motivator** | Results | 32-63 |
| | Relations | 32-63 |
| **Unleader** | Results | 0-31 |
| | Relations | 0-31 |

## Are You Sure?

Now that you **know** what type of leader you are, a word about self-deception is in order. It may well be that the type of leader you have rated yourself to be will more accurately reflect what type of leader you want to be than what type of leader you actually are. In a study of the management of 24 New England child care centers, this author found that directors' perceptions of their own leadership styles were significantly different from what their teachers perceived their styles to be. Teachers generally found directors to be far more authoritarian than directors considered themselves to be (Neugebauer). To check the accuracy of your self-assessment, it may be helpful to have your teachers assess your leadership. This can provide you with valuable insights on how the teachers perceive your leadership behavior.

## One Director's Experience

Mary Jane Blethen, the director of the Golden Heart Child Care Center in Mankato, Minnesota, used the Leadership Assessment Guide to assess her leadership performance. She approached the process with considerable nervousness — she felt quite comfortable with her leadership, but she wasn't sure if the staff felt the same. In fact, when she and her secretary were tabulating the ratings by the staff she found herself being possessed by large doses of both curiosity and anxiety.

Much to Blethen's relief, she found that the ratings came out near the top in most categories. This was very confirming to her. However, there were some surprises, most notably with the item of "Feedback." She considered herself to be a "wonderful" communicator of feedback, but the staff didn't see it that way. They indicated that they received feedback on their performance only once or twice a month.

After discussing the problems in the area of feedback, the staff set as a goal raising the rating for feedback from 5.3 to 6.6 within 12 months. After considering a number of formal feedback techniques, the staff decided to try out a combination of the "DESC" model of feedback developed by Sharon and Gordon Bower and the "Personal Messages" model developed by Marjorie Kostelnik and P. D. Kurtz. During the next 12 months the staff worked on improving feedback using these approaches. At the end of this period they performed the Leadership Assessment Guide rating again and found that the feedback rating had improved to 6.5.

While the new rating fell just short of the goal, staff were satisfied that dramatic progress had been made. Blethen found that the meeting at which the initial ratings were discussed provided a real breakthrough. After she shared the results, the staff members were much more open than in the past in discussing leadership issues. "Using the Guide was a real jumping off point," reports Blethen. "After that, staff really got involved in this process of change."

However, such an assessment is not without potential pains and hazards. To begin with, a director opening herself up to evaluation by her teachers needs to have a fair degree of self-confidence. If you are insecure about your leadership at the outset, and then teachers rate you unexpectedly low in certain areas, this could provide a blow to your ego that you will not soon recover from.

Before jumping in, therefore, you should think about how comfortable you are in your relationships with the teachers, and how able you would be to handle some critical ratings. New directors in particular should shy away from being intensely evaluated until they have had at least a year on the job to get to know the staff and to find a management style that works for them in this setting.

When you are ready to be evaluated, you may want to start by discussing the Guide at a staff meeting so that teachers understand that you need their honest feedback in order to be a better director. Take some time to discuss each item on the Guide so that there is general agreement on the meaning of terms.

The first time teachers actually use the Guide, you might ask them to rate how they would **prefer** leadership to be handled in the center. This will give them the chance to test out the Guide, to see if there are any parts that are still not clear. The results may also be helpful to you as they will spell out what teachers' expectations are for you.

When everyone is ready to use the scale to rate actual center performance, you should pass out one copy of the Guide to each staff member (including teacher aides, cooks, and bus drivers). Have everyone complete the forms anonymously at their own pace.

To tabulate the results, add up all the scores for each item and divide by the number of people turning in the Guide. For example, if seven staff members rate item #1 ("Clarity of Objectives") 2, 3, 1, 3, 2, 2, and 1, the overall rating for that item would be 2 (14 divided by 7).

## Now Comes the Hard Part

When you first read the overall ratings of staff members, you may want to shout for joy or cry in anguish. Most likely you will do a little of both. Your next inclination will be to throw the ratings away and to get on with life. This would be a mistake (unless, of course, your ratings all are perfect 9's). It is one thing to know how staff perceive your leadership, and another to do something about it. To make the most of this opportunity, you need to take some additional painful, yet positive, steps.

**Step 1. Share the results.** At a staff meeting, pass out blank copies of the Guide to all staff members. Then go down the list and announce the overall rating for each item. Try not to express anger, regret, or any other defensive reactions while reporting.

**Step 2. Discuss the results.** Identify three or four of the lowest ratings, and discuss these one at a time. Invite staff members to share incidents or examples of center practices which demonstrate why these ratings may have been low. It would be best if you could play a low key role in this discussion. The more you listen, the more you will learn. You may need to prime the pump — to get the discussion rolling — by asking specific questions about the way you do things. For example, you might ask, "How often do you get feedback from anyone on how you talk to the children?" or "When we had the problem with traffic patterns in the toddler room, did we address it properly?"

**Step 3. Develop a game plan.** Select one or two items that you would like to address as a team. Set specific goals for these items. For example, you may decide to improve the overall rating on "Feedback" from 3.5 to 7.0 within six months. Then brainstorm some strategies for achieving these goals. Put these goals and strategies on paper, and pass them out to all staff members.

**Step 4. Monitor your progress.** Every three months or so, check out your progress. Pass the Guide out to all staff members and have them rate conditions at that point. Discuss whether your strategies are working, or whether you need to rethink what to do to make progress.

## Can You Change?

Leadership style is often viewed as a fixed behavior pattern — a deeply ingrained component of an individual's innate personality. However, an individual's leadership behavior is not static. A leader may utilize a different approach to handling different situations and may handle the same situation differently at different times (Blake).

A Motivator, for example, may handle certain problems more like a Task Master or a Comrade. The type of leader a person is, therefore, is not a single, uniform, unchanging behavior pattern. Rather, it is the net effect of a complex combination of various behaviors. By changing the manner in which you handle specific situations, you can begin to adjust your overall leadership style.

The Leadership Assessment Guide is one tool you can use to identify the strong points and the weak points of your leadership behavior. If you want to improve, you can then use this as an opportunity to work with the staff in setting and implementing strategies for change.

While it is certainly possible to adjust your pattern of leadership, such change will not come easily or dramatically. Yet the rewards are clearly worth the effort.

Improvements in your effectiveness as a leader will inevitably improve the satisfaction you experience on the job, as well as the quality of care children receive in your program.

### References and Resources

Blake, R. R., et al. (November-December 1964). "Breakthrough in Organizational Development," *Harvard Business Review*.

McGregor, D. (1960). *The Human Side of Enterprise*. New York: McGraw-Hill Book Company.

Neugebauer, R. *Organizational Analysis of Day Care*. ERIC Document Reproduction Service, PO Box 190, Arlington, VA 22210.

Prescott, E., et al. *Day Care As a Child-Rearing Environment*. Washington, DC: NAEYC.

Tannenbaum, R., & Schmidt, W. H. (May-June 1973). "How to Choose a Leadership Pattern," *Harvard Business Review*.

Townsend, R. (May-June 1973). *Further Up the Organization*. New York: Alfred A. Knopf.

## Leadership Assessment Guide

Rate your center on a scale of 0-9 for each of the 14 leadership elements listed below. Select the statement which most accurately describes the situation in your center, and place its rating in the blank on the left. If the situation in your center lies somewhere between two of the statements, use a rating midway between the two given ratings. For example, if communications in your center are somewhere between moderately frank and moderately guarded, you might record a rating of 4 or 5 to the element **Communications**.

_____ 1. **Clarity of Objectives**

( 9 ) The center has **clear** objectives which are understood by **all** staff members.
( 6 ) The center has **fairly clear** objectives which are understood by **most** staff members.
( 3 ) The center has objectives, but **few** staff members are **aware** of them.
( 0 ) The center does **not** have **any** established objectives.

_____ 2. **Communications**

( 9 ) Communications flow **both ways** between director and teachers and are **extremely** frank and open.
( 6 ) Communications flow **both ways** and are **moderately** frank and open.
( 3 ) Communications flow **primarily** down from the director and are **somewhat** guarded and cautious.
( 0 ) Communications flow **only** downward and are **extremely** guarded and cautious.

_____ 3. **Ongoing Planning**

( 9 ) Staff members engage in planning on a **weekly** basis to insure that the daily curriculum promotes the center's objectives.
( 6 ) Staff members engage in planning on a **monthly** basis to promote the center's objectives.
( 3 ) Staff members engage in **occasional** planning with **little** emphasis on objectives.
( 0 ) Staff members do **not** engage in planning on a regular basis.

_____ 4. **Creativity**

( 9 ) Staff members are **encouraged** to be creative, to take risks, and to explore their own interests.
( 6 ) Staff members are **allowed** to be creative, to take risks, and to explore their own interests.
( 3 ) Creativity, risk taking, and the exploration of one's own interests are **discouraged**.
( 0 ) Creativity, risk taking, and the exploration of one's own interests are **forbidden**.

_____ 5. **Evaluation**

( 9 ) Center objectives, curriculum results, and staff performance are **continuously** evaluated.
( 6 ) Evaluation occurs on a **frequent** basis.
( 3 ) Evaluation occurs on a **sporadic** basis.
( 0 ) Evaluation **seldom**, if ever, takes place.

_____ 6. **Decisionmaking**

( 9 ) The director seeks input from **all** staff members in making major center decisions.
( 6 ) The director seeks **advice** from **most** teachers before making major center decisions.
( 3 ) The director seeks **advice** from a **few** teachers before making major center decisions.
( 0 ) The director makes all decisions with **no** teacher input.

_____ 7. **Problem Solving**

( 9 ) Problems confronting the center are **always** addressed promptly and decisively.
( 6 ) Problems confronting the center are **usually** addressed promptly and decisively.
( 3 ) Problems confronting the center are **occasionally** addressed promptly and decisively.
( 0 ) Problems confronting the center are **never** addressed promptly and decisively.

_____ **8. Policy Implementation**

( 9 ) Center policies and procedures are enforced with **extreme** consistency and fairness.
( 6 ) Center policies and procedures are enforced with **moderate** consistency and fairness.
( 3 ) Center policies and procedures are enforced with **moderate** inconsistency and unfairness.
( 0 ) Center policies and procedures are enforced with **extreme** inconsistency and unfairness.

_____ **9. Feedback**

( 9 ) Staff members are given constructive feedback on their performance on nearly a **daily** basis.
( 6 ) Staff members are given constructive feedback on a **weekly** basis.
( 3 ) Staff members are given constructive feedback about **once a month**.
( 0 ) Staff members are **seldom**, if ever, given constructive feedback.

_____ **10. Discipline**

( 9 ) Discipline is **totally self-imposed**; staff are fully responsible for controlling their own behavior.
( 6 ) Discipline is **mostly self-imposed**.
( 3 ) Discipline is **mostly imposed from above**; control is exerted mostly through close supervision.
( 0 ) Discipline is **totally imposed from above**.

_____ **11. Staff Development**

( 9 ) **Continuous** efforts are made to upgrade staff members' skills and knowledge.
( 6 ) **Frequent** efforts are made to upgrade staff members' skills and knowledge.
( 3 ) **Sporadic** efforts are made to upgrade staff members' skills and knowledge.
( 0 ) Staff development **seldom**, if ever, takes place at the center.

_____ **12. Staff Motivation**

( 9 ) Staff members are **highly motivated** to perform to the best of their ability.
( 6 ) Staff members are **moderately motivated**.
( 3 ) Staff members are **moderately frustrated** with their work or the center.
( 0 ) Staff members are **highly frustrated**.

_____ **13. Director Motivation**

( 9 ) The director is **extremely** enthusiastic and productive in her performance.
( 6 ) The director is **moderately** enthusiastic and productive in her performance.
( 3 ) The director is **slightly** enthusiastic and productive in her performance.
( 0 ) The director is **not at all** enthusiastic and productive in her performance.

_____ **14. Staff-Director Relationship**

( 9 ) The director is on **warm, personal** terms with **all** teachers.
( 6 ) The director is **friendly** with **all** teachers.
( 3 ) The director is **friendly** with **some** teachers.
( 0 ) The director is personally **isolated** from the teachers.

**Scoring:** Place your ratings for all **odd** numbered elements on the **Results** line, and place all ratings for the **even** numbered elements on the **Relations** line. Add the ratings on each line. This will provide your center's overall rating for the leadership dimensions of results and relations.

**Results** (odd-numbered items) _____ + _____ + _____ + _____ + _____ + _____ + _____ = _____

**Relations** (even-numbered items) _____ + _____ + _____ + _____ + _____ + _____ + _____ = _____

# Being a Boss

**by Roger Neugebauer**

*The effective boss is one who possesses a high concern for influencing people toward the benefit of the organization.*

*Don't try to use your position to make people love you, and don't expect that people will obey you because they love you.*

*A People-Oriented Boss, who cares mainly about stimulating high performance by staff members, provides objective feedback to them, knowing this will help them improve their performance.*

Child care directors come in all shapes, sizes, and styles. One thing you all have in common is a genuine concern for people. As you well know, sometimes this concern for people can get in the way of your being effective as a director. At times you would rather be a friend to the staff members than their boss. You want very much for all staff members to like you and to follow your lead as director because they like you, not because they fear you.

Unfortunately, it can't always work out this way. You find that you are forced to make some decisions which won't please everyone or, on occasion, anyone. You find that no matter how friendly you try to be, staff members are often cautious and somewhat distant in their relations with you, even though they may be open and easy going in their relations with each other. Sometimes it seems like the harder you try to please everyone, the more they resent it.

What you are experiencing is "status anxiety." This is that seemingly inevitable tension — that invisible wall — that arises between director and staff. While this anxiety is a feeling that nearly all directors experience at some point in their careers, it is also a feeling that can be successfully dealt with.

This article describes a number of approaches that are guaranteed to fail, as well as many that are likely to succeed, in relieving status anxiety. Before reviewing these suggestions, you might want to take a few minutes to assess how well you are succeeding in balancing your desire to be a friend and your need to be a boss. The more of the following questions you can answer with "yes," the better. Then try out some of the suggestions that follow, and check yourself out in six months to see if you are making progress.

## How Do You Rate As a Boss?

1. When you enter a room of staff members, does conversation continue?
2. Are staff meetings chaired by you lively and honest?
3. Is staff turnover, especially for key people in your center, very low?
4. Do staff members regularly come to you for advice?
5. Do staff members freely voice conflicting opinions on center issues?
6. When a decision is made, do staff members faithfully carry it out?
7. Although gossip seldom reaches you, do you always hear about center problems before they become crises?
8. When you delegate a task to a staff member, do you stop worrying about it?
9. Do staff members freely give you feedback on your performance?
10. When you encounter staff members unexpectedly outside the center, do they appear to be genuinely pleased to see you?

## How Not to Be a Boss

When confronted with the dilemma of trying at the same time to achieve your desire to be a friend and your need to be a boss, many solutions present themselves. Not all of them will yield equally satisfactory results. The five approaches described below are guaranteed not to work.

### The Benevolent Boss

Sometimes one's need to be loved is so strong that all other demands take a back seat. The director giving in to this need, trying the Benevolent Boss approach, seeks to make everyone on staff love her. She strives to be perceived as everyone's buddy, as just one of the gang.

The Benevolent Boss uses her position and personality to try to please everyone. She is overflowing in praise and sparing with criticism. She seeks to win staff members over with favors — going out of her way to provide supplies teachers ask for; bending the rules for individuals experiencing personal problems; overlooking deficiencies in job performance; loaning her books, her car, her money. The personal lives of staff members become a major concern of hers. To keep everyone happy, this amiable administrator never overlooks an opportunity to throw a party.

### The Disappearing Boss

One temptation for a director who feels uncomfortable with the trappings of power is to play down his authority and play up his likeability. This is an exercise in "status stripping" — whereby the director tries to disregard all the symbols of his status and authority (Zaleznik).

The Disappearing Boss eschews all appearances of pretension and privilege. He uses the cheapest desk available, and his chair is the oldest (and preferably the most uncomfortable) in the center. A spartan motif prevails throughout his office — if he has an office at all (some uneasy executives locate themselves in some dimly lit corner or in a breezy entryway). In dress, he is as nondescript as possible — he's an annual fixture on Exchange's "Worst Dressed Directors" list.

In his behavior, the Disappearing Boss likewise deemphasizes his power. He answers his own phone and types his own letters. In staff meetings he avoids sitting at the head of the table. He doesn't issue orders, he makes requests. He consults with everyone before making any decision. When there is controversy about an issue, he avoids making a decision altogether, hoping the problem will go away.

### The Workaholic Wonder

Another approach to ameliorating the effects of being the boss is for the director to work twice as hard as anybody else. The Workaholic Wonder convinces herself that staff members will be less likely to resent her authority if she earns their respect through hard work. She comes in before anyone else, is the last to leave every day, and lets it be known that she comes in on weekends. Not only does she refuse to delegate any of her tasks, but she insists on taking over the grubbiest of the teachers' jobs, such as picking up at the end of the day and cleaning the bathrooms.

These three approaches may do wonders for assuaging the director's sense of guilt over her special status, but they are shortsighted attempts to deny or obscure reality. Sooner or later they are bound to backfire. When the Benevolent Boss is forced to make an unpopular decision, Santa Claus will be exposed as just another boss, and her efforts to win popularity will be viewed as pure phoniness.

On the other hand, the Disappearing Boss and the Workaholic Wonder may be so successful at downplaying their status and authority that when the time comes to make a hard decision everyone will question their right to do so (Prentice). Rather than increasing the director's respect among staff members, these last two approaches are more likely to convince them that their boss is not operating with a full deck.

Another potential ill effect of these approaches is that attempts to avoid making unpopular decisions will do more to undermine staff morale than will the decisions themselves. If the director bends the rules for certain individuals, or overlooks their poor performance, other staff members are likely to become upset at this unfair or inequitable treatment.

Directors who continually avoid making hard decisions are likely to stimulate apprehension among staff members as they try to determine where the organization is heading and what is expected of them. Studies by David C. McClellan tend to support these conclusions. He found that managers who place their need to be liked above all other considerations tend to have subordinates who feel that they have very little personal responsibility, that organizational procedures are not clear, and that they have little pride in their work group. Their employees feel ". . . weak, irresponsible, and without a sense of what might happen next, of where they stand in relation to their manager, or even of what they ought to be doing" (McClellan).

### The R2D2 Boss

An entirely different approach to resolving status anxiety is to try to perform like a robot — to take all feelings out of the process of managing. The R2D2 Boss is resigned to the conclusion that it is not possible for a boss to gain the friendship of his staff members. He therefore strives to perform his job in a very efficient, businesslike manner.

R2D2 focuses his attention on the goals of the center, and views the staff as a tool for accomplishing them. He makes specific assignments to all staff members and closely monitors their performance. Violations of rules and deficiencies in performance are dealt with quickly, fairly, and predictably. Time is viewed as a precious commodity not to be squandered on socializing and chit chat.

### The Tyrannical Boss

Finally we have the boss who has completely thrown in the towel on human relations. Believing that staff members view all friendliness as a sign of weakness, the Tyrant seeks to rule with an iron hand. Staff members will be made to obey her not because they like her but because they fear her. Rules and assignments are spelled out in great detail and posted everywhere. Failures to comply with these requirements are dealt with swiftly and harshly.

It should come as no surprise that these last two impersonal approaches to being a boss are doomed to failure as well. These directors are clearly not inhibited by concerns about whether subordinates will like them, nor are their subordinates uncertain about what is expected of them. However, they make staff members feel like cogs in the machinery or slaves in the galley.

In studies of more than 5,000 organizations by Rensis Likert, it was found that totally "production-oriented" managers were inaccessible, autocratic, and punitive. They were not good delegators. Their units were plagued with low morale and low productivity (Rogers).

## How to Be a People-Oriented Boss

The Benevolent Boss, the Disappearing Boss, and the Workaholic Wonder described above demonstrate (in overstated terms, of course) that a boss preoccupied with his need to be liked cannot succeed. On the other hand, R2D2 and the Tyrant make clear that a preoccupation with "production" is not a healthy response to status anxiety either. So where does the answer lie? According to David C. McClellan, the effective boss is one who possesses a high concern for influencing people toward the benefit of the organization. This concern ought to be greater than her need to be liked by people, as well as her concern for production (McClellan). She is a "people-oriented" boss. Her prime objective is to motivate members of her staff to work to their full potential to achieve the goals of the organization.

There is no set formula for becoming a People-Oriented Boss. Your management style will be influenced by the size and structure of the center you manage as well as by your own personality and previous experiences with authority. However, a variety of studies have found that successful people-oriented bosses do have in common the ten characteristics described below.

### #1. Be Realistic

There is no denying that your being a boss does affect your relationship with your subordinates. There is a maxim in the study of human behavior which describes this situation: "love flees authority." Where one individual has the capacity to control and affect the actions of another, the feeling governing this relationship tends to be one of distance and (hopefully) respect, but not one ultimately of warmth and friendliness (Zaleznik).

This does not mean that directors must resign themselves to a total lack of friendliness. In fact, if a boss cannot get along comfortably with subordinates, he will never be able to do his job well or enjoy it (Caplow). From having visited hundreds of child care centers across the country, this author has observed that many of the most effective directors do have warm relationships with their staff members. However, underlying even these relationships is a noticeable constraint. The role of the boss, even in a small, non-bureaucratic human service organization, brings with it some invisible barriers which can be largely overcome but never totally erased.

Don't frustrate yourself with unrealistic expectations. Don't feel like you are a failure if staff members don't all love you. Above all, don't try to use your position to make people love you, and don't expect that people will obey you because they love you.

### #2. Be Yourself

One way to relieve status anxiety is to establish a firm sense of identity — to know who you are and who you are not, to know what you are capable of and what you are not. Successful leaders exhibit all types of personalities. They are shy, gregarious, laid back, hyperactive, jocular, and humorless. There is no need to try to be someone you are not, to try to change your behavior based on what you think others want you to be.

By establishing a firm sense of identity, by being oneself, a director avoids what Abraham Zaleznik describes as "being buffeted around the sea of opinions he must live within." This sense of identity permits a freedom of action and thinking that is so necessary for effective leadership (Zaleznik).

### #3. Be Consistent

Closely related to the need to be yourself is the necessity of maintaining a constancy in how you present yourself to others. Frequent, unpredictable changes in your behavior are confusing to your staff members. They are entitled to a sense of security that comes from a feeling of reasonable continuity in the responses of their boss (Zaleznik).

Staff members function optimally when they receive consistent signals from their boss in terms of performance standards, personnel policies, work assignments, and program emphases. For example, if a director is continually announcing new program emphases — one month proclaiming "self image" the center's top priority and the next declaring "reading readiness" the number one concern — staff members will become reluctant to invest too much effort or personal interest in any one project for fear it will be wasted.

Consistency in the administration of rewards and punishments is especially important. Employees need to know what efforts on their part will result in known rewards and what acts on their part will lead to known punishments. To be perceived as "being fair" in this regard, a director must adhere to certain ground rules. Staff members should be informed clearly and in advance about their exact work assignments and performance standards. Likewise, center rules and the penalties resulting from their infraction should be made clear at the outset. The director then must be firm and consistent in administering rewards and punishments based on these known expectations (Hackman).

Failure to make expectations clear at the outset will cause uncertainty and frustration. Failure to enforce them consistently will result in hostility and loss of credibility and respect for the director.

## #4. Be a Goal Setter

A key task for any boss is to focus the attention and efforts of staff members on the goals of the organization. The organization can be most successful if all staff members are channeling their efforts in the same direction. Likewise, staff members can be most effective if it is clear where they should be directing their efforts.

One hoped for outcome of focusing attention on organizational goals is the building of loyalty of staff members to the organization. A boss with an overwhelming need to be loved may strive to make subordinates loyal to him as an individual. However, this establishes an unstable base for performance. Employees' willingness to work hard will ebb and flow depending upon their current attitude about the boss. Also when this boss leaves the organization, disorganization often follows. The employees' high motivation, which the boss personally inspired, deflates and they do not know what to do (McClellan). Staff members should be motivated by the challenge of achieving the goals of the center, not by the desire to win the approval of the director or to avoid his displeasure.

To encourage the highest level of commitment to the center, the director should seek to involve staff members in setting the goals. By participating in the goal setting process, employees can help shape goals that they personally care about and have a stake in. The more they perceive the center's goals as coinciding with their own professional goals, and the less they perceive them as only the director's goals, the more they will be inclined to work hard toward their accomplishment (McGregor).

## #5. Be a Feedback Giver

A Benevolent Boss, who cares primarily about having staff members like her, lavishes praise on them, hoping this will make them feel good about her. A People-Oriented Boss, who cares mainly about stimulating high performance by staff members, provides objective feedback to them, knowing this will help them improve their performance.

Praise, even well-deserved praise, has been shown to have only minimal impact on the long-term performance of workers. Objective feedback, on the other hand, gives them data they can use to change their behavior (Drucker). The more employees know about their own performance, the more they are able to adjust it toward accepted performance standards.

There are several criteria for effective feedback. First and foremost, feedback should focus on facts, not opinions. A director should describe for a teacher exactly how she talks to children and let her draw her own conclusions, rather than offering a judgment about whether her conversational style is good or bad. Making a judgment causes the recipient to react emotionally, either with anger or embarrassment, and obscures the important message.

Feedback should focus on behavior, rather than on the person. A director should report to a teacher that "You spoke rather harshly to the children today," rather than "You are too authoritarian." Talking in terms of personality traits implies inherited constant qualities, which are difficult, if not impossible, to change. Commenting on behavior implies that it is something related to a specific situation that might be changed (Lehner).

Feedback should be timely. The closer feedback is given in time to the point at which the behavior actually occurred, the more likely the recipient will clearly remember the incident and put the information to use (Drucker). If a teacher is told that the children were inattentive when she read to them last week, but she can't remember what she was reading, how she was reading it, or what took place just before the reading, she will not know enough about the incident to change her behavior for the better in the future.

Feedback should be given in frequent small doses. People can absorb only so much feedback at one time and put it to effective use (Lehner). Feedback in the form of an annual appraisal which attempts to summarize an entire year's performance in one lump sum can be overwhelming. Feedback which comes in tiny daily bits is easily digested and put to use.

## #6. Be a Delegator

One of the paradoxes of organizational life is that the more authority a boss gives away the more his authority is enhanced (Caplow). Authority can be given away by delegating tasks to subordinates and by granting autonomy to them in the exercise of their day-to-day work.

By assuming greater responsibility within the organization, employees feel more like they are in control of their work and less like puppets on a string. They tend to feel more like they are a significant part of the organization. And they tend to care more about how well the organization performs. The more they respect the organization and care about their performance in it, the more they respect the authority of the leaders of the organization, and the more they value the feedback they receive about their performance from these leaders. As a result, a People-Oriented Boss who grants considerable autonomy to his subordinates is better able to influence their performance.

### #7. Be a Facilitator

A People-Oriented Boss facilitates the optimal performance of his subordinates by providing whatever support they need to do their work. This support needs to be provided in a variety of ways. The director needs to provide staff members with the equipment and supplies they require. He needs to ensure that the environment they work in is safe and pleasant. He needs to do all he can to provide them the compensation and benefits they deserve and require.

In addition to providing these basic types of support, a boss needs to be able to support the professional development of staff members. Two ways to do this which have already been discussed are granting employees autonomy and providing them with feedback. Another is to provide them with appropriate training opportunities and materials. Finally, a director needs to support the professional development of staff members by being available to listen, to review, to advise, and to counsel. He needs to be a resource of last resort in problem solving. He needs to be a trusted source of expertise. He needs to be able to stimulate people's thinking and self-analysis. In short, he needs to be able to do whatever is needed to facilitate the development and performance of his subordinates.

### #8. Be Communicative

That invisible barrier between the boss and her staff tends to play havoc with the flow of communications in a center. A director must be aware of how communications are affected by this barrier in interpreting communications that she receives and in framing messages that she transmits.

One common problem that develops is that directors tend to overrate the effectiveness of downward communications. They become so immersed in all the details of current administrative hassles and crises that they tend to forget who they told about what. After a while they tend to assume that the staff must be aware of what is going on.

More often then not, staff members have only picked up bits and pieces of information about current administrative issues. Having only partial information, the rumor mill tends to fill in the gaps with exaggerated, typically alarmist versions of what is going on. Worse yet, when the data received is sketchy, staff members tend to feel that information is being withheld intentionally. This contributes to undermining the respect for and authority of the director.

Being aware of this scenario, a director should make a regular practice of reporting to staff on the status of current administrative issues. Never assume that subordinates are aware of everything you are, and never assume that staff members won't be interested in certain issues. In terms of downward communications, it is usually wise to err in the direction of overkill rather than keeping employees guessing and grousing.

Upward communications are usually even more sluggish. Information tends to be well filtered before it reaches the director's ears. Since no one wants to be the bearer of bad news, negative information about the organization tends to flow upward much less routinely than does positive information.

Likewise, while personal information and news about staff members tends to flow freely among staff members, it seldom flows upwards. Staff members are often reluctant to share personal information with directors for fear that this information will be held against them in some way. Thus, as Caplow observes, a director ". . . can never hope to understand the office love affairs that are crystal clear to everyone else in the organization" (Caplow).

While a director can do very little to become a part of the center's network of news and gossip, there are specific steps she can take to encourage the upward flow of organizational information. One of the most effective ways is to encourage it by taking action. When a teacher reports a heating problem in her room, take immediate steps to do something about it. When a teacher suggests that one of the center's curriculum goals may be too ambitious, bring this issue up at the next staff meeting to see if there is general agreement about this. If there is, abandon or modify the goal accordingly. The more that staff members see that their input makes a difference, the more they will be willing to share both negative and positive information with the director.

In addition, the director should open multiple channels of upward communication. A director might encourage written communications for those times when she is not available or for staff members who may be reluctant to share negative information on a face-to-face basis.

Likewise, the director could reserve time in staff meetings for staff members to report their news and views. Or the director could schedule private talks with individual staff members on a regular basis to discuss their successes, their problems, and their concerns. The more avenues a center provides for communication to take place, the less likely it is that important messages will be withheld or get lost in the cracks.

### #9. Be Visible

It is very easy for a director to remove herself from the day-to-day life of the center. Directors spend so much time in meetings, both at the center and away from it, and tend to get so involved in paperwork and phone communications that they become invisible to staff members. This pattern can be heightened when a director, in the throws of status anxiety, starts avoiding encounters with staff members which make her feel awkward.

It is often necessary for a director to take deliberate steps to increase her visibility at the center. It may help to set a specific time of the day to take a stroll through the classrooms. A director could from time to time take the opportunity to actually work in the classrooms. When crises erupt in the center, the director should make an immediate appearance and offer whatever leadership or support is needed (Caplow).

### #10. Be Open to Feedback

A large measure of a director's status anxiety comes from not knowing how he or she is perceived by subordinates. According to Theodore Caplow, "The usual behavior of a normally ambivalent subordinate is to display his affection and conceal his resentment in the presence of his superior." As a result, a director has a very difficult time getting accurate feedback from the staff on how his performance is perceived and received.

This is a normal situation and should not alarm the director. But she should not allow herself to be lulled into the illusion that she is universally loved (Caplow).

To keep in touch with reality, a director can initiate specific actions to elicit feedback on her performance. She should communicate to staff, both in word and deed, that she welcomes and values their feedback. When staff members offer her negative feedback, she should resist the urge to become defensive. The surest way to discourage honest feedback is to challenge or argue with staff members whenever they deliver painful messages. Listen carefully to what they have to say and then thank them for helping you.

A director can also utilize more formalized procedures for soliciting feedback. In a staff meeting the director can ask staff members to provide anonymous written ratings of her performance. There are a variety of forms which have been developed for this purpose. Or the director can develop her own form. She could ask staff members to rate her performance in areas she identifies on a scale of 1 to 7. By totaling and averaging these ratings she could get an idea of how staff members are perceiving her performance in these areas.

Another approach would be to utilize the critical incidents technique. The director asks staff members to write down two examples of incidents that made them feel good about her performance and two which upset them. By compiling all of these incidents, a director may detect some real patterns — certain things she does which seem to work and others that are causing problems.

## References and Resources


Caplow, T. (1976). *How to Run Any Organization*. New York: Holt, Rinehart, and Winston.

Drucker, P. F. (1974). *Management: Tasks, Responsibilities, Practices*. New York: Harper and Row.

Hackman, J. R., & Suttle, J. L. (1977). *Improving Life at Work*. Santa Monica, CA: Goodyear Publishing Company.

Lehner, G. F. J. (Summer 1978). "Aids for Giving and Receiving Feedback." *Exchange*.

McClellan, D. C., & Burnham, D. H. (March-April 1976). "Power Is the Great Motivator." *Harvard Business Review*.

McGregor, D. (1960). *The Human Side of Enterprise*. New York: McGraw-Hill Book Company.

Neugebauer, R. (January 1979). "Are You an Effective Leader?" *Exchange*.

Neugebauer, R. (May-June 1982). "Leadership." *Exchange*.

Neugebauer, R. (November 1980). "Make Communications a Two-Way Street." *Exchange*.

Prentice, W. C. H. (September-October 1961). "Understanding Leadership." *Harvard Business Review*.

Rogers, C. (1977). *On Personal Power*. New York: Dell Publishing Company.

Zaleznik, A. (July-August 1963). "The Human Dilemmas of Leadership." *Harvard Business Review*.

# Growing a Vision: Growing Your Staff

**by Margie Carter**

Last week I walked into a child care center office and found a co-worker standing behind a seated director gently rubbing her shoulders and offering reminders to breath deeply as the director faced the computer. This comforting scene was quickly followed by an incessant ringing of the telephone, a teacher yelling for help with a child who had just vomited, and a parent in tears with the news of being "downsized." I went off in search of a mop.

It's no secret that child care directors wear far more hats than your average saint. No wonder that heavy weight frequently translates to a chronic stiff neck and tight shoulders. The program referred to here is regarded as one of the best in our city. They are accredited and have a highly capable director and staff and more financial stability than most small centers. Still they experience the ebb and flow of crises that plague most child care programs.

Somehow they manage to not only hold on during this roller coaster ride, but to enhance the quality of their program as they come over each hill. I want to pinpoint what accounts for this tenacity, because what Hilltop Children's Center and others like them have achieved is worth talking about.

## Working with a Vision

Programs that stand out are not only focused on checklists of quality indicators and best practices, but have their eye on the prize — a clear vision of where they want to be.

When I teach child care management classes, we begin by clarifying the difference between a manager and a leader. A manager is focused on the people, problems, and tasks at hand. A leader tends to these things, but brings them into focus through vision building. Susan Gross describes it this way:

"What we mean by purpose is the end or result at which an entire organization is aimed. Purpose is the organization's driving force and reason for being. It is always translatable into vision — that is, an image shared by the organization of what the world or society or an environment or community would look like if that purpose were realized."

Gross is describing something different than uniting a center around the self-study for accreditation, as important and rewarding as that might be. She is suggesting using our imaginations, not our checklists, defining dreams that linger with us as we move through our days of stress, chores, and "to do" lists. It has to do with how we cultivate our hearts, approach interactions and decisions. Gross goes on:

"The most potent ingredient in organizational effectiveness is a clear sense of purpose shared by every member of the organization. Organizational problems, including nasty interpersonal conflicts and wrenching internal schism, can literally begin to dissolve when people in an organization rediscover the depth of their common vision."

Visions can't be handed down like a mission statement or a memo. The ground has to be prepared, seeds have to be planted, and tender shoots have to be protected from destructive pests and early frosts. Here are some strategies toward that end.

## Strategy:
### Ask "Why are we here?"

Over time people can lose sight of their real passion for this work, or overlook the idea of even working with a passion. During a meeting of community college field instructors, Jeannie Turner asked us to begin by briefly sharing why we first wanted to be a teacher. I wondered if our answers would seem like old hat. To the contrary, the question sparked an outpouring of longing for continued play, spontaneity, and acceptance; desires to heal from negative experiences; hopes and dreams for changing the world by treating children differently. The energy in the room was electrifying and deeply satisfying.

Hilltop Children's Center asks this question of its staff in a number of ways throughout the year. Each time around the answers get deeper and more fully developed. "Why are we here?" is not a rhetorical question for these teachers. It is a simple but effective inquiry to explore and grow a collective vision over time.

## STRATEGY:
### Interview parents

Each family enrolling a child in your center has hopes and dreams for their children. This is easily overlooked as we negotiate schedules, fees, and lost socks. Find ways to coax it out of families. Put something in your application form that asks about their hopes for their child as they form relationships with caregivers. During intake interviews or orientation visits, respectfully raise questions that get to values and longings they have for their children.

At Hilltop there is a bulletin board that features different families every month. Interviews and photographs tell a story of what this family wants others at the center to know about them. During the winter holidays at Kidspace Child Care Center, the parents are given mat boards to create a visual story of how they celebrate the season. Each of these strategies involve families and staff in expanding the way we think about ourselves and the possibilities for our lives.

## STRATEGY:
### Encourage keepers of the vision

When programs are steadily building a vision, it seems worthwhile to listen to all the staff voices and find in each special elements of the vision you want to craft together. Rather than discouraging what sound like far-fetched ideas, flush them out for possible pieces that could be worked on. Encourage each staff person to be as passionate as he or she can be in promoting and keeping that vision alive.

For years Hilltop teachers have bemoaned their lack of outdoor space and the limitations of their rooms located in a church building. During a vision building discussion, they offered the idea of tearing down walls or moving to a new building. Their director could have just rolled her eyes and told them to get real. Instead, she listened and nodded and encouraged them to keep generating ideas for how they'd like things to be.

Teacher passion to overcome the factors inhibiting their vision led them to knocking down some of the emotional walls they had constructed. Within a month, they moved to a new level of trust, respect, and collaborative teaching. Their physical space was reconfigured to create an art and discovery studio. They transformed their classrooms with a number of large plants, driftwood, rocks, art work, flowing fabric, and new lighting, creating a rich sensory environment that invites curiosity and discovery for both adults and children.

## STRATEGY:
### Create maps, symbols, and representations

Some people build a vision with words, while others work with images, symbols, and concrete materials. Make sure you provide opportunities for your staff to express themselves in ways not dependent upon verbal expression.

A new addition to Hilltop are beautiful autobiographical display boards staff members made for their entry way. They were given a piece of mat board with their name and a photo of themselves and asked to create a representation of what they would like others in the Hilltop community to know about them. The results were stunning, both in content and aesthetic quality.

## STRATEGY:
### Develop a vision statement together

At a staff retreat, Hilltop director Leslie Howle asked people to help her rewrite their mission statement. It became clear that what they really wanted was a public declaration of the vision they were building. People began tossing out some word associations and phrases that represented what they longed for Hilltop to be. From there we built sentences and a few short paragraphs.

Here's the statement that now guides their work and graces the comings and goings of each day.

**Hilltop Children's Center**
***A Learning Community for Children and Adults***

*Where children are valued for their ability to do meaningful work, their wonder and curiosity, their perspectives, and ability to play —*

*Where families are valued for their bonds and traditions, their ability to play, their commitment to work, home, and community, and their dreams for their children —*

*Where staff are valued for their vision, their delight in children, their skill, heart, and knowledge, a commitment to families, and an ability to play —*

*We cherish what we learn from each other.*

## Reference

Gross, S. (July 1987). "The Power of Purpose." *Exchange*.

# ARE YOU TRULY PROFESSIONAL?

**by Roger Neugebauer**

*8:30 AM — "Hello, this is Dr. Klinger's office calling to remind Roger about his 1:00 PM appointment today. Please be on time."*

*12:15 PM — I arrive, sign in, and start filling out a two page medical history — the same one I filled out last year — and one page description of reason for visit — sore knee.*

*1:20 PM — I am escorted into an examination room.*

*1:45 PM — Nurse arrives and asks me about my medical history and the reason for my visit — ignoring forms I just filled out. She takes my pulse.*

*2:05 PM — Dr. Klinger drops in for two minutes — asks why I am here and a few questions about my medical history. Leaves.*

*2:15 PM — Doctor returns, examines my knee for two minutes — says he needs an x-ray.*

*2:35 PM — Nurse comes in, takes me down the hall for an x-ray, and returns me to the examination room.*

*2:55 PM — Nurse comes in and pins up the x-ray.*

*3:10 PM — Doctor returns, spends 15 seconds studying the x-ray, writes me a prescription, tells me to stop running for a few weeks, and to be sure to stop at the reception desk on the way out to settle my bill.*

What is aggravating about this story is not that it is unusual, but rather that it is so very usual. In fact, I am sure all 27,000 *Exchange* readers can share similar, and even more serious stories. What strikes me about this story is that whenever a group of child care folks start bemoaning their plight, we conclude that we need to have child care perceived as a profession — like the medical profession.

Although I have experienced many considerate and competent doctors, on balance I do not perceive the medical profession as a model to which we should aspire. Doctors have done an effective job in demarcating a body of knowledge that must be mastered by candidates before they are admitted into the profession. Unfortunately for consumers, expertise in communication and customer service appears to be optional components of the doctor curriculum.

In child care, we have nearly the opposite situation.

Excellence in communication and customer service is widely understood to be a prerequisite of quality care. No one in our profession would consider it acceptable for staff to withhold information from parents about their child, for staff to treat parents' time and insights as unimportant, or for so many staff to be involved with the care of one child that no one really knows the child. Establishing a bond of trust among staff, children, and parents is considered essential.

On the other hand, we have not come to agreement about the specialized expertise required of teachers and directors. We all agree that specialized training is critical, but there are as many views on the content of this training as there are training institutions.

In recent years, many encouraging efforts to establish credentialing systems and to standardize training content have been launched. Hopefully these efforts will lead to greater overall expectations for director and teacher training, profession-wide agreement on essential components of training, and greater recognition by society that child care is indeed a profession.

While these efforts are taking place, there is much every director can do to build his or her own professionalism. To do so, one need not look outside. Instead we should look within our profession for inspiration. By stimulating the diffusion of the best practices and most ethical behaviors of current practitioners, we can uplift the professionalism of all directors.

## The Hallmarks of Director Professionalism

I have observed center directors in action for over 20 years. From this experience, I recognize that director professionalism is not a rare commodity. Even though child care is not widely acknowledged to be a profession, it is blessed with a great number of center directors who hold themselves to professional standards as demanding as those in any other profession. These standards can be expressed in the way a director values, in word and deed, self, children, parents, staff, community, and profession.

### I. Valuing One's Self

- Continually learning how to perform at a higher level;
- Constantly evaluating one's performance;
- Keeping fit so as to maintain a consistently high level of performance; and
- Keeping one's personal life separate and significant.

### II. Valuing Children

- Treating children as worthy individuals;
- Respecting children's privacy;
- Providing a physically and psychologically safe environment for children; and
- Mounting a coherent, stimulating, and joyful curriculum that is based on the best current thinking in child development and education.

### III. Valuing Staff

- Respecting all staff members as professionals;
- Providing just compensation for all staff;
- Protecting the rights of staff members to criticize the organization, challenge personnel decisions, and lobby for better working conditions;
- Respecting staff members' rights to privacy;
- Delivering frequent feedback to staff on their performance; and
- Creating continual opportunities for staff to grow.

### IV. Valuing Parents

- Acknowledging parents as the primary caregivers and final decision makers;
- Respecting parents' insights about and wishes for their children;
- Respecting differing family structures and lifestyles;
- Communicating intensely and frequently with parents about the experiences and behaviors of their children;
- Respecting parents' rights to privacy; and
- Welcoming parents to observe, participate in, and help to shape the program.

### V. Valuing the Community

- Keeping informed about developments and trends in the community;
- Evaluating whether one's organization is in touch with community needs;
- Coordinating with and supporting other community organizations; and
- Advocating for the needs of all children.

### VI. Valuing the Profession

- Supporting the efforts of effective professional organizations;
- Promoting public understanding of the professionalism of the child care; and
- Working to improve the quality of all programs.

These are indeed demanding standards. From our collective experiences, it would seem directors who guide their performance accordingly can truly be considered "professionals" who are improving the image of our "profession."

# Developing Your Skills

## Chapter 2

# When You Are the New Director — Finding Your Way with Staff

by Linda Riepe

*"Congratulations, you are the new center director!" This phrase generally causes a wide range of emotional reactions from a large number of people. The new hire certainly will be filled with excitement, anticipation, good ideas, and the desire to make meaningful contributions. Most likely, that excitement will be coupled with nervousness and anxiety about how to get off on the right foot. Other people are also reacting to the pending change. Among existing staff, the hiring committee is hopeful that they made the best choice and the entire group experiences nervousness as they anticipate the transition in leadership.*

Replacing the director of a program affords everyone involved an opportunity for growth. An excellent program can be taken to new heights. A program facing difficulties may find that change energizes burned out staff, providing them with the courage to face problems. New leadership certainly brings new ideas and energy into a program, but energy and ideas may not be enough.

Unfortunately, while change can and should be positive and meaningful, many programs suffer and deteriorate during the period of staff transition. If the change is not handled well or the new director is insensitive to the natural anxiety of the group, existing staff can inadvertently, or deliberately, set up traps that get in the way of new ideas, viewpoints, and progress. The stumbling blocks that cause problems are set in place by the fears and personal insecurities of existing staff.

Whatever a situation may be, good or bad, we all live in comfort zones. Those zones trap us into hanging on to that which is familiar and can have a stifling impact on potential growth. For many people, a new leader shakes them out of their work-related comfort zone, tapping into insecurities. Once that process is in place, worry and anxiety color communications and interfere with the potential effectiveness of the new person. It really is not the person so much as the position and the power of the position that are troublesome. It makes little difference if the job is filled from within existing staff or from outside the organization, the change itself is fertile soil for the development and growth of problems.

When you are the new person, navigating your way through these thinly veiled pitfalls can be a harrowing experience. It is the nature of the human condition to allow insecurity to create problems where none exist. Anxious staff may worry about personal job security or possible policy changes the new person may want to make. If the new leader comes from within, prior conflicts or allegiances become a factor, each creating a unique set of problems. If the leader comes from outside the program, she is an "unknown quantity."

While no leadership transition is likely to happen seamlessly, the following road map (with appropriate caution signs) can prevent wrong turns, dead-end streets, and serious speed bumps, allowing the director to avoid some of the roadblocks along the way.

First, having an understanding of the problems commonly associated with leadership change is a critical piece. If you understand the natural anxiety issues that concern staff members, it can keep you on course in the face of resistance. To not have this understanding complicates problems and increases tension. The knowledge about staff needs also minimizes reactivity.

If a new director is going to survive and thrive, it is useful to move into a new job with some degree of caution. That is not to say that you should hide in an office for fear of saying or doing the wrong thing. What it does mean is that you allow time to observe the existing operation and fully develop an understanding of current center culture. By taking time to learn firsthand what works and does not work, you demonstrate your respect for ideas and work that has come before you.

Even the worst organization will have functional components and talented people. A good manager will find those strengths and utilize them in the best interest of the center. By taking time to observe, getting acquainted with people, and looking at the big picture, you will have the opportunity to establish a solid beginning and lay the foundation necessary for the development of trust.

If work needs to be done to improve the operation, it is critical to involve the individuals who will be directly impacted by the changes. It is clear that individuals who are doing the front-line jobs or working in the problematic areas have feelings and ideas about the underlying causes of problems. They may well be your best source for seeking solutions.

Even in a situation where they have not known what to do, their involvement in the process is critical to future success. It is much the same as the problem solving process we use with children. Expecting anyone to adapt to rules or changes designed by others and handed down simply does not work.

One approach for getting off on the right foot with staff, regardless of the problems you may be facing, is to plan a full staff meeting fairly early in your employment. By gathering all of the players into a given space, you have the opportunity to formally greet everyone and to share your plan to do observations and your vision for how you will work together with everyone at the same time. This is a great way to avoid the natural inclination of staff members to lend their own interpretations to your words as they talk to others.

During this meeting, you could point out what your initial observations have revealed. Be sure to point out what appears to be working well before you mention areas of concern or suggest any changes. In some situations, you will already be charged with the task of making a specific change and the staff may know that to be the case. Regardless, bringing the staff into the process early is critical to the development, success, and management of any change.

After a reasonable observation time has passed, meet again to define your task(s) with the staff. Engage their assistance in clarification of the nature of problems. This is true at all times, but critical in the beginning when your own newness may give the impression that you don't understand or appreciate the big picture. Remember that staff may have a level of understanding about the problem beyond what is clear to you.

Granted, staff members may be too close to the problem to have complete objectivity. If they have been doing battle with issues for a long time, they may need the director's facilitation skills to bring clarity to the discussion.

Once the problem has been defined, you can begin the process of jointly developing solutions. It is most desirable to use some form of decision by consensus. If you don't have experience with that process, many resource models are available. If you have the good fortune to begin a job with a problem-free program, a similar approach can be used to highlight program strengths and encourage staff to continue their good work. It can also be a time to consider potential areas of growth or expansion.

When staff members see for themselves that you are not a dictator, they will experience a collective sigh of relief. You will have a solid footing for starting the working relationship and establishing an atmosphere of trust. Be aware that the staff will continue to watch your actions. They need to see for themselves if you will do what you say. Demonstrate to them that your words are followed up with actions. Those actions may come in the form of completing assigned tasks, providing any needed support and encouragement to individual groups, or arranging for resources.

The history of the previous director's actions, both good and bad, will be a part of the environment. You may be following in the footsteps of a trusted and adored friend, or a feared dictator. "Trust me" as a statement is an inadequate way to gain the trust of staff. Respect and trust will have to be earned.

Style issues can also get in the way of acceptance from others. A great deal of study has been done in the arena of personal styles. Clearly, differences in style and how various styles work together should not be overlooked. By understanding our own personal style along with the styles of coworkers, we have the opportunity to adjust our approach and create more reasonable and appropriate expectations from others.

It is particularly helpful when all individuals in a work environment have some exposure to, and understanding of, style issues. Many initial barriers can be broken down during an in-service on this topic. Routine communication problems, such as assigning motives to others' actions, often relate to something as simple as a style difference.

Finally, the personality characteristics and behavior of the director are an important component for successful leadership. The need for using ethical means to reach ethical ends is a benchmark for leadership. Everyone must know that they will be treated fairly, that confidences will be honored, and that personal needs will be considered whenever possible.

The integrity, or lack thereof, of the person in charge sets the tone for the organization. Every aspect of your performance and your personal style play into that tone. We know that risk taking is part of making progress and moving to new heights. Staff members are reluctant and unlikely to take those risks if they do not trust the integrity and ethics of the management person.

Regardless of what problems the organization may face, the leader must be willing and able to operate as an ethical model. In day-to-day interactions, a leader needs to have the ability to be a good listener, to control her own reactivity, and to avoid interfering with the productivity of others.

Much of what is needed in finding your place as a new director has to do with the passage of time. Only real experiences with the staff will allow you to demonstrate your value and trustworthiness to the center.

If you are the new kid on the block, or an old kid with a new hat, the existing group will initially view you and your actions with reservation and suspicion. Any new supervisor who quickly makes sweeping changes, or announces that major changes are coming down the pike, is pouring fuel on a simmering fire. It is much easier to move people to a new and better place when they choose to walk on their own than if you try to drag them kicking and screaming.

In today's world, the only certainty seems to be change. Your challenge as a program leader is finding ways to manage change yourself and to assist others in the process.

# Power Lines — The Use and Abuse of Power in Child Care Programming

by Pauline Davey Zeece

*The last teacher walked into the room, rushed and five minutes late. All eyes turned to her as the director stopped the meeting and spoke: "I was just about to tell the group that merit pay for the year will be determined by behavior at this meeting!" People laughed tentatively. The director's humor sent a ripple of reactions throughout the group. The incident was quick and unrecorded in the minutes of the meeting, but the effects lingered for a long time afterwards.*

The use and abuse of power impact every aspect of early childhood education programming. Part of the functional and necessary role of a competent director involves influencing the attitudes and controlling the behavior of subordinates on a continuing basis. In every program, a director assumes responsibility for making and enforcing decisions that may not be unilaterally understood or accepted. In every child care setting, one of the supervisory vehicles used to carry out such responsibility is power. Yet the notion of power in child care programs is a curious phenomenon. Without its use in some form, programs would revert to a frightening state of disarray — even grind to a halt. With discussion of its presence or legitimacy, directors may feel uncomfortable and staff members may act defensively. For many programs, power is used but not discussed, a technique to be acted upon but never collectively explored or analyzed. As a result, power usage may be structured or developed in isolation and sometimes abused.

## Power and Ethics

The job of administering a child care program is permeated by ethics. Directors, by nature of their position, are powerful. As such, they affect people's lives and well-being, distribute organizational resources, and design and implement rules and policies. These activities and responsibilities give administrators control over others in a wide variety of ways. Thus, the abuse of power can have ethical as well as business consequences.

## Basis of Supervisory Power

Many years ago, French and Raven (1959) identified five kinds of supervisory power bases: Coercive, reward, legitimate, expert, and referent. This model still guides much of the current thinking and research in the area of power and management so it is useful to apply it to child care.

### Coercive Power

Staff perceive that a director has the ability to punish them for non-compliance or non-conformity (Rahim and Buntzman, 1989).

**Pros:** Coercive power can be very effective in the short term or during crises where quick, definitive decision making is needed. It may be useful when a program is out of control as a director establishes consequences for actions that will not be tolerated under any circumstances (e.g., adult aggression on a child always results in termination).

**Cons:** In the long term, a director who uses primarily coercive power will create an externally controlled staff. Desired behavior often continues only in the presence of fear or anticipation of punishment. Staff's internalized motivation is not fostered — fear, resentment, passive aggressiveness, and powerlessness may appear. All these contribute to potentially weakened, non-productive, or even destructive staff attitudes and behavior.

### Reward Power

Staff perceive that a director can reward them for desired behavior (Rahim and Buntzman, 1989).

**Pros:** Rewards can be a powerful way to mold behavior and influence the attitudes of staff. Rewarding staff appropriately lets them know they are an important functioning part of a child care program. Rewards help people to think of themselves as competent and confident when directors are supportive. Responsible administrators who utilize reward power use a variety of reinforcements to maintain or change staff behavior. They know rewards mean different things to different people.

**Cons:** Reward power does not always influence behaviors in ways a director predicts. Those who are not rewarded may feel anger or resentment; those who are rewarded may feel discomfort or embarrassment. Sometimes highly intrinsically motivated staff may become more dependent on external motivation — decreasing their internal drive to do well or act in the ways a director wants. In a sense, rewards backfire by lessening a staff member's original, natural behavior.

### Legitimate Power

Staff perceive that a director has the right to prescribe and control their behavior (Rahim and Buntzman, 1989).

**Pros:** Legitimate power is supported by staff respect for the position or role of "director as boss" in a program. As such, staff do what they are told, despite their personal convictions, because they believe the director has the right to make and enforce regulations and rules.

**Cons:** Directors may be driven by their right to prescribe and control. They sometimes lose sight of the importance in seeking input from staff. Staff may find themselves in conflict with their beliefs and actions when they obey legitimate power that mandates actions that violate personal beliefs. Having legitimate power does not guarantee having the understanding or knowledge to use it wisely.

### Expert Power

Staff perceive that a director has job experience and/or special knowledge or expertise (Rahim & Buntzman, 1989).

**Pros:** When legitimately bestowed, expert power puts a director in a good position to instruct and lead others. It provides for a bridge between the "what" and "why" of child care programming. Staff comply because they believe decisions and requests are based on competence. Subordinates are most likely to be satisfied with supervision based on expert or referent power than any other kind.

**Cons:** Power based on expertise and knowledge is not tied exclusively to the educational level of an administrator. To use this power base well, a director must understand how these are related to solving the everyday crises of child care programming. A danger arises when either staff or director have an unrealistic view of director knowledge or experience or when a director stops learning in the context of his or her management position.

### Referent Power

Staff identify with a director because of their admiration or personal liking of that person (Rahim & Buntzman, 1989).

**Pros:** Directors operating from this power base are very effective. Oftentimes staff will go to great or unusual lengths to do their jobs well when working under the influence of referent power. The atmosphere in a program is positive — sometimes infectious. Even when hours are long and resources are limited, directors are perceived as acting in the best interest of staff and program. They are seen as inspirational.

**Cons:** Life on a pedestal can be lonely, if not frightening. Referent power creates a leadership style that causes people to follow without always thinking or questioning. The responsibility to do self-checks and monitoring becomes very important. Acknowledgment of mistakes and explanations for decisions and actions help staff to understand why things happen (or don't happen).

## So What Does It All Mean?

The opening incident could be perceived in five different ways, depending on how staff members view the director's management style. In all human interactions, perceptions are subjective and unique. No two people will ever perceive the same interaction in an identical way. Over time, however, a group perception about director style emerges. This is based on the patterns and processes an administrator uses to do the day-to-day work of child care programming. It also involves the way individual problems and crises are managed.

Understanding the group perception about the primary power base used allows a director to anticipate effects and mitigate negative consequences. Rarely, however, does a director rely on only one power base. Combinations are used in connection with different situations involving different personnel. Patterns develop and become more apparent over time.

## Short Circuits to Powerful and Effective Management

Here are some short circuits to effective power usage in child care management:

### Short Circuit #1:
*Do As I Say and Not As I Do*

When administrators mandate and enforce policy for staff, but disregard it themselves, this short circuit occurs. It fosters a sense of resentment and disrespect toward the director, and a sense of detachment from and disregard for the program and its goals. Such behavior often creates a hierarchy of compliance, so that rules are followed according to rank or position. Control becomes relative and tenuous.

**Examples:** An administrator says "No Smoking" but smokes in his office. Punishment for sharing information inappropriately might be levied against a staff by a director who engages in gossip with her program confidants. More subtly, power is abused when a leader says such conflicting things as "I don't care how you feel about this, in this program we will all respect one another."

**Circuit Breakers:**

- What rules and policies/practices are most important to me? Others?
- What exceptions do I make? For myself? For others? Why? How?
- What ways do I have to obtain feedback about my performance? How do I utilize such information?
- Are there any "boss only" behaviors permitted? How did these evolve? What rationale is there for their continuance?

### SHORT CIRCUIT #2:
### *Speak Softly and Carry a Big Stick*

A sense of confidence and competence comes from ongoing experiences of being accepted rather than rejected and of feeling safe rather than threatened. Effective power usage is compromised when a director says all the right things (e.g., "We are here to work together to create a partnership), but engages in punitive and/or vengeful actions when challenged. Such mixed messages not only threaten employees' sense of security but potentially also create fear, anger, and an externally controlled staff. Communication and collective problem solving are hampered.

**Examples:** Some Big Stick bosses may make overt threats, such as "You will do it my way or else." They are more likely to veil their coercive power by using public humiliation, inappropriate humor, or denial of resources to offending subordinates. The key to the abuse here rests in the inappropriate use of power and punishment over others. In one center when this short circuit occurred frequently, a five year old was overheard telling a young friend about the director: "She's always nice when company's here and then she gets mean when they go away."

**Circuit Breakers:**

- What power style do I use most? In what ways? Under what circumstances? With whom?
- Do I change my demeanor or behavior in front of non-staff members? How? When? Why?
- If I advocate cooperation and community building, how do I support achieving it (be specific)? Do I interact the same way with everyone as I work toward this goal? How can I be sure?
- What would be my first reaction to dealing with employees who challenge me? Does this change? Why? How? Is it effective? How do I know?

### SHORT CIRCUIT #3:
### *Lying King (or Queen)*

This is perhaps the most destructive short circuit because it so completely undermines a sense of trust and respect among people. Few (if any) administrators get up in the morning and plan to lie to staff or misrepresent to others. Instead, directors may get caught in a lie when they have made an error they do not want to acknowledge or have discovered an embarrassing event or activity in a program. Sometimes directors misrepresent, rather than tell employees they are unwilling or unable to share information.

Directors who consistently lie will eventually end up being the only ones who trust themselves. Staff learn quickly not to believe what is said and to engage in lying themselves.

**Examples:** Overt lying is easy to identify. A director may under fire lose his temper and tell a staff member one thing in anger, later to learn that personnel policies and regulations were violated. To save face, the director denies the comments. More subtle deception may take place when an administrator tells staff not to tell a parent that medication has been forgotten or inappropriately administered or that a child no longer cries throughout nap time. A director may take sole credit for the work or creative efforts of subordinates. The model of deceit becomes the method of operation for the center and quality erodes as trusting interactions disappear.

**Circuit Breakers:**

- Am I generally truthful to staff? Are there exceptions? Why? When?
- Are staff truthful with parents? Children? Each other? How do I know? Is there a clear payoff for truthful behavior in the program?
- What mechanisms are in place to help staff deal with others (including me) they feel have lied to them? How are these monitored? What level of effectiveness occurs?
- Have I developed a way to help staff understand why some things cannot or will not be shared with them? Does this work? How do I know? Does staff have input? What kind?

## Short Circuit #4:
### *Higher Ups Who Hire Down*

Hiring new personnel provides a wealth of opportunities and challenges to a director and program. A confident, secure, and professional director seeks to hire the best staff possible — even when they may bring more experience or knowledge to a program than the director possesses.

The message to everyone is "We are all teachers and learners here!" Abuse occurs when an administrator excludes from a pool or fails to hire a highly competent person because she or he may assume expert status in the program. Examples: Hire Power Abuse may happen when a director structures a hiring committee that is subtly powerless, or when directors change job requirements in midstream of a hiring process to keep a highly competent (and perhaps professionally threatening) candidate out. Such actions might carry legal as well as ethical consequences for a program.

**Circuit Breakers:**

- What qualifications are needed to do this job? How were these determined? How will they be evaluated?
- What role will I play? What safeguards are in place to ensure there is a check on this role?
- What criteria can I use to develop a hiring process? To identify a hiring committee?
- What policies/processes are in place to ensure ethical conduct? To identify vested interests? To follow legal processes?

## Short Circuit #5:
### *All the Write Stuff*

Words and messages appear everywhere in a child care program. Directors' written words carry as much power as do their verbal ones. Abuse occurs when an administrator uses written communication as punishment or a hidden agenda to seek revenge for being challenged. Overtly hurtful or destructive written communication may be particularly harmful because a staff member may share with others or read it over and over again.

**Examples:** Blatantly inappropriate written communication includes things that are inaccurate, incomplete, or unrelated to the professional dialogue between director and staff. This may occur when a director deliberately omits crucial information or incomplete documents. Subtle (but equally unethical) behavior occurs when written acknowledgments are differential, innuendo is rampant, and/or information is only sporadically supplied to selected staff. Rarely does this behavior go unnoticed by others.

**Circuit Breakers:**

- How/when is written communication used in the program?
- What mechanism is in place to monitor its effectiveness? Is there ongoing feedback from staff about ways to improve it?
- What criteria is used to determine that a negative communication is to be written? Where is this kept? How is such information filed?
- Do I have a recognizable or predictable pattern/style for communicating or responding to staff? What is this? Have I ever had this style evaluated by an objective other?

## Short Circuit #6:
### *The Clique Heard Round the Center*

The larger a program is (or becomes), the more likely it is that there will be incremental levels of an administrative structure. When small programs grow larger, some employees may feel left out or left behind as this structure evolves. Directors may seek out specific staff members to serve as advisors in specific areas; this, too, can be perceived as differential treatment. Yet a director has the right to seek the best possible choice.

Abusive power management occurs when a director forms an "inside" group with some staff, primarily to meet a personal or emotional need. This abuse is exacerbated when the group receives special/unearned privileges or inappropriate information.

**Examples:** Overt director/staff cliques form when people share "inside" jokes, eye rolls, and exclusive center-based information with each other. This behavior goes beyond cordial interaction or friendship because it is often exclusionary or inappropriate. More subtle cliquish behavior may involve less recognized distribution of resources, accolades, or status symbols. Cliques are divisive and destructive.

**Circuit Breakers:**

- What are structures for the formal and informal written information within the system organization?
- How is the written information system monitored? Accessed?
- In what ways is written communication used to inform staff? Parents? Larger community?
- What mechanism do I have to evaluate the subtle and overt impact of my written products on others?

### Short Circuit #7:
### *Being Boss Means Never Having to Say You're Sorry*

Acknowledging errors says to staff that human behavior is understood. It models a mind set in which accountability for behavior begins with oneself. When a director refuses, or is unable to acknowledge or admit mistakes, anger, suspicion, and resentment may surface. Such behavior may also deny directors the opportunity to learn from their own mistakes and help staff to do the same.

**Examples:** Not Sorry bosses are ones who never admit mistakes to others (or sometimes to themselves). They see such an acknowledgment as an indication of weakness or loss of face, rather than a declaration of humanness or an opportunity for growth. Such administrators may blame others and directly or indirectly refuse responsibility for error; they may conveniently forget unpleasant incidents/promises/actions that are viewed negatively by others, or reframe these so that accountability shifts or drops by the wayside.

**Circuit Breakers:**

- How do I deal with the mistakes I make in the context of my job as director?
- Do I tell others directly? Indirectly?
- Do I correlate mistakes to weakness? Ineptness? Incompetence? Strengths?
- Who monitors my successes and failures? How do I get feedback? What do I do when others bring my mistakes to my attention?

## And So . . .

Power and its management go hand in hand with being a director. Used as a weapon, power facilitates the development of a destructive stream of actions and attitudes. Used as a tool, it provides a means to order, regulate, and move a program ahead. Power used wisely and well provides a positive force in child care programming.

## References


Abdel-Halem, A. (1983). "Power Equalization, Participative Decision Making, and Individual Differences." *Human Relations, 36(8)*, 683-704.

Abdel-Halem, A. (1980). "Power Equalization and Work Effectiveness: An Empirical Investigation." *Journal of Occupational Behavior, 1*, 223-237.

Brady, F. N. (1990). *Ethical Managing: Rules and Results*. New York: Macmillan Publishing.

French, J., & Raven, B. (1959). "The Bases of Social Power." In D. Cartwright (editor), *Social Studies in Power* (pp. 150-167). Ann Arbor, MI: Institute for Social Research.

Rahim, M. (1986). "Some Psychometric Properties of Two Measures of French and Raven Bases of Power." *Journal of Psychology, 120(1)*, 465-472.

Rahim, M., & Buntzman, G. (1989). "Supervisory Power Bases, Style of Handling Conflict with Subordinates, and Subordinate Compliance and Satisfaction." *Journal of Psychology, 123(2)*, 195-210.

# Enjoying the Good Lice: Managing Crises

**by Pauline Davey Zeece**

> *"It is what we do rather than what we feel or say we do that reflects who and what we truly are."*
>
> — Leo Buscagalia quoted by D. Lynch and P. Kordis in *Strategy of the Dolphin: Scoring a Win in a Chaotic World,* New York: Ballentine Books, 1988

The first time I ever saw lice hopping from curl to curl on a small child's head was over 15 years ago. The critters were so small and quick (the lice that is) that I had to blink twice before I could process what I was seeing. And when the realization finally struck me, I felt compelled to shift my weight, to scratch my scalp . . . and quite honestly to exit quickly.

To make matters worse, one of the other teachers who had also never seen lice but who believed that "such things only inflicted impoverished people" had systematically checked the heads of 22 children **with the same comb**. By the end of the week, the school was involved in a lice crisis of major proportions. Teachers, staff, children, and families had been afflicted and the local pharmacist had become wealthy.

I am pleased to report that the out-break claimed no long term casualties; everyone did survive. In subsequent times and other places amidst a lice event, I have been more able to act effectively. I now am actually beginning to control my head scratching. You might say that I am learning from lice, or at least from their presence in early childhood programs.

With this in mind, how can administrators learn to manage this and other crises constructively and to use these as opportunities for learning?

## Best Kept Crisis Secrets

■ **Crises happen.**

Crises are a predictable part of life, and therefore a predictable part of child care programming. Quality programming is not necessarily characterized by absence of crisis, instead it is identified by presence of effective crisis management. Accepting that crises **will** and **do** occur is the first step in dealing with them well.

> *The sky is falling, the sky is falling.*
>
> — Chicken Little

Another important part of crisis management is understanding how crisis happens — this can be accomplished by actually charting crisis events. In doing this, a director can develop a crisis pattern or profile for a program. Such a profile typically consists of five W's: what, when, where, who, and why.

**What.** Understanding the **what** of a crisis can be deceptively simple. This is particularly true when crisis is interpersonal rather than programmatic in nature. A cook who walks off the job 30 minutes before lunch or a child with a broken finger is a clearly recognizable crisis. But a group of parents who collectively decide not to support a teacher or a staff person who burns out is less specifically pinpointed.

> *No one is ever old enough to know better.*
>
> — Holbrook Jackson quoted by Jon Winokur in *Friendly Advice,* New York: Dutton, 1990

Really understanding what happens in a crisis entails separating **facts** from **interpretation**. For example, "The cook left the building at 11:30 am today and said she was never coming back" is a fact. "The cook stomped out of the kitchen and quit because she was angry at everyone" is an interpretation. Both bits of information are useful, but in different ways. Collecting facts over time about programmatic crises enables a director to chart events and sometimes to predict and head off disaster before it strikes.

Interpersonal crises may be less easily charted. These may need to be monitored by attending closely to the interpretation of a fact or a collection of facts surrounding a crisis. For example, the fact that "Marba hasn't smiled or spoken to anyone in the center for a week" may be less critical information in dealing with an interpersonal scrisis than the interpretation that "Marba is burning out and has appeared depressed and withdrawn for some time." Most times, crises are handled best when accurate facts **and** interpretation are considered.

*It often happens that we only become aware of the importance of facts if we suppress the question 'Why?' and then in the course of our investigation these facts lead us to an answer.*

— Ludwig Wittgenstein
quoted by D. Lynch and P. Kordis
in *Strategy of the Dolphin: Scoring a Win in a Chaotic World,*
New York: Ballentine Books, 1988

**When.** It should not come as a surprise to learn that more accidents involving young children occur when adults and/or children are tired, hungry, bored, or under undue stress. When you think about it, this includes just about everything that happens to adults and children in a child care setting except sleep. And anyone who has spent time in a naproom can testify that this too can be a hazard area.

Crises then are affected by timing. Right before lunch and nap and late afternoon are prime times for children to get hurt. And hurt children precipitate crises of all sorts. Charting when crises occur in a program can help a director identify critical periods.

Adults can also have identifiable "down times" in child care settings. It would be helpful to learn what contributes to these times in your program. Take a few minutes to jot down the last five crises with which you have dealt. When did these occur? Do you see a pattern? Were these adult or child crises (or both)? What can you learn from understanding the timing of these events?

**Where.** As children and adults learn to live and work with each other in a child care setting, they construct cognitive maps about how the space around them is to be used. What this means for young children is that they develop ideas about where things should happen — this is where I play blocks, this is where I sleep when it is naptime, this is where I run. Crisis looms when there are unclear messages about space usage or when people live and work together for long hours each day in an overcrowded child care setting. Without clear boundaries, both children and adults are more apt to experience difficulties.

In the lab school we have a wonderful patch of mature pine trees which children call the "forest." When weather permits, teachers will often take tents and camp in this forest with children. A minor crisis evolved with the grounds department when the shrubbery around the camping area began to die . . . it appears some children were taking a rustic approach to toileting. Obviously, the cognitive map for camping at school and at home had not been clearly drawn.

On a more serious note, **where** may also contribute to interpersonal crises. Where do you speak with staff or parents when there is a problem? Is it always in the same place? What else happens there? Do you ask staff to trust and share openly in this same place? Is it on your turf or theirs? Or, better still, is it ever in a neutral location?

The last two W's (who and why) fall under the next secret about crisis.

■ **Blame doesn't work.**

**Who.** Blame for the sake of blame builds neither individual character nor strong early childhood programs. Equally important, it has never been demonstrated that self-flogging clears the mind or sharpens the skills of a child care administrator. Thus, the importance of understanding **who** rests in the power of unraveling the roles **everyone** plays during a crisis.

The work of child care is a collaborative effort; nothing happens in a vacuum. The good and bad, the successes and failures, the highs and lows of a program all contribute to its milieu. It might be useful to know who told the cook he was tired of burned food just five minutes before she quit and stormed out. But equally useful to understand would be how every person, as well as the demands of the cook's job itself, contributed to an unmanageable situation for one person.

Charting the who of crises in a program allows an administrator to see a different kind of worker profile. Over time it can be determined if one or two workers are always in the eye of the storm or if others are always the ones to calm the waters and pick up the pieces. Both groups of people need support in different ways.

As your profile begins to develop, look to see where **you** fit. What role do you typically play during crisis? How would workers categorize you if they were developing their own profile?

**Why.** Asking **why** in the heat of a crisis is like demanding that a three year old explain why she stuck a grape up her nose. In both instances, why usually does little to solve the immediate situation or to shed light on a long term solution. Thus, why is best asked after the passion of the moment has subsided and after all the other W's have been processed. This is so because why is the interaction among the who, when, where, and what of a crisis.

When management of crisis is approached in this way, the why of a difficult situation may actually be understood before anyone even poses the question. Understanding the why of a crisis also allows directors to polish their own panic and increase their own effectiveness in dealing with crisis. This occurs when directors:

- take time to understand the role model they set within a program and to learn how their response matches those of others;
- set time for regular "crisis drills" to discuss the merits of solving hypothetical crises in a variety of ways;
- and recognize and reward effective crisis resolution in an ongoing way within their programs.

But this is not to say that every crisis can be accurately anticipated, perfectly dissected, or even clearly understood. There are things that happen in day-to-day life that cannot always be explained; there are also circumstances over which an administrator may have little or no control. Thus, like all of the other W's, why is only one of many tools to be used to better manage crisis.

■ **Not all crises are bad.**

The last best kept secret is that crisis is not always bad. Granted, when children or adults get hurt, when people lose self-respect or self-esteem, when resources or circumstances dictate impossible decisions where no one feels good about the outcome, crisis injures a program. But in other instances, it may actually be instructive or even healthy.

Through effective crisis management, one can come to the understanding that all crises are potential opportunities for learning. As such, directors learn to assign and/or accept responsibility for error without condemning themselves or others and without giving up. They learn to put each crisis on a continuum and to ask themselves: "What is the importance and the consequence of this action today, tomorrow, next month, next year?"

And, finally, directors can learn to evaluate the full spectrum of crisis effects. When crisis damages beyond repair, it brings a special kind of challenge to an administrator. When crisis discourages, it is, at best, cumbersome. When crisis devastates people or programs, it is destructive.

But when crisis fosters close inspection of philosophy, policy, or practice, it is useful. When crisis requires collective ownership of a mutual problem and mandates collaborative solution, it is powerful. When crisis butts heads with apathy and paves the way for meaningful and effective change, it is worth the effort it engenders.

Crises can be crippling if they are not taken seriously. But competent administrators learn to monitor the pulse of a program so as to best understand the magnitude of a crisis and its fall out.

Effective managers then are able to use crisis to learn and to make their programs better and stronger and less vulnerable the next time around.

*The play-it-all pessimists of the world never accomplish much of anything because they don't look clearly and objectively at situations, they don't recognize or believe in their own abilities, and they won't stretch their abilities to overcome even the smallest amount of risk.*

— Benjamin Hoff in *The Tao of Pooh*, New York: Penguin Books, 1982

## References

Hoff, B. (1982). *The Tao of Pooh.* New York: Penguin Books.

Jackson, H. (1990). *Friendly Advice.* New York: Dutton.

Lynch, D., & Kordis, P. (1988). *Strategy of the Dolphin: Scoring a Win in a Chaotic World.* New York: Ballentine Books.

# How Are You Doing? A Center Director Self-Review Tool

by Karen L. Talley

The idea for a Self-Review for directors was born out of two separate Boston Association for the Education of Young Children initiatives. Members of the Committee on Administrative Leadership and the Director's Breakfast Group began discussing the need for director support and professional development. Eventually, seven members of these groups formed a committee to develop a process and related instruments which would fill the needs expressed by their colleagues.

The process itself is completely self-directed and can take as long as you would like. Above all, it is intended to be a private tool. Rate yourself through your own eyes using the General Survey.

A second approach would be to rate yourself through the eyes of those who are knowledgeable of your professional skills. When you are ready to venture out to others for feedback, duplicate the General Survey for distribution. Prior to duplication, place NR next to those criteria for which you do not have direct responsibility. Once the surveys are complete, they should be returned to you for your own personal analysis.

The surveys are for your information only and can be used in any way which fits your needs. We suggest that after you've had a chance to compile the information, you look for a pattern or specific focus area which may indicate a goal for professional development. Then devise and implement a plan of action which would accomplish this goal. A follow-up survey could later be conducted to evaluate your success. To compile your results, enter in the total score at the end of each focus area. Next, determine the number of N and NR scores and subtract them from the total of possible responses. For example, in focus area I. Program, there are 15 possible responses. If one has been rated NR and one rated N, the total score would be divided by 13. Therefore, if the total is 36, the average rating would be 36 ÷ 13 = 2.77.

You may find it helpful to compile the results based on the positions of the evaluators. Teachers' responses could be compared to those of another group such as board members or parents.

This tool has been developed to assist on-site directors in their professional growth. We do not recommend it be used as a basis for employment continuation, for hiring, or for salary determination. Nor do we recommend that this tool be used by executive directors who are not directly responsible for daily operations.

## Director Self-Review General Survey

Using the following key, please rate each question below.

KEY

| | | | | |
|---|---|---|---|---|
| 3 | = | Usually | N | = Not sure |
| 2 | = | Sometimes | NR | = Not Responsible (prior to duplicating, the director will place NR next to those criteria for which others have direct responsibility) |
| 1 | = | Seldom | | |

NOTE — For each section, attach a separate page for comments.

### I. Program

Does the director:

a. communicate the mission to staff and parents? a. __________

b. support developmentally appropriate curriculum? b. __________

c. encourage development of educational goals for all children? c. ________
d. provide adequate materials and equipment? d. ________
e. ensure a clean, healthy environment? e. ________
f. ensure a safe environment? f. ________
g. maintain materials and equipment in proper working order? g. ________
h. support diverse staff and families (including race, religion, cultural heritage, political beliefs, national origin, disability, marital status, and sexual orientation)? h. ________
i. encourage parent/teacher communication? i. ________
j. maintain proper teacher/child ratios? j. ________
k. encourage appropriate staff/child interaction? k. ________
l. support the emotional well-being of children? l. ________
m. encourage healthy food choices? m. ________
n. follow and reinforce program policies? n. ________
o. implement a yearly program evaluation? o. ________

For director's use only: Total ________ Average ________

Comments:
(Please elaborate on both strengths and areas for growth. Be as specific as possible.)

## II. Work Environment

Does the director:

a. foster a positive work environment? a. ________
b. respect people as individuals and shape expectations accordingly? b. ________
c. provide for staff supervision that promotes growth and good teaching? c. ________
d. advocate for personnel benefits? d. ________
e. encourage innovation? e. ________
f. proactively recruit new staff? f. ________
g. hire competent staff? g. ________
h. orient new staff? h. ________
i. communicate clearly defined expectations (including job descriptions)? i. ________
j. inform staff about schedule and policy changes? j. ________
k. develop staffing that provides continuity of care for children? k. ________
l. make her/himself available to staff? l. ________
m. offer opportunities for training and development? m. ________
n. provide for fair, effective staff evaluation? n. ________
o. implement program policies fairly? o. ________
p. provide adequate substitutes? p. ________
q. plan regular staff meetings? q. ________
r. encourage staff retention? r. ________
s. terminate inappropriate staff? s. ________
t. support cooperation and team effort? t. ________
u. greet staff members warmly and show personal interest? u. ________
v. respond to staff questions and concerns? v. ________
w. give staff positive feedback? w. ________
x. welcome suggestions from staff? x. ________
y. share reasons for decisions when relevant? y. ________
z. encourage creative problem-solving? z. ________
aa. help to resolve conflicts among staff members when appropriate? aa. ________
bb. offer support and help as needed? bb. ________

cc. know when and how to assist a teacher? cc. ________
dd. assist each teacher in developing a professional growth plan? dd. ________
ee. allow for flexibility in scheduling? ee. ________

For director's use only: Total ________ Average ________

Comments:
(Please elaborate on both strengths and areas for growth. Be as specific as possible.)

## III. Budget and Finance

Does the director:

a. keep the staff informed of relevant budget issues (impact of enrollment on staff salaries, costs of materials and supplies)? a. ________
b. respond to staff input on the budget? b. ________
c. identify alternative funding sources when appropriate? c. ________
d. participate in budget/finance planning and management? d. ________
e. present a realistic budget? e. ________
f. maintain accurate records? f. ________
g. oversee the bookkeeping system? g. ________
h. manage revenue sources? h. ________
i. monitor expenses? i. ________
j. establish clear financial policies? j. ________
k. communicate financial practices? k. ________
l. promote fair and equitable financial policy implementation? l. ________
m. encourage fundraising when necessary? m. ________
n. maintain inventory records? n. ________

For director's use only: Total ________ Average ________

Comments:
(Please elaborate on both strengths and areas for growth. Be as specific as possible.)

## IV. Public Relations and Community Outreach

Does the director:

a. promote the program in the community at large? a. ________
b. participate in public relations and marketing activities? b. ________
c. clearly communicate enrollment policies? c. ________
d. practice fair enrollment procedures? d. ________
e. develop fair enrollment procedures? e. ________
f. analyze market conditions? f. ________
g. advocate for children and for quality programs in the community? g. ________
h. make good use of program and community resources (including the services of public schools, libraries, and the medical profession)? h. ________
i. foster public awareness of early childhood issues? i. ________

| | | | |
|---|---|---|---|
| j. | network with other directors? | j. | ________ |

For director's use only: Total ________ Average ________

Comments:
(Please elaborate on both strengths and areas for growth. Be as specific as possible.)

## V. Family Relations

Does the director:

| | | | |
|---|---|---|---|
| a. | maintain a positive rapport with the families? | a. | ________ |
| b. | utilize parent suggestions if appropriate? | b. | ________ |
| c. | demonstrate sensitivity to individual needs of parents? | c. | ________ |
| d. | know when to say "no"? | d. | ________ |
| e. | use discretion when discussing a child with others? | e. | ________ |
| f. | help to resolve conflicts with families when appropriate? | f. | ________ |
| g. | inform and support parents on child development issues? | g. | ________ |
| h. | encourage families to participate in the program? | h. | ________ |
| i. | communicate effectively with parents? | i. | ________ |
| j. | provide parental support? | j. | ________ |
| k. | strive to be available to parents? | k. | ________ |
| l. | promote opportunities for parent education? | l. | ________ |
| m. | communicate program activities and events to families? | m. | ________ |
| n. | recommend outside support resources? | n. | ________ |
| o. | support special events — i.e., picnic/pot luck suppers? | o. | ________ |

For director's use only: Total ________ Average ________

Comments:
(Please elaborate on both strengths and areas for growth. Be as specific as possible.)

## VI. Planning and Administration

Does the director:

| | | | |
|---|---|---|---|
| a. | oversee program operations? | a. | ________ |
| b. | keep abreast of program issues as they arise? | b. | ________ |
| c. | handle day-to-day routines? | c. | ________ |
| d. | know what to do in a crisis? | d. | ________ |
| e. | cope with the demands of the job? | e. | ________ |
| f. | maintain a sense of humor and an ability to keep things in perspective? | f. | ________ |
| g. | comply with licensing standards? | g. | ________ |
| h. | manage legal and insurance issues? | h. | ________ |
| i. | keep the board and/or immediate supervisors informed? | i. | ________ |
| j. | meet deadlines? | j. | ________ |
| k. | manage short-term objectives? | k. | ________ |

| | | | |
|---|---|---|---|
| l. | facilitate the development of a long-term vision and goals? | l. | __________ |
| m. | keep necessary and current records on staff and children? | m. | __________ |
| n. | follow through on concerns of others? | n. | __________ |
| o. | provide records and information upon request? | o. | __________ |
| p. | manage time effectively? | p. | __________ |
| q. | facilitate program changes smoothly? | q. | __________ |
| r. | participate in policy development? | r. | __________ |

For director's use only: Total __________ Average __________

Comments:
(Please elaborate on both strengths and areas for growth. Be as specific as possible.)

## VII. Professionalism

Does the director demonstrate:

| | | | |
|---|---|---|---|
| a. | confidentiality? | a. | __________ |
| b. | impartiality? | b. | __________ |
| c. | resourcefulness? | c. | __________ |
| d. | current knowledge of early childhood theory and practice? | d. | __________ |
| e. | appropriate behavior with children — positively, at eye level, with respect? | e. | __________ |
| f. | communication skills? | f. | __________ |
| g. | organizational skills? | g. | __________ |
| h. | flexibility? | h. | __________ |
| i. | democratic leadership? | i. | __________ |
| j. | openness? | j. | __________ |
| k. | self-awareness? | k. | __________ |
| l. | self-confidence? | l. | __________ |
| m. | preparation for meetings? | m. | __________ |
| n. | professional ethics? | n. | __________ |
| o. | informed decision making? | o. | __________ |
| p. | integrity? | p. | __________ |
| q. | responsibility? | q. | __________ |
| r. | advocacy? | r. | __________ |
| s. | membership in professional organization/affiliations? | s. | __________ |

For director's use only: Total __________ Average __________

Comments:
(Please elaborate on both strengths and areas for growth. Be as specific as possible.)

*The following individuals contributed to this project: Linda England, Shirley Gallerani, Chris Giguere, Joyce Hollman, Nancy Jo Kessler, Gerry Pedrini, James Robertson, and Karen Talley.*

*The development of these materials was funded through a grant from New England AEYC.*

# Building and Rebuilding Your Credibility

by Roger Neugebauer

*"What happened to my credibility?" pondered Kathryn. Kathryn had been hired as director of the Hill Street Child Care Center when it was in crisis. The center was broke, its license had just been revoked, and two long-time teachers had just left to start their own center — taking many parents with them. Tempted to quit when she found out how bad the crisis was, Kathryn decided to give it a shot. She worked 60-hour weeks, doing everything from tearing down the old porch (that had cost the center its license) to teaching the three-year-old class, cooking meals, and driving all over town posting ads for teachers and parents.*

After two years, the center was back on its feet; three years later, Kathryn had the center accredited with a long waiting list.

Then one day she observed a teacher hitting a child. In accordance with center policies, she dismissed the teacher immediately. Also in accord with center policies, Kathryn could not disclose to parents or teachers the reason for the termination. Unfortunately, the dismissed teacher was very popular, and she felt no compunction about spreading the story that she was terminated because the director was jealous of her popularity. Pandemonium ensued; teachers were in revolt, and parents threatened to withdraw.

Over the weeks that it took to put out this fire, Kathryn couldn't help but wonder why, after sacrificing everything to save the center, she seemed to lose all her credibility in one afternoon.

Was her predicament fair? Of course not. Was her predicament unusual? Unfortunately not.

For center directors, establishing credibility with teachers and parents is not a one-time event. Credibility must be continuously built and rebuilt. To understand why this is so, it is necessary to understand that establishing credibility is based upon meeting mutual expectations.

## What Teachers Expect of a Center Director

- **Staff expect you to be an expert.** Staff respect a director who knows her stuff, who really understands how to deliver quality child care. They need to know that if they have a problem they can turn to the director and know they will get the support and guidance they need.

- **Staff expect you to know what's going on.** The most frequently voiced complaint about bosses is that they are out of touch with what is happening on the floor. A director loses credibility when teachers perceive (whether correctly or not) that he doesn't understand (or care about) the day-to-day issues they face.

- **Staff expect you to make good decisions.** Most decisions a director makes involve a mix of financial, organizational, and tactical factors, factors that few staff are aware of. For staff to have confidence in their director, they must trust that she is balancing all these factors wisely and making decisions that are in the best interests of the organization.

- **Staff expect you to listen.** Nothing is more demotivating than to believe that others do not respect your judgment. Teachers need to believe that the director values their opinions and takes their input (whether requested or volunteered) seriously.

- **Staff expect you to be fair.** In order for staff to respect you, they need to be convinced that you will treat them fairly when it comes to scheduling, raises, discipline, and attention.

So you can see that there are many areas where a director can slip up and not meet staff expectations, causing a lapse in credibility. But if a director is working hard to meet staff expectations, she can legitimately have certain expectations of her teachers.

## What Center Directors Expect of Teachers

- **Directors expect teachers to be committed to the organization.** You have the right to expect teachers to be loyal to your organization, to behave professionally at work during good times and bad, and to represent the organization well in the community.

- **Directors expect teachers to communicate concerns.** The hardest problems to solve are those you don't know about. Teachers may think they are doing you a favor by withholding bad news (about an upset parent, a child having trouble, or equipment not working), but by depriving you of the opportunity to fix a problem early, they run the risk of it turning into a crisis. For you to succeed, you depend upon staff to share concerns and problems before they are out of control.

- **Directors expect teachers to trust them.** Since you cannot consult every teacher about every decision you make, you need for them to trust your judgment, to give you the benefit of the doubt. If you are looking over your shoulder worrying about how staff will perceive every decision, your effectiveness will be undermined.

## What You Can Do to Maintain Credibility

You are not at the mercy of fate when it comes to maintaining your credibility. You can take an active hand in improving your credibility with some basic common sense actions:

- **Don't fool yourself.** Don't expect that the credibility you have earned from your heroic efforts in the past will last forever. If you take your credibility for granted, you may be in for a big surprise, much as the one that Kathryn experienced. Staff and parents have short memories when it comes to director accomplishments.

- **Keep current.** Your bachelors degree in child development may have been state of the art in 1975, but in case you haven't noticed, the field has moved on a bit since then. I still remember my third grade teacher, Mrs. Boetchen, who taught the same lesson plan on the same day year after year for her entire career. Those first few years it was probably an exciting class, but by the time I came on the scene, it was a bit tedious.

Directors can fall into the same rut, assuming their understanding of child development will hold for decades and as a result allowing their center to fall behind the times. You need to keep on top of new ideas in child and family development or you will not remain on top.

- **Keep visible.** If staff never see you in the classrooms, they will naturally assume you are out of touch. Setting aside specific times every week where you visit classrooms may or may not get you up to speed on the day-to-day issues facing teachers, but it will go a long way toward keeping staff assured that you have your finger on the pulse of the center.

- **Be fair.** Leadership textbooks instruct leaders in training to be scrupulously evenhanded in dealing with staff. "Don't play favorites" are the standard words to the wise. What the textbooks fail to tell you is that in real life you will have favorites. There will be some staff you absolutely worship and others you tolerate only because they seem to hit it off with the children and parents.

If you have such feelings, don't feel guilty — this is normal. What is abnormal, and destructive, is if you let your emotions dictate your treatment of staff — if you are always bending the rules to help the teachers you like and enforcing the letter of the law for those you don't. Once staff members perceive that you grant "most favored teacher" status to an in crowd, your credibility is on the skids.

- **Keep staff in the loop.** Fear of the unknown erodes confidence. Staff become insecure when they feel they don't know where their center is headed and what that means for them. Timely information can reduce most of this anxiety.

Many center directors are martyrs who like to carry all the burdens on their shoulders. If the center is losing enrollment and cash flow projections are troubling, such a director shields her staff from this scary news, hoping to resolve the situation before staff even learn about it. The problem with this line of thinking is that staff usually sense something is wrong and without firm information start worrying about worst-case scenarios.

Just as you do not want staff to protect you by withholding bad news, you should not be overly protective of your staff. Keep them in the loop about where the center is headed, about developments — good and bad. Particularly when change is on the way — when funding is about to be cut, when you are contemplating adding a new classroom, when you are thinking about redoing the schedule — prepare staff early for the change ahead.

- **Don't overstay your welcome.** Not all loss of credibility is subject to repair. At some point in your career, it is possible that staff may start losing confidence in you because you in fact are starting to lose your enthusiasm, or because you are starting to lose your ability to keep up with changes.

The problem is, if you are starting to lose your edge on the job, you are likely to be the last person to know this. While staff will complain freely to each other that you have lost some of your fire and savvy, they may be reluctant to share this feedback with you.

If you have been the director in one place for a long time, you need to find a confidant (someone on your board or maybe an outside consultant) who can evaluate your performance and give you honest feedback. If your confidant reports that your performance is starting to tail off, this indeed may be a sign that it is time to give serious consideration to moving on.

More likely, it may simply be a warning that you need to revitalize your commitment. There may be steps you can take to regain your edge. You can:

- change your focus from the day to day to the long range — pouring energy into developing a long-range plan for the organization.
- spend some time visiting other centers, both near and far, to get new ideas and to restimulate your creativity.
- change your role, turning over administrivia to a trusted assistant, and working less hours as the educational leader.
- recruit a sister center in another nation so that you, the teachers, and the children can enjoy the insights of communicating with peers in a different setting.
- start writing articles for *Exchange*.

Whatever you do, don't take your credibility for granted. Take the initiative — it will not only strengthen your rapport with staff but it may renew you enthusiasm.

# A Director's Lot Is Not a Happy One

**by Henry M. Morgan**

*Many early care and education directors occupy small but stressful domains within their organizations, wedged between staff and board. These positions often lead to what has been called role ambiguity resulting in role conflict.*

I first ran into this phenomenon when serving on my local school committee, wondering why the average life span of a school superintendent in our state was less than three years. School superintendents occupy the same space as child care directors, who are often caught in the same rate of turnover. What is there about these jobs that is so hard? Why do some directors and school superintendents make a career of it and some get caught in the revolving door? What do we know about which behavior in that role creates longevity and which doesn't? I want to explore some ideas with the readers. I hope that many of you will write to me, challenge or agree with what I have written so we can share and learn together.

The generation of these thoughts comes from two books from 30 years ago. While I constantly read the current literature, these remain as classics. The first is Organizational Stress — Studies in Role Conflict and Ambiguity by Kahn, Wolfe, Quinn, and Snoek (John Wiley & Sons, 1964) and the second is The Social Psychology of Organizations by Katz and Kahn (John Wiley & Sons, 1966). There is a lot of good new research on organizations, but I find comfort by referring back to these timeless classics.

Before applying these ideas of role conflict and role ambiguity, let me explain my concept of the role of an early care and education director. Of course, the role will differ with the type of organization — differ but not without similarities. In all forms of early care and education organizations, the director works at the boundaries within the organization with responsibilities internally for children, staff and programs. The director has another set of internal responsibilities to the parents and board. There are also a set of external responsibilities to regulators, funding sources, and communities.

The role conflict develops when we try to determine what makes for success. Is there the same criteria for success with the parents and the board; the same criteria for success with fee-paying parents and fee-absorbing staff; the same criteria for success with state regulation and the costs to parents? These different groups may have quite different perceptions of success. Everyone wants to believe that they are all in it together, primarily because we tend to believe that our perception of reality is truth, and other perceptions are wrong. Hopefully, we can get to a balanced set of criteria which will make everyone happy and there will be no ambiguity and no role conflict, but I don't think we are all there yet. Some are, some aren't.

One management text describes three domains in organizations: (1) policy and strategy; (2) administration; and (3) service delivery. In any organization, there is tension between these different domains. The board, with input from the director, is in domain (1). The director and central administrative staff are in (2). The teachers and other support staff are in (3). The time frames of these three are different: (1) is long term; (2) is intermediate term; and (3) tends to be day to day or week to week. These differences in responsibilities and time frames, along with budgetary constraints, are sources of role ambiguity and conflict.

The director is the one person in the organization with a foot in all the domains. The board (or owner) expects the director to interpret their perceptions to the staff; the staff expects the director to carry their concerns to the board or owner. Each expects loyalty from the director. Neither sees everything the director sees.

In addition to the role ambiguity and conflict, there is another problem for directors. In many organizations, particularly those which tend to be hierarchical, directors have trouble showing any kind of weakness or equivocation to their staff. As leaders, they're looked to by staff and parents for the answers. They don't want to be thought incompetent, but we all are incompetent at some times about some things. Similarly directors have trouble displaying doubts to their boards. The director is hired to be the expert in all aspects of running their centers, managing their staff, developing the appropriate curriculum, meeting all financial requirements, and on and on. The pressure to be omnipotent is draining. So where can a director turn for help? Where can a director show weakness?

In an ideal environment, directors can show vulnerability without fear of recourse from the board or a loss of confidence from the staff. I have been a part of such organizations, but they are rare.

Most child care directors serve several sets of stakeholders. These stakeholders range from parents to staff to children to board and so on. Take the simple case of the trilemma as expounded by my wife, Gwen Morgan. The trilemma is the budget tension among parents' fees, teachers' pay, and staffing ratios. It is actually a systems problem that cannot be solved at the program level. At present, however, it represents competing interests for too-scarce resources in most programs' budget processes.

Raising the salaries of staff would be seen as a victory by the staff, but if this results in significant cost to parents, they won't celebrate the same victory. Higher ratios of staff to children could give an opportunity to use the same amount of income spread over fewer people — higher pay without higher parental cost. *But* wait a minute — what about program quality and licensing requirements?

Higher staff ratios doesn't seem to be much of a victory for anyone, yet that is the primary way that public school costs are kept down. Teachers can negotiate for higher salaries, voters and public servants put caps on budgets. Voila! Larger classes — to the detriment of children's education. The delicate balance of the trilemma requires a tough act for directors with not much chance of a victory for anyone. Managing these stakeholders is one of the major sources of pressure for those in boundary jobs.

Even after there are systems improvements, this budget tension will probably remain as a central issue for decision-makers. I certainly felt the tension as a dean. I wanted to improve the classroom conditions by lowering class size and decreasing the teaching load. A big win for students and faculty but a very dicey situation with my president. As for vulnerabilities, there was no way I would reveal any uncertainties to that particular president.

Boundary jobs are lonely jobs. Where can you let loose and show your vulnerability? Actually these stressful conditions are not reserved for early care and education directors or for school superintendents. I have often been called by executives of large for-profit organization to do consulting. At first I was puzzled. Why are they asking me to spend time with them? I soon realized that there was no one with whom they could share their doubts and vulnerabilities. They knew I would go away and have no impact on their careers. They were simply lonely and insecure, with no one to talk to. I just listened and for that I was worth it. Strange but not unusual.

The Small Business Association of New England has established groups of presidents of small businesses. The presidents meet regularly and share their problems. Many find their problems are not unique but go with the job. Knowing this gives comfort and also leads to cooperative solutions to similar problems. When I was the dean of the School of Management at Boston University (another boundary job), the deans in the Boston area, seven of us, met several times a year for dinner and sharing. In a way we were competitors, but in another way we were in it together.

Another approach was described in an article in the Boston Globe about a year ago. A small unique group of school superintendents in suburban Boston many years ago formed a support system for themselves. I know three of the four and in fact worked with them. They felt the need for support in their professional roles. They began meeting weekly, to share and problem solve common issues in their job. They started out dealing with shared work issues; but as they listened and cared about one another, their discussions went deeper. They also shared deep personal issues. At one point, they were joined by a psychologist who served initially as a facilitator but later abandoned his specialized role and became a peer in the group.

These four men are still supporting one another, still meeting after 25 years. One is now a college president, one has become a financial advisor, one is still a school superintendent at a larger school system, and one remains a professional psychologist. It is unusual for men to create that kind of support. Is this a useful approach for child care directors? What ways are there for getting support and help? There is a big difference between the group of deans meeting to share professional information and problems and the group of four I discussed above. The latter group went far beyond professional issues into very personal issues. I am not advocating one support group over the other, but I am advocating that child care directors look for ways of professional sharing. Knowing you are not alone can be a big help.

There are many ways that support groups get started. Gwen Morgan — who happens to be my partner in life —

likes to tell a story about her very first seminar for directors at Wheelock College. As the one-week seminar drew to an end, the group had bonded and had come to value the opportunity to communicate with one another. "How can we continue this relationship?" they asked. "How can we keep on exchanging information?" One participant declared that it was so important to continue the communication he would start a magazine, *Exchange*. So, thank you, Roger Neugebauer, for this magazine.

I recently participated in a pilot program in New Hampshire created by Dr. Margaret Copeland. Directors from all over the state came together to discuss career development in early childhood education. The participants formed seven action groups to work on projects related to improving quality through credentialing. Three months later, they came together to report on what had happened on their projects.

While outstanding work had been done, the over-riding accomplishment in my eyes was the way that they were communicating with each other. They had joined in a larger purpose, they were committed to improving the quality of child care throughout the state. Those in the higher population districts, like Manchester or Concord, were, with difficulty, meeting regularly. For those in the North Country, above the White Mountains, where the roads are narrow and the distances between directors is great, the Internet has come into play.

I find it astonishing how rapidly the Internet has entered the lives of the child care director. For those long snowed-in months of Northern New Hampshire, it will be a lifesaver. In a small state, these networked directors can do more than support one another, they can make changes in the system.

So let me suggest that your director's job can be much less stressful, much more rewarding, and you will learn a lot if you find a way to share, to communicate, to listen, to let off steam, to hear the steam of your colleagues, to join together to make needed changes in public policies. The underlying concept is to look at the director's job as part of a large system. You have an important part to play — your role — in this big and growing bigger drama of the emerging child development system. You can do some of it alone, but you can do all of it better together.

# Advocating for Children and Families

## Chapter 3

# Advocacy is Everybody's Business

by Bettye Caldwell

> *Professionals in the field of early childhood have been slow to recognize the importance of advocacy. Some consider such efforts to be beneath their dignity. Others do not work as advocates because of a feeling that they are unsophisticated about how the political process actually works.*
>
> — Joan Lombardi

This feeling of powerlessness may come from a perception of just how difficult it is to change either what is done or the way things are done and a resultant apathy about tackling the system. On the other hand, it may come in part from a feeling on the part of personnel in this field that they are not really professionals. As Lana Hostetler poignantly reminds us, many people outside the field do not so view us. If they did, salaries would be higher, and job descriptions would not be on par with custodians and domestics.

This reluctance to develop skills with which to influence the political process — which is what advocacy is — is not found in other professions generally considered higher on the professional totem pole. For example, the American Medical Association is regarded by many students of political science as the effective lobbying organization par excellence. Awareness of the importance of advocacy is spreading to the point where we now have leaders in higher education (Almy; Lombardi) recommending the inclusion of training in advocacy as an essential component of teacher education.

## The Ideological Setting for Advocacy

As Goodnow and Burns have stressed, all advocacy occurs within an ideological context which will significantly influence both how one should advocate and the outcome of such efforts. Presumably, there is always some resistance, or advocacy would not be needed. However, the climate of public opinion is much more favorable for the growth of some advocacy efforts than others. For example, efforts to secure more funding for research on a cure for AIDS would probably meet little resistance, even though some people consider contracting the disease a just punishment for the unfortunate persons who do so. However, the general level of fear about how it is spread and contracted is sufficiently high that such resistance could easily be overcome.

Unfortunately, the climate of public opinion about the merits of early childhood programs is not so uniform. There are hot spells and cold spells and hurricanes and tornadoes. For every person who believes such programs are beneficial to children and families, there appear to be at least two with opposing convictions. As I have stressed repeatedly over the years, the blame for some of this lack of support must be laid at our own feet. We have confused the general public about who we are and what we do by using a variety of labels to describe the field (day care, child care, early childhood education, preschool — and on and on) and then trying to make the case that these services are intrinsically different from one another rather than merely variations on a general theme of quality services needed by children and families and society at large. Furthermore, in attempts to make certain that we do not seem to endorse any program that is not of high quality, we have sometimes made it sound as though most of our programs are of poor quality.

The lack of consensus about the importance of quality early childhood programs will continue to impede advocacy efforts. Until we have more of the sort of evidence that convinces legislators and the general public — money saved, lives changed, families strengthened — we will have to continue our advocacy efforts in an ideological climate that is either indifferent, conflicted, or downright hostile.

## For Whom Do We Advocate?

If we asked that question of early childhood professionals, most would answer without hesitation, "For young children." Or possibly, "For children and families." As long as we think of our advocacy efforts in that way, we feel honorable and altruistic about what we are doing. But, according to our critics, our advocacy efforts for children and families have a way of spilling over into advocacy for ourselves — for better salaries and working conditions. When that happens, we feel guilty and conflicted. Hostetler suggests that we have to overcome such feelings of guilt by recognizing that we can do a better job for children if our own needs are met.

Some years ago, we had a Secretary of Defense named Charles Wilson who had formerly been the chief executive of General Motors. He was noted for what today we would call one-liners. Once, when asked by a senator whether he was recommending some action "because it is good for the United States or good for General Motors," he replied, "Sir, what is good for General Motors is good for the United States." The corollary is clear: What is good for personnel in this field will indeed be good for children and families; and we should never lose sight of that fact. We need not feel guilty about advocacy efforts that also benefit us. There is no way that it can be good for children to be cared for by persons who are overworked, underpaid, and underappreciated; who often cannot afford to play an important role in the lives of the children of other people without causing their own children to suffer economic privation; who constantly have to defend the validity of what they do to persons who at best consider them inconsequential and at worst harmful. In short, there can be no effective advocacy for children without including advocacy for those who help care for and educate them.

## Types of Advocacy

There are at least three types of advocacy to which we should be committed: **personal**, **professional**, and **informational**.

**Personal advocacy**. This is one-on-one advocacy — you and somebody else. Although we may tend to think of ourselves as advocates only when we are contacting our elected representatives, we are also being advocates when we help our neighbors understand what we do, when we correct them (gently but firmly) if they refer to their child care worker as a babysitter, when we get people to think about why their child care costs as much as it does — and about how those workers are enabling them to earn whatever they earn at their own jobs.

Recently, while waiting in the chair for my dentist to work on my mouth, I was correcting galleys on an article I had written. The technician noticed the heading *Child Care*, sighed audibly, and said, "Child care — that's my biggest problem."

Fortunately, I had not yet been anesthetized and could say, "Tell me about your problem." She launched into a diatribe about how much it cost. It was a perfect opportunity for some personal advocacy. I asked her whether she knew the salary of the director of her child's center, to which she replied in the negative. "It is probably less than you make," I ventured, and then went on to tell her that probably two-thirds of the workers in that center made only minimum wage. She was happy when the dentist came in. But so was I. It had been a wonderful opportunity for some personal advocacy.

Unless we represent organizations that have a budget for it, personal advocacy is generally carried out on our own time and must be paid for out of our own pockets. This is undoubtedly another explanation of why early childhood personnel have not been overly active in the realm of advocacy — we have no surplus of either of those commodities.

But sometimes we work in organizations that might not be willing to take the same stand on certain issues that we do as individuals. And many of us work for public organizations that do not allow us to conduct employee-oriented advocacy efforts. In such situations, we have to make it abundantly clear that we speak within our rights as citizens, not as public employees. If we fail to do so, we can generate opposition to, rather than support for, our cause.

I can cite a personal advocacy failure on my part that clearly illustrates the importance of this proviso. Once, when the Arkansas legislature was considering an important bill in the early childhood area, I spoke to our entire staff (teachers, aides, researchers, secretaries) about the importance of the bill and drafted a sample letter that I asked each person to adapt to his or her style and mail. I told them to use their home addresses and suggested that they not mention that they worked on the Kramer Project. As a small token of support for the effort, I bought stamps to use on the letters. Then, in keeping with the pattern of my own life, I had to go out of town.

No sooner had I returned than I received an irate summons from a legislator demanding an explanation of how it happened that "30 or 40 letters threatening legislators had been sent on University of Arkansas stationery and presumably typed by a secretary being paid a University salary."

The part about the threat puzzled me. However, a rereading of my sample letter made me aware of how damaging careless language can be. I had used the phrase *We will note your action on this issue and vote accordingly*. That was interpreted as a threat — and perhaps it was. But I had to do some sleuthing to find out about the stationery and typing. It seemed a well-intentioned secretary asked around a couple of days after the meeting to find out whether people had actually written their letters. Upon finding that almost no one had (and knowing how disappointed I would be to learn that), she had volunteered to type the letter on project stationery for everyone! A beautiful example of personal advocacy gone wrong. About the only thing that saved us was the fact that I could truthfully say, "The state didn't pay for the stamps!"

**Professional advocacy**. When we move from the personal to the professional level, we tend to stop calling the process *advocacy* and refer to it instead as *lobbying*. If we are hesitant about advocating, we are almost phobic about lobbying. But the aim of the activity is still the same — working on the benefits of both children and the professionals who serve them. As Wilkins and Blank state, "While lobbying may sound intimidating, it is nothing more than getting the right information to the right people at the right time."

During my time as a member of NAEYC, it has been gratifying to note the extent to which the organization has become committed to advocacy activities. All issues of *Young Children*, the official journal of the organization, now contain a Public Policy Report, and many issues contain a Public Policy Alert, in which members are urged to take specific action on some important issue. As much important advocacy takes place at the state and local levels, the affiliate groups of NAEYC have been heavily involved.

Of course, there are many other professional groups which serve as advocates for quality early childhood programs — the Child Care Action Campaign, the Children's Defense Fund, and the Center for the Child Care Workforce, to mention but a few. Furthermore, groups such as the American Academy of Pediatrics are now also involved in advocacy efforts in this field. This gradual broadening of our base of support represents a major advance toward greater public acceptance of the field.

**Informational advocacy**. This is an awkward term, but it represents an important category of advocacy. It refers to attempts to raise the general consciousness of the public both about the importance of events that occur during the early childhood period and about the capacity of quality programs to foster growth and development and to strengthen families. It seems to me that, more so than in any field, our public image is at odds with our reality. Until very recently, almost everything that appeared in the public press about child care stressed its negative aspect. That is gradually changing; but it seems as though the whole world is always just waiting for one slip on our part to let all those negative feelings out again.

This type of advocacy actually involves a combination of the first two types. We must get more accurate images into the media, which calls for personal efforts using professional supports — i.e., data which demonstrate the value of what we do. And just as we write articles for scientific and professional journals, so must we be willing to write for popular magazines. Short of that, we can write letters to the editors of our newspapers.

And, as Lombardi reminds us, we must be willing to be visible — to speak to local civic clubs, to be interviewed by the media, to bring opinion influencers to visit our programs, and so on. Only by working diligently to change public attitudes toward child care and early education can we have any hope of getting the critical mass of support we need for our own personal and professional advocacy.

## References


Almy, M. (1985). "New Challenges for Teacher Education." *Young Children, 41*, 10-11.

Caldwell, B. M. (1971). "Day Care — A Timid Giant Grows Bolder." *Saturday Review*, February 20, 1971.

Caldwell, B. M. (1983). "How Can We Educate the American Public About the Child Care Profession?" *Young Children, 38*, 11-17.

Caldwell, B. M. (1986). "Professional Child Care: A Supplement to Parental Care." In N. Gunzenhauser and B. M. Caldwell (editors), *Group Care for Young Children*. Somerville, NJ: Johnson & Johnson Baby Products Company, 3-10.

Goodnow, J. J., and A. Burns. (1982). "Factors Affecting Policies in Early Childhood Education: An Australian Case." In L. G. Katz (editor), *Current Topics in Early Childhood Education*, Volume V. Norwood, NJ: Ablex Publishing Corporation.

Hostetler, L. (1981). "Child Advocacy: Your Professional Responsibility?" *Young Children, 36*, 3-8.

Lombardi, J. (1986). "Training for Public Policy and Advocacy." *Young Children, 42*, 65-69.

Wilkins, A., & Blank, H. (1986). "Child Care: Strategies to Move the Issue Forward." *Young Children*, 42, 68-72.

# Cutting Through the Red Tape — Strategies for Dealing with Bureaucrats

by Roger Neugebauer

*The term bureaucrat conjures up the stereotype of a nit-picking, regulation spouting, heartless, bumbling paper-pusher. Yet bureaucrats no more fit a single mold than do child care directors or teachers. Some are rigid, others are flexible; some are brilliant, others are insipid; some are dedicated, others are self-serving.*

*What gives rise to the stereotype is that certain characteristics of life in the bureaucracy force employees to conform to standard and structured routines in performing their jobs. This article will describe these characteristics and how they affect bureaucrats' relationships with outside agencies. It will then outline some strategies for dealing with the types of bureaucrats child care directors are likely to encounter.*

## Life in the Bureaucracy

**Bureaucracies provide little motivation to work hard.** Individuals typically come to work for bureaucracies sincerely committed to making an impact in their field. However, new employees' expectations of becoming involved in shaping major policies and in planning exciting new programs are soon dashed. New policies and programs are generally developed at the highest levels of the bureaucracy and then turned over to the lower levels to enforce or administer. Lamented one welfare official:

*I hoped to use my expertise to help improve services for children. But instead I spend all my time tracking down lost payments, reviewing budget revisions, clearing audit reports, and running around getting 18 sign offs on contracts. My masters degree in child development is irrelevant; I should have gotten one in paperwork.*

*Bureaucracy is a giant mechanism operated by pygmies.*

— Honore de Balzac

Bureaucracies also provide little recognition for quality performance. Bureaucrats typically are responsible for monitoring or processing a workload of projects, contracts, or programs. If they fall behind in their *production,* they may receive considerable negative recognition in the form of pressure to produce from their superiors.

However, if they manage their work on a timely basis, their work tends to be taken for granted. What the bureaucracy focuses on is quantity, not quality. What is important is how many licenses are renewed or how many contracts are approved, not the quality of care children are receiving in those programs.

Given the emphasis on paperwork and processing, bureaucrats are seldom required by the bureaucracy to exercise their professional skills. If they take an interest in improving quality of services, it is because their own personal standards demand it or because they are receiving recognition or support from outside the bureaucracy for doing so.

A contract representative may work particularly hard to gain full funding for high quality programs, a welfare official may advocate the adoption of a sliding fee scale, or a licensing official might provide technical assistance to centers struggling to survive. Such efforts generally go unrewarded by the bureaucracy.

**Bureaucracies pressure bureaucrats to conform.** Bureaucracies manage routine work best — work to which the established rules, process, and schedules can be applied. When something comes along which causes the bureaucracy to move outside its routine procedures, this causes problems and is resisted.

Thus, a bureaucrat advocating a procedural waiver for an innovative program, or for the revocation of a particularly bad center's license, will likely encounter resistance and resentment. Bureaucrats who regularly push for changes, exceptions, and quality services are soon labeled as troublemakers.

The pressures on a *troublemaker* to conform are considerable. The most effective pressure is that the more a bureaucrat inconveniences his co-workers by seeking non routine actions, the harder it becomes to overcome their resistance and gain their support. A more long term pressure is the fact that superiors will not actively fight for promotions for troublemakers. Those who conform with the routines are rewarded with promotions.

In addition, reassignment of duties is a common ploy for discouraging troublemakers. A social services worker who gets actively involved in advocating rate increases for centers may be reassigned to process Medicaid claims or to work in an undesirable geographic location. Finally, superiors can grind troublemakers into submission by rigidly enforcing office procedures — for example, personal phone calls may be forbidden and pay may be deducted for taking five minutes too long on a break.

*Bureaucracy defends the status quo long past the time when the quo has lost its status.*

— Laurence J. Peter

Not surprisingly, the vast majority of bureaucrats eventually succumb to this pressure to conform. Many spirited *advocates* (see "Four Types of Bureaucrats") have been cowed into becoming *pseudo-advocates* who chant the clichés of their causes but who no longer have the heart to fight the bureaucracy for them.

**Bureaucracies reward outside agencies which conform to their routines and standards.** The treatment outside agencies receive from a bureaucracy is largely determined by the extent to which they conform to the bureaucracy's established procedures. The likelihood of an agency's request being approved often has more to do with the way the agency fills out the forms than with the quality of services it provides. Requests which cannot be handled routinely cause inconvenience to bureaucrats. The tendency for the bureaucracy is to delay acting on such requests, to reject them on a technicality, or to return them for *clarification*.

The treatment an agency receives may also depend upon the extent to which it conforms to unofficial standards for *good* programs. Bureaucracies generally have neither the inclination nor the resources to fully evaluate providers' services. As a result, *quality* judgments are often based upon stereotypes and labels. Oftentimes a program will be reacted to as *good* or *bad* depending upon whether it is for profit or non profit, small or large, part day or full day. In other situations, a bureaucrat may label an agency depending upon his personal relationship with the director, the extent to which the agency complies with his requests, or the physical appearance of the agency's facility. Such labels, once established, are communicated to co-workers and are slow to change.

**Bureaucracies unofficially delegate operational decisions to the lowest levels.** While bureaucrats at the lowest levels are virtually powerless to influence the bureaucracy's policy development, many do exercise considerable control over the day-to-day decisions. First line bureaucrats, those who deal directly with the outside agencies, in large part determine the outcome of requests from these agencies. They seldom have the authority to make any final decisions; but their recommendations on routine, non-controversial decisions are generally adhered to by their supervisors.

Supervisors commonly handle four to ten workers, each of whom may work with ten or more outside agencies. Therefore, the supervisor cannot possibly be familiar with all the requests from all the agencies and must of necessity rely on the opinions of the workers.

First line bureaucrats' strongest power is of a negative kind. While they may have a difficult time gaining approval for requests, they can easily prevent their approval. They can make a recommendation that a request be denied, which will be difficult to reverse unless the requesting agency has supporters in the higher echelons. They can delay processing a request until a deadline has passed. They can pester the agency interminably for additional information or revisions. If all else fails, they can lose the paperwork.

**Strategies for Dealing with Bureaucrats**

**Be a friend — not an antagonist.** For many bureaucrats, the most, if not only, satisfying aspect of their work is their relationships with the organizations and individuals they deal with outside the bureaucracy. If a bureaucrat derives satisfaction from a pleasant professional relationship with a child care center, she will be motivated to work hard to see to it that the center's requests receive fair and expeditious treatment. If she is irritated or offended by the center, she will be more likely to exercise her negative powers.

*I do not rule Russia; ten thousand clerks do.*

— Nicholas I

- Establish rapport with bureaucrats. Don't treat them like impersonal cogs in a giant machine. Show concern for their personal interests.

- Give them a tour of your program. Invite them to lunch with the children. Introduce them to your staff, board members, and parents.

- Keep in touch regularly, not just when you have a problem or need money. Invite them to special occasions (Thanksgiving dinners, annual meetings, carnivals). Send them regular progress reports, newsletters, and announcements.

- Show your appreciation for their work on your behalf. Thank them personally. Write a letter to their supervisor to let them know what a good job they are doing.

- Strive for fairness, not favoritism. If it becomes apparent that you are befriending a bureaucrat in hopes he will ignore a blatant licensing violation or push through an unnecessary budget increase, this will more likely rub his ego the wrong way and cause him to work against you. An attempt to buy a bureaucrat's unquestioning support through wining and dining is also more likely to backfire than not.

**Make bureaucrats your advocates.** Since bureaucrats receive little professional stimulation from pushing

## Four Types of Bureaucrats

### CLIMBERS

- Seek to maximize their own power, income, and prestige through increased rank and authority
- Tend to enforce or ignore agency rules depending upon what best suits their personal interests
- Promote reorganizations and changes which provide them with opportunities to increase their power base
- Insert themselves in the center of decisionmaking wherever possible

### ADVOCATES

- Seek to promote specific causes by fighting on their behalf from within the bureaucracy
- Work to promote decisions favorable to their cause by coordinating pressures from inside and outside the bureaucracy as well as by winning over key decisionmakers
- Bend, stretch, and ignore agency rules on behalf of their cause and look for loopholes or seek revisions in rules which are disadvantageous
- Constantly fight for changes in agency policies and structures which further their causes

### CONSERVERS

- Seek to maximize their security and convenience through maintaining their current position and income
- Escape responsibility for decisionmaking so as not to risk making bad or controversial decisions
- Rigidly apply agency's rules, exercise minimal personal discretion, and try not to rock the boat
- Oppose organizational changes which might threaten their position

### PSEUDO-ADVOCATES

- Sympathize with specific causes, yet are unwilling or unable to promote them in the bureaucracy
- Complain about decisions which hurt their cause but do not work hard to influence them
- Enforce agency rules while claiming they disagree but are powerless to change them
- Constantly talk about the need for changes but do little to actively promote them

*This classification is derived from one proposed by Anthony Downs (see **Credits**) but modified on the basis of the author's experience.*

papers inside the bureaucracy, they often welcome opportunities to become involved in providing technical assistance to service providers. (It's an irony of the field that frustrated bureaucrats long to work in centers where they can be directly involved providing services, while burned out directors seek to move into bureaucracies so they can have a broader impact on programs and policies.) It is especially helpful to get their assistance in shaping projects or proposals which will be submitted to the bureaucracy. Once they have an ego involvement in a request, they are not likely to let it die easily.

- Don't show bureaucrats only your center's bright spots. Share your problems with them and get their advice on solutions. Ask them how other centers they work with are handling these problems.

  It can be particularly helpful to gain the bureaucrat's support when the problem is the result of her bureaucracy's policies or procedures. She may be able to find loopholes, waiver procedures, or other proper means of getting around the problem. If not, having seen the effect of a policy on a center, she may be motivated to advocate from within for changing the policy.

- When preparing requests to the bureaucracy (applications for a license renewal, subsidy proposals, annual financial reports, etc.), seek the advice of the bureaucrats. Twenty minutes spent going over a proposal with a bureaucrat before it is filed may save weeks of delays caused by filling it out improperly, or by not explaining certain sections fully enough. If your center is about to file an unusual request (such as a major midyear budget revision or a waiver request for a particular licensing requirement), the bureaucrat may be able to suggest ways of framing the request which are least likely to cause conflict with the bureaucracy's standard routines and procedures.

- Give bureaucrats opportunities to become involved in major policy debates. Invite them to participate in local coalitions or associations which are active in advocacy around policy issues. If they can be fired up about the importance of certain policy changes, they are more likely to act as advocates for policy reform within the bureaucracy. Advocates within the bureaucracy who are not inspired and supported from the outside soon lose their enthusiasm and become pseudo-advocates.

**Don't become too dependent upon individual bureaucrats.** While it is vital to gain the understanding and support of the bureaucrats who deal directly with your center, it can be a mistake to rely solely on their support. No bureaucrat is going to care about your center as much as you do. While they may support your requests, given the many pressures they are under, they may not push your requests as aggressively as you might wish.

- Become thoroughly informed about how the bureaucracy functions. Find out the names and responsibilities of all the individuals who handle your request. Become thoroughly familiar with the rules and procedures which affect your center. Don't rely on bureaucrats to interpret the rules for you. Find out which rules can be waived and who has the authority to waive them. Talk to other directors and find out the various ways in which unclear rules have been applied.

- Get to know all the decision-makers in the bureaucracy personally. Make a point of introducing yourself to the head of the organization, as well as to the secretaries, auditors,

> *Guidelines for Bureaucrats:*
> *(1) When in charge, ponder.*
> *(2) When in trouble, delegate.*
> *(3) When in doubt, mumble.*
>
> — James H. Boren

### Understanding Bureaucratize

Conservers and pseudo-advocates tend to convey unpleasant news with obtuse stock phrases so as to avoid the inconvenience of having to assuage angry clients. The following examples demonstrate how to interpret such phrases.

*This looks good to me, but I'll have to clear it through the front office.*

**Translation**: Your proposal stinks, and I plan to reject it, but I'd prefer you to think it was my boss who shot it down.

*You mean you haven't received our answer yet?*

**Translation**: I haven't done a thing on your request, but I'd prefer you to think I had and that the post office lost our reply.

*I don't make the rules — I just carry them out.*

**Translation**: I could have fought to get a waiver to approve your request, but it was so much easier for me to simply reject it.

*He'll be in conference all day* or *He's away from his desk now.*

**Translation**: He hasn't even looked at your budget revision yet, but he doesn't have the guts to tell you that.

financial analysts, and other technicians who may handle your center's requests. If they know you personally, it is somewhat less likely they will treat a request from you as just another piece of paper to push. Also, they will be more likely to listen and give you an honest answer when you call in to check on the status of a request.

- Develop a contact in the bureaucracy who will give you an accurate report on the status of your requests. It is best, of course, if you can develop sufficient rapport with the first line bureaucrats who deal with you directly so that they will always give you honest reports. If you are dealing with a climber, a conserver, or a pseudo-advocate, however, you may find that they cannot be relied upon. They may say, for example, that a budget revision is being held up in another office while in fact it has been sitting on their desk for a week. If this is the case, it behooves you to make a friend in the bureaucracy who can provide reliable reports. Don't be reluctant to develop such contacts. You are not seeking inside information — you are seeking information which you are fully entitled to have.

*We can lick gravity, but sometimes the paperwork is overwhelming.*

— Wernher von Braun

**Know how and when to apply pressure.** Oftentimes developing a good working relationship with a first line bureaucrat will not be enough to insure that your center is treated fairly by the bureaucracy. Your license renewal may be rejected over a questionable interpretation of a rule, your child care food program reimbursement claim may be delayed unreasonably long, or you may be required to submit unnecessarily detailed financial reports. In such instances, it may be necessary to apply some pressure on the bureaucracy. However, if pressure is applied at the wrong time or in the wrong place, this could do more harm than good.

- Don't make a cause celebre out of every minor delay and setback. An organization that develops the label of chronic complainer will soon find the bureaucracy turning a deaf ear on its complaints. Regular phone calls to politely inquire on the status of your requests are more likely to prevent routine delays.

- Similarly, if you have developed a good relationship with and are receiving generally good service from a first line bureaucrat, it is not in your best interest in the long run to alienate this bureaucrat by going over his head when an isolated breakdown does occur. A more effective strategy would be to consult the bureaucrat directly. Ask him where the delay or problem is and get his advice on how you can most effectively bring pressure to bear.

- If, on the other hand, you find that you are receiving consistently poor service from the first line bureaucrat assigned to your center, you should request that a different individual be assigned. Ask for a meeting with the field representative's immediate supervisor. Cite specifically how in case after case the bureaucrat in question has failed to act responsibly on your requests, supplied you with inaccurate information, or failed to inform you of deadlines and policy changes.

- When it is time to apply pressure, it is best to attack with facts, not emotions. A display of righteous indignation may be effective in gaining the attention of the head of the bureaucracy; but in the final analysis, it will be the facts you present which will influence her decision.

If you are complaining about unnecessary delays and red tape, you should document the date your request was submitted, as well as the dates you contacted the bureaucracy by letter or phone seeking a status report, who responded to your inquiry, and what they said. If you are protesting an unfair decision, go to the rules and regulations. Demonstrate why the decision was not appropriate. Also cite examples of how in the past or in other jurisdictions the opposite decision was made on similar cases.

- Give the bureaucracy a means of saving face. Bureaucrats, like everyone else, have egos and prefer not to admit publicly that they made a mistake. Superiors don't like to alienate their staffs by publicly criticizing their actions or inactions.

Don't demand that a decision be reversed; rather ask that it be *reconsidered* on the basis of *new information* which you are supplying (even if you are only restating or clarifying what was presented initially). Even be prepared to offer to make some minor changes in your position so that the bureaucracy can announce that a *compromise* was reached. Give them a means of making a graceful retreat.

## Credits


Altshuler, A. (1977). *The Politics of the Federal Bureaucracy.* New York: Harper and Row, Publishers.

Boren, J. H. (1972). *When In Doubt, Mumble: A Bureaucrat's Handbook.* New York: Van Nostrand Reinhold Company.

Downs, A. (1973). "Inside Bureaucracy: Five Types of Bureaucrats," in Harold J. Leavitt and Louis R. Pondy (editors), *Readings in Managerial Psychology.* Chicago, IL: University of Chicago Press.

# Mentoring Advocates in the Context of Early Childhood Education

by Sessy I. Nyman

*Advocates have been a critical component in every social movement that effects change. Whether we examine the Civil Rights movement, the Women's Movement, or the movement to create a public K-12 educational system, movements are made up of individual advocates. Types of advocates and how they create change vary greatly, but what ties them together is their common goal.*

*In the field of early childhood education, we have the foundation for an effective, broad-based coalition of advocates; there is much work to be done. Growing our advocacy community must be a high priority for everyone who cares for the future of young children — one advocate at a time. The work of each and every advocate is critical if we are to reach our goal of high quality early learning and education for each child.*

## Advocates are People Who Bring an Issue to Life

There are no specific prerequisites for being an advocate. Most people advocate for something every day of their lives. It is in our nature when we believe in something or have a passion for the issue. The challenge lies in being an effective advocate — connecting the day to day work to a larger movement.

The Day Care Action Council of Illinois (DCACI) is a statewide advocacy organization, one of the few in the state to have a full time lobbyist who works with elected officials to further an agenda that supports high quality care and education for all young children. DCACI has a broad membership base of child care providers, parents, and other advocates. The strength of the agency does not lie only in its legislative relationships and policy know-how but equally on its grassroots constituency.

In the spring of 2002, the Illinois Child Care Assistance Program faced drastic cuts that would have crippled child care providers and devastated low-income families already struggling to keep their children in high quality programs. Over the course of 10 weeks, thousands of parents and child care providers across the state wrote letters, called their legislators, and rallied at the Capitol. In the end, no cuts were levied against the program — one of very few social service support programs that were not cut in a year of severe budget shortfall.

The key was not the access DCACI had to policy makers, nor was it the relationship DCACI had with community providers and parents statewide. Instead, it was the combination of both that made its advocacy efforts so effective. Individual advocate's actions were multiplied and made more effective because they were part of a larger campaign.

It is most effective when advocates come from a wide array of fields and interests to create a broad foundation for support. With a diverse foundation, an issue is brought to life for a variety of constituencies, in a variety of ways that more people can relate to and understand. Our challenge, as early childhood advocates, is to make the issue of high quality care and education for young children everyone's issue. If it remains only *our* issue, we will never be successful.

In Illinois we have long worked to engage the business community as advocates for early care and education. Because they have a different constituency than either the *typical* parent or provider advocate, they speak from a business, workforce, or economic perspective of why child care matters. They often have networks and friends that early care and education advocates may not be able to access. Clearly, growing our advocacy community in numbers and diversity is critical to broad-based support and long-term change.

Our goal is to make everyone an early childhood advocate: professional advocacy groups, researchers, elected officials, child care providers, pre-school and K-3 teachers, parents, community members, members of the business community, civic organizations, and unions. Many voices singing the same chorus is always more effective in creating change.

## The Role of Mentors

Everyone has the capacity to be an advocate, but to be an effective advocate takes time and support. This is the role of the mentor in building advocates. Mentors can be many things to many people; the key is to be the right thing at the right time.

Any mentor, no matter what the issue or circumstance, needs to recognize the individual capacities of the person they mentor. One of the biggest mistakes a mentor can make is to measure one person against another, or worse, against him/herself. Just as there are advocates from all walks of life, there are individuals with different levels of ability and commitment.

In its simplest form, the role of a mentor is to recognize each advocate's abilities and then build upon them. Understanding the starting point of a potential advocate will define the long process of mentoring the individual's potential.

Consider this scenario: Sylvia was a life-long advocate now in a position to bring others along. She had been a central decision-maker to the children's movement, marched on Washington too many times to remember, established personal relationships with her local and national legislators, and effected change for children for over 20 years. She is a born advocate and wants to nurture future advocates and leaders for children. To her peers and fellow life-long advocates, Sylvia is a natural leader and thus, a natural mentor.

She is excited to share what she knows with others, so they too might become effective advocates for children. However, early on she became frustrated when a mentee did not participate in Saturday meetings, was unable to commit to national trainings, and did not feel comfortable speaking to large audiences. After a short time Sylvia told her mentee that he did not have the qualities to be an effective advocate. She put the fault on the mentee, but the fault was in her skills as a mentor. A huge opportunity was lost.

From the beginning, Sylvia defined the criteria by her personal standards and skills; she did not begin with a clear understanding of the starting point for her mentee's emerging leadership. Instead of building a life-long advocate, she convinced a potential advocate that *he didn't have what it takes.*

To be an effective mentor, it is important to remember that the charge is not to clone yourself, but instead to identify skills and potential in the person you are mentoring and then to nurture the development of those skills. Sylvia could have nurtured the personal relationships the mentee already possessed, set up one-on-one meetings rather than creating large group settings, and built on the personal experience and knowledge of the mentee to help him begin to see his advocacy potential. In time, the confidence of the new advocate grows, and he or she looks for new challenges and opportunities for growth.

Ultimately, a mentor is charged with developing skills in a potential advocate, as well as:

- helping *'beginner advocates'* recognize that they are already advocates, and what they already do, however small, makes a difference.
- helping grow and nurture advocacy efforts — looking not only at skill but context and reach.
- demonstrating to the advocate how his or her efforts fit into a larger movement.
- helping the advocate identify key relationships they currently have, and encouraging them to establish new relationships that will extend the reach and impact of their work.
- supporting the advocate in the pieces of advocacy that are new, until the advocate feels comfortable doing it on his or her own.
- encouraging every advocate to be a leader and continually reaching out to engage new advocates committed to the same goals.

## Part of a Movement

In reality we are all part of a state, national, and even international movement that supports high quality care and education for all children. This is a big concept for many advocates to get their arms around. It is always important to be aware of the larger movement or vision, while at the same time making the issue local and real. When an issue has immediate impact on local children, it is much easier to build a broad base of support.

All advocates must be part of a movement, group, or network that can directly affect public policy. Policy is the primary way to create overarching, long-lasting change. While the work that happens in our neighborhood, our school district, or our town are all important, unless they connect to the larger public policy process, real change will not occur.

## What an Advocate Needs

Passion is the essence, the necessary requirement for advocacy. It provides the essential foundation upon which other advocacy skills can be built. A review of the following list can help gauge an advocate's skill and

## Ten Commandments of Policy Advocacy

Start with a base. Your base should reflect the breadth and diversity of support for your issue.

Work on a bi-partisan basis. This is the only way to avoid gridlock between the two chambers and the executive.

Cultivate a legislative champion in each house. Advocates, grassroots supporters, and lobbyists can only do so much; the sponsor must be a committed advocate when the legislation is debated.

Create a simple message that explains your issue, and then make sure that your supporters repeat it, over and over again.

Develop human-interest stories to demonstrate your points. Do not underestimate the power of anecdotes.

Organize a *creative* coalition in support of the issue. The most effective coalition partners lend an element of surprise; they are not expected to support the issue and may have opposed you before.

Activate your grassroots support. Legislators care most about issues that affect their own constituents. At the state or local level (not Congress), their unique letters or telephone calls create an impression of widespread support or opposition on all but the most controversial issues — on the same theory that ten cockroaches in a kitchen appear to be an infestation.

Be ready to compromise. No policy of government ever looks the same as when it was proposed.

Never lie or mislead a policy-maker about the importance of an issue, the opposition's position or strength, or any other matter. Your word is your bond.

Use the media to focus on public debate and to generate interest in the issue. Legislators and policy-makers are especially sensitive to media approval and criticism.

*Prepared by Julie E. Hamos and Associates, September 1998*

knowledge level, whether the advocate is you or someone you are mentoring. Knowing where you are at the beginning points you in the direction of where you need to grow — this is an important first step in mentoring an advocate.

- **Understanding the issue.** Many advocates understand the issue from their own perspective or experiences. However, in order to build support and ownership of the issue among others, understanding the entire issue, with all its complexities, is critical. It is essential to be able to explain the issue and its importance to people who might not be early childhood professionals or who do not have young children.

- **The context.** Knowing at least part of the history of an issue is critical to mapping out where it will go. Why has ECE emerged today as such an important issue? What has changed to increase demand? How have our expectations changed for young children? What is the role of ECE?

- **Messaging.** The work of creating a message or building support happens in two primary categories:

  1. Creating public will is central to the work of an advocate. If the general public does not support a concept or an issue, then the chances that change will happen are slim. Having a broad range of support and demonstrating need and effect is important in building public will.

  2. Creating political commitment largely depends on the ability to create public will and to make sure elected officials know that the public supports the issue. We do this in a variety of ways, including relationship building, networking, public education, and media exposure. Just as it is important that advocates individually work towards a common goal, so too is it critical that the work comes together in a common message.

- **Relationship building.** Relationships are built over time, by establishing trust, respect, and common interests. Whether engaging an elected official, other advocates, parents, or community members, relationships are crucial to an advocate's success. Understanding that a relationship goes beyond the current issue or campaign is critical for a new advocate.

- **Understanding the players.** Who are the players? They are anyone and everyone you interact with, who cares about your issue, who is effected by your advocacy work, or even who might take a contrary view of your issue. They are also the leaders on your issue — the people making decisions, the people people listen to, and the people who have made a difference in the past. While everyone is important in turning an issue into policy, the players are the faces that the general public connects with the issue.

- **Why should anyone else care?** Early childhood care and education affects every segment of our society. An effective advocate will be able to explain how the issue affects different populations in different ways. The reasons why a parent cares about early childhood care may be different from why the local Chamber of Commerce cares. Both are important. The cost-benefit model of investing in quality early care and education is just as compelling to some legislators as the new research on brain development in infants is to others. By working with advocates from various fields, you learn how to craft your message in order to reach a variety of populations which helps you to ultimately be successful.

Thinking of advocacy skills in these ways will enable a mentor to help advocates recognize their skills and potential, and then to nurture strengths, overcome weaknesses, and understand the context.

## Mentoring Change

Change happens in a variety of ways, and a good mentor can ensure that each venue and opportunity for advocacy is the most effective it can be. As a young person entering the world of community activism and advocacy, I needed the leadership, guidance, and inspiration of mentors so that I could see my potential and the possibilities for change.

It is appropriate to write this article now, as the climate in our nation is not one conducive to highlighting the deficiencies in our various systems. States are facing major budget shortfalls, and critical services like child care and other early learning opportunities are being cut; some to the point of their collapse.

This is also a time of great opportunity for change. There is a national awakening around the importance of early brain development and the critical impact of high quality early learning opportunities for children from birth to five. There is growing concern in the business and education communities that if we don't invest in our very youngest learners, then we can never expect to have successful students and productive professionals in the future.

Now is the time to become an advocate, mentor an advocate, and grow our community of advocates for high quality early learning for all children.

# Organizational Management

# GETTING ORGANIZED

## CHAPTER 4

# How to Prepare a Business Plan

by Keith Stephens

> *"Cheshire-Puss," said Alice, "would you tell me, please, which way I ought to go from here?"*
> *"That depends a good deal on where you want to get to," said the Cat.*
> *"I don't much care where . . ." said Alice.*
> *"Then it doesn't matter which way you go," said the Cat.*
> *". . . so long as I get somewhere," Alice added as an explanation.*
> *"Oh, you're sure to do that," said the Cat, "if you only walk long enough."*
>
> — Lewis Carroll, ***Alice's Adventures in Wonderland***

Whether you are running General Electric or ABC Child Care Center, you will not succeed for long operating like Alice in Wonderland. Every business needs to know where it wants to go, and how it plans to get there.

For most child care operations, if there are any plans at all, they only exist in the head of the owner or the director. I am a firm believer in taking time to formally think through the directions for your child care business, and then committing the results to writing in the form of a business plan.

Having a business plan in place provides you with a starting point, a set of directions to guide your actions and decisions along the way, and a target to work towards. Having a specific goal is what drives most of us to accomplishment.

In addition, having thought through your business, set priorities, and documented your thinking, you will have a convenient vehicle for communicating with the people — staff, business advisors, bankers, etc. — who will help you accomplish your goals.

There is no set formula for writing a business plan. No matter how it is formatted, however, it should provide answers to five key questions:

*Where are we?*
*What threats and opportunities do we face?*
*Where are we going?*
*How do we plan to get there?*
*What do the numbers say?*

## Where are we?

Just like when you use a road map, before you can determine how to get to where you want to go, you have to start by identifying where you are. The description of your current status should address the following points:

- **What business are we in?** What is the service we are selling? (Is it child care, education, family support?) Who are our customers? (Spell out as specifically as you can a profile of your current customers in terms of where they live, how much they earn, where they work, and what they want for their children.)

- **What is our philosophy?** Not only is it important to spell out your philosophy for other people to understand but it also helps each of us to go through the process of making a clear statement about what we are trying to accomplish: what our attitudes are about the needs of children, about the process of education, about the needs of parents, and about our role in terms of the families and communities we serve.

- **What is our track record?** Where are we coming from? How did we get started? How successful have we been to date? What major changes have we made along the way? In putting together your historical data, it can be very helpful to use charts and graphs to depict your progress visually.

- **Where are we now?** This should be a snapshot of the status of your business: assets, locations, enrollments, organizational structure, key personnel, main competitors, and current financial position.

## What threats and opportunities do we face?

Answering the first question will cause you to take a hard look within your organization. This second question will force you to look outside, at forces and trends that may impact your program's future.

- **What threats do we face?** What factors could interfere with the development of our program? Is our lease about to expire? Are any new centers opening up within our service area? Is the availability of qualified staff becoming a problem? Are the demographics of the neighborhoods we serve changing? Are parents being attracted to centers with different philosophies or lower fee scales? Are pending changes in licensing requirements going to increase our cost of doing business?

- **What opportunities are there?** Is there new residential growth taking place that will increase the demand for child care? Are local employers exploring child care options for their employees? Is the developer of the community's new business park interested in having a child care center as an amenity for the development? Could we build a new structure that is a better facility, yet more economical? Are there nearby neighborhoods or communities where the demand for child care is going unmet? Are any national chains interested in buying our business?

- **How do we rate with the competition?** You may find it helpful to analyze your relative competitive position by creating a chart entitled *Competitive Position*. In the left hand column, "Bases of Competition," list the characteristics that customers use to choose a child care center. These might include location, service, staff, program, reputation, facilities, and pricing, among others. In the second column, assign a relative weight to each characteristic on a scale of 1 to 5 (5 being the most important, 1 being the least). Now, list your major competitors across the top, beginning with your organization. For each characteristic, rate each competitor — including yourself — relative to each other with a rating of +1, 0, or -1. For example, if one competitor is relatively strong in terms of *location*, you would place a rating of +1 in the upper part of the box for *location*. If another competitor is average in terms of its pricing, you would place a rating of 0 in the upper corner of the *pricing* box.

Determine a score for each characteristic by multiplying the individual rating by the weight for each characteristic and writing that score in the lower corner of the box. For example, if an organization was rated +1 for location, and you have assigned a weight of 5 to location, the resulting score would be +5. Now, sum up all the scores for each organization to arrive at a total score. Finally, rank each of the competitors in terms of their total scores.

## Where are we going?

This is the focal point of your business plan. After reviewing the current status of your business, set goals for your organization.

There are many ways to express the goals of your organization:

- **Customer objectives**. You may set specific goals for generating new customers, or for reducing customer turnover. Alternatively, you may decide to shift your customer base ("We will increase the share of families enrolled in the center with incomes above $35,000 to 50%").

- **Staff development objectives**. You should take a look at what objectives you need to achieve in terms of recruiting and training staff. For example, such goals might include, "Each staff member will attend one seminar or class on child development each month," or "A gymnastics person will be added to staff by September 1."

- **Program enhancements**. This encompasses any plans to upgrade the operation of your program — such as adding a new playground, remodeling the interior of your center, or equipping your center with a new computer program.

- **Market share**. You should take a look at where you are going to be in the market. For example, if you are in a major city, one of your goals might be to increase your share of the market from 1% to 2% in order to solidify your business base in that community.

- **Growth rate**. Your goals for growth may be expressed in terms of units ("We will add two new centers a year for the next five years"); *enrollments* ("We will increase the number of children enrolled by 100%" or "We will increase the utilization rate of our center to 90%"); or *stability* ("We will maintain the utilization level of our current center").

- **Income objectives**, articulated in terms of *gross revenues* ("We will increase revenues at the rate of 20% per year for the next five years") or *profits* (We will increase center profits by 15% per year"). Since the revenue you collect is a function of the number of customers, the programs, and the rate charged, you may want to establish goals for each of these items ("We will increase the number of children served to 160 by September 30," and "We will add an after-school program serving 25 children by September 1," and "Our rate will be increased 5% on July 1").

- Business ratios. These can become useful as another means of measuring your progress. For example, you might state as your goals "reducing accounts receivable to less than one week's tuition" or "keeping my investment in property down to 50% of my total investment in the business." Expense ratios can be particularly helpful in the month-to-month management of your business. For example, such a goal might be "maintaining supply expenses at 5% of total program cost."

- **Personal objectives**. If you are the owner of the business, you need to be thinking about how the business fits into your own plans. Do you plan to run the center until your children are old enough to take it over? Are you grooming someone else to run the center for you when you are ready to retire? Or are you planning to build up a sound business and then sell it to a national chain? None of these will just happen. You need to recognize these personal issues in setting goals as well.

## How do we plan to get there?

Having written your goals is a major accomplishment. But it is not enough. You need to translate these goals into results by developing and implementing specific *strategies* or *action plans* for making them happen.

If your goals call for considerable expansion, you will need to develop strategies for securing financing, for locating suitable sites, for designing appropriate buildings, and for accelerating your marketing efforts. If your goals call for working more closely with employers, you will need to develop strategies for identifying and making inroads with employers likely to be interested in child care as a benefit.

**People**. No matter what your goals are, however, one area you will certainly need to look at in developing your action plans is people. Having the right people on board at the right time is crucial to the success of nearly anything you want to accomplish.

You need to look at your goals and ask: "Will we need to add people to accomplish what we plan to do?" "Will the types of people we need be readily available?" "What kind of training will be necessary to prepare people for what they will be doing?"

**Structure**. An organizational chart is a necessary part of analyzing your people requirements. Not only does it depict for you how your organization fits together, it also helps you identify key people you will need to bring in and when, or who will need to be upgraded by when, and when their training will need to start if they are going to be groomed from within.

In the business plan you may include more than one organizational chart — one for how your structure looks today and one for how it will look a few years down the line if you are to accomplish your goals.

**Critical elements**. A final step in analyzing your goals is an examination of elements critical to your success — things that absolutely have to be in place in order for you to accomplish your goals. Your business plan should include a listing of the three to five most critical elements. For example, if your intention is to locate new centers on fringes of development, then a critical element for your success will be infill — continued economic growth in communities you will be serving.

## What do the numbers say?

After you have defined your goals and strategies, it is time to assign numerical values to these plans. It is important to convert the plans to cash because cash is what drives the machine. However, it is important to recognize also that the numbers are only one part of the business plan — really the last part. Your budgets and projections are just a numerical statement of goals. If you do everything up front well, the writing of the budget will come easy. All you are doing is taking the thought process you went through and assigning numbers to what you plan to do.

A standard business plan will forecast financial statistics for three to five years. These statistics typically include:

- **Annual income and expense statements**. Forecast the revenues and expenses that are likely to be generated as a result of the goals you have established. Don't forget to assign a cost to training and promotional activities that will be required to implement your goals.
- **Cash flow projections**. These projections are important to do in tandem with your annual budgets because they give a running view of the ebb and flow of income and expenses. They can help you identify points in time when your plans will result in cash surpluses and cash deficiencies. In doing these projections, it is helpful to separate out the cost of doing special projects (such as a major staff training effort or a one shot marketing campaign).
- **Balance sheets**. A balance sheet allows you to take a snapshot of what the business is worth at any point in time. It is a numerical assessment of how much the business owns (how much its assets are worth), how much it owes (how much its liabilities are), and what its net worth is (the difference between its assets and liabilities).

By projecting balance sheets on an annual basis, you can see the strength of the business and how it is changing from one year to the next — you don't really see that if you look only at your income and expense statements or at cash flow projections. They allow you to see when your cash balances are large so you can use this cash to do something else.

- **A statement of assumptions**. In making cost projections, you have to make certain assumptions. For example, you will have to make estimates about interest rates, food costs, and insurance costs. These assumptions will need to be spelled out in your business plan so that someone reading the plan can interpret your numbers.

**A final caution**: Developing a business plan is not a simple process. After you develop your goals and work out the numbers, you may find that you will end up losing money. You may have to go through the entire process several times in order to develop goals that are in line with your resources.

## Q & A about Doing a Business Plan

**Does every center really need to do a business plan?** Without a doubt, every center can benefit from developing their own business plan. This is true whether you operate a chain of six centers, or a single center for 40 children, whether you are seeking outside financing for a major expansion effort, or you are content to remain at your current size. Every business needs to think through in a formal way where it is going and how it plans to get there. Without such a plan, your business will drift from year to year in no particular direction.

**How far in advance should you forecast?** The standard for business plans is three to five years. That is a reasonable time period for most larger centers. A smaller center not looking to expand can probably do just as well with a one or two year plan. In any case, the farther into the future your plans and projections are made, the less reliable they will be. Therefore, while your projections for the coming year can be, and should be, quite specific, there is no point in pinning activities down dollar for dollar or month by month for distant years. For example, your cash flow projections could be done on a monthly basis for the first year, on a quarterly basis for the second year, and on an annual basis after that.

**How often should the plan be updated?** Every year. Very seldom will what you write in your plan today be what you actually implement when you get there. Inevitably, many changes will occur. But annual updates are not too burdensome. Once you have done all the hard work developing the initial plan, tinkering with it to reflect changes should not be too difficult. This is particularly true if you perform this work on a computer.

If major changes occur, however, you may have to update it more than once a year. If you start veering off course significantly, you may find that your business plan is not at all reflective of reality — in which case you may need to chuck it and start all over again.

**Would you do a plan differently if you were using it as a tool for raising money outside?** No! Your basic business plan should be developed just as thoughtfully if you are going to use it to raise money outside or if it will only be used internally. If you do a good job on your business plan, you should only need to add two or three pages to have a package to deliver to outsiders. For example, if you are presenting the plan to your banker, you would probably want to include an initial statement of the kind of money you are looking for and how you plan to use it. If you are looking for investors, you would have more of a sales presentation at the front of your plan, and you might include some analysis of what their return would be.

Even if you do not plan to send your plan outside, you should still package your final product well. The better job you do on the packaging, the more important the document (and the thought processes behind it) becomes. If you have a handwritten, two-page plan with one 13-column scratch pad, this product is probably not something that you would treat as significant for very long.

Your business plan needs to be a working document that you review, access for information, and monitor your progress against on a regular basis. I'm a firm believer in putting it into a good enough format that it takes on some significance to the writer and to other people who should use it.

**Who should be involved in developing the plan?** You will probably need an accountant to help you with the income projections. If you have any other business advisors, you should show them your plans to see if they make sense. In a small organization, board members who are involved in running a center need to be part and parcel in developing the plan.

It is also very important to involve employees. They can be particularly helpful in the evaluation of opportunities and threats — and in coming up with recommendations about what should be done.

Once the plan is completed, you should distribute it widely. My personal preference is to share all the information, even the financial information, with all officers and staff members. Your people are going to make the thing come about and they need to know what is expected and where the organization is going.

One reason to share information is that if the prospects are good, staff members already think they are better, and if prospects are bad, then they think they are good. It is a great asset for the people to know what the facts are, for them to know where the business is going, and what the opportunities are for them.

**How should the final plan be formatted?** The manner in which you commit your plans to print should first and foremost make sense to you. You can simply follow the format that was described above, with sections on the history and status of the organization, threats and opportunities, future plans, and financial projections. Or you can organize the information as a series of goal statements, with background information and action plans spelled out for each one.

However, no matter how the plan is organized, its first page should be your mission statement. While you will not be able to develop this until all other parts of the plan are completed, this statement should be up front as a capsule summary of what is to follow. The mission statement should briefly state: who we are (your markets), what we provide (your services), where we operate (your service area), where we are heading (your goals), and why we are going to be successful (your competitive advantage).

**How pessimistic or optimistic should you be with your financial projections?** When you initially do your cash flow projections, you should strive to be as objective as possible. Try to be realistic in estimating revenues and expenses. Then, since none of us project the future with 100% accuracy, go back and say, "What if the revenues we project are not as great?" or "What if the projects that we want to undertake cost more than we expected?" In other words, go back and take a very conservative look at the cash flow.

Your business plan should include both of these projections — the realistic and conservative one. Chances are, you will end up somewhere in that range.

# Getting Organized: 50 Ideas for More Effective Use of Your Time

by Roger Neugebauer

*Recently I received a note from a former subscriber who commented: "I love* ***Exchange****; but I let my subscription expire because, being a director, I never have time to read it." This really got my adrenaline flowing. I decided it was a problem of crisis proportions if directors were so crunched for time that they couldn't read* ***Exchange****!*

*So in order to help directors regain control of how they spend their time (and to avoid losing subscribers), I pulled together the following list of 50 practical time management techniques. These were selected to deal with the most common time problems of child care directors — too much paperwork, too many tasks, too many crises, too many interruptions, and too little time to relax.*

## Cut Down on Paperwork

Paperwork has become a major source of frustration for child care directors. In fact government researchers estimate that every year four centers are totally buried in a blitz of paperwork and red tape and 3500 directors are afflicted by chronic paper cuts. While scientists have not yet discovered a cure for the common paperwork, there are some techniques for treating its symptoms:

**1. Engage in creative waste basketry.** Be guided by the maxim — "When in doubt, throw it out." Don't kid yourself. If you don't need that brochure on "101 Classroom Uses for Used Egg Cartons" today, you probably won't need it two years from now either. Throw it out. Don't be constrained by a small wastebasket which fills up fast and discourages your urge to purge. Buy a large wastebasket and use it freely.

**2. Don't become a paperwork junkie.** Don't become part of the problem by creating unnecessary paperwork. When you are about to write a memo, draft a report or develop a new form, ask yourself — "What is the worst that could happen if this activity went unrecorded?" If the answer is not too serious or too likely, save the paper. Also, whenever possible, communicate messages to persons outside the center by phone rather than by mail. Most messages can be relayed more quickly and more accurately that way (Mackenzie). When answering letters where a short reply will suffice, jot your answer on the original letter and send it back.

**3. Don't be a copycat.** Resist the urge to photocopy 25 copies of everything that crosses your desk. While many others may have a *right* to know or even a *need* to know about everything you do, let's face it — they probably don't have a *want* to know about most of it.

**4. Master the art of dictating.** Letters can be transcribed about five times faster than they can be written out in long-hand. Additionally, this can be done while waiting for appointments, traveling to and from work, or relaxing in an easy chair at home.

**5. Install a center management software system.** There are a variety of software packages on the market that can expedite your handling of financial transactions, student records, waiting lists, and staff scheduling. Such systems can save time as well as provide you with better, more up-to-date information.

**6. Handle mail once.** Reserve a specific time in the day to devote about 15 minutes to handling the day's mail. As much as possible try to take appropriate action on each letter at once. If a letter requires a short response, don't put it down until you have responded. If the letter requires more involved investigation, strive to at least take one step to move it closer to completion (Lakein). Throw out as much as possible, and label everything else for appropriate filing.

**7. Batch filing.** On the upper right-hand corner of any material that needs to be retained, write the name of the file in which it should go, and place it in a *to be filed* basket. Once every week or so set aside 10-15 minutes to file everything in the basket.

**8. Streamline filing.** The purpose of a filing system is to provide ready access to information you need. Two guidelines apply. First, keep files you use on a regular basis within easy reach of your desk. Keep all other files organized, but out of the way. Second, keep the system as simple as possible. Try to divide your files into as few functional categories as possible. If you set up large numbers of specific categories, when trying to find a particular file you'll not only have to remember the name of the file but also the name of the category. Within each category organize all files in alphabetical order.

**9. Purge files periodically.** Most people just keep accumulating records year after year. They can tell you how much pencils cost them back in 1937, but their offices are so crowded with files that they can't find the pencils they bought last week (Frost). At least once a year you should review your files to see how much can be discarded. Experts in records retention report that 90% of all files are never referred to after their first year. Strive to retain only the correspondence, general reference, and historical files that there is an obvious important reason for retaining. Check with your lawyer and accountant to determine how long legal and financial records must be retained. Once again, exercise the guideline — "When in doubt, throw it out."

## Work Smarter, Not Harder

The key to effective time use is to identify those tasks which are most vital to the success of yourself or your organization and to focus your efforts on completing them. What is important is not how much work gets done, but what work it is that gets done. By concentrating energies on a limited number of high impact tasks, a director can accomplish more in 35 hours than a director who toils for 60 hours over less important tasks.

**10. Compile a *to do* list.** On a single (long) sheet of paper list everything you have to do. Include on this list all tasks from the most mundane (clean desk) to the most critical (hire a new teacher). Don't limit the list to those things that happen to be on your desk at the time. Be sure to include your short and long range goals for yourself (increase reading speed) and for your organization (initiate school age care component).

**11. Set priorities.** Once you have completed your undoubtedly lengthy *to do* list, it is time to rank the tasks on this list in order of importance. If your list doesn't have more than three or four major projects, it may be easiest for you to identify the task that is most important and number it *1*, and then number all other tasks in descending order of importance. If your list is more complex, it may be helpful first to subdivide your original list into three new lists:

List A — Quality Tasks
List B — Survival Tasks
List C — Routine Tasks

Put on List A all the tasks which will be beneficial in upgrading the quality or range of services your organization provides, or in improving your professional skills. Examples of A tasks are: *organizing a series of curriculum workshops for teachers, opening a new infant care component.*

On List B include all the tasks which must be completed on a timely basis to assure the survival or stable operation of the organization. B tasks might include: *filing quarterly tax payments, enrolling ten new families.* Place all remaining tasks on List C.

Finally, within each list number all tasks in order of importance. For instance, the task on List A which will provide the most beneficial impact should be labeled number *1*. Then all other tasks on List A should be numbered in order of descending importance.

**12. Start at the top.** The key to effective time management is to work on your most important tasks first. Having prioritized your A, B, and C lists, you should, therefore, focus your energies in the coming week to accomplishing the tasks at the top of your A and B lists.

You should strive to strike a reasonable balance in the amount of time you devote to A (quality) and B (survival) tasks. Unfortunately, what too often happens is that nearly all of a director's time is devoted to survival tasks.

If your center is operating on the brink of financial disaster, you may barely have time to breathe between crises, let alone work on quality tasks. Even under stable conditions it is easy to defer a quality task — *organizing a workshop on language development in toddlers* — since it doesn't covey the same sense of urgency as a survival task — *performing a cash-flow analysis*. Nonetheless, if you fail to exert leadership in upgrading your center's services, these services may degenerate to the point where the center no longer deserves to survive.

**13. Avoid the activity trap.** It is also easy to fall into the trap of wasting time on non-productive tasks. It is often tempting to avoid difficult high priority tasks by being very busy with routine tasks. Such tasks — *filing letters, answering phone calls, reorganizing the desk* — do require hard work and can yield a sense of accomplishment since many items will be checked off your *to do* list by the end of the week (Odiorne). However this sense of accomplishment will be illusory if the activities fail to contribute significantly toward the survival and upgrading of your center. As time management consultant Alan Lakein recommends, you should strive to work smarter, concentrating your efforts on high priority tasks, not harder, occupying your time with low priority tasks.

**14. Know your limits.** In setting to work on high priority tasks, you should be realistic about how much you can accomplish in the time available to you. You must be prepared to admit that you cannot complete all your work every week. In order to get important tasks done, you must be willing to let less important tasks go undone.

Likewise, you should be realistic in the amount of time you budget for completing high priority tasks. Don't plan to complete the annual budget and redesign the three-year-old room on Monday, when you know that either task could take a full day. You will only be setting yourself up to be frustrated when you fail to meet your deadlines.

**15. Utilize your best skills.** You can get much more work done by sticking to what you do best. One manager, for example, rates each task from 1 to 10, according to how well it matches his best skills. He then works only on the tasks that rate over a 7. The rest he delegates to other staff members or to outside experts who can handle them more effectively than he can.

If the most important tasks confronting you consistently require skills which are not your strong points, and which are not possessed by your staff members, you may need to look for training in those areas or consider restructuring your center's staffing to bring in a person with those skills.

## Control Your Time

The constant swirl of activity in the typical child care center does not naturally allow a director to concentrate undivided attention on high priority tasks. To regain control of your time, it might help to schedule in advance the use of your time. Draw up a blank schedule for your typical week. Mark off any times that are irreversibly committed already. Then consider blocking off your remaining hours as follows:

**16. Get results from prime time.** This is the time in your week reserved for working exclusively on A and B tasks. Ideally the bulk of your time, 15 to 25 hours per week, should be blocked out as prime time. During this time you should concentrate your undivided attention on high priority tasks. To be most effective you should schedule it at times when you are typically most alert and energetic and when you are least likely to be interrupted. Some directors find they can get the most done by coming in at 7 AM, while others concentrate best late in the evenings.

**17. Be available during interaction time.** Since you will strive to avoid all personal contacts, except those which you initiate, during prime time, you need to set aside an hour or more every day (ideally the same time every day) for interacting with others. If your staff members know there will be a time they can talk to you every day, they will be less likely to interrupt you during your prime time.

During interaction time you should return calls you received during your prime time, be available to discuss problems or ideas with staff members, hold staff meetings, meet with parents, schedule meetings with outside parties, or make daily rounds of the classrooms.

**18. Limit routine tasks time.** Set aside a small block of time every week for attacking non-urgent C tasks that must be done. Do as many of the most important tasks from your C list as you can during this time, and then set the remainder aside for the following week.

**19. Utilize lunch time, too.** Coffee breaks and lunch times should be put to productive use as well as work times. If you are working under a lot of pressure, you should work at relaxing during your break times. Get away from the center, read a book, take a walk, or jog. Enjoy yourself, and don't bring your work along.

Some directors find lunch times to be a convenient time to spend alone with individual staff members. Others find that lunch time, combined with nap time, is the quietest time in the center — the time when they are most able to concentrate on A and B tasks.

**20. Reserve crisis time.** The best laid scheduling plans often go awry when the school van breaks down or the lead teacher in the three-year-old room calls in sick 20 minutes before the children arrive. To prepare for these inevitable unexpected crises, your weekly schedule should include some uncommitted hours, especially toward the end of the week. Ideally, these free hours should be scheduled after prime time hours so that if no crises occur you can simply keep on working on high priority tasks.

If you are hit with a major, time consuming crisis, be prepared to sacrifice prime time: but don't then become discouraged and abandon all future efforts to control your time. As soon as possible force yourself to get back to your schedule.

**21. Protect your leisure time.** Child care directors must be prepared to devote certain evenings or weekends to handling unavoidable crises and to attending meetings and conferences. What should be resisted vigorously, however, is falling into the habit of routinely giving up your leisure hours to work. Robbing your leisure time in this way can have a negative impact on your health, alienate your friends and family, cause you to resent your job and drain your energy so that your effectiveness and alertness is reduced during working hours. In addition, falling into the home work habit can become a vicious cycle as you feel less pressure to complete work during the day, because you tell yourself you can get it done at night (Bliss).

**22. Solicit cooperation.** If you are to succeed in setting aside blocks of prime time to concentrate on high priority tasks, you will need to gain the support and understanding of people who frequently interact with you. It is quite possible that staff members will become resentful if you are unavailable most of the time. Before you start your first week on a schedule you set, you should meet with your staff to explain what you are doing and to ask for their cooperation in making it work. If they appreciate what you are doing is in the best interest of the program, they will be more likely to respect your privacy during prime time.

Also, when staff do come to you with a problem, see to it that you are attentive and helpful. Their resentment of your time management efforts is likely to dissipate if they see that you are, in fact, still able to help them with their problems.

Likewise, identify individuals outside the staff who most frequently interrupt you with calls and visits. Ask for their cooperation as well, and advise them when your interaction time is so they will know when you will be available.

**23. Don't expect instant success.** Directors who have been successful in gaining control over the scheduling of their time have found that they did not notice a significant improvement immediately. Even though they may have fully intended to devote 20 or more hours to high priority tasks that first week, they found that once the week began, they were continually distracted by phone calls, visitors and their own procrastination. It was not until about the third or fourth week that they finally were able to log significant numbers of hours of uninterrupted prime time. It may take this long to break old work practices and to get others to adjust to your schedule.

## Fight Procrastination

It has been said — "There's no time like the present for postponing what you don't want to do." Indeed, procrastination is the number one enemy of effective time management. Faced with a difficult or unpleasant task, it is extremely tempting to yield to countless distractions and more enjoyable tasks. The following are some suggestions for dispelling the fascination of procrastination:

**24. Confront yourself.** Much procrastination is unintentional — you allow yourself to be sidetracked without thinking about it. Often such mindless diversions can be avoided by asking yourself — "What is the best use of my time and energy right now?" If the answer is not what you are doing at the moment, stop that and put your time and energy to work on a more important task (LeBoeuf).

**25. Attack ugly tasks first.** When you start the day, it may be most effective to dispense with the most unpleasant task on your priority list first. If you postpone working on this task, you will most likely fret about it all day, thus preventing yourself from concentrating fully on other tasks you attempt.

**26. Create instant tasks.** Sometimes it helps to take a major task you're avoiding and break out some easy sub-tasks which you can readily start. For example, if the major task is filling out income tax reports, instant tasks could include pulling together all the necessary income and expense documents, filling out the identifying information on the forms, or reading the instructions on filling out the forms. Once you get rolling on these *instant tasks*, you might establish some momentum that will carry you well into the major task (Lakein).

**27. Establish familiarity.** It may help to get started on an intimidating task by establishing some familiarity with it. If the task is developing the budget, you might reduce your resistance to starting by reading articles on preparing budgets.

**28. Offer yourself a reward.** Try to give yourself some incentives for completing major tasks. Promise yourself, for example, that when you complete a difficult task at hand you can go out and have a lobster salad sandwich or call up another director you enjoy chatting with.

**29. Put pressure on yourself.** Don't allow yourself the luxury of extra time for procrastinating. Give yourself a deadline for a task that does not allow you any leeway for wasting time.

**30. Take advantage of your moods.** How many times have you said — "I'm just not in the mood"? You should use your moods to your advantage. For example, you may not feel like writing that report today, but you may feel like organizing the next staff training session. Remember those high priority tasks you have been delaying and put your moods to work for you (LeBoeuf).

**31. Complete what you start.** Once you've overcome the inertia of getting started and are rolling on a difficult task, it is a mistake to stop. Try to finish a task or a complete unit of a task in one setting. If you stop, you may well waste additional time getting organized and getting rolling again.

**32. Leave work starters behind.** Sometimes it is impossible to complete a task when you leave for the day or go to lunch or head to a meeting. On these occasions it may help to get right back into the swing of the task you left behind if you stop at a point where the next step is obvious. Then when you return you won't need to waste time trying to decide where to begin.

**33. Close Escape Routes.** Everyone has their favorite routes for escaping from doing unpleasant tasks. These may include wandering into the classrooms to chat with the teachers and the children, reading the newspaper, staring out the window, or leaving the center to run unimportant errands.

To avoid procrastinating in these ways, try to cut off all opportunities to take advantage of them. For example, work somewhere far removed from the classrooms, don't bring the newspaper to work, close the curtains, and don't bring your car to work for running errands. Make it inconvenient to use escape routes (Lakein).

## AVOID TIME WASTERS

"Meetings, visitors and telephone calls are not necessarily unproductive any more than gunpowder is a necessarily destructive substance. It's all a matter of application." (LeBoeuf). Unfortunately, the seeming legitimacy of these common time wasters allows them to eat up large chunks of child care directors' productive time. The following are some suggestions for counteracting the wasteful aspects of these occurrences:

**34. Avoid attending meetings.** Don't go to meetings where there is no clear benefit for you or your organization, or where you have nothing to contribute. Explore alternatives to meetings. For example, a decision by a responsible party can eliminate the need for group action. A conference call may substitute for getting together. Delay holding a meeting until all the facts relating to an action are available. When all else fails send a representative in your place (Mackenzie).

**35. Keep meetings short.** Start meetings on time. Announce the ending time at the onset and stick to it. Schedule meetings near the end of the day so that participants will be eager for it to end. Circulate an agenda prior to the meeting and stick to it. Keep attendance at meetings as small as possible. Be clear at the outset what is to be accomplished at the meeting and discourage sidetracking. Hold meetings in rooms without chairs, or at least with uncomfortable chairs, so that participants will not be inclined to let the meeting last longer than absolutely necessary (Mackenzie).

**36. Discourage drop-in visitors.** While you, as the director, will want to maintain good personal relationships with people you work with, you cannot afford to be continually distracted from accomplishing center business by drop-in visitors.

To discourage prolonged social visits, a number of simple measures may help. Avoid making eye contact with every passer-by. Close your office door when concentrating, or face your desk away from the door. Remove excess chairs and other social amenities from your office to avoid playing the informal host. If someone unexpectedly walks into your office, stand up and confer with him while standing. Such body language usually indicates to the visitor that you're busy and have more pressing things to do. If someone knocks on your door, confer with him outside the office. Once again, the idea is to keep visitors from firmly planting themselves in your office (LeBoeuf).

**37. Meet elsewhere.** When you need to meet with someone, agree to meet in their office. You can control the length of the meeting since you can leave at any time.

**38. Control phone calls.** Avoid taking calls during prime time hours. If you have the luxury of a secretary, provide him with a list of callers to put through and have him take messages from all others. If you must take calls yourself, explain what you are doing and promise to call back at an agreed upon time.

When making calls, if you must ask for someone to call back, give a preferred time. Make a note of the best time to reach anyone you expect to call frequently. Buy a small, three-minute timer and put it by your phone. Every time you get a call or make one, see if you can successfully complete it in three minutes (LeBoeuf).

**39. Get a hideaway.** Some directors have found that when they really need to work undisturbed, they must get away from the center. Some can accomplish most by working at home occasionally. Others succeed by fleeing to a quiet corner in the local library.

## ADOPT TIME SAVERS

While the key to effective time management is being able to concentrate on doing the most important tasks first, there are definite advantages to adopting some time saving techniques as well. Although time freed up by time savers may seem incidental, the cumulative effect can be significant. Each new way to save ten minutes a day gives you more than 60 hours a year of *extra* time.

**40. Learn to say no.** Of all time saving techniques ever developed, perhaps the most effective is the frequent use of the word *no*. You cannot protect your priorities unless you learn to decline tactfully, but firmly, every request for your time that does not contribute to the achievement of your personal goals or the goals of your center (Bliss).

Sometimes it is most tempting to say *yes* when you are asked to do something well in the future when you at last expect *to be on top of things*. Before you say *yes* to a commitment for the future, however, see if you would have time for it now. If you don't have time now chances are you won't later. Say *no*.

**41. Delegate tasks.** A most effective option when you are overworked is to delegate to other staff members some of your tasks. This option, however, is often rejected by directors. Suffering from the classic workaholic syndrome, they believe — "I must do everything myself; no one else here has enough interest, time, knowledge, or ability." This attitude is often wrong on all counts. Not only can delegating relieve some of your workload, it can also provide a change of pace for teachers and give them a greater sense of involvement in the overall life of the center.

When delegating work to other staff members, delegate important work. Don't waste their time and talents on trivial or low priority work. When delegating work, give the individuals involved the full assignment in advance. Don't dribble assignments out piece by piece. Give staff the opportunity to plan and be responsible for a complete unit of work. Then once you've made the assignment, leave them alone; don't be continually looking over their shoulders and second guessing their work (Mackenzie).

**42. Consolidate tasks.** When confronted with a batch of smaller tasks, it is most efficient to consolidate tasks by category and complete them all at once. For example, initiate and return all phone calls during one period rather than sporadically throughout the day. Do all errands at once rather than making two or three trips out of the center each day. Take care of all financial tasks — paying bills, balancing the checkbook, preparing invoices — at the same time.

**43. Read selectively.** This is becoming the age of information overload. Step into any director's office and you will see rows and stacks of books, magazines, newspapers, memos, reports, and bulletins everywhere. There is always too much to read and too little time. The main solution is to read selectively — to zero in on reading that which is most beneficial. With a book or magazine, first scan the table of contents to determine what articles, chapters, or parts of chapters may contain ideas you can use. Then only read those potentially beneficial sections. If nothing of relevance jumps out at you, don't bother with the publication at all.

**44. Read faster.** The extravagant claims of most speed-reading crusaders tend to make the practice appear less than credible at times. Nonetheless, most people could significantly increase their reading speed by adopting the underlying techniques of speed reading. Increase your reading span by taking in groups of words rather than single words. Stop moving your head from side to side as you read. Stop rereading. Start with the second or third word of each line to stop wasting peripheral vision on margins (Mackenzie).

**45. Organize your work space.** Efficiency experts recommend that you should have absolutely nothing on your desk except that which relates to the task you are working on at the time. Most directors would find this somewhat less than realistic. However, the reasoning underlying this ivory tower advice is valid — the more things in your immediate work space, the more you are likely to be distracted from the task at hand. Make a list of all the tools, supplies, books, and files which you utilize on a daily basis. Make sure these items can be reached without leaving your chair. As much as possible remove everything else from your immediate work area.

**46. Make your work space comfortable**. Some directors seem to believe there is some value in working under Spartan conditions. In fact, an uncomfortable work space is only a distraction that serves to hinder productivity. As Michael LeBoeuf observes, "Life is already filled with a more than ample supply of discomforts, distractions and frustrations." Why add more?

**47. Use a pocket diary.** Brilliant ideas and dates and people to remember often occur when you are away from your desk. To keep from losing these key bits of information, always keep a pocket diary / appointment book with you. This will also save you the time of having to sift through dozens of scraps of paper to find that vital note.

**48. Avoid perfectionism.** There is a difference between striving for excellence and striving for perfection. The first is attainable, gratifying and healthy. The second is often unattainable, frustrating and neurotic. It can also be a terrible waste of time. As Edwin Bliss suggests, "Spend a reasonable amount of time on tasks striving for a 'sensible approximation' of perfection."

**49. Carry five minute tasks.** Keep with you a batch of five-minute tasks — memos to write, letters to answer, articles to read, or questionnaires to complete. Whenever you end up having to wait — for meetings, buses, dentists, etc. — pull out these tasks and polish off a few.

**50. Keep fit.** Your ability to work hard over long periods of time is dependent upon your physical vigor. Being in good shape through regular exercise will increase the number of hours you are able to work alertly and effectively during the day (Bliss).

## References


Bliss, E. C. (1976). *Getting Things Done: The ABC's of Time Management.* New York: Charles Scribner's Sons.

Frost, T. S. (1976). *Where Have All the Woolly Mammoths Gone?* West Nyack, New York: Parker Publishing Company, Inc.

Lakein, A. (1973). *How to Get Control of Your Time and Your Life.* New York: New American Library.

LeBeouf, M. (1979). *Working Smart.* New York: Warner Books.

Mackenzie, R. A. (1972). *The Time Trap.* New York: McGraw-Hill Book Company.

Odiorne, G. (1974). *Management and the Activity Trap.* New York: Harper and Row.

# And Away We Grow! A Five Phase Model for Growing a Child Care Business

by Pauline Davey Zeece

*The report to the board was an overwhelming success. Everyone was pleased and excited about the numbers — all slots filled, a long waiting list, and now the go-ahead for the third expansion in a year. Yet the gnawing in your stomach just won't go away. Why do you feel so nervous, even scared, at a time when so many others are telling you "bravo"?*

The answer to your question may be related to one of the best kept secrets in child care program administration. Growing a business and managing it well is difficult, trying, even painful work. It requires a keen understanding not only of where you are going, but where you have been. Growing well takes insight, courage, and information about the nature of growth itself.

In a provocative article on managing expansion, Sharlit and McConnell (1989) propose a five-phase model of business growth: **creativity**, **direction**, **delegation**, **coordination**, and **collaboration**. Each of these phases is further divided into two stages designated as **evolution** and **revolution**.

During the evolution of a phase, growth is relatively calm and predictable. This is often the time when practices and policies are formulated. As the revolution phase begins, the same well-tested, well-received practices may become ineffective, incomplete, or sometimes even problematic.

Following are descriptions of Sharlit and McConnell's five phases of development as these might apply to a growing child care program. See if you can place your own expanding program somewhere along the continuum.

## Phase 1 — Creativity

Phase 1 is where it all begins for an early childhood education program. It is the time when a program and its initial policies and practices are launched. It is also a period when first memories are most likely to be created. It may be the source of a myriad of "remember when" comments heard throughout all other phases of development. These are the "good old days" of a program's history — even when they are not!

**Evolution.** Getting the program off to a good start is the primary goal of this stage. Everyone rolls up their sleeves and pools their resources to ensure a sound and successful beginning. Directors and staff may work long hours for meager compensation — often side by side. Communication is frequent, informal, and staff may feel very close to the director. At this point, the program may be reactive in nature. Clients may directly or indirectly dictate the terms of service provision and impact upon many of the activities surrounding managerial decision making.

**Revolution.** As growth begins, working hard on-line is usually not enough. Additionally, the child care administrator must now use (or acquire if necessary) more specialized knowledge about the actual business of child care programming — personnel, finances, management strategies, marketing. This is the time when leadership approaches and styles become identified and cultivated. A management team approach is implemented in some programs during Phase 1.

*Implications for Directors*

Little matches the excitement of successfully beginning a program. Yet sustained success occurs only when a director is willing to first dig in and then step back. If staff members do not understand why this occurs, they may feel abandoned or even used. Clear, honest, and frequent communicating aids in the successful movement into Phase 2.

Five questions to clarify thinking during Phase 1:

1. Can I really do this?

2. What can I do to make sure that everyone (especially me!) understands the long- and the short-term consequences of all the actions and decisions which occur?

3. How can I help staff to understand how and why my involvement has begun to change?

4. What messages have I given about channels of communication in this program? How do I know that everyone hears and understands about important program issues?

5. What specific information do I need to do my best as we begin this venture? How do I obtain this information?

## Phase 2 — Direction

The direction phase is characterized by a program's first period of sustained growth. During this time the blueprint for more efficient organizational functioning is laid down to deal with the changes and challenges associated with initial development. Some staff members are given increased responsibilities as team or program area leaders and managers. Growth causes excitement and anxiety throughout a program.

**Evolution.** In the evolution stage, Sharlit and McConnell suggest that several changes may appear. Organizational structure becomes more sophisticated as the need to separate program activities increases. Fiscal management, personnel development, marketing, and curriculum development must increasingly be attended to in specialized ways. Job assignments become more specified and communication throughout the program is less spontaneous and more formalized.

**Revolution.** The revolution stage of Phase 2 is oftentimes driven by problems related to the sense of loss or threat felt by employees who do not understand why the functions and familiarity associated with the "good old days" have changed, decreased, or disappeared. As a hierarchy of responsibilities and positions emerges, it is common for adversarial feelings to surface. An "us versus them" agenda may rob the program of its past sense of purpose.

*Implications for Directors*

Administrators caught up in the challenge of rapid growth may not notice that all is not well during this phase. In fact, a director is sometimes the last to know that effective communication has diminished or broken down completely or that guerrilla warfare exists within staff ranks. A director who facilitates communication during growth optimizes the chances for a program to thrive during this period. Building bridges among all program components and employees is an especially necessary activity at this time.

Five questions to clarify thinking during Phase 2:

1. How will changes in organizational structures be best achieved?

2. By what mechanism will job assignments be redefined? What safeguards are in place to ensure that the most competent staff are not just given more work, rather differently defined or expanded assignments?

3. How can the memories of the "good old days" be retained and used to drive the further development of the program?

4. What mechanism is in place to get information **to** as well as from the director? What measures are taken to hear comments and concerns from all employees?

5. Have changes inadvertently developed a special class of protected employees? What other perceptions might contribute to an "us versus them" mindset among staff? How could these be mediated in a constructive way?

## Phase 3 — Delegation

When a rapidly growing child care program reaches Phase 3 in its development, competent directors seek ways to efficiently and effectively delegate more responsibilities. This means that duties across all areas of the program may be turned over to program leaders, coordinators, or middle managers. Staff are recruited and trained carefully to accept such increased responsibilities. Ideally, their activities are monitored, but not policed. They are given the autonomy to make real decisions about real issues affecting their areas. A director serves as a model mentor by providing information, encouragement, and support (of all kinds).

**Evolution.** As the delegation phase evolves, a subtle shift in the primary focus of a director's duties occurs. As staff are put in place to deal with a myriad of operations-related issues **and** to keep the director informed, a director begins to focus more effort on the development of such things as long-range planning, improved market-ing strategies, and continued growth (Sharlit & McConnell). This also may be the time when a director's "open door" policy ends in some programs. In this instance, communication becomes more formal and the era of the memo may be initiated.

**Revolution.** While it may be logical to assume that the loss of direct access to a director may cause staff discord, administrators are also thought to face their own challenges during the revolution stage. The competent, caring director who has built a program from the ground up (or who moved a program forward to previously unknown places) may find himself or herself in the throes of what Sharlit and McConnell term a "control crisis." Often centralized management returns after a crisis. Some directors panic and attempt to make all decisions and demand control over previously relinquished areas.

*Implications for Directors*

Phase 3 can be one of the most difficult times for a director who is highly and personally invested in a program. Giving up control or delegating to those who in turn make poor decisions or costly mistakes while they learn is hard to do. The temptation may be great to say: "Never mind, I'll do it myself; I'll do it my way!" During Phase 3, crises will occur, setbacks will happen, and mistakes will be made. There will always be those rare directors who will be able to retrench and successfully control everything by themselves. But the cost of such control and redirection may be quite dire for the program (and even for the director) in the long run.

Five questions to clarify thinking during Phase 3:

1. How should a director's duties and responsibilities change during this phase? What consequences will these changes have for the day-to-day operations of the program?

2. What mechanisms are in place to ensure that staff have the ongoing resources they need to make good use of their newly delegated authority?

3. What plan is in place to handle crises of all kinds? Who contributes to the development and monitoring of this plan?

4. Under what circumstance would it be necessary for a director to rescind previously delegated responsibilities and assume all control in a program? How would this shift be executed? Monitored? Conveyed to staff?

5. What resources or strategies could a director employ to reassign responsibilities after a crisis?

## Phase 4 — Coordination

When a director works through the control crises of Phase 3 and appropriately and successfully delegates with a child care program, the coordination activities of Phase 4 logically evolve. At this point in a large, growing program, networking between delegated areas and personnel is crucial. The complex and diverse nature of a program's activities require a well-constructed and finely coordinated management approach.

**Evolution.** In the evolution stage, coordination activities facilitate and support formal planning efforts. Sharlit and McConnell suggest that this is the point at which some activities are firmly centralized (e.g., data processing), while others are slowly decentralized (e.g., decision making). The role of the program's administrative team is expanded to include mechanisms to review and evaluate goals, objectives, and long-term outcomes.

**Revolution.** The revolution stage during coordination contains activities which occur typically in many large, evolving bureaucratic systems. A sense of powerlessness may appear in on-line staff who feel their efforts now go unnoticed or that their actions no longer make a meaningful contribution. Equally serious, procedures may take precedence over problem solving. This can be the death knell for innovative thinking or for creative risk taking. Without insightful managerial intervention, a director and a program may become seriously bogged down in its own red tape.

*Implications for Directors*

Sharlit and McConnell advise that the bureaucratic crisis of Phase 4 can be mediated or overcome through the introduction of a more flexible management style. For example, groups, teams, or other areas within a program could be given increased autonomy. At the same time, intergroup protocols could be standardized to facilitate meaningful coordination of efforts. As program coordination is refined, a sophisticated decentralization might be proposed and implemented. This sets the dias for the final phase where true collaborative efforts occur.

Five questions to clarify thinking during Phase 4:

1. What networking system would work best within this unit? What technology would enhance this network? How could such networking tie the program to outside resources?

2. How does this program use formal planning? Can this be improved? In what ways? By whom?

3. What activities benefit most from centralization? Decentralization?

4. How can increased flexibility be introduced into the present management style? What are some of the costs and benefits from doing this? For the program? For the staff? For the director?

5. What else needs to happen in this program to set the stage for successful, collaborative interactions?

## Phase 5 — Collaboration

Sharlit and McConnell predict that, following decentralization, a team approach to problem solving and innovation can be emphasized. A program in this phase is now able to devote much of its creative energy to achieving collective goals and reaching collective success. Systems have evolved and developed within the program which help all staff to see that there is a way in which their voice can be "heard," even if this does not involve visiting with the director herself or himself.

**Evolution.** During the evolution of this final stage, a director may devote resources to ensuring that key managers and employees are working together to facilitate growth in each program area. The connection and trust between director and these key staff is very important, as they are the connection to the pulse of the on-line staff and the client families. For some directors, there may even be a sense of isolation at this point. Yet sustained and meaningful collaborative efforts require the sustained and informed leadership of a visionary director, even when that director feels lonely in her/his leadership role.

**Revolution.** Ideally, in this model, there is no revolution stage in this final phase of development. When people within a program collaborate in productive and meaningful ways, everyone thrives. In the real world of child care program administration, however, there is always work to do — things to learn and change and laugh at when they do not make sense. The point of this model is that there is a place at which directors can hope to be with their program, staff, and themselves. Some of us live in that place as we do this job. Some of us just visit for awhile. Some of us are not even ready to make the journey.

Five questions to clarify thinking during Phase 5:

1. In the ideal sense, how would collaborative efforts occur throughout this program?
2. What rewards are given to encourage and sustain collaborative efforts? Who monitors the distribution of these rewards? What role does the director play?
3. How is information from key managers and program areas utilized? Shared? Analyzed?
4. What technology is used (or could be used) to optimize collaborative efforts? How is this technology shared throughout the program?
5. Can I do this?

## Some Final Thoughts about Growth

Some of the best information about directing an early childhood education program comes from watching the children who have been entrusted to our care. Such is the case with understanding about growth. Like growing children, growing programs are both predictable and unpredictable. Programs are predictable in the stages through which they will pass as they grow. They are unpredictable or different in the time and the rate of their growth.

No program is ever textbook perfect. This means that some parts of this model will be useful and other parts will make little or no sense. The useful parts should be pondered and gleaned and utilized to the fullest. The unuseful parts should be passed over for better information or alternative insights.

No part of a program escapes the trials and triumphs associated with growth. And while such growth is taking place, young children and their families are being impacted in a host of ways. The costs of not growing sanely and soundly may be greatest to those a program serves first.

## Reference

Sharlit, I. B., & McConnell, C. J. (July 1989). "Managing Growth," *Small Business Reports*, pp. 27-33.

# Hide It in Plain Sight

by Edna Runnels Ranck

> *"Now, where is the insurance policy and automobile club card for the van?"*
> *"Are the insurance policies filed under 'Building' or 'Vehicles' . . . or both?"*
> *"I know the folder with the rental agreement must be here someplace."*
> *"The warranty and service agreement should be under 'TV/VCR,' but they're not here.*

If these laments sound familiar, you may want to examine your "file style" and give serious consideration to putting your center's essential documents in systematic order once and for all. Everyone needs a simple, consistent, workable filing system, and busy people absolutely require one to remain efficient and effective (Hemphill, 1992; Ranck, 1995). Child care program directors especially need a flexible but structured means of filing and retrieving documents: the well-being, if not the lives, of children and staff may rest on pulling exactly the right file folder from the drawer when it's needed.

A wide range of details is involved in filing and storing your program's essential documents so that each one is in a place that you know about and that you can find at a moment's notice. Even if you have staff to do the filing, you as the director must know where every document is and how to find it. *It's time; do you know where your essential documents are?*

*Essential documents* are required to prove ownership, to show compliance to predetermined conditions, or to indicate your right to operate the program and its equipment. Often, they are needed in case of an emergency event, such as a van accident; when an immediate decision is required, such as purchasing a new refrigerator at an appliance sale; or when an opportunity for a basic change comes up, such as re-negotiating a mortgage or lease. Essential documents are the legal documents required to operate a business in your community and to meet licensing or occupancy requirements of local or state government. Some essential documents, especially originals, may best be stored away from the program site in a bank safe deposit box.

This article will focus on the filing and storage of essential documents. Important files required for keeping children's enrollment and staff employment records, board minutes and election processes, curriculum materials, correspondence, and archived documents will not be addressed. However, the principles cited here apply to other types of documents as well.

**About state-specific requirements.** Most essential documents have legal and fiscal importance. Since state laws and regulations vary, you are urged to discuss your document issues with the relevant professional — your attorney, accountant, insurance agent, licensing contact, etc.

**About computer files.** Although the world has not yet become the "paperless society" predicted a decade ago, child care programs must also organize their electronic files with care and consistency. Ideally, a center's computer programs should be recorded under the same major categories as the paper documents. Many center-created documents can reside in a hard drive, on back-up disk, and in paper files. *Always back up your important operating documents.*

## One Director's Story

### The Opportunity for Change

Sally was looking forward to her new position as director of the Happy Apple Children's Center. She happily envisioned her first day as she greeted the children and parents at the entrance. She would observe the staff and the children during the morning sessions, learning names and daily routines, and sensing the climate of the program. Lunch in one of the classrooms would highlight the day. In the afternoon, Sally would start a review of the program files and plan her first staff meeting. Here's how that first day actually went:

## Things to Do to Reorganize the Filing System for a Child Care Program

| Things to Do | Person Responsible |
|---|---|
| Conduct inventory of all files and place in a central location. | Director, Head Teacher, Secretary |
| Conduct inventory of office supplies. | Secretary |
| Order additional supplies. | Director and Secretary |
| Determine need for bank safe deposit box and make arrangements with a bank, preferably a complimentary box with the bank in which the program accounts are located. | Director and Finance Officer or Board Treasurer |
| Brainstorm essential document file categories and make a 5″x8″ sign for each one. | Director, Head Teacher, Secretary |
| Identify file cabinet drawer(s) or strong file boxes for storing **only** essential documents. Install a hanging file frame in each drawer and use hanging files. These may be color coded for each category if desired. In black ink, print each file category in BLOCK LETTERS on hanging file label: **BUILDING**. | Director and Secretary |
| Review each file folder to discard duplicates and obsolete documents and to archive necessary items. Allow enough time for this lengthy task; new directors should get advice from long-time staff before discarding documents. | Director and Head Teacher |
| Assign each file folder to one of the file categories. | Director and Secretary |
| In black ink, print each file folder label title in Upper and Lower Case letters: **Insurance**. | Secretary |
| Create an **Essential Document Directory** on a hard drive and a three-ring binder or a special color folder. Place hard copies in the front of the first EDD file drawer. | Secretary |
| Distribute copies of the directory to the head teacher and board president. | Director |
| Maintain the files by making changes as they occur and recording them in the directory. | Director and Secretary |

## Happy Apple Children's Center Inventory and Supply Order (Supply Order items in parentheses)

- One four-drawer letter-size file cabinet with hanging file frames in two drawers and no key for the lock (one matching four-drawer file cabinet with keys and hanging file frames for all non-equipped drawers)
- Hanging file folders and a box of plastic label holders (refill box of label inserts)
- Used letter-size manila folders recycled from earlier use (one box of new manila folders in one-third cut, plain peel-off labels for manila file folder tabs)
- Felt-tip markers in black and blue (red markers as well as additional black and blue markers in different size points)
- Two-inch three-ring binder to use as a file directory (clear plastic sleeves for individual page inserts and separators for each major category)
- Box of blank computer disks (peel-off labels for disks)

6:30 AM: The morning van driver called to report that the van wouldn't start. *"Now, where is the insurance policy and automobile club card for the van?"*

9:30 AM: The mail arrived with a registered, second overdue notice for insurance policy premiums. *"Are the insurance policies filed under 'Building' or 'Vehicles' . . . or both?"*

10:30 AM: The building owner dropped by to ask if the center was interested in renting the room on the second floor for meeting and training space for staff, parents, and board. *"I know the folder with the rental agreement must be here someplace."*

11:30 AM: Anna-Li, the lead teacher in the four-year-old classroom, announced that the TV/VCR had no sound. *"The warranty and service agreement should be under 'Equipment: TV/VCR' but they're not here."*

By the end of the first day, Sally knew she had to do something about the center's filing system. Not only did she need to be able to locate any given document at any given time, but also the secretary, Donna, Anna-Li, and even whoever the next director might be should also be able to find things quickly. That night, Sally made a list of what had to be done to implement a new filing system at the center and who on the staff would do each task (see "Things to Do to Reorganize the Filing System for a Child Care Program" box). The next morning, Sally and Donna conducted a quick inventory of office supplies which they found in five different closets and drawers throughout the center, not counting the office files. They wrote out a shopping list of additional items which Donna phoned in to an office supply store for next-day delivery (see "Inventory and Supply Order" box).

Other items on the order list included paper clips in assorted sizes and wire baskets for temporary storage of file folders while they are in use or when they are ready to be returned to the files.

### Making Change Happen

Because it is difficult to concentrate on detailed filing tasks when the children are present, Sally offered Anna-Li and Donna comp time for working on the next available weekend. On Saturday morning, the three colleagues pulled two large tables into the office and proceeded to set up a new file system that fit the requirements of their program. After brainstorming the major categories they knew they would need, they narrowed the list to four: *Building*, *Equipment*, *Program Operations*, and *Vehicles*. For each category, they made a 5"x8" file card with the category name on it and laid them on the table. Each file folder was assigned to one of the major categories. As they assigned each folder, they sorted the contents. Duplicates and obsolete documents went in the recycling bin. Similar documents were combined into a single file folder. Old but valuable documents went in a separate file box marked ARCHIVES to be reviewed carefully and stored properly later.

Each major category was given a label with a heading handwritten in bold, black all-cap letters and inserted into the plastic holder for hanging files. Each file folder had a peel-off label handwritten in upper and lower case letters. When they finished the task many hours later, they had come up with a full list of major categories and their subcategories for the essential documents in the Happy Apple Children's Center (see "Essential Document Categories" box).

## Managing Paper

Hemphill, a paper management consultant, suggests that people ask four questions about each piece of paper:

1. Do I *really* need to keep this?
2. *Where* should I keep it?
3. How *long* should I keep it?
4. How can I *find* it?

This article assumes a "yes" for question #1 and "for as long as necessary" for #3. If those two are answered fully, then questions #2 and #4 almost answer themselves; if you decide where to keep a piece of paper and maintain a written record of the location, you'll be able to find it at a later time!

## Happy Apple Children's Center
## Essential Document Categories

### — Building —

- Mortgage or lease or rental arrangements and contact person/s
- Insurance for building/contents (theft, fire, storm) and personal injury — agent's name and contact information
- Certificate of occupancy (CO) from the municipality and related permits
- Fire extinguishers and smoke alarms: record of purchase and schedule for servicing
- Contact information and schedule for carpenter, cleaning contract, garbage collection, glazer, heat/air conditioning, locksmith, playground maintenance, plumber, snow removal (if needed)
- Paint, tile, carpet, fabric swatches with contact information

### — Equipment —

- Keep a full inventory list of equipment by site location, classroom, office, kitchen, playground — include date of purchase, cost, depreciation if applicable, source of item and funding
- Prepare a file folder for the equipment in each location: kitchen, office, classroom A, B, C, etc., playground — keep in each folder the information for each piece of equipment: purchase order or donation source, receipt, warranty, maintenance agreement, and operating instructions

### — Program Operations —

- Incorporation papers
- Tax-related papers (tax-exempt letter from IRS, state tax-exempt certificate, corporate filing papers)
- Charitable organization records (if applicable)
- State and local licenses and accreditations (copies posted in visible location)
- Employment-related payments, tax records, payroll information
- Bank statements and account records — bank branch and contact information
- Investment accounts
- Bylaws, including original and each revision
- Attorney contract or agreement
- Accountant contract or agreement
- Medical personnel contract or agreement
- Insurance policies (copies of relevant policies should be in building and vehicle folders)
- Food documents and permits
- Fire drill procedures and record
- Corporate credit card records
- Funding sources, contracts, reports, etc.
- Journal and periodical subscriptions — payment and renewal schedules

### — Vehicles —

- Title or proof of ownership (original in safe deposit box, copy in files) for each vehicle
- Registration documentation and renewal schedule for each vehicle
- Insurance policies (originals in safe deposit box, copies in files) for each vehicle
- Automobile club membership
- Authorized drivers, proof of age, copy of license with photo, etc.
- Service and repair arrangements and maintenance schedule for each vehicle
- Gas/oil credit card (if applicable)
- Parking arrangements in garage or on parking lot

Hemphill's Principle on dealing with paper is: "If you don't know you have it or you can't find it, it is of NO value to you!" (p. 14). In the case of child care programs where lives are at stake, Ranck's Principle takes this statement one more step: *If it is of critical value to your program, you'd better know that each document is accurate, up to date, and in its proper place.*

## This Is a Test!

The following four questions are adapted from Hemphill's (pp. 12-13) paper-management skills survey and will test your knowledge about your own agency's file system. If you can't answer "yes" to the questions, it's time to re-read the article and start revising your filing system!

- I recognize the need to safeguard essential documents for my child care program
- I know which documents are essential to the responsible operation of my child care program
- I know exactly where every essential document is located in my program
- Someone else also knows where the essential documents are located and has a written list of their locations

Probably everyone's grandmother had a saying: *A place for everything and everything in its place*. Hemphill summarizes this old adage in modern terms: "An effective paper management system will help you control what you do with your time and energy and create an environment that is supportive of your plans and dreams" (p. 7). Sally made a copy of this quotation and hung it above the filing cabinets. A system that supports plans and dreams sounds like a good idea to me. How about you? Does your filing system make life meaningful and plans operable and dreams fulfilled?

## A Word of Advice to Directors Starting a New Program

Sally inherited her child care center from a previous administration, warts and all. Although not thoroughly familiar with the entire existing filing system, Anna-Li and Donna were able to suggest which files were important and where they should be filed. Persons preparing to open a new center have the opportunity to start a new filing system that will work for them and their successors.

Use this article as a jumping-off place; purchase a management book or video to get your process started or hire a consultant to assist your efforts in designing the most appropriate filing and storage system for your program.

## Resources

Child Care Law Center (CCLC), 973 Market Street, Suite 550, San Francisco, California 94103, (415) 495-5498 (www.childcarelaw.org).

National Association for Regulatory Administration (NARA), 26 East Exchange Street, Fifth Floor, St. Paul, Minnesota 55101-2264, (651) 290-6280 (www.nara-licensing.org).

National Association of Child Care Resource and Referral Agencies (NACCRRA), 1319 F Street NW, Suite 810, Washington, DC 20004-1106, (202) 393-5501 (www.naccrra.org).

## References


Hemphill, B. (1992). *Taming the paper tiger: Organizing the paper in your life.* Revised and expanded edition. Washington, DC: Kiplinger Books. Useful in understanding why paper encroaches on your space and time and helpful in supplying practical suggestions for bringing about change in your life of paper use and storage.

Ranck, E. R. (November-December, 1995). "Do Will You Remember? Taking a child care program's past into the future." *Exchange, 106*, 91-95. Applies the principles of archiving obsolete but important documents for future reference by child care center staff and board members.

Winston, S. (1978). *Getting organized*. New York: Warner Books. Still practical after over 20 years, Winston offers rationales for why things get messy and unorganized and provides quaint references to typewriters and carbon paper. Winston's other books on the same topic are *The organized executive* and *Getting out from under*.

Yager, J. (1999). *Creative time management for the new millennium.* (2d ed.). Stamford, CT: Hannacroix Creek Books. See Chapters 5 and 6 for information about paper management.

# Transforming Your Computer From Paperweight to Management Tool

**by Chip Donohue**

> *"A child of five would understand this. Send someone to fetch a child of five."*
>
> — Groucho Marx

Take a moment to reflect on the words that come to mind when you think about working on a computer. That's long enough! Now, let me ask you six simple questions.

Are the words that come to mind ones you prefer not to speak in polite company?
_ YES
_ NO
_ DEFINE POLITE

Has your computer become a paperweight on your desk (an office version of the clothes rack your exercise bike at home has become)?
_ YES
_ NO
_ SO WHAT, IT DOES THE JOB (I haven't seen my exercise bike in years)!

Does your home VCR have a flashing time/date light?
_ YES
_ NO
_ SO WHAT, IT CAME THAT WAY

Can you tell the difference between your computer mouse and the cute little pet in the preschool room?
_ YES
_ NO
_ ASK MY CAT

Have you ever said, "Today I'm going to learn how to use this #*$&! thing once and for all?"
_ YES
_ NO
_ NONE OF YOUR #*$&! BUSINESS

Have you ever asked a child of five to show you how to do something on the computer?
_ YES
_ NO
_ I REFUSE TO ANSWER ON THE GROUNDS THAT IT MAY INCRIMINATE ME

If you said "yes" to one or more of the questions above, you are not alone in needing help learning how to use your computer more effectively. These tools are new to us and it is hard to find the time to get to the other side of the learning curve. But the computer can help you improve program management and enhance quality, so the effort is worth it.

*"Computers aren't intelligent, they only think they are."*
— Source unknown

The first lesson to learn about working with a computer is that you, not the computer, are the smart one. Most people will admit to being intimidated by the computer the first time they sat down at it, and many confess that it is not an easy feeling to get over.

But why do we feel that way? This box just sits there waiting for you to do something. Ahh-hah! Therein lies the secret. The computer is waiting for you to tell it what to do, and without your input it is little more than a paperweight (and an expensive one at that) taking up space on your desk. So, there is good news and bad news. The good news is that you really are in control and the computer will do whatever you tell it to. But that's also where the bad news comes in. You have to know what to tell it to do if you hope to have the desired outcome — kind of like with partners and kids. As one administrator said to me recently, "I think my computer and I need counseling."

## Computer Literacy for Child Care Administrators: Don't Leave Home Without It

Managing a child care program involves many complex tasks and daily challenges for administrators — but you already know that. The appropriate and effective use of technology can make these tasks more manageable, improve your responsiveness to parents and families, and enhance program quality. However, surprisingly few administrators possess the skills, or have access to the training and technical assistance needed, to take advantage of the opportunities that computer technology, e-mail, the Internet, and distance learning offer. Perhaps you are one of them.

As managers of small businesses, administrators are confronted with a number of critical issues related to their use of technology, including:

- Limited financial resources;
- Inadequate access to technology, training and technical support;
- Dependence on outdated systems (that obsolete computer donated by a parent a few years ago);
- Limited knowledge and skills;
- Lack of resources and technology training specifically designed for child care administrators; and
- Lack of access to the Internet, e-mail and distance learning opportunities.

A survey of center administrators conducted by the Center for Early Childhood Leadership in 1997 and again in 2000 found that while there has been a dramatic increase in the use of technology as a management tool, many administrators still face these challenges. Time, money, and training were identified by administrators as the biggest barriers to their effective use of technology. Are these the barriers that you face?

Even so, computer use in child care administration is clearly on the rise. According to this survey, 65% of the administrators said they had a computer that was adequate for their needs, up from only 12% in 1997. Nearly half of the administrators surveyed use e-mail on a daily basis, compared to just 10% in 1997, but many administrators reported that they have never used the Internet and only 30% report that they currently have access to the Internet or use electronic mail on a regular basis.

To succeed as a child care administrator in our information age, you need access to technology, specific training, opportunities for on-line learning and professional development, access to the wealth of information, resources and services available on the Internet, and the ability to link electronically with parents and other child care professionals.

A child care program managed by a computer-literate director clearly has an advantage in our highly technological age, and the positive impact on program quality, the staff, children, and parents make an investment in computer technology and training a smart business decision.

## How Do You Get Started?

So what do you need to get started? A *must* for every director is access to the Internet and e-mail. You need to network with other child care professionals across the country, and around the world, and learn new ways to use these tools for communicating with staff, and being more responsive to the needs of parents and families.

You also need a word processing program — it's the application you'll use the most. All of the manuals, reports, newsletters, proposals, and correspondence you write will be easier to manage and look more professional with the use of word processing software.

A spreadsheet program allows you to ask "what if" questions and to do budget projections and manage other financial tasks in powerful ways. Managing records and information is a big part of your job, so you'll definitely need a database program. You'll also want a presentation graphics program, because they are fun to use, and more importantly, they help you create eye-catching presentations and proposals. Many administrators are now using desktop publishing, graphics, and digital imaging software to create brochures, flyers, and other marketing materials that *stand out in the crowd*.

These programs can be found in integrated packages like Microsoft Office and Lotus SmartSuite. In addition to an *office suite* of integrated applications, many administrators like to use a Child Care Management Software package that provides templates and guides for many common management tasks.

It's fantastic to see how administrators are using computers to improve their management and enhance program quality. Start out with a few simple tasks, like writing a letter using your word processing program. Experiment with the templates and pre-formatted documents included with your software to give yourself a jump-start. And follow this simple advice when the going gets rough —

*"To err is human — and to blame it on a computer is even more so."*
— Orben's Current Comedy

## Surfing for Quality: Using the Internet as a Management Tool

The Internet has become part of our lives. We live in a *dot com* world with new ways of communicating, gathering information, and doing our personal and professional business. Everywhere you turn you see web site and e-mail addresses, and going on-line is becoming second nature for children and adults. Perhaps you've even launched a web site for your program. Yet the Internet is still a relatively new phenomenon in our homes and child care centers.

We are just beginning to understand the awesome potential the Internet has to bring us closer together, to provide new opportunities to network with one another, to locate, gather and exchange information, to access resources, and to purchase goods and services. You can also use the

Internet to market your program and to increase your access to training, continuing education, and professional development resources. In short, the Internet allows you to bring the world of early care and education directly to your desktop each day.

Each day the number of resources available to early childhood professionals and parents increases in both quantity and quality. Take the opportunity to explore the Internet to see for yourself the rich variety of resources you can use to become a better administrator and to improve the quality of your program and services for children, parents, and families.

E-mail is another new tool that promises to change the way you communicate. Your parents and teachers now have a means of communicating more efficiently and effectively with one another when busy schedules make face-to-face meetings hard to arrange. And, you have another way to correspond with parents, and parents have new opportunities to seek support and information from other teachers and parents.

On-line learning opportunities for training, continuing education, and professional development are also rapidly expanding. For busy administrators they can provide a convenient alternative to traditional course delivery systems. The best on-line courses respond to the needs, interests, and learning styles of child care professionals, and that makes it easier for busy administrators like you to participate in continuing education and professional development opportunities.

Effective on-line courses create a community of learners in which you can exchange information, share ideas and resources, and develop a network of professional contacts and colleagues. This is particularly important for child care professionals who highly value the time together that face-to-face training programs and courses offer.

Perhaps you've been curious about what you've heard, read, and seen in the media about the Internet. Maybe you've already *surfed* the web. Or, possibly the whole idea scares you to death. However you feel about it, the Internet is here to stay, and the more informed and experienced you are, the better you will be able to take advantage of this incredible information resource to improve your program. Just one note of caution — using the Internet is both challenging and fun, so it's easy to sit down for a few minutes and then wonder where the afternoon went. So, take a little extra time, and give yourself permission to play and explore — the best ways to learn!

*"Anything I've ever done that was ultimately worthwhile . . . initially scared me to death."*
— Betty Bender

## What Are You Waiting For?

*"If at first you succeed — try to hide your astonishment."*
— Los Angeles Times Syndicate

The appropriate and effective use of technology as a tool for management, information exchange, and professional development will enhance program quality and improve responsiveness to parents, *if* administrators have access to the technology, training, and technical assistance they need. Specific technology solutions are needed for this group of adult learners. New strategies are needed to assure equal access to technology, information, and resources available on the Internet and through distance learning.

As you become a more *informed* participant and user of these technologies, I encourage you to reflect on what works well and what could be improved to make these tools more effective for teaching and learning by early childhood professionals. And, think about what is missing — what would make the computer, the Internet, and distance learning more effective for you now, and in the future?

Have fun. It's time to boldly go where few early childhood professionals have gone before . . .

## References


Donohue, C. (2000). *Microsoft Office 2000 for Child Care Administrators: A Technology Training Manual*. Wheeling, IL: National-Louis University, Center for Early Childhood Leadership.

Donohue, C. (2000). *Lotus SmartSuite: A Training Manual for Child Care Administrators*. Boston, MA: Work Family Directions and Wheeling, IL: National-Louis University, Center for Early Childhood Leadership.

Kalinowsky, M. (July / August 2000). Child Care Administrative Software. *Exchange*, pp. 81-88.

Laskaris, N. E. (November / December 1997). Eight Ways to Use the Internet Now! *Early Childhood News*.

Research Notes (Summer 2000). *The Role of Technology in Early Childhood Administration*. Wheeling, IL: The Center for Early Childhood Leadership, National Louis University.

Rothenberg, D. (May 1995). *The Internet and Early Childhood Educators: Some Frequently Asked Questions*. Champaign, IL: ERIC Clearing House on Elementary and Early Childhood Education, ERIC Digest EDO-PS-95-5.

# LEGAL ISSUES

## CHAPTER 5

# Bettering Your Odds of Not Getting Sued

by Abby J. Cohen

*Fortunately, most child care center directors will never face a lawsuit. But in order to avoid one, it is well worth considering how to be prepared for the most serious issues that centers may confront.*

## Suits by Parents for Injuries to a Child

A lawsuit by parents for the death or injury to a child in care is almost always the greatest concern of every center, and this is as it should be. The range in nature and severity of possible injuries is vast. Real-life examples range from failing to supervise a child who falls from a climbing structure and breaks an arm to leaving a child in a van during hot weather resulting in death.

Lawsuits like these are to be avoided not only for the obvious reason of maintaining the well-being of children in care. They are also to be avoided because lawsuits resulting from injuries to a child can be won sometimes even when you are in the right, as a consequence of the sympathy they engender. They also can cost you your ability to keep running a successful operation. Verdicts can be large, insurance may be inadequate or unavailable (if the injury was the result of an intentional act), and center reputations may be irreparably damaged.

There are a variety of ways to minimize the chances that a lawsuit of this nature will be filed.

First and foremost, center administrators and staff must promote open, trusting, and regular communication with parents. This must begin from the very first time the parents walk through the center doors to take a look at the program and continue until the child leaves for another setting. It has been shown that in cases of medical malpractice, trust between the patient and health provider is decisive in determining whether a lawsuit will be filed. When patients trust their providers, even when things go wrong, they are much less likely to sue. When patients don't trust their health providers, they are more likely to sue even when there is no clear basis. It seems quite likely that the same findings would be reproduced in relationships between child care providers and parents. Indeed the author is familiar with several instances in which parents had valid claims and opted not to pursue them because of their generally positive regard for the provider.

Most of the injuries children receive in care are preventable. Just as proper hand washing is the single most effective means of preventing the spread of disease, proper supervision is the single most effective means of preventing injuries of all types. Proper supervision requires the development of policies, adequate training of staff, and the consistent implementation of policies. In one recent and notorious instance, a 14 month old child was inadvertently left in a Virginia child care center as it was locked up for the night. Obviously, this center had grossly inadequate policies and practices for lock-up and supervision of children in care. Their story also underscores the equal importance of regular and consistent communication between and among staff, not jut between parents and providers.

Ensuring sufficient staffing for the number of children being cared for (operating at a capacity that is workable); developing and implementing appropriate discipline policies; and regularly checking toys, equipment, grounds, and other aspects of the facility itself are other means of protecting the center.

In addition to purchasing adequate liability insurance, programs should also purchase accident insurance. In some instances where a child is injured, it may be possible to cover the damages through the accident coverage which is considerably less expensive.

Excellent resources exist which can assist center staff in preventing or minimizing injuries to children in care. Several are listed in the *Resources* section of this article.

## SUITS BY PARENTS OVER SEXUAL ABUSE OF A CHILD

While a lawsuit by parents claiming sexual abuse of a child is really a variation on the type of lawsuit described above, a lawsuit for sexual abuse is far less likely but may be far more damaging. The possibility of such a devastating claim must be dealt with preventively — through some of the policies and practices described below — as well as through developing plans which address how to respond if such a claim is brought to minimize potential damage.

### *Preventive Practices*

Some of the questions which programs should ask themselves *before* they are sued include:

- Are staff having contact with children checked against the state's criminal records and child abuse registry? If checks are not required but available, be certain to conduct them. Are new employees closely supervised during a probationary period?

- Are all visitors required to sign in?

- Are parents informed in a general way about how staff handle sensitive issues which result in actions that could be misinterpreted? These would include such things as toileting practices and the comforting of children by staff, as well as the explicit sexual play, sexual questions, and sexual discussions engaged in by children in care. Are parents informed specifically when sensitive situations arise with their children?

- Are there inappropriate opportunities or locations which allow staff to be alone with children? For example, it should be against center policy for a staff member to take an individual child on errands.

- Are staff well trained in typical and atypical child development and behavior so they are capable of identifying possible signs that a child is being abused?

- In addition to making required reports, programs should document reasonable suspicions of child sexual abuse. In certain instances, allegations of sexual abuse directed at child care staff have later turned out to be a cry for help from a child whose *parent* is the source of the abuse.

- Does your insurance cover sexual abuse claims? If you currently do not have such coverage, consider purchasing it if it is within the means of the program. Now that the child abuse in child care hysteria has died down, such coverage may be more readily and inexpensively available.

### *Minimizing Damage Once a Claim Is Brought*

Every center should plan what it will do if a sexual abuse lawsuit is filed against the center. This would include developing strategies for informing parents, children, and other staff. It will also be critical to develop appropriate strategies to respond to the media. Learn from others who have been through these devastating experiences what has worked and not worked. Poor judgment here could result in additional unwarranted claims against a center including slander, libel, and obstruction of an investigation.

## SUITS BY PARENTS OVER CONTRACTUAL MATTERS

Disputes over admissions agreements are commonplace. This may be the result of failure to include certain important issues in agreements, where both sides *think* they know what policy is in place but fail to explicitly agree. Such issues include fees for late pick-up and payment for days the child is absent. Disputes may also result from poor wording, where the center ascribes one meaning to a phrase while the parent interprets the phrase very differently.

Try to get all important matters down in writing and share these with parents when a child is first admitted. Review the contract with the parents item by item, so that you can document that these issues were discussed and agreed to. The objective is to limit surprises down the road. Parents are much less likely to sue over contracts if they have a clear idea of what the center is responsible for and what they are responsible for *in advance of the time the situation arises*.

Be sure to include a provision which allows for amending the contract with proper notice. All providers learn as they go along about issues they should have included in their initial contracts. Consequently, it will be important to reserve the right to make necessary changes, but this should always be done with sufficient notice to parents that the contract is changing. Any amendments to the contract should again be agreed to in writing.

## SUITS BY AN EMPLOYEE FOR WRONGFUL TERMINATION

Increasing numbers of employees who lose their jobs are choosing to fight their terminations. There are myriad reasons why staff are fired, and many of them will be valid. However, many employers, lacking understanding of federal and state employment laws, will terminate employees in violation of law. For example, while a center might consider making complaints to the licensing entity about perceived violations of the licensing law by the center as insubordination warranting dismissal, some states have general and some states specific (California) whistle blowing statutes which protect employees of licensed facilities for making a report of a possible violation.

Even in states which allow for "at will" employment, which means that any reason is sufficient grounds for terminating an employee (as opposed to states which require "good cause"), an employer may still be found liable if the employer violates its own personnel policies.

It is very important that centers implement their policies consistently. If one employee is terminated because of excessive absenteeism, a center will have difficulty justifying that action if another employee is just as frequently absent and is not terminated.

Centers should also give themselves time to investigate allegations of wrongdoing. Generally, it is wise not to fire someone on the spot, even when allegations are very serious, such as that a teacher hit a child or that an employee was arrested. Instead, it is better practice to immediately put the employee on administrative leave and determine whether termination is warranted. If a center acts too rashly, it increases the likelihood that it will come to a false conclusion, terminating an employee when it is not justified. This is a sure fire method to wind up in court.

There are several other important means of preventing a wrongful termination lawsuit. These include:

- Developing personnel policies with the assistance of persons knowledgeable about federal and state employment (labor) law.

- Maintaining confidential personnel files which carefully document concerns regarding staff and actions taken as a result of these concerns.

## Suits by Parents for Failing to Care for a Child with Special Health Needs

There are increasing numbers of children with special health needs. For parents of such children, the options for care are often extremely limited. However, with the passage of the Americans with Disabilities Act (ADA), all centers are required to *consider* admitting such children, and *actually* admit them when their needs can be met through reasonable accommodations. Some examples of these health needs includes children with severe allergies who may need a possible injection with an Epi-Pen,™ a disposable spring-loaded device (without an exposed needle) with a premeasured dose of epinephrine; children with diabetes who may require daily glucose testing with a blood prick; and children with asthma who may need their medications administered through a nebulizer.

Some centers have refused to make reasonable accommodations required by the ADA and have been sued. The cases generally fall into two categories. One group of cases involves centers which refuse to serve children with special health needs where there is no legal impediment to their making the accommodation other than their own refusal, whether out of ignorance of the law, ignorance of the condition, or fear of liability for performing the service. The other group of cases involves centers which refuse because of a prohibition to provide the service found in their state laws — either in the licensing law or other laws regulating the practice of various health professions (doctors, nurses, respiratory therapists, etc.). The latter centers are put between a rock and a hard place, knowing that to comply with federal law, which is supreme, they may have to violate state law until state law is brought into conformity with the ADA.

To eliminate the possibility of these lawsuits, centers need to revise their policies to ensure that reasonable accommodations will be made available in appropriate cases. In situations where state requirements violate the ADA, centers should support the passage of complying legislation. California and Connecticut have recently made changes allowing child care staff to perform blood pricks for glucose monitoring. Legislation is currently pending in California to allow the use of nebulizers in child care facilities.

When centers provide these services for children with special health needs, they worry that liability will be assumed from the child with the disability as well as from staff and other children in care. To respond to liability concerns arising from the direction of the parents of the child with the disability, centers can request that parents sign releases which may be of some help in some states; in any case, it is better practice to have *all* parents sign releases for the administration of medication rather than requiring this only of parents of children with disabilities. To respond to the liability concerns arising from the direction of staff and the parents of other children, centers should also ensure that they implement universal precautions policies which include the disposal of items which have blood on them.

Chances are good that your center will never experience any of the claims described above; but by reviewing the suggestions offered in this article and making operational changes which respond to these suggestions, you can better your odds that your center will go unscathed.

## Resources


*Child Care Law Center*. "Revised Description of OSHA Regulations on Bloodborne Pathogens."

*Grantsmanship Center Magazine*, "Letting Go," Summer, 1998, pp. 4-8.

*National Association for the Education of Young Children*. "Self-Evaluation for Loss Control."

The National Program for Playground Safety, School of Health, Physical Education, and Leisure Services, Cedar Falls, Iowa 50614-0618. Call (800) 554-PLAY or fax (319) 273-7308; free information on checking the safety of playgrounds.

# Who Can You Trust? Protecting Your Organization From Internal Fraud

by Thomas Lukaszewski, CPA

## Why Worry? — The Extent of Fraud

*Like all of us, you want to believe your employees, co-workers, and partners have the best interests of the business at heart. But you have a "gut" feeling that something just isn't right:*

- *Two or three clients have complained recently that they had already paid their bill when they received another statement for late payment from you.*
- *It seems odd that you have been paying so much more for reimbursing staff for their supplies or out of pocket expenses during the last four to six months.*
- *Your payroll checking account never runs this low over several months. Not to worry, because your payroll clerk is so dedicated she doesn't even take a vacation, especially near payday!*
- *Perhaps you need to change banks — they have been getting on your nerves lately, especially since they have been losing some of your canceled checks during the past few months!*

The above situations are not unusual in large or small businesses. They don't necessarily mean that fraud exists; but they should be warning signs to pay closer attention to what is going on in your business, because they do signal possibilities that foul play is occurring. A large company can often recover from the loss of assets; but for a small company, the consequences can be devastating.

An increase in the use of part time and temporary employees, coupled with increased instability and competitiveness in the job market, all contribute to an increase in employee fraud.

How big is this problem? Organizations such as the Bureau of National Affairs or the Association of Certified Fraud Examiners have estimated that *annual losses* from employee embezzlement may be as high as $20 *billion* to $40 billion, and that white collar crime, which includes several types of fraud, may be as much as $400 billion or more per year!

"But my business is small, and I am there every day. That is just a problem for big companies!" Not so! A major business magazine states that over 80% of all crimes against businesses are inflicted on small businesses.

## Different Types of Fraud

First of all, what is *fraud*? The U.S. Supreme Court has defined fraud as a legal wrong, or "tort," which meets the following conditions:

- a misrepresentation of a material fact
- the perpetrator knew was false and
- made with the intention that the misrepresentation be relied on and that
- the victim did rely on and, as a result, incurred a loss.

It is important to note that the misrepresentation must have been intentional. Misrepresentations made unintentionally or by mistake are not fraud.

The National Crime Information Center calls fraud "a nonviolent crime for financial gain, committed by deception."

There are two broad classifications of fraud:

- **Employee fraud** — which involves the misappropriation of assets.
- **Management fraud** (actually refers to any employee who can manipulate the financial records — not just management), sometimes called "cooking the books" — which involves fraudulent financial reporting.

Some common types of employee **fraud** involve:

- Theft of cash by:

— Diverting cash receipts

— Manipulating accounts receivable by "lapping" (which involves stealing a customer's payment and concealing the theft by applying subsequent payments from other customers to the first customer's account)

— Altering bank deposits

— Stealing or forging checks

— Stealing petty cash

— Disguising thefts as cash payments for supplies

— "Less cash" schemes — This is where a deposit is made but cash is withdrawn on the deposit ticket and only the net amount is deposited

- Abuse of travel or entertainment reimbursements by including personal items, or by submitting different documentation more than once for the same charge (e.g., first an airline ticket, later a credit card receipt)

- Payroll schemes such as:

— "Ghost" employees — In this scheme, nonexistent employees are created, fake records are set up for them in the payroll system, and they are "paid" along with the regular employees

— Paying more hours than actually worked

— Employees writing extra checks to themselves (usually where one person prepares the payroll with little or no supervision)

— Keeping a terminated or retired employee on the payroll for one or two extra periods — Here the perpetrator then steals the extra checks, forges the endorsement, and cashes or deposits the checks

Note that the above are by no means a complete list as there are many ways in which fraud can be committed.

**Management fraud** involves the intentional misstatement or omission of financial statement amounts or disclosures to deceive users of the financial statements. Here, either fictitious transactions are recorded, valid transactions are omitted, or accounting rules are intentionally not applied properly. These schemes may involve falsifying, altering, or manipulating accounting records or source documents such as invoices.

## Why would such a situation occur?

- Perhaps the owners approved an unrealistic budget, and the staff needs to inflate the revenues or decrease the expenses to be rewarded with bonuses or to even meet these goals just to keep their jobs.

- Perhaps the organization needs to borrow money to make improvements to their programs or to stay competitive. The incentive here might be to inflate their assets or reduce the liabilities on the books so the lender will be more likely to approve the needed funds.

- In smaller businesses, there may be pressure to increase tax deductions to minimize taxes, perhaps by charging personal expenses to the business.

Again, there are many other reasons why management fraud might be committed. The above is just a partial list.

In all of the situations where fraud exists, research done in this field by criminologists, psychologists, and other business disciplines have determined that three key factors are usually necessary for fraud to result:

- **Pressures facing the person**, whether stemming from financial hardship; personal habits such as drugs, alcohol, or gambling, which may result in financial pressures to commit fraud to support these habits; or work related pressures such as feelings of being overworked and underpaid, which may prompt a person to want to "get even" with the employer by committing fraud.

- **Perceived opportunity to commit fraud**. This situa tion usually occurs where conditions such as the following exist:

— Poor internal controls such as weak segregation of duties

— A rapid turnover of employees

— Constantly working under crisis conditions

— Absence of mandatory vacations

— Failure to consistently enforce standards and policies or to punish violators

Some conditions under which such opportunities exist include the use of many banks, inexperienced accounting staff, frequent change of auditors or legal counsel, or transactions between related parties.

- **The person's integrity**. Even if the worker is under severe financial pressures, and is in a position to have the opportunity to commit fraud, the person will not do so if their personal integrity is high — it will prevent them from committing the fraud.

## How to Protect Your Organization from Fraud

**Establish an effective internal control system**. This is perhaps the most important deterrent to fraud. Two of the most important aspects of an effective internal control systems involve:

- Setting a tone, or developing a policy which lets employees know that the unauthorized use of the organization's assets will not be tolerated.

This policy should be communicated in a serious but non threatening manner. Most importantly, management must be prepared to follow through in implementing this policy; it will not be effective if violators are not dismissed or prosecuted. Effective managers can accomplish this while fostering a positive atmosphere of teamwork. A workforce developed in such a manner can contribute substantially to an organization's success.

Center leaders play a key role not only in enforcing this policy but as importantly in modeling compliance with it. If staff members perceive that the center director is using a staff vehicle for personal use, making personal phone calls on the center line, or being loose about work hours, they will get the message that it is okay to bend the rules.

- Segregation of duties — that is, making sure that the responsibility for authorizing transactions, recording transactions in the books, and having access to assets should be performed by different people in the organization. In many small businesses, this becomes difficult as there are often not enough employees available to accomplish this. Where this is not possible, adequate control can be accomplished by the direct involvement of the owner/manager.

In the areas dealing with cash, for example, the owner can sign checks, review and make the bank deposits, review all bank statements and reconciliations, and monitor duties. In general, if the employees know you are actively involved in the security of your business, they are less likely to attempt fraud.

**Pay attention to unusual behavior by employees.** Psychology research indicates that when a person commits a crime, he or she often becomes overcome by emotions of fear and guilt. This usually displays itself in unusual behavior such as increased drinking, smoking, defensiveness, suspiciousness, etc. These types of behavior do not indicate that fraud exists; rather, it is the unexplained changes in behavior that arouse concerns, such as angry people suddenly become nice and vice versa. Caution should be used regarding probing employees' behavior without sufficient cause, as this may lead to charges of harassment.

**Frequent tips or complaints.** Often fraud is detected when customers, employees, friends, or managers complain that something is wrong. Customers complain because they feel they have in some way been taken advantage of. Fellow employees may feel jealous or angry when they see a sudden extravagant life-style change, or a soured friendship can be acted out in anger or blackmail.

Although the motives of the person complaining may be suspect, the allegations usually have merit that warrant further investigation.

**Review bank reconciliations for old, reconciling items.** Thefts of cash often cause reconciling items on bank reconciliations. For example, where receipts on the books do not appear as bank deposits on the same day, it could mean that the funds were diverted. Missing checks could indicate they were made out to unauthorized payees. Transfers between bank accounts should be reconciled on the same dates. A deposit in transit on one account might be listed as a reconciling item but never actually be deposited.

**Excessive "void" transactions.** Perhaps cash is received for extra services such as late fees, the receipts are diverted, and the office copy of the client's receipt for payment is marked "void." Here, observations of unusual transactions occurring during particular employee's shifts are coupled with interviews with staff as to names of children who stayed late, followed up with a comparison of cash receipts records indicating whether those parents paid the required fee.

**Many thefts of cash deposits** can be discovered by comparing the entries in the cash receipts register for the day with that day's bank deposit ticket.

**Periodic *surprise* cash counts** of imprest petty cash funds is an effective way of determining cash shortages in the fund.

***Confirmations* of accounts receivable** is another effective detection method used in discovering fraud involving cash. Periodic statements should be sent to parents showing all billings and payments on your records asking them to indicate whether the record is correct.

**Reviewing *write offs*** of customer receivables as uncollectible may lead to information indicating the employee diverted customer payments for their own use.

Many types of payroll fraud can be detected by **examining the organization's payroll records, payroll checks, employees' lists, and personnel files.**

For example:

- If fictitious employees are suspected, determine whether the same social security number may exist for the same employee or whether two different employees have the same address. Further, examine canceled checks for unusual or second endorsements. Note any checks that were cashed rather than deposited (generally a bank adds a code marking indicating that the check was cashed rather than deposited). Have a high ranking officer physically distribute paychecks to each worker and follow up on any unclaimed checks.

- To determine if too many hours are being paid, trace the hours to time cards or other internal records used to track hours worked. Recalculate the gross pay if the worker is paid on an hourly basis. Trace gross pay rates to proper authorizations and employee contracts.

**Expense account reports should be reviewed** for reasonableness, and dates and details of the charges should be compared to other company records indicating the employee should have been on business for the organization during those time periods.

Establishing a positive and effective internal control system, creating an attitude that management is involved and aware of what is happening on an ongoing basis, maintaining an accounting system with built in audit trails, and following up when questionable situations arise — all of these will go a long way to protecting your organization from becoming a fraud victim.

# Teacher Aides and Other Dangerous Instruments — Lessons in Legal Self-Defense

by James Strickland and Mark Levbarg

*Editor's Note: For the last several years at meetings of the Association of Trial Lawyers of America, the association has dedicated a special section to child sex abuse. Frequently, those sections have focused on ways to more effectively represent the plaintiff against schools, child care centers, and other types of child care facilities. The following article uses information drawn from those and other meetings to serve as a starting point to develop relevant risk management and program improvement plans.*

1 **ACCIDENT REPORT**
2 The party of the first part, hereinafter referred to as "JACK,"
3 and the party of the second part, hereinafter referred to as
4 "JILL," while in the care of a child care provider, hereinafter
5 referred to as the "DANGEROUS INSTRUMENTALITY,"
6 were recklessly allowed to ascend a grass covered elevation
7 composed of rock and dirt, hereinafter referred to as "HILL,"
8 for the purpose of obtaining, securing, or procuring a liquid,
9 hereinafter referred to as "WATER," which they were to
10 convey in a receptacle, hereinafter referred to as
"THE PAIL" . . . *

Life — especially for child care providers, does seem to get "curiouser and curiouser." As the insurance industry continues to selectively narrow your coverage, trial lawyers develop new and better ways to construct lawsuits against child care providers. In the new improved lawsuit, the curious part is that the wording will be designed to avoid the exclusions in your insurance policy, and won't sound like a description of "what actually happened."

The good attorney representing an injured child on a contingent fee basis must find theory of recovery that involves a defendant who has insurance. Finding that coverage and a liability theory that will avoid the policy exclusions is like shooting at a moving target. Insurance coverage keeps changing.

For example, several years ago insurers began to exclude "child abuse" from policies. Plaintiffs' attorneys responded by suing providers for "negligent hiring." The insurance industry then wrote policies that excluded "negligent" or "wrongful" hiring.

Plaintiffs' pleadings responded by suing child care providers for "negligent failure to train." When the insurers excluded that, trial lawyers, bloodied but unbowed, reworded their pleadings to focus upon "negligent failure to supervise." Now, that too is often excluded from coverage.

When many states passed deceptive trade practices legislation for protection of the consumer, plaintiffs' attorneys began wording their pleadings to make allegations under the various states' consumer protection acts. Now, the insurance industry has excluded most possible deceptive trade practices from coverage in most states.

## Teachers As "Dangerous Instrumentalities"

The naive child care provider caught in the middle of these word games might begin to wonder, "What next?" We have attempted to answer that question. Some of the answers may appear bizarre to you at first glance. In a world where insurance carriers are attempting to avoid paying, attorneys representing injured children have become quite creative. For example, you may prepare for teachers' aides and other personnel being lumped together with pointed scissors, knives, guns, and mace as *dangerous instrumentalities*.

Bizarre? Perhaps not. Some readers have known an aide they would have labeled a "dangerous instrument." If you have ever wished you could fire someone but did not do it because you did not have a competent replacement, you have known a "dangerous instrument." If you have shared stories with colleagues about the "inappropriate" conduct of one of your staff, you have known a teacher or aide who was a "dangerous instrument." If these vignettes are alien to you, you have either been very fortunate or you are new to the profession. If you nodded your head knowingly, you must now become familiar with an old theory of negligence applied in a new way to your profession. From the "Restatement of Torts S 307" (1965), we read the following:

***Use of Incompetent or Defective Instrumentalities***
*It is negligence to use an instrumentality, whether human being or thing, which the actor knows, or should know, to be so incompetent, inappropriate or defective that its use involves an unreasonable risk of harm to others.*

The cited excerpt from a scholarly legal treatise is not a new theory. Courts in every state look to scholarship of the American Law Institute when they determine the course and direction of legal policymaking for that state. So, while you have not yet added "dangerous staff" to the list of hazards to be checked, it would be practical and wise to add "dangerous behaviors" to the checklist. The staff member who appears late or disappears early (placing the provider in noncompliance with staff-child ratios) and the caregiver who chooses the comfort of the shade tree and doesn't move around the playground are as dangerous as the unlocked cabinet which contains the drain cleaner.

You may find it disconcerting that your insurance company is busy designing ways to exclude your coverage while trial lawyers are busy designing responses that will avoid the exclusions. However, a prudent director can use these circumstances to take steps to prepare the organization for potential law suits. If you have not confronted that staff member whose actions or inactions have concerned you, your opportunity is now! If confrontation is difficult for you, blame it on the lawyers. Tell them about this article. Tell them that the lawyers are coming and that it is to their advantage to clean up their act now!

## Child Sex Abuse Allegations

Perhaps the most explosive potential problem for the child care provider is the allegation of "child sex abuse." It should not come as a surprise that the Association of Trial Lawyers of America now includes a member section focused on child abuse. While you may see this attention as threatening, trial lawyers see it as a way of staying abreast of a new emerging field of tort law, and as a way of encouraging safer child care.

As a media event, the report of child abuse in child care is juicy and newsworthy; as a courthouse event, it raises the specter of both civil litigation and criminal charges. When criminal charges are pending, the prudent plaintiff's attorney will cooperate with the District Attorney's Office and provide all the investigative aid that he or she can muster. The plaintiff's attorney may attempt to affect any plea bargain attempt on behalf of his minor client. An interesting twist occurs when the plaintiff's attorney may try to discourage the District Attorney from taking a plea bargain where your staff member pleads "guilty." A guilty plea may amount to an admission of "intentional" misconduct. The child's attorney who discourages the District Attorney from accepting a guilty plea is not an altruist convinced of your employee's innocence. He merely seeks to avoid your insurance policy exclusion for intentional misconduct.

You face the following dilemma if you think your staff member intentionally endangered or harmed a child. If there is any foundation for your suspicion, you must discuss it with your defense attorney. Remember that a jury finding of intentional misconduct would probably void your insurance coverage. While this means that the plaintiff's attorney would be less interested in you, it also means that you may face personal exposure to liability as an uninsured defendant. Your defense attorney should discuss with you any potential conflict he or she may have. Remember the attorney was hired to defend you by your insurance carrier. It could be in the insurer's best interest for your employee to plead guilty. In fact, attorney Jerry Spence recently intimated on the Charles Grodin talk show that a recent notorious "au pair" case resulted in an insurance carrier driven guilty plea.

Your defense attorney should be able to explain to you why your organization and each person named within it as a defendant was sued. You should understand that it is the duty of the child's attorney to try to find someone who has some true connection to the event under a viable legal theory and who is also insured.

There will be people in your organization with important information who would prefer to remain silent. The plaintiff's attorneys are well aware of the reluctance of witnesses to unpleasant events to involve themselves. They may sue individuals in order to help generate witnesses. They may attempt to exploit areas of potential conflict between your staff members and your organization. A good trial lawyer will have investigated the potential liability of every possible defendant before filing the suit.

The prospect of a skillful plaintiff's attorney, working in tandem with the District Attorney, naming all the warm bodies standing near the injured child as defendants and driving wedges into your organization is frightful. It can terminate friendships and destroy families. Well in advance of any problems, train your staff, parents, and board members. Tell them what to expect.

## Board Member Liability

In large child care organizations, executives or members of the board of directors may be shocked when they are sued. They will not understand how they could be liable when they "have done nothing." If there is a central lesson to our presentation, it is that you must understand the ironic truth that one can be found negligent in dealing with children exactly because one has done nothing.

Unfortunately, it is often true that it was negligent for the board of directors of the child care operation to have done nothing and it is often easy to prove. Some boards consist of family members of the director; board meetings may be very informal. If there is a concern, it may be suppressed for the sake of family harmony. That harmony will be severely disrupted when a suit is filed.

In other instances, the board members may be community or parent volunteers. While the board meetings may be more formal, issues of fundraising dominate and usually occupy far more time than reviewing and determining supervision and training policies. In still other organizations, board meetings degenerate into fights over whose friend or relative is to be hired (or whose enemy is to be fired).

The plaintiff's attorneys now have a fairly good idea of how child care works. You can expect the plaintiff's attorney to subpoena copies of the agendas of board meetings and the minutes. Also, expect copies of all written records to be subpoenaed — staff meeting agendas, minutes, records of training sessions, personnel files, memos, appointment books, children's records, licensing agency monitoring reports, even records of long distance telephone calls.

The injured child's attorney will be looking for anything that will prove that you knew a problem existed and did little or nothing to resolve it. In fact, you may have occupied yourself with matters which the jury would consider trivial, while allowing hazardous conditions to continue until a child was hurt. You may have fiddled while Rome burned, or so it will seem.

Do not conclude that we are suggesting you should not keep records. You must. However, be careful that the records you keep include information useful to management rather than gratuitous by-play.

## Negligent Decisions

Have you ever hired an applicant for employment having checked all but one of the applicant's references? Have you ever left open a two or three year period in an applicant's life after checking references? The plaintiff's attorney is often amazed at what he finds in investigating because the investigation covers that one previous employer or those three missing years.

In child care, many young women change their name each time they marry, divorce, or remarry. Have you checked the applicant under all of her previous names? The plaintiff's attorney must and will.

It is often very difficult, time consuming, and expensive to obtain a perfect reference check of past employment. However, if you don't make every reasonable effort to try, you must anticipate that a plaintiff's attorney will make an issue of your efforts, if it is to the advantage of the injured child.

The plaintiff's attorney and the jury will be able to spend hours or days dwelling upon, analyzing, scrutinizing, and dissecting a decision that you took minutes to make. If you had as much time to make decisions as they will to analyze them, you would still be pondering which cereal you want for breakfast.

You can't slow time and ponder every decision, but there is something that attorneys and jurors do that you can do. You can occasionally stop and reflect on past decisions. Is there a pattern that you had not noticed? If so, would a jury see that pattern as positive or negative? Taking time, at least annually, for reflection and review is one of the best risk reduction strategies we can recommend.

When it is done right, the process should include everyone: janitors, cooks, teachers, aides, caregivers, members of boards of directors, parents, even major contractors and past employees. If there is something to be amazed about (whether positive or negative), it is much better that you discover it.

This risk reduction strategy is extremely important for organizations or institutions where there is a risk of a suit alleging sexual abuse or molestation of a child. The child's lawyer will be working very hard to prove that your staff selection process was seriously flawed, not from sinister motive to destroy your career, but to find someone who in some way contributed to the injury of the child who also has insurance coverage. A judgment against an individual pedophile will not afford insurance coverage.

Trial lawyers know that child care centers are especially vulnerable if they suffer rapid staff turnover. Former employees are a wealth of information (much of which is hostile to, or critical of, your operation). A former staff member may be very willing to reveal information to a trial lawyer or on a witness stand that she would not readily share with you while in your employ. She reasons that, after all, you were the director, the owner, the boss. Knowing what was going on was your job — your responsibility, not hers.

## Former Employees

There are practical steps for you to take to lower the risk that you will be surprised by the testimony of a former employee. It is a sign of effective management in any business or industry when employees feel free to discuss their job concerns. It makes sense to establish a formal exiting procedure for all employees. While making sure that you have the keys to your building returned, you should learn if the individual noticed any situations (not previously reported) where a child may have been injured, abused, molested, neglected, or endangered. If the exiting employee responds that she has noticed these situations, you must request the details in writing and you must follow up.

One of your first follow-up questions should be, "Why didn't you tell me (or your supervisor) about this when it happened?" If a staff member refuses to participate in the accident review or fails to mention important observations and then later appears as a witness against you, your attorney will have some ammunition for cross examination and will be able to argue that you did your best to discover and correct the problems. We should point out that a staff member who refuses to participate in the accident review has raised the red flag for you.

## Building Parental Trust

For a child care provider, the importance of open communication with parents cannot be underestimated or overemphasized. Implemented correctly, a parent involvement program will reduce the risk of injury to children and the risk of lawsuits.

You must train each parent to understand that there is a major difference between dumping a load of clothes at the dry cleaners and leaving a child in the care of another. If the dry cleaners damage a favorite pair of slacks, the harm is nominal at worst and repairable at best. If a child care provider is involved in the injury of a child, the damage may be lasting and severe.

Parents should be required to attend an orientation session. The orientation session meeting should be recorded. There should be regular parent meetings with formal agendas and recorded minutes. Parents should be asked to complete a checklist investigation of the child care facility.

All risks and hazards that are known to you should be shared with parents. Please understand that there are risks involved in every childhood activity and that most parents are not looking for a totally risk-free environment. However, the level of mutual trust and respect is raised when parents and child care provider are aware of the same risks and have shared information about these risks.

Really letting the parents in on everything that is going on in the center may frighten you — "What if they find something they don't like?" "Won't the parents try to run my business and be a nuisance?" Take heart, involving parents really works! Far more frightening than an involved parent is the uninvolved one. The parent who believes that you should do the parent's job as well as the provider's job and holds you to an unrealistic standard for both is not doing the child or you one bit of good.

Any good parent involvement program will be candid. Candor is especially important when your center is found in violation of state or local licensing regulations. A careful review of sometimes conflicting licensing regulations will often support allegations of negligence. The attorney for an injured child will learn about violations during his investigation.

It is much better that the parents know about violations as they occur. If the violations are numerous or frequent, the process of telling the parents will force you to improve. From a risk management prospective, a center that informs its parents of violations won't be risk free, but it will have eliminated suspicion and distrust as a litigation source.

Another aspect of eliminating suspicion and distrust with parents requires you to inspect your promotional literature in a new light. Have your own lawyer review the material looking for information which might be considered "deceptive" under your state's consumer protection legislation.

Detailed information about establishing parent involvement risk management programs; useful analytical tools, such as sample forms for the exiting procedures; and further training is available from:

Human Services Risk Management
818 East 53rd Street
Austin, Texas 78751
(800) 222-4051

Before stereotyping all plaintiffs' attorneys as "the enemy," try asking your local trial lawyers' association for training. The state trial lawyers' associations and most trial lawyers would prefer a safer environment to more lawsuits (and view litigation as just one means to that end). You can find experienced trial lawyers in most metropolitan areas who will volunteer to lead information panels or lecture provider groups on the courtroom perception of child care issues.

Some trial lawyers experienced in child care litigation have even testified for provider associations at legislative and administrative hearings on licensing, regulation, and funding. Do not overlook ATLA and your state trial lawyer association as resources.

We strongly recommend that you consult your attorney periodically and that he be familiar with both day care and liability laws in your state. Remember:

12 Jack, the party of the first

13 part, fell in a direction

14 opposite from up (i.e., down)

15 and, in doing so, sustained an

16 injury commonly known as a

17 broken crown; and Jill, the

18 the party of the second part,

19 sustained similar life-

20 threatening injuries by

21 falling, rolling, or tumbling

22 after.

Jack and Jill healed quickly. Their parents immediately sued the child care provider, obtained an unreasonably large settlement from the child care provider's insurance company, from which the plaintiff's attorney deducted his contingency fee. The insurance company raised its rates, excluded broken crowns, and everyone but the child care provider lived happily ever after.

---

*Paraphrased from *Legal Guide to Mother Goose,* "The Jack and Jill Case," by Don Sandburg, Price/Stern/Sloan, 1979.

### Self-Defense Strategies

| Plaintiff's attorney might . . . | Child care provider should . . . |
|---|---|
| Claim that staff member was a "dangerous instrumentality." | Warn staff that their actions (or inactions) could result in their being termed a dangerous instrumentality. Document unsafe, imprudent actions (inactions) of staff and take necessary personnel actions. |
| Join forces with the District Attorney's investigation. | Warn staff in advance that in the beginning it might look like everyone is against them. Develop a plan on what support accused staff members may expect from the center. |
| Agree that the acts were unintentional. | Be aware that a plaintiff's attorney is not necessarily doing you or your staff a favor — intentional acts are usually not insured, so chances of a large settlement are decreased if the acts are intentional. |
| Threaten to sue everybody even remotely related to the case, then try to drive a wedge between defendants. | Within limits bounded by truth and ethical behavior, ask your affected staff to cooperate with your defense attorney. The investigation you conduct into the incident with or on behalf of your defense attorney should not be hampered by lack of cooperation from staff. |
| Expect institutional defendants, including churches, youth organizations, and related groups, to underrate their culpability — to not fathom how they could have any liability. | Work with boards of directors and policy groups to stay on target in reviewing and making policy — neither delegating everything to the director nor trying to run all administrative functions. |
| Subpoena agendas, minutes of board of directors meetings, staff meetings, training sessions, memos, phone logs, appointment books, and other files and records. | Keep good records. Check with your attorney about the kind of gratuitous and careless misinformation that should not be recorded. Information regarding fundraising should be limited to resolutions so that your meeting history doesn't unfairly condemn you as an organization beset with, and overwhelmed by, funding problems to the exclusion of safetyconcerns. |
| Spend a great deal of time reviewing management decisions looking for patterns which would prove negligence. | At least annually, take time to review your own management decisions. Ask all staff, board members, parents, and others involved to help look for things that you had not noticed or which might be misinterpreted. |
| Interview past employees and call them as witnesses. | When possible, try to part as friends with all staff. Establish fomal exiting procedures for staff, asking that they share with you any concerns they have about the way children are treated and asking if there were any instances they can remember (but have not previously reported) where a child may have been injured, abused, molested, neglected, or endangered. Where possible, obtain such concerns in writing. |
| Attempt to prove that you participated in deceptive practices by promising safety or security for children and then not exercising due diligence in that safety or security. | Have your attorney review all advertising or promotional trade materials. Establish an active parent involvement risk management program, and keep parents well informed of providing problems. |

# Risky Business

by James Strickland

*"The child care industry is especially vulnerable" or so declared the Wall Street Journal in an article about liability insurance for child care. That special vulnerability is caused by the length of the risk. The statute of limitations does not run out as quickly for children as it does for most adults. Children have the right to sue up to the time they reach the age of majority (and, perhaps, some years thereafter).*

If the youngest child in your care is age three and the age of majority in your state is 18, your liability risk will extend for 15 years (or more). The liability for the service long outlives the service. That makes the child care industry reasonably unique and "especially vulnerable."

You don't want your retirement going to pay off a settlement for the tike who crashed a trike a decade and a half ago. So you probably have purchased the correct type of liability policy. That would be the type that covers you for those things that *occurred* while you were paying the premiums — *even if you have long since closed your doors, canceled the policy, and stopped paying the premiums, OR even if you are still in business but just happened to have changed insurance companies.*

If you are only now learning of the long lingering liability risk associated with child care and you have no idea of what your liability policy covers, then you are in good company. Most child care professionals shy away from these issues. They are best left to other professions, RIGHT? Just thinking about being sued can be so threatening to some people that they go to some interesting lengths to avoid facing the responsibility for their own fate. Take Mabel, for example, the center director who would have considered it an extravagance to pay an attorney. Nevertheless, she did run up a psychic hot line phone bill of several thousand dollars (on the center's phone bill). It is a true but sad story because the psychics failed to inform her that she would be fired.

It might not be as entertaining, but forget the psychic and start with your attorney. Do this in a formal, as opposed to an informal, setting and PAY for the consultation. You should *start* with your attorney because he or she has some knowledge about the laws in your state that you should consider *before* purchasing liability insurance. Also, he or she knows (or can most easily find out) the type of suits and size of judgments against other child care providers in your state. But that does not mean that attorneys know about child care — most don't! It is going to be your job to bridge the gap between what your attorney knows about the law and what you know about child care.

Have your consultation in a formal setting because the issues are complex. The questions and answers are easily misunderstood and you are likely to be making decisions based on this consultation which will have significant long-term financial consequences. So it is preferable to have these consultations confirmed in writing.

You should pay for this consultation because it is something of value to you. Also, you have the potential of sustaining damages should the advice lead you to an incorrect decision. Your chances of holding your attorney responsible may be improved if you have *paid* for the services.

AFTER you have obtained the information from your attorney, you are then ready to start where most people start — with an insurance agent. But you are still not ready to make the purchasing decision. What insurance you buy and how much of it you buy will depend on the answers you get to your questions.

It is important to have your questions handled formally, and having this done in writing always provides you with a more reliable record and can help reduce the chances of misunderstanding. The agent's compensation usually is provided as a commission or a percentage of the premium paid for the coverage. However, the same issues as with your attorney apply. You need to be able to hold the agent responsible for the information provided you. This is a complex field and in most cases agents are competent. Nevertheless, errors are made. According to some texts, as many as two-thirds of the claims brought against the errors and omissions coverage can be traced back to agents' lack of understanding of the risk they are insuring.

The following questions are designed to promote that understanding, but don't expect quick yes or no responses. Ultimately, some of the questions might not be answerable. However, asking them will start a useful dialogue between you and your attorney and insurance agent.

## Questions for Your Attorney

- What is the statute of limitations in this state for damages sustained by children? What if the child thinks he or she was molested as a child but only rememberd a psychological injury well after becoming an adult?

- If the child's parents should sue me and there is a settlement or judgment, could the child still sue me later?

- What are child care providers in this state sued for most often?

- What is the usual size of the judgment against child care providers who have been sued in our state?

- For those cases against child care providers which have been settled out of court, is there any way for you to find out or estimate the size of those settlements?

- Since child care is a rather unique type of risk, the possibility of disputes over coverage and settlement remains a possibility. What happens when a liability insurance company denies coverage or refuses to settle a claim in this state?

- To what extent does the Americans with Disabilities Act (ADA) apply to me or the facility I am responsible for? For example, if I am supposed to serve children with disabilities, and doing that requires that I give the disabled child more attention, it means that I have to give the other children less attention which increases the potential risk of a child being injured.

  Profit margins in the child care industry are notoriously slim, so I probably couldn't afford to hire more staff.

  I also need your advice on the extent to which the ADA applies to me in making employment decisions. For example, what risks do I face if I were able to find enough money to hire the extra staff needed and someone with a disability significant enough to affect his or her ability to safely care for the children should apply for the position?

- The *state* stipulates the maximum number of children per caregiver, so staff attendance and fitness for duty are significant issues. Also, the caregivers in our workforce are frequently young women of childbearing age or older women who have raised their families, meaning they are likely to need to miss work to care for sick children or aging parents. Finally, the work itself will occasionally require major physical acts that are absolutely necessary but NOT part of the daily routine (running to save a child, lifting and carrying a 40+ pound child). What about the liability and regulations I face under the workers' compensation laws and the Family Medical Leave Act (FMLA)?

- Some states have laws which limit the liability of churches, non-profit organizations, etc. Would my operation be covered under such a law and in your opinion does the law provide sufficient protection to affect the amount or type of insurance I should purchase?

- Are there any things about the laws governing use of motor vehicles, or officers and directors, or other risks that I haven't mentioned that you think I need to consider coverage for?

- Would you have any additional advice that might help me in making a decision about purchasing liability insurance?

## Questions for Your Insurance Agent

- We occasionally take the children on field trips and/or have other activities away from our primary location. I have heard that because of that I probably need commercial general liability (CGL) coverage as opposed to owners', landlords', and tenants' coverage. Do you agree with that, and are there other reasons that I might need the CGL coverage?

- Childhood injuries are so common that they might be considered *accidents* for which no one was really at fault. However, I have read that if the injury is the result of an accident where no one is claiming negligence the normal liability insurance coverage would not even pay for the medical expenses. However, not having medical expenses covered could make the parents mad enough to sue me. So does your policy cover medical payments?

- We transport children and I understand that I need to have a separate policy that covers that. Is that correct? Also, I understand that both my general liability coverage and my policy that covers risks related to transporting the children may have exclusions. Occasionally the same exclusions may exist on both pollcies, so there might be a gap in coverage. For example, what would happen if a child were injured while we are loading or unloading the van? Which policy would provide coverage if the van were loaded, but not yet moving and still in our driveway, and one child should injure another or if one child should injure another while in transport?

- Being accused of abusing or molesting a child is always a possibility in child care. Does this policy provide coverage should that occur? If it does, are the policy limits the same for this as for the rest of the coverage? If it does not, would it at least reimburse the cost of the attorney should the charge prove to be unfounded?

- We might lease copiers and kitchen equipment. If they should be damaged, am I covered for suits from the lessor? If not, how would I get coverage for losses like that?

- The turnover rate among child care workers is normally very high. Even the small child care center is making several employment decisions a year, each of which has the potential of being contested. Also, the turnover means that at any one time there is a reasonably large portion of the staff that are new (not yet fully trained). There is a significant potential for misunderstandings which could give rise to suits brought by employees. Does this policy cover me for suits brought by employees against me?

- Child care centers are places where staff interact with parents, so staff are occasionally called upon to report what they witness a parent doing. A parent could take exception, claiming that the staff member has libeled or slandered him or her. Does this policy cover that?

- Of all the types of different policies, which ones cover my employees if they are sued?

- We occasionally use volunteers. Does the coverage you might propose for us protect them? Also, what if a volunteer sues me, does this policy provide coverage for that?

- We serve food in our facility and we may have a rummage sale or bake sale. Does this policy have a *product liability* exclusion? Would the activities I described be excluded?

- Leases usually contain hold-harmless clauses. Does this policy have a *contractual liability* exclusion and does that exclusion apply to leases? If it does, could that be used by the company as a reason to deny claims arising out of anything having to do with the maintenance of the center or a flaw in the building or premises? Should I ask my landlord if he/she has OL&T coverage?

- Child care centers always seem to have plumbing problems. What if a toilet overflows onto the sidewalk and someone slips, or the septic tank overflows and runs onto nearby property and the neighbor's prize dog drinks it and dies. Am I covered, or would such things fall under the policy's exclusion for pollution-related acts?

- What if there is a verdict that involves punitive damages? Does this policy cover punitive damages?

- I am not sure what directors' and officers' insurance covers that is not covered in the other policies, or if the coverage even applies to the way my operation is set up. Why would we need D&O coverage?

- Given the types of coverage we are already discussing and considering obtaining, what would be the reason for me to consider purchasing excess liability coverage?

- I know that some facilities are offering prepaid legal services as a fringe benefit and as additional protection for legal fees should criminal charges ever be filed in conjunction with a child abuse allegation. I understand that usually liability insurance will not even pay legal fees for allegations of criminal activity such as child abuse. Is prepaid legal coverage sold in this state?

- Since we serve children, I am concerned about suits that might be brought well after the center is closed or I no longer have any connection with it. Of the policies you are proposing for us, could you tell which ones would provide coverage for things that happen during the period I am paying premiums, even if the suit itself is brought years later?

- Is there any additional type of liability coverage that we have not discussed which you would recommend?

# Structuring the Organization

## Chapter 6

# ARE YOU RUNNING A CENTER OR BUILDING AN ORGANIZATION?

by Joan Dunn Antonsen, Jan Silverman, and Pauline Work

*Ten years ago, centers serving 100 children were an anomaly. Today, not only are 100 child centers commonplace, but centers serving 200 and even 300 children in one location are no longer atypical. Likewise, local, regional, and national child care chains have experienced unprecedented growth in this same decade. In short, this has been a period of dramatic change for child care centers — a period of dramatic growth.*

*When a 50 child center doubles its capacity in five years, or when a single center branches out to offer care in five different locations, more is changing than the number of children being served. In a period of expansion, relationships among individuals within the organization undergo dramatic, often wrenching changes. Similarly, the relationship of the organization to the community it serves changes — to the satisfaction of some segments in the community, and to the dissatisfaction of others. In the article that follows, the authors address the problems that occur when a center grows and changes but the center's management does not.*

## THE CASE OF THE INDISPENSABLE ENTREPRENEUR

Henrietta brimmed over with pride the day her baby, the Duck Duck Goose Day Care Center was highlighted on a local TV newscast as the "sterling example of how child care would work in a perfect world." Indeed, Duck Duck Goose was Henrietta's baby and, indeed, it was exemplary.

Henrietta got her start caring for six preschoolers in her home. As her reputation as a loving caregiver spread by word of mouth, Henrietta found it necessary to move the program out of her house, to rent increasingly larger store fronts and church basements, and to hire more and more teachers to supplement her efforts. Before long, Henrietta recognized her ultimate dream as she obtained financing to design and build her own facility. What made this rapid expansion possible was not only Henrietta's loving attention to the children but also her warm relations with the parents, her uncanny memory for details, and her seemingly endless capacity for hard work. Even though Henrietta now employed over 20 teachers, she still tried to spend a few hours every day in the classrooms to be with the children, to work with the newer teachers, and to maintain control of the center's curriculum. While the center now served over 100 families, Henrietta still remembered all the parents' names and shared in their joys and sorrows.

> *The problems of managing a growing organization are not insurmountable, but they do become more severe as the rate of growth accelerates, and organizations that grow very rapidly are often managed so badly that they ultimately collapse.*
>
> — Theodore Caplow, in *Managing an Organization*

Even though Duck Duck Goose now operated on a $400,000 budget, Henrietta still ran it by the seat of her pants. She kept items needing immediate attention on top of her desk, bills to pay in the top left drawer, receipts in the bottom left drawer, and payroll records in the bottom right drawer. What kept this shoe box accounting system from self-destructing was Henrietta's memory. She never forgot to deposit payroll taxes, never let a parent get behind in fees without a gentle reminder, always paid bills on time, and always remembered when a teacher was due an annual increment.

However, keeping Duck Duck Goose alive and well required a heroic effort on Henrietta's part. She was on the scene to handle every crisis, she seldom took a vacation, and she routinely put in 60 hour work weeks.

After carrying on like this for 20 years, and loving every moment of it, Henrietta decided she would like to retire from her job when her husband retired from his. She appointed the head teacher to take her place, and looked forward to a well deserved life of leisure. Six months later, she was back working 60 hours a week at Duck Duck Goose, as her replacement was blown away by all the administrative details. Now Henrietta had to work harder than ever to straighten out the mess.

## What Went Wrong

In a nutshell, what went wrong was that Henrietta was so busy running her center that she failed to build an organization that could run without her. Henrietta's case is, of course, fictional; but it is borrowed closely from real life. All too many directors, both of non profit and for profit centers, are so gung ho about making their centers bigger and more profitable that they never get around to making them stronger and more adaptive. Here are some of the mistakes directors such as Henrietta make:

*To stay on the upward growth curve requires a broadening of the management talent base — some effective staffing that adds up to a well rounded functional team.... The manager must begin getting results through others.*

— Steven C. Brandt in *Enterpreneuring*

- **The Wonder Woman Syndrome** (also known as **The One Man Band Syndrome**). This syndrome consists of one part egoism ("This is my center"), one part over-confidence ("I can do everything"), one part condescension ("If I want it done right, I'd better do it myself"), and one part masochism("60 hour weeks — I love it"). Wonder Woman protects the center with her heroic efforts. She meets every crisis head on, she resolves every conflict, she makes every decision, she soothes every disgruntled parent, she unplugs every clogged toilet.

Being Wonder Woman is a demanding job, but it is not without its rewards. Feeling indispensable can be rewarding. Members of the organization can also provide lots of strokes for working so hard on behalf of the center.

However, by doing everything herself, Wonder Woman fails to allow her staff to grow. Never given full responsibility for anything important, staff members fail to develop any administrative skills. Never allowed to make decisions or to think for themselves, staff members fail to develop any sense of responsibility.

- **The Bigger is Better Syndrome**. If a director succeeds in expanding a one room child care center into a system providing care in five locations, that magnitude of achievement can be a heady experience. This sense of progress can easily obscure a deterioration in quality of services.

In a center's headlong effort to expand, hiring and training standards may be relaxed, the spontaneity and creativity of the staff may be lost, and communication with parents may become more cold and businesslike. The very qualities that gave the center a strong reputation in the community and enabled it to grow in the first place may be disregarded as the center attempts to capitalize on its reputation, thus sowing the seeds for the organization's eventual decline.

- **The Stegosaurus Syndrome**. Dinosaurs were the peak performers of their era; but when conditions changed, they fell on hard times. Likewise, many directors excel in a particular environment but fail to keep pace when the ground rules change.

This failure to adapt to changing conditions is the result of a critical shortsightedness. For example, a typical Stegosaurus director was extremely effective at attracting public monies to his center in the 1970s. He was a prolific proposal writer, an artful negotiator, an efficient administrator of government contracts, and a skillful report writer. Yet, when government funding started to dry up, he was not able to look ahead and identify other funding sources to nurture, other markets to explore. As a result, his center gradually went under.

## Building an Organization

The difference between a director who is running a center and one who is building an organization has been summarized as the difference between being an administrator and being a manager. An administrator is a very good technician — he can capably carry out all the day-to-day tasks involved in operating the center. But his focus is narrowly on the here and now — "What do I need to do to keep the center afloat this week?"

The manager's focus, on the other hand, is always two steps ahead. She is able to look beyond the day- to-day details and see the broader picture. She is attuned to shortcomings in the daily performance of the center, to current opportunities for the center to make an impact, and to future trends that may affect the center.

So assuming that you aspire to be a manager and to build your organization, where do you start? Here are four not-so-simple tasks to get you well on your way:

## Task 1: Building a Managerial Team.

Henrietta made herself indispensable — Duck Duck Goose couldn't run without her. The goal of an aspiring manager should be to make yourself completely dispensable. You should strive to surround yourself with people who take over major portions of your job. Building this managerial team involves three separate steps:

- **Analyze your workload**. Make a list of all your jobs — those that you spend most of your time on as well as those you believe you should be doing but never seem to find the time for. Now organize them into functional categories. Theodore Caplow suggests, for example, that in a growing organization there are at least three managerial jobs that need to be done: running the existing organization, supervising the expansion, and coping with the unpredictable problems that expansion creates. On the other hand, you may chose to divide your responsibilities along more conventional, functional lines, i.e., financial management, staff supervision, planning, marketing, etc.

Finally, study your categories and see how many of them you could give away. Identify those functions that someone else could do as well as you could, if not better, and those that would be the best investment of your time.

- **Identify potential team members**. Obviously not everyone on your staff, nor everyone you could recruit off the street, is capable of performing at a managerial level. In building a managerial team, you need to find people who are capable of functioning on their own, who are willing to take risks and make difficult decisions, and who are eager to grow. Just as importantly, they should share your vision of where the organization should be headed, and they should be people you are comfortable working with closely on a day-to-day basis.

You should make every effort to seek out managerial talent within your own organization. Before making a long term commitment to someone who you believe has managerial potential, test them out by upping their routine responsibilities, or by giving them a challenging one-shot assignment.

- **Delegate**. The only way to develop your managerial team is on-the-job training. If you cling to your Wonder Woman habits, you will prevent anyone else from sharing your load, or ultimately taking over for you.

Delegating is a painful, risky process. To help make it work, and to prevent disasters resulting from premature overload, you should release responsibility gradually. Start by assigning routine parts of a function, such as the bookkeeping task of the financial management function. Explain the task very carefully, and be readily available for questions and suggestions. Then assign the budding manager moderately difficult and clearly defined problems to solve (Which health insurance plan should we go with? How can we schedule staff in the afternoon?), and ask her to bring the options to you for a final decision.

Once a team member has demonstrated ability at these lower levels, it is time to turn over a larger piece of the action to her and ask that she periodically keep you informed about what she is doing and what decisions she has made. Finally, you can turn over the full responsibility for a function and say, "You're on your own, don't bother me."

The first stages of delegation can require a lot of time, patience, and tolerance. However, when you get to the final stage, when you have groomed someone so well that you can rely on her totally, the amount of support this provides to you makes the entire effort worthwhile.

The easiest way to sabotage the delegation process is to allow end runs. Let's say, for example, you have delegated fee collection to a head teacher, and one of the parents comes to you asking for more time to pay her overdue fees. The easy thing for you to do would be to make a decision on the spot like you always used to do. However, this would undermine the authority of the head teacher in the eyes of the parents, and demonstrate to the head teacher that you aren't really taking the delegation seriously. As a rule, once you delegate, don't vacillate.

## Task 2: Building an Administrative System.

One sure way to add stability to a program in the process of change is to avoid making the same decisions over and over again. Formal policies and procedures should be worked out for dealing with common problems and questions.

Procedures should be worked out, put in writing, and distributed to all staff for handling typical problems, such as a child becoming sick at the center, a teacher calling in sick at the last moment, a bus breaking down on a field trip, a fire breaking out in the center, or a furnace going out in midday. Likewise, regular schedules and flow charts should be worked out for routine functions. For example, it should be decided who gets what financial reports on what days, or who handles inquiries from parents checking out the school, and how such inquiries are handled.

The routinizing of administrative functions does smack of bureaucratic red tape. Certainly if procedures become too rigid, they can take the life out of an organization. But given a healthy dose of common sense, committing routine procedures to paper does add a degree of stability that is important in an organization undergoing change. The center shouldn't be thrown into an uproar every time a problem arises and the director is not there to deal with it. Working out administrative systems also saves a lot of time and energy that is otherwise wasted on continually reinventing the wheel.

## Task 3: Tuning In to One's Environment.

Increasingly, child care centers are at the mercy of forces beyond their control. A decision in Washington, DC, to up the production of Stealth bombers may cause child care subsidies to be slashed. An inflammatory article in the local paper about a child care scandal clear across the country may add to a center's enrollment woes. A shift in the local employment structure may wreck havoc with a center's traditional customer base.

Directors who are not alert to such events and trends may allow their centers to be jeopardized by an unexpected threat, or to miss out on a new opportunity. Therefore, a director who desires to build a strong organization needs to tune in to what's happening outside the center as much as what's happening within the organization. The following are some means of keeping informed:

- Keeping in close contact with the parents. As an organization grows, it is very easy for the director to become increasingly isolated from the parents the center serves. It is critical to counteract this by structuring into one's work week some time to talk to parents, to keep in touch with their current needs and concerns.

- Tracking changing needs in the community by maintaining records of phone inquiries. Data on needs and means of those currently in the marketplace is an excellent barometer of changing local needs.

- Watching your center's financial trends. Knowing where you've been, what programs are making money, what programs are losing money, etc., is a strong indicator of where you should be heading.

- Volunteering to speak to local employer and parent groups. The questions you are confronted with in these sessions will keep you in touch with community concerns about child care.

- Participating in a directors' group. Comparing notes with other directors will allow you to check out your hunches about trends and changes.

- Discussions in staff meetings and board meetings about people's perceptions about community needs and developments increase the numbers of eyes and ears you have working for you.

*Adaptive managers must adapt swiftly to immediate pressures — yet think in terms of long-range goals. Above all, the adaptive manager today must be capable of radical action — willing to think beyond the thinkable: to reconceptualize products, procedures, programs, and purposes before crisis makes drastic change inescapable.*

— Alvin Tofler, in *The Adaptive Corporation*

## Task 4: Maintaining a Long Range View.

To be effective in building an organization, you need to have some idea of what you are building toward. What do you want your center to look like in five years? Who will it be serving? What services will it provide? What needs to happen to realize this vision? To develop long range action plans:

- Do plenty of "what if" planning. With your staff or board, do some brainstorming about potential scenarios and possible plans. Ask, "What if we . . . opened a new center in the suburbs? . . . offered a computer camp? . . . doubled our fees?" Explore the best/worst outcomes for each scenario.

- Establish some long range goals. Spell out what you would like your center to be doing in five years and what you want it to look like. Then outline a plan of action — lay out what needs to happen during those five years to move your center from point A to point B.

- Take some risks. Seldom will a plan of action come with a guarantee of success. If your center is to keep pace with changing needs, you will need to act at times when you can't be sure of what will happen. In those cases, you will have to trust your own judgment and be willing to make some mistakes. When you shrink from taking risks, you stop growing. Conversely, the more risks you take, the more you accelerate your learning, and the better you get at making judgment calls.

- Never give up. As you try out new ideas to meet changing needs in the community, you have to expect that some of them will succeed, that some of them will fail, and that none of them will succeed forever.

If you are content with running a center, you will continue to plug away at accustomed ways of doing business. However, if you want to build an organization with a future, you need to be continually open to new ideas and new directions.

# THE FOUR CHALLENGES TO SUCCEEDING IN A FAMILY BUSINESS

**by Roger Neugebauer**

*My husband and I decided that child care was the perfect business for us. We thought we could provide a valuable service for families and that child care would be an easy business to start. We were right on the first score and dead wrong on the second.*

— Husband and wife owners of a child care center

There are probably over 20,000 family operated child care centers in the United States. In addition, a large share of the vendors serving the early childhood profession are run by husbands and wives. Most of these owners are highly motivated by their pride in providing much needed services. Yet most would probably admit that if they had known how very hard it is to succeed in launching a business in this arena they might have directed their energies elsewhere.

This article will provide insights from 18 husbands and wives on dealing with four major hurdles they confronted in operating a family business. The families interviewed are typical of the spectrum of families currently operating child care businesses. Some have been in business less than five years, others more than 50. Some are husband and wife teams, some involve parents and siblings, and some involve three generations as well as other extended family members.

NOTE: Since the issues addressed are so personal in nature, we have elected to forgo our normal practice of crediting interviewees for their ideas directly in the article. Instead, we have listed all contributors at the end of this article.

## CHALLENGE #1:

### Keeping the Business From Consuming Family Time

*We'll be at our daughter's school play and find ourselves talking about a problem employee during intermission; or, at dinner, we'll be asking our son about his day at school, and before we know it we're talking about replacing the rug in the four year old room.*

When family members work in business together, there is a tendency to talk about business issues outside of working hours. And when their shared occupation is the demanding business of child care, their personal lives can easily be totally consumed by the business.

This problem is acute in the start-up years when family members may toil away for 70 to 80 hours a week to make a go of it. (Not only do family members invest all their time in these early years, they usually invest all their savings and a good portion of the funds of other family members.) As the business stabilizes, the absolute necessity to sacrifice family time diminishes, but the temptation to slip into business conversations at all hours still remains strong.

Those interviewed have developed a number of approaches to protecting family time:

✔ **Move the business office out of the home.** Having a separate physical location for the office helps demarcate that the home is where family life happens and the office is where business is transacted. With an office in the home, it is just too tempting to slip in and get a little work done after hours. Some families even stop having business lines ring into their homes. One family moved their home into a rural area away from their business in order to keep their family life relaxed and separate from the business.

✔ **Enforce the rule that business issues will not be discussed on family time.** Many families have adopted a formal rule that, except in emergencies, business issues won't be discussed after hours. If a family member launches into a business topic, the other family members immediately put the brakes on the discussion.

✔ **Schedule family activities first.** It can be helpful to block off family activities (school conferences, family picnics, sporting events, parties, etc.) on the business calendar well in advance, before business obligations gobble up all free time. Some families even block off some open time where there aren't any specific activities, just so the family can hang out together, or take spontaneous mini-vacations.

✔ **Build in vacation time.** If you wait for the proverbial *when things settle down* to take a vacation, it will never happen. Many families schedule vacation time just as meticulously as they schedule vacation time for their staff. Some families block out the same weeks every summer so they can plan well in advance to cover all the bases. Others arrange their schedules so that each family member can take off one day a week.

Taking aggressive steps to put a limit on time devoted to business is necessary for family well-being. After all, what sense does it make to work hard to make life better for other families at the cost of neglecting your own family?

Another reason to be vigilant of your time has to do with your personal well-being. Many of those interviewed stressed the importance of having outside interests to provide a change of pace from the child care business. They found that if they pursue hobbies, recreational interests, or community activities, when frustrations are building with the business, they can set their worries aside and restore their spirits by doing something else they enjoy.

## Challenge #2:

### Sharing Responsibility Among Family Members

*It took us a long time to get our act together. Sometimes, for example, my husband would make a big decision, like promoting a teacher aide, without telling me; and I would get upset. Or sometimes he would say no to a staff member's request and she would ask me and I'd say yes, which really frustrated him.*

When two or more people share responsibility for managing a child care organization, working out a procedure for making decisions is important. On paper, this seems like a simple task; in real life, it's a never ending challenge. Conflict is only one hasty decision away.

Here are some approaches family members interviewed found helpful in sharing responsibilities:

✔ **Carefully divide areas of responsibility.** Nearly all interviewed for this article recommended being very specific in detailing who does what. For example, if one family member is in charge of supervising the teachers and another is in charge of the bookkeeping, who makes decisions about taking advance vacation days or bringing in a substitute?

✔ **Identify those decisions that need to be made jointly.** Many big decisions will spill over all areas of responsibility, and therefore should be made jointly. Again, as much as possible, interviewees recommend preparing a list of the types of decisions that cannot be made solo.

✔ **Put your differing management styles to best use.** Chances are any husband and wife, or any two family members for that matter, will have a different style of managing people, handling crises, or solving problems. Interviewees found it valuable to talk about these differences and to trade off responsibility for handling difficult situations based on whose style is most appropriate. For example, if a new, insecure staff member has unintentionally committed a faux pas, sending the hard-nosed, authoritarian family member to talk to her would not be a good idea. Likewise, sending the spouse with the most kind-hearted disposition to confront a parent three months behind on fees might not do the trick.

✔ **Communicate to staff the division of responsibility.** Make sure staff are very clear about who to turn to for help and decisions. Those interviewed suggested that when staff come to the wrong person for a decision, you should point them in the direction of the right person, even if you know the right answer. Don't allow staff members to appeal a decision from another family member, even if you don't agree with that decision. Once this has happened, the first person loses total credibility.

Many family members recalled having problems when a staff member had surreptitiously asked one family member for a decision after already having been turned down by another family member. They recommended putting an immediate stop to this by letting this staff member know that such behavior will not be tolerated.

✔ **Keep up to date on each other's work.** Family members should be able to fill in for each other in emergencies or when meetings or travel take one person away from the center. To be able to do this, all family members need to have some experience in handling each other's jobs. And family members need to communicate frequently about problems and issues they are dealing with so they won't be caught unaware when filling in for each other.

✔ **Give each other honest feedback.** The best way to keep small misunderstandings from blossoming into major conflicts is to keep talking. Interviewees strongly recommended that if you believe your spouse has invaded your turf, don't harbor a grudge, talk about it. And if you disagree with the way your spouse handled a situation, let him know, in private, your opinion.

One husband and wife team cautioned that if you feel you cannot give negative feedback to your spouse for fear he or she will overreact or get angry, chances are you shouldn't be in business together. If you can't give each other honest feedback, this will handicap your business.

One of the major frustrations of being a center director is that it can be a very lonely job with no one to confide in, no one to lean on in tough times. One of the major advantages of having a family member as a partner is that you don't have to deal with this isolation. By working out a harmonious division of responsibilities, you can support each other, provide feedback to each other, and bring the strengths of a team effort to bear on building a successful organization.

## CHALLENGE #3:

### Involving the Next Generation

*We really wanted our kids to work in the center with us. But all their lives they heard us hashing over center headaches at dinner. So their view of the center was very negative and they didn't want any part of it.*

It's the dream of most husband-wife teams to have their children work with them, and maybe even take over the business eventually. But, in reality, about half the time the children have other ideas. And sometimes when children work in the family business, rather than being a source of enjoyment, it is a source of tension.

Family members interviewed shared these insights on involving the next generation:

✔ **If relationships are rocky at home, they'll not improve at work.** Several interviewees observed that if children are going through a rebellious stage at home, chances are they will carry their attitudes with them if they work in the family business. This is not conducive to a harmonious team effort.

✔ **Forcing children to work in the family business often has negative consequences.** If children are expected to work at the center against their will, their contributions will probably not be as positive as possible, and the likelihood of their staying involved on a long term basis will be lessened. Many parents who allowed their children to opt out of working at the center were pleasantly surprised to find them eager to return years later.

✔ **It is important to relate to children working in the center on an employer-employee basis.** The most common source of tension for sons or daughters working in a center is having their parents discipline or reward them as parents, not employers. Not only does this make them feel awkward among the other employees, but it also makes them feel like second class employees. The parents interviewed reported that it can be very difficult to learn to treat their offspring the same way they treat all other employees. Both spouses constantly need to be reminding each other when their behavior crosses the line.

✔ **Don't supervise offspring directly.** Many parents reported that the best way to avoid unnecessary tension is to have sons and daughters supervised by non-family members. This puts a helpful buffer between family members.

✔ **Have children start working elsewhere.** Several of the parents interviewed required their children to work elsewhere prior to coming to work for the center. In this manner, they can prove themselves and learn about the culture of employment without the complication of family issues. When children come to work in the family business, they are more secure in their abilities and clear in their expectations.

✔ **Be sensitive to the difficult role offspring play.** When offspring work in a center, they are likely to be placed in some difficult situations. If staff are frustrated with a decision or pattern of supervision, offspring may be exposed to the complaints. They can be alienated from their co-workers if they try to defend their parents, or if they are perceived to be spying for the parents. Likewise, they can be put in a bind if staff members ask them to influence a decision of their parents. Parents need to support their children in this environment by not asking them to report on their co-workers, by letting them know they do not want them to act as their defenders or apologists, and by letting staff know that any input on decisions needs to be made directly to them, not through their children.

✔ **Don't discuss personnel matters in front of employed children.** Unless you are grooming a son or daughter to take over the business in the near future, one interviewee cautioned, you should not talk about problems with other employees in their presence. The confidentiality of all employees needs to be respected by employers even with other family members.

## CHALLENGE #4:

### Planning the Future of Your Business

*When we first set up the business, we always assumed that we would turn it over to our kids as their birthright. But gradually it dawned on us that this was not a dream shared by our children. Now we don't know what we will do.*

According to conventional wisdom, only about one out of every three family owned businesses in the United States is passed along to the second generation. From the small sample of family businesses we looked at for this article, it would appear that this ratio will not be exceeded in the child care arena. But whether you intend to turn the business over to your children or to sell it as your retirement fund, careful planning is required. Here is some advice on how to proceed from those interviewed:

✔ **PLAN AHEAD!** Don't leave the disposition of your family business to chance. There are too many stories of couples who intended to sell their center and retire on the proceeds only to discover when the time came to sell that the business wasn't worth nearly as much as they expected.

Whether you are planning to sell your business to your children or to an outside party, setting the business up to sell can take ten years of preparation. In addition, if you don't have a plan in place for the disposition of your business and something happens to your spouse, you may end up losing your entire investment.

✔ **Plan for succession openly.** Many interviewees recommended talking openly with your children to see if they entertain any interest in taking over the family business. If one or more of your children expresses an interest, and you are confident they possess the ability to make a go of it, bring in a business planner to help work out a succession plan. Openly involve the children in developing the plan so that there are no surprises and no misunderstandings. Most importantly, once your children take over, stop your involvement as soon as possible. Don't hang around looking over their shoulders second guessing every move they make.

Interviewees whose children are unlikely to follow in their footsteps were following a number of paths to earn a return on their investment: many plan to sell their businesses outright to a third party, some plan to retain ownership while setting up the business to run itself, and some are bringing in outside investors to grow the business with the idea of eventually selling the entire business or at least their share. No matter which of these roads you travel, there are certain important transitional steps they recommend:

✔ **Determine the potential value of your business.** Don't operate on a wish and a hope. Bring in an outside expert to determine the current value of your business and its potential value in five or ten years. This will tell you whether or when a sale will make your retirement possible.

✔ **Bring in outside advisors.** One common weakness of family businesses is that they tend to be parochial. They are often not open enough to new ideas, to seizing new opportunities, to detecting changes in the environment. To keep your center from getting in a rut, some of the families interviewed have set up boards of advisors. They suggest recruiting a group of outside advisors to fill the gaps in your knowledge — maybe a lawyer, a child development specialist, or a marketing expert. Pay them from $250 to $500 a day to meet with you three or four times a year to evaluate your business and help you strategize for the future.

✔ **Make yourself dispensable.** When a family business is growing, the many hours of overtime worked by family members is critical to the success of the business. However, when it comes time to sell the business, if family members are still working long hours, this can detract from the sale price of the center. If the only reason a center is making any money is because of the extraordinary contributions of the owners, this is not likely to appear to be a very attractive investment.

If you intend to sell the business and retire, or if you want to set the business up to run itself so you can take drawings while acting as absentee owners, you need to groom staff to take your place. This cannot happen overnight. Some of those interviewed suggest that this may require at least five to ten years of careful planning.

### Family Owners Interviewed

**Sandy and Randy Bright**, ABC Child Development Centers, Greeley, Colorado.

**Margie and Scott Butler**, West University Children's School, Tucson, Arizona.

**Roseann and Dennis Drew**, The Sunshine House, Greenwood, South Carolina.

**Roslyn and Vincent Duffy**, Learning Tree Montessori, Seattle, Washington.

**Marcy and Paul Erwin**, Primrose Schools, Cartersville, Georgia.

**Jane and Jim Flanagan**, Flanagan's Preschool Inc., Whitemarsh, Pennsylvania.

**Sue and Jon Jacka**, Bright Start Children's Centers, St. Paul, Minnesota.

**Sharon and Charles Jones**, Woodlands Day Schools Inc., Charlottesville, Virginia.

**Carol and Ken Krysko**, Early Explorations, Encinitas, California.

**Dave Linsmeier**, Children's Programs Inc., Brookfield, Wisconsin.

**Jean and Gene Little**, Creative Child Care Inc., Hurst, Texas.

**Barbara and Charles Loeb**, Children's Place Ltd., New Orleans, Louisiana.

**Joan and Mark Mendel**, Kidstop Early Learning Center, Boynton Beach, Florida.

**Jane and Dawn Peckwas and Kimberly Peckwas Strzelczyk**, Early Education Unlimited, Chicago, Illinois.

**Suzanne and Rick Porter**, Rainbow River/Rainbow Rising Child Care Centers, Hermosa Beach, California.

**Bobbie and Marvin Schneider**, The First Class, Holmdel, New Jersey.

**Missy and John Webb**, Teddy Bear Day Care, Alexandria, Virginia.

**Linda and Bill Wilkinson**, Settlement Inc. Preschool, Bethlehem, Tennessee.

# Making the Partnership Stronger — Working with a Board of Directors

by Cindy Ratekin and Gary Bess

*If you are working with a nonprofit child care center, then you are under the direction of a board of directors. You may have little or no experience working with boards. On the other hand, the board members of your organization may have little or no experience working with child care centers. What is the role of the board of directors, and how can the child care staff and director work with the board to produce the best results for your center?*

*The board of directors and the staff are the two pillars on which a child care center rests. If either pillar is weak, the center runs the risk of an imbalance, which, if not corrected, can lead to major decline — if not altogether toppling — into chaos.*

But why should this happen? Isn't it simply a matter of clear definition of who does what and when?

One answer is offered by Herman and Heimovics (1991), who speak of the assumption that organizations are "unitary, rational actors":

*In many nonprofit organizations the differing perspectives between service delivery and fund-raising units, between paid professionals and volunteers, and between clinically prepared and management-trained staff also make achieving unity difficult.*

This article will focus on the role of the board of directors within nonprofit organizations and how the board and the child care center staff can work well together for the agency.

Let's begin with a questionnaire designed to separate the responsibilities of the board and staff.

The answers, based on commonly applied organizational wisdom, are at the end of the article. If you are unsure as to the correct answer, a clue is to pay attention to key verbs which are often used in differentiating roles and responsibilities for board and staff. Words and phrases such as "approves," "establishes" (as in policy), or "authorizes" generally apply to the board of directors. On the other hand, "implements," "drafts," or "recommends" often pertain to staff functions.

Unfortunately, in some situations, words are used which do not clearly communicate where responsibility rests and thus, at times, ambiguity leads to conflict. The verb "plans," for example, is a function of both board and staff roles, as are words such as "represents," "oversees," and "develops."

These ten questions cover the four most common areas of board responsibility — finances, program planning, resource development, and personnel. Tasks in these areas are often relegated to committees of the board as provided for in the child care center's bylaws. They help to structure the agenda for most board of directors' meetings by organizing reports based on these four domains. They are also areas in which the center director and staff are involved.

## Four Areas of Board and Staff Joint Involvement

There are purposeful, practical, and legal reasons why the board of directors and child care center staff together address the four areas of center responsibility. The following is a brief description of each area and the generally accepted role and responsibility for each party.

- ***Financial Oversight***

A Finance Committee, often chaired by the board treasurer, is responsible for reviewing the agency's income and expenses, balance sheet, investments, and other matters related to the center's financial situation. It is also responsible for submitting the annual operating budget for the center to the board of directors for its approval, and for comparing income and expenses to the approved operating budget.

In most instances, the treasurer or Finance Committee members do not maintain the organization's books, but rely on the center director or an outside accounting or bookkeeping service. It is generally accepted practice for the center to produce a monthly report of income and expenses for the preceding month which, after review by the Finance Committee, goes to the board of directors for approval.

Explanation of unusual items among either income or expenses is often left to the center's director, who is more familiar with the actual transactions than members of the board. It is extremely helpful for the director to have reviewed the reports before the Finance Committee meeting in order to look into any extraordinary situation and to be prepared to explain, for example, why food costs were higher than usual this month or that tuition declined more than 10% from the prior month. The Finance Committee can only monitor how much money comes in and how much goes out; the director must be the one to explain why.

In addition to having responsibility for monitoring income and expenses, the board is responsible for investing the organization's funds in a safe and prudent manner, and for making sure that all money is handled properly. It is best for an agency to have a financial procedures manual, approved by the board of directors, which specifies these procedures. In addition, an annual independent audit will provide assurance to the board and outside agencies, including funders, that the center's finances are properly managed.

- ***Program Planning***

This is one area where the expectation is that staff will lead and the board will follow. But not necessarily. On the one hand, the center staff is expected to be knowledgeable about developments in the field and to advise the Program Planning Committee about how things are going and what program improvements may be possible. On the other hand, however, depending on the background of the board members on the committee (e.g., professionals in the child care field, parents of enrolled children), ideas can be offered from their perspective, which are equally as valid.

Regardless of where the new program ideas are generated, the committee must assess the benefits and risks of each new venture from numerous viewpoints. These include the cost of a new service, the impact of a new service on current services, staffing requirements, promotional and marketing ideas, and whether the new program fits with the center's purpose and, if available, its strategic plan (Ratekin & Bess, 1995).

The Program Planning Committee is the filter through which the center's activities are managed. It is the board's way of assuring itself that services are being provided to families according to standards of quality approved by the board. Just as the Finance Committee conducts a monthly review of income and expenses, the Program Planning Committee reviews the services provided during the preceding month (e.g., average daily

---

For each statement which follows, indicate whether the primary responsibility for the task rests with the board of directors (B) or the child care center director and/or staff (S). If you feel that more than one of the above groups are responsible, list each in order of their share of responsibility:

1. Drafts the center's annual budget for approval _______
2. Establishes personnel policies _______
3. Plans fund raising events _______
4. Approves legal contracts and agreements involving the center _______
5. Analyzes unusual budget line item revenues and expenses _______
6. Recommends possible new service directions for the center _______
7. Is legally responsible for the affairs of the center _______
8. Engages in grant writing to public and private sources _______
9. Prepares reports for funding agencies _______
10. Maintains center's financial records _______

---

attendance, number of new children enrolled, community presentations made) in preparation for reporting to the board of directors.

Sometimes the committee's oversight extends to the center's compliance with grants or contracts where specific measures of performance are set. Many service contracts — especially those funded by government — are audited for proof of services rendered. Just as a financial audit can disallow expenses, a program audit can disallow services that were not provided as specified in the contract. Liability for deficiencies falls on the board of directors. Thus, the committee may request copies of staff prepared reports submitted in compliance with service contracts, in addition to requesting information from staff at its meetings on any issues associated with contract noncompliance.

From the staff's perspective, the Program Planning Committee is the vehicle for testing the board's response to new program ideas. This happens when a center staff member offers an idea to the committee, where it is examined at length, constructively challenged, and shaped, if necessary, for presentation to the board. If the committee supports the proposal, it will take the idea to the board, who will either accept or reject the committee's recommendation. If the committee is not supportive of the staff's plan, the staff member may revise the plan based on the committee's recommendations.

• ***Resource Development***

This is an area of great importance to the child care center. The Resource Development Committee is charged with the raising of funds and other beneficial resources for the organization. Referred to by some agencies as the Fund Raising Committee, the term "resource development" is a broader concept which refers to bringing several kinds of resources to the center. Donations such as equipment and supplies, in addition to volunteer services such as printing or computer consulting, allow for more of the center's income to be spent in other areas.

Though the committee serves as the coordinating body for all resource development ventures, there are separate and clear areas of involvement for center staff and board members. Traditionally, agency staff are involved with grant writing to public and private sources either at their own initiative or in response to formally issued requests for proposals. Although completed by center staff, it is not uncommon for board members to require that the board be informed of, and sometimes to approve of, each grant submission. This requirement can become cumbersome, especially when deadlines are involved. The Resource Development Committee can serve an important role by serving as a liaison between the center staff and board in these situations.

Board involvement in resource development often takes the form of special event planning; individual, business, and corporate solicitations; as well as raffles, product sales, and other forms of community wide fund raising. Though primarily the board's area, staff sometimes play an important role as well in helping to manage the numerous logistical details for each event. A common refrain on the part of staff is that the board does not do enough in resource development, while committee members will complain that they are not supported in their efforts by either the staff or, often enough, other board members.

There is a tendency on the part of board members and staff to assume that constant problems such as inadequate funding have been resolved if a Resource Development Committee is formed. After all, members have divided up the work of the agency by committee and those serving in other capacities are released of direct responsibility for resource development, save for receiving reports at board meetings and attending events.

Unlike other committee assignments, however, the Resource Development Committee requires the personal support of virtually all persons who are affiliated with the agency. For events to be successful, everyone must pitch in and help. Leadership of this kind begins with the board of directors, who should each have contributed to the agency, and extends to the center's staff who, too, should be contributors.

This latter point is sometimes difficult for some staff members to accept. Why should staff contribute to their employer when their compensation is less than what they deserve? The answer is found in an assumption that everyone, including center staff, is inclined to contribute a portion of their earnings to nonprofits of their choice. It is unthinkable that they would not support their own agency in this way. An immeasurable amount of good will is had when board members and staff are counted among active donors.

• ***Personnel Management***

Personnel committees deal with the agency's most important resource — its employees. After all, expenses for salaries, payroll taxes, and fringe benefits in most child care centers exceed 50% or more of the total operating budget. In a very real sense, the staff is our technology, the machinery by which services are delivered. Their skill level, their satisfaction with their employment, and their commitment to the agency and the population which it serves all contribute to their effectiveness.

In another context, however, there are state and federal regulations which govern how staff are to be treated as employees, what they are entitled to receive in compensation and other benefits, and what should be expected in their work environment. If an employee is dissatisfied with an aspect of employment, she or he can file a complaint with the local labor board and/or file a civil suit. In either situation, the board of directors is the liable party.

Given their legal liability, boards of directors sometimes misinterpret their role with regard to personnel matters.

It is the board's responsibility to establish personnel policies which govern the employment of center staff. Personnel policies are made up partly of the legal requirements concerning employment, such as federal wage minimums and work day hours, and also the specific policies of the center, such as vacation and sick time accrual, holiday closings, employee evaluation, and grievance procedures.

The board is also responsible for approving and revising employee job descriptions and for setting salary levels. With the exception of the center director, whom the board hires, fires, and often negotiates separate terms of employment, the assessment of the performance of other employees is the responsibility of the center director or delegated to other staff.

In essence, the board of directors provides the framework within which the staff, through its center director, is managed. The center director is responsible for implementation of the center's personnel policies. All too often, however, board members interfere with the center director's ability to manage the staff — either through giving input (solicited or not) as to performance, passing judgment regarding specific compensation, or soliciting input on "how things are going." By doing this, they have unintentionally communicated to staff that it is appropriate to circumvent the director and go directly to a board member with concerns.

This is not to say that the board and staff should not communicate with one another. There are numerous opportunities for constructive dialogue to occur. On matters of center business or at social events, this is most appropriate. The treasurer should be called by the bookkeeper with regard to financial matters, and members of the Program Planning Committee should be encouraged to meet with project directors to discuss new program plans. With regard to an employee's employment status, however, the line is clearly drawn.

## Conclusion

Working with a board of directors is a rewarding, frustrating, serious, and always challenging experience. But a strong board and a strong staff working together is what it takes to manage a child care center. The four areas of board involvement — finances, program planning, resource development, and personnel — provide a framework for building a strong enduring organization. Now take the quiz again and ask members of your board to take the quiz as well. This may be the start of a stronger working relationship between the staff and board members of your child care center.

## References


Herman, R. D., & Heimovics, R. D. (1991). *Executive Leadership in Nonprofit Organizations*. Oxford: Jossey-Bass.

Ratekin, C., & Bess, G. (1995). "Where We Are Headed — and Why: A Step-by-Step Guide to Strategic Planning in Center-Based Child Care." *Early Education Journal, 23(1)*, 15-21.

Robert, H. M. (1971). *Robert's Rules of Orders Revised*. New York: William Morrow and Co.


## Answers to the Questionnaire

**(based on commonly applied organizational wisdom)**

| | | |
|---|---|---|
| 1. | Drafts the center's annual budget for approval | S |
| 2. | Establishes personnel policies | B |
| 3. | Plans fund raising events | B/S |
| 4. | Approves legal contracts and agreements involving the center | B |
| 5. | Analyzes unusual budget line item revenues and expenses | S |
| 6. | Recommends possible new service directions for the center | S/B |
| 7. | Is legally responsible for the affairs of the center | B |
| 8. | Engages in grant writing to public and private sources | S/B |
| 9. | Prepares reports for funding agencies | S |
| 10. | Maintains center's financial records | S |

# Nine Questions for the Dedicated Board Member

**Exchange Evaluation Instrument**

### 1. Do you understand your responsibilities as a board member?

Being a board member is not an honorary position—it entails serious obligations. The board of directors of a non profit corporation bears final responsibility for the direction and control of the organization. This involves setting goals and policies, overseeing administration, evaluating performance, and monitoring finances.

### 2. Is the board well organized to accomplish its responsibilities?

As volunteers, most board members can only devote a limited amount of time to board work. Therefore, it is imperative that their time be spent effectively. Most of the work of the board should take place in active committees with staff support. Meetings of committees and the full board should keep on task with the majority of time devoted to issues of the highest priority.

### 3. Is there an ongoing board development process?

The board should have in place an ongoing effort to recruit new board members who are committed to the goals of the organization and who bring to the board a full range of skills and perspectives. New members should have the opportunity to participate in a thorough orientation on the activities and structure of the organization and their responsibilities as board members.

### 4. Are board members committed to the mission of organization?

A paramount responsibility of the board is to define the short-term and long-term goals for the organization. These goals should be clearly communicated throughout the organization as well as to the community at large. Periodically, the board should re-evaluate this mission statement in light of changing community needs and resources.

### 5. Does the board closely monitor the performance of the organization?

For board members to effectively carry out their responsibilities, they must keep their fingers on the pulse of the organization. They should keep in touch informally by observing the organization at work and by soliciting feedback from people the organization is serving. In addition, the board should carry out a formal periodic evaluation of the organization's progress toward achieving its goals.

### 6. Do board members make well-informed budgetary decisions?

The budget is an organization's most powerful policy statement. Shaping and approving the annual budget is the most important single task board members are called upon to perform. To carry out this task responsibly, they must be consulted early in the budget development process, they must be given adequate information about the financial and program implications of budget proposals, and they must deliberately weigh budget decisions in terms of the goals of the organization.

### 7. Does the board exercise effective oversight of the organization's financial management?

Board members should periodically review the organization's financial statements to assure that income and expenses are in line with the annual budget, and that assets and liabilities are being responsibly managed. At least annually, the board should determine whether adequate financial controls are in place. In addition, the board must approve and update a plan for the maintenance and insurance of the organization's physical assets.

### 8. Is there a healthy tension in relationships between board and staff members?

Unless a board abdicates its responsibility and simply acts as a rubber stamp for the staff, there are bound to be periods of tension between board and staff members. Often these tensions occur when board members overstep their bounds and inject themselves into the day-to-day operations of the organization. To prevent this, there should be a clear understanding among all parties as to the demarcation between board and staff responsibilities.

Tension can also arise when staff and board members openly disagree about a proposed course of action. While it is helpful if board and staff members can work together in harmony, board members must appreciate that their duty transcends pleasing the staff. A board member is elected by the members of the corporation to represent their interests on the board. Sometimes the interests of the members at large do not coincide with the interests of staff members. In these cases, board members must work through these conflicts and reach decisions in the best interests of the organization. In an effectively functioning organization, such tensions are dealt with openly and professionally, with a minimum of lingering hard feelings.

### 9. Does the board have an effective system for evaluating the performance of the executive director?

It has been said that a strong executive director may be able to carry an organization with a weak board, but that a strong board cannot save an organization from the ill effects of a weak executive director. A board must set clear standards of performance expected of an executive director and commit itself to the ongoing task of evaluating the director's performance against those standards.

***Credits:*** *The title of this form was adapted from a form developed by Terry W. McAdam and the contents from a variety of sources including* ***The Nonprofit Organization Handbook*** *(New York: McGraw Hill Book Company, 1980) by Tracy D. Connors;* ***A Handbook for Day Care Board Members*** *(New York: Day Care Council of New York, Inc., 1984) by Christine Dimock Secor;* ***The Board of Directors of Nonprofit Organizations*** *(Washington, DC: Management Assistance Group, 1977) by Karl Mathiasen, III; and* ***Evaluating the Performance of Trustees and School Heads*** *(Boston: National Association of Independent Schools, 1986) by Eric W. Johnson.*

# To Profit or Not to Profit: That Is the Tough Question

by Roger Neugebauer

*Two working mothers, Jane and Bonnie, were upset when their family child care provider decided to retire. They were frustrated with the lack of good alternatives they had for the care of their children. And in talking to their friends and community leaders, they found that this frustration was widespread. Many families in their community, some well-to-do, others struggling to get by, were in desperate need of good child care.*

Jane, an elementary school teacher, and Bonnie, a middle manager in a Fortune 500 company, decided to do something about this critical community need. They agreed to quit their jobs and start a center that parents could turn to with confidence.

Once they had made this exciting decision, they were confronted with a perplexing choice — should they organize their program as a for profit or a non profit? They consulted a range of early childhood experts on the advantages and disadvantages of the two forms of business and here is the advice they received.

## Ease of Start Up

It is nearly always easier and less expensive to set up a for profit child care organization than a non profit one. If an individual, or a husband and wife, are going into business as a sole proprietorship, all that is required to be in business are a few simple filings with the federal, state, and local governments.

If two or more individuals are setting up a partnership to operate the child care business, the filing of partnership papers with the state government is a bit more complex and may require some support from a lawyer. If one or more individuals or organizations decide to incorporate the center, the steps in pulling together a corporate filing are more complex and can entail $1000 or more in legal fees.

The establishment of a non profit involves two basic steps. The first step, which is relatively easy, is the filing of articles of incorporation with the state.

The second, more involved step is to make application with the IRS for tax exempt status. Securing 501(c)3 status from the IRS is important to a non profit — it means that individuals or corporations can take a charitable tax deduction for donations to the organization. This process can take at least six months and can cost $2500 or more in legal fees.

## Access to Capital

A major disadvantage of non profit status is that it is not conducive to the raising of capital. Private investments cannot be attracted since non profits cannot spin off dividends and cannot be sold to yield returns for investors. Likewise, banks are often nervous about making loans to non profit child care organizations, partly because they do not understand this business model, but also because they dislike putting themselves in the bad public relations position of having to foreclose on community non profits.

In theory, for profit child care ventures have the ability to attract capital. In reality, until a child care organization has established itself as a solid business, it is not likely to easily attract support from investors or bankers. The typical for profit center is initially founded with funds from the founders or the founder's relatives, or with a bank loan personally guaranteed by the founders. However, once a proprietary center establishes a sound track record it gains access to the full range of financial instruments available to finance the growth of any small business.

## Access to Funding

A non profit organization typically does enjoy greater access to funding from public and philanthropic sources. Many public and private grant programs restrict availability to non profits or yield significant advantages to non profits in the award process. In addition, non profits are more likely to be recipients of charitable donations from individuals and corporations.

In recent years, the funding advantages of non profits have lessened somewhat. To begin with, the distribution of public subsidies is shifting. In the past, state and county governments distributed most child care subsidies through large contracts to non profit child care agencies. Today, increasing proportions of child care subsidies are distributed through some form of vouchers where parents are empowered to select their own provider. As a result, for profit providers are benefiting along with non profits from these funds. Today, the greatest share of federal subsidies for child care result from the forgiveness of taxes under the Child and Dependent Care Tax Credit. Parents can take advantage of a federal tax credit, on a sliding scale basis, for child care fees paid to nearly any provider. Non profits enjoy no advantage at all in this funding stream.

While non profits remain the primary beneficiaries of philanthropic funding, this advantage is less pronounced as well. In the past 15 years, the number of families (both fee paying and subsidized) using child care has exploded. However, child care funding by philanthropic organizations, such as foundations and United Way Agencies, has grown more incrementally. In fact, less than one percent of all funding for child care today comes from philanthropic sources (Behrman).

As a result, while in every metropolitan area there may be a few large, long established non profit child care agencies that receive a significant share of their funding from charitable sources, most non-profit child care agencies receive little if any charitable funding. Most small and mid-size non profits lack the skills and resources to compete effectively with larger non profits in the grantsmanship arena.

Employers are a recent addition to the private funding picture. Seeking to gain a competitive advantage in staff recruitment and retention, increasing numbers and types of employers are investing in child care as a valuable benefit. At first, companies typically provided such benefits by setting up a non profit child care program to run a center on or near site. As employers started to realize how complicated it was to operate a center, the recent trend has been to contract out to an existing child care agency to manage child care programs for their employees. In awarding such contracts, employers have tended to favor for profit providers who they perceive to better understand the language and psychology of business operations.

## Exposure to Taxes

By virtue of their legal status, non profit tax exempt organizations are able to avoid exposure to many forms of taxation. If a non profit happens to enjoy a surplus of income over expenses at the end of a tax year, this surplus is not subject to taxation. In addition, non profits enjoy exemption or relief from many sales, payroll, property, and licensing taxes.

Many of these tax savings truly do contribute to the bottom line, particularly as the purchases and assets of the organization grow. However, the largest form of tax relief, exemption from taxes on surpluses, may not be a significant advantage for the average non profit.

To demonstrate this point, it is useful to examine the economics of a typical non profit center and a typical for profit center. Let's look at two organizations serving 80 children, each having a total income of $300,000 and ending up with a 5% surplus at the end of the year. For the for profit center, since it is most likely organized as a sole proprietorship or a Subchapter S corporation, the center pays no taxes on the surplus. The surplus, as can be seen in the table below, is passed on to the owner who pays federal (and often state) income taxes on her salary plus the profit.

**Tax Liability Scenarios**

| | For Profit | Non Profit A | Non Profit B |
|---|---|---|---|
| Center Revenues | $300,000 | $300,000 | $300,000 |
| Salary of CEO | 30,000 | 30,000 | 45,000 |
| Other Expenses | 255,000 | 255,000 | 255,000 |
| Annual Surplus | 15,000 | 15,000 | 0 |
| Taxable Income | 45,000 | 30,000 | 45,000 |

For the non profit center, a range of scenarios are possible. If the executive director of the center takes a relatively low salary ($30,000 in example A), the surplus escapes taxation and is returned to the organization, and the director only pays taxes on her $30,000 salary. On the other hand, if the salary of the executive director is relatively high ($45,000 in example B), the center with the same operating budget enjoys no surplus at the end of the year, and the director pays taxes on her $45,000 salary.

From these scenarios it can be argued that the advantages the average non profit enjoys have less to do with exemption from income taxes than from the low wages it pays. If a non profit elects to pay its employees well (whether the director or the teachers), its surplus will decline and the income taxes paid by its employees will increase.

As child care organizations expand beyond typical size, the tax advantages of the non profit do start to have an impact. On the for profit side, as profits start to increase beyond a modest increase in the owner's salary, tax liability grows at an increasing rate. For the non profit, as surpluses grow, increasing funds are returned to the organization free of taxation.

## Access to Community Support

While tax and funding advantages are often not as profound for the average non profit as expected, access to community support is often more significant. This advantage is most dramatic in terms of occupancy costs. The average for profit center invests nearly three times as much in occupancy costs as does the typical non profit (Helburn). This is a result of the fact that churches and other community organizations are much more likely to contribute free or reduced cost space to non profit centers.

In addition, businesses are more likely to donate equipment, supplies, and labor to a non profit center than a for profit one. In the community, a non profit may benefit from the impression that they are more deserving. All this is not to say that for profits have no chance at gaining community support. A well-respected for profit center does have opportunities to garner community support since child care is currently viewed as a valuable service. For example, office park and residential real estate developers may provide reduced cost rent to for profit child care providers because child care is an amenity that will make their developments more attractive.

## Appeal to Volunteers

As a general rule, it is probably true that a potential volunteer will more likely elect to work in a non profit setting. And there are a number of organized volunteer initiatives, such as the federal Americorps program and similar programs operated by religious organizations, where volunteers are placed in community non profit programs.

However, the days of a broad base of eager volunteers are over. Whether a for profit or a non profit, the realistic potential pool of volunteers is parents of currently enrolled students — at least those few not working full time or in a senior enough position that they can actually afford to take time off. Parental desire to help their children has more to do with personal motivation and time availability than with the legal status of the center.

## Appeal to Teaching Candidates

In the 1970s, a wave of student and parent activists entered the early childhood workforce motivated by their vision of changing the world. Today, not only are such cause-motivated workers in short supply, but in fact the supply of teaching candidates of all types is shrinking. In this climate, factors such as pay and benefits offered, the stability and quality of the center, working conditions at the center, and the charisma of the leader are much more important factors than legal status in recruiting teachers.

## Appeal to Parents

Not only is the legal status of a center not an important selection factor for parents, once parents make their choice they seldom know whether the center they selected is a for profit or a non profit one. Most parent surveys have found that factors such as cost, convenience, safety, and teacher warmth are the most important selection factors.

## Challenge of Management

Conventional wisdom holds that for profit entities are driven to run in a business-like manner and non profits are less motivated to be efficient. In the real world, centers of all types operate at such tight margins that any center that is not operated withsound management skills will fail.

At the extreme ends of the legal spectrum, organizations do require divergent management skills. Large non profit child care systems serving predominantly low income populations are required to exercise skills in grantsmanship, multisource fund management, public contracting, public relations, and supporting families in crisis. Large, national for profit chains, on the other hand, must excel in real estate acquisition, multi-site management, communication, and marketing.

For the bulk of the programs in the middle of the spectrum, small and mid-sized community-based non profits and for profits, the skills required are almost identical. Nearly all of these typical programs derive well over 90% of their income from parent fees and must focus their attention first and foremost on guaranteeing parent satisfaction.

The area where significant differences may arise is in decisionmaking. In a typical for profit center, control is concentrated with a single owner or a husband and wife team. This makes for a simple, if not very rich, decisionmaking process. In a non profit, ownership is maintained by the community of the non profit as defined in the articles of incorporation. This ownership is vested in the hands of a board of directors, who are empowered to set the course for the organization. This introduces more players, and more complicated procedures, into the decisionmaking process, but in theory has the advantage of ensuring that interests of the community are represented in decisions.

The non profit reality is far different. In the child care world, most boards function in an advisory, not ownership, capacity. Board members, whether parents, community members, or business leaders, do not have sufficient time to invest in thoroughly understanding all the legal, financial, educational, political, and demographic issues involved in operating the center. As a result, they by and large defer to the director in decisionmaking. They function more as "boards of directeds."

That is not to say that non profit boards are simply a necessary nuisance. Creative directors use board positions to recruit champions and allies, such as bankers, lawyers,

## Expert Contributors

Although Jane and Bonnie are fictitious characters, the advice reported is real and came from the following highly respected leaders in the early childhood world:

Mary Ann Anthony, Director of Child Care Division, Catholic Charities, Jamaica Plain, MA

Doug Baird, CEO, Associated Day Care Services, Boston, MA

Angela Barnhart, Accounts Coordinator, YMCA of Greater Halifax/Dartmouth, Halifax, Novia Scotia

Bob Benson, former CEO of Children's World Learning Centers, Evergreen, CO

Roberta Bergman, Senior Vice President, The Child Care Group, Dallas, TX

Sue Connor, Educational Consultant, Providence, RI

Cynthia Conway, Director, Westminster Child Development Center, Grand Rapids, MI

Margaret Leitch Copeland, Administrator, State of New Hampshire Child Development Bureau, Concord, NH

Marcia Pioppi Galazzi, Executive Director, The Family Schools, Inc., Brewster, MA

Mary Ellen Gornick, President, The CPA Group, Chicago, IL

Gwen Hooper, Director, Arlington Children's Center, Arlington, MA

Michael Kalinowski, Associate Professor, University of New Hampshire, Durham, NH

Linda Kosinski, Director, Groton Community School, Groton, MA

Gwen Morgan, Founding Director, Center for Career Development in Early Care and Education, Wheelock College, Boston, MA

Joe Perreault, Program Specialist, Army Child Care Services, Arlington, VA

Edna Ranck, Director of Public Policy and Research, NACCRA, Washington, DC

Nina Sazer-O'Donnell, Director of Community-Life Programs, Families and Work Institute, Durham, NC

William Strader, Professor, Fitchburg State College, Fitchburg, MA

Roy Walker, Program Specialist, Administration for Children and Families, Boston, MA

Karen Woodford, President, Summa Associates, Inc., Tempe, AZ

early childhood professors, marketing specialists, accountants, and political leaders.

## Risk to Management

The non profit structure provides limited protection to board members and the director. For example, if the center fails leaving significant unpaid bills, creditors typically cannot go after board members or the director for payment. Liability is limited to the assets of the organization. In addition, insurance coverage can be secured which provides substantial, if not complete, protection to board members acting in good faith from lawsuits arising out of the operation of the center.

On the for profit side, risks are greater. In a sole proprietorship, if a center fails, creditors can usually go after the owner for uncollected debts.

If a center is incorporated, creditors are limited to attacking the assets of the corporation. However, typically the biggest debt a for profit center has is loans taken out to finance the start-up of the business. In many cases, banks will require the owner to guarantee such loans.

## Flexibility to Change

Today, because both community based non profit and for profit centers are primarily customer driven, they are equally sensitive to changes in consumer demand. Non-profit organizations with diverse, talented boards of directors may be more tuned into broader changes in the community or upcoming funding opportunities, but clever for profits also do such forecasting.

When it comes to responding to changes, for profits, with their greater access to capital, may be able to respond more quickly to demand for new or additional services. On the other hand, with the surge of interest by public officials in the lifelong impact of the early years, effective non profits may be able to position themselves to benefit from anticipated new public funding streams.

One way in which non profits are inflexible is in the disposition of their assets. If a non profit is on the verge of going out of business, it can only be taken over by another non profit. If it goes out of business, its remaining assets can only be donated to another non profit.

## Motivation for Leaders

According to conventional wisdom, non profit organizations are mission-driven and for profit businesses are profit-driven. In the real world, motivation is not so simple.

Individuals who are driven solely by the desire for economic gain would likely give child care, with its low profit margins, a wide berth. (In recent years, of course, several child care companies have gone public, resulting in large gains for their founders. However, given the hundreds of thousands of operators who have entered the child care sector in the past decade, one's chances of hitting it big are still extremely low.)

Most child care entrepreneurs have a strong belief in the importance of early education and see their business venture as making a difference for families and children. On the other hand, they do have a strong economic incentive — if their business fails, chances are they will lose their life savings as well as funds they may have borrowed from friends and relatives.

Individuals who aspire to leadership positions in the non profit sector clearly have a desire to contribute to society. Typically as they develop their leadership skills, they also become motivated to become effective in managing the business side of their organization. However, their rewards for success are limited.

If they are successful in growing their non profit into a successful, stable community institution, they can enjoy great satisfaction in this accomplishment. Along the way too, they will undoubtedly receive recognition in their community and their profession. And, as the organization grows, their compensation package can grow (within limits). However, when they retire, they cannot reap any financial benefits (other than a farewell dinner and a gold watch) for their contributions.

## The Bottom Line

Bonnie and Jane are faced with a difficult decision. If their goal was to provide child care in a low income community, they clearly would pursue the non profit route. If their plan was to build up a large chain of centers with the goal of going public, they clearly would pursue the for profit route.

However, their goal is more middle of the road. They want to set up a center for a range of working families. Their best course is not at all clear. On balance, they should probably start with the assumption that they will be opening a for profit business as it is easier to establish and offers more flexibility in changing along the way and disposing of in the end. However, they should test this assumption by reviewing each of the factors above to see if in their particular situation the non-profit route actually offers some significant advantages.

A number of factors may dictate the non-profit path. For example, they may decide that they absolutely cannot afford to risk any of their own money or that of their families. Or, there may be some well-endowed community organizations that are willing to make significant contributions to their start-up efforts.

In any case, their decision should not be made in haste, or based on unexamined assumptions. We wish them luck.

## Resources


Behrman, R. (Ed.) (1996). Financing child care. *The future of children*. Los Altos, CA: The David and Lucille Packard Foundation.

Helburn, S. (1995). *Cost, quality and child outcomes in child care centers: Executive summary*. Denver, CO: University of Colorado.

# Financial Management

# Managing Money

## Chapter 7

# Five Fundamentals of Financial Health

by Mary R. Brower and Theresa M. Sull

*When child care centers are in poor financial health, the quality of care for children can decline, affecting their future success as students and, eventually, as employees. Research demonstrates that by the time children are in second grade, those who attended high quality child care centers have better academic and social skills than children from low quality centers. In addition, the benefits of high quality child care affect children from all socio-economic backgrounds, including families with both high and low income.*

In our list of *Building Blocks in a Foundation of Financial Health* we name at least 40 indicators of good financial management for child care programs, but five stand out as *fundamental* to a program's financial health (see sidebar on page 126). To illustrate these fundamentals, we've used stories that are compilations of experiences in real programs, but none of the following profiles represent actual, individual, child care centers.

## Enrollment is at Capacity, With a Waiting List in Place

Child care centers operate on a tight budget. High quality care is labor-intensive, and requires well-equipped, well-maintained, and spacious facilities. The income adequate to support quality, whether obtained from private-pay families or from public subsidy, is dependent on enrollment. When centers don't consider seasonal fluctuations in enrollment, and don't maintain an active waiting list, enrollment may slip below the program's budgeted capacity, resulting in loss of income.

One center with an enrollment capacity of 35 children, did not maintain a waiting list, instead relying on unsolicited phone calls. For example, the County Department of Social Services (DSS) counted on this center to accept children whenever they called the director. And the center staff were proud that they always had a slot. But when the economic climate of the state suffered, counties experienced funding shortfalls that were passed on to social service agencies.

In August, when four year olds typically move on to public kindergartens, there was no subsidy funding to pick up new families, so enrollment in the center dropped to 18. With its long history of relying on DSS for referrals, this center was unprepared to maintain enrollment with private-pay families. Within two months, the center was experiencing a cash flow crisis. The director continued to make payroll — just barely — but taxes and bills went unpaid, and soon they had growing debt.

Advertise! Keep your program in the public eye, even when enrollment is at capacity.

## Tuition is Based on the Full Cost of Care

Even when programs maintain adequate enrollment, they may be selling themselves short by neglecting to base tuition rates as closely as possible on the full cost of care. For years, one popular center used a sliding fee scale to help low-income families who could not afford the full cost of care. This center also maintained about 75 percent publicly subsidized enrollment, again trying to meet the needs of low-income families in their community. In addition, the private pay rate was set below market rate, which meant that payment from the county for subsidized children was lower than the center's private pay rate.

Although this program had budgeted funds for some scholarships, administrators failed to recognize and record the cost of default scholarships created by the difference between market rates and their private pay rates, not budgeting this difference as a real expense. What's more, the center did nothing to raise additional funds to close the gap between budgeted revenue and the full cost of care. As a consequence, this lack of financial planning resulted in teachers' underwriting these scholarships with their low salaries and lack of benefits.

Because this poor financial management continued for years, this program eventually found itself with delinquent obligations — to the Internal Revenue Service for payroll taxes, to the caterers for children's meals, and to local vendors — to the tune of over $65,000.

Operating in a survival mode, the director sought grant funding for new initiatives that, without adequate planning and a new board-approved budget, cost more than they brought in. Taking on new initiatives, such as Early Head Start and a school-age program, did not improve the financial health of the center because the initiatives were based on projected enrollments that did not materialize. The new programs were not marketed adequately. And children who *were* enrolled — only 25 percent of budgeted capacity — were all subsidized by the county at market rates that did not reach full cost of care.

Compute the full cost of care for each classroom! Compare that cost to tuition charged private-pay families and to market rates paid by agencies that subsidize families.

## Family Fees are Paid on Time

It's essential that programs establish a written policy regarding *what* family fees are due, *when* they are due, and what *penalties* will be imposed when fees are late. Because the staff of child care centers are often made up of dedicated individuals who want to serve children and families, they sometimes take excuses for late fees.

In one program, collecting family fees was an on-going problem. The director and staff were very sympathetic to families with cash flow problems and did not operate under the written policies that parents had signed. Neither the board of directors, nor the bookkeeper, was aware that many parent fees were delinquent. In fact, *several teachers* with children enrolled in the center were among the parents who had not paid their fees. When discovered, the uncollected fees for the prior 12 months totaled in excess of $30,000. By this time, families who owed a lot of fees, some even thousands of dollars, could not come up with the funds, and took their children out of the program, defaulting on payment. This put the center on a financial slippery slope from which it could never recover. After 25 years of serving their community, the program went out of business.

Collect family fees on time and apply penalties when necessary!

## Program's Bills and Taxes are Paid on Time

Good cash management can mean the difference between paying your bills on time and paying them late, incurring finance charges, interest, and penalties. Paying bills late can mean putting your child care program's credit worthiness in jeopardy.

Understanding the cycle of how and when cash flows into your business is the key to managing how and when it flows out. In managing the program's disbursements, administrators should prepare and use a *cash flow budget*. This financial management tool can point out cash shortages due to a drop in enrollment, a delay in food program or subsidy reimbursements, or slow collection of parent fees.

Payroll is usually at the top of any administrator's list of obligations to be paid. And the taxes withheld from payroll should be next in importance. Missing a tax payment deadline can carry heavy financial penalties.

In one program, the director expected positive cash flow based on the annual budget, but by the beginning of the second quarter, the center was in trouble. The program was feeling the effects of under-enrollment, a decreased number of new referrals, and a delay in reimbursements due to a state budget shortfall.

This center did not use a cash flow budget and it failed to react to these changes in the financial climate. Soon the center found its debt increasing each month. The only way the program could continue was by not paying some bills, including taxes. But by choosing to leave taxes unpaid, the program quickly began to owe government fines and interest. Before long, the administrator was contacted by the IRS who had placed a lien on the property held by the center and garnished their subsidy reimbursement. Poor financial management by this administrator and a lack of oversight by the board of directors led this center deeper into debt and put at risk their ability to continue to deliver services.

Always pay taxes! And negotiate credit terms with vendors based on the program's cash flow. Negotiations with avendors can provide additional time to pay bills without jeopardizing the center's credit rating.

## A Cash Reserve to Cover Operating Expenses

One component of every sound budget plan is including some savings for contingencies. A cash reserve can carry a child care program through the inevitable fluctuations in income. A cash reserve may also be needed for unexpected expenses, like new playground surfacing, another child-sized sink, or repair to a weather-damaged roof.

Experts recommend having enough cash to cover three months of the center's expenses. But administrators can begin to build this reserve slowly. Including in their annual budget as little as $100 savings per month can start a center down the road to financial health. It's worth noting that none of the troubled centers mentioned in this article had a cash reserve.

The ribbon running through these five fundamentals is *planning*. Financial planning is not a once-a-year exercise, but an on-going effort.

## Five Fundamentals for a foundation of financial health for Child Care Programs

1. Enrollment of program is at capacity, with a waiting list in place.
2. Tuition is based on the full cost of care.
3. Family fees are paid on time.
4. Program's bills and taxes are paid on time.
5. A cash reserve can cover operating expenses for three months.

Administrators and boards of directors must work together to meet new circumstances and make adjustments when necessary for continued financial health of a child care program. Only by maintaining financial health can a child care center insure the high quality care that children deserve.

## Suggested Reading


Brower, M. R., & Sull, T. M. (November/December 2001). "Is Your Center in Good Financial Health?: Six Symptoms and Some Prescriptions." *Exchange,* 142, pp. 32-34.

Cherry, C., Harkness, B., & Kuzma, K. (2000). *Child Care Center Management Guide* (3rd ed.; revised by B. Harness and D. Bates). Torrance, CA: Fearon Teacher Aids.

Neugebauer, R., & Neugebauer, B. (1997). *Managing Money: A Center Director's Guidebook*. Redmond, WA: Exchange Press.

# Travel Tips for Your Budget Trip

**by Carl C. Staley, Jr.**

*A budget is the equivalent of a "trip plan" expressed in the language of dollars. It is important to accept the reality that if a successful trip cannot be planned on paper it is not likely to happen. A budget is a tool that provides the basis for evaluation of your "trip". As you proceed through the trip you may run into unanticipated problems that require you to adjust your budget. Money that has been budgeted cannot be spent if something happens that results in the reality that the money will not be received, just like you cannot take a planned route when you come to a detour.*

I am going to serve as a travel agent for your budget trip and offer some recommendations to make your trip as smooth as possible. But, as with any trip, it is up to you to make the tough decisions, complete the planning, and implement the plans.

## Advice on Projecting Income

Projecting income for a child care center budget requires hindsight and fortune telling expressed through mathematics. Your budget must take into account past trends (your enrollment trends) as well as future changes (changing constituencies, funding sources, and fees).

- **Determining enrollment experience**. Projecting fee income is not the same as multiplying the capacity of your center times the annual fee per child. This amount is your maximum potential fee income. In reality you will never achieve this income level — you will never have 100% utilization of your center for an entire year. Inevitably there will be days, if not weeks where there will be unfilled spaces in various classrooms. To help planning your budget you can benefit from knowing your recent enrollment experience. The simplest way to do this is to take your actual fee income for the past twelve months and divide this by what your maximum potential fee income. For example, if your fee income for the past twelve months was $112,000 and your maximum potential fee income was $120,000, your utilization rate for that period was 93%. This means that, all things being equal, you should not project for more than 93% of your maximum potential fee income in the coming year.

- **Evaluating enrollment experience**. Of course, your experience in the past twelve months may not necessarily be repeated exactly. You should consider if there were any unusual situations that impacted your enrollment. Was there a dip in the economy? Did state subsidies dry up at the end of the state's fiscal year? Did you get a late start in promoting your summer camps? Did a new center open across the street? Were staff lax in collecting fees so that bad debts mounted? You will need to adjust your projection for next year based on the likelihood of these events recurring. In addition, you may want to calculate your utilization rate for the most recent three months to understand what your current position is.

- **Foreseeing external impacts**. You also need to determine whether any decisions have been made or are contemplated that will impact on your income. For example, are there plans afoot as dramatic as a road closing or the rezoning of the lot next door for a junk yard? In addition, are there many more subtle things happening in the neighborhood such as a gradual aging of the population, an increase in the number of family child care providers, or the expansion of a nearby business?

- **Evaluating the impact of fee policy changes**. Every fee decision and every change in fee policies has an impact on the budget! For example, if you decide to give discounts for second children and to give a free week of care after a child has been enrolled for 25 weeks, these decisions may boost enrollment but also reduce maximum fee income. And when the center charges employees half of the regular fee when they have children enrolled at the center, it is important to determine whether the center should expect to have more employee children than they have had in past years. Finally, and most importantly, if you opt to raise your fees not only do you need to factor in the increased income per child, but you must also make allowance for any potential dip in enrollment due to the higher fees.

- **Evaluate changes in the funding climate**. If your center receives income from outside sources such as a United Way agency, a state subsidy, or a local employer, you need to factor in any changes taking place with these players.

## Advice on Projecting Expenses

Once the projected income has been established, you are going to have to face the real world of child care administration. You will never have enough resources to do everything that you would like to do. You will always be faced with difficult decisions about prioritizing. Here are some pointers to aid your decisionmaking:

- **Categorize expenses**. In projecting expenses, it may help to think about three categories of expenses. Fixed expenses are those that must be met regardless of the number of children enrolled, such as administrative staff, rent and utilities. Variable expenses are those that will increase and decrease dependent upon the number of children in care, such as food and supplies, and to some extent teaching salaries. The third category of expenses are the optional expenses. These are the expenditures that will not be made if income falls short of expectations. It is important to know from the beginning the expenditures that will not take place if a "bridge goes out" in the budget trip.

- **Analyze fixed expenses**. Fixed expenses are ones over which we have no control? Not true. The utility bills for the building can be managed to some degree. Refinancing a mortgage could have a favorable impact on occupancy costs. Good managers have to work to impact budget wherever they can.

- **Prioritizing variable expenses**. Variable expenses are very much subject to priority setting. A merit raise for a teacher, the cost of different field trips, the impact of menu planning are all examples of decisions that impact on variable costs.

- **Deciding about optional expenses**. A center director or a center staff can come up with more ideas for expenditures than will ever be possible. The process by which a center decides which expenditures to include in the budget may be a critical variable in the quality of the center. Staff participation in the process helps staff understand and accept the realities. It also involves more individuals in thinking about creative solutions for getting the most out of the limited funds available. Some of the costs that may be considered as optional expenses are such things as bonuses for staff, the decision about sending several staff members to NAEYC, or that additional piece of playground equipment that you and the staff would like to have. Even within optional expenditures priorities must be set. Some of the priorities are impacted by timing. If things are not going well when a conference is approaching, it is obvious that you should not make that optional expenditure.

- **Maximizing your staffing dollars**. Salaries and wages constitute a major portion of any center budget. Policies about increases must be recognized in the budget. Will the budget allow money for merit increases? Can we plan to schedule staff for additional hours so that planning time can be scheduled when all team members can participate? Could the budget include the projected cost of allowing staff members to use their paid sick leave when they have sick family members who need their care?

- **Anticipating mid-year changes**. When a center is subject to property taxes, it is important to recognize the impact of the property being reappraised at twice the value on which the taxes were paid in the past. It is also critical to recognize that salary increases given in the middle of the year impact the salary line item for the full year.

Budgeting can be a director's best friend. It takes conscious effort to budget, and discipline to follow the budget. A budget can provide the understanding necessary to make it possible for a program to reach difficult goals as well as to be prepared for hard times. A carefully planned budget goes a long way to insuring that your trip is a success.

# Preparing and Using Monthly Financial Reports

by Roger Neugebauer

*The budgets of most child care programs are precarious, with little margin for error. A drop in fee income of only 2-4%, or an unnoticed escalation in utility costs, can have a disastrous impact on a center's financial stability. Child care directors do not have the luxury of being able to wait until the end of the year to deal with balancing the budget. They need to be monitoring the center's financial position continually to catch monetary tremors before they swell into economic earthquakes.*

*One effective monitoring tool is the monthly financial status report. This report gives the director a stop-action view of how closely the center is adhering to the annual budget. It helps pinpoint areas where expenses are exceeding projections or where income is falling behind.*

## Developing the Report Format

There are two main components of the monthly financial status report — the annual budget as projected on a month-by-month basis and an up-to-date record of actual revenues and expenditures. These two pieces of information are summarized and analyzed on a one-page chart (see Table 1 on page 131).

On the lefthand side of this chart are listed categories of income and expenses. In listing these, break out categories that are meaningful to you — don't automatically use the categories from a standard budget form. Don't clutter the chart with minor items such as *Postage Stamps* or *Photocopying*. Rather, consolidate these into more meaningful categories such as *Office Supplies and Services*. On the other hand, you may want to subdivide major categories such as salaries into subcategories which vary independently, such as *Administrative Salaries* and *Program Salaries*.

Ideally, the annual budget, the accounting system, and the status report should all be organized with the same categories so that data can be transferred and compared easily. The financial information can then be presented in four columns. In the first column, Column A, is recorded the actual financial activity of the center for the year to date. For example, Column A in the chart below shows that the Honey Dew Nursery had received $56,400 in *Parent Fees* and expended $71,400 in Salaries as of June 30. This information should be readily available from the center's accounting records.

## Setting Monthly Targets

In Column B is recorded the financial activity for the year to date as it was projected in the annual budget. Column B shows that the Honey Dew Nursery had projected, or anticipated, having received $55,200 in *Parent Fees* and having expended $70,200 in *Salaries* as of June 30.

There are two methods for developing the information for Column B — one simple and one complicated. The simple method involves dividing the amount for each category in the annual budget by 12. This yields a monthly budget. (For a school operating ten months during the year, the annual budget is divided by 10.) When the monthly financial status report is prepared, this monthly budget is simply multiplied times the number of school months which have elapsed in the current year. If, for instance, a center projects collecting $180,000 in parent fees in the annual budget, the monthly budget amount for parent fees would be $15,000 ($180,000 ÷ 12). The projected activity in this category as of June 30 would then be $90,000 ($15,000 x 6). This amount is the target the center will strive to achieve.

This simple method is probably accurate enough for small programs and for programs where enrollment, staff schedules, and major expenses do not vary significantly from month to month. For many centers, however, income and expenses do not flow in and out evenly from month to month. Fuel costs may be much higher in the winter, enrollment may be lower in the summer, subsidized workers may need to be replaced by paid staff six months into the year, etc.

To set realistic targets in these centers, income and expenses need to be methodically projected on a month-by-month basis. To do this, enter the center's annual budget on the lefthand side of a wide sheet of paper. Under *Salaries* list each position separately. To the right make a column for each month. Now go through each income item and determine how much of each type of income will be received each month. For example, if enrollment typically declines during the late spring and summer, the *Parent Fees* income should be lower in these months. If the only major fundraiser is scheduled for September, most *Fundraising* income should be recorded under this month.

Then do the same for all expense items. For administrative and teaching staff who work stable schedules, their salaries should be divided equally over the 12 months. For personnel working part of the year or with variable schedules, their likely salaries for each month should be predicted as carefully as possible. Substitute expenses should be concentrated in months where absenteeism is typically high in your center. If supplies and equipment are purchased in big orders several times a year, these expense items should be attributed properly to these months. If insurance is paid for in quarterly payments, it should be charged to the months when payments will be made.

When the entire budget is analyzed in this manner, the resulting monthly budgets are to be used for the status report. For the June 30 report, for example, the cumulative amounts for each category in the January through June budgets will be entered in Column B.

## Computing Variations

In Column C is entered the difference between Column A and Column B. If the actual amount (Column A) is larger than the projected amount (Column B), the variation is recorded as a positive amount. In the chart below, the actual amount collected in *Parent Fees* income ($56,400) was larger than the amount projected ($55,200), so that the variation is a positive amount (+$1,200), meaning that actual income exceeded that which was projected. When the actual amount is less than the projected amount, the variation is expressed as a negative amount.

While Column C shows the amount of the variation, Column D indicates its magnitude. In this column is recorded the percentage by which the actual amounts vary from the projected amounts. It is computed by dividing the amount in Column C by the amount in Column B and multiplying the dividend by 100 (C/B x 100 = D). Thus when this formula is applied to parent fee income in the chart below ($1,200 ÷ $55,200 x 100), the actual income is found to be 2% above the projected amount. When the amount of variation in Column C is a negative amount, the percentage of variation in Column D will be a negative value as well.

## Interpreting the Report

First check the bottom line. On this chart the bottom line is the *Balance*, the difference between total income and total expenses. In the case of the Honey Dew Nursery, income exceeded expenses by $3,000 for the first six months, so the balance under Column A is +$3,000. This would appear to be cause for celebration. However, moving over to Column B, the balance projected for this date was +$9,000. This means that the school fell $6,000 short of its target for the first six months — a cause for serious concern.

When a significant variation is found in the balance, the next step is to pinpoint the cause. Look at the *Total Income* and the *Total Expenses* categories to see if large variations are apparent. In the Honey Dew case, the actual income ($114,000) only fell short of the projected income ($114,600) by $600 — or by -1%. On the other hand, actual expenses ($111,000) exceeded projected expenses ($105,600) by $5,400 — or by +5%. Clearly the bulk of Honey Dew's problem has to do with higher than anticipated expenses.

To pinpoint the problem more precisely, next examine Columns C and D. Look for income categories with high negative amounts or percentages and for expense categories with high positive amounts or percentages. In the Honey Dew case the most serious problem is with Food expenses which were running 11% over the budget for a total of $1,800 by June 30. Spending under the *Curriculum Supplies* and *Substitutes* categories will also have to be radically altered as these categories are running 75% and 36% over the budget. The amount of deficit incurred in the *Salaries* category is also high ($1,200), although the changes needed to bring salaries back into line are less serious since salaries are only running 2% over the budget.

Even when a center has more money left over than it anticipated, it is still instructive to look for the cause of the surplus. If the surplus is the result of the fact that a large piece of equipment has not yet been purchased, this is only a temporary surplus. This money needs to be set aside for when the equipment is actually purchased. If, on the other hand, the surplus is the result of higher than expected income from parent fees or fundraising, or of lower than projected expenses for substitutes or supplies, this surplus is real. It is money in the bank. It is available for buying new supplies, giving raises, or setting aside in an emergency fund.

## Tailoring the Report

This chart should be modified to meet the specific needs of each center. A center with a small budget could

**Table 1**
**Honey Dew Nursery Monthly Status Report**

| | A<br>Actual Amount as of June 30 | B<br>Budgeted (Projected) Amount as of June 30 | C<br>Amount of Variation | D<br>Percentage of Variation |
|---|---|---|---|---|
| Income | | | | |
| Parent Fees | $ 56,400 | $ 55,200 | +$1,200 | +2% |
| State Subsidies | 40,500 | 40,800 | -300 | -1 |
| Food Program | 16,800 | 17,100 | -300 | -2 |
| Fundraising | 300 | 1,500 | -1,200 | -80 |
| Total Income | $114,000 | $114,600 | -$ 600 | -1 |
| Expenses | | | | |
| Salaries | $ 71,400 | $ 70,200 | +$1,200 | +2% |
| Substitutes | 4,500 | 3,300 | +1,200 | +36 |
| Food | 18,900 | 17,100 | +1,800 | +11 |
| Curriculum Supplies | 2,100 | 1,200 | +900 | +75 |
| Curriculum Equipment | 1,800 | 1,800 | 0 | 0 |
| Office Supplies | 1,050 | 900 | +150 | +17 |
| Occupancy | 11,250 | 11,100 | +150 | +1 |
| Total Expenses | $111,000 | $105,600 | +$5,400 | +5% |
| Balance | +$ 3,000 | +$ 9,000 | -$6,000 | -67% |

probably do without Column D, for instance. A center with a large budget may want to break down the categories, especially the *Salaries* category, into more specific line items, in order to pinpoint variations more narrowly. Centers can also consider adding two more columns to record the actual and projected amounts for the most recent month. If there is a problem category, a review of this category on a month-by-month basis can indicate whether the situation is getting better or worse.

# Guidelines for Fine Tuning Your Salary Schedule

**by Roger Neugebauer**

*In one of my first forays into the child care world, some 20 years ago, I applied, unsuccessfully, for a job at a staff cooperative. All employees at New Morning Children's Center were paid the same hourly wage and shared equally in responsibilities and decisionmaking. The team spirit of the place is what attracted me to it.*

*Even in my brief encounter with the center, it was clear that this team spirit was developing a few chinks. The founders of the center shared a strong commitment to equality of pay and power. However, state licensers looked upon the staff structure with horror and were aggressively fighting it. In addition, as new staff members came on board whose ideologies and priorities did not match the founders, internal enthusiasm for equal pay declined.*

*Eventually, New Morning gave in to the pressures of capitalism and began paying the cook, the administrative coordinators, and the teachers differing amounts. Eventually, too, it changed its name to something like Preschool Prep Learning Center. Eventually, too, it went out of business.*

The moral of this story is never turn down a future publisher who can give you bad press. It also demonstrates that the administration of salaries is not a simple mechanical procedure. Rather, it is direct expression of the values of the organization. How differences in pay are distributed, and the size of these differences, intentionally or unintentionally communicate what the organization values.

Pay differentials are typically spelled out in a center's salary schedule. In research for this article, we analyzed over 100 salary schedules submitted by Exchange Panel of 200 members. In these schedules, four factors were used to measure the monetary value of employees: responsibility, training, experience, and performance. In this article, I will share with you how centers weigh these factors in developing their salary schedules.

## Pay for Responsibility

None of the centers whose schedules were reviewed were staff cooperatives — all centers paid differing amounts for persons carrying out different responsibilities. Pay differences by position are in fact quite dramatic, as can be seen in Table A. A lead teacher typically earns 50% more than a teacher aide, and directors earn 50% more than a lead teacher.

We are not recommending that your center adapt these pay patterns. We are simply reporting what is standard practice in the early childhood arena.

What we are strongly recommending is that you take a close look at your own pay patterns. Do the differences in your pay for different positions truly reflect the value you place on these positions? The way you invest your resources in personnel should support your understanding about what it takes to deliver quality child care.

In the salary schedules we reviewed, for example, it was clear that a growing number of centers have identified the lead teacher as a key to quality. In these centers, lead teachers are paid anywhere from 65% to 85% more than teacher aides.

## Pay for Training

Centers clearly place a value on training. The more training a teacher has, the more she is likely to be paid.

However, how training is factored into salary schedules varies considerably.

About one in four centers build training into job requirements, but offers no financial incentives. For example, a center might require that a teacher aide have a high school diploma, an assistant teacher have at least two years of college, and a lead teacher have a college degree. In these centers, an assistant teacher with a college degree would earn no more than one with two years of college, and a candidate with only a high school degree would not be considered for an assistant teacher position. The majority of centers, however, recognize the value of training in establishing job requirements as well as in setting salaries within job categories. In these centers, an assistant teacher with a college degree would earn more than an assistant teacher with two years of college. As can be seen in Table B, typically a teacher with an AA degree will earn 15% more, and one with a BA degree 25% more, than a teacher with only a high school degree. A master's degree only adds another 5% to one's pay.

Some centers place additional value on education that is specifically related to early childhood education. In these centers, for example, a teacher with an AA degree in early childhood education is valued just as highly as a teacher with a bachelor's degree in an unrelated field (Table B).

In the days when the supply of teaching candidates seemed inexhaustible, there wasn't great pressure on centers to pay more to hire teachers with college training. Directors would rationalize their fiscal conservatism by observing that in their experience college trained teachers often weren't well prepared for the real world of child care.

Research findings now make it clear that teachers with college degrees or college level ECE training will typically do a better job. With the returning shortage of qualified teachers, it would be a mistake for centers not to place high value on college education in establishing or refining their salary schedules.

## Pay for Experience

Three out of every four center salary schedules we reviewed offered some form of annual pay increases. Increases ranged from 1.5% to 5% annually, with the average falling in the 3% range.

These increases tend to be described more as cost of living adjustments than as rewards for improved performance. Experience tends to be a poor predictor of teacher performance. Teachers with more years on the job are not necessarily better performers than less experienced teachers. Therefore, centers are probably exercising good judgment in not investing heavily in longevity.

Cost of living increases, on the other hand, are very important to teachers. With salaries as low as they are, teachers have little cushion against the impact of inflation. Slightly less than half of the salary schedules we reviewed stated that there were no automatic cost of living increases. When funds permit, these centers typically give across the board increases in the range of 2% to 4% to all employees.

### Table A
### Early Childhood Salary Relationships

This chart demonstrates the relationship of average salaries for different positions in early childhood centers, using Teacher Aide salaries as the base. For example, the average Lead Teacher salary is 150% of the average Teacher Aide salary. Based on a review of over 200 salary schedules.

|  |  |
|---|---|
| Executive Director | 320% |
| Center Director | 230% |
| Educational Coordinator | 190% |
| Assistant Director | 180% |
| Lead Teacher | 150% |
| Administrative Assistant | 150% |
| Custodian | 130% |
| Assistant Teacher | 120% |
| Substitute Teacher | 120% |
| Cook | 120% |
| Bus Driver | 110% |
| Teacher Aide | 100% |

Most of the other salary schedules we reviewed treated annual increases regressively, i.e. the higher your salary the lower your annual increase. In some cases, this is done intentionally. Recognizing how low their entry level salaries are, some centers deliberately give employees at the bottom third of the salary schedule a higher percentage annual increase than employees at the top third.

From reviewing salary schedules, we conclude that all centers need to take a close look at their provisions regarding annual increases. First, consider whether you want to lock your center into automatic annual increases for all employees. Especially for your low income employees, automatic increases offer some degree of security. However, if your center is struggling to achieve financial stability, annual increases may not always be affordable.

Second, in granting cost of living increases, you should deliberately decide what your priorities are. Do you want to give an equal percentage increase to all employees, or do you want to give a higher increase to low income employees, or do you want to invest the greatest share of the increases in your top employees?

## Pay for Performance

While a strong case can be made for merit raises, in fact, the concept is not a popular one in this field. Less than one in 15 of the salary schedules we reviewed offer any form of merit pay. Tying pay to performance is often viewed as running counter to the nurturing team spirit we promote in our centers. This case was strongly put by one of our Panel of 200 members (see "No to Merit Pay" box). In addition, many directors are reluctant to attach dollars to performance since measures of performance are so subjective in this field.

Those few centers that do tie pay to performance do so in a variety of ways. The most common approach is a two to four category rating system. One center rates each employee annually as either *unsatisfactory*, *satisfactory*, or *highly satisfactory*. Employees rated unsatisfactory are given no annual increase and are scheduled for close monitoring. Those rated satisfactory are granted a 3% increase, and those rated highly satisfactory earn a 6% raise.

Several of the more ambitious plans we reviewed calibrated their reward systems more finely. For example, employees might be awarded points for attendance, training attended, teaching skills, staff relations skills, and parent relations skills. Employees' annual increases would then be calculated based upon how many points they earned — if they earned 50% of all possible points, they would earn 50% of the maximum possible raise.

One after-school program offered a unique approach. They start all teachers at a low entry level wage. Then, over the course of two years, they rapidly move up those teachers who demonstrate good skills into teaching positions paid above the going rate.

## Putting Together the Pieces

Now the hard part. Once you've decided what your center intends to value monetarily in its salaries, you need to translate these values into a usable salary schedule. Here are some factors to weigh in developing or refining your schedule:

**Simplicity**. Heed *Accounting Law #1* — "Salary schedules inevitably expand to fill every square on the spreadsheet." Resist the urge to make your salary schedule more elaborate than it needs to be. Many small and some not-so-small child care organizations get by with no more than a list of starting salaries for each job category. Every year the director then either decides on giving an across-the-board raise or makes decisions on an individual basis.

**Security**. The main disadvantage with very simple salary plans is that they fail to provide employees with a long range view. Employees who plan to make a career of child care want to know what they can aspire to — What is the maximum salary they can earn? How can they advance within the center? A good salary schedule informs employees about their career options and opportunities.

**Clarity**. Some of the salary schedules we reviewed were incomprehensible. Give your new salary schedule the man-on-the-street test. Have several of your friends who are not involved in child care review it. When they can understand it, it's ready to be unveiled at your center.

**Flexibility**. Some of the salary schedules we reviewed left no room for maneuvering. The steps and levels for all positions were set in stone. Make your plan flexible enough so that you can add positions, upgrade or downgrade positions, or change step sizes without redoing the entire plan.

**Liability**. Before committing to any salary schedule, you should evaluate the long range worst/best case scenario.

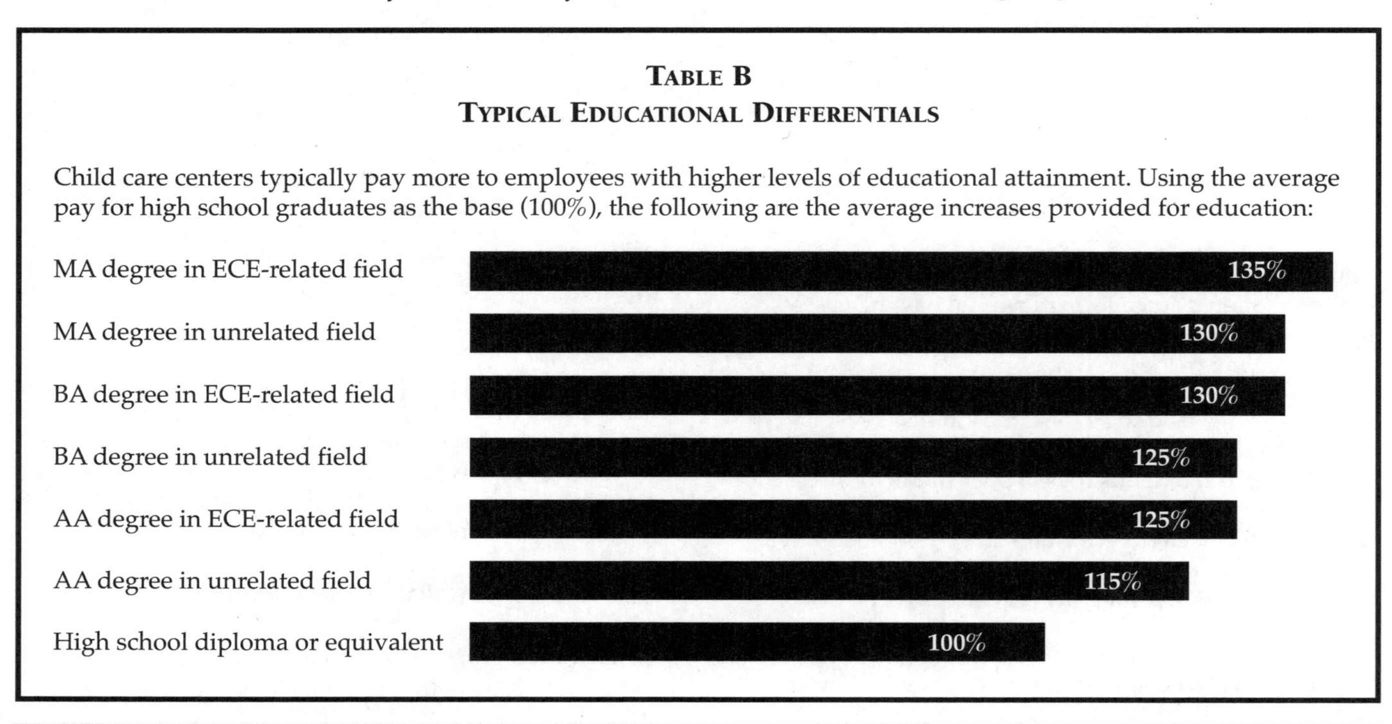

## One View: No to Merit Pay

It is our policy NOT to give merit increases or bonuses. We are aware that this is somewhat of an unusual policy, but our reasoning is tied to our respect for teachers and our philosophy, which understands that quality education comes from a community of professionals working together to serve the needs of the children and families in its care.

Teachers need to be paid the highest salaries possible for the challenging work they do. Our board of directors makes significant efforts to provide maximum funding for salaries and benefits. Teachers get "rewarded" with knowing the salary increase is maximal (ours has ranged from 6% to 8% per year) and that the board and administration are continually working to provide a place where teachers can practice their profession.

We have no teacher aides in the school, only teachers and head teachers, who have supervisory and administrative responsibilities. We have hired them to do the same job (within job classifications), not to do a "better" job than others. Moreover, we believe that a primary obligation of the professional early childhood administrator is to develop team building skills. ECE teachers need to have the skills to be able to work with peers sometimes under stressful conditions.

If we were to try to reward some teachers at a differential rate, it would be very difficult to make a decision that would accurately reflect the precise truth about who deserved what. Merit pay is by nature exclusionary and we believe counterproductive to building a stable, quality environment in which to teach. No matter what criteria "merit" is measured by, if monetary value is assigned individually, team boundaries are crossed, possibly damaged, and probably discouraged. The hierarchical relationship between the administration and the individual teacher is promoted to the exclusion of the teacher's development of complex, sophisticated, and subtle communication with his/her peers. This is the very communication necessary for meeting the complex, sophisticated, and subtle educational needs of young children and their families. This, in our view, is counterproductive to our goal of respecting our teachers as professionals and contrary to our view of what quality education is all about.

*— Susan Britson, Step One School, Berkeley, California*

What if your salary plan works and you totally avoid turnover? What would your total salary costs be three years from now? Five years from now? Can you afford this?

**Relevancy**. At the beginning of this article, I observed that your salary schedule should be a direct expression of your organization's values. Sometimes, however, in developing a schedule you get so wrapped up in the mathematics and logistics that values and goals fade into the background. You should analyze your new or your current salary schedule to see if it truly supports your values. Are the positions that are most valuable to your organization properly rewarded? Are the factors you value the most (training, experience, or performance) rewarded the most?

## Three Types of Salary Schedules

In developing your salary schedule, you have some choices to make. The salary schedules we reviewed fell into three general categories. One in three of these were very simple or basic plans; most of the rest were traditional salary schedules; and less than one in ten fell into the innovative category.

The basic plans were not much more than lists of positions with starting salaries. In some cases, these spelled out the starting, mid-range, and top of the line salary for each position. While these plans are seldom inspiring, they are probably perfectly adequate for small, stable centers.

What we call the traditional salary schedules are grids with multiple levels and steps. Typically, the columns across the page represent different levels of education (high school diploma, AA degree, etc.), and the rows down the page represent years of employment. In some centers, there is a separate grid for each position, while in others all the positions are covered in one mega-grid.

The advantage of these traditional schedules is that they can be easily understood. People are accustomed to seeing salaries presented in grids and can easily figure out where they currently fit in, where they can progress, and what they need to do to get there (complete that AA degree, survive ten years, etc.).

A possible disadvantage is that the beauty of these plans is often only skin deep. The traditional schedule looks very impressive — it looks organized and standardized, and it fills the page with numbers that appear to have been calculated with great precision. Yet some of the most impressive looking grids we reviewed were seriously flawed. Some had steps that increased in erratic non-patterns; some had step increases that were so tiny as to be insulting; and one contained math errors that resulted in the assistant teacher making more than the lead teacher after six years.

A few of the schedules we reviewed were innovative. There were some creative attempts to factor in performance, ongoing training, and participation above and beyond the call of duty. Unfortunately, a few of the most creative plans were also some of the most complicated ones — it would take a computer whiz to calculate all the points and percentages. Overall, however, we appreciated the courage centers demonstrated in blazing new ground with these plans and only wish that we could convince some foundation to fund a study of their impact.

We attempted to capture the best thinking we observed in the 100+ salary schedules we analyzed and present it in two models. These models are presented in Table C, "Traditional Salary Schedule," and Table D, "Performance Based Salary Schedule."

*Before we present these models, a major note of caution is in order: Do not adapt these models in your center! These are presented as starting points only. You need to modify these to incorporate your own values, priorities, and fiscal realities.*

## Model 1:
### The Traditional Approach

This model is in the form of the standard grid with levels going across the page and steps going down the page. Here is how to modify it to your needs:

**Decision 1.** What increments do you want to build into your grid? In Model 1, we set the increases for the levels in 4% increments. These increments typically account for levels of education. We set the increases for the steps, which typically account for annual increases, in 2% increments.

We purposely made the steps smaller than the typical 3% increments to provide more flexibility. When increments are large, the center has an all or nothing choice — you either move an employee up to the next step or you don't. With smaller increments, you can decide to move each employee up one, two, or even three steps a year, or you can move them up one step every six months.

**Table C**
**Traditional Salary Schedule**

| | I | II | III | IV | V | VI | VII | VIII | IX | X |
|---|---|---|---|---|---|---|---|---|---|---|
| 1 | 1.00 | 1.04 | 1.08 | 1.12 | 1.16 | 1.20 | 1.24 | 1.28 | 1.32 | 1.36 |
| 2 | 1.02 | 1.06 | 1.10 | 1.14 | 1.18 | 1.22 | 1.26 | 1.30 | 1.34 | 1.38 |
| 3 | 1.04 | 1.08 | 1.12 | 1.16 | 1.20 | 1.24 | 1.28 | 1.32 | 1.36 | 1.40 |
| 4 | 1.06 | 1.10 | 1.14 | 1.18 | 1.22 | 1.26 | 1.30 | 1.34 | 1.38 | 1.42 |
| 5 | 1.08 | 1.12 | 1.16 | 1.20 | 1.24 | 1.28 | 1.32 | 1.36 | 1.40 | 1.44 |
| 6 | 1.10 | 1.14 | 1.18 | 1.22 | 1.26 | 1.30 | 1.34 | 1.38 | 1.42 | 1.46 |
| | | | | | | | | | | |
| 11 | 1.20 | 1.24 | 1.28 | 1.32 | 1.36 | 1.40 | 1.44 | 1.48 | 1.52 | 1.56 |
| | | | | | | | | | | |
| 21 | 1.40 | 1.44 | 1.48 | 1.52 | 1.56 | 1.60 | 1.64 | 1.68 | 1.72 | 1.76 |
| | | | | | | | | | | |
| 31 | 1.60 | 1.64 | 1.68 | 1.72 | 1.76 | 1.80 | 1.84 | 1.92 | 1.96 | 2.00 |
| | | | | | | | | | | |
| 41 | 1.80 | 1.84 | 1.92 | 1.96 | 2.00 | 2.04 | 2.08 | 2.12 | 2.16 | 2.20 |
| | | | | | | | | | | |
| 51 | 2.00 | 2.04 | 2.08 | 2.12 | 2.16 | 2.20 | 2.24 | 2.26 | 2.30 | 2.34 |
| | | | | | | | | | | |
| 61 | 2.20 | 2.24 | 2.26 | 2.30 | 2.34 | 2.38 | 2.42 | 2.46 | 2.50 | 2.54 |

NOTE: This is an abbreviated model. To save space we have left out Steps 7–10, 12–20, etc.

One disadvantage with these small steps is that it adds to the size of your grid. If you want to include all staff members on the same grid, you may need to include as many as 70 to 100 steps.

We also chose, for simplicity's sake only, to make the increments for the steps uniform throughout the grid. Thus the salaries of employees at the bottom and top of the grid would increase at 2% for every step. What this means is that employees at the bottom end would receive smaller increases in actual dollars and cents than those at the top. You may elect to reverse this by starting the increments at 3% or 4% at the bottom and gradually reducing them to 1% at the top end.

(Note: Throughout this article we refer to salaries and salary schedules in reference to all employees. Many centers actually pay hourly wages for some employees and annual salaries for others. We are not arguing for or against this classification of employees. We use the term salaries as a generic term for all monies paid to staff.)

**Decision 2.** What is your base salary, i.e., what is the starting salary for your lowest paid employee? Once you set this entry level amount, you can translate all the increments on your grid to actual monetary amounts.

For example, using our grid in Table C, if your base salary is $6.00 per hour, the succeeding amounts in row 1 would be $6.24, $648, $6.72, etc. Step 2 amounts would be $6.12, $6.36, $6.60, etc.

**Decision 3.** How much are you going to reward various levels of education? For example, if we were to take the typical educational differentials from Table B, here is how they would fit into our salary schedule:

High school diploma starts at Level I
AA degree would start at Level V
BA degree would start at Level VII
MA degree would start at Level IX

You may elect to value these levels differently or to define the levels differently. Some centers, for example, set levels based on credit hours of college completed. Others factor in CDA status or workshop attendance.

**Decision 4.** Where do you want to set the entry point for each position at your center? If we were to use the typical position differentials from Table A, here is how they would fit into our model:

| | | |
|---|---|---|
| Teacher Aide | = | Step 1 |
| Bus Driver | = | Step 6 |
| Assistant Teacher | = | Step 11 |
| Lead Teacher | = | Step 26 |
| Center Director | = | Step 66 |

As with educational levels, you will need to take the job categories used at your center and place them on the grid based on how you value them.

**Decision 5.** When will center employees qualify for moving up a step or to another level? Do employees move up one step every year automatically, or only if they receive a positive evaluation, or only if monies are available? Do employees progress to a higher level every time they complete a higher level of education?

## MODEL 2:

### PERFORMANCE BASED APPROACH

This model is a variation of some of the innovative schedules we reviewed. It assigns significant weight to a staff member's performance in setting annual increases. Here is how to modify it to your needs, keeping in mind that every point awarded in Steps 1, 2, and 3 is worth 100% of your base rate:

**Decision 1.** What is your base salary, i.e., what is the starting salary for your lowest paid employee? You will use the hourly rate for the base salary in Step 4.

**Decision 2.** What value do you want to assign to each job category in your center? In Model 2, we have used the differentials from Table A. You will want to modify these to reflect your center's values.

### TABLE D
### PERFORMANCE BASED SALARY SCHEDULE

How to Use This Instrument: For Step 1, insert the points assigned for the employee's position. For Step 2, insert the points earned for the employee's highest level of education completed. For Step 3, insert the number of points earned first for years of satisfactory performance at your center, second for the years of above average performance, and third for the years of superior performance. Now determine the employee's new hourly rate by completing Step 4.

**Step 1 — Responsibility** ________

| | |
|---|---|
| Teacher Aide | 1.00 |
| Cook | 1.20 |
| Assistant Teacher | 1.20 |
| Custodian | 1.30 |
| Lead Teacher | 1.50 |
| Assistant Director | 1.80 |
| Director | 2.30 |

**Step 2 — Training** ________

| | |
|---|---|
| AA Degree | .05 |
| ECE-Related AA Degree | .10 |
| BA/BS Degree | .10 |
| ECE-Related BA/BS Degree | .20 |
| Master's Degree | .15 |
| ECE-Related Master's Degree | .30 |

Step 3 — Experience/Performance

Years of satisfactory performance (add .02 points/year) ________
Years of above average performance (add .04 points/year) ________
Years of superior performance (add .06 points/year) ________

**Step 4 — New Hourly Rate Determination**

Multiply total points earned in Steps 1 through 3 times base rate for center.

_____ points x $________ per hour = $________ per hour

**Decision 3.** What value do you want to assign to each level of education? In Model 2, we have used the differentials from Table B. You will want to modify these to reflect to your center's values.

**Decision 4.** How many points do you want to award for different levels of performance? Keep in mind that if you go this route you must find or develop a tool for measuring performance that is viewed by all concerned as fair.

Once you have completed these adjustments, you should test it out. Based on your recent experience, use this format to determine, hypothetically, the salaries of several employees at different levels in your organization. Does this result in salaries that are fair? Does it result in any radical increases or decreases in current pay levels? Can you afford it?

If your test is unsuccessful, keep tinkering with the points or come up with a similar set of steps that fit your needs better.

## A Final Caution

Your organization may well have a salary plan in place, so you may not be interested in going through a big production to establish a new one. That is probably a wise decision. However, I would encourage you to at least take the time to review your current schedule against the key points raised in this article. Make sure that you are getting the maximum positive impact out of the resources you devote to salaries.

## Credits

We reviewed over 100 salary schedules from Exchange Panel of 200 members in preparing the two articles in this series. The following centers' plans were especially helpful :

Central Learning Center, Memphis, TN; Children's Learning Center, Yardley, PA; Children's Programs Inc., Brookfield, WI; Community Children's Project, Jackson, WY; Gertrude B. Nielsen Child Care and Learning Center, Northbrook, IL; Graham Memorial Preschool, Coronado, CA; Gretchen's House, Ann Arbor, MI; Janet Rich Day Care, Rochester, NY; Learning Tree Montessori, Seattle, WA; Moffett Road Baptist Child Development Center, Mobile, AL; The Nursery Foundation of St. Louis, St. Louis, MO; St. Elizabeth's Day Home, San Jose, CA; Wausau Child Care, Inc., Wausau, WI; World Bank Children's Center, Washington, DC.

## References

Ruopp, R., et al. (1979). *Children at the Center*. Cambridge, MA: Abt Associates.

Whitebook, M. (1989). *Who Cares? Child Care Teachers and the Quality of Care in America*. Oakland, CA: Child Care Employee Project.

# COST-BENEFIT ANALYSIS: TOOLS FOR DECISION MAKING

by Gary Bess

*If you are like most child care center directors, you have a healthy respect for your center's bottom line. At minimum, you want to be assured that inflows, revenues that you derive from fees, grants, contracts, and other income-generating activities, is equal to your outflows, your expenses that enable you to remain in the black. But, there may be a time that your inflows do not exceed your outflows, and you find yourself involuntarily dipping into savings, drawing on your line of credit, or cutting costs that may affect program quality.*

Even if your agency is not spewing *red ink*, you are still wise to continuously assess the *cost-effectiveness* of your programs. As an administrator, you have likely made decisions based on your intuitive criteria of cost-efficiency, choosing among alternative approaches that are least costly, and yet provide high quality child care services. Have you, however, put pen to paper to consider the specific costs associated with each alternative approach? Probably, your answer is "no."

## WHAT IS COST-BENEFIT ANALYSIS?

One way to assess cost-effectiveness is cost-benefit analysis, an administrative tool for choosing among several alternative approaches to determine the most economical way to manage a program or service. It provides the "best results for any given resource outlay," thus helping you to determine your program's minimum resource requirements (Levin, 1983).

Said another way, cost-benefit analysis enables you to maximize your efficiency, while achieving your program's intended outcomes. It is also a way of justifying your approach to your board of directors and external stakeholders such as grantors or elected officials, who, like you, have an appreciation for each dollar saved or spent. This article will provide an overview of cost-benefit analysis and how it is used in child care administrative decision making. Perhaps the best way to understand how it can be used is with an example:

ABC Child Care Center was experiencing declining enrollment, the result of layoffs by the primary manufacturing business in town. Parents were withdrawing their children to care for them at home until the economy improved and they would be rehired. The center director's first reaction to declining enrollment was to cut costs by reducing her staff. Though sometimes this is an inevitable response, reductions in staff are more than a proportional adjustment in worker to child ratios. Reductions in quality, effectiveness, and morale can also occur.

With fewer staff, responsibility for secondary activities such as food preparation and cleaning will fall on the remaining workers. Parents who favored one of the laid off workers may withdraw their children, or remaining staff members, fearing that the ax may next fall on them, will find employment elsewhere. Thus, a downward piraling occurs, affecting program quality and efficiency as other valued employees depart.

Fortunately, there are alternatives to this scenario that a prudent director may wish to consider. An analysis of the differences in each approach can help to illustrate the best course of action for the ABC Child Care Center.

**TABLE 1 — HYPOTHETICAL COSTS AND BENEFITS**

| Approach | Cost | Benefits | C/B | Net Benefit |
|---|---|---|---|---|
| Reduce staff proportional to enrollment | $60,000 | $60,000 | 1 | $0 |
| Workforce reduction of 20 percent | $60,000 | $55,000 | 1.09 | –$ 5,000 |
| Increase in fees | $60,000 | $15,000 | 4 | –$45,000 |

**Table 2 — Hypothetical Costs and Benefits, Including Intangible Costs**

| Approach | Direct Cost | Additional Factored Costs | Total Costs | Benefits | C/B | Net Benefit |
|---|---|---|---|---|---|---|
| Reduce staff proportional to enrollment | | $15,000 * | | | | |
| | | $12,000 ** | | | | |
| | $60,000 | $27,000 | $87,000 | $60,000 | 1.45 | -$27,000 |
| Workforce reduction of 20% | | – $18,000 ** | | | | |
| | | $ 7,500 * | | | | |
| | $60,000 | – $10,500 | $49,500 | $60,000 | .9 | $ 7,500 |
| Increase in fees | $60,000 | $12,000 ** | $72,000 | $15,000 | 4.8 | -$57,000 |

*Retraining of employees at $7,500 each.
**Addition or loss of child care slots at $6,000 each.

## How do you analyze costs and benefits?

The cost-benefit approach considers alternatives based on anticipated expenses and their effect on a particular set of financial outcomes (Lewis et al., 2001). Only approaches that target the same outcomes (e.g., an increase in enrollment or stabilization at current enrollment levels) can be assessed together. Also required is a common measure of effectiveness that can be applied to each intervention. For example, the number of child care slots to be retained would need to be established as the outcome for each of the three approaches.

With our focus on adjusting to the loss of income associated with a sudden decline in enrollment, the director would need to consider alternative interventions that address the common measure of enrollment stabilization at the current level.

For example, three possible solutions she could consider are: (a) reduce her child care staff proportional to current enrollment ratios; (b) reduce all workers by 20% (one day a week); or (c) increase fees to help defray fixed operational expenses. Let's look at each of these approaches, assuming hypothetically that we wish to, at minimum, stabilize our decline until the economy improves, which would require a budget reduction of $60,000.

Scenario A would require the laying off of two full-time workers, valued at $30,000 each, for a 12-month savings of $60,000. In Scenario B, a workforce reduction of 20% would yield a near similar $55,000 savings or benefit for the same period, and in Scenario C, the center would net an additional $15,000 a year in increased fees from the remaining families by increasing tuition. Each of these three approaches has corresponding assumptions about costs and benefits as the matrix in Table 1 demonstrates. The first column in Table 1 lists your alternative *approaches* based on the discussion above. The *cost* column represents the loss of annual revenues associated with a declining enrollment.

It could also represent anticipated expenses, if the analysis were to focus on different questions such as which alternative way of delivering lunchtime meals should your agency choose, or which alternative methods of promoting your services (e.g., low introductory fees, ads in local newspapers, or billboard advertising) is most cost effective.

The *benefits* column shows the anticipated changes in financial terms. In this example, the benefit is the cost savings that is equal to the reduction in staff. In other scenarios, however, benefits can be a calculation of new revenues to be received or of estimates of later-life societal cost-savings (Lewis et. al., 2001) that result from your program's intervention (e.g., early identification of children with special needs or parenting education and support). The requirement is to translate anticipated benefits into financial terms, and to be consistent in your calculations across differing approaches.

The column titled *c/b* refers to the ratio of costs to benefits. This is a common measure of cost-effectiveness analysis (Yates, 1996). We ideally want to achieve a statistic that represents either a balance between costs and benefits (e.g., break even), or where benefits exceed costs (<1). The lower the ratio, the stronger the benefit, while numbers greater than one (1) suggest higher costs compared against benefits.

The final column — *net benefits* — shows the financial savings in expenses as a difference between costs and benefits. This represents the anticipated net savings or expenditures associated with each project.

Though there are political as well as financial risks associated with all three approaches, the *risk* of reducing staff proportional to enrollment, no matter how personally troublesome, is clearly the most cost-effective approach based on this analysis. But wait! Does this convey the full picture? There may be another interpretation and course of action when you also consider *additional factors*.

For example, the remaining four staff members may view your decision to lay off staff as "writing on the wall" concerning the longevity of their own employment, and one or two may quietly decide to seek work elsewhere. You know from experience that it will cost you upwards to $7,500 an employee for recruitment, hiring, and training before a new employee is operating at full potential. With workforce reductions you, too, fear that an employee may leave; but, based on your experience and knowledge, only one is likely to leave.

You also know that among the staff to be let go is a newer and well-liked employee — someone, parents have commented to you, is one reason why they have chosen your center over others. If you lay this person off, as you feel bound by the policy of "last hired is the first fired," upward to two parents may also leave, which is valued at $12,000 ($6,000 a year in tuition for each). You additionally believe that by avoiding full layoffs, you will be in a better position to build enrollment and that within the next 12 months, you will be able to increase your enrollment by three children. Being down two staff positions will make it more difficult to increase your census.

The third approach of increasing fees is also not without risk. Some parents may decide to place their child with another agency if fees are increased. We assume in our scenario that two parents will withdraw from our program if fees are hiked.

These additional factored costs must also be considered into each decision as Table 2 demonstrates. In this approach, we see that a workforce reduction of 20% represents the better choice. If the scenario is correct, we actually show a cost-benefit ratio of less than 1, meaning that benefits clearly outweigh costs.

Let's take a look at a second example: Due to increasing costs, XYZ Child Care Center is considering an alternative to its present system of providing lunchtime meals prepared by its staff to 60 children each day. At a staff meeting it was suggested the agency consider hiring an outside company to cater lunches or that beginning with the next program year, parents be required to prepare meals for their child's lunch.

**TABLE 3 — SUMMARY MATRIX OF LUNCHTIME ALTERNATIVES**

| Approach | Food | Staffing | Consumables | Drinks | Total |
|---|---|---|---|---|---|
| Continue Current Lunchtime Meal Program | $15,145 | $13,520 | $1,560 | $780 | $31,005 |
| Engage Catering Company | $21,060 | $13,520 | $ 0 | $780 | $35,360 |
| Requirement that Parents Send Meals | $15,145 | $13,520 | $ 0 | $780 | $29,445 |

**TABLE 4 — HYPOTHETICAL COSTS AND BENEFIT ANALYSIS**

| Approach | Direct Cost | Benefits | C/B | Net Benefit |
|---|---|---|---|---|
| Continue Current Lunchtime Meal Program | $31,005 | $31,005 | 1 | $ 0 |
| Engage Catering Company | $35,360 | $31,005 | 1.15 | — $4,335 |
| Require That Parents Bring Meals | $29,445 | $31,005 | .95 | $1,560 |

Like before, the question is which of these three alternatives is most cost-effective? Should XYZ Child Care Center (a) continue to provide meals prepared by its staff; (b) arrange for catering by contract; or (c) require parents to send a lunch for their child?

Staff discussion concerning each approach identified several hidden costs and benefits. A 12 month review of agency expenditures for food showed that the agency spent $15,925 ($1.25 per child each day) in direct expenses for lunch, including food stuffs, fruit drinks and milk, and paper products. It additionally incurred approximately four hours each day in staff time devoted to meal preparation and cleanup. This was estimated to cost $13,520, or an additional 86 cents each day based on a census of 60 children.

On top of these expenses, there were periodic costs associated with pot, pan, and kitchen utensil replacements, and consumable supplies such as dish washing liquid, paper towels, and gas to shop for food and supplies. This was estimated at an additional $1,560 each year, or 10 cents per child each day. It became clear that the cost of lunchtime meals was $1.98 per child each day when the full costs were considered.

Two catering companies were called to see what they would charge to deliver meals each day. Based on comparable menus proposed by the two companies, it was found that the price per day for each child would be $1.35, which would be inclusive of food and paper products, but would not include drinks, which you knew from your research cost your agency an average of five cents per child each day or $780 each year.

Considering your third alternative — having parents send lunches for their child — you reasoned that you could not rebate to parents the $5,070 in staff time devoted to food preparation as these are fixed staff costs that you would want to retain. But you could adjust fees to account for your annual food expenses of $15,925, minus the five cents per child each day in drinks. The net amount to be adjusted would be $15,145 in annual revenues, or $252.41 a year for each child (84 cents each day).

A summary matrix of the three alternative costs is presented in Table 3.

You may be surprised that in the *food* column for the third alternative — the requirement that parents bring lunchtime meals — includes an expense equal to the first approach of continuing the current lunchtime meal arrangement. This is because forfeiture of income, the $15,145 that parents will not be paying for child care, represents an *expense* in the sense that the agency has willfully incurred this reduction, which is equal to the direct cost of food and related products.

In Table 4, we examine the cost-benefit of each approach based on the summary of *direct costs* drawn from Table 3, and our known *benefit* of $31,005, which is the current total expense of having our staff prepare lunchtime meals. We see from this analysis that the third approach of requiring parents to send their child's meal is the most cost-effective approach based on a *c/b* ratio of .95. Supporters of this approach would also likely argue that the four hours each day in staff expenses that is no longer needed for food preparation, could be reassigned to child care duties.

## Discussion

You have seen that cost-benefit analysis can be a helpful tool for assessing difficult and complex problems. Its rational approach can help quantify and explain to stakeholders and others why you made the decision that you did. It also helps you to define and select the conditions on which to base your alternative choices. There also is a firm bottom line in cost-benefit analysis that we try not to cross: benefits must be at least equal to costs (Levin, 1985).

One difficulty in using this approach, however, is that benefits must be equated in financial terms. We must be able to determine a monetary equivalency in areas where it is sometimes difficult to do so. How do we equate a cost to parenting education or early identification of children with special needs? Well, there are ways to do so, but some may disagree with your assumptions. We can look at public costs associated with child abuse and neglect or serving children with special needs, and suggest that with early interventions, these expenses are sometimes reduced.

It is also important to be clear about your audience when performing a cost-benefit analysis. Are they board members, elected officials, donors, or parents? Again, some may disagree with your assumptions or the values that you place on certain functions. And, even when you are clear as to your audience, you must realize, too, that other audiences may read your report and review your decision. As Levin states: "The importance of determining which audiences one is addressing and for what purposes is that these data guide the level and nature of the presentation and the types of information and analysis that should be forthcoming" (1985, p. 39).

At a time when terms like *logic models* and *evidence-based practice* seem to be directed at raising the bar on administration standards, cost-benefit analysis should be in your toolbox so that when questions are raised — "Is there a less costly way to do this?" or "Is there another better way?" — we know how to respond to these questions.

## References

Levin, H. M. (1993). *Cost-Effectiveness: A Primer*. Beverly Hills: Sage Publications.

Yates, B. T. (1989). *Analyzing Costs, Procedures, Processes, and Outcomes in Human Services*. Thousand Oaks, CA: Sage Publications.

Lewis, J. A., Lewis, M. D., Packard, T., & Souflee, Jr., F. (2001). *Management of Human Services Programs*. Belmont, CA: Brooks/Cole.

# RAISING MONEY

## CHAPTER 8

# Where the Bucks Are: Sources for Funds to Grow Your Child Care Business

**by Keith Stephens**

*Starting a child care business and building it up into a profitable operation requires entrepreneurial skills, hard work, determination to provide a quality service, respect for the consumer, and good luck. And, in most cases, it requires an infusion of money from the outside.*

*Finding the money you need to finance the process of growth can be a frustrating, fruitless experience unless you do your homework. Prior to hitting the streets looking for money, you need to put together a solid business plan which spells out where your business is headed, how you will do it, benchmarks for judging your progress, and why you will be successful. No one will give you money unless you can assure them of what you expect to accomplish — and can demonstrate a reasonable expectation for a solid, profitable return.*

Then you need to identify likely sources of money. There are a wide range of financing alternatives to consider, but each is best suited to businesses at different growth stages. People get in trouble when they pursue the wrong source at the wrong time. Your chances of success are improved by concentrating your energies on a source that is likely to produce results. To help you sort out what sources make the most sense at what point, I have discussed below characteristics of the most common sources of funds for a for profit child care business.

## Tapping Friends and Relatives

Friends and relatives are the money source of first and last resort for entrepreneurs just setting out to make their mark in the world. When all you have is a dream, it is very difficult to attract investments from conventional sources of money. As enthusiastic as you may be about your dream, potential investors will primarily be looking at economic return. Weighted heavily against you are the all too familiar statistics showing that most new small businesses fail. As a result, those starting from scratch must turn to the people who are most likely to be supportive — friends and relatives.

**Advantages:**

- **Friends and relatives are most likely to be receptive** to your plans because they know you and have more reason to be confident that you will succeed.
- **The money will come with fewer strings attached.** Since people close to you will invest in you on faith, they are not likely to insist on placing formal restrictions on how you use the money — or on how you run the business.
- **Most often they will invest for equity only.** This means that you will not be encumbered by a tight repayment schedule or interest payments.
- **You will probably not suffer serious economic repercussions** if your business doesn't pan out and you don't repay the money. Friends and relatives are much less likely than bankers or investors to press for repayment.

**Disadvantages:**

- **The emotional pressure can be overwhelming.** You don't want to fail for the people who are closest to you. The personal embarrassment is greater if your business is failing and you are losing the money and the respect (you assume) of the friends and relatives who were counting on you. For example, if you lose $50,000 borrowed from your parents and it turns out this was their retirement fund, the emotional cost involved can be very, very high. In many cases, complete alienation results.
- **You are not likely to raise as much money** via this route as you would from conventional money sources,

unless you are one of those rare individuals blessed with rich relatives who are eager to part with their money. On the other hand, while the $50,000 to $100,000 that is the most that you are likely to secure from friends and relatives will not enable you to launch a national chain, it should be sufficient seed money to start a single center.

**Other Considerations:**

In most cases, it is best to treat money raised from friends and relatives as an investment in the company. Give everybody stock in the company. If your business is successful, everyone will get a stock dividend or be bought out by someone else (hopefully at a nice profit). If the business fails, they will have gambled and lost.

On the other hand, if for some reason you desire to retain 100% of the stock, you would want to treat the money received as a loan with an agreed upon repayment schedule and rate of interest. While this will place you under a stronger obligation to repay the money, it will enable you to exercise full control of the business.

## Finding an Angel — A Private Investor

An angel is a wealthy individual who you persuade to invest in your business. This approach is similar to convincing a friend to invest, although — since this individual will not necessarily know you personally — your personal credibility as well as that of your business plan will be subject to much tighter scrutiny.

**Advantages:**

- **A private investor will be more emotionally removed** from you than a friend or relative. Your relationship can operate in a more businesslike fashion, without the emotional undercurrents of a personal relationship.
- **An angel will probably not insist on gaining control** of the business. Most likely he or she will not have the time or inclination to become immersed in everyday decisionmaking.
- **You are likely to have access to more money** from a wealthy individual than from friends and relatives.
- **An angel will not necessarily be looking for a quick return**, so you will not be pressured to generate - dramatic profits immediately. More likely, the private investor will be looking for a reasonable return three to seven years in the future when you sell the business or go public.

**Disadvantages:**

- **A private individual will be harder to win over** than friends and relatives. You will need to prove yourself and the viability of your plan.
- **She will want more protection**. One way to structure a more attractive deal for a private investor is to offer preferred stock. A preferred class of stock could offer many privileges to this individual: a stated rate of return, some preference upon liquidation, some preference in terms of dividends (that he would receive dividends before you did, for example), the right to move from preferred stock to common stock, or the right to pick up voting privileges to more actively protect her investment if the business is not doing well.
- **More documentation and more legal work will be involved** in putting the transaction together.
- **The final arrangement will likely be much more tightly structured** than one with a friend or relative. There will be more restrictions on how you spend the money and run the business, such as frequent reporting on your progress, participation in approval of the budget and major fixed asset purchases, limits on expenses, and limits on your salary.

**Other Considerations:**

**How do you find an angel?** By talking to your banker (most larger banks have something akin to an executive banking section for wealthy individuals), your lawyer

### Table 1
### Types of Business Financing

Child care businesses utilize outside financing for two general purposes:

**To finance the business itself:** Money needed for the total operation of the business in order to facilitate growth. This article explores options available for this purpose.

**To purchase real estate:** Financing required for the purchase of land and real property. The real estate serves as collateral. A wide range of real estate financing vehicles are available, such as conventional bank mortgages, loans from insurance companies, and investments made through limited partnership arrangements.

There are two general types of financing available:

**Equity investments:** Money that is invested in your business in exchange for a share of the ownership. Money is invested with the expectation that a return will be realized in the future as the value of one's share of the business appreciates.

**Loans:** Money advanced to a business with a formal repayment schedule. Return is realized from interest charged for the use of the money.

(particularly lawyers in bigger law firms which have contact with affluent individuals), your accountant, and representatives of trust companies and investment management services (that manage assets for other people); by going to the right business meetings and belonging to the right community organizations; and by advertising in the business or classified section in the newspaper. In all these ways you will be seeking referrals which will lead you to an individual who is willing and able to put up the kind of money you need.

## Making a Private Placement

A formalized method of securing private investors is the private placement. Under this procedure, you go out to the business or investment community with a business plan and offer to sell stock in your company. Typically the purpose of a private placement is to attract money from a number of people beyond your inner circle of friends and relatives.

A private placement is a less rigorous procedure for selling stock than a public offering. The rules governing private placements are less involved, and the disclosure requirements less stringent. However, there are specific limitations on how much can be raised in this manner, and who can invest. You will need to consult your lawyer regarding rules and regulations defining these limitations.

**Advantages:**

- **You are spreading the risk.** By selling shares in your company to a number of investors, the degree of risk each one is being exposed to is less than if one individual were making the whole investment. People may be more willing to invest if they know that others are willing to do so also.
- **A greater amount of money can be raised,** in most cases, through a private placement than through private individuals.
- **You can retain final control.** While you are selling shares in your business in order to generate capital, you can normally retain at least 51% of the stock yourself.
- **This is a long-term investment.** Investors are typically looking for a payoff coming not from annual earnings but from resale of the company either to someone else or to the public through a stock offering (so their 3% share in a $1,750,000 company becomes 3% of a $10,000,000 sale). Normally, investors expect a return in a three to seven year time frame. Thus there will not be pressure to achieve an immediate high level of profitability. However, there will be the expectation that the company grow steadily and significantly.

**Disadvantages:**

- **This is not a do-it-yourself project.** You will need to hire a lawyer to prepare a form of prospectus known as a private placement memorandum. In this document you spell out for prospective investors the nature of your company and the business that you are engaged in, the key people in your company, your future plans, your past financial performance and future financial projections, and your money needs.
- **This is not an appropriate vehicle for a small business** planning for modest growth. Even if you perform most of the paperwork and legwork yourself, legal fees can run anywhere from $10,000 to $20,000. With this built in cost of raising the money, it means that for raising anything under $200,000, this would not be a practical vehicle. This is not for single centers looking to add one or two locations. It is more applicable if you are operating three or four centers profitably and can present a creditable plan for growing significantly.
- **This is not an appropriate vehicle for a new business.** Typically you need to be up and running in order to establish credibility. In some cases, primarily in the high tech arena, it can be a vehicle for start-up, but in this case you will need a strong sell on yourself.
- **This is a time consuming process.** It will require that you take time away from your business. This means that you must be able to set your business up in such a manner that it can run without you during this period. If not, you may see your business go down the drain before you get the investment to make it grow.
- **You must be prepared to lose** the time and money you invest in the process. There is a high likelihood that the deal will fall through. Therefore, the legal fees and the time you invest in the effort will go for naught.

**Other Considerations:**

Once your private placement memorandum is complete, you can conceivably sell it yourself by tracking down likely prospects and pitching it to them on a one-to-one basis. You are more likely to experience success, however, if you enlist professional assistance. Often you can find a small local brokerage firm, a local investment banking firm, or a local financial management firm that is willing to take on the sales effort for you. What they end up doing is placing your shares with their clients. Financial planners are a good vehicle for taking your plan and presenting it.

Keep in mind that any investment professional will expect a commission in the 5% to 10% range. In addition, you must recognize that they see a multitude of plans. You must make yours stand out from the crowd. Finding a lawyer who is experienced in doing private placement deals will be most helpful here.

## Borrowing from a Bank

Your friendly neighborhood banker is often the first person you think of when you need money. Unfortunately, you are likely to discover that this friendliness is only skin deep when you come asking for money to grow a business. While banks have tremendous assets at their disposal, they are not inclined to risk these assets on any business that is not already well established. However, at various stages in your growth, bank financing is feasible and desirable.

**Advantages:**

- **Banks are easy to find**. Bankers love to have deals brought to them to look over. (It's amazing how positive they are at the first interview, how difficult they are to deal with after that, and how cold they are when they turn you down.)
- **The methodology for dealing with banks is clearly defined**. From the very start, it is clear what banks will lend money for, what hoops you will have to jump through to get it, and how the deal can be structured.
- **Banks can be very helpful** to you in your business. They have trained people who look at numerous businesses and see how they perform. They routinely analyze your financial statements and compare them with other industries. If you can see these comparisons and the financial ratios they develop on your business, this can be quite useful to you.
- **Banks have several financing vehicles** to employ: working capital loans when you need more money in your business, and have the profitability to support it; asset financing when you want to grow your business, but need money to buy new equipment, etc.; real estate construction funding when you want to construct a new facility or remodel your old center; and mortgage financing when you want to purchase or refinance your property.
- **The amount of money obtainable is limited only by your ability to qualify**. Loans can range from $500 personal loans to commercial loans for billions of dollars. Most independent banks will be limited to the $200,000 to $300,000 range, but this should meet the needs of most center operators.
- **You don't have to give them part of your company**. Banks are not equity investors, they are lenders. They

**TABLE 2**
**FINANCING UNDER DIFFERENT STAGES OF DEVELOPMENT**

| Stage of Organizational Development | Likely Financing Sources |
|---|---|
| **Start-Up Stage** | |
| • Organization is only in the idea stage. | Self, friends, or relatives |
| • No service is being delivered. | Private sources |
| • This represents a high risk investment. | |
| • A limited source of funds is available. | |
| **First Stage** | |
| • Organization is now delivering a service. | Venture capital |
| • It has proven that it can sell in the marketplace. | Private placement |
| • Profitable operations are still at least two years away. | |
| **Second Stage** | |
| • Organization is up and running. | Venture capital |
| • It is marketing its service with a degree of success. | Private offering |
| • It needs funds for expansion. | Public offering |
| | Bank |
| **Third Stage** | |
| • Organization is running well. | Public offering |
| • It is generating steady profits. | Bank |
| • It needs additional capital to continue its rapid growth. | |
| **Mature Stage** | |
| • Organization is running well. | Bank |
| • It is generating steady profits. | Insurance company |
| • It has been able to manage in both up and down business cycles. | Public offering |
| • It generates sufficient cash flow to handle most of its working capital needs. | |
| • Its services are well accepted by the marketplace. | |

will insist upon a tight repayment schedule, not a share of your business.

**Disadvantages:**

- **Banks are very conservative.** Banks are tightly regulated and closely scrutinized, and this forces them to be conservative. A banker is thinking at all times, "What can go wrong?" We, as entrepreneurs, think of all the things that will go well. It is important to know how a banker thinks and tailor your presentation accordingly.

- **Banks rarely give long-term loans.** You can get term loans in the three to five year range, but seldom are they willing to go beyond that (with the exception of mortgages). A common procedure is to write a loan with a five to seven year payment schedule, with a single large payment at the end of every year. This gives them the leverage to review the loan every year to determine if it should be renewed.

- **Banks will closely monitor your business.** They will periodically want to see your financial statements and, if you start falling behind, will ask for more frequent and detailed reports. This can become onerous if your recordkeeping is haphazard or done in an unconventional way.

- **Banks are professionals at collecting money.** In the event you fall behind, they can make it reasonably difficult for you.

**Other Considerations:**

When evaluating your loan request, bankers will take a close look at the three c's of banking: *character, credit,* and *collateral.* Is the person running the business competent and trustworthy? Does the business have a solid credit history? Are there sufficient assets in the business to secure the loan? Almost always, you will be asked to provide a personal guarantee.

These criteria tend to work against businesses just starting out, or those that are struggling. In addition, the stipulation that investments be secured by hard assets can be a problem in child care where there is no inventory, no receivables, and few tangible assets (outside of property) which a bank would view as marketable.

## Pursuing Venture Capitalists

In recent years most of the glamour in venture capital has gone to high tech industries. However, now that growth in this area has leveled off, venture capitalists are looking around for other hot industries. And child care is one industry that has started to attract their attention.

Companies that venture capitalists find appealing are not yet at the bankable stage. Sometimes they are start-up companies, but more likely they are already organized and just starting to show a potential for dramatic growth. What these companies need is an infusion of money to turn this potential into a reality.

**Advantages:**

- **They will help you grow.** Because venture capitalists are in the business of growing companies, they have talent on hand to assist you in managing your business. They are going to be actively involved in protecting their investment.

- **Venture capitalists can make substantial investments.** Because of all the investigative work that goes into making investment decisions, they are not interested in any deal for less than $250,000. Venture capital is not a viable source of money for small companies. It is only a realistic possibility for a business with aspirations of becoming a regional or national chain with around 50 centers.

**Disadvantages:**

- **Venture capitalists are hard to find.** They are not on every street corner like banks. However, lists are available from *Inc.* and *Money* magazines.

- **Dealing with a venture capitalist can be an intimidating process.** They won't know you, and won't have any confidence in what you can accomplish. You will need to convince them that you are worthy of their trust.

- **You will need to sell them on the child care industry** as well as on your business. They won't share your dream. When you say *child care,* they will say *insurance problem.* You will have had to do your homework well to make a convincing case for them to invest in a soft service industry that they won't understand.

- **You will have to give away a big hunk of your company and you will be under the gun to perform.** They will want seats on the board of directors, and they continually will want to know what is going on. You can retain control, but only if things are going as planned. In all likelihood, they will insist upon provisions that will improve their influence over the company if things don't go well.

**Other Considerations:**

A venture capital firm is absolutely going to want to know "How are we going to get out of this deal?" If you can't demonstrate to them, with a high degree of certainty, that within three to five years they will be able to walk away from the deal with a healthy profit, they won't even talk to you.

They are not looking for dividends paid out of profits. They're looking for the return that comes from building a company and then disposing of it. The return they expect from any one investment is in the range of 50% to 60% per year. In other words, if they put in $1 million they would expect $10 million back at the end of five years.

## Approaching Insurance Companies

Insurance companies are not a likely funding source for garden variety child care businesses. The financing vehicles they prefer are suited to massive real estate investments. For the most part, insurance companies won't even talk to you if you're looking for less than $1 million. On the other hand, if you are an established regional chain needing $20 million to build 20 centers at $1,000,000 apiece, an insurance company would be an appropriate vehicle for arranging for that investment in one fell swoop.

While insurance companies will consider some equity arrangements, they are primarily interested in real estate deals. Like banks, they are not risk takers; but because of the size of their investments, they can sometimes offer better interest rates, and they can be somewhat more flexible in how they structure the deal.

## Making a Public Offering

A public offering is a vehicle for mature companies that want to finance growth or a change in ownership. This is a route that would only make sense for regional or national chains with 50 or more centers looking to raise at least $10 million.

Investors in a public offering would be interested in a return on earnings — your profitability is going to determine what price you can get for your stock.

You could have a public offering for a start-up venture, but you would need one of the regional or national brokerage firms to work with you on it, and it is unlikely that you could sell them on the idea. On the other hand, a public offering would be an appropriate route if an individual had built up a chain of 50 centers and wanted to sell them, yet wanted to stay involved in the day-to-day management.

# Developing a Proposal: When Opportunity Knocks, Will You Be Prepared?

**by Craig Boswell**

*It was a dark and stormy night . . .*

*Suddenly, a portly, middle-aged developer burst into my office. "Are you the babysitter?" he barked.*

*As I stood up, graham cracker crumbs fell to the floor. "Yes. Well, not exactly," I stuttered. "We don't consider child care as babysitting," I said, surprisingly bold.*

*"That doesn't matter," he roared. "I'm here because I've heard you're the best in town, and I have a business proposition for you."*

"Please come in and sit down," I murmured while my tongue searched for the last graham cracker crumb. "Oh, sorry, let me move that xylophone. I've been meaning to fix it for the last three weeks," I giggled, in a manner reminiscent of my seven year old daughter.

"Boswell," he said without introduction or salutation, "I'm developing the largest research park this county has ever seen. I have contractual commitments with eight out of twelve large, and I mean large, companies. But the county commissioners are demanding that I provide some amenity parks, with tennis courts and walking paths. They also wanted a day care center," he said in disgust.

"Child care," I said. "We prefer to be called a child care center, not day care."

"That doesn't matter," he roared. "I've heard you're the best in town."

"And you have a business proposition?" I interjected.

"Well . . . yes, that's right," he stumbled with his thoughts. "I'll build this center the way you want it, and CAM charges from the big boys will help pay for your rent."

I was too intimidated to ask what CAM was and who the big boys were. (I found out later that CAM stands for Common Area Maintenance Fee. I think then it should be called CAMF. The big boys referred to the research companies that would be building or leasing the property.)

"So, Boswell, I need an operations proposal with technical and management procedures with a three-year projection. The county has established a review subcommittee that will oversee the proposal review. Oh, yes, they have a consulting company to review the child care issues and the total PUD (Plan Unit Development)."

"Hold it," I bellowed. "You'll have to go a lot slower. This is new ground, and I'm used to single digits and three-letter words."

He laughed, and the corners of his mouth reached to the bottom of his ears. "I don't have time now, but here's my card. Come over to the office where I can explain in detail what I need," he said. "What time can you come next Thursday?" he asked.

"I can come during nap time," I stated without thinking. "One-thirty," I responded after realizing what I had just said.

"Great! I will look forward to discussing this matter in detail with you, Boswell. It has been nice talking to you." He left quicker than he had arrived.

I sat quietly for about ten minutes. Then I began looking for my package of graham crackers.

The developer had presented me with a unique challenge — how to write a proposal in a manner that developers, commissioners, and consultants could understand. More importantly, how would I write a proposal that I could understand?

## Understanding the Proposal

RFP (Request for Proposal) usually comes in written form, ranging in length from 1 to 101 pages. It is a document that outlines a problem and solicits proposals that explain how that problem can be solved. If the problem is how, when, where, and at what cost to establish a child care in the new area, the response could have many sections, and it could take weeks to complete.

An important point to make in the "art" of proposal writing is that most RFP readers are looking for a clean, well-written document that simply tells them what they want to know.

## Things You Need

- ✔ Space to work
- ✔ Uninterrupted time
- ✔ Computer
- ✔ Binding machine and device
- ✔ Copy machine
- ✔ Resource files
- ✔ Calculator
- ✔ Independent reviewer
- ✔ Vision and insight

Many proposal books and seminars advocate a team approach to proposal writing. My experience dictates that team members get in the way and ask stupid questions. My recommendation, therefore, is to sit down with the door shut and have a clear outline (along with a box of graham crackers). Then go for it!

The basic elements of your proposal should stand out when the document is completed. For example:

1. The proposal should be neat, clean, and easy to read.
2. Jargon should be eliminated. Terminology should be defined so the reviewer (builder) knows clearly what you intend by using certain words.
3. Communicate your message without putting the reader in a stupor.
4. Your language should communicate your enthusiasm for this project. Be positive.
5. Use supported assumptions:
   - **a.** describe your organization clearly
   - **b.** document the need in context, by describing how the "national issues of quality child care" relate to local efforts
   - **c.** use tables and graphs sparingly and when you do employ them be sure headings clearly explain what is being presented

**Outline**

**1.0 Executive Summary**
1.1 Introduction letter
1.2 Board of directors' letter (optional)
1.3 History statement
1.4 Management commitment statement

**2.0 Technical Section**
2.1 History
2.2 Management team with organization chart
2.3 Administrative policy
2.4 Management challenge statement
2.5 Time line
2.6 Early childhood quality guideline

**3.0 Management Section**
3.1 Personal and compensation package and job description
3.2 Staffing ratios, staff supervision, and staff retention
3.3 Inservice training guidelines and professional advancement
3.4 Program information
3.5 Philosophy overview
3.6 Curriculum statement
3.7 Explanation of daily curriculum
3.8 Center/parent relationships
3.9 Health and safety
3.10 Children with disability condition statement
3.11 Food program and procedures/menu
3.12 References (at least five)
3.13 Personal resumé

**4.0 Cost Section**
4.1 Marketing plan
4.2 Budget/item description
4.3 Equipment/supply cost
4.4 Proforma — three year projection
4.5 Sample of parent tuition, handbook, registration
4.6 Schedule for obtaining licenses and insurance with cost breakdown

**5.0 Appendix**
5.1 Sample of parent handouts
5.2 Sample of infant information sheets
5.3 Sample of newspaper clipping of school's program
5.4 Sample of medication authorization forms
5.5 Sample of school/teacher evaluation forms
5.6 Sample of posted preschool curriculum outline

This article does not afford me the capability to describe in detail the subtopics of each section outlined above. However, I will briefly review a few.

**1.4 — Management commitment statement** is a subtopic that pledges your expertise to long-term operations, realizing your past experience and future goals in early childhood education and child care operations. Furthermore, it acknowledges the tremendous challenges that lie ahead in the planning, start-up, and long-term operations.

Details and concerns can be elaborated upon — e.g., "Our experience has determined that organizations outside the scope of early childhood education have a difficult and costly time of setting up, operating, and maintaining the type of quality center they envision. A management team that is educated, trained, and experienced can cut through the problems that arise and focus their energy / resources in maintaining the elements that are associated with quality, staff training, low teacher turnover, and a low child to teacher ratio."

**2.3 — Administrative policy.** This section allows for explanation on multiple site operation and the manner of hiring, training, and supervision of middle management and faculty staff — e.g., "During the start-up phase, the executive director will be on site, hiring, training, and supervising the teachers. The on-site director will be trained at our nearest child care center under current child care management. The hiring and training will occur well in advance of children entering the school. After the school is operating satisfactorily, the executive director will maintain an inservice education, monitoring, parent-board participation schedule that is satisfactory to both the staff and the parents and the parent advisory council."

**3.2** — Issues regarding **ratio**, **supervision**, and **retention** will always be foremost on a reviewer's mind. You must provide details on how your child care company can provide solutions to these significant concerns — e.g., "Although the staff turnover rate is a natural issue as it relates to child care, our child care has had the fortunate opportunity to retain most of the staff throughout all its center(s)." The retention is achieved through the following reasons:

✔ Higher salaries than the local average.

✔ Insurance benefits — health, life, dental, and maternity.

✔ Staff child care at a significantly reduced rate. Food is provided free while staff is working.

✔ Paid vacation and ten days for major holidays during the year.

✔ Creative expression through involvement in curriculum.

✔ Inservice training and recognition of completed tasks.

✔ Involvement with an organization where the primary directive is to provide the best learning and caring environment possible for young children.

**4.4 — Proforma** (budget) and three projections are critical information for any developer or banker, but most important for the financial feasibility of the new center. The proforma is used to illustrate the connection between child ratio, teacher salary, staff benefits, cost of living, and parent tuition. Remember to factor in cost of living increase for the staff / faculty and parent tuition increases throughout the next three years.

## General Proposal Checklist

1. Acknowledge receipt of the RFP to developer.
2. Determine qualification and commitments.
3. Consult informally with board of directors, trustees, owners, or husband / wife, etc. to determine your commitment to the new project.
4. Make copies of RFP (used for working copy).
5. Make formal presentation to decision makers in your organization.
6. Decision makers' — e.g., board, trustee, owners, etc. — signatures of support.
7. Plan response time and deadline.
8. Identify and allocate supplies and support.
9. Outline RFP tasks.
10. Secure work space.
11. Develop proposal writing and assembly schedule.

## Proposal Writing Checklist

✔ Cover letter

✔ Letter of support from "decision maker"

✔ Table of contents

✔ Executive summary

✔ Technical section

✔ Management section

✔ Cost section

✔ Appendix

One final thought: Always use the overnight express mail (I use Federal Express). They keep terrific records on time, date, receiving signatures, etc. That doesn't mean that you need to wait until one day before the deadline. However, I've never met a time-compulsive early childhood educator. But you and I both know if it weren't for deadlines, taxes, payroll, board reports, and RFPs would all be sitting on our office floor with the xylophones.

# Fishing for Dollars in Philanthropic Waters

**by Anne Mitchell**

*Every child care director, at some point, has confronted the fact that parents (even well-off ones) just can't pay enough to support good child care services. The savvy director is always looking for new sources of funding and evaluating whether they're worth pursuing. If we could become a United Way agency, would the effort be worth it? What could we do as a fundraiser besides another bake sale? Is buying lottery tickets a good investment? Somewhere in this process, the idea of soliciting foundations comes up. Probably right after you hear that some national child care group just got a multi-million dollar grant from You-Name-It foundation, you think: "Why couldn't we do that?" This article is for you.*

First, let's be clear that foundations are not now (or ever) going to be the direct source of funding that solves the compensation-affordability problem. Foundations are not — and never will be — the main source of funding for any child care center's operation. The direct services or general operating expenses of any organization are almost never supported by philanthropy. The role that foundations play in a field is something like what an entrepreneur does — improve, expand, and innovate. The difference is that foundations do this indirectly through the work of those organizations they fund, rather than directly as an entrepreneur would in operating a business.

Foundations are looking for innovative solutions to problems, promising approaches to improve on current methods, or expansions of successful programs that address a problem. Expanding services for families (adding or starting new programs), improving practice through professional development, linking child care services with other services families need are all examples of child care ideas foundations might consider supporting.

Foundations correctly believe their role in child care is to help the field solve problems and address current needs, not to become a direct funder of services. Given that cautionary note, foundations can and will fund child care if you approach the right ones in the right way.

## The Philanthropic Landscape

Philanthropy comes in many forms, from individual donors to national foundations. This article focuses on philanthropic entities (foundations and corporations) that might support local child care projects. If you want to know how to find major individual donors, that's another story (actually, a set of unique and non-replicable stories). Understanding something about the types of foundations and their basic characteristics can help you identify the right ones to consider pursuing.

All foundations are legal entities designed to give away money for particular purposes to other non profit entities. Many were established with the funds from one individual, one family (or extended family), or one corporation. Others are collections of funds bequeathed by many different individuals and families. Some foundations are restricted to supporting certain types of work or particular geographic areas — either by the will of those who gave the money or the wishes of the current trustees.

Foundations can have a national, regional, and/or local focus in their grantmaking. Some national foundations also have a local grantmaking program to benefit the community they reside in. Community foundations are usually collections of trusts and bequests that are restricted to a specific community. Community foundations often have the word "community" or "area" in their names, e.g., the Rochester Area Foundation or the Marin Community Foundation.

Corporate foundations (or a corporation's annual charitable giving) focus mainly (or solely) on those communities where the corporation has worksites and employees.

Community foundations and corporate foundations with a local focus are probably the most likely to support local child care projects. National foundations with a diverse local grants program may also be supporters.

Foundations can legally only give money to certain types of organizations — almost always a non profit corporation which has tax-exempt status (a 501(c)3 organization). Most non profit child care centers would qualify, but for profit centers generally cannot receive funds directly from a foundation. However, associations of providers such as a family child care association or a for profit directors' association can qualify if the association is incorporated as a non profit and has tax-exempt status.

Generally a foundation establishes a set of program areas, priorities, or strategies that guide its grantmaking. Child care is unlikely to be a distinct program priority all by itself, but child care easily fits into a broader area — such as child and youth development, community building, strengthening families, early education and school readiness, or prevention — which are typical philanthropic program areas.

In larger foundations, each program area is the responsibility of an individual program officer. Smaller foundations may have only one staff person who covers all the areas. In some cases, one of the foundation's directors manages the grantmaking as a volunteer. Knowing whether there is a program area where child care would fit and which foundation staff person handles the area where child care fits are essential pieces of information to have.

Foundations generally make grants based on thoughtful, well-written proposals that directly address the specified issues within a program area. Sending a proposal — no matter how brilliant the ideas in it might be — is not the best way to introduce yourself to a foundation. Very few foundations will read and respond to proposals sent "cold." Some foundations do not accept unsolicited proposals at all — they will return them unread — because they only fund projects that are developed at their request by organizations they select.

Others only accept short letter proposals that follow a specified format. Before you make a move, you must know how each foundation approaches grantmaking and what its requirements are for applicants or grantseekers.

## What Foundations Fund

Given that foundations will not underwrite your center's parent fees, what will they support? Answer: Improvements and innovations that solve child care problems and benefit the wider community. Professional development is a good example. If the community lacks infant care, a proposal from a group of centers to collectively train their infant care teachers in a manner that would institutionalize an infant care course in the community college might be a fundable proposal. Building the infant care rooms might be fundable if you could find a foundation that supports capital projects, so called "bricks and mortar."

Another example is collaborations to expand services. If the community's Head Start grantee and a child care center(s) wanted to jointly provide comprehensive all-day early education, a foundation might fund the planning and start-up phase of such a venture.

Fundraising — no matter whether it is selling raffle tickets or writing a grant proposal — is not begging. You are offering someone an opportunity to support a worthy organization or project and, in the case of a foundation, an opportunity to give away money that the foundation is required by law to give away. Successful fundraising is the combination of four elements:

- a credible, trustworthy person
- with good ideas for feasible projects,
- that match the foundation's goals, and
- will be carried out in an organization that is financially solid and well managed.

Technically, grantmaking is the act of one organization making a grant to another organization. Actually, successful grantmaking is the result of positive human interactions — the foundation officer and the grant seeker establish a working relationship based on good communication and mutual trust that leads eventually to the approval of a grant.

Foundations fund people — people they know, people they trust, people with good ideas. Child care center directors who are active in their community are more likely to encounter potential funders in situations where relationships can be established — such as at community meetings or events — than directors who only venture out to attend an occasional conference with their early childhood colleagues.

## Getting Started

Many people think the first step is to make a list of all the geographically appropriate foundations that have any history of "giving to early childhood." On the contrary, the place to start is with ideas (although research on funders may be needed later). The goal is to make a match between your good ideas and a foundation's goals. Matchmaking is done by people — your ideas will be shaped and changed (improved, hopefully) through your interactions with the foundation officer.

Begin by developing some ideas for projects that would benefit your organization and the wider child care community. This can be done alone, but often goes faster in a small group (if everyone is clear on the task). You might get the local directors' group to brainstorm ideas. After you get a list, pick out the three or four ideas that seem most feasible and write a one-page description of each idea. The "who, what, where, when, why, how" approach used by newspaper reporters is a good way to start. Write down what the project is, why it is needed, who will do it, how long it will last, what results it will have, and what it will cost.

Because human relationships are important in philanthropic fund raising, another good method for getting started is to think about your own networks and contacts in terms of potential funders. Are any of the people you already know potential funders — that is, connected in some way with corporations or foundations? What about your board — who do they know? Some of your board members may well know philanthropic leaders and be willing to discuss child care with them and introduce you to them directly.

Finally, think about your staff and parents. Some of them may have networks that include potential funders.

Chances are, if there's a community foundation in your area, you've heard of it. If not, look in the phone book or go to the library. There are a number of published sources of information about foundations that can help you find those in your geographic area that might consider a child care related request.

Your local library may have the current year's *Foundation Directory* published by the Foundation Center, an information clearinghouse on foundation and corporate giving headquartered in New York City. This directory contains entries for close to 12,000 foundations, giving brief descriptions of their mission and history, total assets, annual grant total, size of an average grant, types of organizations supported, contact information, and any restrictions. The Directory of Corporate Giving has similar entries for over 2,000 corporate grantmakers.

If your library does not have these directories, you can contact The Foundation Center directly at (800) 424-9836. They will refer you to the nearest Foundation Center Library or to a Cooperating Collection.

Another way to access information about The Foundation Center is on the Internet (http://fdncenter.org).

The process of seeking and receiving foundation funding takes time and effort. Think carefully about whether the process is worth the reward before you start. If it were easy, everyone would be doing it. In fact, some child care center directors have successfully negotiated the foundation waters and are willing to share their lessons.

# Keys to Success in Raising Funds

by Roger Neugebauer

*Exchange has surveyed over 100 child care centers about their successful, as well as their unsuccessful fundraising projects. From the experiences of these centers, the ten factors described below have emerged as keys to successful fundraisers.*

## Define Your Purpose

The willingness of staff members, parents, volunteers, and members of the community to give their support to a fundraiser will be enhanced to the extent that the need for funds is clear and important. People need to know that their contribution of time, talents, or resources will make a difference.

Therefore, before launching a fundraising effort, a center should assess whether it is truly necessary and, if so, for what purpose. This intent should then be identified at the outset of any appeals for support. Centers have found that the more specific the purpose can be defined the better. It is easier to generate support for "constructing an outdoor climbing structure" than for "building up the contingency account"; it is more inspiring to contribute towards a "scholarship fund" than towards "general operating expenses."

In child care, fundraisers often have important secondary purposes as well. Centers often utilize these projects to provide publicity for the center and to enhance parent involvement. These purposes should clearly be identified at the outset, also, so that the project can be organized in such a way as to ensure their accomplishment.

A common pitfall here is when a secondary purpose is really the main purpose. Centers sometimes use fundraisers as a device for getting parents involved. This can unnecessarily waste the precious time of parents and can backfire when the parents realize their efforts do not accomplish anything of importance.

## Set a Goal

Centers have found it beneficial to set a target amount to be raised each year. Having a financial goal helps planners to gauge the magnitude of the effort required, and to decide on the type of activities which are appropriate. A center needing to raise $500 would not establish a thrift shop, nor would one requiring $6,000 schedule a bake sale. Having a specific dollar goal is more likely to instill confidence in potential donors that the center knows what it's about. Once the goal is set, it can also help focus volunteers' efforts if they are kept informed about the progress toward that goal. Some centers even post a chart at the center, much like the thermometer of United Way, which shows volunteers how close they are to accomplishing the goal.

## Know the Audience

Who is likely to contribute to your center? The type of fundraising projects a center implements should be appropriate to the project's potential audience. If your center is known by individuals in your community who have abundant financial resources and who believe in what your center is doing, the direct approach may be best. Contact them, explain your need, and ask for a donation.

If, on the other hand, your program is known and supported primarily by individuals with scant financial resources, asking for donations may not be realistic. Instead, it may be more appropriate to offer some goods or services in return for people's contributions.

In planning this type of fundraiser, the potential audience needs to be examined even more closely. Who is the potential audience? What goods or services are likely to be of real interest to them? How much are they likely to contribute? You are operating on shaky ground if you cannot answer these questions with some certainty before planning a fundraiser.

## Make It Fun

Select a project that staff and parents are excited about. Most fundraisers depend heavily upon the volunteer work of staff, parents, and board members. The amount of effort these people are likely to invest in a project relates significantly to the extent they are excited about it. If the chairperson of a fundraising committee decides that a raffle will be the solution to all the center's financial woes, but parents are none too eager to hustle prizes or tickets, chances are the raffle will fizzle.

## Build on Strengths

Try to select a fundraiser that builds on the skills that already exist in the center. Personnel in child care centers have expertise in areas such as child development, child nutrition, children's activities, and parent education.

Examples of fundraisers capitalizing on such skills include children's entertainment series, gymnastics classes, babysitter training and referral, cookbooks for children, and parenting workshops.

A child care center should be most effective and efficient in organizing fundraisers such as these. In addition, such a project can showcase the skills and services of the center to potential supporters and customers.

## Look for Repeaters

Centers surveyed noted several reasons for selecting fundraisers that can be repeated on a regular basis. First, the center can learn from its mistakes. Errors which were made the first time in planning, publicizing, and putting on a project can be eliminated in future reruns, thus saving on wasted energy and resources.

Second, the project will not need to be organized from scratch every time. Press releases, flyers, costumes, booths, or publicity strategies developed the first time can simply be refined rather than reinvented.

Third, the more often a successful project is run, the more effective publicity will be.

## Be Cost Effective

Centers can fall into the trap of thinking that any project that brings in money is worthwhile.

However, such reasoning fails to consider the value of staff and volunteer time expended in raising the money.

People's time should be considered as a valuable resource. It should not be squandered on fundraising projects that generate a small return on time invested.

To calculate the return on time investment (R) of any project, simply deduct all expenses (E) incurred in putting on the project (including the value of paid staff time) from total income (I) of the project, then divide the remainder by the total number of hours (T) spent by staff and volunteers on the project:

$$\frac{I - E}{T} = R$$

To illustrate, consider the case of a spring fair held by a nursery school in New England. This school's staff and parents donated about 475 hours of time (T) planning, publicizing, setting up, and operating the fair — and expended $250 in center funds (E) for booths, food, and publicity in order to raise a total of $850 (I) for the center. Plugging this into the formula, it can be seen that for every hour invested in this project the center earned $1.26 in profit:

$$\frac{\$850 - \$250}{475 \text{ hours}} = \$1.26/\text{hour}$$

Even though the project was a success in terms of raising a significant chunk of money, the return on the investment of volunteers' time was dreadfully low. Bake sales and dinners are often equally wasteful of volunteers' time.

On the other hand, other fundraisers described by directors interviewed for this article brought returns of anywhere from $25-150/hour. Given the fact that such cost effective projects are quite realistic, a center should certainly think twice about engaging in any project which will return less than $20/hour.

## Publicize Aggressively

Centers that have the most success with fundraisers are those which have mastered the art of getting the right message to the right people at the right time.

The first step in an effective publicity campaign is clarifying what is being *sold*. If the fundraising project is a direct appeal for donations, what is being sold is the cause — people are being asked to give money to a cause they believe in.

For an indirect fundraiser, such as a raffle, a bake sale, or a dinner, it is the product or service that is being sold — the chance to win, the cookies, or the meal. The *message* of all publicity should concentrate heavily on what is being sold.

This right message must also reach the right people. Often in membership drives and appeals for donations, certain professionals — such as doctors, who are deemed most likely to contribute to the center — are singled out for calls.

Likewise, a center which offers a noon luncheon in a downtown area sends flyers around to offices in the neighborhood to alert people who eat lunch out. Effective publicity has much less to do with *how much* than it does with *where*. Centers with sound ongoing fundraising campaigns also take great pains to develop extensive lists of known supporters. Included on this list should be former parents, staff, and board members; those who have visited the center; and those who have attended or contributed to past fundraisers. For every fundraiser, this group should be sent a special announcement.

## Maximize Publicity

At the outset of this article, it was mentioned that publicity can be a secondary purpose of fundraisers. In fact, every time you embark on a fundraising initiative you should analyze the publicity opportunities the fundraiser offers. That way you will get extra mileage out of the time and resources you invest in the fundraiser.

A classic example of a missed opportunity occurred when a New England center provided child care at a Women's Fair. The center set up a variety of activities in a corner of the auditorium where the fair was being held. Children were so happy and fully engaged that fairgoers stopped and enjoyed observing the children at the *play area*. This could have provided extremely beneficial publicity with a highly appropriate audience. However, nowhere in the area was the name of the center posted.

## Thank Contributors

After every fundraiser, the center should send a thank you to all who contributed to the project — those who planned it and volunteered time to make it happen, as well as those who donated money, goods, or services. The thank you typically includes a final report on the results of the fundraiser — "We reached 110% of our goal," "We were able to finance remodeling of the infant room," etc. Some centers keep donors on their mailing list for the center's newsletter.

# State-of-the-Art Thinking on Parent Fee Policies

**by Roger Neugebauer**

*There are two fools in every market; one who asks too little, one who asks too much.*
— Russian proverb

*No one wants to make foolish mistakes when it comes to the tricky business of setting parent fees. It's a difficult balancing act, setting fees high enough to adequately reward staff and low enough to be affordable to families. It's no less difficult setting fee policies that are flexible enough to meet the needs of parents under stress yet tough enough to protect the center from financial hardship.*

*To give centers guidance on setting fees and fee policies, we analyzed over 150 fee policies submitted to us by members of the* ***Exchange Panel of 200.*** *In this article, we will share some of the best thinking we discovered in these documents.*

## A Bargain at Twice the Price: Fee Schedules

There is a tremendous variation in the rates early childhood programs charge. In the fee schedules we reviewed in 1993, for example, the daily rate for full day care of a four year old ranged from $7.80 to $31.05. These variations reflect regional cost of living factors, staffing levels, competition, family incomes, and outside support.

In the "Fee Relationships in Centers" box (see page 160), you can see the relationship between what centers charge per day for different services. For example, if Your Average Children's Center charges $20.00 per day for full day care for preschoolers, it would charge $25.60 per day for infants, $23.00 for toddlers, and $9.00 for school-agers (after school only). If Your Average Children's Center charges $20.00 per day for full day care, five days a week, they would charge $13.00 per day for half day care and $23.80 for three days a week care.

The relationship among fees for preschoolers, toddlers, and infants is fairly consistent. However, the differential in fees for preschoolers and school-age children attending in the afternoon only varies dramatically.

In some centers, the after-school fees are as little as 15% to 20% less than preschool fees, while in others they are as much as 75% to 80% lower. Part of this enormous differential depends upon whether or not transportation is included in the fees and whether or not the space is being provided at low or no cost. But even when these variables are factored out, fees for after-school care still vary widely. This would seem to indicate that there is not a common agreement regarding the structure and staffing of school-age programs.

## Cheaper by the Dozen: Multi-Child Discounts

There is also wide variation in the discounts centers provide for the second and third children from the same family enrolled in a center at the same time. Slightly under half of the policies we reviewed made no provision at all for multi-child discounts. In those that did, the amount of discount varied from 5% to 50% for a second child, and from 10% to 66% for the third child.

Some of the typical policies:

*If you have more than one child enrolling in the center, you will receive a family discount. The fee for the second child will be two-thirds tuition, and the third child will be one-third tuition.* — **Colorado Springs Child Nursery Center**, Colorado Springs, Colorado

## Fee Relationships in Centers

In analyzing fee variations, we used the daily fees charged for preschool children (three and four year olds) attending full day, five days a week as the baseline. We found that fees charged for different types of services varied on average as follows:

|  |  |
|---|---|
| **Infants** (full day, five days a week) | +28% |
| **Toddlers** (full day, five days a week) | +15% |
| **Preschoolers** (full day, three days a week) | +19% |
| **Preschoolers** (half day, five days a week) | -35% |
| **School-Agers** (before and after school, five days a week) | -26% |
| **School-Agers** (after school only, five days a week) | -55% |

*Parents enrolling more than one child will pay full fee for the youngest child and be given a 10% discount for each other child.* — **Ebenezer Child Care Centers**, Milwaukee, Wisconsin

*There is a discount for the second child in the family of 20%. A third child could attend at a 30% discount.* — **Euclid Avenue Preschool**, Cleveland, Ohio

Most policies are a little fuzzy as to which children get the discount. Some imply that the discount applies to the most recent enrolling child, while a few indicate that the discount is applied to the child(ren) paying the lowest fees.

## To Be or Not to Be: Charges for Absences

The greatest amount of ink in the policies we reviewed was consumed explaining to parents how and why fees are charged even when the children are absent. Clearly, this is an area where centers have experienced a hard sell. Therefore, it is important that the policy statement on absences be clear and persuasive. Here are some of our favorite examples:

*We are prepared for each child each day whether the child attends or not. There will be no refunds for days absent. Each family will be allowed two weeks of absenteeism with no charge.* — **Hester's Creative Schools**, Inc., Greensboro, North Carolina

*Tuition is the same every payment regardless of days missed due to illness or holidays. Think of this as a yearly commitment for your child, not in terms of days of attendance.* — **Breezy Point Day School**, Langhorne, Pennsylvania

*To assure that we can provide the highest quality of services, it is essential that the financial status of the center remain stable. Expenses cannot be sufficiently reduced to overcome losses due to absenteeism. Therefore, we must require that each family financially support space guaranteed for your child(ren) even if the child is absent.* — **Pow Wow Child Development Centers**, Johnson City, Tennessee

*Please note that tuition must be paid in full without deduction for absences. This is because our staffing and other operational expenses are arranged on the basis of fixed enrollment levels and must be met on a continuing basis. Few of the operating costs of the facility are eliminated when a particular child is absent.* — **HeartsHome Early Learning Center**, Houston, Texas

Centers struggle to develop absence policies that meet the centers' needs for financial stability, yet are sensitive to the needs of families. About half the centers provide discounts or credits for family vacations and/or extended periods of illness. Here are some of the clearer, more creative policies on "approved absences":

*Families enrolled in our 12 month program prior to June 1st of that year are entitled to one free week of vacation. This vacation week is not transferable from year to year. . . . This vacation week is offered on a Monday through Friday service week only.* — **Rainbow Express Preschool**, Lansdale, Pennsylvania

*There will be no credit for absences of one week or less. A $45 non-attendance fee will be charged for the second consecutive week of absence and up to four weeks. Your child's place will not be held after the fourth week.* — **Another Generation Preschool**, Sunrise, Florida

*The vacation allotment has already been figured into your child's contract at the time of enrollment. Your child's regular rate remains the same every month, regardless of when he/she goes on vacation.* — **Gretchen's House**, Ann Arbor, Michigan

*If your child is absent from the center three or more days in one week due to sickness, conditions beyond your control, or pre-approved vacation time, your tuition charge will be reduced by 40%.* — **Children's World Learning Center**, Euless, Texas

Some centers waive fees for absences due to a variety of other causes: "in-patient hospitalization," "death in the immediate family," "court-appointed visitation," "center closings due to inclement weather" (only two centers out of the 150+ waive fees for this reason), "parents on maternity leave," and absences "at the request of your doctor."

## Pay Me Now or Pay Me Later: Payment Terms

With the exception of drop-in programs which charge after the fact for actual hours attended, centers today require payment in advance. Not too many years ago, collecting after the delivery of services was common, and commonly this resulted in major cash flow stresses as expenses were incurred ahead of income.

A slight majority of centers require payments on a monthly basis. This clearly is the low-hassle route as it minimizes the number of collections that must be made. It also gives a center considerable flexibility in managing cash flow. Most centers divide the annual fee into 12 equal payments, although a few invoice each month based on days of service to be delivered. In some communities, however, parents cannot afford to pay 30 days in advance. Therefore, a significant minority of centers collect on a weekly basis.

Some centers give parents a choice of paying on a weekly, bi-weekly, monthly, or semester basis. In these cases, discounts are given to those paying on the longer term basis.

Most centers prefer to receive payments by check — some even have policies against receiving payments in cash. Surprisingly, only a small minority allow payments by credit cards.

## What's Up Front?: Registration Fees and Deposits

At enrollment time, nearly all centers collect from parents a registration fee and a deposit. The primary purpose of these charges is to provide security for the center — to assure that parents are serious about enrolling their children and to cover unpaid fees if a child is withdrawn abruptly.

Registration fees, variously referred to as "application fees," "enrollment fees," and "reservation deposits," range from $15 to $75. We found little correlation between registration fees and service fees — i.e., centers charging the highest fees for child care don't necessarily impose the highest registration fees. For most centers, registration fees are a one-time charge. However, many centers, particularly centers operating on a ten month schedule, impose a smaller "reenrollment fee" every year.

Registration fees are typically non-refundable. One center offers a refund if a child or family encounters an "unavoidable crisis" which forces them to withdraw in the first 30 days. Several centers observed that the registration fee was refundable in special instances "at the discretion of the director."

Security deposits (which are seldom referred to as "security" deposits) range from one week's to one month's fees. Most centers ask a two week deposit and many ask for one month. These deposits are refundable if parents comply with center fee policies. For example, typical statements on deposits read:

*At time of registration, a refundable deposit is required. The deposit is refunded if the family gives the director of the center a written notice two weeks prior to withdrawing from the center. If this notice is not received. the family will forfeit the deposit.* — **Early Childhood Options in University Circle**, Cleveland, Ohio

*A two-week deposit is required prior to a child starting the center program, preferably at registration; however, an alternate payment schedule can be arranged if the entire deposit cannot be paid at time of registration. If a child is withdrawn at the end of the program year, the two-week deposit can be refunded. If a child is withdrawing prior to the end of the program year, the two week notice must be given; but the deposit can only be refunded if a replacement can be found within that two week period.* — **The Children's Center**, New Milford, Connecticut

From a center's point of view, registration fees and deposits are necessary for financial stability. However, from a family's perspective, they can add up to a serious hurdle. If a family must pay up front for a registration fee, a one-month deposit, and the first month's tuition, this could run anywhere from $500 to as much as $2,000 per child.

Realizing the cash flow strain this can cause, some centers try to soften the blow. For example, **The Children's Center** (as noted above) offers to work with families to collect the deposit over time. Another alternative, which is used by other services but not by any of the centers whose policies we reviewed, is to ask parents to guarantee their fees with a credit card. In that way, no money would be collected unless the family defaulted on their fees.

With concern, we noted that none of the fee policies we reviewed included a provision for refunding interest accrued on deposits. If your policy does not address this, you may want to check to see if your policies are in compliance with your state's usury laws.

## This Is the End, My Friend: Withdrawals

Most centers spell out fairly specific policies and procedures for withdrawing a child from the program. These policies are designed to give the center adequate notice so it can collect what is due from the outgoing family and find a child to fill the vacancy.

A typical policy:

*Thirty days written notice is required to withdraw a child from the program. This enables the center to process an application from the waiting list. Payment is required for 30 days follow-*

*ing the withdrawal notice, whether or not the child continues to attend the center during that period.* — **Play and Learn Centers**, Fort Washington, Pennsylvania

Many centers also spell out specific policies for temporary withdrawals due to family vacations or illnesses. Often a center will place a child on extended absence on a priority wait list so that he has the opportunity to fill the first vacancy when he is ready to return.

This issue most frequently arises during summer vacation months. Here is a typical way centers deal with such withdrawals:

*Persons signing a 12 month agreement and wishing to withdraw for the summer months of July and August may do so by informing the center director in writing by April 1 and paying the September tuition by June 1. If the child does not return in September, the tuition is forfeited.* — **The Children's Learning Center**, Yardley, Pennsylvania

## All Dressed Up with Nowhere to Go: Late Pick-Ups

This obviously is another hot issue. Clearly, it is a major imposition on teachers when they must wait until a late parent shows up. And it can be anxiety-producing to young children. Most centers have learned that they must be firm about late pick-ups or it quickly mushrooms. Here are some typical policies designed to discourage lateness:

*Since the center closes at 6 pm, a late pick-up charge of $5 will be assessed for each quarter hour or fraction thereof that a child is left beyond 6 pm. This fee is payable immediately to the employee who has remained with your child.* — **Early Explorations**, Encinitas, California

*Once the center closes, the teacher who remains with children is paid directly by the parent. Charges are $3 for the first five minutes and then $1 per minute. All payments are to be made by the end of the week. If payment has not been made, First Care will pay the staff member and will add twice the amount to our statement.* — **First Care, Inc.**, Glen Ellyn, Illinois

Most centers also recognize that being totally inflexible regarding lateness places even more stress on families already operating on the edge. Here are examples of policies designed to be less burdensome:

*You are allowed three late pick-ups with a maximum tardiness of up to 30 minutes.* — **Pulama Keiki Preschool and Daycare**, Lihue, Hawaii

*If you know you are going to be late, call the center. If is difficult for both your child and staff if a child is left at school without knowing why.* — **Child Care Center**, Evanston, Illinois

*No fees for late tuition or late pick-ups. We trust families will cooperate. Families who are habitually late in paying or picking up their children will be asked to find another early childhood program.* — **St. Elizabeth's Day Home**, San Jose, California

On average, centers charge 75¢ per hour for late pick-ups, and most policies provide that payments be made on the spot to the teacher staying with the child. **The Reston Children's Center** in Reston, Virginia, imposes progressively stiffer penalties, with the first lateness being charged at $1 per minute, the second at $2 per minute, and the third at $4 per minute. **The World Bank Children's Center** in Washington, DC, even spells out that it is the "center's front office clock" that will be used to define lateness.

## The Check Is In the Mail: Late Payments

Another chronic problem for child care centers is collections. People in early childhood education usually are not hard-nosed collectors, so late payments can easily get out of hand if not dealt with decisively.

The better fee policies clearly define when fees are due and when payments become late. Typically, monthly fees are due by the first of the month and become overdue by the fifth of the month. Weekly fees are typically due by Monday and are late by Wednesday.

When fees are late, most centers impose late fees ranging from $5 to $20. One center imposes a late penalty of 10%. If parents are late with their fees several months in a row, or fall more than a month behind (two weeks behind in some centers), directors typically reserve the right to disenroll the child (with any deposit being forfeited).

There are two problems with flat charges for late payments. First, once a payment is late and the late penalty has been incurred, there is no incentive for parents to quickly make amends — whether they are one day late or two weeks late, the charge is the same. Charging interest that accrues on a daily basis makes delays progressively more painful.

Second, late charges may violate state usury laws. States limit the amount of interest you can charge for overdue payments. Typically, the limit is in the range of 1.5% per month. Thus, if your monthly fee is $350, the maximum late payment you could charge would be $5. Review your late payment policies in light of applicable state laws!

Here is an example of a late payment policy that clearly has been developed with legal requirements in mind:

*It is further agreed that any payment which is in default shall bear interest at the maximum legal rate and from the due date until paid. The promiser hereby waives demand notice of presentation. In the event it is necessary to refer this matter to an attorney for collection, it is mutually agreed that the prevailing party shall be entitled to reasonable attorney's fees and that the venue of any action shall be King County, Washington.* — **Learning Tree Montessori**, Seattle, Washington

Another way to avoid bad debts is to confront problems early and work out solutions that meet the center's needs as well as a family's. By encouraging families experiencing financial difficulties to let you know in advance about problems they may have with fee payments, you can often work out a schedule of payments that will help the family, but will also assure the center that payments will eventually be made. Here is one center's approach:

*If your family should have an unusual or emergency type financial problem that may effect the prompt paying of tuition, please call or stop by the office and talk with the administrator or bookkeeper. Often we can work something out until the crisis or emergency subsides.* — **Kirkmont Presbyterian Preschool**, Beavercreek, Ohio

## Roger's Rules for Effective Fee Policies

1. **Don't sell yourself short.** The fees you charge should be based on what it costs to provide a level of quality you can believe in. If you set your fees to be in line with what other centers in your community charge, you may or may not be setting them high enough to cover your costs. If you keep your fees low because you fear that parents may not be able to afford higher fees, you are resigning your center to a mediocre level of quality. Rather, you should set your fees based on what quality care costs and then work hard to find ways to offer scholarships and discounts for families who truly can't afford your program.

2. **Don't set policies you won't enforce.** It is easy to write tough policies to deal with all your problems. However, policies accomplish their purpose only if they are enforced by real people in real life. The cleverest late pick-up policy is worthless if you lack the commitment to enforce it, or if you only enforce it intermittently. And if you have one policy you don't consistently enforce, it takes the teeth out of the rest of your policies.

3. **No small print, no surprises.** Parents won't be influenced by policies they aren't aware of. At intake, carefully review in person your key policies on withdrawals, absences, late pick-ups, and late payments so parents clearly know in advance what the rules are. Many centers require that parents sign a statement or contract agreeing to these policies and, in some cases, agreeing that they were briefed in advance about these policies.

4. **Watch the tone.** In writing policies it is natural to slip into a negative, legalistic tone. This often leads to policies that are far from family friendly. One manual, for example, stated that it was including a strict late pick-up penalty because "inconsiderate behavior by parents forced us to do this." Don't lecture or moralize. Show respect for parents, assume their intentions are good, and take their perspective into account. State your policies in straight-forward, non-judgmental fashion.

5. **Write policies well.** Some of the policies we reviewed were so garbled that we couldn't understand them. Many were littered with misspellings and grammatical errors. Some of the policies were far too complex — one center's policies on vacation credits took four pages to explain and a degree in mathematics to calculate. After you have written your policies, have them reviewed by people outside your staff — center parents, your neighbors, your grandmother. Then quiz them to see if they understand your policies.

6. **Attend to presentation.** Just as a delicious dinner can be diminished with lousy presentation, the best policies can be undermined if poorly presented. If no one on staff has an eye for graphic design, see if you can find a volunteer among your parents to give you some layout and design advice, or lean on your printer for a little free consultation.

7. **Help parents find help.** Some of our favorite fee policies included advice to parents on how to qualify for public subsidies. We were truly amazed by how few centers' policies informed parents of how they could save money with the federal child care tax credit. Make your policies useful tools for parents as well as your center.

# NINE STEPS TO HEADACHE-FREE FEE COLLECTIONS

**by Exchange Panel of 200**

> *"When I started out as a director, I was pretty lax about collecting fees. I was uncomfortable with confronting parents. As a result, we always had quite a few parents who were falling behind and inevitably many who left owing us money. Since then, we have adapted strict fee policies and enforced them consistently. Now we collect over 98% of the fees due to us."*

In surveying members of the Exchange Panel of 200, this was a consistent story — fee collections can cause major headaches, but these headaches can be avoided by taking the following nine steps.

## STEP 1

### SPELL OUT FEE POLICIES ON DAY ONE.

When enrolling a new family, explain to parents how the smooth operation of the center is dependent on all fees being paid on time. Fee payment schedules and procedures should be clearly presented verbally and then provided to parents in writing.

This discussion should cover not only when and how to pay fees but also what actions the center will take when payments are delinquent, and what steps parents can take when they know they will have difficulty paying fees in a timely manner.

To avoid future misunderstandings and to underline the importance of these policies, many centers have parents sign a copy of the fee policies at enrollment. Some centers even require a positive credit check before finalizing enrollment.

## STEP 2

### KEEP IN CLOSE TOUCH WITH PARENTS.

Parents in two situations are most likely to fall behind in paying fees. First, there are parents who are unhappy with the program and therefore feel little motivation to pay their fees on time. Second, families who are experiencing financial difficulties may be too embarrassed to ask for special consideration and, as a result, start falling behind.

One of the most effective steps you can take to avoid fee delinquencies is to maintain good relationships with parents. As director, you need to detect signs of disgruntlement early and deal with them before they get out of hand.

Likewise, if a director is on good terms with parents, they will feel more comfortable approaching him when they are in difficult straits. Directors have found that when they show understanding and work out a formal schedule of deferred fee payments at the outset of a problem, they are far more likely to experience success in collecting fees than when they only find out about a problem after parents start falling behind. In addition, working with parents in advance builds loyalty, whereas confronting parents in arrears often leads to resentment.

Some centers have a small scholarship fund so that fees for families in crisis can be partially subsidized for short periods of time. Some centers lower fees temporarily with the understanding (agreed to in writing) that the amount of the reduction will be made up over a set period of time when the crisis is over. Other centers assist families in securing assistance from public agencies, church groups, or other charitable organizations.

## STEP 3

### TAKE THE PAIN OUT OF PAYING.

The easier you make it for parents to pay their fees, the less likely it is that you will run into problems. Here are steps some centers take to ease the paying:

- Send out invoices with stamped return envelopes so parents can write out their checks and drop them in the mail.

- Provide parents the option of paying by credit card.
- Offer a discount for parents willing to pay well ahead.
- Have a locked box with a mail slot in the entryway so that parents can drop their payments when they pick up their children.
- Have a chair and table in the entryway so that parents can sit down and write out their checks.
- Offer a discount to parents willing to sign up for the automatic electronic transfer of fees from their checking accounts.

## STEP 4

### Collect fees in advance.

Today, most centers require parents to pay for service before it is provided. This makes it easier for the center to keep ahead of the curve on payments.

In our recent survey of Panel of 200 members, we found considerable variation in how such advance payment policies are administered. Some centers collect fees as much as two months in advance; some collect fees the first day of every month; some collect fees on Wednesday for the following week's service; and some collect on Monday for that week's service.

From an administrative point of view, collecting fees for a month in advance is clearly advantageous — there are less checks to process and less opportunities for payments to be late. However, for parents who have low incomes or who are paid on a weekly basis, paying a month in advance may be onerous.

Some centers have dealt with this dilemma by establishing a monthly fee policy and then working out biweekly or weekly payment plans for parents who can't pay on a monthly basis.

## STEP 5

### Collect a deposit.

It is now common practice for centers to collect a security deposit equivalent to two weeks' or one month's fees. This fee is held and applied toward a parent's final fee payment. For centers, this deposit provides some assurance that a family will not leave owing fees.

In instituting a deposit, be sure to investigate applicable state laws. Many states require that interest be paid to parents for deposits while that money is in the hands of the organization.

## STEP 6

### Enforce late payment penalties.

Many centers have successfully discouraged late payments by charging penalties. The range of the penalties charged by Panel of 200 members varies considerably. Most typical is a $5 fee for late payments, although some charge as much as $25. Some centers charge $5 for the first delinquency and $10 for each subsequent offense, while others charge a penalty in the range of 1.5% for overdue fees at the end of every month. Still other centers take an altogether different approach, offering a discount to parents who pay their fees on time.

Factors to keep in mind regarding payment penalties include:

- If you enact a payment penalty, enforce it automatically whenever there is a violation. If you enforce it only occasionally, you will send the message that parents don't need to worry about it.
- Consider a progressive penalty. If you have a one-time penalty, once the fine has been levied there is little incentive to pay up. One center surveyed charges $1 for every day a payment is late, another charges $3 every two days.
- Whatever your penalty is, make sure it complies with state usury laws.

## STEP 7

### Act quickly.

Quickness counts. As one Panel of 200 member recounted, "I have found that I can avoid most serious problems by contacting delinquent parents immediately with a gentle reminder. Once a family falls more than a month behind, they seldom catch up."

For a parent who is late in paying only rarely, a written notice of delinquency will probably suffice. However, for chronic late payers, immediate personal contact may be required. Those who make a practice of not paying bills on time are not likely to be influenced by form letters, no matter how threatening. When negotiating with a parent over a late payment, it is important not to show anger or disrespect. Work at maintaining the dignity of the parent, and your own dignity will remain intact.

## STEP 8

### Stop providing care.

The ultimate penalty, when all remedies have been exhausted, is to stop providing services for families who fail to pay their fees. Most centers have seldom, if ever, found it necessary to exercise this option, as its mere threat is often sufficient to produce action.

Panel of 200 members exercise varying degrees of patience before expelling a family. Most centers stop providing care after a parent falls a month behind, many after two weeks, and some as quickly as one week. Ideally, your deposit policy and your termination policy should be coordinated so that the deposit covers any unpaid balances upon termination.

## STEP 9

### TAKE LEGAL ACTION.

If a parent leaves your center owing you money, you have several approaches to consider to collect the balance due — you can continue pursuing payment on your own, you can turn the debt over to a collection agency, or you can sue in small claims court. Of these options, the first is least promising. If you haven't been able to convince a parent to pay while they were using your services, your chances of collecting after they leave are minimal.

Turning the account over to a collection agency is a painless alternative that may yield some results. Of course, you will have to share at least half of what is collected with the agency. And you need to be careful in selecting an agency because they will represent you in the community. If they use inappropriate collection techniques, this will reflect on your center.

Some centers have had success in suing parents in small claims court to recover unpaid fees. The advantage of this approach is that these courts operate informally — lawyers aren't required, both parties simply discuss the case with the judge. Panel of 200 members have had much success in winning judgments in small claims court.

One drawback of this approach is that winning a judgment does not guarantee payment. One director reported that in two decades they have taken parents to small claims court three times, won all three, and then never collected a penny. Other centers have found it necessary to go to the local sheriff to have judgments enforced.

## SUMMARY

While these nine steps may seem a bit on the extreme side, especially in a caring profession, they do avoid considerable grief and loss of income. Centers that consistently enforce the early steps in the process rarely need to resort to the stronger measures. Centers that demonstrate their willingness to go all the way seldom experience losses. Most importantly, centers that work closely with parents, and support them in times of stress, are rewarded with strong parent loyalty.

## CREDITS

The following members of the Exchange Panel of 200 have contributed ideas to this article: **Judy Chosy**, Smoky Row Children's Center, Powell, Ohio; **Rose Dobkoski**, Encompass Child Care, Green Bay, Wisconsin; **Katheryne Chappell Drennon**, Chappell Child Development Centers, Jacksonville, Florida; **Steve and Polly Eberhardt**, FM Kirby Children's Center, Madison, New Jersey; **Jane Flanagan**, Flanagan's Pre-school, Conshohocken, Pennsylvania; **Betsey Hale**, Tender Loving Care, Pocatello, Idaho; **Carla Horowitz**, Calvin Hill Day Care Center, New Haven, Connecticut; **Debra Imbriale**, Dr. Goldberg Child Care Center, Westwood, New Jersey; **Gail Laskowski**, North Pocono Preschool, Moscow, Pennsylvania; **Jill Hardwick Moore**, Early Learning Center, Champaign, Illinois; **Paula Olson**, Hobson Coop Nursery School, Naperville, Illinois; **Julia Rand**, Kids-Play, Inc., Akron, Ohio; **Roberta Recken**; Fruit and Flower Day Nursery, Portland, Oregon; **Leighan Rinker**, Beginnings Child Care Center, Altantis, Florida; **James Robertson**, Plowshares Child Care Program, Newtonville, Massachusetts; **Linda Tynes**, Enrichment Preschools, Nashville, Tennessee; and **Gail and Doug Wiik**, Breezy Point Day School, Langhorne, Pennsylvania.

# Personnel Management

# PERSONNEL POLICIES

## CHAPTER 9

# AN OUNCE OF PREVENTION: HOW TO WRITE AN EMPLOYEE HANDBOOK

**by Joe Perreault and Roger Neugebauer**

*Hopefully your employee handbook will be the best written document you never use.*

*In an ideal world, you and your employees will work in perfect harmony, with communication flowing back and forth unhindered and work being performed in an exemplary fashion. In this dream world, your employee handbook will gather dust on the shelf.*

*In the real world, however, even the best-intentioned director is going to encounter frustration, anger, and disappointment in working with others. You may fail to clearly explain all center rules and procedures to a new employee, or exhibit poor judgment in denying a raise to an old employee. Teachers may arrive late, take shortcuts with health procedures, or make inappropriate remarks to parents.*

*In the real world, you and your staff periodically will need to refer to an employee handbook to resolve disputes and miscommunications. A well-conceived employee handbook helps soften these bumps and grinds by (1) spelling out what types of behavior are encouraged and discouraged and (2) informing employees about their rights and benefits.*

*In this article, we will provide some pointers on overall organizational issues such as content, the development process, design, and writing style of an employee handbook.*

## COVER THE WATERFRONT

An employee handbook should be more than just a listing of rules and rewards. It should serve as a one-stop source of answers to any questions that might arise regarding one's employment. The sample table of contents included in this article demonstrates the range of issues that some centers include in an employee handbook.

In reviewing dozens of personnel documents developed by child care centers, we noted that their most common weakness content-wise was a failure to provide employees with a sense of the history and mission of the organization. At a minimum, an employee handbook should open with a statement of the goals or philosophy of the organization. Such introductory comments provide an important framework for all the rules and procedures that follow.

Manuals that provided the broadest array of information even pulled together descriptions of center routines — procedures for health and safety, problem solving, field trips, emergencies, abuse reporting, grievances, telephone answering, and center visits. Having all such procedures located in one place makes it easier to find than if they are scattered about on various memos and bulletin boards.

## REACH OUT FOR IDEAS

No matter who makes the final decisions on personnel policies and procedures — whether it be an owner, a board of directors, or a center director — these decisions will be improved if ideas from a variety of perspectives are scrutinized during the development process.

Obviously, employees affected by these decisions can offer valuable insights. Their opinions on the fairness of policies and procedures should be considered before decisions are made. In addition, their opinions on whether the writing is comprehensible are important. If procedures are described poorly, they will not be followed. The fact that a procedure makes sense to the person writing it up is not a measure of how well it will be understood by those who have to carry it out.

It is also useful to do some brainstorming about what needs to be included in an employee handbook. You might ask every member of the organization (teachers, substitutes, cooks, secretaries, and janitors) to write down five "what if" questions that the handbook should answer. For example, people might ask, "What happens if I have sick leave left at the end of the year?" or "What happens if a snowstorm hits in the middle of the day?" or "What happens if a newspaper reporter calls for an interview?"

It may also be stimulating to take a look at the personnel manuals of other child care centers. This might give you some alternatives to consider on thorny policy questions, as well as some ideas on content and design. However, you should avoid borrowing policies word for word from other manuals without modifying them to fit your unique circumstances.

You should also have a lawyer review your handbook before it is printed. He will need to check whether your policies and procedures are in compliance with applicable laws. He might also provide useful advice on whether what you propose is too vague or cumbersome, and whether you are leaving yourself enough flexibility.

Finally, you should have someone who knows your organization very well review your handbook to see if it consistently reflects the style and values of your organization. If your management style is firm and authoritative, your employee handbook shouldn't sound like it was written by Abbey Hoffman.

Likewise, if you run a freewheeling, do-your-own-thing operation, your handbook shouldn't read like the Marine Corps' drill sergeants' rule book. The dissonance between what you say in writing and what you do in real life will confuse and frustrate employees.

## Make It User Friendly

Research by the American Management Association found that the major criticisms of employee handbooks by users are problems in finding information, and in understanding what is said. The way a handbook is organized and written will in large measure determine if it helps or hinders the supervisory process. Here are some suggestions for ensuring that the messages you want to convey in a handbook are communicated:

- Start with a detailed table of contents. An employee with a question on reimbursement for travel expenses shouldn't have to wade through the sections on benefits, attendance, and compensation in order to find an answer. She should be able to find out where to look in the table of contents.

- Number pages consecutively throughout. In other words, don't start numbering over with each section (A1, A2, A3 . . . B1, B2, B3 . . . C1, C2, C3, etc.). This type of numbering makes it easy for editors who need to insert frequent updates, but it is user hostile. How can you turn quickly to page E23?

- If your handbook is more than 20 pages long, consider using some device to visually differentiate major sections. Print each chapter on differently colored paper or use chapter dividers with plastic tabs. Find the book *A Sign of Relief* (New York: Bantam Books, 1984) and see the devices it uses to help make its first-aid information quickly accessible.

- Make it easy on the eyes. Have your final product printed on a letter-quality printer. Choose an easy-to-read type font. Leave plenty of white space on every page. If your resources are limited, spend your money on high quality printing rather than on fancy paper or deluxe binders.

- Don't make it cumbersome to read. The personnel documents we reviewed were printed in all shapes, sizes, and formats. Of all of these, two set-ups seemed to work best. Letter-sized sheets, three-hole punched, to go in a three-ring binder were our first choice. In this format, the pages lie flat — you don't have to hold the pages down to keep from losing your place; updated pages can be easily replaced; and you can insert other center documents in the same binder for convenience.

Our second choice was letter-sized sheets stapled together in the upper left-hand corner. This format worked well for shorter documents because pages can easily be turned. If you choose this format, it works best to print only on one side of the page.

- Use consistent formatting for all center documents — parent handbooks, operations manuals, curriculum guides, business plans. All your documents will be easier to access if the same formatting, style, and organizational logic is followed. This also lends a more professional tone to your efforts, and gives them more credibility.

- Write like you talk. Just because you are writing a manual doesn't mean you have to lapse into unintelligible bureaucratize. After you write a paragraph, read it out loud. If it sounds stilted and clumsy as you talk it, that's how it's going to come across to someone reading it.

- Make it lively. Inject zest into your writing by leading off with a punch, attending to the cadence of your sentences, and sticking to active, colorful words.

## Typical Contents of an Employee Handbook

I. **Introduction**
   A. Table of contents
   B. How to use this handbook
   C. How the handbook is updated

II. **Welcome to Hippety Hop Child Care Center**
   A. History of Hippety Hop Child Care Center
   B. Philosophy of Hippety Hop Child Care Center
   C. Goals and mission statement of Hippety Hop Child Care Center
   D. Organizational structure of Hippety Hop Child Care Center

III. **Terms of Employment**
   A. Categories of employment (i.e., permanent full time, permanent part time, temporary part time, probationary, substitute, etc.)
   B. Job descriptions
   C. Hiring (posting vacancies, screening procedures, hiring of relatives, physical exams and other pre-employment requirements, and non-discrimination statement)
   D. Compensation (salary plan, timekeeping, pay periods, pay days, overtime)
   E. Supervision and evaluation
   F. Discipline and termination
   G. Voluntary resignation
   H. Grievance procedures

IV. **Expectations of Employees**
   A. Attendance (hours, absenteeism, lateness, inclement weather days)
   B. Staff development (participation in meetings, planning, and training)
   C. Interactions with children (guidelines for interactions with, and discipline of, children)
   D. Interactions with adults (guidelines for written, in person, or telephone communication with parents, staff, board members, visitors, media representatives, vendors, and public officials)
   E. Problem solving procedures
   F. Health and safety procedures
   G. Field trip procedures
   H. Emergency procedures
   I. Reporting requirements (injuries and accidents, suspicion of abuse, safety concerns)
   J. Other requirements (outside employment, dress, eating, smoking, telephoning, leaving premises)

V. **Benefits for Employees**

   A. Time off (holidays, vacations, personal leave, sick leave, jury duty, parenting leave, disability leave, leave without pay)
   B. Bonuses and awards
   C. Insurance (health, life, dental, Social Security, workers' compensation, unemployment, etc.)
   D. Other benefits (breaks, meals, uniforms, travel reimbursement, tuition assistance, reductions in child care fees, retirement plans, etc.)

- Make the organization abundantly clear. Use headlines and subheads as a road map for the reader to guide him to the exact information he wants as directly as possible.

- Don't sound like a nag. No one enjoys being beat over the head with page after page of rules and restrictions. Set a positive tone by opening with an upbeat summary of the strengths and goals of your organization. Stress the positive environment you are striving to establish for parents, staff, and children. Wherever possible, state your policies and procedures in terms of the positive behaviors to be emulated, rather than the negative behaviors to be avoided.

## Create a Living Document

Writing an employee handbook is hard work, plenty of hard work. You don't want to go to all this trouble if the handbook is going to fall into disuse in six months. Make sure your work stands the test of time by making it easy to update. Here are some suggestions:

- The best way to extend the life of any manual is to develop and store it on a computer. That way, when sections require revision, all you have to do is bring up the portions in question on your computer, make the necessary changes, and print out the new version of the page, chapter, or section.

- Whenever you make a change to the handbook, replace at least an entire page. Don't circulate attachments or appendices intended to supersede sections that remain in the manual. Such updates are messy and confusing.

- Enter the effective date on the bottom of every page in your handbook. This minimizes confusion as to which is the current information.

- Do not include in the body of your handbook information that changes frequently or which is explained in detail elsewhere. Package your handbook in a binder with front and back pockets.

## A Final Caution

An employee handbook is not the cure-all for employee headaches. Having policies and procedures spelled out clearly in writing doesn't guarantee that they will be carried out.

Look upon the handbook as one means of communicating the policies, procedures, and priorities of the center to employees. To ensure that all staff are performing appropriately, you need to supplement written guidance with an active orientation, ongoing staff development, and responsible supervision and monitoring.

A well-written employee handbook is an important cornerstone of an effective supervisory process. It sets sights, clarifies expectations, and establishes ground rules. Hopefully, all other components of the supervisory process will work so well that this handbook will seldom be used.

# Developing Your Employee Handbook: Job Descriptions

**by Joe Perreault and Roger Neugebauer**

*A job description is a simple but complete description of the duties involved in the performance of a particular job. If used properly, a job description can be an effective tool in the supervision of the individual employee. An employee handbook is useful because it covers a wide range of topics the employee needs to know, but a job description zeros in on the one job the employee is most interested in — his own.*

*The job description tells the employee what is expected and to some degree offers guidance on how to perform the job. It can be used to orient a new worker or in the ongoing supervision of an employee. Because the job description is a clear statement of duties, the employer can also use it to hold the employee accountable for performing the job satisfactorily.*

A job description contributes to effective center management in other ways, too:

- Before filling a staff vacancy, it is important for people involved in the hiring process to read the job description to be certain that potential candidates meet all the qualifications the job calls for.
- The job description is used to determine the dollar worth of the job. That is, information about education, experience, and the nature of the work contained in the job description are the basis for deciding the salary of anyone hired to work in the job.
- Some directors review job descriptions as part of a process to develop a yearly training plan for staff.
- Job descriptions can be used to document compliance with state or federal personnel laws.
- Finally, the total set of job descriptions in the center helps clarify roles. A complete list of jobs is a composite of all the major duties at the center, and it ensures that all duties are assigned and helps eliminate overlapping job responsibilities.

## Getting Started

The simplest way to write a job description is to collect job descriptions from other child care centers similar in size and organizational sponsorship to your own. Job descriptions vary from center to center in terms of how much information or how detailed a description of duties is included. Some centers use the employee handbook or a center policy manual to describe job expectations that are common to all employees and do not need to include this information in each separate job description. In other cases, the job description is the only document being used by the center to convey a written message about job expectations so each job description is lengthy.

Another factor influencing the content of job descriptions is the age and organizational maturity of the center. Brand new centers typically have short job descriptions. Usually a new director has little time to write job descriptions and needs just enough information to determine which candidates qualify for each vacancy. A new center usually describes each job in general terms because there is a need for staff to be flexible while the new center gets off the ground.

In a more established center, job descriptions tend to be more specific about expectations and duties. In these settings, the director is more likely to be using the job description as a supervisory tool. Staff may even have requested more detailed job descriptions because clear job descriptions represent a clear and orderly process of assigning duties and evaluating jobs. Assuming that your center has or is willing to develop an employee handbook, the authors believe a well written job description should be from one to three pages in length. It should be fairly detailed, although it is not possible or desirable to identify every single duty that the job entails.

## What to Include in the Job Description

All job descriptions have certain basic elements:

**Job title.** The job title is simply the name your center chooses to give to a certain job or class of job. Most organizations try to develop job titles that are simple and descriptive of the nature of the job. That is why a director of a child care center is called a *director*. It is simple and to the point.

Deciding on the job titles in a child care center is relatively easy. There are some points to consider, however.

Each job title in the center should be sufficiently different from every other job title so the average person can tell the difference. For example, most centers think that the employee in each classroom who has primary responsibility in that classroom has a more responsible job than any other employee(s) who works in that same classroom. Thus the person who has overall responsibility is usually called the *teacher*, *lead teacher*, or *head teacher*, while anyone else in that room is called an *assistant teacher*, *teacher's aide*, or *aide*.

A job title should convey a positive image about the job. Some people think the title *custodian* is a more positive title than *janitor*. Some people think that the title *food service worker* is a more positive title than *cook*. Sometimes the discussion of what title to use seems frivolous. Actually, the debate is almost always based on a sincere attempt to tell an employee his job is important and contributes to the professionalization of the child care industry. Be prepared for a little healthy debate on job titles.

**Job summary.** A job summary is a brief description highlighting the general characteristics of the job. It is usually three to eight sentences in length. It indicates clearly what the employee must do and includes sufficient information to identify the major function and activities of the job. When announcing a job opening, the job summary is often quoted to job applicants or printed in newspaper advertisements.

The job summary usually contains a statement defining who is the immediate supervisor of the employee. For example, the job summary of the cook might say "the cook reports directly to the director," or the teacher aide summary might say "the teacher aide will be supervised by the head teacher." Acknowledging the supervisory line of authority helps the employee know who to go to with a question or how to get clarification about a specific job expectation.

**Description of duties.** The description of duties is a more detailed statement of what is necessary to perform the job. It lists all major tasks, particularly tasks for which the employer intends to hold the employee accountable. Sometimes the description deliberately identifies job duties that may not be pleasant as a way of forewarning the employee that this is a required duty. Sometimes tasks which are performed infrequently but which are important are included.

**Job requirements.** This portion of the job description identifies any qualifications a person must meet in order to be hired for the job. Some qualifications may be determined by the child care licensing standards in your state. Be sure to write every one of these qualifications into the job requirement section. Most qualifications, however, will be determined by you, based on your knowledge of what education, experience, and personal qualities are required to do the job well.

It is important to have education and experience requirements on most jobs, but it is wise to avoid writing requirements in such a way that the position is hard to fill. To avoid this dilemma, job descriptions often specify several different combinations of education experience that could meet the job requirements.

"But it's not in my job description."

Sooner or later an employee is going to make this statement as a way of implicitly or explicitly refusing to perform a task you have asked her to do. Even if the duty is not specifically mentioned in the job description, don't despair. Unless your job descriptions are negotiated as part of a collective bargaining agreement with a union, they need not be absolutely inclusive. It is gen-erally recognized that a job description identifies a range of duties that is normal for that particular job but does not cover every single duty that will be required. The duties listed are illustrative rather than exhaustive.

Many job descriptions include a general statement "and other duties as required" as a way of putting the employee on notice that certain other duties will be required. Whether you add this statement or not, you do have the right to expect an employee to perform duties not specifically stated in the job description.

Furthermore, a child care center is a living organism where conditions change from time to time; and job duties will, of necessity, change, too. An employee who says "It's not in my job description" may be raising a reasonable question about new responsibilities that have been added, making it hard to fulfill all the responsibilities of the job. It may be time to reassess duties and rewrite job descriptions.

On the other hand, "It's not in my job description" may, in fact, be a refusal to perform a duty. If that is the case, a discussion of the language of the job description probably will not help the situation. It is time to step away from the written tools of supervision and use your very best interpersonal skills to find out what really is the problem and how you can work with the employee to change his attitude and motivation.

## Summary

A job description conveys to the employee the importance of the job to the overall success of the center. A job description is a brief statement usually one to three pages long. It cannot convey as much information as an employee handbook, but it is the one written document that speaks directly to an employee about her particular job. For this reason, a well written job description can contribute to effective employee motivation, and it is an important tool in the supervision process.

## Sample Job Description

**Head Teacher**

The head teacher is responsible for the supervision and management of a classroom in accord with the goals and curriculum plan of the Hippety Hop Child Care Center. The principal duties of the head teacher include: develop action plans, carry out activities on a daily basis and evaluate the effectiveness of child development activities, supervise staff assigned to assist in the classroom, ensure the safety and physical well-being of the children, maintain regular communication with parents, and contribute to the effective operation of the overall child care center program. The head teacher reports to the child care center director.

**Description of Duties**

- Plan and conduct an effective child development program to meet the physical, social, emotional, and intellectual needs of each child. This should be done based on the goals and general curriculum plan of the Hippety Hop Child Care Center.
- Ensure that child care routines are carried out in a manner that is prompt, hygienic, and consistent with the good child development principles. This includes routines related to diapering, potty training, hand washing, tooth brushing, eating, napping, and transitioning between activities.
- Ensure the safety of children through constant supervision, effective arrangement of space, proper maintenance of equipment, and regular practice of fire drills and other emergency procedures.
- Operate the classroom in compliance with all child care licensing standards, paying particular attention to ensure that standards prohibiting corporal punishment are obeyed.
- Provide supervision to all staff assigned to the classroom and include staff in planning and child development assignments.
- Create a pleasant, inviting classroom atmosphere in which children feel comfortable and secure.
- Provide positive guidance to help children develop the ability to be self-disciplined.
- Provide experiences which promote individual self-expression in conversation, imaginative play, and creativity.
- Provide a variety of language stimulation activities.
- Provide experience involving thinking skills such as generalizing, classifying, sorting, and problem solving.
- Provide a variety of opportunities to help children develop and understand appropriate relationships with others.
- Ensure that parents receive adequate information about their child's experiences at the center through daily contacts and regularly scheduled parent conferences.
- Maintain written records designed to evaluate each individual child as well as the class as a whole.

*(continues)*

- Contribute to the operation of the center by participating in staff meetings and sharing information gained through attendance at workshops and professional reading.

- Work as a member of a team to ensure continuity of curriculum and a high standard of quality in all classrooms in the center.

## Job Requirements

**Education and Experience**

A college degree in child development or early childhood education and at least one year of experience teaching in a part-day or full-day program for preschool children; or

A college degree in an appropriate human service or education field (e.g., psychology, special education, music, social work) including some courses in child development, and at least two years teaching in a part-day or full-day program for preschool children; or

An associate degree in child development or early childhood education and at least two years experience teaching in a part-day or full-day program for preschool children; or

A child development associate credential and at least three years experience teaching in a part-day or full-day program for preschool children.

**Personal Qualities**

Must be physically able to perform the job of a teacher of young children. Must have a warm, supportive attitude toward children. Must be reliable. Must be flexible in receiving assignments or adapting to changes in the program. Must be willing to accept supervision in order to improve work performance.

# Developing Your Employee Handbook: Leave Policies

by Joe Perreault and Roger Neugebauer

*In developing your center's employee handbook, you are continually striving to reconcile the personal needs of employees with the day-to-day realities of operating your center. No section of your handbook better exemplifies this balancing act than the policies regarding time away from work.*

*All workers need opportunities to restore their physical and emotional health and to deal with personal and civic responsibilities. At the same time, in order to provide a quality service, a child care program needs to maintain a high level of continuity in its staffing. The center's leave policies should, therefore, seek to fulfill employees' need for time off in a way that maintains a consistent staffing pattern.*

*Finding the right balance is not easy. Since no two centers share exactly the same mix of resources, goals, educational philosophies, and management styles, there is no ideal set of leave policies that will work in every center. In fact, in reviewing employee handbooks from over 50 child care organizations in preparing this article, we found over 50 unique versions of leave policies.*

In this article, we will outline for you the many choices that you will need to make — the questions you will need to answer — in molding leave policies to meet the needs of your center. In addition, we will share examples of the varied policies that centers have adopted. (Note: Centers whose leave policies are cited are listed at the end of this article. We have not credited excerpts specifically since, taken out of context, they may not fairly reflect a center's overall posture.)

## Vacation Leave

**How much vacation time should be offered?** Centers typically grant full-time employees between five and ten days of vacation time per year, with the average closer to ten days. The number of days granted increases as employees accrue years of service, usually at the rate of one additional day per year.

**Should part-time and temporary employees be granted vacations?** Some centers grant vacation time only to full-time employees. However, as it is becoming harder to recruit qualified staff, more centers are offering such benefits to help attract solid part-time staff. Often vacation time for part-time staff is granted in proportion to hours worked. For example, a teacher working half time would be granted one half the vacation time of full-time teachers.

**When can vacation time be taken?** For new teachers, there is often a probationary period during which vaca-tion time cannot be taken. Typically this waiting period is 90 days but extends as long as six months in some centers. In most centers, new teachers still accrue vacation credit during this period.

Most centers require that time taken off for vacations be approved in advance, and some even restrict the times during which these vacations can be taken. Some examples:

*Vacations shall be planned for the mutual convenience of the staff and the center. In deciding preferences for vacation time, the primary consideration will be the necessary coverage of the center's services. Otherwise, position and seniority of service, as well as mutual agreement among staff, will be considered.*

*Requests for vacation should be made at least one month in advance in writing. These requests will be granted on a first requested, first received basis. No more than two employees in each group may take a vacation at any one time. Employees are encouraged to spread their vacations throughout the year and cooperate in planning their vacations so that everyone may use the periods best suited to their needs.*

*Vacation must be taken at Christmas time or between June 1 and August 15.*

**Can vacation time be used in advance or, conversely, not used and carried over from year to year?** Most centers require that vacation time must be earned before it is used and that it must be used in the same year that it is earned. Some centers allow time to be carried over, and some even provide that employees can be paid for unused leave upon termination. Frequently, directors have authority to grant exceptions in unusual circumstances. Some examples:

*Vacation leave is to be utilized on a yearly basis based upon anniversary of employment. Leave not utilized by anniversary date must be forfeited.*

*Unused vacation leave may be carried over to the following year to a five day maximum. Accumulated vacation pay, up to a limit of two weeks, may be paid upon termination of satisfactory service if notice is received two weeks in advance.*

**How will vacation time be calculated?** To avoid confusion and disputes, the method of calculating how much leave an employee has earned should be spelled out clearly. It is recommended that this method be as simple as possible. (These points apply equally to all forms of leave.) For example, some centers grant one half day of leave at the end of each pay period. Others credit the employee with one or two days of leave at the end of every full month of service completed by the employee.

## Sick Leave

**How much time off for sickness should be offered?** Centers typically offer full-time employees from seven to twelve days of sick leave per year. Some offer sick leave to part-time employees on a prorated basis. One center offers sick leave to all employees ". . . at the rate of one hour earned for every 21 hours worked."

**For what purposes can sick leave be used?** Most centers restrict the use of sick leave to instances where the employee is physically unable to perform. Other centers allow it to be used more flexibly. Some examples:

*Sick leave may be approved for personal illness or injury, for an employee who is required to take care of an illness in one's immediate family, or for an employee who has been exposed to a contagious disease which might endanger fellow employees or children.*

*Sick leave may be used for illness of the employee, illness of a minor child residing in the employee's home, for a doctor's appointment which cannot be scheduled during off hours, in the event of a death or serious illness in the immediate family, and for absence due to pregnancy.*

**How will the appropriate use of sick leave be verified?** Many centers insert language and procedures into employee handbooks to protect against the abuse of sick leave. Many require an employee to notify one's supervisor in advance of using sick leave and to provide a doctor's verification of illness for extended periods of leave. Some examples:

*An employee who will be absent shall notify the director before scheduled starting time on the first day of illness (or the night before if possible) and each successive day. Request for sick leave for a medical, dental, or optical examination shall be submitted to the director as far in advance as possible.*

*Approval of sick leave is not automatic. An employee requesting sick leave must notify his/her supervisor of the nature and expected duration of the illness or injury. Employees must keep their supervisor informed about their condition and the probable date of their return to work. Employees who do not keep their supervisor so informed are subject to disciplinary action or termination.*

*Any employee missing work for health, mental, or emotional reasons can be required by the supervisor to supply a doctor's statement confirming the condition and/or the recovery. The supervisor, not the doctor, has the responsibility and authority to determine if an employee is sufficiently recovered to return to work and if the doctor's written confirmation is sufficient to justify sick leave being authorized.*

*Any unapproved sick leave taken on the day preceding or following a center holiday shall result in no pay for the holiday itself.*

*It must be expressly understood that excessive time out for sickness hurts the quality of our program and, therefore, cannot be permitted. If, in the director's judgment, an employee's absences are excessive, counseling, probation, and/or termination with cause will result.*

**Can sick leave be used in advance or, conversely, not used and carried over from year to year?** Most centers provide the director with the authority to grant sick leave in advance when circumstances merit. In addition, most centers allow employees to accumulate sick leave and carry it over from year to year (this practice is more common than allowing employees to carry over annual leave). The amount of sick leave that can be accumulated ranges from 20 to 132 days, with most falling in the 30 to 50 day range. About half the centers surveyed pay staff members for unused sick leave upon termination.

## Personal Leave

In recent years, there has been a movement toward personal leave. This is a catch-all leave category that employees can use for personal reasons that don't fit into any other leave categories. Some centers grant vacation leave, sick leave, and personal leave; other centers grant vacation leave and personal leave; and some centers have gone so far as to consolidate all leave into one overall personal leave category designed to cover the entire range of an employee's needs for time off.

Proponents of personal leave argue that it sets up a more professional relationship with employees. They are no longer required to play the *calling in sick* game, or dip into precious vacation leave, when what they really need to do is care for a sick family member, entertain visiting relatives, meet with their lawyer, or take a day away from work to restore their emotional energy.

Opponents, on the other hand, argue that loosening leave policies in this way encourages employees to take more days off. These fears tend to be misplaced. Personnel studies have consistently shown that the amount of time off that employees take is much more dependent upon their satisfaction with their work environment than it is upon the strictness of the leave policies. In other words, employees who are unhappy with their jobs will take as much time off as they can, and employees who are highly motivated will take little time off.

## Leave Without Pay

**Under what circumstances will an employee be granted leave without pay?** There are two general categories for leave without pay — voluntary and involuntary. Voluntary leave without pay applies when an employee needs to take time off for an extended period and does not have enough vacation or sick leave to cover this time. In this category, centers typically include leave for serious illness, pregnancy, education, or other urgent personal reasons.

Involuntary leave without pay is charged when an employee is absent from work without authorization (for example, if an employee failed to show up for work and didn't call in ahead of time as required by center policies) or when the director determines that the employee is unable to carry out his/her responsibilities (for example, if an employee was ill or injured).

**What restrictions apply?** Many centers restrict leave without pay to full-time employees who have been with the center for a minimum period of time. This time period ranges from six months to two years. Centers usually require that the employee request such leave 30 to 180 days in advance in order for the center to find a replacement. Some centers place a limit of anywhere from three months to two years on the length of a leave of absence.

**What benefits does an employee retain while on leave without pay?** In most cases, employees on leave without pay status do not accrue annual leave or sick leave, nor do they earn credit toward length of service salary increments. Some centers specifically state that an authorized leave without pay will not constitute a break in service in determining continuing eligibility for seniority and the retirement plan.

Some centers maintain the employee's medical insurance coverage up to three to six months, while others require that the employee bear the full cost of premiums in order to maintain coverage while on leave. An employee placed on leave without pay due to a job-related disability may be eligible for compensation under the Workers' Compensation Act.

**Is the employee guaranteed a job upon return?** Centers tend to be guarded in the language they use in this area:

*If during your leave of absence it becomes necessary to fill your position, we will make every effort to return you to a similar position at a similar hourly rate. However, we cannot guarantee that a position will be available.*

## Other Forms of Leave

**Jury duty.** Centers allow employees time off with pay when they are summoned to serve on a jury. A typical policy reads:

*Employees called for jury duty will be paid the difference between their regular base salary and the amount received as compensation for jury duty. A copy of the summons must be presented to your supervisor as soon as it is received. The center reserves the right to request an exemption from jury duty for an employee. No leave is charged for jury duty.*

**Military leave.** Federal law requires that employers provide employees leave for certain forms of military service. One center's policy:

*Employees who present official orders requiring attendance for a period of active military duty will be entitled to military leave with full pay, less that paid for military service, for a period not to exceed two weeks.*

**Bereavement leave.** Most centers grant employees up to three days of leave with pay to attend the funeral of an employee's or spouse's immediate family member (spouse, children, sister, brother, parent, grandparent).

## A Final Caution

The purpose of this article was to outline the range of choices you should address when developing your center's leave policies. Since labor laws vary in all states and localities, this was not intended to provide legal advice. Before adopting your policies, you should have your lawyer review them in terms of applicable local, state, and federal labor laws. While centers have a great deal of latitude in the policies they develop, in certain areas — such as maternity leave, disability, jury duty, and military leave — legal restrictions will apply.

## Sources of Examples

Central Learning and Day Care Center, Memphis, TN; Child Care Center, Evanston, IL; Child Inc., Austin, TX; Children's World Learning Centers, Golden, CO; Day Nursery Association, Indianapolis, IN; Episcopal Child Day Care Centers, Jacksonville, FL; Handicapped Children's Association, Johnson City, NY; Ithaca Child Care Center, Ithaca, NY; Jane Addams Day Care Center, Toms River, NJ; Janet Rich Day Care Center, Rochester, NY; Mercy Child Development Center, Des Moines, IA; Mercyhurst Child Care Center, Erie, PA; Moffett Road Baptist Child Development Center, Mobile, AL; Neighborhood Centers Association, Houston, TX; Nursery Foundation, St. Louis, MO; Ohio State University Child Care Center, Columbus, OH; Playcare Child Care Centers, Rochester, NY; Presbyterian Child Development Center, Wellsboro, PA; Rainbow Chimes, Huntington, NY; Reston Children's Center, Reston, VA; Summit Child Care Center, Summit, NJ; The Learning Center, Jackson, WY; and United Day Care Services, Greensboro, NC.

# Developing the Employee Handbook: Grievance Procedure

by Joe Perreault and Roger Neugebauer

*At the heart of every grievance are fundamental questions about the rights and responsibilities of employment.*

*Usually when a group approaches an employer with a complaint, they are unhappy with a center-wide decision or with a broad question of the employer's attitude to employees.*

Hippity Hop Child Care Center used to be such a nice place to work. But lately things haven't been going so well. Several employees seem to be unhappy. As it turns out, they have different complaints:

Mary took two days off to attend a funeral. When she returned, the director told Mary that the days off would be without pay. There is no funeral leave policy at the center; vacation leave must be requested two weeks in advance. Mary thinks the policy is unfair since she had earned several vacation days.

Anne, an aide at the center, has a new lead teacher who has been critical of her work. Recently, the lead teacher told Anne that they will no longer meet together to plan. From now on, the lead teacher will plan and conduct all teaching activities. Anne will be responsible for clean up after activities and supervision of the children during meals, naptime, and bathroom breaks. Anne has always been treated as an equal by other lead teachers and resents this new definition of duties.

Lynne, Karen, and Jackie are teachers in the toddler group. They are feeling a growing resentment toward the teachers in the preschool group. From their perspective, the preschool room is consistently given more supplies and equipment than the toddler room.

## Why a Grievance Procedure Is Necessary

Hippity Hop may sound like a director's nightmare. But keep in mind, it's a nightmare for the employees, too. At the heart of every grievance are fundamental questions about the rights and responsibilities of employment:

- Does an employee have a right to question the decision or actions of the employer?
- Are there some decisions an employee is automatically entitled to question and others that an employee can question only if the employer grants permission?
- If a grievance is of a very serious nature, should an employee be given an opportunity to communicate directly with the owner or board of directors rather than through the normal chain of command?
- If an employee has a right to express a grievance, how can the employee be given a "fair" hearing and protected from being punished for exercising that "right"?

Most employers recognize there are times when an employee's grievance needs to be heard. It may be that a decision affects the employee negatively and the employer is not aware of the full implication of the decision. It may be that an individual supervisor is acting contrary to the intention of the organization. Yet, how does an employer acknowledge these potential failings of the organization and give the employee a chance to petition for a change? The employer must make an enlightened decision, one that spells out the rights of an employee to air a grievance and which set limits on the kinds of grievances and the extent to which a grievance will be heard. These issues should be clearly spelled out in the center personnel policies in a section entitled "Grievance Procedure."

## What Is a Grievance Procedure?

A grievance procedure is simply a written statement informing employees that they have a right to express complaints and a right to expect the employer to review and respond to the complaint. The grievance procedure is generally designed to address two basic issues:

1. **Interpretation of personnel policy.** No matter how clear the personnel policies, there are always judgment call situations, as well as new situations which do not seem to fit the written policies. Because these possibilities exist, the grievance procedure usually allows an employee to seek interpretation or review of personnel policies when necessary. In some grievance procedures, the language is more open-ended, allowing the employee to question other kinds of center decisions which have a clear relationship to the employee's specific job.

2. **Employee-supervisor conflict.** Incidents of sharp disagreement between an individual employee and the immediate supervisor occur in child care as in all work settings. A grievance procedure accepts that reality and explains how an employee can appeal a decision or action of the supervisor to a level of supervision higher in the organization. If there is no clear way to express a grievance, there is a danger that a weak supervisor becomes a petty dictator and the director or owner will not be aware of the problem.

Acknowledging the employee's right to file a grievance also implies an employee responsibility. The employee should use every means possible to resolve the conflict directly with the supervisor before resorting to the center's grievance mechanism. In some personnel policies, the employer includes a description of the purpose and process of supervision as a way of emphasizing how disagreements should be resolved routinely.

For a sample grievance procedure and statement of supervisory policy, see "College Avenue School Grievance Procedure" (page 184) and "The Supervisory Process" (above).

## The Supervisory Process

Employees at the Hippity Hop Center can expect consistent, direct, and constructive information from their supervisor about their work. Supervisors are responsible for helping staff develop the skills and abilities necessary to function successfully in their positions.

After completing the probationary period, employees are assumed to possess the basic skills and qualities necessary for their position. The goal of supervision for these employees is to assure that these skills and qualities are reflected in day-to-day activities, to promote personal and professional growth, and to insure that the center's policies and program philosophy are effectively carried out.

The basic elements in the supervisory process include:

- A clear statement of what is expected through job descriptions and written center policies.
- An opportunity to participate in establishing individual goals.
- A regular mechanism for reviewing information about job performance, including regular meetings with the supervisor or an annual written employee evaluation.

## What Should Be Included?

The grievance procedure is basically the description of a process: It should state who can initiate a grievance. Most centers allow any employee to initiate a grievance, although some centers limit this right to full time employees (as opposed to part time or probationary employees). Some centers allow the employee to file the grievance verbally but most require a written statement before the grievance can be formally reviewed. Describing who should receive the grievance is important, especially in larger child care organizations. Should it be the educational coordinator, director, owner, board of directors, or who?

The next issue is how the complaint will be reviewed. Usually a hearing is held within a specified number of days. The employee is allowed to present the grievance fully. In supervisory disputes, the supervisor is also present and is given equal opportunity to explain the situation. Some grievance procedures stipulate that only the employee is allowed to be present at the hearing, while others allow the employee to have witnesses (for the purpose of presenting information) or an advisor present.

In some policies, the employee is responsible for proposing a "remedy." That is, the employee must describe the change or action which needs to occur in order for the grievance to be resolved.

The procedure should also assure prompt employer action by stating when a decision on the grievance will be made. Usually the hearing is held within one or two weeks after the grievance is filed, and a final decision about the grievance is made as soon after the hearing as possible.

Finally, the grievance procedure may offer a means of appeal. For example, in some centers the director is expected to make a determination on all grievance issues. If the employee is not satisfied with the director's decision, the employee may then appeal to the board of directors (or owner).

## Handling a Group Grievance

If a grievance is filed, it will most likely arise from the interpretation of personnel policy or a supervisory dispute. But what about the example of Hippity Hop where a group of teachers have a grievance? Hopefully, these circumstances will never occur at your center, but you do need to think about how to handle such a grievance.

Usually when a group approaches an employer with a complaint, they are unhappy with a center-wide decision or with a broad question of the employer's attitude to employees. There are lots of possible examples. The issue could be salaries, staff scheduling, a decision to open or close a particular classroom or program, or favoritism of one group of staff over another by the director.

Often when grievance procedures are established, the owner or board does not envision using them to cover a group situation. Although the interpersonal dynamics of a group grievance are complex, the principles for handling the grievance are similar to any other individual grievance and can be used to give the group a fair and objective hearing.

Some centers address the issue of group grievances in personnel policies, although not necessarily directly. These centers include statements which talk about communication, decisionmaking, or even conflict resolution. For example, they might describe the purpose of staff meetings, how often staff meetings are held, and what role staff is expected to play. They might also discuss how staff are involved in making certain kinds of program decisions related to curriculum, equipment, or other decisions affecting daily work or the long term success of the center. These statements show staff that they will be listened to. They describe the appropriate time and place to raise questions or state disagreements. The more these mechanisms are provided, the less likely that the center will be caught by surprise some day with a group grievance.

## College Avenue School Grievance Procedure

**Initiation of Grievance**

- Any permanent employee or group of employees (group may include probationary employees).
- Any parent or group of parents with a child or children presently enrolled in the school.
- Any employee or group of employees of College Avenue Baptist Church.

The complaint must be submitted in written form and signed by all complainants. It must be specific and with documentation of complaint or grievance and with a list of steps already taken to solve the problem.

**To Whom Complaint is Addressed**

- The initial grievance must be presented to the director in writing. A reasonable time for solution of a grievance must be agreed upon by the director and complainants. A third and neutral party may be called upon to negotiate this time line.
- If no resolution is forthcoming, the grievance may be taken to:
  — the Minister of Education of College Avenue Baptist Church and/or
  — the Children's Committee of the Christian Education Council of College Avenue Baptist Church.

Either of these parties must respond in writing to the complainants within one working week with an outline of their planned course of action. This may include follow-up study, conference with director, or a specific action.

**Follow Up**

- The written grievance must be responded to with a written proposal for solution and within a period of 15 working days.
- All staff involved in this procedure are guaranteed no undue retaliatory action.

**Grievances That Apply to This Procedure**

The following are complaints that are valid grievances:

- Breach of licensing regulations.
- Detriment of health and safety of children and/or staff.
- Breach of fair labor standards.

*Reprinted from* ***Staff Handbook*** *of the College Avenue School in San Diego, California — Kathryn Prickett, director.*

# Recruiting and Selecting Staff

## Chapter 10

# Selection Interviews: Avoiding the Pitfalls

by Roger Neugebauer

*The interview is the most frequently used — and most frequently misused — staff selection tool in child care. Nearly all child care centers use interviews as a major part, if not the only part, of the process of evaluating the employment suitability of job candidates. Indeed, the interview can provide an employer with useful insights on the qualifications of prospective employees. However, the interview is the most complex of all selection techniques. Centers employing it can encounter any of a number of pitfalls. This article will outline the most frequently encountered pitfalls and will describe techniques for avoiding them.*

## Pitfall #1

**Attempting to assess too much.** The interview can be an effective technique for assessing some — but not all — job qualifications. While a candidate's performance in an interview may give a reliable indication of her skills in relating to adults, it sheds little light on her ability to relate to children. To rely solely on an interview to evaluate the suitability of a candidate is placing too much faith in this technique. It is put to best use when used in conjunction with a variety of other techniques such as observations and reference checks.

The interview is most effective in assessing the knowledge, attitudes, and personality of candidates. Even in these areas, however, the interview can only be effective if it is used to assess candidates in terms of a limited number of job qualifications. When interviewers are asked to assess candidates on more than a half dozen factors, they begin to suffer from information overload, and the reliability of their judgment begins to plummet (Shouksmith). Therefore, it is critical at the outset to isolate no more than six key job qualifications to be probed in interviews. It may be helpful to review the full list of qualifications for a job and to distinguish between those which are essential and those which are nice to have but not critical. Then, during the interview, concentrate attention on the "must have" and not on the "nice to have" qualifications (Jensen).

## Pitfall #2

**Attempting to interview too many candidates.** The interviewers had just completed interviewing ten candidates for the position of director in two nights. When they met to select the best candidate, they spent most of their time not objectively weighing the qualifications of each candidate but just trying to unscramble who said what. This incident is not atypical. The more candidates interviewed, the harder it is for interviewers to retain distinct impressions of each of them.

There is, on the other hand, a real advantage in seeing as many candidates in person as possible. This lessens the likelihood of a candidate with the ideal personality for a job falling through the cracks simply because she lacks skills in putting together an impressive resumé. One way to solve this dilemma is to converse with all candidates who possess the minimum job requirements in a brief (five to ten minutes) screening interview.

The purpose of this interview is to outline the nature of the job — its duties, rate of pay, hours, etc. — to the candidate and to secure from the candidate clarification about information on her resumé. From this personal interchange, the interviewer should be able to eliminate from further consideration all candidates whose preparation and/or personality is clearly unsuitable, as well as those who are no longer interested in the job described. The interviewer should also be able to spot those candidates with unimpressive credentials who nonetheless appear to possess the appropriate personality and temperament for the job.

Information overload can also be minimized through judicious scheduling. To give interviewers sufficient opportunity to digest and retain information about candidates interviewed, no more than three interviews should be scheduled for one sitting. Allow 45-60 minutes for each interview, with breaks of at least ten minutes between interviews.

## Pitfall #3

**Failure to establish rapport.** At the outset of an interview, a candidate is likely to be uptight and nervous. Until he relaxes and feels comfortable with talking frankly, he will not present a realistic impression of himself.

Certain details can be arranged to help relieve tension prior to the interview. When the candidate arrives for the interview, he should be made to feel immediately welcome either by having someone greet him or by having a notice posted indicating he is in the right place and that someone will come and get him when it is time for his interview. If there is time, the candidate might be offered a tour of the center.

The candidate should be personally escorted into the interview room and introduced to the interviewers while they are standing. If there is more than one interviewer, the candidate should be seated so that he can easily see all the interviewers, yet not feel like he is on display himself. With one interviewer, both parties should be seated in comfortable chairs, preferably not on opposite sides of a cluttered desk. After the candidate is seated, there should be a pause which allows him to catch his breath and get his bearings.

To help the candidate *warm up*, an interviewer should get the candidate talking with some easy, non-threatening conversation or questions. This should not be small talk about the weather as this will heighten the tension as the candidate waits for the ax to fall. The interviewer could start with some point of common interest from the resumé — "I went to North Dakota State also. How did you like it there? — or with a series of specific, easy-to-answer questions. Do not rush this phase of the interview as the interchange will not be open and frank until rapport has been established. Then once you are ready to begin in earnest, brief the candidate on what the interview will be like so he knows what to expect.

### Examples of Questions Found to Be Effective in Interviewing for Teaching Positions

How would your discipline of a five year old differ from that of a three year old?

What is the difference between directing children's play and facilitating it?

What would you do when a parent tells you to discipline a child in a way you believe to be wrong?

How do you handle the child who bites? . . . who doesn't like you? . . . who is experimenting sexually? . . . who is abused at home? . . . who is ridiculed by other children?

How do you handle transitions? . . . nap time? . . . lunch time?

What kinds of additional training will you need to be successful as a teacher?

What qualifications do you have which will contribute to your success as a teacher?

What would you like to learn to do that you cannot do now?

What aspects of teaching do you like most? . . . least?

Where did you gain your most valuable experience for teaching?

In your last job, when did you feel most effective? . . . least effective?

What work would you like to be doing five years from now?

What do you expect your references to say when we call them? Why?

## Pitfall #4

**Having too many interviewers.** The most common pitfall in child care selection interviews is the *Spanish Inquisition* syndrome — bringing candidates before a panel of four to ten inquisitors. It is hard enough for a single interviewer to establish rapport with a candidate. When there are two or more interviewers, it becomes much more difficult, and when there are four or more, it is usually impossible. As a result, there is "a loss of sense of intimacy, a diminution of empathy, a confused interviewer, and a consequent inhibition of communication" (Lopez). In a panel interview setting, it is also much more difficult to proceed in an organized fashion, to carry out a line of questioning to completion, and to ask spontaneous follow-up questions.

There are, nonetheless, occasions when, for either political or programmatic reasons, it is necessary to have more than one interviewer. An alternative to consider in these situations is the serial interview whereby one candidate is interviewed by a number of interviewers individually in sequence. Each interviewer covers different job qualifications or aspects of the job. In the end, all interviewers meet to share their impressions and findings.

## Pitfall #5

**Failure to provide enough structure.** Research on selection interviews has uncovered many shortcomings of informal, unstructured interviews: They are highly inconsistent and highly susceptible to distortion and bias (Pursell); the same materials are not covered for all candidates; interviewers tend to talk more than interviewees; and interviewers tend to make their decisions early in the interview (Stewart). In addition, interviewers tend to spend more time formulating their next question than listening to what the candidate is saying (Goodale).

For best results, most personnel experts recommend a well-prepared for, semi-structured interview format. Prior to the interview, the key job qualifications to be probed in the interview should be identified, and one or two open-ended introductory questions should be developed for each qualification. After the interview has progressed through the rapport-building stage, the interviewer should introduce a job qualification with one of these open-ended questions, and then follow up with specific spontaneous questions which seek clarification of issues raised in the candidate's initial response.

## PITFALL #6

**Being swayed by general impressions and stereotypes.** Interviewers often are struck by a single aspect of a candidate's personality or background or by a single statement and allow this single factor to determine their overall assessment of the candidate. For example, the physical appearance of a candidate, especially one who is very thin, fat, short, tall, good looking, well dressed, or poorly dressed, will often color an interviewer's judgment about a candidate (Jensen). Interviewers also tend to be influenced more by unfavorable information revealed by a candidate than by favorable information; and the earlier in the interview the unfavorable information is disclosed, the greater its negative impact (Stewart).

To keep such biases and distortions from undermining the selection process, interviewers need to be encouraged to concentrate on gathering specific pieces of relevant evidence about candidates' qualifications, rather than general impressions. One way to do this is to spend some time prior to the interviews reviewing the job qualifications so that interviewers are well aware of what information to probe for. A second approach is to provide training on effective listening skills (see Nichols).

## PITFALL #7

**Failure to record information.** By the end of an interview, interviewers generally have already forgotten 50% of what was said. By the next day, 85% has been forgotten (Nichols). Therefore, even though it may be somewhat distracting or discomforting to the candidate, it is critical to record information during the interview.

The best method is to tape record interviews. When doing this, tell candidates at the outset that the interview will be taped and for what purpose. A candidate may feel uptight with being recorded, but generally after the first few minutes everyone tends to forget about the recorder and converse normally.

The next best method is to take notes onto a format prepared in advance which provides spaces for each qualification. When taking notes, however, it is necessary to avoid telegraphing what you want to hear by stopping to write whenever the candidate says something of interest. Instead, the interviewer should make a mental note of valuable points and record these when attention shifts to another interviewer or point in the discussion. In either case, after the interviews, the interviewers should take a few minutes to record their reactions.

## PITFALL #8

**Asking discriminatory questions.** Interviewers are barred by equal employment opportunity guidelines from asking questions that can lead to discrimination on the basis of race, religion, age, sex, marital status, arrest record, handicaps, or national origin. Questions such as the following are not legal:

- Do you live with your parents?
- Who will watch your children while you work?
- How do you get along with other women?
- Do you have any physical disabilities?
- Where were you born?
- Have you ever been arrested?
- How would you feel about working with people younger than yourself?
- Does your religion prevent you from working weekends?

This does not mean, however, that no questions can be asked about these subjects. They can be asked in reference to bona-fide occupational qualifications. For example, although a candidate cannot be asked "Are you a U.S. citizen?," the question "Can you, after employment, submit verification of your legal right to work in the United States?" is acceptable (Jensen). Centers which are uncertain about the legality of their selection procedures should contact their state's Equal Opportunity Commission.

## PITFALL #9

**Failure to sell the organization to the candidate.** Interviewers can become so preoccupied with assessing the candidates that they may not be aware of the impression they are making on the candidate. It is counterproductive to select the best candidate in the batch if that candidate is so turned off by the image the

## More Dos and Don'ts for Selection Interviews

- To encourage a candidate to be open, praise her for answering questions fully.
- To be sure you understand a candidate or to probe for more details, restate what she told you, but in an expectant tone — "You say you have had difficulty working with aggressive parents. . . ."
- Use silence to draw candidates out. People tend to be uncomfortable with silence in a conversation. When a candidate stops talking but has not supplied enough details on a point, don't rush to fill the void. Wait for the candidate to speak up.
- Don't do all the talking. The more you talk, the less you learn.
- Don't ask questions which are answered in the resumé.
- Don't telegraph what you want to hear by describing the philosophy of the center at the outset or by asking leading questions — "Do you believe in open education?"
- Don't reveal your reactions or feelings either through gestures, expressions, or remarks. This may cause the candidate to clam up or tailor her remarks to suit you.
- Don't debate issues with the candidate or seek to give advice.
- Don't ask trick questions. You cannot encourage the candidate to be open and frank if you are being devious yourself.
- Don't rely on general questions about teaching philosophies. How a candidate describes her approach in theory and how she performs in practice often bear little resemblance. Specific situational questions — "What would you do if . . ." — may be more instructive.
- Don't allow the interview to get sidetracked on an interesting but non-job-related tangent.
- Don't let the candidate take control of the interview.
- Don't allow the candidate to sense your impatience.

organization conveyed during the selection process that she turns down the job offer.

Throughout the interview process, all candidates should be treated warmly and professionally. Appointments should be clearly made and adhered to. Candidates should be made to feel welcome when they arrive and respected when they depart. Having a well-structured interview not only yields more information about the candidates; it also shows the candidates that they are dealing with a professional organization and that the organization takes the job under consideration seriously.

Near the end of the interview, time should be set aside for describing the organization and the job to the candidate. Questions from the candidate should be welcomed at this point also. In describing the job and answering questions about it, however, care should be taken not to oversell it. If there are negative aspects of the job (low pay, a split shift, or a recent history of staff turmoil), these should be discussed with candidates. The interview should be viewed as the first step in negotiating a contract. A new employee's commitment to the center may be seriously undermined if the center can't deliver on promises made or expectations aroused in the interview.

At the close of the interview, the candidate should be told the process that will follow and when and how she will be notified of the decision. Unless a candidate clearly lacks some basic job qualification, no indication should be given at this time about whether or not the candidate is likely to get the job.

## References

Goodale, J. G. (July 1981). "The Neglected Art of Interviewing." *Supervisory Management*.

Jensen, J. (May/June 1981). "How to Hire the Right Person for the Job." *The Grantsmanship Center News*.

Lopez, F. M. (1965). *Personnel Interviewing: Theory and Practice*. New York: McGraw-Hill Book Company.

Nichols, R. G. (November 1980). "Improve Your Listening Skills." *Exchange*.

Pursell, E. D. (November 1980). "Structured Interviewing: Avoiding Selection Problems." *Personnel Journal*.

Shouksmith, G. (1968). *Assessment Through Interviewing*. Oxford, England: Pergamon Press, Ltd.

Stewart, C. J., & Cash, W. B. (1974). *Interviewing: Principles and Practices*. Dubuque, IA: William C. Brown Company, Publishers.

# Observing Teaching Candidates in Action

by Roger Neugebauer

*"We found that everyone loves children in the abstract, but will they love them eight hours a day in the classroom?" Thus Nancy Alexander explained the reason her center in Shreveport, Louisiana, instituted a policy of observing all teaching candidates before they were hired. At first, when teachers were selected strictly on the basis of their performance, she found that there often was a wide variance between how individuals described their child caring skills and how they actually performed in action. By observing likely candidates working in a center, Nancy Alexander was able to much more reliably assess them. As a result, she nearly eliminated hiring mistakes.*

This experience is not unique. Most child care centers and nursery schools now include observations as an integral part of their selection procedures. To provide readers with ideas on how to conduct an effective observation, *Exchange* surveyed eight child care organizations which have experienced positive results with this staff selection technique. The results of this survey are summarized below.

## Before the Observation

An observation can provide a reasonably reliable forecast of a candidate's likely performance if it is properly prepared for. This preparation should center around the identification of what you hope to learn about candidates in the observations.

You probably can generate a long list of qualifications you would like to find in your ideal teaching candidate. Some of these, such as *level of training*, can be reliably measured by a resumé review; and others, such as *knowledge of child development*, can be assessed well in interviews. Many others, especially those relating to personality traits and teaching style, can only be assessed by observing the candidates in action. Identify about a half dozen of these qualifications or traits that are most critical to the accomplishment of your center's curriculum goals. Don't attempt to assess too many or your attention will be dispersed in too many directions to effectively measure anything.

For each trait, identify some specific indicators to look for during the observation. For example, if an important qualification is *positive interaction skills*, helpful indicators of this might be *maintains eye contact at the child's level* and *listens patiently to children*. At the end of this article are listed 29 such indicators that the surveyed directors found to yield insightful data on the candidates.

Thoroughly discuss the list of qualifications and their indicators in a staff meeting. Make sure that anyone who will participate in observations understands what to look for. Make any revisions that come out of this discussion for improving or clarifying the list. Then print it up in a checklist format to hand to observers before each observation to be sure the traits and indicators are attended to.

With this degree of preparation, observation can be a more reliable staff selection technique than the interview. It would be desirable to be able to observe all candidates who meet the center's minimum training and experience standards. This might enable you to identify candidates who don't have impressive formal qualifications and who do not express themselves skillfully in the interview but who, nevertheless, are naturally gifted in interacting with children. Unfortunately, observations are time consuming and a bit disruptive to the flow of classroom activities. Therefore, most centers tend to use observations sparingly — only observing the top two to five candidates from the interviews. If this is the approach your center must take, follow your hunches from time to time. Include among those to be observed candidates who didn't fare well through the interview stage but who you have a gut feeling may do well in practice.

Bea Ganson, a director in Abilene, Texas, is able to get a maximum use of observations by requiring all candidates to serve as paid substitutes before they can be hired. Thus she can observe many candidates over a period of time before making selection decisions.

## During the Observation

One teaching candidate, upon inquiring at a center about a job, was immediately assigned for his *observation* to care for 15 children in the nap room by himself. Many of the children could not be comforted by this *stranger*, and most of the others took the opportunity to test him. The result was chaos. The candidate had a miserable experience and never considered returning to that center, and the center didn't get the foggiest picture of what the candidate was like as a teacher.

For the best results, the center should schedule observations carefully. Centers have found that observations should last at least two to four hours to get a reliable picture of a candidate. Shorter periods do not allow candidates enough time to get acclimated.

Time of day is also critical. Nancy Alexander schedules interviews during a free play period rather than a group activity time so that candidates are more likely to get involved with the children rather than sitting back and observing an activity. Peg Persinger, a director in Eugene, Oregon, tends to assign candidates to the most challenging groups to really test their skills. Most directors also assign candidates to work with teachers they would actually be working with if they were hired, so that the current teachers can assess whether this is someone they would be comfortable with.

In any event, try to have all candidates for a single position be observed by the same staff people. Barbara Day, a director in Edmonton, Alberta, recommends scheduling all observations for a single position in the same week so that the memories of the first candidates won't fade by the time the last ones are observed.

For the candidate to present a true picture of herself, she needs to be as relaxed and comfortable as possible. For the candidate to be interested in working for the center, she needs to have as pleasant an experience as possible. Both these requirements call for the director to take specific steps to put the candidate at ease about the observation and to ease her into it gently. Start by telling all candidates from the beginning that they may be expected to participate in an observation. When scheduling interviews, tell them exactly what will be expected of them, how long the observation will last, and what the class is like that they will be in.

On the day of the observation, the director should escort the candidate into the room and introduce her to the teaching staff and the children. At this point, Barbara Day leaves the candidate, and the supervisor (or head teacher) leads the candidate on a brief tour of the room.

The candidate's involvement in the activity of the room should be allowed to expand gradually. Most centers allow for a 30 minute *warm-up* period in which no official observations are made. Candidates under observation at the North Pocono Preschool in North Pocono, Pennsylvania, are encouraged by director Gail Laskowski to start their four hour observation by observing what is going on for a while, then working with the teachers for a while, and finally working on their own when they feel comfortable doing so.

Many centers ask the candidates to plan and present a specific 20-40 minute activity for the children. Karen Miller, Evergreen, Colorado, has found that if some of the less experienced candidates are not given such a specific task, they tend to sit around, giving no hint of their potential. Staff should go out of their way to cooperate with the candidates in providing materials and assistance for the activities. Give the candidates every opportunity to do their best.

During the observation, it is best not to heighten their sense of being followed by all eyes. The director should not pull up a chair and formally observe the whole period. Gail Laskowski simply makes a point of being in the area with a purpose often during this period. The teachers should also go on about their business and not take notes or talk about the candidate in her presence.

On the other hand, the staff should not ignore the candidate but should be alert to her performance. While observers should take note of a candidate's general demeanor, they should most keenly observe how he handles specific incidents. The data they should be trying to collect is not general impressions but as many small pieces of evidence as possible — especially pieces of evidence relating to the indicators identified beforehand.

## After the Observation

There should be a definite closure to the observation. The director should return to the room to retrieve the candidate, or the head teacher should thank her and ask her to report back to the director. At this point, Barbara Day invites the candidate to share her reactions. These reactions can be very revealing. The candidate's impressions of specific incidents can disclose a great deal about her knowledge and philosophy. For example, the candidate may talk about the *misbehavior* of a certain *troublemaker* when in reality this child's behavior was well within normal bounds. This may be a clue to you that either this candidate is not tuned in to child development or else that she may have a more restrictive approach than you prefer. If the candidate shares only general reactions, it may be useful to prod her memory with open-ended statements about specific incidents.

After the candidate leaves, all those who observed her should take the first opportunity to record their reactions. Gail Laskowski has all observers rate the candidate on a selection criteria matrix and then include some narrative comments.

Then, as soon as possible, while the experience is still fresh in everyone's minds, the observers should meet together to share their assessments. The director should steer this discussion away from generalities. One way to do this is to read through the list of traits and their indicators. For each indicator, ask observers to describe specific incidents where this indicator was demonstrated in a negative or positive way. If the indicator relates to the candidate's success in integrating children into the group, the observers would describe a candidate's various attempts to do so and the outcome of the attempts. By reviewing as much specific evidence as possible, the observers will eventually have a reasonably solid basis for deciding whether or not to hire the candidate.

Observations can add a strong element of reliability to staff selection decisions. However, this technique does not guarantee that all mistakes will be avoided. Charlene Richardson, director of the Child Development Center in San Diego, places new employees on a three month probationary status. During this period, she carefully monitors their performance using the same procedures as in the selection observation. Such pre- and post-hiring observations do require considerable effort on the part of staff members; but in the long run, they assure a more consistent program for the children.

## What to Look For

The directors surveyed for this article identified the following performance indicators as ones they have used with the best results. Overall, the indicators that were cited most frequently related to the way the candidates relate to the children. As Nancy Alexander explained, "We want to see if they treat them as sweet cutesies or as thinking human beings." In this vein, the most popular indicators were tone of voice, eye contact, body language, and listening skills.

**Physical Appearance and Personal Attitude**

- Does she use positive body language?
- Is her tone of voice appropriate?
- What are her facial expressions as she interacts with children? Is she animated, angry, or "bored to tears"?
- Does she maintain eye contact at the child's level?
- Does she dress appropriately, "as if she expects to sit on the floor and have tempera paint spilled over her?"
- Does she convey an overall sense of enthusiasm?
- Is she having fun or is she tense and resentful?

**Interaction Skills**

- How does she react when children approach her?
- How does she answer children's questions?
- Does she listen carefully and patiently to what children tell her? How does she signal interest in their communications?
- Does she appear comfortable talking to children?
- Does she serve as a good language model?
- How does she help integrate children into the group?

**Direction and Control**

- Does she maintain control? How?
- How does she show tolerance for child-like demands, impatience, mood swings, self-assertion, negativism, exuberance, angry feelings, tears, and testing behavior? How does she guide children at such times toward adequate coping and socially acceptable behavior?
- Does she allow children to resolve their own conflicts?
- How much are children allowed to diverge from her directions?
- If a child has lost control, can the candidate accept the child's feelings and help him regain control? Does she retaliate or offer alternatives? Does she tear the child down or build him up?
- Does the candidate use a positive approach — "Blocks are for building." — or are her directives negative — "Don't throw that block."

**Teaching Skills**

- Is she actively engaged or merely babysitting?
- If she brings in an activity, is it appropriate for the age group she is working with?
- Is she able to follow a schedule while still remaining flexible?
- Is she able to adjust to unforeseen incidents?
- How well does she hold the interest of the children?
- How well does she arouse children's curiosity?
- Does she move around the room to help children and show interest in what they are doing?
- Does she provide an appropriate balance of unstructured and structured activities?
- Does she demonstrate a willingness to learn herself? Is she open to new ideas? Does she ask questions about particular activities and materials?
- Does she work comfortably with other staff in the room?

# SUBSTITUTES — WE'RE THE REAL THING!

by Bonnie Neugebauer

*The life of a substitute is not an easy one — the very word suggests someone who is not the real thing, someone we must put up with for the interim. The word, usually shortened to "sub," even sounds awful — rather short and low.*

*Yet it would be hard to come up with a person more sought after than a reliable, effective substitute care-giver. Early childhood programs will desperately search — even beg, borrow, or steal — to find a substitute. But on the job, substitutes often feel neglected, even exploited.*

As I worked as a substitute teacher in early childhood programs, I discovered that I sometimes felt most valued before I entered the center. An affirmative response to a plea for help resulted in all sorts of joyful, enthusiastic gratitude — I was made to feel important and helpful. After I began my day's work, I often found myself abandoned, saddled with the worst jobs, and floundering to really take care of children with minimal information and support.

To give a sub his or her due, I would like to focus attention on some often forgotten truths about life as a substitute:

## A SUBSTITUTE IS A REAL PERSON

This seems like a pretty straight forward point; but if you are not given a bathroom break, then someone has forgotten that you are real. It's awkward to be unsure, fumbling; but there is much that a center can do to enhance the effectiveness and foster the sense of belonging of the substitute.

## A SUBSTITUTE HAS REAL NEEDS

**A substitute needs to understand the context.** No one works effectively in a small, isolated space. Without some sense of the big picture, all of us tend to lose our sense of direction — we feel lonely, unsupported, forgotten.

A first time substitute needs a tour of the center. Show her where different age groups meet and how various rooms and spaces are used. Point out the bathroom. Introduce him to other staff, making special note of people he can turn to for specific kinds of help. Help him see how all the pieces of your program fit together. This is also a good time to fill a substitute in on the center philosophy and a few important rules.

*Leslie, the director, mails a substitute packet to me, with the appropriate forms for me to fill out. She asks me to arrive 15 minutes early so that I have time to ask questions and read the routine and instructions for individual children before I begin working.*

**A substitute needs to feel competent in his working environment.** Have someone orient the sub as to where supplies and equipment are located. Clearly define procedures for using and returning toys and equipment. Outline expectations for end of the day clean up. Look at the center from the substitute's point of view when labeling mats and storage and designing charts for routines.

*A good way to tell if a classroom is efficiently planned and well labeled and organized is to watch a sub at work. How many fumbles to diaper a child? How many false starts in the search for scissors?*

**A substitute needs to feel the flow.** Map out the routine for the day so that the substitute feels on top of things rather than scrambling behind. Children usually have a pretty good sense of the flow, so they can be helpful. However, a substitute who is dependent on the children for basic information feels vulnerable.

*In this program there are nappers, half nappers, and no nappers, which I learn the hard way. My assignment is to get about 18 children to sleep. The mats are already positioned, thanks to the departing teacher. As the children come in from outdoors, we sort through pillows and blankets, do the shoe and bathroom routines, read stories, and relax to soothing music. Just as peace is settling over the room, Paul begins to cry, "I'm a half napper. I'm not supposed to come in yet."*

**A substitute needs to know how to prepare.** Before the sub arrives, she should know exactly what to bring.

*A group of 25 three and four year olds is having lunch outdoors in the sunshine. It's a beautiful day, and the children are enjoying all the nooks and hidey places in the bushes for small lunch groups. In this program the children bring their own lunches — no one told me to bring one, so I hungrily join the conversation at the picnic table.*

Once you have given instructions, don't change the rules.

*I am asked to bring an art activity for pre-kindergartners, but find myself in the three year old room. I don't know where any of the supplies are. Jonathan wants to paint, but I can't find any paper. Finally I discover a stash of old letterhead and tape a sheet to the easel.*

*Several times I arrived at a program at the appointed day and time to the surprise of the director who had forgotten that she had hired me.*

**A substitute needs to know your expectations.** Clearly define your expectations for how the substitute will function. Make it easy to fit in and feel competent.

*The infant room enjoys a ratio of one caregiver for three babies. Kay is in charge with Rose as her assistant. So I am assigned to care for Caitlin, Graham, and Zoe. Special instructions for each baby are posted near the daily chart. Nap times are staggered, so that most of the time I am watching only two babies. All time not spent in routine care is to be spent playing with the babies.*

**A substitute needs to feel respected.** Once you have hired her, support her in doing her job.

*Nap time. I tell the children that I will read them a story, we will listen to a tape, then we will drift off to sleep. After nap time I promise to read another story. I'm just to my favorite part of* ***Where The Wild Things Are*** *when Pauline walks by. "That's not how we do it! Play a record for them."*

**A substitute needs to be identifiable.** Make sure that everyone else knows that the sub is a sub. Knowing this will enable parents and staff to adjust their expectations and respond supportively. No one wants to be put in a position of feeling embarrassed or inadequate.

*I am asked to arrive during nap time, so I sit quietly in a room of sleeping children. It's hard to stay awake. I can hear noises overhead as other groups are working away. A teacher comes by to check that all is well. A mother arrives to pick up Gina. I don't know the names of these children! I don't know where Gina is and I can't find her.*

Post a notice on the door identifying the substitute — who she is replacing and the hours she will work. Be sure she wears a name tag that clearly identifies her to parents as a substitute — this enables parents to refer to her by name.

**A substitute needs to belong.** This is one of the trickiest issues to resolve. A substitute is a temporary part of your program so the issues of belonging are different. There is no history, no peer group (in a way), no future.

Somehow you must make the substitute feel that there is a place for him in your program — even if for only a day. Being sensitive to his needs, clear and generous with your introductions, and supportive in your expectations will help you accomplish this goal.

If you are nurturing a long term relationship with a substitute, consider ways to include her in your staff meetings, training sessions, and staff and parent social occasions. The more a substitute feels part of your program, the more committed she will be to continuing her role or becoming a permanent employee.

Part of belonging in an early childhood program is being able to call children by name. Devise a way of helping a substitute learn the children's names quickly. The best idea I've encountered is to put masking tape name tags on all the children before the sub arrives. Include the children who will be on the playground if that is to be part of the day's duties. Children expect immediate name recognition; having to refer to a wall display just doesn't work.

And perhaps most important and most often overlooked, give your substitute time to say goodbye. Often subs just disappear during nap time or into another responsibility. Making sure that substitutes mark their place with children bestows respect on the feelings of both.

**A substitute needs to be a *sub*-stitute.** A sub should not be expected to replace a regular teacher in knowledge and ability to perform without time to learn and observe.

Do not ask a sub:

- to diaper a child who is wary of strangers until they have had a chance to get to know each other,
- to take all responsibility for playground duty unless that is the job you have outlined beforehand,
- to take the children outside the center unless accompanied by regular staff,
- to administer medications,
- to work all day without a break,
- to perform all the onerous tasks — unless you never want to see him again,
- to know policies and procedures if you have not given her the opportunity to learn them, or
- to instantly take the place of a regular staff member in knowledge and ability to perform.

## A Million Dollars for Sam's Other Shoe!

*an excerpt from the diary of a substitute*

3:00 PM. My afternoon assignment is the Panda Bears (the three year old room). I walk into a blur of activity. Several children on risers are watching a squirrel's antics through the window. One boy is clutching his blanket and crying, "Daddy, daddy!" One child in the midst of it all is sleeping.

Brenda, the morning Panda Bear teacher, announces, "Hi friends, this is Bonnie. She's going to be with you for the afternoon. Isn't that great?" No one responds. Brenda ticks off the names of the children: "This is Caitlin, and Quinn, Drew, Renko, Sam, and Emily (sleeping) . . . oh, you're not going to remember them anyway!" She pulls me to the side. "This is Drew (the boy with the blanket). He's new and having a rough time. And you have to watch him. He's always wandering off. Usually I find him near the bathroom. And this is Jennifer, our teen aide. Sometimes she needs guidance in how to talk to the children. So keep an eye on her, too."

Brenda shows me the schedule:

| | |
|---|---|
| 3:00 to 3:15 | wake up |
| 3:15 to 3:30 | snacks |
| 3:30 to 4:00 | stories |
| 4:00 to 5:00 | playground |
| 5:00 to 5:30 | free play / parents begin pick up |
| 5:30 to 6:00 | clean up |

"Oh, and by the way, I can't seem to find Sam's other shoe." Brenda looks at her watch and rushes out the door.

I offer to put the laces back in Caitlin's shoes, but she refuses help, not at all sure about me yet. The cook brings in squares of cornbread and cups of milk. There aren't enough for everyone so Jennifer goes off to find more. Snacks are quickly devoured and everyone is asking for more. Emily sleeps on. Quinn is struggling with her shoes and socks. Renko insists on another piece of cornbread. Drew wants more milk. There isn't any more milk. I help Quinn with her socks. Jennifer shoves Emily gently with her foot, "Wake up, Emily." Emily sleeps on. Sam is walking around with one shoe. As his weight shifts from one foot to the other, he notices: "Shoe?" He looks at me, and I quickly scan the room for hiding places.

I put out Duplos for the children who have eaten, clear some of the mess away, give my piece of cornbread to Renko, and look around for Drew. He's not there. Jennifer is sent to find him, as I begin to search for the shoe. Caitlin and Sam are squabbling over the Duplos because they each want to use the same piece for the tail of an airplane. Jennifer returns with a crying Drew. I hold Drew in my lap, arbitrate the Duplos dispute, and give Jennifer verbal instructions to take over the shoe hunt.

Emily finally wakes up and looks around, bewildered. Jennifer helps her with shoes and socks and gives her her snack. Drew joins the Duplos play. I look for the shoe.

It is now 3:45. We must be back in by 5:00 for parent pick up. Sam cannot go out without his shoes. The kids are getting antsy. I find two empty glue containers, a bag of paper scraps, and a stash of raisins, but no shoe. Jennifer is reading to Emily. I'm getting frantic. "Forget story-time, Jennifer! Help me find the shoe!" My perspective is slipping.

I see a certain look in Renko's eye and feel an instinctive need to involve the children in the hunt. "Does anyone have an idea where Sam's shoe might be?" Jennifer: "I'm sure none of them would hide it; and besides, they're not smart enough to do something like that." I send Jennifer to the office to ask for a spare shoe of any sort so that we can go outside and begin to rally the children to the bathroom. Drew (surprise) is already there.

Now no one wants to go either to the bathroom or to the playground. The office can find no shoe. Okay, so we won't go outside. Jennifer plays Duplos with some children, and I get out **Caps for Sale**, one of my favorite readalouds. Jennifer comes over to listen. "What caps are on top of the grey caps?" I ask. Jennifer responds: "The red ones." "Oh, you've heard this story before, Jennifer. Does anyone know where the monkeys are?" Jennifer: "In the trees!"

Every now and then someone stops by to see how I'm doing, asks about Sam's shoe, looks around a bit and leaves. We're obviously into problem ownership. So we spend the time until 4:40, now and then looking for the shoe. I get out my collection of jar caps and bottle lids and the children enjoy sorting through and playing with them. Jennifer decides the shoe could be in the sleeping mats so she sorts through all the mats, piling them all in the center of the room as she does so. While she is looking, Drew makes another trip to the bathroom.

We get out markers and scissors and glue. For a few minutes, everyone — even Drew — is happily absorbed in artistic endeavors. The stack of paper quickly disappears, so I lift the roll of butcher paper in the corner — and out rolls Sam's shoe!

Hurray! We have ten minutes of outdoor time left. To hurry them on with coats, I suggest we make a list of things we'll look for outside:. "Let's see if we can find a slug, and what else? A worm, a round stone; and anything else? A puppy." Jennifer: "We'll never find all of those things." As I button Drew's coat, I easily notice that he has had a bowel movement. "Jennifer, do you want to diaper Drew or take the others outdoors?" She pats me on the shoulder, "He's all yours."

## Prepare a Substitute Information Packet

If possible, mail this packet to the substitute so that he can come prepared. Include the following information:

**Expectations —**
- Hours and days to be worked
- Pay rate and how payment will be made
- What to do upon arrival — whom to report to, where to stow personal items
- Breaks — when, where, how
- Age group of children

**Basic rules —**
- Smoking
- Telephone privileges (include staff phone number if applicable, when phone can be used, any special dialing procedures, whether incoming calls can be accepted and where messages will be posted)
- Food (any special foods that may or may not be eaten) also times when it's acceptable to eat

**Guidelines —**
- Discipline — time out/cool off, etc.
- Drop off and pick up procedures
- Health issues, list of children with special health considerations — food allergies, medications (who and what to administer)
- Curriculum — which activities are fixed and which are open to choice

**Responsibilities —**
- Daily routine
- Any activities or materials that the substitute should bring/prepare
- Clean up — how to know when work is done

**Directions —**
- How to get to the center by car or bus
- Which door to enter
- Where to park

## A Substitute Has Hidden Potential

Just like everyone else, a substitute will need to talk about her experiences in your program. It's been a stressful day and whether it went well or not, your substitute will be eager to share her adventures. Whom she chooses to talk to and what she chooses to say is up to her but not totally out of your control.

**Think of a substitute as a marketing tool.** Whether you like it or not, your substitute is going to be doing some word of mouth marketing for your program. Armed with the information he has gathered — facts, impressions, experiences — he will be talking about you. Make sure that your substitute feels part of your program so that he feels invested and speaks from that perspective. If you give a sub the opportunity to share his experiences and insights with you, he leaves your center feeling valued and will be more likely to put the best light on things.

**Think of a substitute as a short term, inexpensive consultant.** During her day in your program, the sub will have gathered all sorts of impressions. Because her perspective is different, she will see different things. Some of her observations will be valuable and some will be irritating. But all of her observations will give you information about your program.

*Anika's parents arrive during their lunch hour to be with their six month old. She is sitting in an infant seat, playing with the mobile overhead. Her parents crouch down beside her and talk to her. They play with her fingers, but they do not pick her up. Why?*

You might even offer to pay a substitute for an additional half hour of time to ensure that she will fill out a questionnaire about her day. Or, if time is possible, pay a substitute for a few minutes of direct feedback in conversation with you.

Of course, the substitute carries her own baggage, so you must keep this in mind. Some comments will point to bias, inexperience, or attitude — you can put these into perspective and still find the insights and truths in this one person's feedback.

**Think of a substitute as a resource.** If you know of special interests and talents, encourage the substitute to share them in the classroom. She might be a gardener, a storyteller, a carpenter, or a musician. This is a wonderful opportunity to bring new experiences to the children; and it gives the sub a special way to become part of things.

A substitute usually has knowledge about other programs in the community. Ask her how other centers solve particular problems and accomplish specific activities. Encourage her to share her valuable expertise.

## A Substitute Responds to Love

If you love your substitute, make it as easy as possible for her to be effective. Prepare a substitute information handbook (see box), orient her on site, give her support on the job, and let her know that her good work just might have saved your day. A good substitute is indeed the real thing — a necessary and valuable component of a quality child care program.

| KEY: |
| --- |
| G — Good |
| A — Average |
| P — Poor |

# Observation and Evaluation

## Substitutes or Prospective Staff

Applicant's Name ____________________

Observer's Name ____________________

Age Group ____________________

Date ____________________

| **Observations of applicant** | **G** | **A** | **P** | **Example** |
| --- | --- | --- | --- | --- |
| Punctuality | | | | |
| Demonstrated initiative | | | | |
| Aware of children's abilities | | | | |
| Aware of health and safety | | | | |
| Ability to set limits | | | | |
| Calm in transitions | | | | |
| Encouragement of self-help in children | | | | |
| Warm, friendly, fair with children | | | | |
| Communication with adults | | | | |
| Respectful of individual children | | | | |
| Group management | | | | |

| **Indicate your conclusion about applicant** | | | ✔ | **Example** |
| --- | --- | --- | --- | --- |
| Experienced and good with children | | | | |
| Book knowledge but no experience | | | | |
| With training, will be good with children | | | | |
| Not what we are looking for | | | | |
| Need to see more | | | | |
| I would like to work with this person | | | | |

✍ Additional comments:

# Hiring the Right Person

by Annette Cannata Heng

*Hiring the right teacher doesn't have to be challenging if it's done with calculated care. In fact, it can be most rewarding and can be as simple as knowing your ABCs — Applications, Behavior-based interview, Conversation . . . .*

Part of being an early childhood leader is filling vacant teaching positions. For some, it happens more often than desired, but the fact remains that selecting the right teacher is critical for your center. The parents, children, and staff depend on your ability as a leader to select the right person.

We cannot always predict when an opening is going to occur, but we can prepare ourselves so that when it does happen, we know what steps to take. In other words, you can never sit back and get too comfortable when it comes to retaining a *fully staffed* center. Life involves change and certainly a child care center is no exception.

## STEP 1
### Applications

Once you receive a candidate's resume or application (whichever applies) it is important that you review it carefully. There are minimum requirements for each state's regulations, but coupled with that are the requirements set by you and your center.

- What is the person's background, education, and work experience? For example, if you are hiring a teacher to work with two year olds, you may want to review the candidate's work experience and identify what age children they have worked with in the past. If they have worked at a summer camp with school-age children, you may want to consider if this would be a good match. However, you can think bigger than just that one position. Could this applicant with school-age experience fit in another room by replacing a currently employed teacher? Could that current employee match your needs in the two-year-olds' room?

Making the right match is extremely important to a successful hire. Will this applicant, based on their background, education, and experience, match the needs of the particular program you are hiring for? These are things you should be thinking about when reviewing a person's resume. Does this mean the person cannot match well with different experiences? Absolutely not. In fact, they may enhance the program. These are questions you should ask and jot down in preparation for the interview:

- What is the mix of children in this classroom?
- What are the needs, desires, and challenges?
- Who will the person work with?

## STEP 2
### Behavior-Based Interview

When it is time to interview your candidates, it will be important to ask open-ended questions that require a behavioral answer.

- Tell me about a time when . . .
- Describe specifically how you have . . .
- Give me an example of a time when . . .
- Describe your role in . . .

For example, let's say that in the two-year-olds' classroom you have a few very demanding parents whose expectations for a quality program are high. The parents are very vocal with their concerns and desires. You may ask the question, "Give me an example of a time you dealt with a demanding parent." Or, let's say that the two-year-old children of this particular classroom are very high energy and spirited. (Have you ever seen the two-year-olds' room not have high energy and spirited children? Anyway, this is for example's sake!) "Tell me about a time that you worked with a group of *high energy* children."

As you ask these questions, you should listen for specific examples and if you do not get them, re-ask the question and patiently wait. You may need to probe for details by asking additional or follow-up questions. Behavior-based questioning will help you identify whether the applicant has certain qualities that will strengthen your program or conversely, uncover weaknesses that can ultimately hurt your program.

#### Conversation Is the Secret

It is really important to put the candidate at ease by having a conversation versus a drilling session. Remember that in interviews you should do only 20 percent of the talking, and the candidate should do 80 percent. You will find that as you talk *with* the candidate, they will tend to be more relaxed. A relaxed candidate is more inclined to allow their *true self* to come through. If you think about any relationship that is long lasting, the start of that relationship was during a comfortable conversation.

You may discover through a more casual approach that the candidate may tell you things that are potential *red flags*. Red flags are those things that you hear a candidate say that may be a potential problem. For example, a candidate may reveal a past experience that does not demonstrate their ability to work well with others.

If the position that you are hiring for requires teamwork and collaboration, this red flag may be an indicator for you to further explore teamwork with the candidate. Often red flags lead to validation of a concern. The idea here is to try to discover these indicators early on, prior to hiring. If you choose to hire a person with red flags, then you can also form a training plan for the candidate, that specifically addresses their potential weakness. (This however, is only recommended if the red flags are minor in nature.)

If you decide during your one-on-one conversation with a candidate that he or she may work well with your center, then you can move to the next step. (This next step is highly encouraged.)

## STEP 3
### Demonstration

Once you narrow it down to the final candidate or candidates, it is important that you see them in action. Have them interact with other teachers in your center. How do they present themselves? Are they friendly? Do they ask questions? Do they seem interested in the teachers? Leave the candidate alone with the other teachers and have them share experiences. (Prior to this happening, you should advise your current staff that you value their opinion and will be bringing the candidate into their classroom to observe and interact.) Watch to see how they react to the children. Do they smile? Get down on the children's level? Offer to get involved?

The key to the retention of any employee is making every attempt to connect them with the center.

The time spent talking, interacting, and observing will be time well spent. Over the years as I have interviewed teachers about their longevity in a center, the question I ask is, "Why have you stayed here at this center for so many years?" The answer most commonly given is "because I have a connection here and it is like a family."

During the demonstration stage, your staff and the candidate are connecting. The time spent during this most important stage of the interview is critical to you in making an educated decision.

## STEP 4
### References

The final and most exciting stage . . . your decision to hire. Obviously, for any potential hire you must obtain references. In today's world, references are becoming more difficult to obtain; however, the children in your care deserve nothing but the best. Checking or confirming references is very important to ensure that the person has done what they said they did (verification of employment). It is important to ask:

- Have you observed this person working with children? (Verify they have experience working with children.)
- Would you rehire this person? (Verifying quality of work.)

When interviewing a candidate, you might want to ask questions to cover these categories as outlined in the *Interviewing Guide* utilized by Children's World Learning Centers:

- Action orientation — task- or process-related
- Innovation
- Integrity
- Practical learning
- Problem solving
- Rapport building / sensitivity
- Reliability
- Planning / organization / work management
- Teamwork
- Knowledge of early childhood education
- Tolerance for stress
- Safety mindedness

## STEP 5
### Educated Offer

After following all the steps above, ask yourself two questions:

1. Would I entrust my own children to this person's care? (If you don't have children, think about a child you care about — niece, nephew, cousin, friend.)

2. Would I want to work side-by-side with this person?

By asking these two questions, you are further validating your decision to hire. If the answer to either of these questions is no, then you may want to seriously question your decision to make an offer. We can't always know if we have hired the right person, but we owe it to the center's reputation, the staff, the children, and ourselves to do our homework completely before the decision is made.

# Hiring and Retaining Male Staff

by Bruce Cunningham

> *"We advertise for teachers all the time but no men ever apply."*
> *"We have one male teacher but I'm afraid he'll leave our program."*

Directors who make these comments acknowledge the challenges in hiring and retaining male staff. While there are relatively small numbers of well-qualified men who can teach young children, there are also effective ways of recruiting them.

Hiring men requires a change in recruitment strategies, and retaining men requires a change in workplace practices. Yet an intentional approach to recruiting and supporting male staff can be successful — and the results can make your program more diverse and responsive to the needs of young children.

## Advertising for Men

Due to the cost of classified advertisements, most programs keep the wording to a minimum, speaking only to the most important or required qualifications of education and experience. When additional descriptive words are used, it is to acknowledge something about the nature of the work — such as using the word *energetic,* which speaks to the physically demanding nature of the work in the most cheery way possible.

Occasionally, other descriptors are used, and these most commonly include *nurturing, caring, affectionate,* and *gentle.* These are important characteristics, and most programs have many staff who exemplify them. However, if you are interested in attracting men and diversifying the characteristics of your staff, consider using words that are more attractive to men. These words include *physically active, outdoors, fun,* and *socially important work.* Many men think in terms of this last phrase to rationalize the low wages they receive.

Advertising directly for male staff with the words *Men wanted* is unacceptable to most newspapers. Yet it is an acceptable practice to add a line to the advertisement that says *Men encouraged to apply.* The reason for this is that the standard for child care positions is women and this line draws the attention of the advertisement to a target audience of men without excluding women.

Such a line is similar to other frequently seen phrases such as *Equal opportunity employer, Committed to workplace diversity,* and, particularly in higher education, *Women and minorities encouraged to apply.* However, in this case, the intent is not one of affirmative action — to provide employment opportunity to members of a group who have previously been excluded. Instead, the intent is to provide children with the presence of men. The additional cost of this phrase will likely be the cost of adding one more line to the classified advertisement — the price of which will vary from newspaper to newspaper.

Most classified advertisements are placed under the categories of *day care, child care, preschool, teachers,* or *education.* These are appropriate places for the position but are not the first places many men tend to look. An alternative strategy is to place advertisements in categories that men will be more likely to see. These categories include *activities coordinator, recreational supervisor, playground supervisor, computer applications with children,* or *general labor.* The idea is that an entry level position of teacher aide or teacher assistant in many programs has important but very general qualifications.

Advertising the position in a way that will bring it to the attention of men is a first step in getting men to apply for the position. This idea need not be deceptive when the advertisement also includes more detailed information that is also given to potential applicants making phone inquiries and to those actually applying.

Another strategy for placing advertisements is to seek out alternative publications in the community. Many larger cities, for example, have a men's organization that distributes a newsletter with articles about men's issues, events, gatherings, support groups, and other services of interest to men. While the circulation of these publications will be small and not approach the circulation of a daily newspaper, the readership will be almost entirely male.

## Asking the Right Questions

In a job interview, it is important to ask questions that elicit information about the qualifications of the applicant. Yet, when a man is interviewed, particularly by a panel of women, he may be reluctant to admit a lack of experience or he may not recognize relevant experiences that apply to the position. The women who are interviewing the man may subconsciously believe that a man is not entirely capable of working with young children and may not ask enough probing questions.

In this situation, general questions such as *Tell me about yourself* will not reveal the most important kinds of information. More specific questions that lead applicants to speak about relevant experiences are needed, and these include:

*Have you worked around young children or youth before? Have you been involved. . .*

- *in sports as a coach or referee?*
- *in swimming lessons or as a lifeguard?*
- *as a playground supervisor or recreational supervisor?*
- *in a church youth group?*
- *as a counselor at a summer camp or an outdoor school?*
- *with a scouting group?*
- *in babysitting younger siblings or neighborhood children?*

When the man answers yes to one of these questions, it is important to follow up with more probing questions to find out how the involvement in these activities applies to the position. Such questions include: *What kinds of things did you do? Did you . . .*

- *plan activities?*
- *teach a skill?*
- *supervise children? how many? what ages? for how long at a time?*
- *enforce rules? discipline children? break up a fight?*
- *keep written records? attendance? scores? an activity log?*
- *care for equipment? what kind of equipment?*
- *meet parents? explain activities to parents?*

## Retaining Men

Once men are hired, it is important to retain them. Many men who are the only man on a staff of women experience feelings of isolation (Nelson & Sheppard, 1992). Yet men will stay in an environment they feel is equitable, safe, values men, and supports them in personal and professional growth.

If you have a man on staff, make sure the assignment of tasks to men and women is equitable. For example, are male staff able to work with all age groups of children rather than just the older groups of children? Do male staff have the opportunity to work with different groups of children or is the man placed with the children most in need of guidance in the assumption that he will provide the guidance that is needed? Are men automatically scheduled to spend more time on the playground than female staff? Men may enjoy spending more time out of doors but often resent being automatically expected to do so.

Think about other job-related tasks such as taking out the garbage, lifting heavy objects, and changing light bulbs in high places. Of course, men will do these things but will certainly resent always being expected to do so.

Consider whether men are allowed the same freedom in their individual teaching style as are women. Many male teachers develop a style that includes activities that are more physically active, louder, messier, and involve more humor, joking, and silliness. This style is appropriate under the broad umbrella of developmentally appropriate practices and can be a valuable addition to the styles of other teachers in a program.

Men will continue to work in an environment in which they feel safe and protected. Many men feel they are but one false accusation away from having to leave a satisfying career working with young children. It is important to have policies that protect men — and all staff — such as those specifying that no staff person is left alone with a child.

Men also feel protected when they receive support from their supervisors. This is particularly important when parents raise questions about the appropriateness of a man doing certain tasks such as diapering infants and toddlers. A supervisor can use such an opportunity to educate the parents by referring to the policy that speaks to the importance of men as competent caregivers. This kind of support affirms the status of a man as a valued member of the staff who can and will perform all tasks required by the profession.

## Valuing Men

Male staff are inclined to stay in a work environment that values men. Images of men — such as fathers with children — on posters, bulletin boards, and other wall decorations reflect this importance. Magazines in a staff lounge, a parent lounge, and a lobby area should reflect the interests of men as well as women. Work uniforms can be modified or adapted to emphasize that men are staff members, too. Social activities among staff can include talk and activities that are also of interest to men. A good way to examine the workplace environment is to spend some time answering the question *What would our program look like if half the staff were men?*

Another way of examining the overall environment is to consider the degree to which it is *father friendly* (McBride

### Getting the Word Out

A variety of other strategies can be used to attract men. These include:

- Encourage your staff to recruit applicants for vacant positions. This word-of-mouth advertising can be effective when linked to cash incentives. Typically such incentives include a cash reward to the employee at the time the person he/she referred signs a contract. Another reward (sometimes split between the two employees) may be made when the new employee, in this case a man, completes a probationary period.

- Establish a resume bank of potential male applicants. Invite currently employed men and men in teacher training programs to submit resumes and then inform them as positions become vacant.

& Rane, 1996). A key idea here is the amount of father involvement your program has generated. For example, *Do as many fathers come to parent activities as mothers?* The attitudes and practices that support the involvement of fathers are the same kinds of things that will retain male staff (Levine, Murphy, & Wilson, 1993).

It is also important that men see the topic of men intentionally included in staff training activities. For example, when diversity is addressed — in any of its many forms of parent involvement, staff working relationships, and multicultural/anti-bias curriculum — make sure the topic of men is included in the discussion. Address and challenge the common assumptions that all evils in our society are the fault of men. Explore the significant contributions men make to child development; debunk the many stereotypes of men as being uncaring or inherently untalented to care for young children.

Examine how our society does not always favor men in that the vast majority of the homeless, alcoholics, substance abusers, and victims of violent crime are men — and that men have a shorter life expectancy than women. In sexual harassment training sessions, make sure that the discussion and the examples given do not always assume that the harasser is a man and the victim is a woman.

Men will want to stay in an environment where they have opportunities for personal and professional growth. Men who are just beginning in the field will appreciate flexibility in their work schedule and tuition support to continue their education. Men who have been in the field for some time will appreciate opportunities, encouragement, and freedom to undertake interesting projects, such as working with different age groups of children to develop new teaching skills, planning innovative curriculum activities or materials, becoming more involved with parent-involvement activities — perhaps in the form of a father and child event or ongoing series of father and child activity nights.

Male staff also feel less isolated when they have the opportunity to interact with other men in the field. The presence of more than one man on a staff and the presence of fathers and male volunteers has a snowball effect which makes the environment increasingly friendly towards men. Consider sponsoring a group of male teachers who wish to meet on a regular basis by providing space for a meeting, or supporting the publicity of such a group through a mailing, or providing a continental breakfast or refreshments for such a meeting.

Finally, it is important to support worthy wage and cost, quality, and affordability initiatives. One of the reasons many men give for not entering or for leaving this field is the low wages. Men, and all staff, need to know that this is an issue that is being addressed.

## References

Levine, J., Murphy, D., & Wilson, S. (1993). *Getting men involved: Strategies for early childhood programs*. New York: Scholastic Inc.

McBride, B., & Rane, T. (1996). Father/Male involvement in early childhood programs. *ERIC/EECE Digest*, EDO-PS-96-10.

Nelson, B., & Sheppard, B. (1992). *Men in child care and early education*. Stillwater, MN: nu ink press.

## Acknowledgments

Several individuals contributed to this article by previewing earlier drafts and offering additional ideas and feedback. They are: Bryan Nelson, Wendy Roedell, Bruce Sheppard, Gregory Uba, and Steve Weber.

# Supervising and Developing Staff

## Chapter 11

# Orienting Staff Right From the Beginning

by Marlene Weinstein and Joe Allen

*Orientation is a beginning. Through the orientation process, you begin to mesh the skills and information an employee brings to the job with your ideas about meeting the organization's needs. Orientation provides the information necessary to get started in the right direction so that the newcomer can assume full and competent responsibility for the job as soon as possible.*

*Orientation enables a new employee to develop an understanding of her relationship to the other employees and to the mission of the organization. It is the process by which the new employee gets her bearings and discovers her place in the overall organizational environment.*

*An employee's first days on the job present the director with unique challenges, as well as singular opportunities. Those first days are often anxious ones for employees, as they feel like strangers in their new surroundings. One task of orientation, therefore, should be to make the new employee feel welcome, to make him feel at ease. But during those first days, the new employee is also most eager to learn and to do well. Never again will he be so receptive to information you give him about the organization and his role in it. Therefore, an orientation program should capitalize on this zeal. It should instill in him a commitment to the goals of the organization and start him off right with proper work habits.*

## Common Evaluation Pitfalls
**(and Some Common Sense Solutions)**

### Pitfall #1

**Hit or miss orientation.** The new teacher arrived at the center and was ushered into the director's office where she waited patiently for ten minutes while the director finished his phone call. The director took the teacher on a tour of the center, stopping off along the way to deliver a message to one teacher and discuss a scheduling problem with a second one. Then back to the office where the director rambled on for another hour about the center and its personnel policies amidst numerous phone interruptions.

For all too many teachers, this is the extent of their orientation. A haphazard tour and introduction. The information this conveys about the center and the teacher's role in it is sketchy. The image this conveys of the center is one of disorganization. The message this conveys to the new teacher is that her value to the center is not very high.

**Solution:** For every position, whether it be the bus driver or the head teacher, the center should develop a specific orientation plan. This plan need not be an elaborate one, but it should spell out what points are going to be covered, by whom, and when. This way, important information will not be left out and, coming in an organized format, it will be much easier for the new employee to digest. Specific periods of time should be set aside for the orientation so that the person doing the presenting can devote full attention to the process. Time should be taken at the outset to preview the goals of the orientation and at the end to evaluate whether, in the mind of the new employee, these goals were met.

### Pitfall #2

**Hidden agendas.** Often, supervisors see orientation as a chance to make a pitch for their own special interests, to improve on some aspect of the job done by a predecessor, to develop some kind of particular supervisor/supervisee relationship. Or they may be so eager to make the new employee feel excited about the center that they will gloss over serious problems or paint an overly rosy picture.

Newcomers, too, may have the idea that orientation is the time to make an impression, to make sure people are glad they hired her. Both perspectives are understandable and to a certain extent unavoidable. However, if either party gets preoccupied with these hidden agendas, this may cause important pieces of information about roles and relationships to be distorted or misconstrued.

**Solution:** Orientation should be an honest, informative experience for all participants. At some point in the first day, it should be pointed out to newcomers that it is natural to feel on the spot at the outset. They should be assured that no one will hold them to high performance standards until they have had the opportunity to get their bearings.

At the same time, the person, or persons, doing the orientation should be forthcoming about center shortcomings and problems, particularly about those that will impact upon the new employee's job. For example, if the teacher a newcomer is replacing was fired against the wishes of the parents, she should be told about this so she doesn't construe any lingering hostility of the parents as being directed toward her.

### Pitfall #3

**Information overload.** In her first three days on the job, the new teacher was introduced to all the children, all the parents, and all the staff members. She was asked to read the personnel policy manual, the parent manual, and the center's curriculum plan. In addition, the director lectured her for one hour a day on the history and philosophy of the center. Unfortunately, the teacher reached her saturation point by noon of the first day, and the last two days she simply struggled to act as if she cared. The bottom line is that the newcomer was bored silly, very little information was effectively communicated, and everyone's time was wasted.

**Solution:** To avoid information overload, orientation should be given in small doses spread out over several days or weeks. It is most effective to give the new employee an opportunity to spend some time on the job as soon as possible, before her enthusiasm ebbs, and to alternate periods of orientation with periods of work. This provides a change of pace between learning and doing; it provides an opportunity to see in action guidelines, policies, and procedures mentioned in the orientation; and it gives the newcomer a chance to ask questions about problems she encounters on the job.

## Useful Orientation Techniques

There are a number of techniques which can be employed to increase the effectiveness of an orientation. Different people learn in different ways, so it is important to use a range of approaches for communicating information. This also makes the orientation a lot more interesting. The following are some techniques which have been used with success by child care centers:

**Pre-arrival orientation.** Even though orientation officially begins on the first day of work, you can effectively use the time between offering a job and having the newcomer start. Begin by making the telephone call in which the job is officially offered a warm, welcoming one. Then send a letter confirming the particulars of the job once it has been accepted. Include starting date and time, work schedule, salary and salary contingencies, and job requirements (for example, a satisfactory health assessment, a driver's license, or completion of certain course work).

Before the new recruit arrives, you may also want to send her information about the program and the job. While you should avoid overwhelming a newcomer, it is often before the first day that there is the most time and interest in reading program philosophy, policies, and history.

**The warm welcome.** On the first day, be certain the newcomer feels expected and welcomed. Someone should be there to greet him, and there should be a sense that things are ready for his arrival. Some centers put a welcome sign on the front door so the newcomer feels welcomed and staff and parents are also aware of him.

**The introduction.** Shortly after the newcomer arrives, the director should welcome her and explain how the orientation will proceed. She should be given a written outline of the evaluation schedule so she knows what to expect.

**The facility tour.** Staff should know the facility in which they work, including any areas which are off limits. Consider distribution of a floor plan if the facility is especially large. Be certain to take at least a brief tour through every room.

In addition to the basic room-by-room tour, also take a more detailed tour to learn the little things that enable a person to function at that site. A written list of the information covered in the detailed tour should be developed. Such a list can be made by carefully observing everything in the facility (include offices, closets, file drawers, keys) and identifying everything an employee has a reason to know about. Chances are they should know just about everything you will see. With a list organized by room, it can be a handy reference for the employee. Include information like where spare keys are kept, how to find the plumber's name and number in a hurry, where the emergency contact information is located, where personnel files are kept and what is in them, where the coffee is kept and who pays for it, etc.

**Group orientation.** When more than one new staff person is beginning at the same time, a group orientation is worthwhile — even if all participants have different positions. It is not only a more efficient use of time but it affords participants an opportunity to get to know other colleagues and feel less on their own. Moreover, each person's questions and comments enrich the experiences for all. It allows for reinforcement of information through discussion which otherwise could not happen.

**Modeling.** This technique will occur with or without specific planning. While words and handouts are valuable, actions are the means through which the newcomer will really learn about the program and the people in it. Think about what you do and how well it meshes with the information being given. It is reasonable to identify ideals (e.g., what you hope will be observed), but when you know the observed activities and information are different (e.g., staff are not complying with the hand washing rules when you observe), it must be acknowledged and discussed. Otherwise, the newcomer will not only know that the ideal is not met but will know not to trust your information.

**Rotating presenters.** Instead of having the director or head teacher responsible for the entire orientation, it helps to pull in other staff members to share their perspectives. This provides a welcome change of pace for the newcomer and also gives them a chance to meet, in a more than cursory fashion, other staff members.

**Observation and participation.** As noted above, actual participation in the life of the center is one of the most effective techniques for learning information during orientation. Any orientation plan should include ample opportunities for both observing and participating. Keep in mind that to participate one does not have to be in charge of a group of children, cook a meal, or drive the bus. There are lots of little ways to participate. Actually using the sign-in, opening the file drawer to locate an item, using the telephone, or attending a meeting are all ways to get right in and do things. Where participation is not feasible, consider discussing topics while the information can be observed.

Follow the rule *see one, do one, teach one* for effective learning. Plan observations followed by participation, followed by some chance for newcomers to tell you what they experienced.

**Apprenticeship.** When a new teacher begins to work, having her work closely with a skilled teacher can facilitate learning about the job. This apprenticeship experience should cover the full range of activity a person will be doing on the job. It works best when specific tasks are planned in advance (e.g., new cook will spend one hour with departing cook preparing snack and will walk through all steps). The supervisor and co-worker would do well to discuss these plans and their respective roles for the apprenticeship in advance.

In addition, provision for continual feedback should be planned during the apprenticeship period. *How am I doing* is what every newcomer wants to know (in fact, all employees want to know the same thing). Take time to let them know how they are doing. Reinforce the efforts and behavior you find effective and identify areas where there is difficulty.

**Written materials** are perhaps the least effective means of primary orientation, but they are extremely effective support for other techniques. Try to have each component of the orientation backed up by written materials. For example, after the new staff member has been introduced to all the other staff members, she should be provided with a list of all their names and positions so she won't have to be embarrassed about forgetting a name.

It is helpful to provide a notebook or folder for all of the material given. Encourage note taking on the handouts and reinforce their value by actively referring to specific information on them.

Be sure written materials are really readable. Use subheadings, visually break up long prose pieces, and consider outlines, charts, pictures. Other written materials can be readings in books. If you find certain published materials to be right on target about some point, it is appropriate to require certain readings (and discuss them). They can be recommended, too, but then be certain your real expectation is only that they *may* be read.

One good way to individualize an orientation is to identify readings which address a newcomer's personal interests or concerns. You might also ask them what books they have found helpful or interesting in the past to better inform you about their knowledge base and interests.

**Audiovisual aides.** To cover information about child development or nutrition, consider using a film. A slide show covering important aspects of the day at your center or a videotape of the room in which a newcomer will be working can both be very effective. You might use a photo album depicting important parts of the program or a tape-recorded commentary for photographs or slides. Or you can use a tape recorder for a self-guiding tour of the facility.

**Special experiences.** If you have the luxury of several days for orientation, try to provide some special experiences which may not be part of the daily routine of the job but which can be part of the job at times. It may be a chance to observe other agencies, attend a relevant workshop, meet with parents, review children's records in depth, observe other rooms at the center, or develop materials for the job.

**Review.** Whenever possible, build on information covered earlier and refer back to the agency's philosophy to give it more tangible meaning. Such review is a good technique for reinforcement and helps identify what in the mass of information being shared is really important. It also gives specific definition to some of the clichés we all tend to use differently.

Throughout the entire orientation period, be sure to include specific opportunities for feedback, follow up, and continued information sharing. In particular, be certain to schedule a time to review the first several weeks' experience on the job with the newcomer.

## Content of the Orientation

Content for the orientation should be the information one needs to function in the organization in general, and in one's particular job from day to day. One good way to begin thinking about content for the orientation is to ask current staff members what they found helpful and/or problematic in their own orientation and what they think is important to include for others.

Generally, the following topics should be covered at some point in the orientation:

**Goals and philosophy.** Whether or not the interview process provides employees with information about the center's purpose and philosophy, written materials about both should be given as soon as possible after the job is offered. Frequent reference should be made to the philosophy during the orientation, and specific time to discuss it should be planned.

**History, funding, and politics.** A review of these topics will generally highlight the constraints on the program and provide a context for many of the policies. While the discussion need not be lengthy, employees should know how and why the program is as it is, and how their job is affected by the information given. Which money pays for what and the relative security of the job (programmatically and financially) should be made clear. There will always be future issues about salaries, purchasing policies, and other items revolving around money. A sound foundation of information about the program's funding will provide the best hope for handling those questions effectively.

With regard to politics, identify the people, programs, and political forces significant to your program. Employees should know how to keep abreast of political developments, how to participate in the political activity affecting the agency, and what constraints are placed on their own political activity.

**Community.** Identify the community in which the agency is located and the relationship between the two. Who are community leaders? Any community foes? Where are the resources in the community? What about places to eat, shop, or take care of other errands on breaks? Consider giving a map of the neighborhood or even taking a tour if community information is especially significant for the job.

**Personnel policies.** Hopefully your personnel policies are in writing and are clearly written. Hand these out and then review, in depth, the employee's benefits and *exactly* how they are earned/accrued, as well as those parts which have been especially important or troublesome in the past. New staff should sign and return a document indicating receipt of personnel policies.

**Program policies.** Although the details of every policy and regulation affecting the program cannot realistically be discussed during orientation, be certain copies of the policies are given, highlighted, and reviewed for questions (the newcomer should be expected to read them). Sensitive issues, such as confidentiality and child abuse reporting, should be singled out for discussion. Also, given current concerns about sexual abuse, there should be a frank discussion of agency procedures designed to protect children from being sexually abused and teachers from being wrongfully accused.

**Health and safety procedures.** To emphasize the center's concern for maintaining a healthy and safe environment for children and adults, time should be set aside to review these procedures in detail.

For all policies and procedures, be sure to discuss underlying principles. Knowing the reasons underlying certain rules enables employees ultimately to function more independently and more effectively, and to do the job in a manner supportive of agency philosophy even in unexpected circumstances. In addition, seize every opportunity to turn a real experience into a chance to illustrate what a policy means or how it works.

**The facility.** Fully acclimating the newcomer with the center is an integral part of any orientation. As indicated above, the center tour should include all parts of the center and not just the room where the employee will be working.

**The staff.** In addition to being introduced to other staff members and being given a list of their names, the newcomer should be given a clear picture of the center's organizational structure. She should know the people who are in each position and a little bit about the job they do. For staff with whom the newcomer will be working closely, some time to meet with them directly should be allotted if possible.

**Communication procedures.** Generally, you should plan to discuss (with written back up) telephones, staff mailboxes, and parent mailboxes as major communication sources. In addition, remember to discuss bulletin boards, meeting schedules and content (and how agendas are established), conferences, and things that are handled via informal discussion.

To be complete, any orientation should relate the informal as well as the formal communication procedures. Must one always have an appointment to see the director, or is a knock on the door sufficient? Can you give work directly to the secretary, or does it go to someone else first? What about discussing ideas with the cook or making a request of the custodian? How is a complaint made? How do I keep people informed of my contacts with parents, or does it matter?

**Caregiver routines.** When a newcomer is not a caregiver, it is important to provide an opportunity to observe and discuss child care routines and philosophy. That person should know how her job is affected by the routines of the child care program and she should be conversant with the primary activity of the program.

**The job description.** The content of the specific job a person is hired to do should also be covered. Be sure to clarify what performance expectations go with the job, how performance will be evaluated, and how training and support will be provided.

Employees must know their *rights* as well as their *responsibilities* for each aspect of their job. Be certain to identify both.

Hopefully these suggestions will help you in developing an orientation plan. An effective orientation sets the stage for a successful working relationship between a new employee and the ongoing staff. While ongoing training and evaluation are needed to keep this momentum going, orienting staff right from the start can make a big difference.

# Self-Motivation: Motivation at Its Best

by Roger Neugebauer

*The director of Mother Goose Child Care Center was concerned. Incidents of lateness and absenteeism among her teachers were increasing. The teachers had stopped planning activities in advance and showed little enthusiasm in working with the children. They also complained continually about everything from inadequate equipment to low wages.*

*She decided that what was needed to improve staff performance was to tighten discipline. She required teachers to submit daily lesson plans for her approval. She had them sign in and out and deducted pay for lateness and unexcused absences. She kept a closer watch on the classrooms and reprimanded teachers who were sloughing off.*

*The results were mixed. Lateness and absenteeism declined, and lesson plans were being developed; but teachers' attitudes became even worse. They complained more and acted as if working in the classroom were a drudgery.*

*Next the director tried the opposite approach. She sought to cheer the staff up by granting them wage increases, setting up a comfortable teachers' lounge, and holding occasional staff parties.*

*Once again she was disappointed. Although the staff acted happier and complained less, they still exhibited little enthusiasm in their work with the children.*

## The Jackass Fallacy

One reason the director's remedies failed is that she was operating from overly simplistic notions about what motivates people to work hard. She acted as if the teachers were naturally lazy and irresponsible, as if they could only be made to work hard through fear of punishment or promise of rewards. This carrot and stick approach may work perfectly well in motivating a jackass, but it is wholly inappropriate in motivating people. As Harry Levinson, creator of the *Jackass Fallacy* analogy, explains:

"As long as anyone in a leadership role operates with such a reward-punishment attitude toward motivation, he is implicitly assuming that he has control over others and that they are in a jackass position with respect to him. This attitude is inevitably one of condescending contempt whose most blatant mask is paternalism. The result is a continuing battle between those who seek to wield power and those who are subject to it."

## What Does Motivate Teachers?

This author interviewed 64 child care teachers about what satisfies them and what frustrates them in their work. In reviewing the major sources of satisfaction (see summary on page 211), it can be seen that they relate directly to the *content* of the teachers' work. These factors — observing progress in children, relationships with children — result directly from the way teachers perform their work. On the other hand, the major sources of frustration — rate of pay, supervision, personnel policies — relate to the *environment* in which the work is performed.

Based on similar findings in studies in a wide variety of professions (see Herzberg), organizational psychologists have reached a number of conclusions on what can be done to motivate workers. When the environmental factors are not adequately provided for (i.e. when pay is low or the environment is oppressive), workers will become frustrated. However, when these factors are adequately provided for, this will usually have no important positive effect — these factors do nothing to elevate an individual's desire to do his job well. The content-related factors, commonly referred to as *motivators*, on the other hand, can stimulate workers to perform well. They provide a genuine sense of satisfaction.

A director seeking to bolster the sagging morale of her teachers, therefore, will have only limited success if she focuses solely on the environmental factors — increasing pay, improving physical arrangements, making supervision less rigid. If the teachers' lounge is renovated, teachers may become less frustrated, but they won't necessarily work harder on the job because of this change. To truly motivate the teachers, a director needs to focus her attention on restructuring the teachers' jobs so that they can derive more satisfaction directly from their work.

## Examining Motivators More Closely

But how does one go about restructuring a teacher's job to take advantage of these motivating factors? Taking a cue from organizational psychologists, a director should strive to meet the following criteria in restructuring a job (Hackman):

1. **Meaningfulness.** A teacher must feel her work is important, valuable, and worthwhile. If a teacher believes her work is unimportant, it won't really matter to her whether or not she does it well. If she believes her teaching does have a significant impact on children's lives, she will work hard to see that the impact is a positive one.

2. **Responsibility.** A teacher must feel personally responsible and accountable for the results of the work he performs. If a teacher is simply carrying out the plans and instructions of a supervisor, he will derive little personal satisfaction when things go well. If he has complete control over the planning and implementation of daily activities in his room, he will know that when children are thriving it is due to his efforts.

3. **Knowledge of results.** A teacher must receive regular feedback on the results of her efforts. If a teacher exerts a major effort on an activity but receives no indication as to whether or not it was successful, she will gain no satisfaction. A teacher can only derive satisfaction from the positive results she knows about.

The remainder of this article will be devoted to describing specific examples of how to apply these criteria.

## Clarifying Goals

Before teachers can be satisfied with the results of their efforts, they must be clear as to what results were expected in the first place. The center must have goals which teachers can use as yardsticks to evaluate their accomplishments. To be effective, a center's goals must:

1. **Be compatible with the personal goals of teachers.** Teachers will work hardest to accomplish organizational goals which are most similar to their own goals. Some centers achieve a close fit between organizational and personal goals by involving the teachers in developing the goals at the beginning of the year. Other organizations accomplish this by holding planning conferences between the director and individual staff members. In these conferences the employee outlines her personal interest and career goals. The two then develop ways in which the individual can work toward the accomplishment of her goals and the organization's goals at the same time (McGregor). For example, if one of a teacher's goals is to develop her creative movement skills and one of the center's goals is to stimulate children's imaginations, the teacher might be assigned to develop and use movement activities which challenge children's imaginations.

2. **Provide a moderate challenge to teachers.** Experiments have shown that most workers respond best to goals which are moderately difficult to achieve (Gellerman). The goal must not be so ambitious that it cannot possibly be achieved, nor so easy that it can be accomplished with little effort. Such moderately challenging goals should be established for the program as a whole (for example, to double the amount of cooperative play among the children) as well as for individual children (i.e. to help David control his temper).

## Encouraging Self-Control

A key to outgrowing a jackass style of management is shifting control over teachers' performances from the director to the teachers themselves. Ideally, a teacher and a director could agree upon a set of goals for a classroom at the beginning of the year. The teacher would then be fully responsible for planning and implementing daily activities to achieve these goals. At the end of a set time period (the less experienced the staff the more modest the goals and the shorter the time period) the teacher would be held accountable for having accomplished the goals. The teacher would work hard, not because he was being closely watched by the director, but because he was personally committed to achieving the goals.

Centers have developed many ways of supporting teachers in controlling their own performance. One center has the teachers write and periodically revise their job descriptions and the rules for various classroom areas. Another provides teachers with sufficient petty cash so they won't have to keep running to the director to request money to buy routine supplies and equipment. A third has teachers bring problems with children before their peers so that teachers can learn to solve their own problems.

## Major Sources of Satisfaction and Frustration

In a survey of 64 teachers in 24 New England child care programs, the following were identified as their major sources of satisfaction and frustration in their work. (They are listed in order of frequency.)

| Sources of Satisfaction | Sources of Frustration |
|---|---|
| 1. Observing progress in children | 1. Rate of pay |
| 2. Relationships with children | 2. Prospects for advancement |
| 3. Challenge of the work | 3. Physical work environment |
| 4. Pride in performing a service | 4. Style of supervision |
| 5. Relationships with parents | 5. Number of hours worked |
| 6. Recognition shown by staff | 6. Inflexible personnel policies |

Not all teachers will be willing or able to function so independently. Some will always feel more comfortable having someone else take the lead and issue directions. Other teachers may be ready to accept responsibility, but not for a full classroom. These teachers could have their self-control supported by being assigned full responsibility for a small number of children, for a certain activity area, or for performing a specific function (such as offering support and encouragement to children).

## Providing Feedback

When teachers were asked what satisfies them, they happily cited incidents such as: "When children beam after finally accomplishing a task"; "Seeing examples of children's cooperative play steadily increase"; or "When a parent comments on how a child's behavior is dramatically improving at home thanks to the school."

Given the high motivational impact of incidents such as these, a director should give high priority to seeing to it that they happen as often as possible. To get an idea of how a director might do this, the hundreds of motivating incidents supplied by teachers were analyzed. The majority of these incidents were found to fall into three primary categories which are listed below. With each category, ideas are listed which a director can use to encourage that type of motivation.

**1. Immediate reactions of children to an activity or to accomplishing a task.**

- Help teachers develop their skills in observing children's subtle signs of change or satisfaction.
- Ask teachers to list incidents of children's reactions and changes (pro and con) on a single day or week. This will force them to be alert for such feedback which they may otherwise be too preoccupied to notice.
- Periodically ask parents for incidents of children's progress or follow through on school activities. Pass these on to the children's teachers.
- Recruit volunteers to teach so that teachers can occasionally step back and observe what's going on in the classroom.
- Provide feedback to teachers focusing on effects of teaching on children rather than on the teachers' methods or styles.
- Set aside a time on Fridays when teachers can pause to reflect on what went wrong and what went right during the week. Devote occasional staff meetings to having teachers share their good experiences from the week.

**2. Warm relationships established with the children and their parents.**

- Provide times and places where teachers can have relaxed intimate conversations with individual children.
- Make teachers responsible for a small number of children so they can get to know each other better.
- Before the school year begins, have teachers visit children's homes to establish rapport with the families.
- Encourage families to keep in touch with the center after their children *graduate*.
- Assign each teacher responsibility for maintaining regular communications with specific parents.
- Bring in volunteers at the end or beginning of the day so that teachers can have informal, uninterrupted conversations with parents.

**3. Indications of the long-range progress of children.**

- Make teachers responsible for long periods of time for complete units of work. If teachers' responsibilities are continuously shifting from one group of children to another, or from one curriculum area to another, they will never be able to attribute any long-term changes in children primarily to their own efforts.
- Keep diaries of children's behavior so that changes in children can be tracked.

- Videotape classroom activities periodically and compare children's behavior as the year progresses.

- At regular intervals tabulate the number of incidents of specific behaviors which occur in a set time period to determine if there are any changes in these behaviors.

- Conduct tests on the developmental levels of children throughout the year.

- In regular parent conferences, with teachers present, ask parents to discuss changes they have noted in their children's behavior.

## Promoting Staff Development

One of the most important ways a director can help motivate teachers is to provide them with opportunities to improve their skills. The more skilled teachers are, the more likely they are to experience, and be rewarded by, incidents of success. The director should help teachers identify their specific training needs and secure appropriate training resources. These resources may be in the form of reading material, in-house staff training sessions, or outside workshops and courses.

## Encouraging Broader Involvement

Most teachers will tend to feel better about themselves, as well as more excited about their work, if they are involved in their profession outside the classroom. If teachers are involved in the overall management of their center or in children's advocacy efforts in the community, they will get a stronger sense of their efforts being an integral part of a vital profession.

At the center level, teachers' involvement can be broadened by keeping them continually informed on the status of the organization as a whole, by assigning them limited administrative responsibilities, as well as by involving them, wherever feasible, in major center decisionmaking.

Centers have also experienced positive results from encouraging their teachers to become involved in professional activities outside the center. Such activities might include participating in advocacy coalitions, working for professional organizations (such as NAEYC chapters), or promoting various child care alternatives in the community. Active teacher involvement in these areas will also relieve some pressure on the director to be the agency's representative on every committee and function.

## Motivation — A Final Perspective

The message of this article is that teachers are their own best source of motivation. If a teacher's work is properly structured, she will be motivated by the results of her own labors, not by external rewards and punishments manipulated by someone else. The director's prime concern should therefore be with helping the teacher achieve control over and feedback from her work.

This is not to say, however, that the director need not be concerned with environmental factors such as wages, personnel policies, and physical environment. Highly motivated teachers will be very tolerant of unavoidable inadequacies in these areas. However, if conditions deteriorate markedly, especially if this appears to be due to the indifference of *management*, teachers' motivation will rapidly be cancelled out by their growing frustration. Therefore, in motivating teachers by concentrating attention on job content, the director should not ignore the teachers' basic needs.

## References and Resources


Gellerman, S. W. (1963). *Motivation and Productivity.* New York: American Management Association.

Hackman, J. R., & Suttle, J. L (1977). *Improving Life at Work.* Santa Monica, CA: Goodyear Publishing Company.

Herzberg, F. (January-February 1968). "One More Time: How Do You Motivate Employees?," *Harvard Business Review.*

Levinson, H. (January-February 1973). "Asinine Attitudes Toward Motivation," *Harvard Business Review.*

McGregor, D. (1960). *The Human Side of Enterprise.* McGraw-Hill Book Company.

Neugebauer, R. *Organizational Analysis of Day Care.* ERIC Document Reproduction Service, PO Box 190, Arlington, VA 22210.

# CREATING ENVIRONMENTS WHERE TEACHERS, LIKE CHILDREN, LEARN THROUGH PLAY

by Elizabeth Jones

> *An individual has got to do his own sequencing and make his own connections.*
>
> *You want people who are working with children to be decisionmakers and to feel competent about their own role.*

People who are concerned with providing good environments for young children are often very clear about what young children's needs for learning are. They really believe children learn through play — through making changes in a rich environment. They go to a whole lot of trouble to set up such environments for children.

Administrators of programs for young children, especially if they have been teachers previously, tend to focus on the learning needs of the children and to overlook these same needs in the adults they supervise. I learned this from Chris Morgan, who as director of a children's center in Hayward, California, came to the realization that "my responsibility is to the adults in this setting. If I make a good learning environment for them, then they'll make a good learning environment for the children. The adults are the people I have to set up the environment for."

Administrators really need to think of the needs of adults in much the same terms in which they, as teachers, thought of the needs of children. Adults need to be safe, they need to have enough resources to work with, and they need to be encouraged to play.

## PLAYFUL LEARNING

When a child is learning through play she gets to explore — there isn't a predetermined end product. She has an idea or notion of a direction she would like to pursue and she is free within broad limits to do so. Her motivation comes from within herself as she interacts with the possibilities in the environment.

Administrators responsible for training staff often find themselves trying to motivate members to learn what has been predetermined that they must learn. But if you want people to stay excited about their jobs, there has to be some opportunity for them to explore, to be decisionmakers, to say "This is what I want to do next." That's playful in the very best sense. Children become active learners through play, and so do adults.

Dave Riley, consulting for Butte County CDA, implemented this concept through a consultation model which I believe could be used by administrators as well. What he mostly did was to come in as an observer. He would spend the day seeing what was going on, writing detailed factual notes, and sharing these with the teachers at the end of the day. This sharing immediately raised their questions and comments. Then he'd ask questions like: "What things do you like that you are doing? What things don't you like that you would like to work on? What's your next strategy for any problem you're having that you want to deal with?"

If teachers were having trouble inventing strategies and solutions and asked for help, Dave often relied upon storytelling. He had hundreds of stories in his head, based on teaching situations he had observed. He used these to describe how other teachers handled similar problems. He deliberately presented them as examples, not as prescriptions. It was up to the teachers to find something in the experiences of others to hook onto and decide "Oh, if that's the case, then maybe if I tried this, this would happen."

At the end of each session Dave would ask the teacher to make a commitment to working on her strategy before their next session. This underscored the importance of the decision making process by which the teachers decided what it was they cared about and what they wanted to do about it.

This consulting model is a good example of a basic approach to working with adults. The trainer says to the trainee: "What do you want to do? How do you want to go about it? What resources do you need from me? When shall we talk about it again?" And then at the following meeting: "What did you do? How did it work?" This is a continual planning and evaluation process with the initiative coming from the trainee. The trainer assumes the role of a mentor in this process. He is saying, "Hey, I'm prepared to help you do what you are committed to doing."

## Closed Means — Open Ends

This playful approach will not work the same for all teachers — and for some it may not work at all. Many teachers, especially newer ones, will get stuck way back at the question "What did you want to do?" Bill Baker, early childhood coordinator for Alameda County (CA) Schools, taught me a useful approach to this problem when he was on the Pacific Oaks faculty. He describes learning situations as involving both ends — where you're going — and means — how you're getting there. Means and ends can be either closed or open. You can have closed means and closed ends, closed means and open ends, open means and open ends, or open means and closed ends. Each combination has a different effect on the learning process.

Many tasks for learners involve closed means and closed ends — both the goal for learning and the procedure for learning it are carefully prescribed in advance. "Learn this material in order to pass the test." "Teach this lesson in this way and we will evaluate what happened." This approach is useful as a way of letting people check out their competence at something, but it has disadvantages as a learning process. The trouble with many such tasks is that either people can't do them very well or else they don't fit in well with where people are at. Tasks of this sort become unenjoyable labor. Where teachers spend most of their time at such tasks, they are likely to develop the attitude *What do I have to do to satisfy that person over there — the enemy?* instead of taking responsibility for their own work.

Not only does the closed means-closed ends approach inhibit motivation, it is also often ineffective in terms of results. You can teach a lot of information which adults can pick up and say and do partly. But all of us learn so selectively that a supposedly efficient closed-means closed-ends process is unlikely to be effective in teacher training. While you're telling someone how to do something, there will be 25 other things going on in that person's head. An individual has got to do his own sequencing and make his own connections. He will only hear as much of what you say to him as he can do something with.

I have had much more success in using closed means-open ends tasks to get people started. I give directions which are very specific — "Go find a partner and tell her six things about yourself." So it's very explicit as to what they are supposed to do, but what comes out of it is wide open. It's not "Go find a partner and work out answers to these five math problems." There's permission to open once you've gotten started.

As an administrator with a new teacher, you might say, "Today, go mix three colors of paint, put them out on the easel, and see what the children can do with them." The task starts closed but it gives teachers a chance to begin plugging in their own curiosity and their own questions. Essentially you are trying to get the play process started, for both children and teacher.

If you are experienced at all, you will have some notion of what you want teachers to learn most quickly. Once you have selected a starting point, you let teachers make their own choices as to where they want to go with it. You are not giving up on quality standards for programs by allowing people to make their own choices. You are simply trying to legitimate the sequence of choices this individual wants to make. Once you've done this, you don't have to worry about motivation.

Most people, including grown-ups, will make good choices for themselves if they are really trusted, supported, and given enough time. The only point at which you would intervene is when an individual gets stuck or is persistently not making choices that you see as essential. You are always free as the trainer to say, "It's my turn. Today I'm going to tell you what to do."

For example, you may have a teacher whose communication skills leave a great deal to be desired and who isn't choosing that direction to work on. At some point you might say, "Look, I think you're ready to work on a goal I'd like to set for you and these are some ways I'd like you to go about it." You then have to decide whether or not you are giving this person a choice or making a non-negotiable demand. In extreme cases, you might even have to say, "If you're not ready to work on this, I'm going to recommend that you be fired."

Mae Varon, as a preschool teacher at Pacific Oaks, used a related approach in helping her practicum students set goals for themselves. At the beginning of one semester she listed ten possible goals and asked students to add two of their own. She then had them prioritize these 12 goals for themselves. She provided quite a bit of pre-structure, she didn't ask them to invent a dozen goals. However, the ones that students put at the top of their lists were up to them. Then she said, "You can work on the top three on your list — for this semester, ignore the rest." In effect, she was saying, "Pick a manageable number of goals for yourself and I will hold you accountable for them."

## The Inquiry Model

A friend of mine, teaching child development, was trying to figure out how to teach Freudian theory. It occurred to her to ask the class what they knew about it. They knew quite a lot — some of it accurate, some of it not. But by the time they had it all down, the class had an experience base to build from.

As an administrator, you can do the same thing; you can assume that the adults are competent. There is, in fact, quite a lot of competence there, and some will be self-fulfilling if you assume it's there.

When confronting a new issue or problem, for example, you may want to start with the staff. You will eventually, as a group, start asking quite specific questions. At this point you could bring in an expert to supply specific answers if that's what is needed.

But I don't think you bring in experts until you've got questions for them. It's a real drag to have experts come in telling you things all the time. While you're supposed to be listening, you're doing your shopping list in your head because the question wasn't one you had asked. You should only bring someone in after you as a staff have already established yourselves as knowledgeable. Then afterwards you can argue about whether the expert was right. (The demythologizing of outside experts is probably a useful thing for staff to experience.)

You want people who are working with children to be decisionmakers and to feel competent about their own role. I think you add expertise in little increments as people say, "I want to know these specific things."

To be this kind of administrator, you ask questions more than you give answers. You employ an inquiry model. You keep asking: "What do you think?" "Why do you think this way?" "What are you going to do about it?"

You don't behave this way at all unless you trust the latent potential of your staff. If you are basically convinced they are unknowledgeable and unmotivated and that you are the authority, this approach will never work.

## Open Communication Channels

To support learning in your center, it helps to set up a very clear communication structure so that you keep getting feedback. When I lead groups, I always try to get some written feedback, as well as oral. In my classes I often communicate back and forth with students through folders. (Each student has a folder kept in an accessible place.) I may take time and ask: "What worked well for you today?" "What didn't you like?" "Take ten minutes and write it down." Then I write responses to their comments in their folders.

I know of administrators who have done this as well. One told me, "I tried this and it really worked. They really did write." Each staff member had a folder in the office. No one was required to write so many words per day, but they were guaranteed a response from the administrator every time they wrote anything.

The reason for encouraging such writing is that it offers one more chance to communicate. In centers, teachers and administrators are often so busy that their schedules don't allow frequent opportunities for face-to-face contact. When a teacher has something she wants to tell the administrator and knows she won't catch her today, one thing she can do is to write a note. You don't do this instead of face-to-face contacts, you do it in addition.

You are trying to build a very lively communications network. Sometimes you give very explicit tasks: "Write down what your goals are for yourself and prioritize them. Then we'll talk about them." Sometimes you ask staff simply to relate incidents: "Please tell me the best and the worst things that happened this week." To be a good administrator, you have to know a lot about what's going on, and this is one more way of insuring that you do.

Written staff communication adds a new dimension to the administrator's job, and administrators who don't like to write probably can't do it. Some teachers will not want to write, and that needs to be okay.

Also, in a very small center (with a staff of three or so), you probably need not bother with writing. But by the time a center gets up to a dozen people, you're not going to be able to talk to everybody, and written communications become more important.

## Peer Supports

I would be very inclined as an administrator to try to build peer groups — to make people accountable to their peers as to how they are expending their time, and not just to the administrator. You want to give people all the opportunities you can to be supports and communicators for each other. Among other reasons, that relieves you of a lot of responsibility. If people are supporting each other, you won't have to do it all as the administrator. Furthermore, it will always happen that there is somebody on the staff who can support someone else better than you can. There will also be staff members who know more about certain problems than you do; everyone benefits if you make use of their knowledge.

It is not enough to say, "We are all resources for each other." You have to structure so that it will happen. You might do networking on what people's goals are. In a staff meeting you could go around the room and ask everyone as specific a question as possible about their work toward their goals — for example, "What have you done in the past week to accomplish your goal to learn how to do music with children?" With this structure, staff are free to choose their own goals and decide how to accomplish them, but they can't do it privately. They have to be accountable to their peers by saying, in effect, "I'm being a responsible team member and these are the things I'm doing."

Another way to encourage communication networks is to have written communications be not just between staff and the director but among everybody. In my classes, for example, folders are open to everyone. (Particular notes can be marked confidential if desired.) Students are free to read others' folders and to make comments on them. Initially they often have trouble with this openness; they feel as if they are eavesdropping. But eventually we get all sorts of complicated conversations going in the folders, with notes upon notes in the margin.

I've also seen a complaints-compliments approach to children's communication work well in an elementary school setting. To apply this method at the center level, an administrator could ask each staff member to write a complaint to somebody and a compliment to somebody else and to put these in their folders.

In whatever structuring you do, you need to be sensitive to how different staff members will react. If the teacher aides are intimidated by the head teachers, you may find it works best to have the aides meet separately for these types of activities. If people are reluctant to open up in large groups, you make a point of dividing into smaller and smaller groups (down to pairs if necessary) until communication is flowing.

You can also structure with the tasks you assign. If you ask nice big intellectual questions, the most sophisticated people in the group will dominate the discussion. If you don't want that to happen, you might narrow the focus by asking, for example, "What happened to you yesterday with a child that you didn't understand?" If you want everybody to talk in a discussion, you must structure so that it will happen. Generally, you will want to tighten up to make things happen at the outset, then loosen up as communications start to flow.

Typically, these types of activities generate all kinds of interactions. People end up sharing professional problems and giving and receiving all kinds of advice. It's a mutual growth process. You want to build enough levels of communication among staff so that they know each other well and care about what happens to each other. If they feel safe together, if they are resources for each other, they will be able to take the risks involved in playful learning. Adults do learn through play; and where they are learning, children are likely to be learning, too.

## References


Jones, E. (editor). (1993). *Growing Teachers: Partnerships in Staff Development*. Washington, DC: NAEYC.

Morgan, C. L. (1983). "Journal of a Day Care Administrator," in S. Stine (editor), *Administration: A Bedside Guide*. Pasadena: Pacific Oaks College.

Riley, D. (1983). "Observation and Story-telling: Useful Tools in Preschool Consulting," in St. Stine (editor), *Administration: A Bedside Guide*. Pasadena: Pacific Oaks College.

# When Friction Flares — Dealing with Staff Conflict

by Roger Neugebauer

*"Aside from the harm an uncontrolled conflict does to an organization, your inability as manager to control it may lead to your overthrow, either by angry contestants or by impatient bystanders."*
—Theodore Caplow

*"Your job in resolving personality conflicts between your subordinates is to make the person involved in the conflict aware how his or her behavior is adversely affecting others, and how it is thereby adversely affecting the operation."*
—Thomas L. Quick

*"It is not best that we should all think alike; it is difference of opinion which makes horse races."*
—Mark Twain

These are the times that try directors' souls — when arguments erupt over the cleanup of shared space, when staff meetings turn into acrimonious debates over lousy working conditions, when two teachers every day find new pretexts to prolong their personal feud.

Wouldn't it be wonderful if you could wave a magic wand and all this disharmony would disappear? Unfortunately, in a demanding, interaction-intensive profession such as child care, where pressures and feelings run high, conflict is inevitable.

There is no way a director can, or even should, drive all conflict out of the life of the center. The challenge is how to manage dissension so that it contributes to the growth, and not the deterioration, of the organization. The following are some guidelines for accomplishing this.

## Encourage Healthy Conflict

Asking a center director to foster conflict is like asking a yuppie to shop at K-Mart. However, in a creative organization, the clash of ideas and opinions keeps the organization growing and improving. In a creative organization, the types of healthy conflict described in the "Signs of Healthy Conflict" box happen all the time.

As a leader in your organization, there are a number of steps you can take to promote healthy conflict:

- **Don't let your ego run amuck**

I recently participated on a committee of teachers and board members tussling with the growing need for infant care. For months we hotly debated whether the center should offer infant care, where we could locate it, and how much we would have to charge to provide a high quality program. When we presented our recommendations to the full board, a lively discussion ensued. Finally, the director took the floor and stated that she didn't believe children that young should be in a center. After her statement, the discussion sort of petered out until finally a motion was made and passed to table the recommendations indefinitely.

This director had no intention of throwing a wet blanket on the debate — she assumed she simply was expressing her views as one member of the board. What she failed to take into account was that the opinion of the leader of any organization is packed with positional power. As a leader, unless you work hard to undermine your authority by behaving like a fool, your opinions may exert an overwhelming influence on discussions.

If you want your staff to express their opinions, be it in meetings or in one-to-one discussions, you must exercise discretion in expressing your own opinions. This is not easy.

Most directors I have met over the years tend to be take charge people. They care deeply about the success of their centers and take it personally when things go wrong. Their egos are heavily invested in their work, and they like to have things done their way.

Take charge directors often do unintentionally put a damper on the clash of ideas in their centers by jumping in with a position on every issue. Particularly if a director

## Signs of Healthy Conflict

Conflict among staff in a center can be constructive if it . . .

- generates new ideas, new perspectives
- provokes an evaluation of organizational structures or center design
- brings individuals' reservations and objections out into the open
- heightens the debate about pending decisions or problems
- forces the reexamination of current goals, policies, or practices
- focuses attention on problems inhibiting performance at the center
- energizes staff — gets them actively involved in the life of the center

has strong verbal skills, she can easily dominate any discussion.

If you value the expertise and insights of your staff members, you need to keep your ego in check. Resist that very natural urge to voice your opinion on anything and everything — at least until everyone else has had their say.

**• Beware the peacemaker**

Often within families there is an unspoken rule that one should not express angry feelings. On the surface this creates a placid appearance. But the result is that anger continues and festers, potentially causing long term emotional difficulties for family members.

The same scenario can play itself out in organizations. When emotions erupt at the center, a peacemaker (maybe the director, maybe not) will rush in and urge everyone to calm down and keep their angry feelings in check. Once again, this may still the waters, but it often leaves conflicts unresolved. Suppressed anger can eat away at staff morale and, if allowed to intensify, can result in an even greater explosion later on.

A wiser, though often less pleasant, course for a director to take is to foster an environment where the true expression of emotions is tolerated. In the long run this results in a better working climate because conflict can be brought out in the open where it can be dealt with and resolved.

On the other hand, you don't want to create a haven for hotheads and chronic complainers. You need to follow three basic rules in dealing with expressions of anger . . .

First, don't answer anger with anger. If you respond to anger in kind, emotions can quickly escalate out of control.

Second, listen. When a staff member is letting off steam, don't interrupt, argue, or explain. Let them get the feelings out of their system as much as possible before you intervene.

Third, ask questions. To move a discussion toward a constructive stage, ask specific questions to clarify the cause of the problem and then start the exploration of solutions.

**• Don't take it personally**

You want to create an atmosphere in your center where all staff members feel free to voice questions, concerns, and objections — where healthy conflict flourishes. You want your staff members to be confident that they can confront you openly over organizational issues and not worry that you will hold this against them.

You can, of course, tell people that you welcome their critical comments, and write them memos assuring them that this is true. But the bottom line is that people won't believe this until you demonstrate your tolerance in real life.

In part, this requires a significant sell job on yourself. You must believe that you and your center will benefit from the clash of ideas and opinions. When a debate flares over teaching practices, the use of common space, the center's ratios, or other program issues, you must truly view this debate as an opportunity to improve the program. If you are not comfortable with conflict and criticism, your body language will surely send out warning signals to staff members that their comments are not being well received.

You can also demonstrate that you welcome open discussions by rewarding people who take risks by saying what they think. At the end of a heated, maybe even emotional, debate in a staff meeting, acknowledge that the discussion may have put many participants under stress, that you appreciate everyone's honesty and openness, and that you believe that the program will be the better for having dealt with the issues at hand.

If individual staff members appear to be particularly upset by a confrontation, take pains to reassure them in private that you bear no grudge toward those who disagree with you. Thank them for expressing their views. Smile and behave normally towards them.

## Discourage Unhealthy Conflict

Not all conflict is positive. A dispute over an organizational issue which is ignored by the director can deteriorate into acrimony and bring down staff morale. A personal feud which erupts between two or more staff members can distract participants from doing their jobs.

One important challenge for any director is to distinguish between healthy and unhealthy conflict. When conflict exhibits manifestations such as those listed in the "Signs of Unhealthy Conflict" box, you need to intervene.

**• Don't allow conflicts to escalate**

Often it is tempting to ignore a minor flare up among staff members and hope that it will fade away. Sometimes this may work, but more often than not the "hands off" approach backfires.

An outbreak of hostility can eat away at staff morale and productivity. The longer you allow it to rage out of control, the more likely your credibility as a leader will be undermined as well. You must act quickly to contain damaging conflict. It is especially helpful to intervene before a private feud has boiled over into a public feud. Once positions have been taken in public, it will be harder to get disputants to back down for fear of losing face.

• **Be a mediator, not a judge**

When faced with a conflict among staff members, you may quickly develop an opinion about who is right and who is wrong. Your temptation will be to end the dispute immediately by playing the role of the judge and declaring a winner. More often than not, you end up being the loser in this case, no matter how wise your decision. The winners believe they were right all along, and therefore owe you no thanks; and the losers end up bitter because you made a stupid or biased decision.

You are better off in the long run to play the role of an impartial mediator working with both parties to hammer out a compromise that all can support. In this case, both parties feel they had a hand in shaping the outcome and will be more committed to making it work.

• **Match your response to the severity of the conflict**

In the case of a minor squabble between two or more staff members, you may find it sufficient to communicate to the individuals involved that you recognize that a problem exists and that you expect them to work out a resolution themselves. Give them a deadline; check back to make sure they followed through.

If the individuals can't work out their own problem, you may need to bring them together in your office and force them to confront the issues causing the conflict. Ask each individual to state their perception of the problem and then their suggestions for a solution. Your role is to lead them to agree on a solution.

In some cases such a face-to-face thrashing out of the issues may work. When emotions are running high, however, a confrontation may actually escalate the conflict. When one angry staff member confronts another in your presence, this may cause both parties to intensify their feelings. In order to save face, they may harden their positions.

In this case you may need to play more of the role of a third party intermediary. Interview each party to the conflict in private and ask them to explain the facts of the dispute as they see them. Then present to each disputant, in as objective a manner as possible, a description of the other party's perception of the problem. Take the opportunity to point out inconsistencies in either party's positions — they are much more likely to agree to a "clarification of the facts" with you than with the other party. In some cases, this clarification process may be enough to end the dispute.

If not, ask each party to propose potential solutions. Find commonalties among the solutions and see if you can gain agreement on those points by proposing them to each disputant separately. If necessary, suggest solutions of your own. In any case, work step by step to an acceptable compromise.

• **Focus on behavior, not personalities**

Your job as a leader is to make the organization succeed. Your concern in any personal feud, therefore, should not be on trying to bring harmony to a relationship gone sour, but on preventing the conflict from interfering with the functioning of the organization.

As a caring person your natural inclination will be to want everyone on your staff to be on friendly terms at all times. However, unless you are a trained psychologist, you are not likely to be successful in changing people's attitudes toward each other.

But in focusing on behavior patterns you are more likely to have success. Point out to disputants how their behavior is hurting their own performance as well as interfering with the performance of others. Don't allow yourself to get caught up with their personal issues. Focus your attention and theirs on changing their detrimental behavior.

## Signs of Unhealthy Conflict

Conflict among staff in a center can be destructive if . . .

- one person or faction is bound and determined to emerge victorious
- focus of the debate changes but the adversaries remain the same
- discussion never moves from complaints to solutions
- staff members start taking sides
- parents or other outside parties get drawn into the debate
- continuing acrimony starts to erode staff morale
- dissension continues even after a decision is hammered out
- debate focuses on personalities, not issues

Conflict is as normal a part of the life of a child care center as Legos and finger jello. By being out front in dealing with conflict as it occurs, a director can create a positive force out of the daily clash of ideas, opinions, and personalities.

## Resources

Caplow, T. (1983). *Managing an Organization.* New York: Holt, Rinehart and Winston.

Quick, T. L. (1977). *Person to Person Managing.* New York: St. Martin's Press.

# Creative Staff Training Is Key to Quality

**by Karen Stephens**

*Director to director, let's talk turkey about program quality. No matter how spiffy and chic our child care center building may look, no matter how high techy we're able to equip and supply classrooms, and no matter how much money we can spend for public relations and advertising promotions — a program's quality is determined by staff attitude and performance — first, last, and always.*

Staff are the most valuable, and temperamental, of program assets. Whether interacting with children, parents, or each other, how well staff meet their job challenges ultimately makes or breaks a program's image and reputation. Our programs are only as good as the staff we're able to hire, retain, support, and consistently motivate to high performance.

Without the strong underfooting of wise, committed staff who possess professional skills, program quality quickly slips down a slippery slope. Even our newly built, avant-garde child care buildings will be little more than warehouses. Void of energized and talented staff, any building is merely a shell where potential for engaging childhoods evaporates into thin air. In the wake are left hollow memories, not sustaining, life affirming ones. That abysmal picture shortchanges children and families, and most certainly robs the future of a stable society.

Today's status quo of working conditions, wages, and benefits in child care, means that keeping a good staff is a continual challenge. But we can't let that distract us from investing in the staff we DO have. The best investment programs ensure staff are consistently — and creatively — trained so they'll continue to be fascinated by their work with children.

There are a variety of ways to keep staff in step with skilled professional practice, such as funding conference or workshop attendance. Some programs subsidize costs for continuing formal education, often by obtaining corporate/foundation grants or participating in government quality enhancement initiatives. Some directors can even build budgets that include an on-site consultant for individualized, ongoing training support.

Considering resources, there are still a lot of directors who have no choice but to provide training themselves. For typical topics, like child abuse reporting procedures, that's fine. But if your training involves asking a staff to change or try new ideas, it's hard to be a prophet in your own land. To enhance training vitality and variety, experienced directors often swap training responsibilities for their respective staff — a bartering system so to speak. It you make the right match, it works.

However you arrange it, training must be a priority for every program, regardless of how programs vary in terms of staff turnover and staff qualifications. Through training you'll help your staff maintain their resilient, good hearts and also develop their keen minds.

With that said, the following are steps to make staff training well-targeted, creative, and useful. When training proves successful, the staff's work life becomes more enriching and satisfying. And to be sure, well trained staff greatly increases the odds that your child care building will be filled with the joy of cherished childhood memories in the making. Bottom line, that's what program quality should be about.

## Identify Training Needs

- Select training topics based on job descriptions as well as current staff experience and qualifications. Training will impact staff performance most when it is tailored to members' current needs. A new, inexperienced staff require different training than a staff with lots of seniority.

- Review licensing requirements which stipulate mandatory training topics. Plan topics in response to improvement suggestions from recent licensing visits.

- Compare program operation with accreditation criteria for high quality. A formal self-study using

NAEYC accreditation criteria is very helpful in spotting staff training needs, even if your program doesn't pursue accreditation.

- To pinpoint training needs, observe staff performance regularly through announced as well as unannounced visits. While observing, note exceptionally skilled staff so they can become resources for mentors or peer trainers.

- Survey staff to find out suggested training topics, preferred methods of training delivery and best times to hold training. Ask staff what they are excited to learn more about!

- During evaluations, ask staff to reflect on skills or knowledge that need bolstering. Cooperatively draft a plan for professional development that responds to those needs.

- Analyze recent parent comments and concerns to reveal training needs. Staff, volunteers, or lab students also make insightful comments that infer training needs.

## Select Training Topic and Define Target Audience

- Select participants based on the work you did in Step 1. For instance, you might want to offer training on understanding and responding to biting incidents in the toddler room. That would define your target audience as well.

- Formulate a desired training group size. Tough, touchy, or confidential topics call for a smaller group size. Other topics may involve the whole staff. When all staff are in attendance, break into small groups when possible so more people get a chance to speak. And remember, your group size will influence how you deliver training.

- Decide who will be required to attend versus who will be invited to attend. Toddler teachers may be required to attend a training on biting; but other staff may appreciate being included — plus they can provide insight. In the case of biting, infant caregivers could give insight on a specific child's development prior to his enrollment in the toddler room. That sharing leads to peer mentoring and team building between classroom assignments.

## Define Training Goals

- Write down desired performance outcomes that will result from training. Be as specific as you can. A vague, general goal doesn't get you good results. Share your goals with the staff and encourage them to *buy into* training by identifying their own goals as well.

- Identify content knowledge and skills staff need to meet desired outcomes. To increase the chances of successful training, break outcomes down into steps that are realistically achievable.

- Anticipate a timeline for achievement of training goals. Estimate how many training sessions will be needed to ensure staff competence. If you set a timeline, include staff in the process so they can invest energy and commitment. This also helps prevent overwhelming staff with expectations too high for immediate mastery.

## Select Methods of Presentation and Activities

- Plan and implement training that is as hands-on and interactive as possible. For long-lasting learning, experiential training is absolutely the way to go. Everyone learns best by doing.

- Whenever possible, interject training with humor. Allow the time and freedom needed for imagination and brainstorming to work its magic. For instance, if you want training to boost staff's creativity quotient, engage them in activities that will require them to practice resourcefulness — whether it is using blocks, art supplies, makeshift music instruments, dramatic play materials, or whatever.

- Vary training activities based on the time you'll have in each session and how many training sessions the topic needs for thorough coverage. Marathon training sessions can overwhelm and fatigue staff. Processing time is needed for training content to sink in and make sense. If you offer a two hour session, break it up in the middle with a relevant video or engaging music during which members can snack on refreshments and move around.

- Plan activities that appeal to a variety of learning styles. Don't limit yourself to lecture or half your staff will tune out — especially if you train after a long day of work. Following are examples of alternatives to a lecture format training:

    - Stage a mock magazine news show (like *20/20* or *Dateline*) so staff can *interview* each other on the pros and cons of topics, like use of computers with young children.

    - To explore all angles of a topic, include role-play when possible, such as staff acting out the scenario of a parent arriving after closing time.

    - Read to the staff a relevant children's book and use reactions to guide discussion. *The Kissing Hand* by Audrey Penn or *Owl Babies* by Martin Waddel are both great lead-ins to separation anxiety discussions.

- Prior to a meeting, have staff record answers to *reflection* questions designed to put them in a receptive mindset for training. If training is on nature education, ask staff to reflect on nature adventures they experienced during their childhood and ask them to share them with others.

- Hold a poster session where staff highlight *before and after* photos that relate to the training topic, such as room arrangement, learning center development, or curriculum documentation.

- Post mural paper on the training room walls. Have staff *web out* or list ideas to discuss that relate to the training topic. For instance, toilet training requires staff to consider child development, parent expectations, personal biases, communication with parents, changing table particulars, family cultural beliefs, pros and cons of Pull-ups, and so on.

Allow the staff to decide where discussions should begin. They can also identify resource materials and local *experts* to help them explore the topic.

## Provide Good Training Resources for Future Use

- No one remembers everything they experience during training. Provide a meeting agenda and outline to refresh memories after training. Folders of resource references also help staff revisit training ideas or explore them more deeply. Provide a video on the training topic that staff can check out when questions arise. Web sites to refer to are becoming increasingly popular. And don't forget to identify skilled team mentors whose expertise can be tapped for support.

## Evaluate Training

- Evaluation of training is critical. Both the director and staff should decide if training was worthwhile or a waste of time. Evaluation helps you plan future training events that will be well received and influential on staff performance.

  Ask staff to give written feedback on training strengths and weaknesses as well as organization and delivery. Ask them to cite a few concepts, tips, or ideas they picked up that could immediately be put into practice.

- Evaluate training success by observing classrooms to see if practice has changed. Also interview parents and team staff to determine if training made an impact. Don't forget, go right to children and ask them their opinions. Children are incredibly honored to be a *focus group*.

## Finishing Touches: Infuse Training With Meaning

In today's hurried schedules, everyone's time is so precious. Time spent in training inevitably means staff are losing time with their own families. Recognition of that personal sacrifice, and appreciation for the dedication it confirms, should motivate directors to infuse staff training with as much meaning as possible. Show staff respect by making sure training is worthwhile and valuable. Disrespect is shown if we treat professional development as merely *putting in time* to meet minimum licensing standards for inservice hours.

- Arrange the training room in anticipation of staff. Have adequate materials set out and ready to use on time.

- Create comfort for a relaxed sense of community and commaraderie. Seating should be comfy and scaled for an adult's body. Room temperature should be cozy — not too cool or too hot. Natural lighting or even *mood* lighting lifts spirits. Candles add warmth and ambiance, as can simple wind chimes or background music. Fresh flowers or a bubbling table top fountain contribute beauty and harmony. Such small things are easy to overlook, but they really do show respect — and they make a big difference. Quality is in the details, even ones we often take for granted.

- Nourish the body as well as the mind — provide your staff with food! Refreshments should be tasty and even fun, and always encourage socializing.

- Provide participants with a focus object they can hold and manipulate. The best focus objects symbolize something about the training and its intent. Here's one of my favorites focus object strategies:

When training participants arrive, there's a small selection of mirrored pebbles at each seat. As the group gathers, I encourage them to make designs with their pebbles and to show them off to each other. They can keep the pebbles during the training in case they get fidgety.

I begin the training session by sharing my personal philosophy of teaching — whether with children or adults. I envision myself as a pebble — a pebble with some knowledge about kids and some experience with them.

Whenever I share my insights, I envision my pebbly-self dropped into a pond. I make a ripple that hopefully circles out widely to make a positive impact on all it touches — the training participants and the children in their care in particular.

At the end of the training, just before participants leave, I hand each one a mirrored pebble to keep — a talisman if you will, to remind them of what they learned and of our shared commitment to children and families. I tell each person they're a pebble, too, able to share their knowledge with others so life is better for us all.

Yep, I'm a sucker for symbolism and sentiment. Luckily, there are many simple items that can symbolize useful metaphors for our field.

Choose symbols that relate well to your specific training topics. Here are some suggestions:

- A packet of garden seeds or a simple daisy reminds staff to bloom with confidence.

- A tiny container of playdough reminds them to be flexible during times of change; silly putty suggests that humor is a great way to maintain perspective.

- A bottle of bubbles reminds staff to manage stress by taking time to play on their own. (Or if staff are in the habit of complaining, bubbles can remind them to lighten up!)

- A lucky penny reminds staff an optimistic attitude can help change take place easier.

- A candle sheds light on new opportunities.

You get my meaning. Use your imagination. Trust it to inspire you and you'll come up with a wonderful symbolic token to infuse your training with meaning.

Now, I don't know about you, but I'm going to the hobby store to buy some more mirrored pebbles!

# What Do Teachers Need Most From Their Directors?

by Margie Carter

> *"Perceptions are powerful regulators of behavior that can influence teachers' level of commitment to a center. In fact, people's perceptions of events may be more important than reality because individuals act according to their interpretation of events."*
>
> — Paula Jorde Bloom, *Circle of Influence*

Over the last eight months, I've been doing an informal research project. Nothing scientific. No statistical analysis. Just keeping my ears finely tuned and asking a few focused questions as I work with child care teachers at their program sites and in seminars at conferences. There is now an established process called "participatory research," but I can't claim to have been even that systematic in my inquiry. Mostly, I've just been trying to carefully listen for what management styles, dispositions, and skills engender confidence and respect from staff toward their director. Are there particular philosophies, policies, decision-making and communication systems that influence teachers to stay at their workplace longer, despite inadequate salaries and benefits?

What I've consistently heard from teachers reflects the research behind several important publications in our field:

- Paula Jorde Bloom's two books, *A Great Place to Work: Improving Conditions for Staff in Young Children's Programs* and *Circle of Influence: Implementing Shared Decision Making and Participative Management*
- The Center for the Child Care Workforce (CCW) publication, *Creating Better Child Care Jobs: Model Work Standards for Teaching Staff in Center-Based Child Care*

Bloom discusses her research on how the interplay between people and the environment, and between work attitudes and group dynamics, supports the professionalism of an organization. In discussing the concept of organizational climate, she says: "Although it is not clear whether climate or satisfaction comes first, job satisfaction seems to be higher in schools with relatively open climates. These climates are characterized by a sense of belonging, many opportunities to interact, autonomy, and upward influence." (1997)

More recently, through the efforts of the Center for the Child Care Workforce, early childhood program staff themselves have been developing an assessment tool, the Model Work Standards, which highlights the components of work environments that are linked to quality for children in our programs. This tool is a welcome addition to our field and substantiates Bloom's point:

"One valuable insight gained during an assessment of employee attitudes about their work environment is the sharper understanding of where perceptions differ between administrators and employees. One of the more common findings, for example, is that directors often believe they give far more feedback to their staff than their teachers perceive they get. Another common difference is found in the directors' and staff's perceptions regarding staff involvement in decisions about practices to be followed in the center . . . directors typically rate the climate more favorably than do teachers." (1997)

The impetus for my own investigation into what teachers want from their directors stems from continually hearing examples of differing perceptions between directors and staff in their rating of the work environment. It strikes me that because directors work so hard and under such stress, they are sometimes reluctant to welcome staff perspectives on what needs changing if there aren't resources or time to commit to an issue. However, I've discovered that when directors welcome feedback on how the work environment feels, they unlock the potential for creative problem solving. A tool such as the Model Work Standards helps directors clearly see where their program should be headed. As with accreditation criteria, it can serve as a weather gauge for the organizational climate and a concrete reference point for budgeting and/or grant writing.

In *A Great Place to Work*, Paula Jorde Bloom is instructive about the dimensions of an organizational climate that need tending to in our early childhood programs. She is also quite persuasive in Circle of Influence, detailing the value of shared decision making and participative management. What she says in these two publications outlining her research is what I have been hearing in my informal, yet careful listening work with teachers.

As I ask, "What do teachers need most from their directors," either as a direct question to them or as I focus my listening and watching, I consistently hear a call for tending to the physical, social, and emotional environment of the program. These are my categories for their ideas, different from but interrelated to the research message from Bloom and the Center for the Child Care Workforce.

## Offer Genuine Respect and Trust

The words "trust" and "respect" easily roll off our tongues, and our heads nod when we hear them, but what do these words look like in action? Teachers say they usually feel respected when someone really listens to them, trying to understand and be responsive, rather than just placating. Some talk about "being trusted to succeed," even if they falter or "goof up."

But they are quick to add that respect and trust means being given the time, support, and tools they need, not leaving them alone to sink or swim but neither hovering or micro-managing. "When I'm really listened to and taken seriously, I feel validated and respected." Others use the word "empowered" along with trust and respect. One teacher commented:

"Empowerment can be a bogus word. No one can give you your power, but they can disempower you, taking away your self-trust and respect. When your director trusts you, you are motivated to use your power to learn and get it right."

Some teachers claim that directors only show trust and respect to staff members who agree with them. This clearly undermines what Bloom refers to as "collegiality" in naming ten important dimensions in an organizational climate. Posting a sign or announcing "We will all respect each other here" irritates some teachers. You can't mandate trust and respect. These feelings have to be developed over time with accumulated experiences to confirm or counter our initial impressions.

Trust comes more quickly when we work from both our heads and our hearts. As we become clear about our values and ideas, and learn to communicate them with a blend of honesty and empathy, respect for different points of view can grow. We don't have to become best friends to trust each other, but we do have to have mutual respect and be able to count on each other if genuine trust is to grow and thrive.

## Work With a Vision

It's striking to hear teachers describe the contrast between directors who work with a vision and those who settle for how things are. The word "vision" isn't always used, but they excitedly describe how their director really inspired them to work at the center, how "she's usually got a twinkle in her eye," is always "showing us pictures or little quotes to expand our thinking," or "keeps her eye on the prize even when our budget comes up short." Perhaps some of this is related to the dimension Bloom calls "innovation" or "goal consensus. Teachers can sense when directors are moving their program forward toward a bigger dream, even as they are thwarted by the crisis of the week. The climate is quite different than one limited to following the rules and regulations or resigning the program to the limitations of the moment.

Teachers acknowledge that directors with big dreams can sometimes overlook the trees for the forest. They can get caught up in grant writing, meetings in the community, or calls and visits to their legislators and neglect a child, parent, or teacher requiring immediate attention, film waiting to be developed, or a promised professional training opportunity. Most teachers don't just want to be kept informed of where the director is heading; they want a role in shaping a vision for the program. When they are offered this involvement, their energy and talents can be tapped and their commitment to the program grows. This is a very different experience for staff than merely delegating responsibility for some tasks the director can't get to. Teachers not only want to work with visionary directors, they want to dream and plan along with them.

## Share the Decision-Making Process

"I hate it when our director has made a decision and then goes through the motions of asking for our input. It's a waste of time and makes me resentful." CCW's Model Work Standards have several components which address this common sentiment from teachers. Their categories of communication, team building, and staff meetings, as well as decision making and problem solving, offer important descriptions of what teachers deem as necessary in a quality work environment. Bloom, in turn, has devoted a book in her *Director's Toolbox* series to the topic of implementing shared decision making and participative management. Circle of Influence outlines principles and values that support collaborative decision making and offers guidelines for determining decision-making processes and avoiding pitfalls. Bloom says:

"It is not enough to embrace the beliefs and values surrounding participation. Organizational structures and processes must be adapted so that staff and other stakeholders have the power and capacity to participate actively in decision-making ventures."

Teachers want clarity in the process for making decisions about things which impact their ability to do their jobs well. Many want more than that and are eager to be mentored in understanding the big picture and learning consensus-building skills. They want their directors to offer strong leadership in getting all voices to the table. Teachers are intuitively clear about the difference between autocratic and democratic leadership, often mentioning the way their director succeeds or fails to facilitate the group dynamics so that everyone has power and input and teachers cultivate their own leadership skills.

## Reject a Scarcity Mentality

Related to working with vision is the idea that teachers don't want their directors to just settle for how things are. They need to see and hear their directors pushing ahead with improvements in their compensation and working conditions.

A wonderful example of this can be found in an article by Carl Sussman, "Out of the Basement: Discovering the Value of Child Care Facilities." Sussman's specific focus is a story of a Head Start director with a vision to create an inspiring new building, but the lessons for directors are even broader — what I call rejecting a scarcity mentality. Sussman puts it this way: "To conserve energy for the educational tasks at hand, many teachers and administrators learn to live with modest expectations. They avoid disappointment by sacrificing their vision . . . (they) need to cultivate the cognitive dissonance of living with inadequate facilities while harboring an ambitious vision that could sustain a greatly enhanced program."

Teachers have many ways of describing the scarcity mentality they experience in their directors, be it excessive penny pinching, power holding as if there's only so much available, failure to network and connect with outside resources, or repeated responses to new ideas with a "They won't let us" or "No way! We can't afford it." They describe directors who inspire and sustain them with contrasting responses such as "Let's see how we could make that work" or "You're pushing me beyond what I know how to do but I want to take up that challenge."

## Tend to the Physical Environment

The typical early childhood program is situated in a less than ideal space with more limitations than we know what to do with. In his article, Sussman describes our situation this way:

"Years of budget balancing and widespread acceptance of inadequate facilities has desensitized providers to their environment and created chronically low expectations."

In his article, he goes on to describe how the physical quality of a center can influence the way teachers interact with children and has the potential to reduce staff turnover rates. Indeed, one of the component areas of the Model Work Standards is the physical setting, where what teachers need for the children and themselves is delineated.

Most early childhood programs don't draw on the research from other professions about the impact of space, light, and color on behavior. We often furnish our programs with little attention to aesthetics or imagination. Across the country, many early childhood programs have begun to look alike, a mini-replica of an early childhood catalog. Usually there are child-sized tables and chairs, primary colors, an abundance of plastic materials, commercial toys, and bulletin board displays. You have to search to find soft or natural elements, places where adults as well as children can feel cozy, alone or with a friend. The smell of disinfectant often floats in the air. Have we forgotten how a cluttered or tattered environment quickly seeps into our psyche? Do we know how a sterile and antiseptic climate shapes our soul?

Caregivers, teachers, and children are spending the bulk of their waking hours living their lives together in our programs. The way we organize the space, create traffic and communication patterns, furnish and decorate all affect the experience people have in our buildings. When I listen for what teachers want from their directors, there is always something about improving the physical environment. In our book, *The Visionary Director*, Deb Curtis and I offer scores of ideas for creating an environment for adults that not only meets their needs but parallels what we want them to be providing for children: softness; beauty; order; reflections of their interests, culture, and home life; things to discover and invent with; a place for personal belongings; and so forth. When directors give attention to the physical environment, it nourishes everyone involved and creates an on-going sense of possibilities.

## Walk Your Talk

Again and again, teachers tell me there's nothing worse than a director who doesn't walk her talk. Promises without follow through, martyring oneself rather than modeling self-care, making excuses rather than making things happen are all behaviors that erode trust and respect. If you say you want more diversity in your program, then you must change the things that are keeping your program homogeneous. When you articulate a vision for your program, you must grow your way into it with how you set priorities and goals, create an environment and organizational culture, harness resources, and conduct human interactions. Listening to what teachers need from their directors can be a superficial endeavor or one which deepens understandings and broadens possibilities. It also contributes to a more stable, committed staff.

## References and Recommended Resources

Bloom, P. J. (1997). *A great place to work: Improving conditions for staff in young children's programs* (Rev. ed.). Washington, DC: NAEYC.

Bloom, P. J. (2000). *Circle of influence: Implementing shared decision making and participative management.* New Horizons, PO Box 863, Lake Forest, IL 60045-0863, (847) 295-8131.

Carter, M., & Curtis, D. (1998), *The visionary director: A handbook for dreaming, organizing, & improvising in your center.* St Paul, MN: Redleaf Press.

The Center for the Child Care Workforce (1998). *Creating better child care jobs: Model work standards for teaching staff in center-based child care.* The Center for the Child Care Workforce, 733 15th Street NW, Suite 1037, Washington, DC 20005-2112, (202) 737-7700, fax: (202) 737-0370 (ccw@ccw.org).

Sussman, C. (1998). "Out of the basement: Discovering the value of child care facilities." *Young Children, 1,* 15.

# DEVELOPING YOUR TEAM

## CHAPTER 12

# The Art of Building (and Re-Building) Staff Unity

by Karen Stephens

*Like an unrelenting poacher, it comes again — poised to pounce in the forefront as the latest crisis for you to solve. Without asking your consent or blessing, it usurps line one (and two, and three) of your already backed up to-do list — and right at your busiest time of year (which for a child care director means ANY time of year)! The predator — staff turnover. Its encroaching shadow announces the impending demise of the delicate balance of respect, cooperation, and loyalty that you have (at long last) seen gel among your staff. Now staff turnover demands that you start the gelling process all over again. Yes, it's time to adopt another member into your child care family.*

*Assuming you have performed a miracle and found a highly qualified individual who will accept very "unqualified" pay, your first staff turnover challenge awaits you — how to help the newcomer AND the existing staff through the adjustment process. But buck up! You can do it! (After all, haven't you already had a lot of practice?)*

*In the following article, I'll share some tricks of the trade to add to your arsenal of skills for coping with the fallout from staff turnover. I hope the ideas will ease your whole staff through another go at the "bonding" process.*

## Staff Turnover Affects Continuing Staff

For everyone, staff turnover can be very intimidating and energy draining. Why? Including new personnel inevitably means change; change means discomfort. (Change ranks high on the Richter scale of stress — ask any Californian!) Overcoming discomfort associated with change-induced stress is work, emotional work — work that means addressing our insecurities related to self-identity and interpersonal relations. Staff members wonder — will their new partner be better than themselves, will she show them up, will the parents or children like her better, will she take over? Worse, will she make things harder than they already are? Directors CAN facilitate the process of integrating new staff so it limits staff stress as much as possible.

## Skills for Integrating New Staff

Integrating new staff members takes commitment, determination, and patience. Building staff cohesiveness requires not only effort, but that most precious commodity . . . time — time for relationships to grow; for commonalties to be recognized (and individual quirks affectionately overlooked); for attachments to form; for respect to be earned and granted; for compassion and helpfulness to overcome turf protection, self-centeredness, and latent concerns of inferiority.

To be sure, it is harder to integrate new staff into some programs more than others. In programs riddled with established cliques, competition for the allegiance of a new staff person can be fierce. This is when a director's patience can be taxed to the max!

The process of staff integration is an art because it requires a sensitive, creative touch. It is a science because it requires a director to make judicious decisions regarding delicate issues that affect staff's egos and perceptions of their abilities. When new staff join your ranks, time for purposeful observation and reflection is required. It takes a keen eye and alert ear to identify strengths and weaknesses of new and continuing staff members. By reflecting on firsthand observations, directors can match personnel strengths and weaknesses so they complement each other.

Directors must employ the skills of flexibility and acceptance when accommodating individual preferences, pet peeves, and personality idiosyncrasies. By example, directors can subtly set limits and boundaries which can prevent current staff from ostracizing new staff because of differences. Increasingly, directors must help staff members learn to not only cope with but to capitalize on diversity among staff!

Directors need to cultivate the skills of creativity, imagination, and resourcefulness to develop strategies and techniques for team building. The ability to set the stage and then step back and let staff work out their own co-worker relationships is critical. No director can WILL staff unity — it must be fostered and continually nurtured like any other type of social relationship.

## Role of Friendships in Staff Relationships

I know, I know. The old adage says that work and personal life should be kept separate — that prickly baggage like emotional friendships should not be relevant, or welcomed, in the work setting. Social relationships simply "muddy up the waters" of a business-like environment. In some business circles, personal friendships are seen as a hindrance to be avoided, not an asset to be cultivated.

But child care is a labor intensive business. And, after all, one of the purposes of our field is to assist in "people-making" for today's and tomorrow's society. How can we perpetuate a philosophy that disregards individual personal relationships? (After all, Dr. Katherine Read did refer to preschool education as a "human relationships laboratory.") Dare we scoff at the validity and importance of our own profession by relegating friendship to being on the fringes of work, rather than an important ingredient in providing quality care? Should friendship only be purposefully nurtured among children, and not staff? Is that being a good role model for children trying to learn social skills?

I believe respectful and, yes, caring friendships are an integral and necessary component among a child care staff. A cohesive staff, who consider themselves friends, is vital to successfully meeting program goals! I have simply found the old adage about keeping friendship out of the workplace outdated. I have seen child care staff become like extended family members to children and each other. I believe this benefits society as a whole, as well as individual programs. I have never found the distance of isolation more comfortable than closeness of caring support. I believe caring support is an outgrowth of friendships developed among staff members.

Over the years, I have observed many teams of teachers. Some appeared very dissimilar in teaching style and personality, and yet their classroom contributions melded seamlessly. I think the common ingredient in those successful "odd couple" match ups was an underlying affection for each other as human beings.

Maintaining a friendship is a strong motivator for cooperation, flexibility, and courtesy (valuable social skills for any business employee). In fact, Karen Miller, in her book *More to Do with Toddlers and Twos* (Telshare Publishing, 1983), states that — based on a survey she conducted — one of the primary reasons caregivers stay in child care, despite its low paying wages, is because they don't want to leave behind close relationships they have formed with co-workers. Directors, are we getting the hint? Apparently promoting friendships can help reduce staff turnover!

## One More Plea for Friendship Building

True friendship provides the cushion of acceptance that is so often needed when a work environment is as people-filled as child care. After all, where there are intelligent, impassioned people, there are bound to be divergent opinions and issues of disagreement.

How tolerant people are of differences of opinion, and how committed they are to work those differences out through negotiation and compromise, is directly related to how important maintaining the personal as well as work relationship is to them.

Let me give you an example. I know of one team teacher who is definitely NOT an early morning person. But the minute her teaching partner announced her pregnancy, she volunteered to take the mother-to-be's opening shift so she would have more time in the morning to get her infant ready and transported to the child care home provider.

If I had imposed this schedule change, I might have appeared to be showing favoritism or expecting more flexibility from child-free staff members than from working parent staff members. Lucky for me, and the working parent, a friendship nurtured over several years existed. It began as a professional relationship and then, as a result of shared work experiences, deepened to a personal friendship.

If the friendship had not developed within the context of work, I doubt such a compassionate team teacher attitude would have been so forthcoming. The result of flexibility was reduced stress — for everyone.

## Setting the Stage for Positive Employee Relationships: Specific Strategies

**✔ Start BEFORE the Beginning**

When interviewing for new staff, include some members of the existing staff whenever possible. Participation could include observing a candidate's classroom teaching style, taking notes during an interview, or simply reviewing resumés or applications. Seek feedback from current staff on the pros and cons of hiring each interview candidate. Certainly, you will want to make it clear that the ultimate decision is yours, but their feedback will be considered in your decision making process.

Why did I recommend including staff in these ways? First, they might gain compassion for you. They will see for themselves that when looking for a qualified and experienced employee, "pickings" can be pretty slim out there! (Excuse my midwestern colloquial terminology, but I can't get it out of my blood or vocabulary.) Secondly, you will be showing your commitment to building a staff that is unified in its approach. Thirdly, it is respectful of current staff. Extra eyes and ears never hurt when you are trying to avoid picking a rotten apple. (Oh, no, there I go again!)

And, lastly, when staff help select a candidate, they are bound to be much more eager to welcome that person aboard. They will be motivated to ensure the candidate's success as a functioning staff member. After all, they don't want to own up to a hiring mistake any more than you do!

**✔ Organize a Mentor System**

Include current staff in integrating new personnel into the staff by asking them to serve as a mentor (a title that recognizes knowledge and ability as well as connotes respect). Mentors can help new staff members with basic orientation, such as where to find the first aid kit. More importantly, mentors can introduce the new staff member to all employees, including the bus driver, custodian, groundskeeper, and nurse.

Mentors can also bring life to program goals and philosophy. Certainly, staff handbooks and staff orientation meetings play a role in staff integration. But these can rarely replace the excitement and commitment conveyed by an enthusiastic mentor. Mentors are in the position to refer new employees to current staff members with special skills in such areas as conducting smooth transitions, developing creative learning centers, or planning activity-based circle times. In this way, mentors can specifically point out role models for new employees.

Mentors can also be "safe havens" for new employees with lots of questions. It is much easier to risk appearing stupid in front of one person than it is to risk it in front of a large staff meeting. New employees may also be shy about asking questions of a direct supervisor who will ultimately evaluate them at the end of their probation period. In the long run, it is better to get new employees' questions answered, whether it be by you or a mentor. An employee with information gaps can unintentionally cause communication or procedural problems for your program; this hinders integration as well as overall staff morale.

**✔ Involve Your Parent Board**

Encourage board members to visit new staff members' classrooms to introduce themselves. Make sure names of new staff are announced at board meetings and parent events. Having the board president send a personal note of welcome can go a long way in engendering a sense of belonging.

**✔ Organize Staff Parties**

Whether you hold it in your home or have it catered in a local park pavilion, parties are great ice breakers! When people laugh together, friendship is not far behind! And, by all means, always have food at the party. I've never failed to see chocolate desserts cause unbridled excitement! If they have nothing else in common, a love of chocolate can begin to break the ice among new and existing staff! Of course, full blown parties aren't necessary. Simple get-togethers at a local restaurant are also helpful during the "getting to know you" stage.

**✔ Celebrate Work Anniversaries**

Surprise a new staff member on her three month anniversary with your program. Try to find out if the staff member collects some special item, i.e., anything with cows on it. Buy her a small gift to add to her collection. Give her the present during a snack time, or hide it in an unlikely place so she will find it unexpectedly. Be sure to enclose a congratulatory note. Honoring a work anniversary with an item that has PERSONAL meaning to the staff member is a small but very effective way to show staff you are glad they are aboard. When you can't offer the pay you would like, thoughtfulness goes a long way!

**✔ Establish Center Committees**

As soon as an employee is hired, assign her (or ask her to volunteer) to serve on a committee. It may be a committee to select multicultural toys or plan a training workshop. The process of working with others informally on a committee gives staff members a chance to know each other away from the classroom.

When committee members delegate tasks and work on goals, a sense of commitment, cooperation, and pride in teamwork is developed. Dare I mention that professional friendships may begin to develop?

**✔ Send a Group to a Conference**

Even a day trip gives staff members a chance to know each other better. Driving in the car, eating a lunch, browsing through an exhibit hall, grabbing a cool drink in the hotel restaurant are the settings in which individuals feel most comfortable revealing themselves to others.

Believe me, I've seen shy people bloom when away from the constraints of the child care schedule! And it never fails to be a delight to witness! . . . Oh, and most relevant to this article, it seldom fails to spark the beginning of a you-know-what — a fulfilling staff friendship.

**✔ Staff Meeting Partners**

Assign partners to contribute to or lead a discussion on an agenda item. For instance, a new teacher and veteran teacher (my politically correct way of saying "old" teacher) may address plans for obtaining free materials to enhance the play yard.

**✔ A "Who Is It?" Scavenger Hunt**

Provide a list of questions geared to help new staff members meet veteran staff members. Wisely selected questions can help new staff members gather information on veteran staff's unique talents or interesting personal history. Give the staff person a month to find out all the answers.

By the end of the month, she should have met plenty of new people and hopefully will feel less like an outsider on an established team. Suggested questions: Who has twins? Whose grandfather was a famous folk singer? Who makes the best chocolate mousse? You get the idea.

**✔ Encourage Parents to Welcome New Staff**

Introduce new staff members in the center newsletter. Provide a profile. Include not only previous experience and training but also personal interests. For instance, if you mention that a new staff member plants native wildflowers or reads mystery books, you are sure to trigger at least one parent's interest so they are inclined to strike up a friendly conversation with the new staff member. Note in parent newsletters the hiring date anniversaries of all staff on an ongoing basis.

**✔ Encourage Parent-Staff Communication and Cooperation**

New staff often enter a new job with trepidation. He may be concerned whether the children or parents will accept him, especially if he is replacing a very popular teacher, cook, aide, or bus driver. Find as many ways as you can to reassure the new staff member by encouraging friendly interchanges with staff and parents.

Night time family events provide ideal opportunities for this. You can also encourage parents to volunteer in the classroom and participate in field trips. Parents should be encouraged to drop in during snack, lunch, or story time. These interchanges will most likely build parents' respect for your staff's abilities, as well as encourage more relaxed, friendly communication and cooperation.

## A Final Wish

Well, there you have it. You are a little more prepared to respond to the next strike from that grim reaper, staff turnover. May it strike seldom — for your staff's and, most importantly, for the children's sake.

# Step-by-Step Guide to Team Building

by Roger Neugebauer

*According to management consultant Peter F. Drucker, the team concept of management is ideally suited to a knowledge organization — an organization that trades in ideas, concepts, and services. Such an organization — and a child care center clearly falls into this category — can extract maximum performance from its workers by managing them as important players on a team rather than as faceless members of the staff.*

*Recognizing the potential value of a team approach to the management of a child care organization, this article describes a step-by-step process for building an effective team.*

Developing a staff of individuals into an effectively functioning team can be a rewarding experience. When a staff is functioning as a team, team members' interrelationships can be supportive, satisfying, and stimulating. Team members will be motivated and enabled to use their talents to the fullest.

Unfortunately, team building is not a quick and painless process. In fact, a center should not even consider making the effort to engage in team building unless all participants are aware of how it will affect them:

- For the leader (whether this is the director, a coordinator, or a head teacher), this means being willing to delegate a considerable amount of authority to the team, being patient when it initially takes the team longer to accomplish a certain task than it would for you on your own, and being able to accept that not everything is going to be done your way. For the leader, it means functioning more as a facilitator than as a boss.
- For subordinates, this means being willing to accept some leadership responsibilities, being more concerned with the interests of the team than with your own interests, and being able to be open and caring in your relationships with other team members. For subordinates, this means functioning as an active participant in the process, rather than as a passive follower of orders.

## The Team Building Process

The team building process described below is designed specifically for the child care setting. Built into it is the assumption that the organization is strapped for time and resources — that staff members do not have a lot of free time to devote to process, and that the organization cannot afford to send the entire staff away for weeks at a time to engage in team building exercises.

In addition, it takes into account the probability that, at the outset, staff members will be unwilling and unable to jump right in and assume significant levels of responsibility.

As a result, the following five step process is designed to be implemented gradually and flexibly. It can be carried out over a period of months as part of regular weekly staff meetings. It can allow various staff members to participate at varying levels of responsibility. And it provides a check to make sure that everyone is satisfied with how the process is working.

### Step #1 — Set achievable goals.

According to Troy D. Bussey, having clear goals is the key factor to team effectiveness. "Mutually agreed upon goals," he observes, "constitute a cohesive and energizing force for all members of the team."

To have this energizing force, the goals should meet these criteria:

- They should be understood and accepted by all team members. The best way to make this happen is to have all team members participate in the goal setting process. One technique for doing this is outlined in "High Participation Goal Setting."

- They should be challenging yet achievable. If goals are too difficult to achieve, team members will soon give up trying, and their motivational force will be lost. Likewise, if goals are too easily accomplished, there will not be much challenge.

- They should be measurable. If at all possible, the team's general goals should be translated into specific yardsticks against which progress can be measured. For example, the goal *To instill a cooperative spirit in children* could be specified as *To increase the incidence of cooperative play by 25%*.

- They should have diverse time frames. Especially at the outset of the team building process, there should be one or two goals that can be achieved within a short period of time, such as *To redesign the toddler room so as to reduce the noise level*. By achieving some goals fairly quickly, individuals will be more inclined than ever to work together as a team to achieve its long term objectives.

**Step #2 — Clarify roles.**

Team members work most effectively together when their roles are clear and reasonably free of conflict. Ideally, each team member should know what tasks she is responsible for, as well as what tasks each other member is responsible for.

An opportune time to clarify roles is just after going through the goal setting process. At this point, there should be some sense of excitement about embarking on a new venture. Team members should be more open than normal to reexamining and redefining their roles.

To clarify roles at this point, team members first should brainstorm about all the areas of responsibility that the team must assume if it is to accomplish its new goals. For example, team members may list such things as . . .

- developing daily plans;
- developing curriculum activities;
- redesigning the classroom;
- selecting curriculum materials;
- buying curriculum materials;
- cleaning up the classroom; and
- supervising student teachers.

After the list is completed, each area of responsibility will need to be formally assigned to one or more team members. The more team members participate in this assignment process, the more accepting they are likely to be of the final breakdown. In any event, the team leader will need to exercise final judgment in cases where team members can't agree, or in cases where team members, due to their inexperience, are biting off more than they can chew.

## High Participation Goal Setting

When attempting to involve all team members in the goal setting process, the most skilled and most assertive team members may tend to dominate the process. If this is likely to happen in your center, you may want to consider employing a variation of the *Delphi Technique* to set goals. This technique assures that all individuals have an opportunity to get their views before the team. The process works as follows:

- Have each member of the team anonymously write down what they believe should be the top two or three goals of the center.

- Read through all these statements, eliminate duplicates, and compile them into a single list.

- Circulate this list back to all team members with the instructions that they select from this list their recommendations for the top three center goals.

- Count how many times each goal is selected and then present the top three or four vote getters to the team at the next staff meeting. At this meeting, team members should discuss these potential goals, agree on which ones make sense to tackle at the same time, and make suggestions as to how these might be stated more clearly.

- Write up the agreed upon goals based on the comments in the meeting and pass these statements out to team members for their final review.

- At the next staff meeting, make final revisions and formally approve the goals. Write up the approved goals and distribute copies to all team members.

In addition to these formal roles relating to the accomplishment of team goals, there also exists an entirely different set of informal roles. These roles relate to the internal functioning of the team. For example, in order for a team to function well, someone on the team needs to accept responsibility for harmonizing relationships among staff members, for encouraging less assertive or experienced team members to participate actively, and for initiating action when a problem or opportunity exists.

While it does not make sense to assign these roles formally, the team leader should continually monitor team functioning to be sure that all necessary roles are being performed by someone.

### Step #3 — Build supportive relationships.

At the beginning of each year, Clare Cherry challenged each of her teachers to see to it that each of the other teachers had the best year teaching that they'd ever had (Cherry). This type of cooperative spirit is exactly what is needed to make a team work. In an effectively functioning team, each team member draws strength from the personal satisfaction of being a part of a caring group of individuals, as well as from the professional support provided by team members.

However, it is very easy to say that team members should care about each other and support each other, but it is not so easy to make this happen. While the team leader cannot require team members to be supportive, she can structure situations that encourage this to happen, and she can remove obstacles that often prevent it. Here are examples of approaches that some directors have found effective:

- **Feedback training.** In a survey of child care centers in New England, "lack of feedback on my performance" was identified by teachers as their greatest frustration (Neugebauer, 1975). The same teachers indicated that the persons they most would respect feedback from are the teachers they work with. Unfortunately, teachers often lack the skills and inclination to give useful feedback. To stimulate the flow of feedback among teachers, it may be helpful to provide training to teachers on how to give effective feedback (see "References and Resources").

- **Team resource people.** Betty Jones has observed that it is easy for a director to view herself as the final authority on everything, when in fact in many areas there are other staff members who know more than she does (Jones). To tap the expertise that exists among team members and to get team members into the habit of looking to each other for support, instead of always relying on the team leader, some centers have found it helpful to designate different members of the team as resource persons for specific topics, such as music, large motor skills, aggression, or language. These people will be designated on the basis of their current skills and interests, and they will be expected to do some extra research to keep up to date.

- **Best-worst incidents.** In a team where there is not yet a great deal of trust and openness, it may be difficult for team members to know enough about the needs and feelings of their peers to provide them support. One approach many centers use to encourage team members to open up is the *best-worst incidents* approach. At a team meeting, the leader asks each staff member to relate the best thing that happened to them at the center the past week, as well as the worst thing.

An infinite variety of variations on this theme could be used: What is the toughest problem you have solved this week and the toughest you have yet to solve? What parent comment made you feel best this week and which one made you feel worst? Not only does this technique give all team members an easy way to share their victories and receive some positive strokes, it also gives other team members ideas on how they can provide some support.

### Step #4 — Encourage active participation.

One of the positive features of the team approach to management is that it can take maximum advantage of the abilities and knowledge of individual team members. However, this utilization of member resources does not happen automatically. A team leader needs to be resourceful in encouraging all team members to contribute their ideas, opinions, and energies. Here are some suggestions:

- **Spotlight challenges.** The creative talents of a team are more likely to be unleashed if there is a specific task to focus on (Uris). The team leader can stimulate team members by pointing out a specific problem that is of major concern to the center (the frequency of accidents on the climbing structure) or an opportunity of high potential (the growing demand for drop-in care in the community).

- **Provide a fertile environment.** Creativity seldom involves the creation of a totally new idea. Organizational theorist James March has observed that "most innovations in an organization are a result of borrowing rather than invention." Put another way, creativity involves combining conventional ideas in unconventional ways.

Therefore, the team leader should ensure that team members have rich and varied experiences to draw upon. This would involve such steps as providing a wealth of reading materials in the teachers' lounge, encouraging team members to visit other centers, and making it possible for them to attend classes and workshops.

- **Demonstrate interest.** Nothing kills the enthusiasm of individuals in developing a new idea more quickly than the realization that no one else is interested in it. If one or more team members are working on a new room arrangement, parent communication form, or nap time routine, the team leader should support their efforts by demonstrating an interest in what they are doing, as well as by bringing it to the attention of the entire team.

- **Offer help when needed.** Not all individuals have an equal ability to come up with an inspiration, to flesh it out, and to develop it into a ready-to-implement product. A team leader needs to be sensitive to the creative styles of various team members. She needs to be able to jump in and offer a helping hand to those who can only come up with gleam-in-the-eye stage ideas, while standing aside and letting others run their ideas through to completion (Uris).

- **Foster a permissive atmosphere.** All team members need to feel that their ideas and contributions are welcomed and valued. The team leader needs to nurture a climate in the team that is accepting of new ideas — no matter how outlandish they may initially appear.

Spiro Agnew loudly decried the *instant analyses* of television news commentators. While one may suspect that he was more upset by the content of their analyses than their speed, his concern does highlight the discouraging aspect of immediate critical reaction. If a team member lacks confidence or assertiveness to begin with, he will certainly be doubly reluctant to expose his ideas to the team if he knows they will be criticized, ridiculed, or ignored.

That is not to say, of course, that all ideas should be accepted no matter what. Certainly every proposal should be subject to careful, objective scrutiny by the team before implementation. However, such a critical examination should only take place after the contributor has had the opportunity to explain it fully, and even try it out if possible.

- **Allow for individual interests.** According to organizational psychologist Harry Levinson, an organization is best served when it "permits people to seize and develop those challenges that most excite their curiosity." In spotlighting challenges for the team, the team leader should not restrict attention to a single problem but should delineate a wide range of opportunities for useful innovation. Being able to follow one's interest is more likely to stimulate a flow of ideas than being restricted to a problem that is critical but of little interest.

### Step #5 — Monitor team effectiveness.

You can't build a house without occasionally stepping back to see if all the workers' efforts are resulting in a solid, salable product. Likewise, you can't build a team without periodically monitoring to determine if progress is being made.

Two types of monitoring are of value. First and foremost, the team should be evaluated in terms of whether it is accomplishing its goals. It can be very rewarding for team members when they see that their cooperative efforts are really making a difference. This can provide all the more incentive to work hard at making the team work. Conversely, it is vital for team members to know as soon as possible if their efforts are not moving them closer to the accomplishment of their goals. The sooner

## Common Team Problems

- **Role ambiguity**. Sometimes certain areas of responsibility are left out in never-never land. Everyone knows that they exist but no one knows whose responsibility they are. This often happens with menial responsibilities that nobody wants to touch, such as cleaning up the classroom at the end of the day and keeping the book and toy shelves well organized. Sometimes it can occur with very important tasks that are hard to find time for. Everyone on the team may believe that researching new ideas or evaluating the curriculum are important, but if no one is specifically charged with carrying out these tasks, they just don't get done.

- **Role conflict**. Conflict can occur when two or more team members believe they have responsibility for the same task. A teacher and a director may both believe that it is their responsibility to bring a major concern with a child to the attention of his parents. When this occurs, both team members may end up expending a considerable amount of energy outwardly arguing about whose job it is, or inwardly dealing with anger and frustration. This energy drained off unproductively into the conflict is energy that could more profitably be invested in accomplishing the team's goals.

- **Intergroup conflict**. Conflict can also occur between groups of individuals, i.e., between teams. If the staff of a center is divided into two teams, one serving the preschool children and one serving the infants and toddlers, these two teams may come into conflict over the use of space, over money for supplies, or over use of the kitchen facilities. This is a behavior that very often occurs in the early stages of team building in larger organizations. Team members become so loyal to their own team that anyone on the outside is looked upon as a competitor. This *we-they* attitude is encouraging to the extent that it shows that some *esprit de corps* is beginning to develop among team members. However, in its extreme form, it can be harmful to the organization as a whole.

## What Is the Optimum Team Size?

There are no hard and fast rules about what is the best size for a team for it to function most efficiently. Organizational psychologist Peter F. Drucker suggests that if a team has more than 15 members (the maximum size of aboriginal hunting teams), it becomes unwieldy. Teams larger than this tend to exhibit a lack of clarity, little sense of responsibility by team members, and an over concern with internal procedures and politics.

Although small teams seem to work best, they can also become too small. They should not be so small that team members collectively do not possess all the skills needed to perform their common tasks. Nor should they be so small that team members fail to exhibit a diversity of experiences, talents, and perspectives.

they know their efforts are misdirected, the less time they will waste before making necessary corrections.

Monitoring progress against goals, or program evaluation, can take many forms. Ideally, the team should be able to express its goals in measurable terms so that there can be some direct yardstick of progress. For example, a team's goal might be expressed as *reducing incidents of aggressive behavior by 30%*. At the beginning of the year, someone could observe the number of incidents of aggression occurring in a classroom over a set period of time. Then, every two or three months, a similar count could be made to see if the number of incidents of aggression is actually declining.

More often than not, however, goals in early childhood settings are not measurable. In these cases, the team must rely on less direct indicators of progress — parent satisfaction surveys, comparisons of behavioral descriptions from diaries, period observations by outside consultants, etc. While such techniques may not yield any cut and dried indications of progress, they can provide team members with significant amounts of helpful feedback.

The second type of monitoring which a team can and should engage in is the assessment of team functioning. At least two or three times a year, team members should take time out to assess how well they are working together as a team. The longer the gap between assessments, the more likely it is that minor shortcomings will degenerate into major problems.

Monitoring of team functioning need not be a complex process. Typically, what happens is that team members anonymously rate the team using a checklist of functions and then discuss the findings and their implications at a team meeting.

As can be seen from the preceding discussion, getting a team approach launched and up to speed is not a simple process. It requires time, patience, and the willingness of all involved to open themselves up to new ways of working and relating to each other. However, in a profession that demands so much creativity, so much flexibility, and so much in terms of interpersonal skills, the team approach offers an excellent vehicle for achieving peak performance.

## References and Resources


Bussey, T. D. (January/February 1984). "Building a Winning Team." *Nonprofit World Report*.

Cherry, C. (1991). "Promoting Harmonious Staff Relationships." *Fostering Improved Staff Performance* (Reprint #3). Redmond, WA: Exchange Press.

Drucker, P. F. (1973). *Management*. New York: Harper & Row, Publishers.

Jones, E. (1990). "Creating Environments Where Teachers, Like Children, Learn Through Play." *Developing Staff Skills* (Reprint #7). Redmond, WA: Exchange Press.

Levinson, H. (1968). *The Exceptional Executive*. Cambridge, MA: Harvard University Press.

March, J., & Simon, H. (1958). *Organizations*. New York: John Wiley and Sons.

Neugebauer, R. (November 1983). "Assessing Team Performance." *Exchange*.

Neugebauer, R. (1991). "Guidelines for Effective Use of Feedback." *Fostering Improved Staff Performance* (Reprint #3). Redmond, WA: Exchange Press.

Neugebauer, R. (1991). "How to Stimulate Creativity in Your Staff." *Fostering Improved Staff Performance* (Reprint #3). Redmond, WA: Exchange Press.

Neugebauer, R. (1975). *Organizational Analysis of Day Care*. Arlington, VA: ERIC Document Reproduction Service.

Uris, A. (1976). *The Executive Deskbook*. New York: Van Nostrand Reinhold Company.

# Planning Staff Meetings

by Margie Carter

*One of the biggest challenges child care programs face is finding a suitable time, space, and budget for all staff meetings. With all the varying work shifts in a program, getting everyone to attend a meeting and paying them for this time requires a logistical genius, not to mention slippery budget configurations.*

Surprisingly, large agencies often seem to have a better time of it than smaller programs do. School districts, Ys, and multi-service agencies tend to plan their annual calendars with staff development and meeting days in mind, and they don't renege in spite of the inconvenience this may cause the families they serve. Large or small, the programs most successful in carving out regular meeting time for staff set their calendars for the year and have persuasive rationales and policies for parents, along with clear expectations for staff attendance.

Some do this with a consistently scheduled early closure once a month, while others close quarterly for a staff development day. When programs hold evening all staff meetings, they often make use of a floating substitute for the week of the meeting so that each staff member gets comp time for these required extra meeting hours. A consortium of child care directors serving low income families decided to collectively close their programs the last few days of the week before the Labor Day weekend to do some individual program and community-wide staff training.

However we configure it, the gyrations required to gather our staff together for a meeting creates an imperative to consider this time as precious and to use it well. In my view, thoughtful planning and organization of our meeting time and space should parallel the process we want the teachers to bring to their work with children and families. The *process* we use in gathering our staff together can be as significant for our staff development as any *content* we might hope to cover during the meeting. When directors create a thoughtful model for adult learning, teachers experience first hand the deep respect and thoughtful planning we want them to offer the children.

## Be clear about the purpose and structure of your meetings

Sometimes we gather our staff together to review important program considerations, make decisions, or strategize on how to best support a child, family, or staff member. Other times our meetings have the structure of a workshop focused on a particular topic, for instance, health and safety practices, promoting literacy, or child guidance. There are occasions when we gather together primarily for social time, perhaps celebrating an accomplishment, holiday, or person we want to honor.

It seems a terrible misuse of our precious gatherings to use them primarily for the business details of staff schedules, reminders of regulations, or important announcements. This information could be better delegated to smaller team meetings, bulletins, or routing slip memos. There are occasions when staff input or involvement in important decisions works best in a meeting where all points of view can be heard and differences negotiated. (Paula Jorde Bloom's little book *Circle of Influence: Implementing Shared Decision Making and Participative Management* offers great ideas for how to think about this.)

In our book *The Visionary Director*, Deb Curtis and I offer a triangle framework for thinking through and organizing your work as a director into three comprehensive areas: managing and overseeing resources, systems, policies, standards; teaching and coaching with a focus on your staff as learners; and building and supporting community within your program and between your program and the wider community. You can plan staff meetings with the triangle framework in mind.

### Managing and overseeing tasks for meetings:

- Creating a system for agenda development and the meeting structure
- Arranging the schedule and environment
- Creating the development of and coaching system for your Code of Conduct or Ground Rules for Meeting Behaviors
- Managing a system for recording and documenting meeting discussions, decisions, and activities
- Monitoring the group process and dynamics
- Tracking responsibilities, decisions, tasks, odds and ends
- Using evaluation systems and planning needed changes

### Teaching and coaching tasks for meetings:

- Using staff meetings for learning and development (rather than business announcements)
- Focusing time with hands on, meaningful learning experiences
- Providing for individual learning styles and collaborative thinking experiences
- Coaching with developmental stages and milestones in mind
- Using facilitative questions to promote self-reflection

### Building and supporting community tasks for meetings:

- Creating a climate for all voices to be heard and respected
- Providing opportunities to get connected through shared experiences
- Practicing the recognition and valuing of different perspectives and communication styles and negotiating differences
- Exploring ways to connect with the wider community
- Celebrating significant events

## Planning meetings for learning and connecting

You can provide effective training during staff meetings if your primary goal is to offer a learning process for the adults, rather than trying to convey information. Time devoted to active learning in staff meetings conveys the importance you place on thinking and growing, and develops your program as a learning community for adults as well as children.

### Strategy: Do skits rather than announcements

I saw a wonderful example of a director turning *reminders* into a playful learning and community building activity. Concerned that some new staff hadn't been working during the summer in her program, director Susie Eisman at Hilltop Children's Center wrote headings of key topics she wanted to review on pieces of paper, i.e. field trip safety, summer sun health issues, playground first aid, communications with families. Small clusters of staff members were given one of these topics, asked to brainstorm a list of concerns to plan for, and then weave these into a skit to present to the whole staff.

Rather than a yawn-filled hour of a long list of guidelines, teachers were treated to a fun-filled time of discovering their creativity, shared knowledge, and values. Months later they were still talking about that hilarious way Lisa played the devil's voice in Jason's ear trying to get him to ignore the safety guidelines for transporting children on field trips, and how Kit reminded the child stung by a bee how to avoid trauma for the bee as well.

### Strategy: Explore different values

Teachers benefit from examining and naming the influences on their own values and preferred practices. It is useful to do this in a context stripped of a *right or wrong* tone. A simple way to do this is to write on separate pieces of paper possible opposing viewpoints on policies and practices and then post them around the room. Ask everyone to find one viewpoint they wish to discuss, go to that paper, and talk with others there. They don't have to agree with the viewpoint, but they should have strong sentiments they want to discuss. Possible ideas for the papers include: children should call adults by their first names; children should primarily be offered limited choices and non-negotiable guidelines from adults; children should have to try at least one bite of all food served; parents should be immediately told when their children break a rule.

In the debriefing discussion following the talk at the different papers, acknowledge that sometimes teachers are asked to carry out practices different from their own belief systems, or there may be a difference between a family's practice and that of the program. Exploring the values and belief systems underlying practices with children can result in new learning and a willingness to accommodate a different viewpoint without judgment or negation.

### Strategy: Invite neighborhood kindergarten teachers and principals

In today's climate of outcomes-based education and high-stakes testing, it is easy for schools and child care programs to point a finger at each other. Why not, instead, try to build a relationship and some mutual understandings between your staff and that of the schools your children typically move on to? Invite the kindergarten teachers and principals to come hear stories of how your children are learning through play. Share documentation of in-depth projects, transcriptions of children's conversations, and other evidence of their learning process. Ask to hear the teachers' and principals' frustrations and concerns and ideas for building stronger connections between your programs. Consider including parents and some of your graduates to contribute to this meeting as well.

### Strategy:
### Do a self-assessment of recent meetings

To explore this idea of having your staff meetings parallel what you want the teachers to be doing with the children, reflect on your last three meetings. Creating three columns on a paper with the dates of each meeting as the headers, quickly jot down the agenda for each and a summary of how time was spent, the tone, focus, and primary voices that were heard. Consider these questions as well:

- Was the space well-organized, comfortable and inviting?
- What kinds of choices did the staff have about how time was spent?
- In what ways were people able to deepen their relationships and experience being part of a community?
- How were staff given opportunities to construct their knowledge about something worth learning?
- In what ways was their learning or experience made visible?

Looking over your answers, do you feel your staff had a meaningful learning experience and deepened their connections with each other, the program philosophy and vision, or possibly the value of their work to the wider community?

# Mentoring Teachers . . . A Partnership in Learning

by Patricia Berl

*Training advice is easy to find these days. Books, videos, workshops, and seminars are everywhere. But ask a university professor, CEO, or master teacher how they acquired the knowledge and skills to successfully perform their jobs and they will rarely say they were guided by traditional methods of instruction. Rather, today's leaders, whether in the boardroom or the classroom, point to inspiring mentors, who were pivotal influences in helping them recognize and develop their own capabilities to excel (**Wall Street Journal**, 2002).*

Within classroom settings, mentors can be the key to unlocking and developing teachers' talents. For many educators of young children, the very essence of teaching is a process of continual inquiry, discovery, and renewal. Yet, most teachers rarely have time in their daily teaching to reflect upon what happens in their classrooms, document their work, or study their own teaching practices. Through regular observations and discussions with a skilled mentor, teachers can begin to refine teaching practices, acquire new competencies, gain insight, and become more confident and effective educators.

Mentors can counter the pull of comfortable and ingrained classroom routines by helping teachers analyze and examine the tacit understandings that have developed around familiar practices (Terell, Klein, Jewett, 1998). With a mentor as a guide, a teacher, whose usual methods may not be working in a particular situation, can step back, reframe, change, or take a more experimental approach in her teaching. Through discussions, observations, and self-reflection, mentors encourage teachers to make new sense out of familiar situations and uncertainties and respond successfully to challenges.

## What is a mentor?

The term mentor originates from the Greek mythological hero, Odysseus, who, prior to setting out for an extended journey to Troy, entrusts the education of his son, Temelecus, to his loyal friend Mentor. Odysseus instructs Mentor to tell the son all he knows. Modern usage defines mentoring as "to coach, tutor, train, give hints, or prime with fact." Training applications in industry and education use the term mentoring interchangeably with coaching. But regardless of the term used, the fundamental concept is the pairing of reflection and apprenticeship, when an older or more experienced individual passes down knowledge of how a task is done to someone who is less experienced.

## A Learning Partnership Over Time

The focus of mentoring is on the acquisition of knowledge, core competencies, and career development. Framed within the context of an extended relationship over a longer period of time, mentors create a learning partnership between themselves and the individual, fostering feelings of competency, recognition, learning, accomplishment, and high performance. Through a series of supportive interactions teachers acquire knowledge, perspective, and self-awareness from their direct engagement with a mentor. Mentors, in turn, stimulate the teacher's own introspection, primarily through questions that facilitate insight or change in a teacher's behavior or perception, leading the way to greater skill, awareness, and defined outcomes. Timothy Gallwey, Harvard educator and tennis expert, describes mentoring, "as a way of unlocking a person's potential to maximize their own performance. It is helping them to learn rather than teaching them" (Whitmore, 2002).

## Let the Learning Begin...

Gloria Steinem, noted feminist author, asserts, "The first problem for all of us men and women is not to learn, but to unlearn." Mentor relationships are effective because they help us to do just that. They challenge our thinking, causing us to critically reflect upon our current practices, moving us to action and transformation.

Mentoring works because it evolves from core principles of adult learning theory (Bell, 1998).

First, adults are motivated to learn as they develop needs and interests that learning will satisfy. In mentoring, we begin with the teacher's needs and interests as the appropriate starting points for setting goals.

Second, adult orientation to learning is usually life or work-centered. Mentor relationships begin with defining the focus of the relationship around life-and/or work related situations, not academic or theoretical subjects.

Third, experience is the richest resource for adult learning. Mentoring involves active participation in a planned series of experiences. Knowledge and competency are derived from the analysis of those experiences and their application to work and life situations.

Fourth, adults have a deep need to be self-directing. The characteristic style of mentors is to engage individuals in a process of inquiry, analysis, and decision-making, rather than to directly transmit knowledge and then evaluate the protege's conformity to it. Mentors encourage self-directed, independent, and collegial interactions over more hierarchical relationships.

Fifth, as individual differences among adult learners increase with age and experience, mentoring is well suited to make use of optimum provisions for differences in learning styles, pace of learning, content, culture, ethnicity, religion, gender, urgency, context, career life cycle, and aspirations.

## Getting Started

The process begins with the mentor inviting the teacher to identify "What do I want to learn, to change, to happen?" The mentor facilitates by helping the teacher explore the current situation and identify what the teacher is doing and what could ideally be done. This *reality check* is achieved through insights the teacher derives from discussions, observations, feedback, and self-reflection.

Next, the mentor and teacher explore the current situation and define a desired goal or outcome. The mentor asks, "What would be the most helpful thing for you to take away from this session?" Once a problem or goal is identified, the mentor encourages the teacher to consider options, alternative strategies, or new courses of action. Questions such as "What can you try?", "What happens if...?", or "What else could you do?" frame the discussions and observations by the mentor. Once a goal is identified, the teacher implements the new plan, evaluates, modifies, and reflects back upon the results.

In facilitating goals or desired outcomes mentors should consider the following:

- An understanding of the principle issues.
- A vision or description of the desired outcome.
- A decision as to which way to proceed.
- A clear idea of the action steps.
- An agreed upon time frame for meeting the goal.
- An outline for the month that each can follow.
- A defined schedule for meeting.

Effective mentors are excellent observers who possess the ability to quickly assess and understand the teacher's skill level and needs. They are able to target their discussions and coaching to what is important to the teacher, developing rapport, and validation. While some mentors may be responsible for supervising others in the organization, it is best if the mentor is not a direct supervisor of the teacher, since supervisory relationships can easily introduce an evaluative quality to the feedback, hindering open communication and risk taking.

## From Feedback to Insight

It has been said, "There is no wisdom like frankness." Leading management consultant and author, Ken Blanchard believes that honest feedback is critical to changing behavior. In the book, *Empowerment Takes More Than a Minute*, Blanchard writes that, "People without information cannot act responsibly. People with information are compelled to act responsibly." Without information, people cannot monitor themselves or make sound decisions. (Blanchard, Carlos, & Randolph, 1996). For Blanchard, sharing information through feedback is the first key to empowering people in organizations. It allows the individual to understand his or her current situation in clear terms. Sharing information through feedback builds trust throughout the organization and helps people to gain a greater sense of responsibility and ownership of their situations. Mentors encourage and facilitate the sharing of information by asking questions, probing, and helping to spark ideas that compel the teachers to search for answers and new perspectives.

## Leading With Questions

Effective mentors lead with questions, not answers. In the popular best seller *Good to Great*, author Jim Collins cites numerous examples of CEOs who create successful work climates by engaging their employees through questions. By opening up conversations with questions like, "What is on your mind?" or "What should we be concerned about?" leaders create a climate of open communication that allows the current business realities and struggles to bubble to the surface, be identified, discussed, and understood (Collins, 2001).

Like the CEOs in *Good to Great*, mentors, too, query teachers with open ended and probing questions that increase awareness and understanding. Here are some examples of questions mentors can use to help teachers reflect and gain insight (Whitmore, 2002):

- What is the hardest/most challenging part of this for you?
- What criteria are you using?
- What would be the consequences for you and others?
- What advice would you give to a friend in your situation?
- What would you gain/lose by doing/saying that?
- If someone said/did that to you, what would you feel/think/do?

- What would success in this challenge look like to you?
- What would be the first step you would need to take? Why?
- What should happen next?

In guiding teachers, mentors are careful to reflect back what they heard the teacher express and summarize points. This ensures correct understanding and reassurance that the learner is being fully heard and understood. Through discussion and analysis, mentors can validate the teacher's perspective as well as bring differing views to the discussion.

## Choosing a mentor

A successful mentor program depends upon creating a climate of mutual trust, patient leadership, and emotional maturity. It requires a shared commitment of both time and goals. The following characteristics are important to keep in mind when choosing a mentor:

**Balance** — Because the mentoring partnership is grounded in mutuality, interdependence, and respect, emphasis is given early on to role clarity and expectations.

**Respect** — Partners recognize their differences while respecting their common needs and objectives. There is a spirit of generosity and acceptance rather than a focus on rules and rights.

**Truthfulness** — Mentors work hard to give feedback in a way that is caring, frank, and compassionately straightforward.

**Trust and acceptance** — There is a climate of experimentation, risk taking, and freedom to fail. Error is accepted as a necessary step on the path from novice to master.

**Optimism** — Mentors see teachers in terms of their future potential, not just past performance. They believe that people possess more capability than they are currently expressing (Whitmore, 2002).

**Self-directed** — Mentors follow the interests of the learner, monitoring how that relates to the problem or inquiry at hand. By refraining from asserting one's own interests, mentors gain the trust and confidence of the teacher since their interests and needs are respected.

**Support** — Good mentors don't rescue, they support. They resist the temptation to demonstrate a preferred way and instead steer the learning into a supportive direction through questions and observations. While mentors may on occasion demonstrate a technique, they continually ask themselves, will my demonstrations increase or decrease the learner's independence?

**Acknowledgement** — Mentors set aside time to reflect on the learner's success. They ask the teacher what made it successful, so that the individual can capitalize on it and experience a positive change process that is self-sustaining (Holliday, 2001).

## Applications

As a practical form of professional development, mentoring lends itself to a myriad of applications including improving team communications, pinpointing the specific cause for an undesirable behavior, conducting classroom observations, addressing classroom management issues, implementing a new curriculum, conducting child assessments, resolving staff or parent conflicts, preparing for accreditation, or succession planning.

In responding to the ever present challenges of retaining quality staff and providing continual professional development, mentoring becomes an invaluable tool for developing the human assets within a center. Simply stated, mentoring is about fostering and developing a professional disposition toward lifelong learning.

Mentoring, when executed well, becomes a way of thinking, believing, and being. It is a process through which teachers can become reflective practitioners, capable of mentoring others. More than just a partnership based on good synergy, mentoring can become a catalyst for learning, high achievement, and personal fulfillment.

## References

Bell, C. R. (1998). *Managers as Mentors*. Austin, TX: Bard Press.

Blanchard, K., Carlos, J., & Randolph, A. (1996). *Empowerment Takes More Than a Minute.* San Francisco: Berrett-Koehler Publishers.

Collins, J. (2001). *Good to Great*. New York: Harper Collins Publishers.

DeSena, J. (2002). Business Consultant and Speaker. Discussion. Jim DeSena, MBA, CSP, is a nationally recognized authority on leadership. He is the author of *Take the Lead and Win* (McGraw Hill, 2003), and president of Performance Achievement Systems, Inc. His web site, www.salesleaders.com, provides free articles, reports, and resources. He can be reached at 800-4321-WIN.

Holliday, M. (2001). *Coaching, Mentoring & Managing*. Franklin Lakes, NJ: The Career Press.

Hymowitz, C. (2002). "Effective Leaders Say One Pivotal Experience Sealed Their Careers." *Wall Street Journal*.

Tertell, E. A., Klein, S. M., & Jewett, J. L. (1998). *When Teachers Reflect*. Washington, DC: National Association for the Education of Young Children.

Whitmore, J. (2002). *Coaching for Performance*. London, UK: Nicholas Brealey Publishing.

# Appraising Staff

## Chapter 13

# Monitoring, Measuring, and Evaluating Teacher Performance

by Kay M. Albrecht

*Although every director would agree that teachers need to be regularly evaluated, many find little time to do it. Nevertheless, there are a number of good reasons to monitor, measure, and evaluate teacher performance:*

- *to identify good teachers so they can be recognized and rewarded for their excellence;*
- *to identify poor teachers so they can be counseled into a more appropriate career choice;*
- *to identify teaching skill deficits so they can be improved through training.*

The critical first step is to establish your program philosophy. It is impossible to determine evaluation criteria until you are in touch with the philosophical principles which guide your program. Include your staff in the process of establishing your philosophy, particularly if you do not have a written philosophy to guide you.

The philosophy statement that emerges as staff members consider their beliefs about children, families, and programs will guide you in all of your efforts. Not only will it guide your behavior, it will also clearly articulate to parents what they can expect from your program. Because parents know what to expect from your program, they are more likely to be satisfied.

The next step is to identify the teaching behaviors that support your philosophy, as well as those that are in conflict with it. For example, if you believe that children need security and nurturance in the care and early education setting, you will value teachers who respond to children needing affection and security by comforting, stroking, and soothing them.

Teachers who use these skills are demonstrating philosophically compatible teaching behaviors. Teachers who respond with comments like "big boys (girls) don't cry when they fall down" are showing insensitivity to children's needs and are demonstrating philosophically incompatible teaching skills.

When developing your competency list, include categories of behaviors such as professional skills (reading professional publications), personal skills (punctuality), interactive skills (bending or stooping to the child's eye level, calling children by their names), parent relations skills (communicating to parents necessary information about the child's day) and peer relations skills (avoiding nonproductive conversation with co-teachers while on duty).

As you go about describing the behaviors which you want teachers to demonstrate, avoid the inclusion of behaviors you cannot see, like *seems to understand children.* Instead, choose behaviors that can be easily observed in the natural setting of the classroom. *Sees that children are dressed appropriately for existing temperatures throughout the day* is a competency that can be readily observed on the playground or perhaps at nap time.

It is also important to limit the number of skills you identify to a reasonable number. While you want your observations to provide you with a measure of teacher performance, you do not want it to be cumbersome and unmanageable.

Finally, put the skills identified into a usable format. A checklist is often the easiest. Listing the skills down one side of a page allows you to take anecdotal notes about the skills and behaviors on the other side of the page. Having a usable format will facilitate the gathering of supportive data through observation. Be sure that your format allows you to easily identify which skills you have not seen demonstrated and need to observe for or plan to address through training.

## Monitoring Classroom Behavior

Monitoring the classroom behavior of teachers is the most difficult part of the process because it is usually perceived by directors as time consuming. The following suggestions may help:

- Set up a schedule for monitoring skills. Observe in the natural setting of the classroom where teachers are regularly assigned.

- Share with teachers the intent of your observations, what you are observing, and the schedule of your observations. If teachers know in advance that you are observing for particular philosophically supportive teaching behaviors and that you plan to observe them more than just once, they will be more likely to see the process as positive and less likely to be intimidated by your observations.

- Vary the time of the day during which you observe. If you observe only at transition times, you are likely to miss certain key skills. On the other hand, observing the way a teacher handles transitions is an important piece of information to have. One or two observations in the morning, one or two at transition times, one observation during outdoor play, and one observation in the late afternoon would be a good basis for beginning the feedback dialogue.

- Vary the length of your observations. During interest or learning center time, there may be opportunities to observe many teaching skills. In this case, a 10 to 15 minute observation may be required. Observing the storytelling skills of a teacher may require only three or four minutes of observation.

- Observe all the time. This is the most important thing to remember. As directors manage by walking around, they see a great deal of teaching behavior taking place. When you go into a classroom to get the lunch count, look around to see what skills the teacher might be demonstrating. By capitalizing on observation moments like these, you will easily gather documentation of skills without extensive time dedicated to the process.

- Resist the tendency to reach a conclusion after one or two observations. You are looking to see which of the identified teaching skills are a part of the teacher's behavior over a period of time. Teachers may handle situations differently depending on a variety of variables. Observing more than once will allow you to differentiate those behaviors which are a part of a teacher's repertoire and those which are emerging or not present.

- Record what you see. Take notes during your observation in an anecdotal or running diary format. In order for the information you gather from your observations to be useful, it must be based on what you see rather than the way you feel about what you see. For example:

*Miss Jan looked up from her story to see Jon and his mother at the door. She stopped her story and said, "Excuse me, children, I'll be right back. Jon is here and I need to say hello to his mother." She walked over to the door, stooped down to Jon's level and said in a pleasant voice, "Good morning, Jon." Then she looked up at his mother and said in a pleasant voice, "I hope you enjoyed the holidays. Jon was looking forward to Christmas at his grandparents. I hope he'll tell us about it later." Looking back at Jon, Miss Jan said, "You can join me in the library center for a story if you like. Say goodbye to Mommy and I'll help you put your things in your cubbie." Miss Jan and Jon walked toward his cubbie as he waved goodbye to his mother.*

This anecdotal report gives a number of clues to this teacher's skills. We know that she stoops to the child's eye level to interact, greets both parents and children upon arrival at the classroom, gathers information from the parent to use in individualizing her interactions, is aware of the activities of the entire group even when dealing with part of it, and so on. The brief interchange may have taken only two or three minutes and may have been observed as the director was returning from escorting a new family to an adjoining classroom. By focusing on the gathering of anecdotal information, it is possible to avoid the biggest roadblock to the system — making judgments based on inaccurate and/or incomplete information.

## Providing Feedback to Teachers

Now that you have gathered documentation of the teaching skills, provide feedback to each staff member. To be effective, feedback must be regular and directed. It is often possible to provide feedback to teachers informally. A brief comment at nap time about the sensitive handling of a classroom conflict provides the teacher with immediate information about how you view her skills. Sharing how you handled a similar situation may provide a teacher with some new ideas about how to handle the situation if it arises again. It may also be possible to make a brief positive comment about what you observed when teachers were not involved directly with children.

As valuable as informal feedback is, it cannot substitute for formal feedback in a constructive setting. New teachers need feedback early in their teaching experiences, as often as once a month. More experienced teachers need formal, structured feedback at least two or three times a year.

During the feedback session, the director should share with the teacher the information she gathered during her observations. The exchange of information is most helpful if it is specific. A brief recount of the skills you observed when Jon and his mother arrived at the center would be a good way to begin.

Share the competency strengths you observed first. Talk about the skills that are in place. Give several examples from your notes. Be sure to include the subtle messages received from tone of voice, facial expressions, and body language.

Identify the one or two skills that you did not see demonstrated or that were inappropriately demonstrated. This discussion will be the real guts of the feedback conference. It should provide the teacher with information about how you perceive her behavior as well as how you would like to see it changed. Both pieces of information are crucial. Giving feedback is not enough. It must be accompanied with specific guidance on how to change the behavior in question.

## Following Up With Training

Sometimes the appropriate guidance cannot be given in the feedback conference alone. If this is the case, a training plan must be developed. The purpose of a training plan is to identify how the teacher will go about modifying her behavior or learn new teaching skills. The basis of the training plan is the director's evaluation of the teacher's weak skills. It should include the specific skills to be developed and improved, the training methods to be used, and the responsible person.

Because you have observed the skills of all of your staff members, you may be able to identify a teacher who has excellent skills in an area another teacher needs to improve. If this kind of situation can be developed, both teachers may benefit. One may benefit from the opportunity to improve her teaching skill; the other may benefit from the personal satisfaction of being recognized for having superior skills.

Directors may also be in the position to provide the needed training themselves. Because they have invested time in carefully monitoring, accurately measuring, and thoroughly evaluating each teacher's performance, training can be specific, timely, and efficiently accomplished. Also, training is better received because it is not a repetition of information skilled teachers already have. As a result, directors can be confident that their limited training time is well spent and effective.

As difficult as it is, we all must recognize that some staff members may not have the motivation or ability to develop their teaching skills to the desired level. In these cases, the director must face the difficult task of terminating a staff member. Supported by the specific knowledge collected in the monitoring, measuring, and evaluation process, the director can be certain that she has made the proper decision and has treated the staff member fairly. Without the documentation, directors may tend to avoid confronting inappropriate behavior to the detriment of young children.

It is human nature to want approval from our supervisors and peers. It is the director's job to be certain that messages of approval relate to real behavior and not to the absence of feedback. Setting up systems to carefully monitor, accurately measure, and thoroughly evaluate teacher competence will assure that teachers get the kind of approval that increases their motivation, job satisfaction, and commitment, and positions them to grow and develop as individuals and teachers.

# GUIDELINES FOR EFFECTIVE USE OF FEEDBACK

**by Roger Neugebauer**

*One of the most critical challenges facing a child care director is improving staff performance. A variety of tools are available to help a director meet this challenge — in-house training, annual appraisals, workshops, conferences, college classes, training films. One of the least glamorous of these tools — providing feedback — is, in fact, the most effective.*

*With proper feedback, teachers can better control and improve their own performance; without proper feedback, teachers operate blindly, not knowing when their efforts succeed or fail. According to George F. J. Lehner, ". . . feedback helps to make us more aware of what we do and how we do it, thus increasing our ability to modify and change our behavior. . ." (Lehner).*

Just how blindly teachers operate without feedback was demonstrated in a study at the University of Michigan (McFadden). Twenty preschool teachers were interviewed about their teaching philosophies and methods. They all expressed attitudes favoring a nonauthoritarian, nondirective approach by the teacher. They preferred to show verbal concern and approval rather than disapproval. This was how they described their teaching. Yet, when they were actually observed in the classroom, their behavior was quite different. Observers found their classrooms to be predominantly teacher controlled and teacher centered. Their statements to children characterizing support, approval or encouragement were fewer than ten percent of their total statements (Schwertfeger). Without feedback teachers may well be operating with false assumptions about the nature of their behavior and its effect on children and parents.

But as anyone who has tried to give advice to a teacher about her teaching style well knows, being effective at giving feedback is not an easy task. The natural tendency is for teachers to become defensive when feedback about their performance is presented. This reaction occurs when the receiver perceives a threat to her position in the organization, to her standing in the group, or to her own self-image.

When individuals become defensive, they are unlikely to accept, or even hear, feedback that is being offered. Instead of focusing on the message, a person reacting defensively ". . . thinks about how he appears to others; how he may be seen more favorably; how he may win, dominate, impress, or escape punishment; and/or how he may avoid or mitigate a perceived or an anticipated attack" (Gibb).

Defensiveness is increased when the receiver perceives feedback to be critical. As Douglas McGregor observes, "The superior usually finds that the effectiveness of the communication is inversely related to the subordinates' need to hear it. The more serious the criticism, the less likely is the subordinate to accept it" (McGregor).

Since teachers need feedback to improve their performance, it is important that a director become skilled at giving feedback that is helpful in a way that does not arouse their defensiveness. The following are recommendations on giving effective feedback:

- **Feedback should focus on behavior, not the person.** In giving feedback, it is important to focus on what a person does rather than on what the person is. For example, you should say to a teacher "You talked considerably during the staff meeting" rather than "You're a loudmouth." According to George F. J. Lehner, "When we talk in terms of 'personality traits' it implies inherited constant qualities difficult, if not impossible, to change. Focusing on behavior implies that it is something related to a specific situation that might be changed" (Lehner). It is less threatening to a teacher to hear comments about her behavior than about her traits.

- **Feedback should focus on observations, not inferences.** Observations are what we can see or hear in the behavior of another person. Inferences are interpretations we make based on what we hear or see (Lehner). Inferences are influenced by the observer's frame of references and attitudes. As such they are much less likely to be accurate and to be acceptable to the person observed. Inferences are much more likely to cause defensiveness.

- **Feedback should focus on descriptions, not judgments.** In describing an event a director reports an event to a teacher exactly as it occurred. A judgment of this event, however, refers to an evaluation in terms of good or bad, right or wrong, nice or not nice. Feedback which appears evaluative increases defensiveness (Gibb).

It can readily be seen how teachers react defensively to judgments which are negative or critical. But it is often believed that positive judgments — praise — can be very effective as a motivational and learning tool. However, studies have shown that the use of praise has little long-term impact on employees' performance (Baehler). Often praise arouses defensiveness rather than dispelling it. Parents, teachers and supervisors so often "sugarcoat" criticism with praise ("You had a great lesson today, but. . . .") that "when we are praised, we automatically get ready for the shock, for the reproof" (Farson).

- **Feedback should be given unfiltered.** There is a tendency for a director to sort through all the observations she makes of a teacher, and all the comments she receives about a teacher, and to pass along that information that she, the director, judges to be important or helpful. This filtering of feedback may diminish its value to the teacher. According to Peter F. Drucker, "People can control and correct performance if given the information, even if neither they nor the supplier of information truly understand what has to be done or how" (Drucker).

- **Feedback should be given in small doses.** George F. J. Lehner has observed that "to overload a person with feedback is to reduce the possibility that he may use what he receives effectively" (Lehner). Accumulating observations and comments to share with a teacher in periodic large doses may be efficient for the director in terms of time management, but it may make the feedback too voluminous for the teacher to deal with effectively.

- **Feedback should be given on a timely basis.** If a teacher is given feedback about an incident in her classroom on the day that it occurs, she is much more likely to benefit from this feedback than if it is given to her days or weeks later. When feedback is given close to an event, the recipient is likely to remember all aspects of the event clearly, and thus is able to fit the feedback into a complete picture. When feedback is far removed from the event, the event will be less well remembered and the feedback will make less sense.

An extreme, but not a typical, example of untimely feedback is the annual appraisal. An annual appraisal is an effort to give feedback about performance over the past 365 days. Not only does this concentrated dose of feedback cause information overload, it also is offered at a time removed from the behavior itself. As such it "is not a particularly effective stimulus to learning" (McGregor). Studies have shown that to be effective, performance appraisals "should be conducted not annually, but on a day-to-day basis" (Levinson).

- **Feedback should be given to the teacher as his tool to control his own performance.** A teacher is much more likely to benefit from feedback if it is given without strings attached, to use as he sees fit. If a director provides feedback ("The children were restless during circle time today") and then offers advice on how to use it ("I think you should have it earlier in the day"), the teacher is very likely to react defensively over this effort to control his behavior. "The real strength of feedback," according to Drucker, "is clearly that the information is the tool of the worker for measuring and directing himself."

- **Avoid giving mixed messages.** Through their bodies, eyes, faces, postures and senses people can communicate a variety of positive or negative attitudes, feelings and opinions. While providing verbal feedback to a teacher, a director can communicate a conflicting message with her body language. For example, when verbally communicating a nonjudgmental description of a playground scene, a director may be telecasting very disapproving signals to the teacher with the tension in her voice or the expression on her face.

When presented with such mixed messages, a teacher invariably elects to accept the nonverbal message as the director's true meaning. As a result feedback gets distorted, and an atmosphere of distrust is created. "Right or wrong, the employee feels that you are purposely hiding something or that you are being less than candid." (Hunsaker).

To avoid communicating mixed messages, you should not give feedback when you are angry, upset or excited. Wait until you cool down, so that you can keep your emotions under control as you talk. Also you should develop the habit of monitoring your voice tone, facial expressions and body language whenever you give feedback. Being aware of your body language can help you keep it consistent with your verbal language (Needell).

- **Check for reactions.** Just as you give feedback, the recipient signals her reaction to it with her body language. You should tune in to these signals as you talk. As Phillip Hunsaker recommends, "Constantly be on the lookout for nonverbal signals that indicate that your line of approach is causing your employees to become uncomfortable and lose interest. When this happens, change your approach and your message accordingly" (Hunsaker).

- **Be open to feedback yourself.** To develop an effective working relationship, you need feedback from your employees on their reactions to your behavior as much as they need feedback from you. According to organizational psychologist Harry Levinson, "In a superior-subordinate relationship, both parties influence each other, and both have a responsibility for the task."

In order to accomplish this task, they must be able to talk freely to each other, and each must have the sense of modifying the other. "Specifically, the subordinate must be permitted to express his feelings about what the superior is doing in the relationship and what the subordinate would like him to do to further the accomplishment of the task" (Levinson).

- **Encourage a team approach to feedback.** As director, you have a myriad of important tasks in addition to upgrading staff performance. Therefore, it is not possible for you to free up enough time to provide staff members all the feedback they need to improve their performance. In order to provide an ongoing flow of feedback information, you need to enlist all staff members to be feedback givers to each other.

First, you must create an atmosphere in your center that encourages staff members to accept responsibility for helping each other improve.

Second, you need to train staff members on the proper ways to give feedback. Feedback given in a judgmental, personal or untimely fashion can be devastating and can poison interpersonal relations. Training can take the form of reviewing the guidelines discussed above in a staff meeting, by doing some role-playing, and by having staff members give each other feedback on how they give feedback.

Most of all staff members can learn to be effective feedback givers if you serve as a good model in the way you give feedback.

## References


Baehler, J. R. *The New Manager's Guide to Success.* New York: Praeger Publishers.

Drucker, P. F. (1974). *Management: Tasks, Responsibilities, Practices.* New York: Harper and Row, Publishers.

Farson, R. E. (September-October 1963). "Praise Reappraised," *Harvard Business Review.*

Gibb, J. R. (1971). "Defensive Communications," in David A. Kolb (ed.), *Organizational Psychology: A Book of Readings.* Englewood Cliffs, NJ: Prentice-Hall, Inc.

Hunsaker, P. L., & Alessandra, A. J. (1980). *The Art of Managing People.* Englewood Cliffs, NJ: Prentice-Hall, Inc.

Lehner, G. F. J. (June 1978). "Aids for Giving and Receiving Feedback." *Exchange.*

Levinson, H. *The Exceptional Executive.* Cambridge: Harvard University Press.

McGregor, D. (1960). *The Human Side of Enterprise.* New York: McGraw-Hill Book Company.

Needell, C. K. (January 1983). "Learning to Level with Employees." *Supervisory Management.*

Schwertfeger, J. (1972). "Issues in Cooperative Training," in Dennis N. McFadden (ed.), *Planning for Action.* Washington, DC: NAEYC.

# Managing Teacher Performance While Walking Around

by Kay M. Albrecht

*Every director knows that much of her time is spent on the move — checking on the timbre and staffing of classrooms, responding to crying or especially noisy episodes, giving messages to teachers, checking the status of supplies, and attending to numerous other details. It often feels like nothing has been accomplished because there have been so many interruptions and distractions!*

On the other hand, directors who spend time in and around their centers, who are visible, who are seen as empathetic to teachers' needs and the demands of the classroom, who help out on occasion when times get tough, and who provide technical assistance in problem solving, are viewed by teachers as both supportive to the teaching role and successful in the director role. Figuring out how to manage performance while walking around is a good strategy for insuring that the day will not pass by without accomplishing something. Capturing the time spent on the move, making it count, can have positive consequences for program quality and teacher satisfaction.

**Develop a note taking system.** Gathering and retaining information is the first step in managing it. As directors move around their centers, comments are made by teachers, problems are identified, information about families is mentioned, and observations about teacher competence and performance are noted. Few directors can keep all this information straight and remember what needs to be done with it when they get back to their desks.

A good note taking system is a must — portable, accessible, and ALWAYS at hand. Some systems that might work include a clipboard with blank paper, a steno book, or a message pad.

One enterprising director who heard this suggestion uses a telephone message book. The result is two copies of any note — one to keep and one to pass on to the appropriate person to take action (such as the janitor, the cook, or another teacher), to file for later action (like ordering more paint or contact paper), or to use as part of the competency data collected for teacher conferences.

How will teachers feel about you taking notes as you pass through? At first there may be some sensitivity. Discuss what you are doing and why with teachers before you begin to take notes.

Then, make sure your first few notes are ones that result in action, like making suggestions on how to deal with a child's behavior or fixing broken equipment. Over time, teachers will become accustomed to you collecting information in writing. One note of caution — this note taking system should not take the place of formal request systems like maintenance requests or vacation requests. It is designed to help the director capture the useful information that is available for the taking as she walks around the center.

**Make the time spent walking around serve a purpose.** As they walk around, directors are gathering information — if not directly, then indirectly. Often, such observations serve to pinpoint "problems" and to identify training or management needs. By focusing the time spent walking around, the type and range of information gathered can be broadened and the usability of information collected increased. When viewed as an opportunity to observe a teacher's competence in a certain skill area, to gather information about classroom dynamics (either between children or among staff), or to identify training interests or needs, walking around becomes a powerful information gathering tool.

At least two strategies for focusing the time spent walking around come to mind. One entails starting the day with an agenda. A long list of action items might be on your list — checking the status of classroom cleanliness, looking for cues about teacher satisfaction (or dissatisfaction), reviewing equipment needs, observing teaching teamwork, evaluating the effectiveness of transitions from indoors to outdoors, observing the play of a child who is having problems. Use your note taking system to prompt your observations by writing down your agenda and checking off the items as information is collected.

A less directed technique borrows from child development observational strategies — take anecdotal notes as you walk around, pausing for two or three minutes here and there to make sure your notes are thorough.

Anecdotal notes have some advantages — they are records of what you see, not of what you think about what you see. The distinction is a useful one because it prevents drawing conclusions based on limited information and saves the analysis of the observation for a later time. Anecdotal notes create opportunities for you to gather information across time, preventing snap judgments and premature conclusions. The disadvantage of anecdotal notes is that they require further work. Analysis of the notes must take place to synthesize, draw conclusions, identify training needs, and so on.

Do something with your notes. A major pitfall to accomplishing anything as a director is the overwhelming feeling that everything must be done by one person. The conclusion of every walk should result in action.

If your walk identifies additional work needed by the custodial crew, copy your observations, add the necessary instructions to fix the problem, then route the message to the custodian. If you identified a teacher training need, drop your notes into the teacher's file to include in her next competency evaluation. Taking action promptly reduces the number of things on your plate and allows you to feel a sense of accomplishment.

If you chose to make anecdotal notes, doing something with your notes is a two-step process. The first step is to analyze your notes, drawing conclusions and identifying implications. The second step is doing something with the analysis.

Don't get bogged down in the analysis step. Some anecdotal notes serve only as documentation of impressions, confirmations of perceptions, or examples of experiences and can either be kept together in a file or sorted out into classroom files for future reference.

Use walking around time as a chance to increase communication. In busy centers, communication among teachers and between directors and teachers is often a casualty of the time crunch. Seizing moments as you walk around can substantially increase the amount of communication that occurs, particularly if you time your moments well.

A personal example — a preschool teacher recently submitted her resignation. The day after I got the resignation, I spent about 20 minutes with the rest of the preschool teaching team after most of the children were asleep. I asked questions about the characteristics and skills the teachers wanted to see in a replacement. I asked them to think about it overnight and returned the next day for about 10 minutes at nap time to continue the discussion.

On the third day, I went back again and asked the teachers to commit their thoughts to paper — 15 minutes later, I left the classroom with a list of the personal and competency requirements for the vacant position from the teachers' perspective.

Another note of caution — if you plan to use walking around time for increasing communication, it must be well timed. Interrupting a busy teacher in the classroom to increase communication will not be well received. Instead, enter as an unobtrusive observer and wait for a free moment. Or, become familiar enough with each classroom's daily schedule to identify when teachers are likely to have a few minutes of time to talk to you.

Managing while walking around is a technique for keeping in touch — with children, staff, and your facility — and for connecting yourself to the day-to-day happenings of the center. It is also a technique for gathering and managing the tremendous amount of information available through observation. Further, it can increase the amount and quality of communication between you and your teachers.

# Assessing Staff Problems: Key to Effective Staff Development

by John M. Johnston

> *Knowledge of how staff members view their own work-related problems can be a valuable asset for the staff development planner. If staff members realize that they are working toward solution of their problems, they are more likely to buy into the staff development process.*

Staff represent an important responsibility and a major problem area for many child care administrators (Johnston, McKnight). Providing appropriate professional improvement activities and then involving staff in those activities is particularly troublesome for many directors.

Some directors try to solve this dilemma by taking sole responsibility for making staff development decisions. Others set up a staff development committee comprised of staff representatives and themselves. In contrast, some directors utilize the *everybody for themselves* approach and, with little direction, simply mandate that staff will engage in professional improvement activities. Other directors use the *catch as catch can* approach and organize their staff development program around whatever workshops, classes, or speakers pop up in the community from month to month.

To be most effective, staff development activities must have a clearly established goal, must be meaningful for those involved, and must be actively valued by administrators. Rather than taking advantage of whatever is available, staff development efforts must be thoughtfully planned in relation to the operation and goals of the center. We know that, like the children with whom they work, teachers are unique individuals. If staff development is to be a meaningful process, then new ways to individualize staff development efforts must be explored.

Finally, administrators must realize that if employees are expected to take staff development activities seriously, so must the administration. Staff development is too important to expect that the often low paid, marginally trained and motivated teachers will take part in them in their spare time. Real improvement in staff development will require careful planning to insure meaningful, personalized activities for which teachers receive release time or appropriate compensation.

## A Problems Based Approach

One approach to providing meaningful, individualized staff development activities with clear objectives and goals is based on identifying the day-to-day problems which staff experience as they go about their work. After decades of research and practice, Cruickshank maintains that if you can identify what teachers feel their problems are, you have accomplished the first step in helping them manage or solve those problems. Armed with this important understanding of how staff view their work-related problems, you will be better able to design staff development activities which address these problems.

Knowledge of how staff members view their own work-related problems can be a valuable asset for the staff development planner. If staff members realize that they are working toward solution of their problems, they are more likely to buy into the staff development process. Staff motivation to be actively involved in professional development efforts will be enhanced if they have meaningful input into the planning process. If they realize that the results of staff development activities may lead to reducing or eliminating frequent or bothersome problems, they will be less likely to look upon staff development activities as an intrusion into their already crowded job responsibilities.

There are two basic approaches to identifying staff problems:

**Inferred problems.** In the inferred problems approach, supervisors, staff development planners, or directors infer from their own perceptions, knowledge, or experience what problems staff are experiencing. One basic drawback to this approach is that it assumes that administrators understand how staff members perceive and experience their unique job requirements. Perhaps more seriously, the inferred needs approach may subtly communicate to staff that administrators lack confidence in staff members' ability to know what their own problems are.

**Expressed problems.** In contrast, the expressed needs approach to identifying staff problems assumes that staff members can be one reliable source of information about how they themselves view the difficulties they face in performing their assigned work responsibilities. Knowledge of how staff members view their own abilities and shortcomings is an important key to successful staff development planning. When working with children in our centers, most of us believe that we facilitate development best by *starting where the child is.* It is equally important to realize that when planning for staff development we must begin where the staff member is.

## Identifying Staff Problems

Recent research on the problems of early childhood teachers (Johnston) is based on the psychological definition that a problem is an expression of an unmet need or an unfulfilled goal (Cruickshank). In other words, if we want something and cannot have it, then we have a problem. Given this definition, then, within each problem a staff member describes is at least one unmet need or goal—something the staff member wants. Below is an example of a problem reported by one day care teacher:

*Out of approximately ten children in the room, when clean-up time comes around, there always seem to be two or three children who don't cooperate. On Friday, one boy wouldn't help (and he hasn't been cooperative lately), so he was given a time out. After that, he helped; however, that isn't always true for him. Another child didn't help and we just talked to her one on one and that was sufficient. That doesn't always work with her either. It seems as though if one child continues to play or starts to pick up and then gets sidetracked and plays, then a few other children do the same.*

From this example, most would agree that what the teacher wanted was for the children to clean up when she asked them to. Having identified the teacher's goal that was being interfered with, we are now in a position to understand that this teacher has a problem getting children to clean up when they are asked.

During the past two years, over a thousand written problem descriptions such as the example above have been collected from child care staff members from all over the country.

Next, these diary-like descriptions were synthesized into problem statements by a jury of child care teachers, teacher/directors, and directors—all of whom were responsible for staff development planning. After synthesizing and eliminating duplicates, the remaining 102 problem statements were used to develop the Prekindergarten Teacher Problems Checklist (PTPC). This checklist was then used by 291 early childhood teachers from 23 states. Analysis of the checklist responses allowed us to determine which problems were (a) frequently occurring, (b) bothersome, (c) both frequent and bothersome, and (d) neither frequent nor bothersome (Johnston). We were also able to identify seven major problem areas which exist for prekindergarten and child care teachers. Finally, it allowed us to revise the PTPC to include only the most important teacher problems.

## Seven Staff Problem Areas

1. **Subordinate staff relations.** Teachers report more problems related to supervision of subordinate staff than any other problem area. Teachers report problems such as getting staff to follow through on assigned responsibilities, getting staff to be on time for their shifts, and getting staff to recognize and act on children's needs in an appropriate fashion. Teachers want to provide for communication among their staff and report problems getting staff to work in a cooperative fashion. Teachers want to be effective in recruiting, training, directing, evaluating, and providing feedback to their staff. They report problems finding time to adequately supervise staff, particularly when they are responsible for children.

2. **Control and nurturance of children.** Teachers report control problems such as getting children to learn and follow room rules and routines, getting children to participate and pay attention during group time, getting them to clean up when asked, and getting them to share or take turns. Teachers also report difficulty understanding and knowing how to respond positively to the frequently aggressive behavior of young children.

Nurturance problems are related to the goal of helping young children resolve concerns which impair their complete and secure participation in the center's program. Teachers report nurturance problems such as involving the passive child in activities, helping new children adjust to the program, helping children deal with their fears and fantasies, and helping children become less dependent upon adults.

3. **Remediation.** Teachers report remediation problems such as knowing how to help the special or atypical child, helping parents of special or atypical children recognize and adjust to their child's needs, and helping parents understand and deal appropriately with their child's behavior. Teachers want to protect children and report problems knowing how to counteract a child's negative home environment and knowing if parents are abusing or neglecting their children.

4. **Relations with supervisors.** The most internally consistent problem area reported by all groups of teachers was relations with their supervisors. Teachers report problems getting their supervisors to treat them fairly, to respect their professional judgment, and to include them in the decisionmaking process for their class-

rooms. They also report problems getting their supervisors to give them program guidelines or job expectations and then to give them feedback about their job performance.

5. **Parent cooperation.** Teachers report problems getting parents to follow program routines and center policies and procedures such as not bringing a sick child to the center or dropping off and picking up their children on time. Teachers have problems enlisting parent cooperation with toilet training efforts and are specifically concerned about dealing with parents who, in order to meet enrollment requirements, say their child is toilet trained when the child is not. Teachers also report problems getting parents to follow procedures and policies with respect to enrollment, fee payment, attendance, and providing required information for files.

6. **Management of time.** Teachers reported problems finding time away from children for planning, cleaning, and other non-teaching tasks. They have difficulty managing their time so they do not spend personal time doing necessary classroom or administrative chores.

7. **Management of routines.** Teachers have problems being able to enlist the support of parents and directing staff to most effectively manage the many routines of a program. They report problems managing toileting or toilet training routines, rest or nap time, and mealtimes.

## Using the Checklist

The revised **Prekindergarten Teacher Problems Checklist** (PTPC) contains 60 items, including all problems which were found to be significantly frequent, significantly bothersome, or both frequent and bothersome. The highest ranking problems from each of the seven problem areas were also included. The attached PTPC may be duplicated and used to identify areas for staff development planning.

Have your staff rate the extent to which each statement represents a problem they experience. Using a 1 to 5 scale, write 1 if the statement is not a problem, 2 if it is a small problem, and so on up to 5 if the statement represents a serious problem. Staff may then go back and make a list of all problems they rated 5 (serious problem). Then have them make a second list of those problems rated 4 (difficult problem). These two lists form the basis for a personalized improvement program for that staff member. In individual supervisory conferences, the administrator and the staff member may cooperatively agree on resources and strategies for reducing or eliminating these problems.

The PTPC may also be used as a basis for staff development plans for the whole center. Use a blank PTPC as a master sheet and record each person's rating for each item. Next, compute the average score for each item. The items with the highest average score represent problems of importance to the staff as a whole. In all likelihood, each teacher will have some problems which are not shared by others. Several teachers may share the same problem; these can form the basis for a small group staff development activity. Other problems will be shared by most staff members and will form the basis for center-wide activities.

Each of the 60 items on the checklist may be categorized in one of the seven broad problem areas. Individuals may use their lists of serious and difficult problems to determine if their problems seem to cluster in one particular area. Similarly, the ratings for the staff as a whole can be compared to these categories for further guidance in planning.

The seven problem areas can also provide a framework for organizing staff development resources. Files of useful books or articles can be organized under each heading. Similarly, speakers, workshops, and classes can be identified and organized under the appropriate category, thus facilitating future planning. Successful and promising practices employed by various staff members to reduce or eliminate their own problems can also be organized by these categories, forming an accessible idea bank and support network.

Use of the PTPC as an aid to identifying needed areas for staff development will provide staff members with a mechanism for meaningful input into the planning process. Since each problem on the PTPC, and hence the problems and problem areas identified by using the PTPC, represents teachers' perceptions of their own work-related problems, there is greater likelihood that staff will be motivated to engage in staff development efforts based on these problems. Finally, since the problems identified represent goals already held by the staff themselves, the chances that meaningful professional development will take place will be increased.

## References

Cruickshank, D. R., & Associates. (1980). *Teaching is Tough.* Englewood Cliffs, NJ: Prentice-Hall, Inc.

Johnston, J. M. (1983). "The Perceived Problems of Prekindergarten Teachers." Milwaukee, WI: University of Wisconsin-Milwaukee (ERIC Document Reproduction Service No. ED 231 525).

McKnight, B. (1992). "The Perceived Problems of Tennessee Child Care Administrators." (Dissertation, University of Memphis).

## PREKINDERGARTEN TEACHER PROBLEMS CHECKLIST

*Instructions: Preface each problem statement with the phrase "I have a problem . . ."*

_____ 1. Getting children to do what I ask them to do.
_____ 2. Controlling the noise or energy level in the room.
_____ 3. Understanding the reason for children's problem behavior.
_____ 4. Getting parents to supply accurate, up-to-date information for our files.
_____ 5. Getting children to share or take turns.
_____ 6. Providing for communication among staff.
_____ 7. Getting parent cooperation in solving their children's center-related problems.
_____ 8. Orienting new staff to all aspects of the program and their job.
_____ 9. Knowing how to handle children's aggressive behavior.
_____ 10. Getting parents to drop off or pick up their children on time.
_____ 11. Dealing with a child who cries or whines frequently.
_____ 12. Promoting effective mutual communication between home and center/preschool.
_____ 13. Getting staff to follow through on assigned responsibilities.
_____ 14. Getting parents to keep their children home when they are sick.
_____ 15. Getting children to clean up.
_____ 16. Motivating myself to be involved in outside professional activities.
_____ 17. Dealing with parents who say their child is toilet trained when he/she is not.
_____ 18. Providing adequate staff to meet all program needs.
_____ 19. Knowing how to help the special or atypical child.
_____ 20. Spending personal time doing necessary classroom tasks or administrative tasks.
_____ 21. Contending with interruptions while I am working.
_____ 22. Meeting the required staff-child ratios at all times during the day.
_____ 23. Getting children to learn and follow room rules and routines.
_____ 24. Finding time away from children for planning and preparation.
_____ 25. Getting children to use words and not hit others when they are angry.
_____ 26. Getting parents to follow policies on enrollment or fee payments.
_____ 27. Keeping children's attention during group time.
_____ 28. Getting parent cooperation with toilet training.
_____ 29. Getting children to sleep or rest quietly without disturbing others at nap time.
_____ 30. Working with an ineffective supervisor.
_____ 31. Getting parents to provide appropriate clothing from home.
_____ 32. Finding effective substitute staff.
_____ 33. Feeling positive toward a child who frequently misbehaves.
_____ 34. Getting my supervisor to respect my professional judgment.
_____ 35. Being able to stay home when I am sick.
_____ 36. Keeping one child's problem behavior from affecting other children.
_____ 37. Finding workshops that are appropriate to my level of skill and knowledge.
_____ 38. Meeting an individual child's needs without neglecting the group.
_____ 39. Getting children who are toilet trained not to wet their pants.
_____ 40. Helping parents understand and deal appropriately with their child's behavior.
_____ 41. Getting staff to model appropriate behavior for children.
_____ 42. Getting staff to work in a cooperative fashion.
_____ 43. Helping parents of special or atypical children recognize and adjust to their child's needs.
_____ 44. Getting parents to come to scheduled events or conferences.
_____ 45. Getting my supervisor to give me feedback about my job performance.
_____ 46. Getting my supervisor to include me in the decisionmaking process for my classroom.
_____ 47. Knowing how to counteract a child's negative home environment.
_____ 48. Meeting the needs of the children when the room is short staffed.
_____ 49. Working with equipment or facilities which are in poor condition.
_____ 50. Getting all children to participate in group activities.
_____ 51. Knowing if parents are abusing or neglecting their children.
_____ 52. Finding time for cleaning and other non-teaching tasks.
_____ 53. Involving the passive child in activities.
_____ 54. Getting staff to recognize and act on children's needs.
_____ 55. Dealing with unfair criticism from my supervisor.
_____ 56. Meeting the needs of all children in a multi-age group.
_____ 57. Giving adequate attention to the special or atypical child without neglecting other children.
_____ 58. Getting staff to understand and deal appropriately with young children's behavior.
_____ 59. Dressing and undressing children for cold weather outdoor play.
_____ 60. Understanding the public attitude that child care is babysitting.

**Prepared by John M. Johnston, University of Memphis.**

# EVALUATING STAFF PERFORMANCE: A VALUABLE TRAINING TOOL

**by Margie Carter**

*In teaching a child care management class and doing on-site training and consultation in early childhood programs, I've seen directors struggle to find a performance evaluation form that meets their needs. Most feel that some kind of checklist is all they have time for, yet most forms of this type aren't comprehensive enough to address all the areas of concern.*

*I collected scores of evaluation forms and reviewed them with directors. With their feedback I then drafted a form for them to field test.*

The most significant change from the original draft to the one on the following pages is a change in the rating scale used. Originally I had columns for conventional categories such as Outstanding, Excellent, Good, Average, Poor. Directors reported that they found these too subjective and hard to distinguish.

Reinforcing the notion that we need to base evaluations on observable evidence, I then revised the form with the rating scale indicated in the key — how often this attitude and behavior is observed: Frequently, Occasionally, Never.

"Attitude" can be a subjective consideration, so it is especially important that examples which substantiate your rating be noted in the space provided. It is most useful to note specific examples with dates and descriptive details.

This requires a director to be highly organized in keeping an ongoing log of teacher observations. Some have found that keeping a copy of the evaluation form in the staff member's file allows them to quickly note a periodic observation from which to later base an evaluative rating. Others just keep a single log of periodic observations of teachers and then transfer that onto evaluation forms as needed.

The following form is now widely used in the state of Washington. Many directors have a staff member use it for self-evaluation and then compare forms in their evaluation conference. The director then summarizes the discussion in the space provided, along with the identified strengths and areas for improvement. Together the director and staff member develop and document the action plan for goals in the coming period. This is then referenced during the next evaluation cycle.

A process and form of this nature enhances the purposefulness of the evaluation process and the professionalism of those involved.

# Staff Evaluation Form

Employee ______________________ Evaluation period ______________________

**KEY - How often observed: F = Frequently O = Occasionally N = Never**

**General work habits** F O N

1. Arrives on time ___ ___ ___
2. Reliable in attendance ___ ___ ___
3. Responsible in job duties ___ ___ ___
4. Alert in health and safety matters ___ ___ ___
5. Follows center's philosophy ___ ___ ___
6. Open to new ideas ___ ___ ___
7. Flexible with assignments and schedule ___ ___ ___
8. Comes to work with a positive attitude ___ ___ ___
9. Looks for ways to improve the program ___ ___ ___
10. Gives ample notice for absences ___ ___ ___
11. Remains calm in a tense situation ___ ___ ___

- **Examples of behaviors observed:**

______________________________

______________________________

______________________________

______________________________

______________________________

**Attitude and skills with children** F O N

1. Friendly, warm, and affectionate ___ ___ ___
2. Bends low for child level interactions ___ ___ ___
3. Uses a modulated, appropriate voice ___ ___ ___
4. Shows respect for individuals ___ ___ ___
5. Is aware of developmental levels/changes ___ ___ ___
6. Encourages independence/self-help ___ ___ ___
7. Promotes self-esteem in communications ___ ___ ___
8. Limits interventions in problem solving ___ ___ ___
9. Avoids stereotyping and labeling ___ ___ ___
10. Reinforces positive behavior ___ ___ ___
11. Minimal use of time out ___ ___ ___
12. Regularly records observations of children ___ ___ ___

**Attitude and skills with parents** F O N

1. Available and approachable with parents ___ ___ ___
2. Listens and responds well to parents ___ ___ ___
3. Is tactful with negative information ___ ___ ___
4. Maintains confidentiality ___ ___ ___
5. Seeks a partnership with parents ___ ___ ___
6. Regularly writes journal entries for parents ___ ___ ___
7. Holds parent conferences on schedule ___ ___ ___

- **Examples of behaviors observed:**

______________________________

______________________________

______________________________

______________________________

**Attitude and skills with class** F O N

1. Creates an inviting learning environment ___ ___ ___
2. Provides developmentally appropriate activities ___ ___ ___
3. Develops plans with goals from observations ___ ___ ___
4. Provides materials for all key experiences ___ ___ ___
5. Provides an appropriate role model ___ ___ ___
6. Anticipates problems and redirects ___ ___ ___
7. Is flexible, responsive to child interests ___ ___ ___
8. Is prepared for day's activities ___ ___ ___
9. Handles transitions well ___ ___ ___

- **Examples of behaviors observed:**

______________________________

______________________________

______________________________

______________________________

______________________________

**Attitude and skills with co-workers** **F O N**

1. Is friendly and respectful with others ___ ___ ___
2. Strives to assume a fair share of work ___ ___ ___
3. Offers, shares ideas and materials ___ ___ ___
4. Communicates directly, avoids gossip ___ ___ ___
5. Approaches criticism with learning attitude ___ ___ ___
6. Looks for ways to be helpful ___ ___ ___

- **Examples of behaviors observed:**

______________________________

______________________________

______________________________

______________________________

______________________________

**Attitude and effort toward professional development** **F O N**

1. Takes job seriously, seeks improvement ___ ___ ___
2. Participates in workshops, classes, groups ___ ___ ___
3. Reads, discusses handouts distributed ___ ___ ___
4. Sets goals for self in development ___ ___ ___

- **Examples of behaviors observed:**

______________________________

______________________________

______________________________

______________________________

______________________________

- **Summary of discussion from evaluation conference:**

______________________________

______________________________

______________________________

______________________________

______________________________

- **Identified strengths and leadership for center:**

______________________________

______________________________

______________________________

______________________________

______________________________

- **Goal or improvement sought for next period:**

______________________________

______________________________

______________________________

______________________________

______________________________

- **Agreed upon action plan to meet goal:**

**1.** ______________________________

______________________________

______________________________

______________________________

**2.** ______________________________

______________________________

______________________________

______________________________

**3.** ______________________________

______________________________

______________________________

______________________________

**Employee** ______________________________

**Date** ______________________________

**Supervisor** ______________________________

**Date** ______________________________

# Program Development

# Evaluating Your Program

## Chapter 14

# Program Evaluation: How to Ask the Right Questions

by Marjorie Kostelnik

*In every early childhood program there are numerous decisions to be made. Administrators responsible for overall program functioning have to make choices about which agency goals to emphasize when; what program activities to maintain, change, or eliminate; and how resources will be allocated among the related but sometimes competing interests that exist within their organizations.*

*Teachers in the classroom have to make similar types of decisions regarding the programs they carry out with children. Thus, both administrators and teachers are decisionmakers. As such, they require relevant information to help them make informed choices from among the alternative courses of action available to them. The purpose of program evaluation is to provide such information to the people who need it.*

## The Process of Evaluation

Program evaluation usually consists of six steps:

1. Formulating meaningful evaluation questions;
2. Designing a means for gathering the information necessary to answer the evaluation questions;
3. Collecting relevant data;
4. Analyzing the data;
5. Reporting the findings to the appropriate parties; and
6. Using the information gained to determine a course of action.

From this outline it can be seen that generating credible evaluation questions is the foundation of the evaluation process. Elaborate procedures that answer queries no one cared about in the first place, or that respond to less important questions while ignoring more pressing ones, are meaningless. Likewise, data that is gathered indiscriminately may answer no questions at all, proving equally worthless.

To avoid these pitfalls, program decisionmakers (or outside evaluators) must first determine what questions could be asked about the program and then select from those the ones people in the organization most want to know about.

## Categories of Evaluation

Although the appropriate starting place for any evaluation is to list a wide array of questions to consider, simply devising them at random is not effective. Important aspects of the program may be overlooked or less meaningful dimensions given greater attention because the applicable questions are more obvious or easier to generate.

A more purposeful, comprehensive approach is to formulate questions that correspond to the following program dimensions — effort, performance, process, adequacy of performance, and efficiency.

**Effort** refers to the inputs or resources used by the program. The ultimate effort question is "How much money, time, material goods, and human energy is expended in an attempt to achieve organizational goals?"

**Performance** focuses on output, that is, the results of effort. The relevant questions for this dimension are, "How much money, time, materials and human energy is expended in an attempt to achieve program goals?"

**Process** is the manner in which efforts are translated into performance. When decisionmakers ask, "How were program activities carried out?" and "Were they implemented as planned?," they are inquiring about this aspect of the organization.

**Adequacy of performance** defines how much progress toward the goal is enough. Questions in this realm are concerned with what level of performance is sufficient to consider the program a success. Adequacy is a relative dimension, and the standards that define it are subject to change over time.

For example, programs may establish lower expectations for adequacy when they are first underway and then raise their standards as they become more established. Thus, a program may aim at serving at least five percent of the eligible population in its first year, then gradually work toward serving at least 20 percent by the end of the third year of operation.

**Efficiency.** Once it has been established that a program adequately meets its goals, the final dimension to consider is efficiency. Within this category, evaluation questions center on whether there is a better method by which the program can achieve the same results. Hence, decisionmakers might ask, "Is there a cheaper, easier, less time consuming way to effectively meet the needs of our clients?" or "What are the merits of alternative A in comparison with alternative B?" "Is the program operating in the most effectual manner possible?"

## Guidelines for Formulating Evaluation Questions

Writing credible evaluation questions takes practice. Program decisionmakers and other evaluators will find the task easier if they follow the guidelines listed below.

- Make sure you have a comprehensive understanding of the program's goals, activities, and context before formulating your questions. Refer to formal program documentation and consult with program sponsors, staff, and clients to expand your knowledge of the program. Do not assume because you have been with a program for a long while that automatically you will know what questions to address without taking into account the information and perspectives offered by others. If you are new to a program, be especially diligent in seeking out such input.

- Identify several evaluation questions related to all five program dimensions discussed in this article. While you may ultimately focus on only one dimension, it is best initially to cover all of them to be sure to gain a comprehensive picture of the program.

- Avoid mistaking effort for performance or adequacy. At times program decisionmakers erroneously assume that effort data will indicate that program goals have been achieved. For example, a director may reason that having five staff members available to work with children (evidence of input) automatically means that children are learning more (evidence of output). The latter can only be determined based on a performance question, such as, "Do children who participate in the program show a significant increase in their social skills by the year's end?"

- Do not overlook the process dimension. Because effort, performance, and adequacy questions often have easily quantifiable answers, it is tempting to focus on these dimensions to the exclusion of process. Yet knowing to what extent program activities are implemented as planned, as well as what changes are made and why, sheds light on how effort and performance are related. Answers to process questions also help to determine whether the content of a procedure should be changed or if changes should occur only in the manner in which it is implemented.

- Address performance and adequacy questions prior to concentrating on those related to efficiency. It is natural for program participants to want to compare alternatives and programs. Yet such comparisons lack substance if there is no clear evidence that an alternate strategy or substitute program is clearly capable of meeting its goals. Efficiency questions are based on the assumption that the alternatives one has in mind are all viable, albeit differing, means of achieving the same result.

- Phrase each evaluation question as a specific item to be measured. Broad questions, such as "Is my teaching effective?" or "Is the program spending its money wisely?," are too difficult to answer as stated. Although the responses to such queries represent the information decisionmakers ultimately want to know, they are too general to be evaluated in this form. Instead, questions such as these must be broken down into smaller, more specific, and hence more measurable items.

Decisionmakers must decide what exact behaviors/events demonstrate effective teaching or wise use of monetary resources. Once these have been determined, effective evaluation questions can be developed.

## Summary

Which questions decisionmakers eventually choose to have answered depends on program priorities; time; and the human, material, and monetary resources available for the evaluation. In most cases, only a few are selected for investigation at any given point. Some decisionmakers will decide to obtain depth of knowledge by concentrating on one particular dimension and so will focus only on a subset of questions related to it. Others will prefer a more generalized approach, picking one question from each category. Whichever method the decisionmaker pursues, it is important to point out that simply obtaining the answers will not conclude the evaluation.

Numbers and descriptions of phenomena do not make decisions, people do. Thus decisionmakers will still have to make judgments regarding the information they receive. They will have to consider the weight of the data obtained, in conjunction with their own experience and in relation to the social and political context of their program. Hopefully, however, these judgments will be easier to formulate because the right questions will have been asked.

## Examples of Comprehensive Evaluation Questions

### *Program Level*

1. **Effort:** How much money was spent on gross motor equipment this year?

**Performance:** What kinds of gross motor equipment were purchased with the money spent?
To what extent did staff members use the equipment?

**Process:** What background will staff members have to have in order to use the gross motor equipment purchased?
How interested has the staff been in developing children's gross motor skills?
What content areas of the curriculum receive reduced attention as teachers devote more time to physical development?
What adjustments have to be made in the physical environment to accommodate teachers and children using the new gym equipment?
To what extent will factors related to storage and cumbersomeness of the equipment effect teachers' use of it?

**Adequacy:** How much gross motor equipment is necessary?
How often must staff members use the equipment?

**Efficiency:** Could the same increase in children's gross motor skills be obtained other than through the purchase of new equipment?

2. **Effort:** How many in-service opportunities were made available to staff over the last six months?

**Performance:** How many staff members attended the various in-service events held during the last six months? What was their reaction to each event?
Do teachers respond differently to workshops that are required versus those that are optional? If so, how?
To what extent do teachers use what they learn via in-service training in their work with children?

**Process:** Were there in-service workshops carried out entirely as "planned"? (e.g. Did the speaker actually arrive? Did the projector work? Did the speaker present the information staff expected to have covered?)
To what extent were the topics chosen of interest to the staff?

**Adequacy:** What percentage of staff must attend each in-service?
How much transfer of training from workshop to classroom must occur?

**Efficiency:** Are there better ways to transmit new information and skills to program staff (e.g. videocassettes to take home versus center-bound workshops)?

3. **Effort:** How many parent events were held?

**Performance:** How many parents attended the parent events?
Which events had the greatest attendance?
What topics did parents indicate they were most or least interested in?

**Process:** How much influence do parents have over the subject and format of parent events held at the center?
To what extent does the format of individual parent events allow for two-way communication between parents and staff members?
What kind of effective climate is evident during various parent events?

**Process:** How much influence do parents have over the subject and format of parent events held at the center?
To what extent does the format of individual parent events allow for two-way communication between parents and staff members?
What kind of effective climate is evident during various parent events?

**Adequacy:** How many parents must attend and what must their reaction be?

**Efficiency:** Are there simpler methods of parent involvement that would yield results similar to those currently in use?

4. **Effort:** How much time went into planning and carrying out the Fun Fair?

**Performance:** How many people from the community attended the Fun Fair?
How many people who attended the Fun Fair had never attended before?
What was the reason participants gave for coming to the Fun Fair?
How many inquiries regarding programs and enrollments did centers receive as a result of families attending the Fun Fair?

**Process:** Were the program's Fun Fair activities carried out as planned?
What was the attitude and demeanor of individual staff members during the time they worked at the Fun Fair?
Do all staff members who are supposed to devote hours to the Fun Fair actually do so?
Was the overall Fun Fair carried out in a way that supported or detracted from the program's participation in it?

**Adequacy:** How much early childhood literature must be passed out? How many new enrollments obtained?

**Efficiency:** Is there a way to participate in the Fun Fair that is less burdensome to the staff?

## *Classroom Level*

1. **Effort:** How much time is devoted to teaching children gross motor skills each day?

**Performance:** What kinds of gross motor activities did teachers develop?
How many children participated in the gross motor activities held each day?
How many children improved their gross motor skills?
Which skills showed the greatest gains, which the least?
Which children participated most frequently, which least often?
Is there a link between the number of minutes children participate in gross motor activities and their degree of motor skill proficiency?

**Process:** Were children enthusiastic or reluctant to participate in motor skill training?
Were the activities carried out as planned?
To what extent do teachers believe in the importance of gross motor skills?
What kinds of attitudes about physical development did teachers exhibit as they worked with individual children?
What factors influenced teachers' choice of which skills to emphasize and which to deemphasize?
How often do teachers praise children during the activities?
What do teachers do when children demonstrate difficulty learning a particular skill?

**Adequacy:** How much time is devoted to gross motor activities?
How much improvement in children's gross motor skills must be evident?

**Efficiency:** Is the current approach to teaching children gross motor skills the best?

2. **Effort:** How often are the children reminded to brush their teeth each day?

**Performance:** How many children remember to brush their teeth after one reminder a day?
To what extent did children increase their understanding of the value of oral hygiene as a result of participation in the program?
Do children increase the number of times they brush their teeth at home?

**Process:** How important do teachers think it is that children brush their teeth after eating?
What procedures for children brushing their teeth were put into effect in the classroom?
What else is going on in the classroom during the time children are supposed to be brushing their teeth?
To what extent do children understand why oral hygiene is important?

**Adequacy:** How few reminders to brush teeth per child must be given?
How many families must report increased brushing at home?
What minimal knowledge of oral hygiene must children display?

**Efficiency:** Is there another way to teach children to brush their teeth that involves less teacher time?

3. **Effort:** How frequent are parent conferences offered during the year?

**Performance:** How many parents requested a conference?
How many parents actually came to their scheduled conference?
How long did each conference take?
How many parents asked for a follow-up conference?

**Process:** How comfortable do teachers feel about conducting parent conferences?
In what ways do teachers make parents feel welcome at the conference?
What is the content of a typical conference?
What do teachers do when parent concerns do not match their own?
How do teachers react to parental criticism/praise/disinterest during the conference?
How does the teacher's feelings about the child influence how he or she presents information to the parent during the conference?

**Adequacy:** What percentage of parents who request a conference must actually get one?
How many follow-up requests from parents must be satisfied?

**Efficiency:** Are phone conferences more or less effective than in-person ones?

4. **Effort:** How many hours do teachers put into planning weekly activities?

**Performance:** What kinds of activities do teachers plan?
How often are planned activities actually carried out?
Are there content areas teachers plan for more often than others? If so, what are they?

**Process:** What factors influence teacher decisions to change an activity or eliminate it all together?
Why do teachers plan many activities for certain content areas and only a few for others?

**Adequacy:** How close a match should there be between planned activities and the ones actually implemented?
What is an appropriate balance among the content areas represented in teachers' weekly plans?

**Efficiency:** Is there a format for writing weekly plans that would be quicker and easier for teachers to use?

# Looking at the Quality of Early Childhood Programs

**by Lilian G. Katz**

*There are many ways to assess the quality of a program for young children. One is to look at it from the top down; another is from the bottom up. Both views are important.*

### A top-down view of the quality of a program

When we enter an early childhood setting as adults and attempt to assess its quality, we look at such characteristics as:

- the quality and quantity of space per child;
- the quality and type of equipment and materials;
- the adult/child ratio;
- the number of toilets, fire safety provisions, etc.

In addition, we should also consider the quality of teacher-parent relations and ask such questions as: Are they usually respectful? Supportive? Open? Inclusive? Tolerant?

These positive attributes are relatively easy when teacher and parents like each other; come from the same background; share culture, values, language, and goals for children. Almost anyone can do that. But to build such positive respectful and supportive relations with parents who are different from us in these ways requires professionalism, which requires training and experience.

To be professional means to respond gracefully rather than defensively in moments of disagreement. It means also to develop relationships not on the basis of personal preferences and impulses, but on the basis of professional knowledge and judgment, and to make them problem-centered, rather than personal.

Furthermore, the top-down view should include an examination of staff relationships. We could ask:

- Are they supportive rather than contentious?
- Are they cooperative rather than competitive?
- Are they accepting rather than antagonistic or even hostile?
- Are they trusting rather than suspicious?
- Are they respectful rather than bossy?

Dissension among the staff of the program can drain energy away from the main focus on children, their families, and their needs. Again, to relate well to colleagues we like — with whom we agree — who share the same goals, background, culture, language, and values is relatively easy. But to be respectful of those with whom we disagree or from whom we are different requires professionalism, and that usually requires knowledge, judgment, and training.

### A bottom-up view of the quality of a program

The characteristics of a program that really predict its outcome are the answers to the bottom-up question, which is: What does it feel like to be a child in this environment?

Obtaining answers to this question is not easy! It requires making the very best guess one can about how each individual child in this group experiences the program. We can proceed by asking about the environment on behalf of each child:

- Is it welcoming rather than merely captivating?
- Do I belong in the group rather than merely have a good time?
- Am I usually accepted by adults rather than scolded?
- Am I taken seriously rather than just precious or cute?
- Am I usually accepted by some peers rather than isolated, neglected, or rejected?
- Is this environment usually involving rather than entertaining?
- Are the activities meaningful rather than mindless?
- Are the activities engaging rather than amusing?
- Are the activities interesting rather than boring?
- Do I usually come here willingly rather than reluctantly?

It seems to me that only when answers to most of these questions are positive can we assume that the quality of the program is worthy of our children.

# Do You Have a Healthy Organization?

by Roger Neugebauer

*For a body to be healthy, a myriad of bodily functions must operate in perfect harmony. Likewise, for an organization to be healthy, a complex array of interpersonal and administrative functions must be addressed simultaneously. A serious deficiency in any one function can throw the others out of balance and undermine the organization's overall ability to perform.*

*Organizational psychologists have begun developing instruments for giving organizational checkups. Their diagnoses pinpoint areas of stress and malfunctioning.* ***Exchange*** *has analyzed several dozen of these instruments in terms of their applicability to the child care setting.*

*The following "Organizational Health Checklist" incorporates 34 criteria for an effective child care organization selected from these instruments. This battery is by no means complete — some instruments include several thousand factors to be assessed — but, in the author's opinion, it includes the major factors an administrator in this labor intensive, resource poor field should be concerned with. Anyone wishing to explore these criteria in more detail should refer to the resources listed below.*

In rating your organization against these criteria, several cautions should be kept in mind. First, the criteria as stated represent the optimum level of functioning for a healthy organization. It is unlikely that any organization could perfectly satisfy every criteria at one time.

The criteria should be viewed as goals to strive toward, not as minimal standards. The purposes of the criteria are to help you identify your organization's strengths and weaknesses and to enable you to develop strategies for improving the performance of your organization.

Second, you should keep in mind that as administrator of your organization your perspective on these criteria will be far from objective. So, in addition to rating the center yourself, you should seek to have members from different vantage points within the organization, as well as knowledgeable outside parties, perform the rating. By comparing ratings from these various perspectives, you will probably get a more accurate reading on your organization's health.

## Organizational Health Checklist

**Instructions:** Rate the organization's performance on each of the criteria below on a scale of 1 to 5 with 5 defined as "organization satisfies the criteria to a high degree," and 1 defined as "organization does not satisfy this criteria at all."

### Planning and Evaluation

___ 1. The organization has identified what it is in business for — it has developed a manageable list of specific goals for the curriculum and for the organization as a whole.

___ 2. Members of the organization helped shape these goals, are well aware of them, and are motivated to achieve them.

___ 3. Strategies for accomplishing these goals have been implemented. The organization pays more than lip service to the goals — its daily activities are directed toward achieving them.

___ 4. The organization has developed an ongoing process for evaluating progress toward achieving its goals.

___ 5. Evaluation findings are acted upon — strengths identified are supported and weaknesses are remedied. The organization does not shy away from abandoning low performing activities and unachievable goals.

### Motivation and Control

___ 6. All staff members take the quality of the organization's services seriously.

___ 7. Staff members exercise self-control over their own performance — they are motivated to perform well out of their commitment to achieving the organization's goals, not out of fear of punishment or desire for financial rewards.

___ 8. Staff burnout is minimized by giving staff members considerable responsibility for managing their own work, by providing variety in their work assignments and training opportunities, and by offering whatever support they need to perform well.

___ 9. Staff members accept the value of constructive conformity to necessary organizational rules and procedures.

___ 10. Staff members perceive salaries and fringe benefits as being administered equitably and fairly.

### Group Functioning

___ 11. Staff members feel they are a part of a group and have a sense of loyalty to the organization.

___ 12. Staff members freely cooperate. They share resources, ideas, and experiences.

___ 13. Staff members feel comfortable enough in the group to openly express their feelings. The exchange of negative, as well as positive, feedback is accepted and encouraged.

___ 14. Conflict over personal issues is dealt with directly through confrontation or negotiation rather than by smoothing it over or ignoring it.

___ 15. Communication flows freely and accurately in all directions — plans, problems, decisions, and developments are shared freely by the director; and problems, suggestions, and criticisms are routinely brought to the director's attention by all employees.

### Staff Development

___ 16. The organization assigns high priority to the staff recruitment and selection process so as to assure that the staff has sufficient skills to accomplish the organization's goals.

___ 17. The organization's leadership has complete confidence in the skills of staff members and makes every effort to tap these skills to the fullest extent.

___ 18. Staff members help set their own training objectives and strategies and assume responsibility for carrying them out. The organization's leadership supports their efforts by providing, whenever possible, the resources they require for self-development.

___ 19. Staff members continually provide each other with objective feedback on the effects of their performance and behavior. Performance appraisal is a daily, not yearly, occurrence.

___ 20. Staff creativity is encouraged by providing an idea-rich environment and by fostering a permissive atmosphere for brainstorming and experimentation.

## Decisionmaking and Problem Solving

___ 21. Problems are identified and addressed early — before they get out of hand.

___ 22. Staff members most directly affected by, or involved with, a decision either have responsibility for making the decision on their own or have major input before a decision is made.

___ 23. Parents' opinions are solicited regarding decisions affecting their children.

___ 24. Decisions, once made, are communicated to all affected members of the organization and are implemented in full.

## Financial Management

___ 25. The organization develops a formal annual budget. The budget is viewed as a means of accomplishing the organization's goals for the year. It is based on a realistic projection of the expenditures required to achieve the goals and the revenues likely to be generated.

___ 26. The organization has a sound accounting system which incorporates adequate safeguards against mismanagement and theft and which generates required reports on a timely basis.

___ 27. Monthly financial status reports are utilized to monitor the actual implementation of the budget.

___ 28. The organization carries out a routine schedule for property and equipment inspection and maintenance.

## Environmental Interaction

___ 29. The organization is effective in collecting information on new ideas and new resources, as well as in processing this information for use in developing the organization.

___ 30. The organization has an ongoing plan for marketing its services throughout the community.

___ 31. Members of the organization actively participate in efforts to influence public policy decisions which impact on the organization.

___ 32. The organization is effective in securing adequate financial and in-kind resources from public and/or private sources.

___ 33. The organization maintains its autonomy by drawing resources from a wide range of external sources, thus not becoming overly dependent on any one source.

___ 34. The organization is alert to changes in consumer needs, political moods, and economic conditions so that strategies can be developed in time for reacting to these changes.

# Out of the Box Ideas for Evaluation

by Roger Neugebauer

*As talk heats up about the concept of director credentialing, attention will be focused intensely on how to evaluate the competence of a director. From observing directors in action and from reviewing current research on center quality, I have learned that there are key indicators of director effectiveness that do not lend themselves to standard evaluation formats. In Part I of this article I am presenting five hard indicators — measures that can be quantified. In Part II, I will present five soft indicators — measures that are more subjective.*

## — Part I —

### Turnover Rates

Most recent research has pointed accusing fingers at turnover as a major deterrent to center quality. Frequent turnover causes anxiety among children and parents. It also undermines team building and program development efforts.

Staff turnover rates reported in recent studies range anywhere from 37% to 41% nation wide, meaning that typically one third of all teachers need to be replaced every year. But turnover is not a given. While some centers struggle with turnover rates over 400%, many centers in these studies experienced almost no turnover.

Clearly, centers that pay significantly higher salaries have lower turnover rates. However, in my experience, centers operating under the same financial and environmental constraints can have dramatically different turnover rates. In centers where the director is a good leader, where staff morale is high, teachers want to stay. To me, a firm indicator of director effectiveness is a staff turnover rate below 10%. Another would be a staff turnover rate that is consistently improving year after year.

However, while all would agree that high turnover undermines quality, it may also be true that near zero turnover is not the ultimate goal. Teacher longevity is not always an indicator of teacher performance. While some teachers may improve on the job every day for 20 years, others may become set in their ways or less inspired in what they do. An effective director is equally conscientious in supporting and supervising the work of experienced and inexperienced teachers.

### Staff Absenteeism

In centers where staff morale is low, staff not only leave more often but they also find more ways to be away from the center. Staff absenteeism typically rises and falls in inverse relationship to staff morale.

Since center leave policies and scheduling practices are so varied, there is no single measure of absenteeism that will work for all centers. What needs to be measured is the frequency with which staff take unplanned or unexpected leave.

One useful indicator is sick leave. If teachers use 100% of their sick leave allotment in a year, this is a strong indicator of organizational malaise. In centers with highly committed staff, directors often need to convince dedicated teachers to take sick leave when they are ill. As a benchmark, a director should be given credit if sick leave usage falls below 50%. A second indicator would be leave without pay. For part-time staff, not showing up for scheduled work often means no pay. Here the measure would be the percentage of scheduled hours where staff failed to appear. This standard needs to be higher — if part-time staff fail to appear for more than 20% of scheduled work time, this is a probable sign that something is amiss.

### Occupancy Rates

Since centers operate so close to the margin, a small difference in an occupancy rate can make a big difference in resources available to enhance quality. Moving a center from an 85% to a 90% occupancy rate can have a huge impact on the availability of curriculum resources, the amount of staff training, and the staffing ratios at the beginning and end of the day.

To a large extent, occupancy rates are affected by factors outside of the control of directors. The state of the local economy, the supply of child care in the community, the rates charged by other centers, and trends in the population of young children all impact occupancy.

However, operating within these constraints, an effective director can do much to improve occupancy. To begin with, the effective director keeps in touch with changing consumer needs. In addition, she knows how to recruit new parents and how to retain them once they commit. Effective directors may also be skillful in negotiating service contracts with local employers or public agencies.

The only fair way to measure director performance in this regard is to compare occupancy rates of centers within a community — information which may be available through the local resource and referral agency. Variances of 5% or more most likely can be attributed to director performance. If center occupancy is 5% above the community average, this is a strong indication that the director is doing a good job.

I absolutely do NOT recommend equating occupancy with licensed capacity. In some states, licensing standards are so inadequate that if a center is filled to licensed capacity it may be dangerously overcrowded or understaffed. Each center must set its own objectives for full enrollment based on quality considerations, not licensing standards.

## Staff Resources

The most significant, and least surprising, findings of recent research focus on the importance of staff. Highlighted in various studies as key determinants of quality are staff/child ratios, staff wages, staff training, and staff education. No single one of these factors consistently emerge as THE key indicator of quality. Different studies have highlighted the importance of different factors. A way out of this might be to look at all of these factors in the aggregate — to look at the amount of staffing resources the center is investing per child.

To arrive at a useful indicator requires a bit of tedious, but not complicated, arithmetic. Put your hands on your financial report for the most recently completed month. Add together the total costs paid out for people working in the classroom. Include the earnings of other staff such as the director or the cook for any time they spend with the children, the cost of staff benefits and substitutes, any monies expended on staff training, and a value for the time of volunteers working in the classrooms.

Now compute the total number of child-hours your program provided during the month. For example, if in the past month 40 children attended your program for 160 hours each, you would have provided 6400 child-hours that month.

Now divide the total monthly staffing costs by the total monthly child-hours. The result represents your staffing costs per child-hour.

The recently completed Cost, Quality and Child Outcomes in Child Care Centers study found a significant relationship between staffing costs and center quality. In poor centers, staffing costs averaged $1.03 per child-hour; in mediocre centers, $1.39 per child-hour; and in high quality centers, $1.82 per hour.

These figures provide a useful yardstick of center quality once they are adjusted for cost of living increases (data were collected in 1993). If your staffing costs per child-hour are above $2.00, this is a strong indication that yours is a high quality program. If your costs are in the range of $1.50, your quality may be mediocre at best. If your costs are well below $1.50, your center is probably not a safe place for children.

It may appear unfair to hold the director responsible for staffing costs. Clearly, many factors come into play. Woeful licensing standards in a state may drag down market rates, thus putting a severe limit on funds available for salaries. Likewise, a cautious sponsoring agency, board of directors, or owner may resist efforts to increase wages.

However, the center director is the focal point of leadership. The center director bears ultimate responsibility for what goes on in the center. To provide appropriate staffing levels, she must accept responsibility for advocating with politicians, bureaucrats, sponsors, board members, and owners. She must be capable of hustling resources to supplement fee income. And, finally, she must demonstrate leadership in strategically targeting available resources.

## Curriculum Resources

When we visit centers, one of the saddest sights we see is children with nothing to do — children pushing and shoving in the playground because they have nothing to play with, children lying listlessly on the classroom floor because they are bored with the few puzzles and books available.

Childhood should be a time of joy and discovery. There is no excuse for early childhood programs with environments that fail to stimulate children's delight and curiosity.

A simple way to test if a director is providing inspired leadership in this area is an audit of the classroom equipment. At any time of the day, how many choices do children have? Do they have choices for play outside; choices of books to read; choices of ways to combine, build on, and work together on play materials?

This last measure provides a good transition to part two of this article because, although it must be worked out in terms of number of toys in the classroom and dollars in the equipment line item, I am reluctant to offer any dollar levels or quantity thresholds as with the previous measures. There simply must be sufficient resources to engage children's spirits. In the next section, I will delve into some even softer, subjective measures.

## — Part II —

I have proposed five non-traditional yet quantifiable indicators of director competence. Now, I will push the envelope a bit farther by proposing five unmeasurable and unconventional evaluation opportunities.

### Return Rates

Financiers measure the success of their investments by their return rates — the percent of profit an investment returns. Centers can measure their success by another form of return rate — the rate at which families return to the center.

For directors who have been in charge for less than ten years, there is only one return rate that applies — the frequency with which families return to the center to enroll their subsequent children. If families routinely enroll additional children in a center, this is a probable sign that the center is doing something right. I emphasize the qualifier probable because for parents the convenience of having children in one location may weigh heavily in enrollment decisions.

For directors who have been on the job for 12 or more years, a second return rate comes into play — people who graduated from a center returning to work as teachers. If a teenager who spent a significant portion of his early years at your center applies for a job, this is a strong indication that your center provided a positive experience for that child. No qualifiers here — this is 100% good news.

Now, for the veterans in our profession, directors who have been on the job for more than 20 years, there is a third return rate — people who graduated from a center returning to enroll their own children. Once again, this return rate is a solid indicator that the children in your center are having a memorable and positive experience. What more perfect testimonial could there be than to have attendees of your program wanting to share this experience with their own children?

### Discipline Problems

At early childhood conferences, workshops on discipline or classroom management are always packed. This gives the impression that discipline problems are inevitable in centers. However, when I visit well-managed centers with effective teachers, discipline is a non-issue. Good teachers know how to structure the environment and present activity choices so that children are continuously engaged.

The amount of time devoted to discipline in meetings with teachers is, therefore, a reliable indicator of the experiences children are having in your classrooms. If discipline continues to be a nagging issue, this likely indicates that children are bored and uninvolved and are venting their frustrations through anti-social behavior.

### Child Views

In the business world, companies typically assess their performance by checking the opinions of their customers. Likewise, child care centers frequently survey parents as one means of gauging their performance. This feedback is always useful. If a large number of parents have concerns about your program, you absolutely need to know about this so you can take action.

On the other hand, if your parents express general satisfaction, this does not necessarily mean it is time to break out the champagne and celebrate your success. The recent national study, *Cost, Quality and Child Outcomes in Child Care Centers*, found that parents are not very accurate evaluators of quality in centers. Parents in the study consistently overrated the quality of care their children were receiving.

A seldom explored alternative might be to survey children in the center. They often spend more time in your center than you do, so certainly their attitudes about the place should carry some weight.

Of course, surveying children as consumers of your services requires some creative questioning. Asking four year olds to rate the quality of your center on a scale of 1 to 10 would not yield particularly helpful results. On the other hand, it may be useful to ask them what they most like to do at the center, what they like most about their teachers, and what they don't like doing. Such questions have the potential of yielding patterns of responses that are instructive about children's experiences.

### Affection

In a recent *Exchange* survey, directors rated "abuse accusations against your center" as the threat that concerns them most. Such concerns have caused many teachers to avoid physical contact with children.

This, of course, is terribly wrong. Centers need to head off accusations of abuse by working hard to develop trusting relationships with parents, to encourage them to share even the smallest concerns before they mushroom into big concerns, to assure them that staff are carefully selected and well supervised, and to invite them to visit unannounced at any time. The worst possible response is to withhold affection from children.

From time to time, it is instructive to take an affection audit at your center. Walk around casually and observe how often you see teachers showing affection to children either by physical contact, body language, or direct communication. If you see a great deal of appropriate affection being exhibited, take this as a good sign; if there is very little taking place, you need to figure out why and do something about it.

## Laughter

Child care centers should be joyful places for children and adults. When I visit a center where everyone is quiet, reserved, or — even worse — somber, red flags go up. I hate spending long periods of time with people who are unhappy, and I can't imagine spending day after day, week after week in such a depressing environment.

While you are walking about the center doing an affection audit, keep your ears open for laughter, too. Children and staff do not need to be laughing all the time, of course. There are many occasions where people in the center will be appropriately involved without laughter, such as when a child is deeply engaged in an activity or when a teacher is talking to a child about something that is troubling her. On balance, however, every hour in every classroom should yield a great deal of happiness.

## Reviewers

Thank you for critical reviews of this article to: **Diane Adams**, Madison, WI; **Richard Clifford**, Chapel Hill, NC; **Robert Lurie**, Morristown, NJ; and **Stephen Sternberg**, Ann Arbor, MI.

## References

Helburn, S. W. (editor). (1995). *Cost, Quality and Child Outcomes in Child Care Centers*. Technical Report. Denver, CO: Center for Research in Economic and Social Policy, University of Colorado at Denver.

Whitebook, M., et al. (1989). *Who Cares? Child Care Teachers and the Quality of Care in America*. Final Report of the National Child Care Staffing Study. Oakland, CA: Child Care Employee Project.

Willer, B., et al. (1991). *The Demand and Supply of Child Care in 1990*. Washington, DC: NAEYC.

# PLANNING FOR PORTFOLIOS

by Connie Jo Smith

*Teachers of young children have been keeping samples of classroom work and stuffing them in folders for many years. The act of collecting work samples to evaluate progress and share with parents during conferences has been around a long time, yet the significance of assessing child progress has increased; and the process of collecting work samples has become sophisticated. Terminology has evolved and an enhanced version of the traditional child folder is now referred to as a portfolio, which is often used as an authentic performance based assessment.*

It is becoming common for teachers to create a professional portfolio for demonstrating their own classroom knowledge and skills. Teachers may include photographs of their classroom environment, sample lesson plans, newsletters or other written communication to parents, a videotape of working with children, and certificates of achievement or appreciation. The teacher portfolio may be used for reflection and growth, to request college credit for experiences, for job applications, or for performance appraisal. Authentic assessment for teachers is important, too!

## PORTFOLIO BASICS

What is a portfolio? Portfolios include diverse information from various sources to demonstrate a child's growth and development. Selected samples of children's work over time generally constitutes a major portion of the portfolio. To supplement the children's work, teacher observations and checklists become an important part of the portfolio. Information from parents or guardians is also frequently included. Results of screening and assessment instruments may be added to create a more complete picture of each child.

Children's work samples may include some of the child's best work as well as typical work. Daily activities and special events can be documented. Children's progress may be illustrated by their original work, photographs of activities or products, audiotapes of singing and interactions, and videotapes of events. Portfolio samples may also incorporate computerized samples of paper work, scanned pictures and photographs, as well as digitized video and audio clips.

For a balanced assortment of children's work, samples from all domains of development can be gathered. Consider ways to document emotional, social, physical, cognitive, and language development. Looking across all curriculum areas will extend the diversity of the work samples collected, thus increasing the value of the portfolio. Think of ways to show children's work in math, science, health, visual arts, music, social studies, physical education, and literacy.

*Reaching Potentials: Transforming Early Childhood Curriculum and Assessment* (1995) indicates appropriate goals in each curriculum area for young children. Evaluating each child's progress towards these goals can be accomplished by creating a portfolio that grows with the child's knowledge and skill. Individualized goals can be developed after establishing a baseline for each child in each curriculum area.

### MATH AND SCIENCE

Photographs of children's block construction is a typical way to demonstrate where they are in their understanding of math and science concepts. Graphs and charts completed by children may also contribute to math and science knowledge evaluation. Photographs or observations reflecting a child's involvement with activities, such as playing store, may also be helpful in tracking children's math and science skills.

### HEALTH

Practicing health habits such as brushing teeth and washing hands can be captured with photographs or video. Audio or videotaping of informal discussions with children can reveal their understanding of health issues. Recording how children use health props in the centers also provides useful information about health knowledge.

### Visual Arts

Documenting visual arts skill is perhaps most common. Maintaining art work created by children allows one to see their ability to use different media and represent their thoughts and feelings. Original drawings, paintings, weaving projects, clay sculptures, constructions, and other products can be kept, or work can be videotaped, photographed, or photocopied for analysis.

### Music

Audio or video recordings of children participating in music activities can be useful for assessment. Teacher observations can also address children's participation in singing, playing instruments, or dancing. Children may be involved in creating songs which can be dictated to an adult or recorded in some way for full effect.

### Social Studies

Specific social studies skills, such as mapping, can be documented by gathering or copying maps developed by children. Recording children's descriptions of physical characteristics of the environment can also be used to evaluate social studies skills. Checklists or rating scales addressing social skills may also contribute to evaluation in this area.

### Physical Education

Physical education skills can be measured through motor checklists or rating scales as well as open teacher observation. Videotapes of physical activity can provide valuable information for reviewing development in children.

### Literacy

Portfolio entries may contain stories, poems, or songs children dictate. Audio or videotapes of children telling stories, reciting poems, singing, or having a discussion will be instrumental in assessing literacy and language. Sample writing created by children should be added to the portfolio. Writing might include signs, notes, names, lists, or other messages they wish to convey.

## Portfolio Enhancements

Analyzing children's work and adding evaluative remarks about the skills and knowledge demonstrated enhances the work sample (Gronlund, 1998). The process of work sample selection, and the completion of checklists, observations, and work sample comments, are most effective for assessment purposes if those involved in the activities have strong child development knowledge and understand stages of development.

Teacher comments, combined with the samples over time, provide valuable information for assessing what the child has learned. Teacher commentary can be added directly to the work sample, affixed on a sticky note, attached with a note card and paper clip, or entered on a work sample comment form.

Ongoing observations by teachers can augment the portfolio. Observations of children working alone, in small groups, and in the large group will produce worthwhile evidence of activities and progress. Observing at different times of the day will provide a better sampling of each child's interests and abilities.

Systematic observations involve watching children for a particular reason and selecting the most appropriate method for gathering and recording information (Beaty, 1990). One example of narrative observation is anecdotal notes. Although this method allows for many details, the content and quality of information is dependent upon the skill of the composer. A rating scale is frequently used to indicate the degree to which specific traits or behaviors are present. Use of checklists is also routine for observing children to determine if specific behaviors or abilities are seen. Logs may be kept to track children's involvement in activities, favorite books or songs, and other relevant information. Rating scales, checklists, and logs may be teacher-made or commercial products.

Parent input can strengthen the portfolio. Family members can contribute work samples from home for the portfolio. Questionnaires completed by parents and guardians may add another dimension. An invitation for parents and guardians to review and comment on their child's work will also enrich the effort.

By considering the results of screening along with other portfolio contents, a more complete measure of the strengths, needs, and progress of each child is provided. Screening tests take a brief look at a child's ability and indicate if further diagnostic testing is merited (Mindes, Ireton, & Mardell-Czudnowski, 1996). Since a screening is a brief assessment, it should only be used as a starting reference point.

## Portfolio Management

How are portfolios managed? Whether made by the classroom teacher or on a center wide basis, several decisions must be made about portfolio management. Teachers may collect work in folders, pizza boxes, envelopes, plastic cases, or other file containers. All portfolio entries should be dated and filed chronologically. Materials may be divided into categories for better organization. Some centers utilize the computer for storing all portfolio work to minimize the need for physical storage space and easier organization.

Determining the curriculum goals to focus on for assessment will serve as a basis for deciding what types of items to collect, the number of items to accumulate, and time frames for gathering portfolio entries. The media used to document progress or capture work samples might include audiotapes, videotapes, photographs, photocopies, or other means. Staggering the date for collection and observations may distribute the work load over time, making the exercise manageable. Tracking charts may be used to ensure that each child has a variety of items in their portfolio and that the collection addresses a sufficient number of developmental and curriculum areas at all times (MacDonald, 1996).

Policies will also need to be determined regarding the future of the portfolio records. Some programs give the portfolio to the family at the end of the year. In some situations, the portfolio is kept as part of the child's permanent record while enrolled. Still other times, the portfolio may be sent with parent approval to the child's next classroom. Confidentiality procedures should be established and followed regarding portfolio assessment work.

Why use a portfolio approach? Portfolio assessment facilitates the integration of curriculum and assessment (Meisels, 1995). Documenting children's progress based on what they are doing every day in their natural classroom environment provides a realistic measure of their abilities, interests, and needs. Assessing in this way encourages appropriate curriculum use where children are encouraged to be active learners (Grace & Shores, 1994).

## References

Beaty, J. (1990). *Observing Development of the Young Child (Third Edition)*. New York: Merrill.

Bredekamp, S., & Rosengrant, T. (editors). (1995). *Reaching Potentials: Transforming Early Childhood Curriculum and Assessment Volume 2*. Washington DC: National Association for the Education of Young Children.

Grace C., & Shores, E. (1994). *The Portfolio and Its Use*. Little Rock, AR: Southern Early Childhood Association.

Gronlund, G. (1998). "Portfolios as an Assessment Tool: Is Collection of Work Enough?" *Young Children, 53* (3), 4-10.

MacDonald, S. (1996). *The Portfolio and Its Use: A Road Map for Assessment*. Little Rock, AR: Southern Early Childhood Association.

Meisels, S. (May 1995). "Performance Assessment in Early Childhood Education: The Work Sampling System." *ERIC Digest* EDO-PS-95-6.

Mindes, G., Ireton, H., & Mardell-Czudnowski, C. (1996). *Assessing Young Children*. Albany: Delmar Publishers.

# Program Evaluation for Child Care Professionals

by Theresa M. Sull

*An evaluation can sound like an unexciting or even an intimidating event, but evaluation is an ongoing and necessary process in the life of a child care professional who has mastered child development or early childhood education, and then keeps up with any new developments.*

Consider the case of another professional, your family pediatrician. Wouldn't you expect your doctor to be up to date? If your pediatrician finished her training in, say, 1970, and then never read another journal article or took another course, she could not be current with new drug therapies or diagnostic technology. You probably wouldn't trust her with your children's health because the field of medicine has changed so much in the last 30 years.

Parents have the right to expect that caregivers entrusted with the future of their children be professionals who are current in the knowledge base of their field. Ongoing evaluations of the child care program and the child care staff ensure that the program and the people involved remain current.

Any evaluation is easier when the process starts with thoughtful planning. The *Evaluation Planning Worksheet* (Figure 1) can be filled out by individual teachers or directors or used as a tool to help program staff coordinate evaluation efforts through small group brainstorming.

## Identifying the Object of the Evaluation

Before we undertake an evaluation, we must first decide exactly what it is that we are going to evaluate:

- The entire child care program?
- Health and safety routines?
- A specific part of the program that is funded by a grant?
- Playground equipment?
- Curriculum?
- Only the literacy or science education portion of the curriculum?
- Parent involvement in the child care program?
- The supervision of teachers?
- The performance of teachers themselves?
- Director performance?
- Progress of the children?

This list demonstrates that many different aspects of a child care program *could* be evaluated. Instead of focusing on the whole program at once, it is wise to narrow the focus of your evaluation to a subset of program characteristics. Before you can narrow your focus you must know **why** you are conducting this particular evaluation.

The purpose and **type** of evaluation are interwoven. Evaluations can be categorized as either **formative** or **summative**. *Formative* evaluation is conducted to provide information to improve a new or ongoing program. To ensure a healthy program, the program budget should somehow address the financial and personnel costs of ongoing evaluation.

*Summative* evaluation is conducted to determine, after it's all over, how well a program has worked. Summative evaluation is usually required to justify expenditures to a funder or to enable a director to report to the board of directors on the program's success at year's end.

## A Teacher-Designed Assessment

To evaluate the literacy program in her preschool classroom, a teacher keeps track of the number of books that the children look at during free choice. She carries a clipboard during free choice on Mondays, Wednesdays, and Fridays for three weeks. She learns that, on average, two children look at two books each.

After a trip to the public library, she begins to add three borrowed books to the shelves each Monday and puts three old books in storage. After three weeks of rotating books she once again records book use during free choice over a period of three weeks. She finds that, on average, four children are choosing three books each day, a 200% increase in book usage.

When the board reads her report, the data presented convinces them to allocate funds for new books on a quarterly basis.

When you have chosen the object, the purpose, and type of your evaluation, jot those down on the *Evaluation Planning Worksheet*.

## Making Value Judgments

Looking at a formal definition of evaluation, we see that the process involves making value judgments. When we make **a value judgment**, we ask ourselves, is the object of our evaluation *good? Needing improvement? bad? better? worse? poor? adequate? excellent*? These value words are meaningless unless we ask questions like, *better or worse than what*? Or, *good or bad according to what standard*? In other words, we need an object of comparison, or some **criteria** for making a value judgment.

Families may judge a program by whether or not the program's philosophy of child rearing matches their own or whether the tuition is affordable. Funders, however, will use entirely different criteria for judging a program, such as the relationship of the needs assessment to the program goals as outlined in a grant proposal.

Smith and Glass (1987) identify five different types of criteria for evaluation: *effectiveness, efficiency, fairness, acceptability*, and *aesthetics*. The following list provides some examples of ways that child care professionals might use one or more of these criteria.

*Effectiveness* could involve the cost effectiveness of a child care center's meal service program, the effectiveness of the hygiene routines in keeping rates of illness down, or the effectiveness of the school-age program in meeting children's academic, physical, and social-emotional needs.

*Efficiency* compares some attribute to an outcome. For instance, higher adult:child ratios might have the attribute of being inexpensive; but, high ratios are not *efficient*, if they result in the outcome of a less intellectually stimulating environment for the children. Diapering routines might become very quick, another attribute; but, quick diapering won't be efficient if the outcome is that illness spreads more quickly because hands aren't thoroughly washed.

*Fairness*, or justice, could involve questions about whether the program staff respects all children, including those of different ethnic or economic backgrounds, or those with disabilities. Fairness might also involve questions about teachers' salaries or the distribution of the work load at the center.

*Acceptability* refers to consumer satisfaction. For instance, how satisfied are parents with the curriculum that their children experience; how happy are children with the activity choices provided in the playground; or how satisfied are staff with the facilities that meet adult needs, such as restrooms, coat closets and adult-sized chairs.

*Aesthetics* involve qualities of beauty, unity or harmony of the program. Some programs, such as those based on the ideals of Reggio Emilia, Montessori, or Waldorf education, typically place high value on aesthetics.

In choosing criteria for judging value, we ask ourselves, what questions do we want answered by this evaluation? Questions about developmental appropriateness, cultural relevance, or even the amount of fun that happens, can be addressed through evaluation. The criteria to be used should be noted on the Evaluation Planning Worksheet. A value judgment is only meaningful if we know why, and by what standard, we judge.

## Gathering Evidence

Our definition of evaluation indicates that value judgments must be based on **evidence**. We gather evidence for evaluation using **assessments**. Assessment tools include surveys like attitude surveys or consumer satisfaction surveys, systematic observation using criterion-based checklists and scales, and naturalistic case studies with anecdotal records. The evidence, referred to as data, falls into two main categories: **quantitative** and **qualitative** data.

*Quantitative* data collection results in numbers, like amounts that you can count or percentages that you can report. Numbers are usually easy to interpret so they make your reports more meaningful.

You can turn your classroom observations into quantitative data by systematically counting the activity of interest over several weeks and then computing an average. For example, you could justify buying new books for the classroom library with data showing that rotating books

## FIGURE 1 • EVALUATION PLANNING WORKSHEET

Name ______________________________ Date ______________________

I plan to evaluate: ______________________________ to find out:
(name of program or one aspect of the program)

______________________________
(questions to be answered)

Why? ______________________________
(purpose of evaluation)

The type of evaluation will be: (circle) formative and/or summative

I will use the following criteria to judge the program: ______________________________

______________________________
(effectiveness, efficiency, fairness, acceptability, aesthetics)

The type of evaluation will be: (circle) quantitative and/or qualitative

Why? ______________________________

I will use the following assessment tools: On the following dates:

1)______________________________ ______________

2)______________________________ ______________

3)______________________________ ______________

4)______________________________ ______________

The evaluators will be: ______________________________

The informants will be: ______________________________

Our stakeholders are: ______________________________

The format of the evaluation report will be: ______________________________

The report will be distributed to: ______________________________

out of storage causes children to choose more literacy experiences (see box).

Surveys scored on a Likert-type scale are another common way to obtain quantitative data.

You can create your own surveys using the sample items (Figure 2) as models. Staff can respond to surveys about the training they attend, about working conditions, or about the quality of the program.

Families can be surveyed to provide valuable information concerning their needs and their experiences in the program. Using more than one assessment instrument can broaden the focus of an evaluation. Published assessment instruments can yield valuable data to inform of program improvement. The Environment Rating Scales (ITERS, ECERS-R, SACERS, and FDCRS) created by Thelma Harms, Richard Clifford, and Debby Cryer are being used in many states, and in several countries outside the United States, to evaluate child care environments.

These instruments have proven to be reliable measures of quality in child care settings. Longitudinal studies have shown that children cared for in higher quality child care, as measured by the scales, do better socially and academically than children cared for in lower quality facilities (Cost, Quality and Child Outcomes Study, 1999).

Several other published instruments, such as the accreditation instrument of the National Association for the Education of Young Children (NAEYC), the Head Start Performance Standards, and the Child Development Associate Credential (CDA) guidelines, can all provide quantitative data on the quality of a the child care pro-

(program staff) or by **external evaluators** (for example, NAEYC validators or assessors for a rated license). It's a very good idea to perform adequate evaluations *internally* before any external evaluator is involved. Consultants who specialize in evaluation, such as quality improvement specialists at the local Child Care Resource and Referral Agency, can assist programs with internal evaluation.

Decisions about which **informants** to use are also made. Will you talk to parents or even give parents a survey?

## FIGURE 2 • SAMPLES OF LIKERT-TYPE SURVEY ITEMS

**Please circle your level of satisfaction with the training:**

| | Unsatisfactory | | Adequate | | Excellent |
|---|---|---|---|---|---|
| Trainer's communication skills | 1 | 2 | 3 | 4 | 5 |
| Organization of the meeting | 1 | 2 | 3 | 4 | 5 |
| Usefulness of the handouts | 1 | 2 | 3 | 4 | 5 |

**Please circle your level of agreement with the following statements:**

| | Strongly Disagree | Disagree | No Opinion | Agree | Strongly Agree |
|---|---|---|---|---|---|
| Literacy curriculum in the preschool classroom is age appropriate | 1 | 2 | 3 | 4 | 5 |
| Child care center playground is safe for toddlers | 1 | 2 | 3 | 4 | 5 |
| Quality of care that my child receives at the center has improved since September | 1 | 2 | 3 | 4 | 5 |

gram. *Qualitative* data is harder to interpret but sometimes easier for the audience of the evaluation to understand. Qualitative data includes records of observations, anecdotes, or narratives about what is happening in the environment that you're studying, or what steps you are taking to improve your program. What assessment tools will you use for your evaluation? Both qualitative and quantitative data are used in formative *and* in summative evaluations. Note on the *Evaluation Planning Worksheet* whether you plan to collect quantitative or qualitative data, or both.

Usually, several assessment tools are used to perform one evaluation. For example, a child who is being evaluated for special needs will be assessed in all the developmental areas, including gross motor, fine motor, speech and language, self help, and social skills.

Evaluation of a program may include assessing the physical plant, curriculum, health and safety routines, communication patterns, administrative effectiveness, financial health of the organization, experience of the staff, and staff levels of education.

To use assessment tools, decisions must be made about who the evaluators are or who will administer the assessments. Evaluation can be conducted by **internal** evaluators

When a program's effectiveness is being evaluated, assessments may include surveys administered to child care teachers, to parents, and maybe even to kindergarten teachers who observe children after they leave the child care center.

Evaluations also have **stakeholders**, those people or groups of people who have an interest in the program being evaluated and the evaluation results. Who might these stakeholders be? The board of directors, the church that houses the center, a funding agency, the parents, the corporation under which auspices the center operates, the community at large? How will they be included in a needs assessment prior to the evaluation? How will they be involved in the evaluation itself? How will they be informed of the results of the evaluation?

If an evaluation is to be useful for program improvement, it must be done well, performed in the most thorough manner possible given the constraints of time and money.

A thorough evaluation is an intense and time consuming process, but, it is well worth the investment. High quality programs are constantly evaluating and improving. Good as they are, they can always be better, just like the professionals who run them.

## References

Harms, T., Clifford, R. M., & Cryer, D. (1998). *Early childhood environment rating scale* (Rev. ed.). New York: Teachers College Press.

Peisner-Feinberg, E. S., Burchinal, M. R., Clifford, R. M., Culkin, M. L., Howes, C., Kagan, S. L., Yazejian, N., Byler, P., Rustici, J., & Zelazo, J. (1999). *The children of the cost, quality, and outcomes study go to school: Executive summary*. Chapel Hill: University of North Carolina at Chapel Hill, Frank Porter Graham Child Development Center.

Smith, M. L., & Glass, G. V. (1987). *Research and evaluation in education and the social sciences*. Englewood Clffs, NJ: Prentice-Hall, Inc.

# Accreditation Strategies, Benefits, and Practical Tips

**by Eileen Eisenberg**

*Have you ever tried to assemble a swing set? Your neighbors have the red and white, candy cane version that is the gathering place for the children on the block. It's a rather large structure with swings, ladder and slide, four-seat glider, and acrobat rings. You decide to purchase a similar one for your backyard. It comes unassembled. You methodically lay out all the parts and quickly glance through the instruction booklet. Terms like struts, u-bolts, strap hinges, fish-plates, gussets, and wing nuts flash before your eyes; diagrams illustrating steps A through Z appear overwhelming. What have you gotten yourself into? You will need guidance from a friend with experience, a do-it-yourself primer, appropriate tools, time, and patience.*

The comparison of assembling a swing set to working through any accreditation process seems highly unorthodox. Yet, the basic principles are quite similar. You need the appropriate *knowledge base* to form a philosophy enabling you to achieve a consensus of goals for your center. Is your staff familiar with terminology such as anti-bias, cultural diversity, open-ended questioning, portfolio assessment, and individual education plans? We've heard from directors that to survive an accreditation process you need *support* from mentors, colleagues, consultants, administrators, boards, and parents. You need a *timeline* that creates a structure and focus for the process. Lastly, to ensure that your program is built on a strong foundation, you need to create an *environment of trust and respect* between administration, staff, and families.

## Strategies for Persevering

I interviewed directors and asked how they kept the enthusiasm of their staff alive during the months of self-evaluation and self-study. They have shared some of their strategies:

- **Identify the strengths of your program**. A director / teacher of a church-based preschool asked teachers to rate their classrooms assessing four areas of teaching practices — interactions between staff and children; curriculum; health, safety, and nutrition; and the physical environment — using tools from *Blueprint for Action* (Bloom, Sheerer, & Britz, 1991). The results of these observations formed the basis of a rich discussion applauding the positive energies of the staff. Beginning on a positive note eases the way to discuss areas of concern.

- **Examine areas of weakness**. Believing his staff would benefit more from observing exemplary practices than "just talking about it," the executive director of an inner-city agency partnered with an accredited center. His teachers visited the center, observed in classrooms, and talked extensively with the director and her teachers. Mentoring relationships naturally formed. Changes in curriculum, daily scheduling, and interactions with children were made as a direct result of these exchanges.

- **Form staff committees to create plans for improvement**. The owner / director of a mid-size center reported that her teachers chose to critically examine their existing room arrangements, to assess the safety of the outdoor play space, and to take an inventory of their classroom materials. "It would have been quicker for me to make decisions, but seeing the teachers working together as a team was well worth the extra time."

- **Observe in the classrooms to refine goals**. A director of a large suburban center put all the teachers' names in a box. Teachers drew names and exchanged places for a day. The next week the assistant teachers also randomly switched rooms. An independent consultant and the director took turns observing in the classrooms. The consultant gathered information from everyone and facilitated conversations with teaching teams about the observations.

- **Encourage teachers to increase their personal professional development by funding tuition reimbursement for early childhood classes and conference attendance**. The director of a newly opened center in a small town sponsored all her teachers' attendance at the local junior college classes on accreditation and family support. Teachers even received cash bonuses when they completed the courses.

- **Provide professional resources and create a space available to teachers to access these materials**. The director of a Head Start program created a staff library/lounge in an unused storage area. A couch, area rug, poster, plants, coffee table, and a lamp provided a cozy feeling to the room. Teachers chose to purchase resource videos, books, and magazines on art, science, music, and literacy.

- **Document the changes made through pictorial displays including enhancements to the physical environment, changes in room arrangements, and snapshots of parent and staff workshops**. Teachers in a corporate child care center created a picture board to represent their *Ten Components of Quality*. A parent in a non-profit child care center displayed the pictures he captured in a collage resembling the old Victorian home which houses the center.

- **Celebrate along the way**. Universally, all directors report that they provide food at every staff and parent meeting. Others purchase small gifts of plants, notepads, or t-shirts; sponsor a festive dinner or evening out; distribute gift certificates (donated by local merchants); and write personal notes to show their appreciation for a job well done.

The greatest stumbling block for directors working to improve the quality of their programs is staff turnover. Some directors become so discouraged that they stop the accreditation process altogether. Others refuse to give up: "How I kept my sanity with constant staff turnover is a miracle. Once, four people left in one month. We had to begin the retraining process all over again. I was just too stubborn to quit!"

## Benefits of the Process

Directors share their reflections on the long-term benefits of working through an accreditation process:

- **Promote team building**. A consultant/trainer directed us to write a mission statement. As a group, we debated our philosophy and desired outcomes for children and families.

- **Refocus curriculum**. Teachers were presented with options for choosing a particular philosophical approach to the design of their curriculum. The results produced a critical look at how children scaffold their learning, how teachers set up the environment, and how to approach the evaluation of children's progress.

- **Establish health and safety training**. Every teacher has attended CPR instruction, has learned how to use a fire extinguisher, and now implements proper hand-washing procedures.

- **Formalize the parent organization**. With the assistance of a mini-grant, we created a series of parent workshops that enabled parents to come together on a regular basis — including a theme *soup* evening, *goop* activity night, and an introduction to *Second Step Training*.

- **Strengthen communication with parents**. Parent surveys indicated we needed to better inform parents when their children were ready to be transitioned (from infant to toddler rooms). We now have formalized opportunities for parents to spend time with the new caregivers before the children change rooms.

- **Strengthen teacher/parent relationships**. Teachers complained that parents never came into the classroom to see their children's work. They felt unappreciated and that their efforts were going unnoticed. A double row of cubbies divided the two classrooms. In order to draw the parents into the classrooms, the sign-in/sign-out sheets were relocated to the top of the cubbies next to an inviting bowl of apples or a platter of cookies. Amazingly, parents began to take notice of the activities and make encouraging comments to the teachers.

- **Promote cultural sensitivity**. Recognizing that our center serves a diverse community, our parent handbook, policies, procedures, and newsletters have been translated into Mandarin and Spanish as well as English. We also provide simultaneous translation at all parent meetings.

- **Renovate an existing space**. The process provided us with the incentive to *clean house*. We created teachers' storage lockers in a once cluttered attic and a teachers' resource room in an old kitchen, resurfaced the outdoor play space, repainted and recarpeted the entryway and stairs, and washed windows throughout the center.

- **Change furnishings and materials**. We recognized the need to add age-appropriate toys for the infant room, recognized the lightweight chairs in the toddler room had fostered accidents and needed to be replaced, and purchased additional riding toys to reduce the waiting time for preschoolers.

## Practical Advice

Lastly, directors share practical bits of wisdom:

- **Learn how to delegate and get everyone involved**. The more staff and parents become part of the process, the more invested in its success they will become.

- **Listen carefully to your staff and your families before making decisions.**

- **Find time and space away from children for staff meetings**. Make every effort to find coverage during nap times or provide incentives for staff to meet when the center is closed. The larger the center, the harder it will be to schedule meetings. In this situation, create teams of teachers (for example, put all the infant/toddler teachers on one team). Let the teams choose their own leaders and convene their own meetings. Provide these new leaders with appropriate management training. Monitor their progress and help them stay focused.

- **Look into the mirror before you criticize others**. Do you want your teachers to clean up their classrooms? Examine your office. Do you want your teachers to extend their education and attend conferences? Look at your training schedule. Do you require teachers to communicate often and appropriately with parents? Refer to your last staff memo or staff meeting agenda. Remember to welcome staff and thank them for a good day.

- **Learn to make tough decisions**. Sometimes it is necessary to terminate a staff person who has not proven to be suitable to work with children. Sometimes it is necessary to release a family from your program if you cannot provide them with the appropriate services. Most situations only worsen. Don't procrastinate. Document your observations and act on your decisions.

- **Be prepared for the on-site validation or verification visit**. Organize your documents and feel comfortable with the materials. Spruce up your center by doing necessary maintenance and removing clutter. Present yourself as confident. Welcome the review team as you would guests in your home.

- **Above all, have patience and maintain a sense of humor**.

As director of an early childhood program, you cannot be expected to assemble a swing set all by yourself nor should you be expected to independently guide your program through a self-evaluation process that results in lasting change. Reflect on the ideas offered by your fellow directors; they are worth trying.

## References

Bloom, P. J., Sheerer, M., & Britz, J. (1991). *Blueprint for action: Achieving center-based change through staff development*, Lake Forest, IL: New Horizons.

Eisenberg, E. (1999). Taking the leap. *Exchange*, November/December.

Eisenberg, E., & Rafanello, D. (1998). Accreditation facilitation: A study of one project's success. *Young Children*, September.

# SHAPING YOUR CURRICULUM

## CHAPTER 15

# What Should Young Children Be Learning?

by Lilian G. Katz

*Recent research on intellectual and social development and learning is rich in implications for curriculum and teaching strategies for early childhood education. Unfortunately, educational practices tend to lag behind what is known about teaching and learning. This digest discusses curriculum and the methods of teaching which best serve children's long-term development.*

## The Nature of Development

The concept of development includes two dimensions: the normative dimension, concerning the capabilities and limitations of most children at a given age, and the dynamic dimension, concerning the sequence and changes that occur in all aspects of the child's functioning as he grows. It also addresses the cumulative effects of experience. While the normative dimension indicates what children can and cannot do at a given age, the dynamic dimension raises questions about what children should or should not do at a particular time in their development in light of possible long-term consequences.

In many preschool programs and kindergartens, young children are engaged in filling out worksheets, reading from flash cards, or reciting numbers in rote fashion. But just because young children can do those things, in a normative sense, is not sufficient justification for requiring them to do so.

Young children usually do willingly most things adults ask of them. But their willingness is not a reliable indicator of the value of an activity. The developmental question is not "What can children do?" Rather, it is "What should children do that best serves their development and learning in the long term?"

## Learning through Interaction

Contemporary research confirms the view that young children learn most effectively when they are engaged in interaction rather than in merely receptive or passive activities. Young children should be interacting with adults, materials, and their surroundings in ways which help them make sense of their own experience and environment. They should be investigating and observing aspects of their environment worth learning about, and recording their findings and observations through talk, paintings, and drawings. Interaction that arises in the course of such activities provides a context for much social and cognitive learning.

## Four Categories of Learning

The four categories of learning outlined below are especially relevant to the education of young children:

- **Knowledge**. In early childhood, knowledge consists of facts, concepts, ideas, vocabulary, and stories. A child acquires knowledge from someone's answers to his questions, explanations, descriptions, and accounts of events as well as through observation.

- **Skills**. Skills are small units of action which occur in a relatively short period of time and are easily observed or inferred. Physical, social, verbal, counting, and drawing skills are among a few of the almost endless number of skills learned in the early years. Skills can be learned from direct instruction and improved with practice and drill.

- **Feelings**. These are subjective emotional states, many of which are innate. Among those that are learned are feelings of competence, belonging, and security. Feelings about school, teachers, learning, and other children are also learned in the early years.

- **Dispositions**. Dispositions can be thought of as habits of mind or tendencies to respond to certain situations in certain ways. Curiosity, friendliness or unfriendliness, bossiness, and creativity are dispositions or sets of dispositions rather than skills or pieces of knowledge. There is a significant difference between having writing skills and having the disposition to be a writer.

  Dispositions are not learned through instruction or drill. The dispositions that children need to acquire or to strengthen — curiosity, creativity, cooperation, friendliness — are learned primarily from being around people who exhibit them. It is unfortunate that some dispositions, such as being curious or puzzled, are rarely displayed by adults in front of children.

A child who is to learn a particular disposition must have the opportunity to behave in a manner that is in keeping with the disposition. When that occurs, the child's behavior can be responded to, and thus strengthened. Teachers can strengthen certain dispositions by setting learning goals rather than performance goals. A teacher who says, "I want to see how much you can find out about something," rather than, "I want to see how well you can do," encourages children to focus on what they are learning rather than on their performance, and how others will judge their performance.

## Risks of Early Academic Instruction

Research on the long-term effects of various curriculum models suggests that the introduction of academic work into the early childhood curriculum yields good results on standardized tests in the short term but may be counterproductive in the long term. For example, the risk of early instruction in beginning reading skills is that the amount of drill and practice required for success at an early age will undermine children's dispositions to be readers.

It is clearly not useful for a child to learn skills if, in the process of acquiring them, the disposition to use them is lost. On the other hand, obtaining the disposition without the requisite skills is not desirable either. Results from longitudinal studies suggest that curricula and teaching methods should be designed to optimize the acquisition of knowledge, skills, desirable dispositions, and feelings.

Another risk of introducing young children to academic work prematurely is that those who cannot relate to the tasks required are likely to feel incompetent. Students who repeatedly experience difficulties may come to consider themselves stupid and may bring their behavior into line accordingly.

## Variety of Teaching Methods

Academically focused curricula for preschool programs typically adopt a single pedagogical method dominated by workbooks, drill, and practice. It is reasonable to assume that when a single teaching method is used for a diverse group of children a significant proportion of these children are likely to fail.

The younger the children are, the greater the variety of teaching methods there should be, since the younger the group is, the less likely the children are to have been socialized into a standard way of responding to their environment, and the more likely it is that the children's readiness to learn is influenced by background experiences which are idiosyncratic and unique.

For practical reasons, there are limits to how varied teaching methods can be. It should be noted, however, that while approaches dominated by workbooks often claim to individualize instruction they really individualize nothing more than the day on which a child completes a routine task. Such programs can weaken the disposition to learn.

As for the learning environment, the younger the children are, the more informal it should be. Informal learning environments encourage spontaneous play and cooperative effort. In spontaneous play, children engage in whatever play activities interest them. Cooperative effort occurs when children engage in such activities as group projects, investigations, and constructions.

## Conclusion

Spontaneous play is not the only alternative to early academic instruction. The data on children's learning suggests that preschool and kindergarten experiences require an intellectually oriented approach in which children interact in small groups as they work together on projects which help them make sense of their own experience. These projects should also strengthen their dispositions to observe, experiment, inquire, and examine more closely the worthwhile aspects of their environment.

## For More Information


Donaldson, M. (1983). "Children's Reasoning," in M. Donaldson, R. Grieve, and C. Pratt (editors), *Early Childhood Development and Education*. London: The Guilford Press.

Dweck, C. S. (1986). "Motivational Processes Affecting Learning," *American Psychologist* 41:1040-48.

Katz, L. G. (1986). "Current Perspectives on Child Development," *Council for Research in Music Education Bulletin*, No. 86:1-9.

Katz, L. G. (1985). "Dispositions in Early Childhood Education," *ERIC/EECE Bulletin* 18. Urbana, IL: ERIC Clearinghouse on Elementary and Early Childhood Education.

Morgan, M. (1984). "Reward-Induced Decrements and Increments in Intrinsic Motivation," *Review of Education Research* 54:5-30.

Schweinhart, L. J., Weikart, D. P., & Larner, M. B. (1986). "Consequences of Three Preschool Curriculum Models Through Age 15," *Early Childhood Research Quarterly* 1:15-46.

# Curriculum That Matters

**by Margie Carter**

*This fall with a new school year underway I've been heartened to see many programs rethinking how they do curriculum planning. Maybe it's because of the growing interest in emergent curriculum, the project approach, and the schools of Reggio Emilia. I also think there is something intrinsically unsatisfying for teachers who repeat the same curriculum themes year after year.*

In their book *Emergent Curriculum*, Elizabeth Jones and John Nimmo describe how easily curriculum can become "canned" or "embalmed," losing any real meaning for the children or teachers. I see this as a reflection of the larger "going through the motions" syndrome which plagues our educational system as a whole and has become a general coping mechanism for a society gone awry.

Commercial interests in the name of education are competing for our precious dollars and attention as well. The lure of cute prepackaged bulletin board displays, costumes, and activity books gives us a sense of "doing right by our kids." They're like *happy meals* for preschool.

Well-intentioned parents and caregivers want youngsters to get a "head start," have fun, and be entertained while learning their "lessons." But before long teachers end up scrambling to meet someone else's expectations, resulting in curriculum plans that have little to do with the true lives or interests of those in their care. When someone other than the teachers is designing how their rooms should look and what they should do each day with the children, I question whether we have curriculum that matters.

## STRATEGY:

### Assess who lives here

Frequently I'm asked to assess a program's learning environment, curriculum planning, or methods of individualization to determine their in-service training needs. I walk through classrooms, hallways, the playground, and, hopefully, a staff lounge and work room, looking for signs of "who lives here?" and what is important to them. All too infrequently do I see an environment that has grown out of the lives of the children, their families, and caregivers.

When I see sets of look-alike art projects on the bulletin board, I'll ask individual children to show me which one is theirs. They rarely can. To me, this says a lot about a center's efforts to individualize and about their success in building authentic self-esteem in children.

Likewise, when programs continually shuffle children and teachers to keep ratios in line, I check to see if the staff can tell me something about a given child. There are times when they don't know each of the children's names, let alone their developmental progress or interests to build curriculum around. This isn't the "fault" of the teacher, but rather the result of ill-conceived policies and notions about providing a quality experience for children.

I encourage program directors to regularly observe and tally the number of commercially designed displays and curriculum activities compared with those that come from the children or the lives of their caregivers. Bring this data to a staff meeting where you pose the question, "If someone used this list of observations to speculate on what people in our program value, what conclusion do you think they'd draw? Does that accurately represent what's true for you? If not, how could we develop better evidence of who lives here? What changes are needed in our policies and priorities?"

## STRATEGY:

### Consider curriculum as how we spend our time together

Many people tend to think of curriculum as the activity they describe in little boxes with time blocks or subject areas. In early childhood programs, this might mean a daily arts and crafts project, some music, and a story to read. Some take it further and plan for learning centers or interest areas, which might include materials and activities around a topical theme or school readiness concern. The daily chores of living together — greeting, eating, playing, cleaning up, and going to the bathroom are seen as things limiting our time for "real curriculum."

For young children, curriculum is everything that happens, including the transitions, spills, spats, and naps. Hopefully, engaging projects that continue over time are part of the curriculum as well, but projects are only part of the complex story of what is being learned in our programs. Remember that your environment, interactions, food, spiritual and physical energy are all included in what you offer as curriculum.

Have teachers write out their daily schedules for children. Then, pass out sheets of colored sticky dots and ask them to put a green dot beside everything on the schedule that is child-initiated, designed, or directed. Put blue dots beside the times that represent "holding patterns" — transitions which involve changing, ending, or waiting. Wherever there are teacher directed or dictated times, add a red dot. When you're done, discuss what you discover. Any surprises? Whose needs are reflected in the blue and red dots? Are you satisfied with the general quality of how the day is designed to meet children's needs?

## STRATEGY:
### Reconsider how money is spent

If we consider curriculum as "everything that happens" and if our learning environments are to reflect the interests of children, then shifts in our budget line items might be in order. Cameras, film, audio and videotape recorders are probably a better investment than cartoon characters and worksheets. Putting money into landscaping our playgrounds back into natural environments makes more sense than buying more plastic toys. Large rocks, hills, creeks, trees, and pets will engage children in hours of significant curriculum, influencing the likelihood they will become scientists, archeologists, artists, and veterinarians.

Fill your staff room with magazines on architecture, computer graphics, botany, and the arts. Create a scavenger hunt contest for who can locate free or low-cost sources of "loose parts" for your classrooms and environments. Seek out in-service training from those outside the early childhood field who could expand our thinking and enrich our sense of possibilities — theater stage set designers, landscape architects, improvisational artists, photographers, and physicists.

## STRATEGY:
### Discover new sources of curriculum ideas

When it comes to ideas for curriculum projects, initially stay away from activity books. These are better used after a project is underway and you are seeking ways to enrich it.

The project approach differs from the typical preschool approach of having weekly themes. The idea is not to keep kids busy or please parents with a potpourri of little activities. Rather, projects should be chosen for their relevancy to the children's lives, for their potential to extend over time, engaging children in discovery and moving them to more complex forms of investigation and representation.

Have staff work together in teams to consider possible sources for project ideas. Ask them to divide a sheet of paper into quadrants. In the upper left hand corner, have them list any requirements in terms of mandated curriculum components or learning outcomes that may be imposed on teachers. (There are a number of these in a typical Head Start or school district program.)

In the upper right hand section, list themes that seem intrinsically interesting to children from your observations and knowledge of child development. Try to get to themes underneath the obvious topical ones. For instance, why do dinosaurs seem to always engage children's interests? Why super-heros? Themes of power and adventure, living and dying, risk and safety preoccupy preschool children. What projects might help them pursue these themes in ways that are meaningful and concrete?

In the lower left hand corner, list passions that you as a teacher have. What interests do you pursue, what consumes your time outside of work? Sometimes teachers have to be coaxed to discover this. Maybe it's a hobby, a collection, a new skill, language, or sport they are trying to learn. If they are genuine, teachers' passions are often of great interest to children. Sharing them in concrete ways helps to build relationships. This gives children a way to learn about role models, apprenticing, and coaching.

The lower right hand corner of the paper can be used to list things in the community and children's families that are being talked about or coming up: a special event or celebration, a birth or death, natural calamities, or predictable excitements.

As you assess these lists for their compatibility with your values and appropriateness for the children in your group, also consider how all the items in the "required" quadrant could be met through projects that could be developed from the other three lists.

## STRATEGY:
### Revamp your requirements for curriculum planning forms

Typically curriculum plans get developed, turned in, and posted prior to the week they begin. When using an emergent or project approach, a curriculum web of possible ideas can be generated and then materials and activities can be mapped out in a skeleton form. The initial project idea may emerge from observation and discussion of children's interests, questions, and developmental themes. It may come from one of the lists generated above.

The schools of Reggio Emilia inspire us to launch a project with a "provocation." Plan for a discovery or initial engagement with some aspect of the project idea. The curriculum then gets co-created by the children, teachers, and family involvement.

With this approach, programs must abandon the typical requirement to complete a planning form with activities all decided in advance. It's important to acknowledge that most of the documentation will follow the activity, not precede it.

Ask teachers to experiment with curriculum documentation formats that work for them. Provide guidelines about what type of information should be included and, for those who want it, make some examples available. After several months of experimentation, hold a staff meeting to see if there is one invention everyone is ready to adopt or if planning formats should continue to be at the discretion of the individual or team.

# Brain Research and Its Implications for Early Childhood Programs

**by Pam Schiller**

*Neuroscience research has supported several key factors that have a direct impact on how we interact with young children. The findings are simple, easy to understand, and for the most part, they reinforce what we have known intuitively, from our own experience, and what we were taught in child development classes. The following is a list of the most relevant findings and some suggested implications for child care centers and preschool environments.*

## FINDING 1:
## Brain Development is Contingent on a Complex Inter-Play Between Genes and Environment

There is no longer the debate between whether our learning is more dependent on nature or nurture. It is clear from the research that nature lays down a complex system of brain circuitry, but how that circuitry is *wired* is dependent on external forces such as nutrition, surroundings, and stimulation. The environment plays a major role in brain development. There are several supporting pieces of research that provide solid information we can use when designing early childhood environments.

### Environmental Implications for Early Childhood

- Rest and nutrition influence brain function. Children need restful sleep at night and they need daily naps. The brain uses sleep time to do its housekeeping and to reorganize itself. Children need diets rich in protein (meats, nuts, cheese), fatty 3 acids, and selenium and boron (leafy green vegetables). Offer children the opportunity to learn about the value of eating healthy foods. Make sure your snack menus contain more complex carbohydrate items like fruit and less simple carbohydrate items like cookies and cakes.

- Offer water frequently during the day. Thirsty brains can't think. Allow children to bring water bottles to school if they are in classrooms without easy access to water. Serve water with lunch and at snack time.

- Children learn better in environments where they feel safe. It is difficult to learn when we do not feel safe. If we must constantly guard ourselves from danger we have little ability to focus on other things.

- Toys and equipment can be selected based on information gained from the research. For example, using the windows of opportunity as a guide we see that problem solving is wired during the first four years of life. We want to supply toys that encourage this skill. For an infant this might be a Jack in the Box or a Busy Box. For a toddler or preschooler it might be puzzles and blocks.

- Children are focused on cause and effect relationships during the first few years of life. Offer toys that reinforce this concept.

- Offer toys and equipment that are multi-sensory. The more senses involved in a learning situation the more likely the child is to process the information.

- Pay attention to what we are learning about colors. Bright colors make us more alert. Darker colors calm us. Infants notice red, blue, and green first. Start with these colors in your nursery or infant room.

- Novelty causes the brain to be more alert. Rotate your toys. Offer homemade games. Rearrange your classroom every three or four months. Use novelty in moderation. Too many changes at one time may be disconcerting to children.

- Children need adequate space for motor development. Motor development is at its peak during the preschool years.

- Include plants in the environment. Plants increase oxygen and the brain needs oxygen to stay alert.

- Use aromas to create your atmosphere. The aroma of peppermint, orange, and cinnamon make us more alert. Chamomile, lavender, and rose calm us down. Add aromas to paints and play dough. Place potpourri bags (out of the reach of children) in the classroom.

- Provide stimulation but don't over stimulate. Too much stimulation, i.e. things hanging from the ceiling, walls covered from ceiling to floor and so forth, make it difficult for children to focus.

## FINDING 2: EARLY EXPERIENCES CONTRIBUTE TO BRAIN STRUCTURE AND CAPACITIES

The quality, quantity, and consistency of stimulation will determine to a large extent the number of brain synapses that are formed and how those connections will function. This is true for both cognitive and emotional development and the effect is life long. Experience is the architect of the brain. In the early childhood classroom we have the opportunity to fashion experiences through our choice of curriculum that will enhance the wiring of the brain.

### CURRICULUM IMPLICATIONS FOR EARLY CHILDHOOD

- Remember emotions and intellect walk hand in hand. Coordinate experiences that nurture both the social-emotional development and the intellect.
- Select curriculum that includes activities that allow time for focus and reflection.
- Make sure activities and experiences are multi-sensory whenever possible.
- Allow for the opportunity to follow the interest of the child. We all learn best when the information is of interest to us.
- Recognize the value of repetition. Brain connections are strengthened and sometimes replaced or expanded by repetition.
- Intelligence is in large part our ability to see patterns. Use a curriculum that encourages children to find and build onto patterns.
- Include music and movement. There are a number of research studies that support the value of music and movement. Both help children develop a sense of patterns. Singing has many benefits. It helps develop language, reduce anxiety, keeps us feeling happy, and enhances auditory discrimination.
- Use assessment as a guide. Children learn from practice but not without some form of feedback. Assessment provides a structure for helping both caregiver and parent to know how and when to provide feedback.

## FINDING 3: EARLY INTERACTIONS AFFECT BRAIN WIRING

Children learn in the context of important relationships. Brain cell *connections* are established as the growing child experiences the surrounding world and forms attachments to parents, families, and caregivers. Warm responsive care appears to have a protective biological function, helping the child weather ordinary stresses and prepare for the adverse effects of later stress or trauma. Non-responsive care, absence of care, drug abuse, and trauma can all have an adverse effect on the child's emotional well-being.

This finding has critical implications when it comes to both the staffing and the retaining of staff in our centers and schools.

### STAFFING IMPLICATIONS FOR EARLY CHILDHOOD

- Hire the best. Look for those special people who are patient, talkative, loving, attentive, and happy. You can train the "head" but not the "heart." Make a list of attributes you expect to find in an employee and stay committed to not settling for less.
- Think of ways to retain staff. There is no profession with more turn over than the child care profession, and there may be no profession where it is more disruptive and damaging. Little things you do — like visiting each classroom each morning when you arrive and greeting each staff member by name — help create a caring climate. Highlighting staff members' personal and professional accomplishments make them feel special and valued.

Being empathetic when personal challenges arise help employees feel like part of a team. Develop a list of things you can do that help make up for the stress and low salaries encountered by caregivers.

## FINDING 4: BRAIN DEVELOPMENT IS NON-LINEAR

There are certain critical periods that are conducive to developing specific skills. Although learning continues across the life cycle, there are windows of opportunity during which the brain is particularly efficient at specific types of learning. For example, children are receptive to second language learning from birth to ten. Children are particularly in tune with music between the ages three to ten.

This information is helpful to both parents and caregivers. Knowing when children are most receptive to learning certain skills and information impacts the way we interact with them. It is important that child care staff be trained to use the windows of opportunity.

### Training Implications for Early Childhood

- Make staff training a high priority in your center or school. Find creative ways of providing release time for training. Perhaps you can offer time off during the holidays when enrollment is down.

- Plan for new employee training to include information on child development and on the windows of opportunity.

- Make sure your regular staff training includes training on the windows of opportunity. Encourage staff members to share examples they have seen in their classrooms.

- Remember that training needs to be continuous. Adults learn in the same way children do. We take new information and match it to existing understanding. Make adjustments. Try out the new information. If it still makes sense we use it. This requires continuous updating and follow-up.

- Find ways to recognize staff members who seek their own training. Give them time off. Acknowledge them in your newsletters or on a bulletin board. Continuous training is the tool of the early childhood professional.

## What Are We Learning?

*What is brain research? Thanks to new imaging technology used in neurobiology we can actually look inside the brains of living children and adults. We can see the brain in action — how it grows, how it acts, and how it reacts. What we are learning is astonishing and is making a major impact of how we view early learning.*

The brain is the only unfinished organ at birth. It will continue to evolve throughout our lives. The primary task of the brain in early childhood is the connection of brain cells. Babies are born with 100 billion nerve cells, called neurons. Every neuron has an axon that sends information out to other neurons and several dendrites that receive information from other cells. As axons hook up with dendrites, trillions of connections called synapses are formed.

During the first three years of life, an infant's brain will forge an estimated 1,000 trillion synapses. It is experience that will forge the connections of neurons. Neurons that are used will strengthen and those that are unused will eventually disappear. You might think of this like roads on a map. Those that are used become highways and those that are not used just fade away. According to neuroscientists sometime near the onset of puberty the brain will prune away all unused or replaced pathways. By late adolescence about half of the 1,000 trillion synapses of the three year old will be discarded. The brain will continue this strengthening and pruning process throughout our lives, but it is at its height between birth and puberty.

The quality of experiences and relationships in the first three years of life has a deep and lasting impact on how the brain gets wired. The richer the environment is — the greater the number of interconnections that are made. The larger the number of interconnections — the faster and more meaningful learning will be. Interactions (relationships) are also shaping children's brains. During the first year of life the baby is developing trust. Trust is the foundation for all relationships. The more loving and responsive the caregiver is, the greater the foundation for later social interaction. Both experiences and interactions are shaping little ones' brains and designing the neural architecture that will influence how they will handle all future experiences. If an infant gets too little stimulation, affection, language, and human contact, the development of the brain that depends on those experiences will be deterred or will fail to progress.

## FINDING 5: A Child's Brain is Two and a Half Times as Active as an Adult's

Children's brains have more synapses and the density of synapses remains high throughout the first ten years of life. Children are biologically prepared to learn.

Finally, after years of scraping for funding, advocating for appropriate programs, stating over and over how significant early experiences really are, we have scientific proof on our side.

But we also have a challenge. How do we make sure that this new information is translated appropriately? How do we hold on to what we know is right for children? How do we make the most of this opportunity?

### Communication Implications for Early Childhood Professionals

- Involve parents in your center or school. It's the best way for them to see the application of appropriate practice. Hold seminars. Send out newsletters and copies of news articles that spread the word about the research.

- Help keep the brain research information in front of the public. Write letters for your local paper. Create your own brochure or use this article to help spread the word. Display children's artwork in local malls or banks. Write a sentence or two about how children's drawings and paintings impact their brain development. Do the same thing when you display children's work in your centers or schools.

- Speak to the Rotary, the PTO, the League of Women Voters, and so forth. Many of these groups are eager to help — they just aren't as exposed to the research as you are.

- Include a session on brain development research in your conferences and seminars. It is important that we help each other understand what the research findings are and how they impact early childhood classrooms.

- When brain research findings are applicable, use them as support for legislative causes. Help make sure your senators and representatives understand the impact of legislation.

## What Can You Do?

We no longer need to debate the critical importance of the early years in a child's life. We don't need to second guess how much influence the environment plays in early development. We don't need to defend developmental programs over academic programs. We have clear and concrete evidence for designing programs that best benefit the development of young bodies, spirits, and minds. The evidence is here.

However, nothing will change until we as a profession embrace the research. It validates all the practices in early childhood we hold dear. It is a gift — a tool we have worked without for too long. Make it part of your life. Turn the findings into applications. Your actions will speak volumes. Every change you make will help teach all those who come in contact with you — parents, children, and other professionals. Over time, each application will become part of our culture. We can create a better beginning for all children and each of us, in our own way, can lead the way. Start today.

- Stay abreast of the new brain research information. Be sure you understand it. Use it to promote the healthy development and learning of every child. Use it to support what you do.

- Remember what you know, through intuition, experience, and education. Apply the new information to test your current practice.

- Teach others!

- Examine your environment on a regular basis to determine that it is in concert with what we are learning.

- Hire only the best. Make sure the *heart* is there and commit to teaching the *head*. The caregivers in our centers are contributing architects to each child's future.

## References


Begley, S. (1997). "How to Build a Baby's Brain." *Newsweek*. Special Edition, 28-32.

Carnegie Corporation of New York. (1994). *Starting points: Meeting the needs of our youngest children*. New York: Author.

Families and Work Institute. (1996, June). *Rethinking the Brain: New Insights into Early Development*. Executive Summary of the Conference on Brain Development in Young Children: New Frontiers for Research, Policy, and Practice, University of Chicago.

Handcock, L., & Wingert, P. (1997, Special Edition). "The New Preschool." *Newsweek*, 36-37.

Jensen, E. (1998). *Teaching with the Brain in Mind*. Alexandria, VA: ASCD.

Nash, M. "Fertile Minds." (1997, February). *Time*, 48-56.

"Your Child Birth to Three." (2000, Special Edition). *Newsweek*.

Ramey, C. T., & Ramey, S. L. (1999). *Right From Birth*. New York: Goddard Press.

Schiller, P. (Spring 1999). *Start Smart: Building Brain Power in The Early Years*, Beltsville, MD: Gryphon House, (800) 638-0928.

Schiller, P. Turning Knowledge Into Practice. *Exchange, 126*, 49-52.

Schiller, P. The Thinking Brain. *Exchange, 121*, 49-52.

Schiller, P. Brain Development Research: Support and Challenges. *Exchange, 117*, 6-10.

Sousa, D. A. (1995). *How the Brain Learns*. National Association of Secondary School Principals, Reston, VA.

Sylwester, R. (1995). *A Celebration of Neurons: An Educator's Guide to the Human Brain*. Association for Supervision and Curriculum Development, Alexandria, VA.


## Web Pages:

- www.iamyourchild.org
- www.zerotothree.org
- www.naeyc.org • www.nccic.org

# Opening Doors to Activities That Include ALL Children

by Whit Hayslip and Lisbeth Vincent

*Ms. Adana ends music time with the last verse of "Oh, Johnny" with her group of preschool-age children and says, "Today we have some special choices in the interest areas. In the library corner there's a new book and tape about a camping trip. We have a collage in the art area with macaroni, cotton balls, and glitter sticks. The sand and water table is filled with colored sand and we have some new purses in the house corner. There are bananas to slice in the cooking area. Think about where you would like to play, and you can make your choices."*

*Carlos stands in the middle of the rug looking out the window. Ms. Adana bends down to him and says, "We need to figure out what you would like to do today. Would you like to listen to the tape or play in the house corner?" As she speaks, she turns him toward each choice. She takes his hand and he begins to walk to the house corner. She goes with him to the area and reminds him to tell the other children he would like to join in. He points to a doll and says, "Baby." Jessica, another child in the group, says, "You can be the daddy and I'll be the mommy," and the play begins.*

*LaTanya walks to the collage table, but all four chairs are filled. She announces, "I want to make one, too!" Her classmate, Don, says, "There's no room. Remember, you have to wait for an empty chair." LaTanya answers, "Tell me when you're done."*

*Four children gather at the sand and water table to play. Susie stands at one end repeatedly scooping up the colored sand and letting it run through her fingers. After a minute Ms. Adana suggests that Bill slide a water wheel under the falling sand. The other two children see how well it works for one to pour while the other holds the wheel, and they set up their own teamwork. Ms. Adana verbally describes what is happening. Bill asks Susie to trade and hold the wheel while he pours. He helps put her hand in the right spot so the wheel will stay upright.*

*Ms. Adana keeps an eye on the other activities and notices that Carlos has left the house corner for the cooking area where he and three other children are cutting up bananas with small plastic knives. Lee uses a knife with a handle wrapped in masking tape to make it bigger and easier to grasp. The group works with a buzz of conversation, mumbled at times, as they are eating the banana slices as fast as they cut them.*

The staff at this center has a genuine understanding of the concept of "developmental appropriateness." Activities are geared to the children's chronological age, while allowing adaptations for individual variations in interest, development, and experience. The activities let children be the initiators of their own play and interactions, while providing adult support when needed to individuals and to the group as a whole. This ability to respond to both age and individual needs is at the heart of the National Association for the Education of Young Children's definition of "developmental appropriateness." It is what enables child care programs and staff to provide supportive, nurturing environments to the wide variety of children who make up today's preschoolers.

Some of today's children have special needs related to their developmental rates of learning and learning styles. For example, in the vignette, Carlos is showing delays in communication and problem solving skills. Susie has been diagnosed with autism and shows differences in her social interactions with peers and adults. Lee needs adaptations made to fine motor materials due to cerebral palsy. These children all need individualized attention to be successful in the room. However, other children need this attention though they are not disabled or developmentally delayed. Developmentally appropriate programs accept that all children need individual attention to grow and learn.

A major reason that this center has been so successful in applying developmentally appropriate practice and meeting the needs of a broad range of children is related to its effort to create a predictable, nurturing environment for all children. Staff realize that for children to feel safe and develop trust in the center they need to know what will happen and when. They need a predictable environment where adult behavior is consistently supportive, activities are routinely carried out, and children are allowed to make choices and have a sense of control. The work of Diane Trister Dodge has illustrated the important role of clearly designated areas with well defined options in supporting children's ability to make choices.

Trying out new things in play is a risk, and children will only take those risks when they have developed a sense of safety. Children with special needs can rely on the program's predictability for that sense of safety, even if they are not as able as their peers to express their wants and needs or participate in the more complex choices the center offers.

Another important ingredient in the center's success with inclusion is creating an environment that is rich with open-ended activities and materials. These materials allow a broad range of children to successfully play together at their different levels of skill and development. Classic examples of open-ended materials are blocks, play dough, and clay. Others being used at the center in the vignette include collage, sand, and the house corner props. With these types of materials, children can use their personal concepts, skills, and experiences to bring meaning to the activity. They can play together at an activity and yet pursue their interests at their own rates. In evaluating materials for this quality of open endedness, it may be helpful to use the following criteria.

## Open-Ended Materials

- The process is more important than the product. The doing is more important than the result.
- Activities are flexible enough to allow different children to participate at their individual developmental levels.
- There are no specific starting or completing points.
- There is no right or wrong way of doing the activity.
- The activity may be made simple or complex.
- The child may find varied ways of doing the activity.
- Initially, the child might not know where it will end.
- The most important thing is that, whatever the result, it is an expression of that individual child.

As the introductory vignette illustrates, however, these open-ended materials alone will not create a center rich in play for a broad range of needs. Often children need help with their play. Child care providers who work in inclusive centers tell wonderful stories of how often this help is given from one child to another. In the vignette, Jessica, Don, and Bill perform crucial roles in the play of Carlos, LaTanya, and Susie. They serve as models, help define limits, and give both focus and extension to the play.

It is essential that staff take time to watch the play and together decide how much adult involvement is required for specific children to be productively involved at their developmental level. In the book Mainstreaming: Ideas for Teaching Young Children, Souweine, Crimmins, and Mazel offer clear frameworks and specific examples for this involvement. Stating it simply, if a child has a low level of participation in the play activity, it would suggest a need for a higher level of adult support.

This support may take many forms. Some children need changes in the physical environment, others need more verbal cues, and others need emotional comfort. Whatever the form, as the child's level of participation gradually increases, there is a corresponding decrease in this adult support. Smilansky developed a similar structure for supporting dramatic play called "play training" and wrote of moving from more obtrusive to less obtrusive intervention as the child becomes more engaged. Both approaches require careful and ongoing observation to allow the adult to respond to the changing child, and both approaches are appropriate for use with the wide range of children in a center.

Experienced early childhood professionals know that even with the most wonderful environment and the best staff facilitation, problems will still arise. As with typical children, there will be times when it is difficult to successfully integrate a certain special needs child into the play of the center. Although it may be helpful to consult with outside experts, often the solutions can be generated by the staff. Child development specialist Ruth Pearce developed a planning model that has been highly successful in centers. When staff sense a problem, she recommends the use of the following five steps and corresponding questions.

## Problem Solving

### Observe and Pinpoint

- What is the problem?
- When does the problem occur?

- Where does the problem occur?
- With whom or what does the problem occur?

### Analyze the Problem

- What is the child telling you?
- What are the expectations for the child?

### Design an Intervention

- Should the environment be modified?
- Can the staff's method of working with the child be modified?

### Evaluate the Intervention

- Observe the child
- Analyze the intervention

### Decide Future Course

- If you are dissatisfied, modify the intervention.
- If you are satisfied, continue the plan.

The success of this problem-solving model has come about because of its emphasis on focused staff observation and planning. It is not dependent on either magical solutions or highly technical training and techniques. It is well documented that when programs make time for this kind of observation and planning, they can flourish with the inclusion of special needs children.

Helping young children with special needs to participate in the activities at a center contributes not only to the well being of families, but also to the inclusion of individuals with disabilities in our society. Parents report that successful inclusion during the preschool years is a cornerstone of their children's formation of friendships and participation in the community. The sense of belonging that the child develops in the center leads to positive self-esteem and acceptance. Early childhood advocates remind us that the child with special needs is a child first. Meeting the needs of diverse children is what quality early education has always been about. Accepting and, in fact, celebrating and cherishing children's differences is the foundation of our work.

## References


Bredekamp, S. (editor) (1987). *Developmentally Appropriate Practice in Programs Serving Children Birth Through Age 8, Expanded Edition*. Washington, DC: National Association for the Education of Young Children.

Dodge, D., & Colker, L. (1992). *The Creative Curriculum for Early Childhood, Third Edition*. Washington, DC: Teaching Strategies, Inc.

Smilansky, S. (1968). *The Effects of Sociodramatic Play on Disadvantaged Preschool Children*. New York: Wiley.

Souweine, J., Crimmins, S., & Mazel, C. (1982). *Mainstreaming: Ideas for Teaching Young Children*. Washington, DC: National Association for the Education of Young Children.

# Children Need Rich Language Experiences

**by Elizabeth Jones**

*Human beings are the animals that talk. Everywhere, they have invented languages with which to remember experiences, plan ahead, and communicate with each other. A child's learning to talk — and, later, to recognize print as talk written down — is a major milestone in her relationships with her family and community; she becomes a "member of the club" of people who use words with each other. If she goes to child care, the adults there will determine, in large part, the language experiences she has during her day, even though they won't be participants in all of those experiences.*

**Adults greet children.** Friendly words are an important welcome to each child, each day; children need to hear their names spoken warmly. They need to see their names written, as well; children learn to recognize the shape of their name, and thus to read it, long before they know the sounds of the letters it's made of.

**Adults engage children in conversation.** Genuine questions (to which the child knows the answer and the adult doesn't) about family events spark conversation just as they do among adults: "Is your grandma visiting you?" "Is your baby better today?" "Is that a new jacket?" When the child takes the initiative — "My birthday's tomorrow!" — the adult responds with shared pleasure.

**Adults give children information** they want or need — "The red paper is on the bottom shelf." "It's time to wash your hands now." "Mama will come back; she always comes back."

**Adults provide experiences worth talking about**, and many opportunities for children to talk spontaneously with each other. These experiences include both the daily — things to play with, food to eat — and the special — celebrations and field trips and attention to street repairs and thunderstorms and things that break down and have to be fixed. Planned or unexpected, all such things are potential language curriculum.

**Adults model useful language while mediating conflicts.**

*"Marcos, what do you want to tell Dulcie?" the teacher asks.*

*"I don't like her. She's a dumb-dumb," sobs Marcos.*

*"You're mad at Dulcie. Can you tell her what she did to make you mad?"*

*"Hit me," says Marcos, sadly.*

*"You hit me first," says Dulcie, reasonably.*

*"Marcos, did you hit Dulcie?"*

*He nods.*

*"Why?"*

*"My hole!" he wails. "She messed my hole!" He tries to hit Dulcie again.*

*"What hole?" asks Dulcie, genuinely puzzled. "I didn't mess no hole."*

*"Can you show Dulcie your hole, Marcos?"*

*"Here!" he shouts. "It was right here, and I digged it and digged it. . . ."* (Jones & Reynolds, 1992, p. 27)

**Adults read stories from books.** Books are a source of delight, wisdom, and useful information. Children being read to and looking at books themselves discover that literacy is a skill worth mastering.

**Adults share songs, chants, and poems**, play games with words, and respond appreciatively to children's word play. Language is a set of sound patterns as well as of meanings, and spontaneous play with its rhymes and rhythms is one of the many ways children begin to learn the phonics useful in reading.

**Adults re-tell to children the stories of their lives together**, letting them know that *their* actions and words are the stuff of stories too.

*"Once upon a time," said Joan to her small class of three year olds, whom she had called into a snug circle as their going camping play was coming to an end, "there were one, two, three, four, five, six, seven, eight children who went camping together." "Me!" said Charlie excitedly. "Me, too!" said Alicia.* . . . (Jones & Reynolds, 1992, p. 125)

**Adults set the stage for children's own storytelling,** keeping in mind that young children are not at their most competent when they're expected to talk in teacher-directed settings like show-and-tell or recall. Children's language is liveliest when their bodies are in action and they haven't been waiting for a turn. Nor are all their stories told in words; *The Hundred Languages of Children* (Edwards et al., 1993) includes dramatic play, block construction, drawing and painting, and many more. In all these modes, children represent their understandings of how the world works and where they belong in it:

*"Here's the driving place. These go with the car. No, get off, I have to drive. We have to get our cars fixed. I have to drive, this is 'mergency."*

*"Hey, help do this, fireman. This is gonna be a hook and ladder to catch people. This goes on the fire truck 'cause that's the water."*

**Adults respect the importance of *private speech*** in early development. Young children talk to themselves as they go about their daily activities, using language as a means of directing their own attention and behavior. (Berk & Winsler, 1995) It's important that children not be shushed very often; they need to think out loud.

**Adults respect children's home language.** The child whose family speaks a language not spoken by the child care staff isn't language-deprived, he's potentially bilingual; and bilingualism is an asset in a diverse and changing world. Staff need to learn basic vocabulary in the other language, just as children do, and staff hiring policies should take the community's languages into account.

**Adults stay alert to naturally occurring opportunities to teach concepts** and vocabulary to children, rather than *playing teacher* in developmentally inappropriate group lessons like this one:

*There were 19 four year olds sitting in square formation around the edge of the rug.*

*Teacher (showing tray): "What do you think is in this?"*

*Some children: "Lemons."*

*Teacher: "How do you think lemons taste?"*

*Some children: "Sour."*

*Teacher passes tray. The first few children don't want a lemon. Teacher (somewhat impatiently): "Oh taste it. It's fun to taste; you just need to lick it."*

*Teacher (tastes lemon): "Mmm, it is sour. What else is something that tastes sour?"*

*A child: "Apples."*

*Teacher: "Sometimes, but not all the time. Green ones can taste sour. What else?"*

*A child (echoed by others): "Grapes."*

*Teacher: "Grapes really aren't sour, although sometimes they aren't real sweet. How about pickles?"* (Daniels, 1988, p. 137)

Here the teacher, continually fishing for the answers she wanted while denying the validity of the children's ideas, got much more language practice than they did. If the taste of things is important to discuss with children, why not do so at the lunch table, a natural setting for conversations about food as a topic of mutual interest?

**Adults acknowledge that face-to-face talk provides better language experience than TV.** Children get enough of TV and videos at home, where adults are busy with other tasks or may want to watch themselves. Further, videos turned on in child care are often arbitrarily turned off when it's time for something else; they're used as a time filler rather than as a story to be paid attention to from beginning to end. Looking at books would be more appropriate, because children do it at their own pace; however, if book-looking happens only at brief transactions and is never given time as a serious activity, children get the message that it isn't very important.

**Adults use transitions as *teachable moments*** both smoothed and enriched by interesting activities. Songs, chants, finger plays, and movement games all focus children's attention and add to their language. Classification games stretch children's thinking as well: If you played in the sand today, raise your hand. If you played in the playhouse, raise your hand. If you played in the blocks, raise your hand. How many boys played in the blocks? How many girls played in the blocks? How come there weren't any girls in the blocks? (With this question, you may well get genuine language experience — lively conversation about a significant issue. If that happens, there goes your smooth transition.)

Games can be designed to move the children to the next activity: "If you're wearing red, stand up and go sit at the table." "If you're wearing stripes, stand up. . . ."

**Adults reflect** on all the things they do, examining their potential for enriching children's language. They need to remember that play time is the most important language opportunity in the day, and provision for it thoughtfully. Children's language will draw on all their family and community experiences *and* on their experiences in child care: What's here to talk about, who's here to talk with, and what are the interesting events in our shared past and our anticipated future?

## REFERENCES


Berk, L. E., & Winsler, A. (1995). *Scaffolding Children's Learning*. Washington, DC: NAEYC.

Daniels, B. (1988). "Digression: A Lesson Where Children's Language Was *Not* Enhanced." In E. Jones (editor), *Reading, Writing and Talking with Four, Five and Six Year Olds*. Pasadena, CA: Pacific Oaks College.

Edwards, C., Gandini, L., & Forman, G. (1993). *The Hundred Languages of Children*. Norwood, NJ: Ablex.

Jones, E. (1992-1993). *Observation Notes: Play and Language Development (Volume V)*. Pasadena, CA: Pacific Oaks College.

Jones, E., & Reynolds, G. (1992). *The Play's the Thing*. New York: Teachers College Press.

# Playing the Day Away

**by Susan J. Oliver and Edgar Klugman**

> *"It is in playing, and perhaps only in playing, that the child is free to be creative."*
>
> — D. W. Winnicott, *Playing and Reality*, Routledge (1989)

## Play: As Natural As Breathing

Think about all the young children who have passed through the doors of your child care program over the years. Each one is an individual, a special young person who approaches the world in his own unique way. Yet there are some behaviors that nearly all children have in common — activities that come to them as naturally as breathing and eating. Anyone who knows the world of children will agree that *play* is one of those behaviors.

There are compelling developmental reasons for a child's instinct to play. Play is the way a child explores his world, builds skills, exercises his imagination, and learns through experience.

"All play means something," wrote the Dutch historian Johan Huizinga in *Homo Ludens*, his pre-World War II seminal study on the social function of play in western culture. "It goes beyond the confines of purely physical or purely biological activity. It is a *significant* function — that is to say, there is some sense to it."

## Play IS for Keeps

At *Playing for Keeps* (www.playingforkeeps.org), we believe that play makes a *lot* of sense, especially for young children, and its developmental benefits are crucial to good outcomes for children. To borrow a playful phrase of childhood: play, itself, *is* for keeps.

Play for all young children is in all the environments where they spend their time, including home, child care, preschool, cultural institutions, and other community settings. We use the term *constructive play* to describe the type of developmentally appropriate, productive, nonviolent, and fun activities that give young children a strong base for building gross motor, fine motor, cognitive, social, sensory, and emotional skills — the kind of skills that will increase their chances for success in elementary school and beyond.

## What is *Constructive* Play?

Our concept of *constructive play* has been shaped through input from several leading scholars and practitioners who specialize in infant, toddler, and preschool development and education. For many years, researchers have studied the role of play in the growth and development of children. They have found that constructive play — like food, love, care, and hope — is an essential building block for healthy children and a critical part of the foundation children need to lead well-adjusted, happy, and productive lives.

Constructive play is characterized by the following qualities:

- It is safe, wholesome, and nonviolent.
- It stimulates children to develop skills and positive relationships.
- It inspires children to learn more about themselves and the world around them.
- It encourages and enables children to fully realize their potential.
- It encourages creativity.
- It helps develop a child's personality.
- It makes learning fun.

## The Benefits of Play

Jerome Singer, Ph.D., professor of Child Studies at Yale University and member of the Playing for Keeps' board of directors, notes that learning through play is intrinsically motivating for both children and adults. "Play can miniaturize a part of the complex world children experience, reduce it to understandable dimensions, manipulate it, and help them understand how it works." (Singer & Singer, 2000.)

A significant body of research conducted over the past generation has articulated a long list of specific benefits that play provides for children. Among the benefits noted in various publications by Singer (1994), Sara Smilansky, Ph.D., of Tel Aviv University, Edgar Klugman, Ed.D. (1990), professor Emeritus at Wheelock College, and others, are the following:

- development of motor skills
- sharpening of the senses
- development of empathy and the ability to express emotions
- understanding and practice of sharing, turn taking, and other peer cooperation skills

- increasing control of compulsive actions and learning to accept delayed gratification
- building ordering and sequencing skills
- increasing the size of the vocabulary and the ability to comprehend language
- increasing concentration skills
- learning to navigate assigned roles
- development of capacity to be flexible
- expansion of imagination, creativity, and curiosity
- reducing aggression

## Today's Play Landscape

If play is so central to healthy development why is there a need to study it, talk about it, and promote it? Won't children do whatever they need to do on their own?

Unfortunately, access to constructive play — especially the type of unstructured free play that does so much to nurture creativity and the imagination — is not a simple matter for many of today's children. Why? It has to do with the lifestyles we have given our children and the fact that not all play is created equal.

Early childhood caregivers and teachers are welcoming children into their classrooms who may bring play habits and experiences unknown to earlier generations. Those working with children in early childhood settings should be aware of the play landscape on which these kids have been nurtured, because it may impact the type of developmentally appropriate learning the children are prepared to do. Here are a few of the realities:

- **Increasing "screen time."** A recent study (Jordan & Woodard, 2001) published by ZERO TO THREE, the National Center for Infants, Toddlers, and Families, reports that the average two to three year old spends more than four hours a day in front of a screen (television or computer). One in six children in that age group have a television set in his or her bedroom. New *play* products for very young children include a *toddlerized* remote control to make channel surfing easier for little kids and *lapware*, which is computer games designed for children as young as nine months to play while sitting in an adult's lap.

  Public television is targeting children as young as 12 months in some of its programs. A toddler living in the average American home is living in a setting with a television operating for six hours a day. For the toddler, much of that television is background noise and visuals while they continue to spend 40% of their time engaged in social activities and 32% of their time engaged in play, according to a study authored by Daniel R. Anderson and Marie K. Evans (Anderson & Evans, 2001). While the child might not be actively absorbed in the television at all times, the background noise and the peripheral motion can disrupt the ongoing play schemes and language development of the child. Moreover, the supervising adult generally is focused on the television even if the child is not, and is, therefore, not available to play with the child.

- **Limited outdoor play time.** While a child can certainly learn some things while watching television or playing on computers, there are other important developmental activities that simply cannot happen when a child is in front of a screen. The gross motor activity and social play that happens most easily in outdoor spaces is increasingly difficult for today's children to experience. Many parents and caregivers make decisions based on the perception that we live in an unpredictable, dangerous society, and therefore, children need to be heavily supervised while playing outdoors. According to the National Association for the Education of Young Children, the many demands on parents and the limited time they have for supervising play makes it increasingly difficult to fit unstructured outdoor play into a child's day (www.kidsource.com/kidsource/content4/school.recess.html). In addition to missing out on valuable developmental experiences, limited outdoor play affects children's physical well-being. Experts believe that children do not get enough exercise today and this is cited as a leading factor in the rise of childhood obesity (Dietz, 1999).

- **Exposure to violence.** While the good news is that today's children have access to a wide variety of play materials to fit a wide variety of interests and abilities (e.g., classic toys, *high-tech interactive* toys, board games, video games, computer games, the internet, and more), the bad news is that some of these forms of play expose children to violent themes and content frequently, and at very young ages. A recent study conducted at the University of California at Santa Barbara found that most violence to which children are exposed is glamorized and sanitized — usually initiated by "good" characters who are likely to be perceived as attractive role models (www.mediaawareness.ca/eng/issues/violence/resouce/reports/ntvs3.htm). Few examples of violence show children any long-term consequences. "These patterns teach children that violence is desirable, necessary, and painless," said Dr. Dale Kunkel, associate professor of communication at UCSB, and a senior researcher for the study.

- **Overscheduling and overfacilitating.** Today's children may demonstrate new play patterns due to their relative lack of experience with unstructured free play. A recent University of Michigan study found that the average child's free time (i.e. after eating, sleeping, and structured educational activities) has dropped from 40% to 25% of their day in the last generation (www.isr.umich.edu/src/childdevelopment/timerep.html). In many parts of our culture, children are in formal, scheduled, adult-driven activities like sports programs and lessons earlier than ever before.

  For many, play with peers takes place in play groups that have been arranged by their parents and that are highly supervised by the adults in attendance. Despite the increased participation of mothers in the paid labor force, children aged three to 12 are spending 24% more time with their mothers and 21% more time with their fathers than they did a generation ago (www.umich.edu/~newsinfo/Releases/2001/May01/r050901a.html). While this is, in general, a positive development, it stands to reason that children who develop the habit of having a readily available adult arbitrator may not develop the same independent problemsolving skills that children allowed more unstructured play might achieve.

## Consequences for Caregivers and Early Childhood Programs

These trends point to the possibility that many children entering child care and early childhood programs are coming with different play habits, skills, and expectations than in the past, and that the caregiver's or instructor's role in making constructive play experiences available is all the more crucial for children's healthy development.

If a significant part of the natural instinct to play has been directed to television and computers, it stands to reason that some of the time those children could have been spending on more traditional play activities richer in developmental benefits has been lost. If adults have facilitated most of the play the child has so far experienced, children may need to be challenged to work out conflicts on their own and explore their own unique creativity.

## Link Between Constructive Play and Good Outcomes for Children

It is often said that play is a child's work. While today's preschoolers may present new challenges that require creative responses from caregivers, constructive play remains a standard for good practice in early childhood settings. The National Association for the Education of Young Children (NAEYC) defines developmentally appropriate play as best practice for early childhood, and several major early childhood curricula are built on the philosophy that play is the natural way for children to learn. For younger children, organizations such as ZERO TO THREE advise parents seeking child care programs to look for a healthy, play-based environment — whether the family is choosing home-based care or center based care.

The consequences of constructive play in a child's earliest days and years are powerful. "The benefits of rich play experiences during the preschool years are extensive and address academic goals for reading and writing, math, science, social studies, and the arts," note Diane Trister Dodge and Toni S. Bickart in their popular guide *Preschool for Parents*. "Several decades of research show that high-quality programs that aim to strengthen social and emotional skills through play have positive effects on all aspects of children's development — including cognitive or intellectual development. What's more, these positive effects are long lasting."

Play, then, is nothing short of a unique — even magical — tool for caregivers of our infants, toddlers, and preschoolers. "The activities that are the easiest, cheapest, and most fun to do, such as singing, playing games, reading, storytelling, and just talking and listening, are also the best for child development," says Jerome Singer. This is good news for those dedicated to the healthy development of our youngest children.

Watch upcoming issues for more information about the research basis for, and practice of, constructive play. And in the meantime, be generous with your time and imagination as you nurture those creative young children in your care. Remember . . . they can't help themselves — they MUST play!

## References


Anderson, D. R. & Evans, M. K. (October/November 2001). "Peril and Potential of Media for Infants and Toddlers." Washington, DC: *Bulletin of ZERO TO THREE, (22)*, 2.

Dietz, W. H. (March 19, 1999). Kids obesity linked to TV. American Medical Association Press Conference. Report by US Centers for Disease Control and Prevention.

Dodge, D. T. & Bickart, T. S. (1998). *Preschool for Parents*. Naperville, IL: Sourcebooks, Inc.

Huizinga, J. (1955). *Homo Ludens*. Boston: The Beacon Press.

Jordan, A. B. & Woodard, E. H. IV. (October/November 2001). "Electronic Childhood: The Availability and Use of Household Media by 2-to-3-Year-Olds." Washington, DC: *Bulletin of ZERO TO THREE, (22)*, 2.

Klugman, E. & Smilansky, S. (1990). *Children's Play & Learning: Perspectives and Policy Implications*. New York: Teachers College Press.

Singer, J. L. & Singer, D. (June 1, 2000). *Make Believe Play Boosts Learning and School-Readiness in Preschoolers, Yale Study Finds*. Office of Public Affairs at Yale.

Singer, J. L. (1994). "Imaginative play and adaptive development" in Goldstein, J. H. *Toys, Play, and Child Development*. Cambridge, England: Cambridge University Press, 1994.

Winnicott, D. W. (1989). *Playing and Reality*. New York: Routledge, 1989.

# Priorities for Health and Safety in Child Care

by Susan S. Aronson, MD

*Many health related activities deserve the time and attention of child care staff, parents, and children; but no child care program can do everything. Because of limitations of funds and personnel, as well as physical and curricular constraints, choices must be made. Further, a completely infection-proof and injury-proof child care program would not meet children's needs. Cognitive, social, and emotional growth requires limited risk taking. Health promotion activities must be integrated with other program objectives. How are these choices to be made?*

One approach is to give attention to the topic or issue which circumstances bring to the fore. With this approach, a crisis serves as the stimulus for corrective action. Those who use this approach are doomed to suffer. A more rational approach is to set priorities by using the collected experience of others to focus available resources. Planning ahead helps avoid crisis.

## Managing Risks

One basic aspect of health and safety is risk management. The boundaries of acceptable risk define what is safe. Risks can be measured by the frequency and severity of harm associated with a given situation. Data collected on deaths and visits to medical facilities can be used to focus preventive efforts on those situations where the probability of injury is greatest.

Risk management efforts in child care programs should be focused on three areas: minimizing injuries, preventing and managing infectious diseases, and modifying features of the environment which affect health. In all three areas, insufficient data are available from child care settings to compare the magnitude of risk in the child care setting with the risk of harm to the child in other settings. As evidenced by high rates of injury and illness among young children cared for at home, young children are injury prone and need protection in any setting. In the child-oriented environment of a child care program, adults should strive for safety both to protect children who are in care and also to protect safe practices for parents.

## Minimizing Injuries

Although no systematically collected data have been published on the incidence of injuries in child care programs as a whole, studies of selected programs suggest priorities for prevention. In a study conducted by the author of insurance claims from policies covering 14,502 children, two-thirds of all injuries for which payment for medical care was requested occurred on the playground. Of these, by far the most common and most severe injuries were associated with the use of climbing equipment. Other products associated with frequent and severe injury included slides, hand toys and blocks, indoor floor surfaces, motor vehicles, and swings.

The specific reason for the injuries could not be determined in the insurance study because the claim forms did not include enough detail. However, using common sense, combined with the recommendations of the US Consumer Product Safety Commission, the US Housing and Urban Development Department, and the National

Highway Transportation Safety Administration, seven corrective actions can be recommended to reduce injuries from the products which turned up as troublemakers in the child care study:

1. **Climbers, slides, and swings used in child care should be modified to reduce the hazardous use of these play structures:**

   - Limit the maximum climbing height to no more than six feet.

   - Mount climbing structures over at least an eight inch depth of loose fill material such as shredded tires, pea gravel, or pine bark to help absorb impact.

   - Space playground equipment far enough away from otgher structures and child traffic patterns to prevent collisions.

   - Cover sharp edges and exposed bolts.

   - Teach children how to play safely on playground equipment.

2. **Gross motor play and block building activities require close supervision.** Because the playground accounts for a large share of the injuries, staff must be especially vigilant during large muscle play time. This part of the curriculum not only provides opportunities for children to let off steam and build gross motor skills but is also a time to learn safety rules to avoid injury.

3. **Certain architectural features of child care facilities like doors and indoor floor surfaces can be modified to reduce risk of injury.** Doors can have slow closing devices and beveled edges to reduce their finger pinching potential. Vision panels which expose the presence of young children near the door are helpful. Open floor areas can be broken up into smaller units by furniture placement to limit running where it is unsafe.

4. **The majority of motor vehicle injuries are preventable through use of age appropriate seat restraints and close attention to pedestrian behaviors, driver training, drop-off and pick-up routines.**

5. **A systematic study of injury in each child care program can identify other high risk areas so additional preventive strategies can be developed.** Individual child care programs can control hazards by collecting and routinely reviewing reports of *near misses* and minor injuries in the program. Merely filing a report in the child's record will not prevent a recurrence of the incident.

6. **The staff of child care programs need training and resources to change hazardous conditions.** By focusing on the common causes of significant injury in the age group served, the training should examine hazard control measures needed for each activity in the facility, playground, and on trips. In addition, the staff must be proficient in first aid and emergency procedures so that when injuries occur complications can be minimized.

7. **In planning staff/child ratios, enough adults must be accessible to the children at all times to handle an emergency and to safely evacuate children in an emergency.** For infants, a practical limit on staff/child ratios is imposed by the number of pounds of child one caregiver can remove from the building in a single trip. Enough staff must always be on hand to handle children who are unable to help themselves, including during staff break and nap times. Staff/child ratios for emergency evacuation are generally coincident with the higher ratios recommended for quality care.

## Controlling Diseases

Young children who are brought together in groups for care have increased exposure to infectious diseases in a manner analogous to a large family. However, child care programs which implement appropriate health and safety policies help prevent transmission of infection by requiring that children receive needed immunizations and routine health care and by giving parents and children day-to-day instruction bout hygiene, nutrition, and management of minor illness.

Much of the current scientific information on infectious disease problems in child care is based on retrospective evaluations of outbreaks. Many of the comparative studies of the incidence of infectious diseases in center care versus home care incorporate reporting bias. Few studies have evaluated the specific characteristics or practices of child care settings which promote or inhibit transmission of infectious disease. Without objective measures in controlled studies, no accurate assessment of the relative risk of infection from child care attendance can be made.

Studies of outbreaks have provided useful information on how to control the spread of diseases in the child care settings. Outbreaks of gastroenteritis, bacterial meningitis, hepatitis A, and vaccine-preventable diseases have been examined in child care programs. For general control of infectious disease agents in child care, most experts recommend routine hand washing after contact with urine, respiratory, or other body secretions. Exclusions of ill children does not seem particularly helpful except in cases where distribution of infectious material such as eye secretions, stool, or vomitus cannot be restricted. Cohorting of ill children to stop the mixing of adults and children from one group with those of another is also suggested.

New developments on the infection prevention horizon include the use of new vaccines to prevent childhood diseases which are suspected to be more common or more easily spread among child care children. Children in child care who are between the ages of 18 months and five years of age should be considered for the *Haemophilus influenzae* type b (Hib) vaccine which became available in 1985. Because children under 24 months may not be protected by the currently available vaccine, a second dose may be needed by these children. Soon a rotavirus vaccine may be available which will help prevent a common cause of diarrhea in cooler months.

Child care personnel, health professionals, and parents are concerned about the correlation between entry into child care and the frequency of illness. In the one study where this issue was examined, the overall burden of respiratory infection was not greater for children in child care, but there was a shift of illness to younger ages. Many parents and even some health professionals who are for children are unaware of the high frequency of respiratory infections among young children in any setting.

In the Cleveland Family Study conducted in the 1950s, children who were cared for in their own homes had an average of 6.7 common respiratory infections per child per year in the first year, increasing to 8.3 per child per year during the second year of life. By four to five years of age, children at home were still experiencing 7.6 respiratory illnesses per year.

The Frank Porter Graham Child Development center in Chapel Hill, North Carolina, infants in child care had 9.5 respiratory illnesses per year; but the incidence dropped steadily thereafter. Beyond the first year of life, children in child care had a lower incidence of respiratory infection than the children in the Cleveland home reared group. By age five, the incidence of respiratory infections for these children who had been in the same child care program since infancy was only 3.8 per year.

In a recently presented study, the Centers for Disease Control surveyed the occurrence of respiratory disease by telephone in randomly selected households in Atlanta during the summer months of 1985. Parents of children in child care reported more colds and more ear infections in the two weeks before the surveyor's call than did parents of children not in child care. The meaning of these data is unclear since the survey depended upon parental reporting rather than examination of the children. Further, the timing of the survey was during months when respiratory disease is less common.

Whether child care increases the risk of illness during the fall and winter months when respiratory disease agents are everywhere remains to be seen. Whether parents who are aware that their child's illness might result in exclusion from child care are more likely to notice and report signs of disease than other parents is also not known.

The challenge of infectious disease control in child care is to reduce transmission in the child care setting without losing the developmentally stimulating features of the curriculum. Based on our present level of knowledge, useful measures to consider include:

- Assign soft cuddly toys to individual children where possible.

- Sanitize mouthed objects by washing them with detergent and water; rinse them with water and give them a dip or rinse in a sanitizing solution (one quarter cup of bleach diluted in one gallon of water, made fresh daily, is an inexpensive sanitizing solution recommended by the Centers for Disease Control).

- Establish routines for hand washing for staff and children.

- Establish routines for handling fecally contaminated materials and surfaces.

- Enforce mandatory immunization for child care participation for children, staff, and volunteers. Systems must be in place to make sure immunizations remain up to date.

- Establish reasonable, scientifically supportable policies for excluding children with transmissible infection. Considering the lack of evidence that exclusion for respiratory infection makes any difference, the decision about permitting a child to remain in child care with respiratory illness should depend on the availability of the parent to provide sick child care and the ability of the child care staff to provide the extra attention that an ill child requires.

  On the other hand, most programs will find it prudent to exclude children with frequent loose infectious stools because they pose a significant risk for transmission of infectious disease if they remain in the program. More liberal use of stool cultures and parasite evaluation for children in child care may be indicated to identify cases where a public health risk exists. All loose stools are not caused by infectious disease agents. For practical purposes, exclusion might be considered when a child is having twice or more his/her usual frequency of stools with a liquid consistency which are not easily contained in a diaper. If the pattern persists or appears in other children in the child care group, laboratory investigation to identify the nature of the pathogen is appropriate. Other infections such as lice, scabies, conjunctivitis, and impetigo require the same precautions as are in common use for school children.

- Arrange for every child care program to have easy access to health consultation. Health consultants are needed to provide technical advice about the nature of an infectious disease problem and suggest control measures to use.

- Provide at least yearly inspection of every child care facility (not just the kitchen) by a qualified sanitarian who is armed with suggestions or inexpensive ways to modify problems identified at the child care site. There should be no exemptions from health and safety inspections because of religious affiliation or any other reason.

## Managing Environments

No data is available on the extent to which adverse conditions in child care contribute to disease. In fact, how such conditions contribute to illness in the general population has not been well studied. Conditions such as excessively dry or excessively humid air probably play a significant role in body defense.

In the winter, outdoor air is cold and can hold little moisture. When this dry air is heated, it can hold more moisture, but has few sources for this water. Living plants and animals need moisture to carry their body secretions, many of which protect against invasion by unwanted infections. When body surfaces lose moisture into dry environmental air, increased susceptibility to infection may result. On the other hand, with excess humidity, molds and other fungi may grow. Sensitive individuals may become infected with mold and fungus infections or react to the presence of such substances with allergic symptoms. Humidity can be controlled by inexpensive equipment which adds or removes water was needed.

Many other environmental conditions may strain body resources. Living where someone smokes, uses a kerosene heater, or improperly vented wood stove has been found to be associated with increased incidence of respiratory disease. Use of chemical cleaning agents with a residual odor may adversely affect those who are sensitive to such agents. Odor intolerance and allergic diseases affect more than half the population at one time or another. In the child care setting, minimizing prolonged, repeated, and unnecessary exposure to odorous and noxious substances, including smoke and personal perfumes, seems reasonable.

Noise pollution is a particularly common problem in child care where the joy of play may drown conversational tones and interfere with a child's ability to hear distinct speech sounds. One study of children who lived in a high rise building erected over a major highway found that children who lived closest to the constant highway noise did not develop speech and language skills as well as those who lived farther away. This finding suggests that constant noise may adversely affect the development of communication skills.

Environmental modifications which may help control noise pollution in child care include use of sound absorbing materials wherever possible. Carpeting can be used as wall and floor covering except in areas where sanitation dictates otherwise. Lightweight sound sponges are available which may be installed like blocks of ceilings and walls to capture and deaden the din. Contoured surfaces and partitioned areas help, too. Sound engineers can often suggest creative and inexpensive improvements for the child care setting. Free advice on how to obtain help with acoustical and other safety and health problems is available on request from state offices of the Occupational Safety and Health Administration Consultation Project.

## Promoting Health

In child care, several significant opportunities for health promotion merit attention. These include: routine or check up health services, nutrition, dental health, mental health and child development, and general health education. Preventive investments in children can gave lifelong benefits. Public health authorities have just begun to recognize the opportunities to foster health for children by outreach to child care programs. As this awareness grows, child care directors should find it easier to obtain advice from health professionals.

**Routine health services.** Check up visits provide the opportunity for health professionals to offer advice to parents to prevent illness and injury and to identify problems when they are most easily corrected. The schedule recommended by the American Academy of Pediatrics for routine health care visits is based on the need for specific issues to be discussed at critical points in development and on the likelihood that certain problems will be discoverable at particular ages. The details of the schedule, including the recommended content for each of these visits, is documented in manuals available for sale by the AAP (call 800/433-9016 for details about cost and availability).

**Nutrition.** With one to two meals and one or two snacks as part of the routine day care schedule, nutrition is a large component of the child care program. Head Start studies showed that preschool nutrition programs can reduce the incidence of anemia among children in the program as well as among their families. This extension of the benefits of good modeling by child care programs to benefit other family members highlights the health promotion power of good child care. Menu modeling, feeding techniques, the integration of eating with social development, sanitation, and management of food resources are integral parts of nutrition.

**Dental health.** With so many meals and snacks being served daily, dental hygiene is a natural component of health promotion activities. In addition, depending on the availability of fluoride in local drinking water supplies, children can be encouraged to receive appropriate fluoride supplements at home or in child care. Many parents are still unaware that when children receive proper doses of fluoride while their teeth are growing, the teeth will incorporate the fluoride into the enamel for a lifetime of resistance against tooth decay. With proper doses of fluoride during the time of tooth formation, children with have less than half the dental cavities they would otherwise suffer in their lifetime.

**Mental health and child development.** Readers of this magazine do not need to be reminded about the opportunities available in child care programs to foster psychosocial development of children and their families. Child care is a family support service which can foster the healthy development of normal children in normal families. In addition, child care is an environment where family stress can be recognized and reduced by directing parents to sources of help. Using early intervention and appropriate curriculum and care, child care can serve as a hub to draw professional, community, and social supports to families engaged in the critical task of raising the next generation.

**Health education.** Child care programs model child rearing practices for parents, many of whom have had little child care training themselves. Because of the trend toward small families, few adults of child bearing age have seen an infant move through weaning or toilet training. Many do not know how to differentiate minor from more serious illnesses or how to manage cuts and scrapes to minimize infection. Outdoor play and fresh air are undervalued; worry about exposure to cold or rain is excessive. When parents become more knowledgeable, competent, and confident, child care programs help families provide better care for their children.

While child care cannot do everything for everyone, by concentrating on the more significant health promoting and risk reducing measures, much can be accomplished. No program will ever achieve perfection. By continually reaching for improved quality, child care can have a positive impact on family life and the development of healthy children.

# Food as Shared Living-and-Learning

by Nadine L. McCrea

*I still vividly recall the food tasting experiences of a small group of children with special needs that I worked with years ago (McCrea, 1981). One boy was chronologically about age eight but mentally an infant; he was difficult in every sense of the word, including being a very fussy eater. However, when we (children, parents, and I) made Chinese steamed buns and fried rice one morning, he ate every grain of rice in his bowl and he ate them one by one with chopsticks! Everyone was astonished that he even ate the rice, let alone all of it and with chopsticks. Similarly, years later when I worked with staff and children at a local child care centre, I found that both children and educators were more adventurous tasters if they were actively involved with foods across a foodcycle.*

*This article presents a philosophical and practical approach to food and food learning for young children and the significant adults that they interact with. The focal ideas discussed below represent* ***food as*** *. . . being shared with others, being everywhere and everyday, and being viewed and explored across a foodcycle within both families and early childhood education settings. Several interactive workshop tasks are provided for encouraging early childhood directors and staff to consider these ideas about food and to try out some of the possibilities.*

## Food is 'Everywhere' and 'Everyday'

We begin with a philosophical approach that conceptualises **food as** . . . an everyday source of healthy learning for young children. This approach represents 'food-in-the-broadest-sense' and places such food everywhere around us. This means that young children live via eating foods and they learn from multiple food experiences that happen in homes and early childhood services, in gardens, and local communities. Similarly, food living-and-learning opportunities happen every day as young children along with their parents and educators:

- prepare foods and eat a meal;
- plant and care for a herb garden;
- co-read classic stories like *Stone Soup, Green Eggs and Ham, The Very Hungry Caterpillar*, or any number of recent picture books that incorporate aspects of the cycle of food from gardening to eating to recycling (McCrea, 1994); or
- decide to explore ideas about any number of food-related artifacts, concepts, and processes.

This **food as** . . . approach is something like Bess-Gene Holt's (1988, pp. 79-81) now classic personal ecology framework and distance-from-self wheel, with food being the living-and-learning medium conceptually, physically, and socio-emotionally. Children are at the center of Holt's personal ecology framework; and I maintain that the ways children ' . . . (are) interrelating, interweaving, and interacting with phenomena . . . ' (Holt, 1988, p. 79) ought to be everywhere, everyday, and shared with others. This living-and-learning approach is as much about adults' values and beliefs (see the workshop ideas) as it is about their daily food practices in homes and early childhood services. The **food as** . . . approach can be designed, carried out, and monitored by educators using a 'foodcycle' (McCrea, 1994; Appleton, McCrea, & Patterson, 2001, pp. 49-54) with parents being actively involved.

If foodcycle events are carefully arranged through interactions, communications, active involvement, and joint decision-making, many contemporary concerns that parents and educators have about children eating enough (too little or too much versus a variety and balance of foods) may well disappear. One might ask why these concerns of parents and educators would disappear. The response is — if young children are regularly and actively involved in all aspects of food reaching our dining tables, they are usually more committed, more willing, and more interested in tasting their handiwork.

## What is Shared and How?

When a shared living-and-learning approach to food education focuses on a cycle of food origins, uses, and reuses, a number of planning and curriculum issues arise. These issues vary from educators' values and beliefs, to the environmental features of early education settings, and on to educators' daily practices. We can begin looking at what is shared and how by considering several understandings or principles that might underpin the design of food curricula. Such principles provide both reasons for, as well as ways to explore foods from gardening to waste recycling. And so, relevant learning principles may well:

- encompass and link children's knowledge (including their abilities), attitudes and behaviors, or actions;
- value cooperation among adults, and between adults and children involved in food events;
- support gender awareness and cultural equity within foodcycle events;
- facilitate empowerment of both adults' and children's food lifeskills;
- define food opportunities holistically and in context as part of both sensitive real life and desirable early education;
- respect the natural and human world with shared caring across generations;
- balance opportunities between multi-sensory and multi-developmental avenues;
- propose interactions and expectations based on interdependence between adults and children, with guided participation in the shared social capital of foods; and
- provide hands-on active learning which considers individuals, plus accounts for social responsibility, integrates areas of child development, and links content across early childhood curriculum (McCrea, 1994).

An early childhood education foodcycle draws children and adults into shared explorations of food: producing, processing, purchasing, preparing, partaking, and waste processing. These food stopping-points can be explored directly (for example, by planting nasturtium seeds in containers near the kindergarten entry) or more indirectly (for example, by reading a picture book about herbs during storytime or bedtime). Often, children from about age two can participate meaningfully. In keeping with the above principles, a brief sampler of foodcycle options is outlined below to assist educators as curriculum designers:

*Producing foods* may include children's involvement in sprouting mung beans, planting mustard-and-cress seeds, or transplanting vegetable and flower seedlings in a garden plot. The related tools and containers are important artifacts.

*Processing foods* may involve children directly with the sun-drying of apricot halves, making dill pickles, steaming Chinese savory buns, or even curing green and black olives. This stopping point brings back to life a few historically family-based food processing events; and the end products may become gift-giving items from children to family and friends.

*Purchasing foods* might include a few children and an adult sharing the experience of buying fruits and vegetables from a corner grocery shop, selecting continental sausages from the butcher's counter, or hunting and gathering cultural-ethnic food ingredients from the shelves of a delicatessen.

*Preparing foods* can include working with raw and cooked ingredients. For example, children may participate in cutting fruits for a fruit salad, spreading mashed avocado on personal slices of toast, or hand juicing orange halves for an individual fresh juice beverage. Here, there is a focus on awareness of varied and balanced meals across several days or a week. The social potential of food tastings and meals is important, too. There is a sensitive attention to incorporating cultural styles, food combinations, and ethnic seasonings. Culinary equipment and utensils as well as the processes of applied science (edible chemistry and physical changes) that occur during food preparing and food packaging are central to these socio-physical activities.

*Partaking of foods* could involve children in selecting and eating either small snacks mid-morning, a smorgasbord self-serve lunch, or an intimate mid-afternoon of cheese cubes and apple rings. The mid-morning and mid-afternoon snacks could take place during dramatic play at a home corner table or under a tree outside. These could be occasions for sampling various ethnic dishes. The atmosphere and expectations surrounding eating and the table are vitally important considerations.

*Processing wastes* from any food preparing and partaking activities may involve children in feeding stale bread to bantam chickens, composting fruit and vegetable scraps for future gardening mulch, recycling aluminium cans and glass bottles, or feeding newspaper and plant food scraps to worms in a see-through aquarium worm farm. In addition to recycling organic wastes from meals, this foodcycle approach incorporates the idea of minimising the non-organic, artificial wastes linked with foods in most contemporary societies. Thus, at the shopping stage, purchases take account of the most natural, the least processed, and minimally packaged (Davis, 1996; McCrea, 1996).

**Food as** shared living-and-learning across a whole cycle of food represents one way of closing the gap that many children and adults are part of today. This gap exists for

## How to Use This Article to Train Teachers by Nadine McCrea

**Listed are a few interactive workshop ideas for director support, early childhood staff professional development, and parent education.**

1. *My food memories — ideas from staff members' and parents' childhoods*: Start with a large sheet of paper and create a clustering brainstorm or *spider web* of your childhood food rememberances that are rich linkages of foods, every-day events, and familiar people (see the 'Little Nadine' example). You may recall fond food experiences and some less pleasant ones. Think about how you felt then and your feelings now. What issues are raised here in terms of your parent or educator roles with young children.

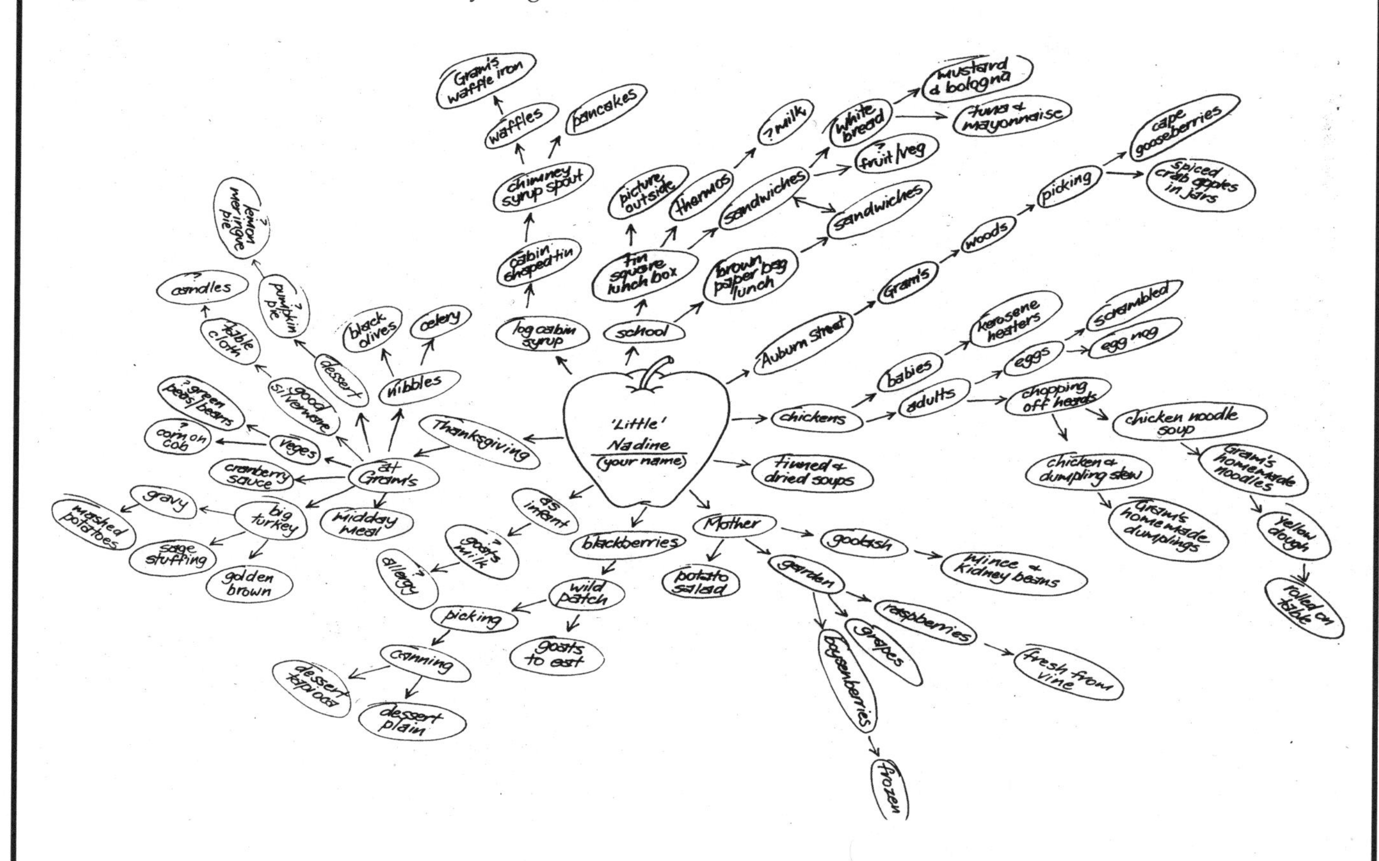


2. *My beliefs, your beliefs*: In a small group, share your beliefs and values about the purposes and roles of foods in our lives. What implications are there for the daily practices in your early childhood program?

3. *Our policies and management processes*: Outline the food living-and-learning policies and processes that currently exist within your early childhood program. Identify the origins and rationales for these. Compare and contrast your policies as well as any related leadership and management issues with those of at least one other early child-hood service. Have ideas arisen that you want to investigate and then consider making changes? (Note: Chapter 5 of *Do Carrots Make You See Better?* includes policies, a management process, and other decision-making ideas.)

4. *A curriculum planner*: Work with one or two other educators to create a curriculum planning framework that takes into account the philosophy and approach described in this article. Remember this is a planning document and a framework, rather than a lock-step intention that may disregard staff, children, and parents and their social and cultural backgrounds. Explore relevant ideas in the book: *Educating the Global Village* (Swiniarski, L., Breitborde, M., & Murphy, J. 1999).

**Ideas for a curriculum planning framework:** Such a planning framework can include a broad aim about food education based on your philosphy and values. It may contain various objectives about food-health, integrated learning concepts, and active processes for children's learning. Key resources and indoor and outdoor learning spaces may be noted. Then, educators build upon this planning framework in response to the seasons and their children's interests, ages, and cultural experiences.

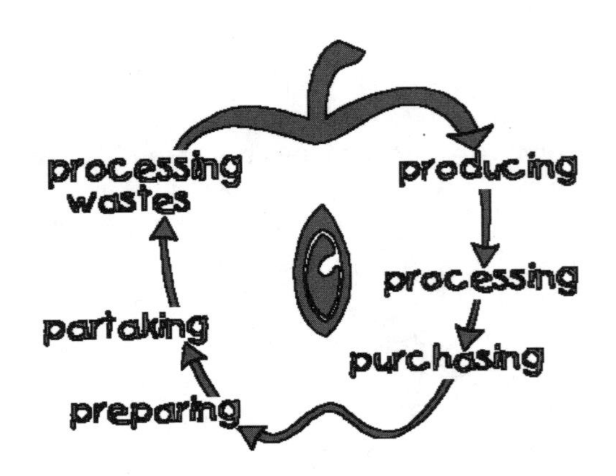


most urban people in developed countries and it means we are totally unaware of and certainly not part of our food source processes. This near-and-distant gap reveals how close we are to foods we eat but still distant; and how far we are from the origins and layers of work that bring our daily food to the table. For me, this concept means that what is described here is real and realistic food education, not scientific nutrition studies. The approach touches on food concepts across everyday family life and daily early childhood education. It is about natural objects, artifacts, and processes. It encompasses exploring such ideas as human bodies, our senses, physical and chemical changes to foods, plus temporal and spatial elements related to foodcyles. The approach is centered around cooperative responsibilities, with adults teaching and also learning. It happens through having choices and making decisions.

## A Synthesis

Much of our challenge with *nutrition* today is that it is not real for parents, educators, or children. Our daily eating and our related health status are about actual foods or dishes; and they can be made most relevant and interesting for adults and children through shared food-cycle interactions. We are all so far removed from what foods mean socially and culturally, where they come from, and how they get to the shelves of supermarkets. Trying to be closer to foods in these foodcycle ways may well encourage both adults and children to understand and care more about what they eat and when, where, and why they eat. In essence, food learning compared to other curriculum areas is unique learning, as there is no way of separating our food understandings, beliefs, and actions when we are creatures of habit in complex social and cultural settings. Thus, food is shared living-and-learning from early childhood on.

## References

Appleton, J., McCrea, N., & Patterson, C. (2001). *Do carrots make you see better? A guide to food and nutrition in early childhood programs.* Beltsville, MD: Gryphon House.

Davis, J. (1996). 'Early childhood environmental education.' *Educating Young Children,* 2 (4) pp. 38-39.

Holt, B. G. (1988). *Science with Young Children.* Washington, DC: NAEYC.

McCrea, N. (1994). *Early Childhood Foodcycle Learning — Revealing food beliefs, happenings and management in three child care centres.* Unpublished Ph.D. Thesis, University of Queensland, Australia.

McCrea, N. (1996). 'Being sustainable gardeners and wise consumers from an early age: Helping care for our environment.' *Educating Young Children,* 2 (4) pp. 10-12.

McCrea, N. (1981). 'A Down-Under Approach to Parent and Child Food Fun.' *Childhood Education, 57* (4), pp. 216-222.

Swiniarski, L., Breitborde, M.L., & Murphy, J.A. (1999). *Educating the Global Village, including the young child in the world.* Upper Saddle River, NJ: Merrill.

# The Art of Leadership
## Managing Early Childhood Organizations

# Working with Parents

### Chapter 16

# Places for Childhoods Include Parents, Too

**by Jim Greenman**

*"Parents are welcome at any time." In a good child care center, this is the right thing to say, the politically correct policy — valuing parent presence in the center. "We believe in partnerships with parents." Equally important, equally correct — implying a belief in some parent power. But do we believe it, really? Do we ALL believe it, all the time? And do our practices and environment back up our ideology?*

## Parent Involvement

Parent involvement is an all-purpose term that encompasses parent boards, volunteering, parent education, fundraising, and the daily exchanges of information. One center's parent involvement places parent action and presence safely on the perimeter — board meetings, special events, and donations; another center has parents intimately involved in center life and decisionmaking around their own child.

What is parent involvement in child care? In discussions with teachers, there is general agreement that it includes much information sharing, parent support by good child rearing and cooperation, some volunteering, special events, donations, and perhaps participation on an advisory board. With some prodding, less so with infant staff, staff may recognize that an important role for parents is advocating for and influencing the care their child receives. Sharing information is one thing, sharing power quite another, and the idea makes many professionals very uneasy.

Confusion over parent roles is understandable because schools, including preschools, rarely accorded the parent a role that incorporated influencing the program's response to their child. The parent's job was to support the professionals. But child care is a different institution. The parent's job is to raise their child, be the expert on their own child, and make sure the child is cared for in accordance with their values and standards.

What is the best child care that money can buy? When Mr. and Mrs. Bigbucks look for child care, they may hire a nanny or seek the specific care they want from programs in their area. They expect control over little Blake's care, not just information about the care Blake received. Their purchasing power backs up their parental prerogatives. They may want advice and education from the child care professional(s), but they certainly expect it will be given respectfully with full awareness that it is their choice.

Quality child care is care that is individualized to the child and the family and education that empowers the child. The best centers work hard to also empower the parents, to help parents feel in control over their child's care. It is a true collaboration that recognizes the prerogatives and constraints of both partners.

Parents approach the parent/staff relationship with some child care guilt and a confusion of messages about what to look for in quality child care. Staff, who often work with children because they feel more confident with children than adults, bring the insecurity that accompanies low pay and status and the same uncertainty about "what is right." Both groups usually come from an individualistic culture not great about sharing love and intimacy. It's not easy. Often staff feelings and perceptions develop that work against a partnership. Those feelings are a natural outgrowth of the complex relationship and are present in nearly all programs.

## "They"

Parents easily become "they" or "the parents," not a collection of individuals. In every population, there are a range of individuals from near saints to clear sinners. We usually use the annoying and problematic behavior of the least agreeable to create our "they" that we rail against or reprove with knowing condescension. The parent who is willing to place their child in care for 60 hours a week — who works part time and pays for facials — defines the "they," along with the chronically late parent, the one who forgets the diapers, the "whiner," and the one who wants her infant toilet trained. When some staff get together and talk about parents, one wonders whether they are talking about a mutant species. Note, however, the bark is worse than the bite. Many staff who rail against parents actually behave in sensitive and accommodating ways when interacting with parents.

This tendency to create "theys" is certainly not limited to child care workers. It is a natural phenomena that has to be fought, an occupational hazard of service related professions.

## "They Don't Tell Us What Is Happening at Home"

As a consultant, I sat in the teachers' meeting at the small center and listened to them share about the children and families.

"What about (two year old) James? He seems to be having a hard time and acting out a lot," asked the director.

"I found out through a mutual friend that his parents are struggling and may split up," his teacher, Jane, responded. "It explains a lot. I wish his mom had told us. How can we help their kids if they don't tell us what's happening at home?"

I asked the staff what they would have done if they knew what was going on with James' mom and dad. They replied that they would have tried to give him "more," and they would have understood more.

I asked Jane, "Suppose you were going through a messy divorce and you were under a lot of stress. And suppose you weren't getting along with Alice (the associate teacher) because she was on edge because she's drinking too much. Should we put out a bulletin to the parents — TO ALL PARENTS: The children in Jane's class may behave differently at home because of problems at child care. Jane's divorce and Alice's drinking have resulted in some tension and breaks in the normal routines, but don't worry because care is still good and their on-the-job performance is acceptable. Just please try and give your child some special attention because he/she may be feeling a little insecure. We thought this information might help explain your child's behavior."

It is tempting to justify knowing all the details of a family's private life because it will help us "understand" or "teach" a child. But we have no RIGHT to know the ins and outs of family life, any more than they have a right to know about our private lives as a means to monitor program quality or better understanding. For the most part, what we need to know is that a child like James is under some unusual stress and needs us at our most supportive best. Much of the time it makes little difference in our response whether the stress is due to family problems, fitful sleep, mild illness, or all the other sources of children's stress. What we do is try to offer flexibility, warmth, and nurturing. If a child is older, perhaps it may help the child to talk about the situation. But in that case, let the child or parent decide.

Respect for parents demands that, unless the situation is one of abuse or neglect, the parents control what information they wish to share. If we come to know something about the family, as professionals we should ask the parents if they mind before sharing the information with colleagues or supervisors. In the case of James, discussing his family situation as a staff, based on gossip and without parent permission, is no less unprofessional than a group discussing a teacher's private struggles. When we have a relationship based on mutual respect and confidence, many parents trust us with information about their private struggles.

## "They Don't Care"

In child care, we often take OUR institutional limitations as givens, certainly not as signs we care less about the children. Ratios, center size, foods served, the limits of our services, staff turnover — "Sorry, welcome to the real world of today's child care." We usually honestly can say we are doing our best. We'd like to do more — have better ratios, more one to one, more field trips, use fewer substitutes, but the budget gets in the way.

With parents, we are not always so willing to accept their givens. Yet parents' real lives — long work days; the need to find some time for themselves; money problems; a difficulty sorting out what is the right thing to do in a diverse, guilt-inducing, materialistic culture — easily brings out the judgmental in us (particularly if we haven't had to face the world as parents ourselves). "They don't care" or "they don't care enough" is perhaps the most common hidden thought that lurks in the minds of many child care workers every time they look for extra clothes, cope with a sick child, or regret the poor turnout at an open house. Followed by, "I wish they would get some parent education," as we put together an image of the child's family life based on the child's behavior, our disapproving glimpses of parent-child interactions, and reports from the home front.

As a director, I made sure the parent handbook had a section asking that parents label their children's clothing because "don't they realize how many clothes we have to go through and how alike all the clothing is?" As a parent, I inconsistently labeled my kid's clothing because "don't they realize how many clothes kids go through and what it takes to label each pair of socks?" As a parent, I missed open houses, regretfully, and committed all the parent sins, still caring deeply about my kid.

## "They Won't Leave Us Alone"

The flip side to "they don't care" is "they care too much" about some things. James' mother, Gloria, was a walking negative stereotype of the mother on welfare — high school drop out, overweight, poorly dressed, erratically kept appointments, rarely provided an extra set of clothes for her children, a mother of three, and only 22 years old. More so, she had been reported to the state for suspected child abuse for what looked like a burn on her child's bottom — which turned out to be impetigo. When she got upset with the center about James' care or had questions about his education, one could always sense from the staff an underlying "how dare you challenge us on our care decisions." The more questions, the more staff outrage. Some of her questions / concerns:

- When will James be taught to read?
- Why does he get so dirty?
- How did he get that bruise?
- How could he lose two shirts and a shoe?
- Why do you let James get away with so much?

Gloria was loud and seemed ill at ease and pushy to the staff. Because of this, many staff didn't recognize that her questions and concerns were nearly always appropriate, never frivolous.

Megan's mother, Jane, was nearly the opposite of Gloria — a 42 year old psychologist and Megan was her only child. She was usually late picking up Megan and often was slow responding to staff requests. When she asked questions or had concerns, and she asked many questions (similar to Gloria's), staff response was less "how dare she" and more "what a typical neurotic older yuppie parent." As with Gloria, Jane's questions and concerns, while numerous and often minor, were never off the wall.

The parents' job is to look out for their child, to monitor their care, and to advocate for quality care and education. Both Gloria and Jane did this, better than many "nicer" parents. When parents are persistent or assertive, they may well be obnoxious (at least to us) and we begin to use stereotypes to discredit them. What staff have to understand is not that parents' concerns or questions are always valid — a parent request or complaint may be ill-founded — but making the request or complaint is a parent acting responsibly.

## Mutual Respect: A "Why Not" Approach

One way to characterize the approach is that all requests are met with a non-defensive attitude and "why not" thinking, an approach that grants the parent request legitimacy. When parents ask us for a change in their child's routine, a special activity, or a different way of doing things, we genuinely ask ourselves, "why not?" This is different than a customer-is-always-right approach. It is not an automatic yes. There may be many legitimate "why nots" that lead to a no — for budget reasons, the complexity of group life, we don't know how, staffing, etc. We have no reason to be defensive about our givens that lead to our limitations.

The outcome of a "why not" approach is not unmanageable complexity, but thoughtful care and a foundation of mutual respect and, in most cases, increased trust that we are professionals thinking through good care. The non-defensive "why not" rubs off on the parents and begins to characterize staff relationships as well. Equally important, a "why not" approach leads to innovation and better care.

# Making the Most of Parent Conferences

by Katherine Koulouras, Mary Lynn Porter, and Sheri A. Senter

**Director**: *"Well, Nancy, I'm afraid I've got some bad news for you. From what I hear, your son Ronald is biting everything that moves, and he's got everyone upset. Two of my teachers have threatened to quit (one of whom, to be perfectly honest, I'd just as soon would leave anyway), the kids flee in panic whenever he comes near, and Mrs. Dole (who tends to complain about our every little foible) is threatening to pull her precious Robert out unless Ronnie stops biting him. You need to make him stop."*

**Parent**: *"I can't believe this. He never bites at home. What are you doing to him?"*

**Director**: *"It's clear to me that there are unresolved conflicts in his familial environments that are being repressed and redirected at substitute antagonists in an external setting. You've really got a screwed up kid on your hands. Could you wait a minute while I handle this call?"*

Hopefully, this does not sound anything like the parent conference you just held Thursday night. Hopefully, this does not sound like any parent conference you have ever held. In this brief interchange, the director has made about every mistake that can be made in a parent conference.

Undoubtedly, many things can, and do, go wrong in parent conferences. But, if handled properly, there is so very much that can go right.

You can establish rapport with a parent who has just been zipping in and out. You can put to rest the anxieties of a nervous parent. You can learn more about the child's life outside the center. You can communicate to the parent what her child is like in the center — his strengths and weakness, his joys and sorrows. You can brainstorm to come up with ideas to help a child overcome his weaknesses and to build on his strengths. Most importantly, you can build a bond of trust that cements a sound working relationship for the balance of the year.

For everything to go right in a parent conference, it must be well planned and thoughtfully executed. The following are guidelines for planning and executing effective conferences:

## Be Prepared

- ***Carefully consider who are the appropriate staff members to be included in each conference.***

The teacher who works with a child on a daily basis is clearly the one who will have the most to offer about the child's life at the center. She is a logical choice to be at the conference.

However, if this teacher is new and not comfortable with running a conference alone, or if the director has worked with other children in the family over the years and can provide a broader perspective, it may be helpful for the director to attend the session as well. One potential outcome of parent conferences is for the relationship between the parent and the teacher to be strengthened.

If this happens, ongoing communication and cooperation will be enhanced. For this reason, even if the director attends a conference, she should be careful not to take over and not to undermine the role of the teacher.

In centers where there is a head teacher/teacher aide setup, it may be wise to involve the teacher aides in conferences. Often aides have a low self image and are insecure in the presence of parents. Having aides participate in conferences may just help establish the beginning of a relationship with parents.

• ***Prepare for each conference by familiarizing yourself with the child and the parent.***

To make a conference a meaningful experience for all involved, it is important to put together as complete a picture as possible of what the child's life is like at the center. Conferences can be much more effective if the participants already have established more than a casual relationship.

Ideally, throughout the year teachers will have been making anecdotal notes about significant events for each child — accomplishments and disappointments, good times and bad times, favorite activities and least favorite activities, efforts to relate to the other children and their dealings with adults.

To supplement the ongoing recording of information, it may be helpful to schedule specific sessions to observe each child deliberately. Teachers may find it helpful to use a preprinted observation form identifying specific points to observe.

At the same time, it is helpful to make a deliberate effort to get to know the parents. Conferences can be much more effective if the participants already have established more than a casual, "Hi! How's it going?" relationship. Also, the better you understand the parents, the better you will be able to present any difficult messages. For example, if you have seen that a particular parent is very insecure about his parenting, you might raise any concerns you have about his child in a much different manner than with a parent who seems abundantly secure.

• ***Train staff members on how to carry out effective parent conferences.***

The dynamics of parent conferences are complex. Situations requiring superior communication skills arise frequently. Mollifying an angry parent, discussing a child who is experiencing considerable difficulty, and dealing with a parent who overreacts to everything you say are but a few examples.

It is wise to prepare for such situations by conducting some informal training each year before conferences begin. The most important area to focus on in this training is communication skills. Important topics to address include how to convey unhappy messages, how to elicit information and feedback from parents, how to be an effective listener, and how to curb defensiveness.

While discussions on the fine points of communication will be helpful, nothing is a better teacher than experience. Meeting with other teachers and the director, prior to the time of the parent conference and sharing concerns that need to be discussed with the parents during the conference, will provide the teacher the opportunity to gain insights and skills from their experiences. Role playing can also be used to give staff members an opportunity to put these fine points into practice. A further improvement on this would be to videotape the role playing sessions so that all parties to the play can see themselves in action and determine where they need to improve.

• ***Specify what you hope to accomplish with each and every conference.***

Every time you walk into a parent conference, you should have a clear idea of what your objective is. It may be as ambitious as to work out a plan for helping a child who has severe behavior problems, or as modest as to establish a stronger relationship between teacher and a parent. If you don't have a specific goal for a conference, you will be wasting everybody's time.

On the other hand, keep in mind that it is possible that your goal for the conference may be suddenly changed by a parent's comment indicating a current problem affecting the family at the present time. If this new concern is foremost on the parent's mind at the moment, you need to be flexible enough to focus first on this concern.

## Set the Stage

• ***Provide feedback to parents on an ongoing basis.***

Avoid the temptation to turn a parent conference into a surprise party. The news that you share with parents in a conference should be a detailed analysis of an old story, not a shocking scoop. Ideally, you should be sharing anecdotes, questions, concerns, and observations with parents on a daily basis, so that when they come to the conference they will already have a good idea about what will be discussed.

• ***Do everything you can to make conferences convenient, casual and comfortable.***

One way to underline the point that conferences are designed for parents is to display sign-up sheets at the center for several weeks so that parents have the opportunity to select conference times that fit their schedule. After the sign-up period, you can call all those who didn't sign up and work out a time with them. Your schedule should provide for choices at all times of the day to take into account parents' varying work schedules.

The schedule should also allow sufficient time so that each conference can, at a relaxed pace, cover all center and parent interests and concerns. A conference of less than 20 minutes, for example, may only provide enough time for a run down of how the child is doing at the center, with little or no time to learn about the child's life outside the center.

The setting for the conference should be comfortable and distraction free. If you are able to clear all the files, magazines, and puzzle pieces from the chairs and desk top in the director's office, you may be able to provide a reasonably comfortable setting; but telephone interruptions will be inevitable.

Another way to cut down on distractions is to make sure that you have everything you will need for a conference on hand when it starts. If you have to halt a conference to go out and hunt for a file or a name, this will lend a disorganized feeling to the proceedings and may cause aggravation to parents on a tight schedule. Having refreshments on hand is another way of reinforcing a casual, caring tone in a conference.

- ***Concentrate on setting parents at ease at the outset of the conference.***

You should never assume that parents will take a conference lightly. Although conferences may be old hat to you, to parents they may be a venture into the unknown. Parents may be anxious about what will happen, or at least uncertain about what is expected of them.

Start every conference on a positive tone, even when there is negative information that needs to be conveyed. "I'm glad we're having this conference, because we really want to work with you to provide the best possible experience for your child" is an infinitely better lead off for a conference than "Well, Nancy, I'm afraid I've got some bad news for you!"

It is also helpful, at the outset, to give a preview about what will happen in the conference. Not knowing what is going to happen, or whether they will get an opportunity to speak their mind, can be discomforting and distracting for parents.

Don't waste time with meaningless small talk, but don't just jump in with the heavy stuff either. To break the ice in a low stress, on-task way, you might start off by describing an amusing or touching anecdote involving their child, or by asking how their child responded to a recent activity.

## Lead the Way

- ***Inform parents about their child's life at the center by sharing specific examples.***

The most effective way to communicate verbally how a child is doing at the center is to paint a picture with a paletteful of anecdotes and specific observations. Sweeping generalizations ("Winifred is progressing nicely" or "Annie's gross motor skills are developmentally appropriate") tend to be vague and open to broad interpretation.

Examples of a child's work can add variety to a conference. However, such items should be used to illustrate a point you are trying to make, and not simply as show and tell gimmicks.

Some centers have gone high-tech, adding a video element to their parent conferences. These centers use VCR cameras to record short, typical scenes in a day in the life of a child at the center. This movie can then be played back on a TV for the parents as part of the conference. Centers using VCRs in this manner have reported excellent reactions from parents.

- ***Speak in plain English***

"Tossing fancy Piagetian phrases about comes easy. What is really impressive is explaining a complex behavioral issue in plain English."

When commenting on a child's behavior or developmental attainment, you should stop and check periodically to be sure you are not jargonizing. Ask parents to restate for you their understanding of key observations you have made.

In a parent conference, a teacher commented that a child was experiencing difficulty with fine motor coordination. Given the age of the child, this was a perfectly normal situation. However, the parent perceived this to be a serious deficiency and immediately went out and bought three different types of scissors for her child to practice with. If this teacher had stopped to test the parent's understanding of her point, this episode of panic could have been avoided.

- ***Listen actively to parents to understand their concerns, their observations, and their impressions.***

A parent conference is most successful when it is a two-way conversation, not a one-way presentation. You need to work almost as hard at eliciting parent feedback as you do at presenting your side of the story.

Parents may well come to a conference with questions or complaints about your center. If they are not offered an opportunity to air these concerns, or if they perceive that their concerns were dismissed too summarily, they will leave the conference dissatisfied, if not angry.

Even when parents have no specific comments to voice, you should utilize this opportunity to learn more about the child. Ask the parent: *What does he tell you about the center? Does anything upset him? What does he seem to most enjoy about the center? What does he most enjoy doing at home? Does he behave differently at home than at the center? Does he have to deal with different rules and expectations at home than at the center? What are your primary hopes for him? What are your primary concerns?*

By gathering this type of information, you can get a broader picture of the child's world. You can get a more complete perspective on why he behaves the way he does at school. For example, if you discover that a child is harshly disciplined at home, this may help you understand why she fails to respond to the positive discipline approaches you employ at the center.

The most effective way to elicit information and opinions from parents is to utilize active listening. With this technique you are trying to get inside the head of the other person, to understand their point of view, to see things as they see them. In listening, your goal is to fully understand what is being said, not to make a judgment on it or to come up with a clever response.

When the parent makes an important point, restate your understanding of what she just said ("Do I understand you to say that your son comes home upset on days when his regular teacher is absent?"). If you do not understand what the parent said, this gives her an opportunity to explain her point more fully. In the end, you should better understand the parent's point of view, and the parent should feel like she got her point across.

- ***Present child behavior problems as challenges requiring joint problem solving.***

Inevitably, when you adapt the "You have to do this" approach for dealing with behavior problems, it doesn't work. About all it accomplishes is to make parents defensive, embarrassed, or angry.

A more active approach is to say, "Here is a challenge your child is presenting, what can we do about it?" This reinforces the attitude that the center's staff and the parents share a mutual concern for the well being of the child.

For this approach to work, your desire to hear the parents' suggestions must be genuine. If you ask for their ideas, but then propose a solution that you obviously had decided upon even before the conference, your insincerity will inevitably show. You will then lose the respect and support of the parents.

- ***Offer ideas, resources, and referrals as suggestions, not prescriptions.***

The spirit of joint problem solving will dissolve if you suddenly decree, "Now here's what I think you've got to do with Ronnie." This clearly conveys the message that it's their problem, not a mutual challenge.

Ideally, when a parent comes to accept that there is a problem requiring some action, he will on his own come up with some approaches to try out. However, if he can't think of anything to try, or if his suggestions are clearly unworkable, you can at that point offer some suggestions of your own ("Maybe we could both try . . .").

Clearly offer your ideas as suggestions, open to discussion, not as commands to be carried out. If at all possible, offer more than one suggestion so that you leave the parent some opportunity to make a decision.

If a parent is deeply concerned about something her child is undergoing, you might offer suggestions on articles or books to read that are relevant to that matter. If a problem is severe enough, you might also offer names of specialists to consult. In offering referrals, however, do so only if the parent is clearly reaching out for help, and be careful to offer several choices wherever possible.

Conclude the problem-solving portion of the conference with a plan of action. What has each party agreed to try to resolve or change the situation? What will you do if this doesn't work?

- ***Close the conference on a positive note.***

Each conference should have definite closure. Summarize what was discussed and what was decided at the meeting. If you have agreed to a specific plan of action, set a time for meeting again to review progress. Most importantly, conclude with a positive statement ("I'm really glad we had this opportunity to talk. I'm confident that the steps we've agreed to will result in real progress.").

Your personality, sincerity and closs relationships with your parents will bring ease at the conference and successful attainment of goals for the child.

# GRANDPARENTS AS PARENTS — UNDERSTANDING THE ISSUES

**by Steven M. Thaxton**

> *Watching my friends and colleagues interact with their grandchildren, I realize that I have my own fantasies of what it will be like to be a grandparent some day. . . . The grandchildren come over once a week or more to visit, we share our words of wisdom, play with them, and spoil them as much as we can. We do this as part of our culture, and as part of seeing our familiar roots move to the next generation.*

We develop bonds with our grandchildren that are very natural and unlike our bonds to our own children. Sometimes we see in our grandchildren our own children. It is like reliving their childhood. It is a special relationship; and, for many grandparents, one that is very tender, very intimate, and very sacred.

However, society continues to change, and the rules we once knew as family values, family traditions, are different. For many, the fantasy of being a grandparent is very different, much more latent with emotional issues in terms of how they see grandchildren, how they see the bonds with their own children, and how they see future generations.

I began working with grandparents when, as a school principal, I was suddenly faced with a whole new population of parents — they were grandparents. I had worked closely with foster parents, aunts and uncles, young parents, old parents, and other family members, and even friends who had been left with young children to raise. But, for some reason, the grandparents that I began talking with were different. They had different questions, different needs, different strengths.

The more I came to know them, the more I realized how much society had changed. The grandparents I was working with were people under a great deal of stress and were themselves at risk.

I began asking grandparents about their situations. And I began to understand that while the economics and housing situations may be different, the issues of emotional strengths and weaknesses are the same for all grandparents, regardless of income, educational background, or cultural background.

Here are some of their stories (names have been changed):

## DAVE'S STORY

*After raising four boys, all one year apart, and working to put all four through college, my wife and I finally retired. Our vision was to buy a small house in northern California, near our oldest son. We wanted to be near our grandchildren.*

*My son and I always had a fairly good relationship, or so I thought. The first year after we moved, our relationship with our grandchildren was difficult. They seemed different when we saw them on a more frequent basis. This was very different from when they came to visit. But my son explained that they were having financial difficulty; I just thought eventually it would work out.*

*My son was in a big corporation and on the way up. My daughter-in-law was a college educated woman working as a secretary and not too happy with her work situation. She began to withdraw; she lost weight, and was home less and less frequently.*

*Then one Saturday evening, the bomb hit. The grandkids were staying with us for the weekend, as my son and daughter-in-law were going to San Francisco for a business conference. At 2:00 AM, I answered the phone call that changed my life. It was the police. My daughter-in-law had overdosed and was dead. My son was in jail for selling and possession of drugs — not alcohol, but cocaine. I was in shock, stunned, totally devastated.*

*Telling an eight, six, and four year old that their mother was dead and that their father was in jail was not something I ever thought I would have to do, or could do. But I now had to take responsibility. My grandson, age six, asked right away: "Where are we going to live?" "Who is going to take care of us." "When is my dad coming home?" My other two grandchildren were in shock. My wife was in shock. This is not something that happens to a middle class retired family. This is not how I thought spending time with my grandchildren would be. This was not my idea.*

*Well, it is now three years later; my grandchildren are eleven, nine and seven. The legal issues have been overwhelming. It has taken all of this time to sort out the custody rights. But our choices were either to have full custody or have them in a foster home. How could I sleep at night knowing that my three young grandchildren were being raised by someone I didn't even know, and that I would have to perhaps give up my rights to see them or have anything to say about how they were raised? I couldn't do that to them. They were the victims, not responsible for what happened.*

*Last year my wife said, "I am leaving. I can't take it anymore. I raised my children. I did my part. I don't want to live like this any more." I haven't seen or heard from her since. So I am now 62 years old. I am a single grandparent. After 43 years of marriage, raising four children, I am doing it all over again. The hardest part is answering the questions of my grandchildren. "Why did my mom die?" "When is my dad coming back?" "How come grandma left?" "What happens to us if you get sick?" "Why are you crying, grandpa?"*

*I sometimes don't have many answers, and sometimes I wish I could run away. But I have an obligation to these three kids. They are part of me. They are my future now. I don't go see my son in jail any more. I can't do it. After my wife left, it was just all too painful. Too many reminders. I need a lot of help. I give the kids a lot to do. Perhaps more than they can do. But I am doing the best I can.*

## Renee's Story

*My story is very simple. My son is dead. He died of an overdose two years ago. He left me with two children, ages three and five. I don't know where their mother is, nor do I care. I was a social worker. I used to tell people what to do to get their lives together. I used to think that the only people who did drugs were deadbeats and low lifers. My son was a college graduate. I am so very angry. Sometimes I have to leave the house.*

*Being an African-American woman who raised children by myself, my job was to see that my children received an education and found jobs to support themselves. I was supposed to enjoy my grandchildren on weekends. My son was supposed to raise his own children.*

*I used to tell people that the system was there to be used. I was part of the system! I used to tell my friends that these people I deal with just don't get it. They have everything, they just need to start using the system in the correct way. What was the matter with them? Well, now I am on the other side of the system. All that has been offered to me is the suggestion to join a support group. I don't need a support group. I need respite care for my grandchildren. I need time to take care of myself at least once a week. I want my life back.*

## Doris and Richard's Story

*Our story is like so many others we have heard. We have a beautiful granddaughter. Her mom is in and out of drug rehab centers. Until we found our daughter two years ago, our granddaughter didn't have much of a chance. Our daughter will probably always live like she does. She goes into drug rehab for a few months, comes out clean, and then comes home and tells our granddaughter she is back for good. Then something happens, and she is back on drugs.*

*The hardest part is dealing with our granddaughter. She wants to know if her mom will ever come back. Are we always going to take care of her? When her mom does come back, she has trouble in school. Last year, her teacher was not very supportive. But this year, guess what? When I walked into her classroom the first day, the teacher was an older lady. I thought, "Oh here we go again." I explained to the teacher that I was her grandmother and we were raising her as best as we could; but sometimes when her mom comes back, she has some trouble.*

*This woman looked at me and gave me the biggest smile. She said, "Don't worry about that. See that little girl over there?" She pointed to a girl about five playing at a table. She said, "Well, that's my granddaughter. She lives with me, and I am raising her as best as I can, and when her dad (my son) shows up, she has some trouble, too. So don't worry about your granddaughter. I understand more than you think." I just started to cry. I was so happy that I didn't have to go through all that explaining again. I don't think I could take talking to another principal and teacher about our situation. It is just too hard.*

*My husband and I feel so discriminated against sometimes. Young people shy away from us. They don't always let their children come over to play with our granddaughter. I think they are scared of us. Maybe they think the same thing will happen to them. And maybe it will.*

*We are from Mexico. We came here with our families and worked in the fields. We went to school and worked in labor jobs all our life. We had a good life. We own our home, we had friends, we wanted to travel. Every time I see a motor home or an airplane taking off, I think that I should be doing that. I really love my granddaughter, but I feel cheated. I see my friends taking vacations, taking those trips we always talked about.*

*We have started to work together with the school. They listen to us now. We know what our granddaughter can do, and what works. Her teacher understands us and talks to us about her granddaughter. It has made a big difference. They are really trying.*

The most startling aspect of interviewing and talking to grandparents is their undying love for their grandchildren. They talk about how wonderful the children are, and how much they want for their lives to be better; they know the children's lives will be better since they are living with their grandparents. They can provide consistency and loving relationships that the children are missing with their parents.

But there is also a sadness with the grandparents. They have not had time to mourn the loss of their own children. They worry constantly about what will happen to their grandchildren if something happens to them. They worry about medical problems and legal issues, and how these will affect their grandchildren. They talk about their lost lives. They talk about how the years were supposed to be. They talk about the cruises and vacations they had planned to take, and they talk about how different children are today. They tear up when they talk about their adult children. There is failure in their voices.

Grandparents talk about how the schools are very discriminatory. They talk about being the oldest people at parent meetings, and how hard it is just to get through some days. As one grandfather said, "I have never cried so much over so many different issues. Sometimes it's little things that my grandchild does to remind me of my son, and sometimes it is when the social worker tells me I don't understand children. I get angry, and sad, and feel alone. Then the only thing I can do is just cry."

## What can we do?

What responsibilities do we as directors and teachers have to the grandparents? And how can we make them feel a part of systems that are unfriendly to their needs?

- ✔ As educators, we need not to be judgmental. We must realize that many grandparents have been put in a no choice position by our systems. Some grandparents do not understand regulations or how systems work. Plan to spend time with grandparents to explain programs, policies, regulations, and the availability of services.

- ✔ Grandparents question rules and regulations and ask why. Plan to spend time with grandparents answering their questions about the system, school, or program. Grandparents need time to understand what types of services a system offers, and how to utilize those services.

- ✔ Become a partner with grandparents. This is especially important with special education programs. Grandparents may have different expectations than professionals. It is important to give them relevant expectations as to what changes will occur with their grandchild. Grandparents know a great deal about their grandchild. They may not know why children act a certain way, but they can explain what types of behaviors are exhibited.

- ✔ Take time to listen to the grandparents' stories. Grandparents, like all parents, need to be able to tell their stories to someone. Many grandparents have been through very traumatic experiences. They need emotional support. They need to know the person they are working with has some understanding and empathy.

- ✔ Allow grandparents to participate. Grandparents need and want to be part of the program. This means finding out their strengths and letting them participate at their own levels.

- ✔ Ask grandparents what they need and then assist them in getting what they need the most. If respite is what is needed, help them find respite care. Be specific in helping.

- ✔ Give grandparents timelines when you will get back to them. Deliver what you promise. Help them understand the system, and work with them.

Being a grandparent in the 90's can be frightening. Grandparents have different issues. Depending on their age and attitude, some grandparents have not adjusted to all the changes in child rearing practices. And, for some grandparents, the issues of grieving the loss of their own children have not been totally resolved. They need time and understanding.

We must remember that many grandparents today are raising our future leaders — the leaders who will be our next presidents, senators, lawyers, truck drivers, teachers, painters, bartenders, trades people, fire fighters. We need to give them assistance, patience, and time in order for them to raise productive members of our future society.

For information about support groups and for further assistance, write to: Grandparents Who Care, 1 Rhode Island Street (Division Street), San Francisco, CA 94103, or call (415) 865-3000.

# Working with Angry Parents – Taking a Customer Service Approach

by Patricia A. Phipps

Parent: *The nerve of you! Charging me $15 for being 30 minutes late to pick up Alex. You know I am always here by 6:30. Something came up at the last minute that could not be avoided, and traffic was heavier than usual.*

Director: *But you don't understand, Ms. Jenkins. I have to enforce our policies. The staff person who waited here with Alex has to be paid overtime.*

Parent: *Well, take it out of all the times I paid and Alex was not here. We pay a fortune to have this child in this program. I think you are being very inflexible. What about all the times I picked up Alex early in the day or brought muffins, cakes, and cookies in for the staff? I didn't ask you to pay for the time and money involved in these situations.*

Director: *That's unfair of you, Ms. Jenkins. This is a totally different issue; and if I break the rules for you, then I have to break them for everyone.*

Parent: *Well break this — as of tomorrow, I am taking Alex out of this program and you'll be losing more than the $15 I am still not going to pay!*

Sound familiar? Unfortunately, there are probably more times than we would like to count in which irate parents have become furious with child care directors or staff — sometimes justifiably so, and sometimes not. Whether or not the parent is justified or not is not the issue. The focus of your actions and responses should be on how to achieve a "win-win" resolution to the conflict, especially when the parent is angered beyond the point of reasonable thought.

Since working with angry parents is an inevitable task that directors and staff must face from time to time, it is important that you understand how to make these verbal exchanges as positive as possible — in other words, how to make them as customer friendly as possible.

Child care personnel don't often view parents and children as customers. Let's look at four definitions of who customers are and see if these definitions hold true in families with children enrolled in your program.

### Customers . . .

. . . are people who buy products and services from you.

. . . are not dependent on you — you are dependent on them.

. . . are not interruptions of your work. They are the purpose of it. You are not doing them a favor by serving them — they are doing you a favor by giving you the opportunity to serve.

. . . are not persons to argue with or match wits. Nobody ever won an argument with a customer.

Is your definition of *customer* similar to the four listed above? Your definition of who your customers are shapes every interaction you have with parents. If parents are not viewed as customers, chances are they are not receiving everything they are purchasing from your program.

Do you know what parents want from your program? Below is a top 10 list of what parents want from their child care programs.

### Top 10 List of What Parents Want from Their Child Care Programs

10 Understanding and empathy for the challenges they face in their lives

9 Assurance that their family values, beliefs, and customs are being supported

8 Information on how to support, enrich, and extend what you are doing in the program to the home

7 Happy faces on children and staff

6 Input on program decisions

5 Regular communication about their child's progress

4 A positive "feel right" atmosphere

3 Assurance that attention is being paid to their child

2 An enriched learning environment

1 A safe, healthy, clean facility serving nutritious foods

When you know what parents expect from your program and every effort is made to provide it, you significantly decrease the probability of having to face angry parents. This is called proactive customer service.

### Developing a Proactive Customer Service Plan

In order to ensure that your families' needs and expectations are being served, a proactive customer service plan should be developed. This plan should become an integral part of your program. Components should include:

- **Survey parents.** To determine the needs and expectations of the families enrolled in your program, regular feedback should be gathered. This information can be obtained using a variety of survey methods. Survey methods are simply the different processes you can use to collect feedback from your families. The four main methods are: written questionnaires, telephone surveys, focus groups, and face-to-face interviews.

Although it takes a little more work and coordination, you get the best survey results by using a combination of different survey methods to poll your parents. Combining focus groups with written questionnaires, combining one-on-one interviews with telephone surveys, or employing any other combination of methods provides the best mix of general and specific feedback, as well as qualitative and quantitative data (Leland and Bailey, 1995).

Families who are no longer enrolled in your program can also provide meaningful information. When possible, conduct exit interviews with families leaving your program. Ask them what you could have done to have better served them.

- **Survey staff.** Sometimes staff have more opportunities to interact with families than the director might and can provide valuable information concerning the needs and interest of families. The same survey methods as outlined above can be employed with staff. Including staff in your data gathering also helps them to understand the importance of having a proactive customer service plan.

- **Mission statement with a focus on commitment to quality service.** A mission statement should include what principles or beliefs you are pledging to adhere to with regards to your families and staff.

- **Collect information on lost customers, wasted time, and reduced morale.** Even thought these might be seen as intangibles, a dollar figure can be placed on what it costs when you lose a family. The cost to market and recruit new families is more complex than just the cost of placing an ad in your local paper.

- **Train staff in customer relations skills.** A comprehensive and well-executed training program is ecessary to achieve consistent improvements in the services provided to families. It is critical that all staff participate in customer service training, not just those who work directly with parents or children. Customer service is not just the responsibility of a limited group of people in your program, it needs to be the way of life for everyone in your program.

- **Director training.** In order to support staff efforts in providing optimum customer service to families, program leaders must also engage in ongoing professional development opportunities in areas such as team building, delegation, and coaching.

- **Orientation process for new staff.** As new staff are employed in your program, a key element of the orientation process should stress customer service. The practice of delivering quality customer service should be part of everyone's job description.

- **Reward and recognize staff.** Your customer service plan must also include a strategy for rewarding service excellence if you want it to become part of your program's culture.

No matter how hard you try, inevitably the time will come when a parent will express his frustrations through anger. At this point, conflict resolution strategies must become part of your customer service efforts. The following five-step approach will help diffuse angry parents so that the both of you can come to a "win-win" resolution.

1 **Let the parent vent and listen attentively to what she is saying.** When parents are upset, they want two things: First, they want to express their feelings, and *then* they want their problem solved. Trying to resolve the situation without first listening to the parent's feelings never works. While you don't want to interrupt parents when they are venting, you do want to let the parent know that you are listening to her.

2 **Express empathy to the parent.** Giving a brief and sincere expression of empathy works wonders to calm an angry parent. Letting parents know that you understand why they are upset helps to build rapport with them. Examples of empathic phrases are:

- "I understand how frustrating this must be."
- "I can see why you feel that way."
- "I'm sorry about this."

3 **Begin active problem solving.** You can begin by asking questions that help clarify the cause of the parent's problem. First, ask yourself, "What does this parent need, and how can I provide it?" Next, ask the parent specific questions; and as you do, be sure to listen to everything she says — and don't jump to conclusions. Asking questions helps you to gather the information and check the facts.

To make sure that you understand the situation, you might mirror it back to the parent by saying, "What you are saying is that Kim's dress was torn yesterday, and the afternoon staff could not give you an explanation."

4 **Mutually agree on a solution.** Once you gather all the facts, you need to work with the parent to come up with an acceptable solution to the problem. If you haven't already discovered what will make her happy, ask. It may be necessary that you delay coming to a solution until you take time to do the behind-the-scenes work necessary to solve the problem. In this case, make sure the parent knows exactly why you are asking her to wait and how long it will take for you to get back to her. Finally, when you both agree on how to resolve the problem, explain the steps that you will take to implement the solution.

5 **Follow up.** You can score big in customer service by following up with parents — by phone, e-mail, letter, or face to face — to determine if the solution worked. If you find out that he is not satisfied, continue to look for another more workable solution. Effective follow up also includes correcting what caused the problem. It might even mean reexamining and adjusting your policies. By spending time solving internal service delivery problems, you prevent them from occurring in the future.

Working with angry parents is not an easy task; however, it is one that would rarely occur if proactive customer service is an integral part of your program. In order to do so, these basic actions must be in place:

- Expand your definition of service.
- Reconsider who your customers are.
- Develop a customer friendly attitude.

These actions are not necessarily easy to do. It will take ongoing commitment and practice; but in the long run, they are much easier than having to confront angry parents.

## Reference

Leland, K., & Bailey, K. (1995). *Customer Service for Dummies*. Foster City, CA: IDG Books Worldwide, Inc.

# Dialog to Understanding Across Cultures

**by Janet Gonzalez-Mena**

*Some child care directors and staff are experts at handling two children squabbling; but when tensions arise between themselves and parents, it can be a different story. Conflicts may come up around program policies or maybe it's just a small practical matter like bibs on toddlers. Behind the conflict may be differing notions of what's best for children, or for a particular child. When professionals find themselves in such a conflict with a parent, it's a good idea to ask if this is a cultural conflict.*

Sometimes what a parent wants doesn't make any sense to the professional. In that case, professionals have to listen, really listen, to parents. To do that listening, they have to step down from their place of power and put themselves in the role of learner. It's not easy for most professionals to accept that their knowledge has limitations, especially when what the parent is telling them doesn't sound reasonable.

Let's play that out. A parent comes with what seems a small complaint. Her toddler gets food on his clothes. Her solution: spoon feed him. The director has a different solution: a bib. Spoon feeding doesn't make any sense to the director. She talks about the importance of self-help skills, independence, and individuality, then considers the matter finished. The mother smiles, says thank you, and leaves. Problem solved. But is it?

What if the mother has overwhelming concerns about whether her child is being nurtured enough, and the complaint wasn't really about dirty clothes at all? Or what if the mother doesn't believe in independence and individuality? Instead, her goal is interdependence. Spoon feeding is an important part of that goal because in her mind it creates a closeness that is lacking when children feed themselves.

The smile and the thank you did not indicate that the parent agreed but were merely social conventions that the parent felt the situation called for. What the director experienced as a small complaint could in reality be a very large cultural difference. Furthermore, the mother's acquiescence to the director's quick solution could be the habitual response of a woman who has experienced a lifetime of oppression. A more privileged and powerful parent might have refused to be dismissed so quickly.

The way to find out these things is to open up an on-going dialog. To do that, the professional has to genuinely want to understand the complaint and everything behind it. She has to let the parent know that she will listen and not discount or criticize. The parent may not trust her at first until she proves she is sincere about wanting to under-stand. If the professional is white and middle class, she needs to also be open to the idea that the power she represents may make it difficult for this mother to trust her. It may take a lot of work at relationship building before a dialog about important issues can take place.

Part of the dialog involves taking a good hard look at your own attitudes and biases and realizing that you might have a monocultural viewpoint. You have to be open to seeing the parent's perspective without judging it. You have to tell yourself that the parent is speaking her own truth, even if it is not yours. Ask questions as a way of understanding rather than as a way of trying to convince the other person of your truth.

Let's look at a different kind of situation that needs cross-cultural understanding and knowledge. A Vietnamese child arrives in the morning with bright red streaks on his neck. When his teacher questions him, he explains his mommy "coined" him. The teacher has never heard of coining and goes to the director who has never heard of it either. Luckily they decide that they need to understand more before picking up the phone and calling the child abuse authorities. When they investigate, they learn that coining is a Vietnamese health measure involving putting a special kind of ointment on the skin and rubbing a coin back and forth.

It may be hard to understand why a health measure doesn't look healthy. But that's an outsider's perspective. Imagine if you moved to a country where they had never heard of immunizations. What would be the reaction to sticking needles in a baby's arm if no one knew about DPT shots? The practice seems abusive if you don't understand it, especially in the face of the resulting red lump on the arm and fever.

Of course, in the name of listening, professionals mustn't throw out judgment entirely or forever. For example, a caregiver in dialog with a parent of a newborn who is telling her to put her baby to sleep on her tummy would need to say something about the research on Sudden Infant Death Syndrome (SIDS). It's the professional's responsibility to share information about the risk factors of prone sleeping.

What makes conflict situations hard is that most child care practices don't have proven risks. They aren't clearly right or wrong. Differences in practices often depend on differences in priorities, and many of those priorities reflect cultural differences. Sometimes professionals get in a situation where they feel so strongly that they are right that they can't see another view. It takes humility and willingness to see another perspective besides one's own.

Dialoging is an approach to conflict that is more effective than arguing. Arguing has to do with persuasion — with winning and losing. Dialoging is different. Rather than trying to convince someone of their viewpoint, people engaged in dialog try to understand the other perspective. The idea is not to win but to find the best solution for all concerned. Dialog levels the playing field and helps the parties in conflict negotiate an agreement without either side *giving in.*

Dissonance is where growth takes place. Professionals need to be able to problem solve in ways that make differences manageable. Some problems can't be solved, in which case both professional and parent need to develop conflict coping skills. Even though harmony may be a goal, it's not a final state but merely a temporary condition. Professionals have to recognize the richness that comes from an environment where there are differences and disagreements. Only when professionals acknowledge that diversity is good, necessary, and provides growth will they be able to effectively respond to children and their families enrolled in early childhood programs. Only when they learn to dialog effectively will they be able to respond equitably to differences, whether cultural or not.

# Community Relations

# MARKETING YOUR PROGRAM

## CHAPTER 17

# Marketing Strategies That Work in Child Care

by Bruce Schon and Roger Neugebauer

*Marketing is often viewed as a tactic to which no self-respecting child care provider would stoop. Certainly anyone who has shopped for a car and experienced the sex-on-wheels ads, the slick sales pitches, and the high-pressure bargaining is aware that marketing practices often are highly objectionable.*

*Yet, marketing is, in fact, an appropriate, even necessary, activity for child care programs. Child care centers must publicize their services so that families who need these services can find them. Additionally, centers that depend upon parents' fees to meet their budgets must actively recruit children to operate at full capacity.*

*To say that centers need to market their services is not to say that they must engage in slick or high-pressure tactics. This article will attempt to demonstrate that child care programs do have a variety of options available to them in honestly promoting their services. Four guidelines to use in developing a marketing strategy will be outlined, and a number of techniques for implementing this strategy will be described.*

***Guideline 1. Adapt your marketing approaches to the varying stages of readiness among families in the community.***

Not all families in your community are equally ready to entrust their children to your center's care. Some are totally unaware of the existence of your program. Others are aware of it but not especially interested in it. A smaller number are interested in it but undecided about enrolling their children. Parents, in other words, are in different stages of readiness to sign up for your services. An effective marketing strategy must include specific approaches to families in each of these stages.

## Promoting Awareness: Let Them Know You Exist

***Guideline 2. Concentrate your publicity where parents needing child care services are most likely to perceive it — when they are actively looking for child care or when they are in settings which require them to use child care.***

- **Know Your Consumers.** Everyone in town doesn't need to know about your center. What matters is that you get the word out to those families who need the services you offer. In order to communicate to these potential users, you first need to identify who they are. One means of identifying your audience is to focus on consumer characteristics. In each of the categories below, identify for whom your services are most appropriate:

**Parent characteristics** — Working parents, single parents, teenage parents.

**Child characteristics** — Infants, preschoolers, school-age, special needs.

**Program characteristics** — Families seeking caretaking, developmental activities, socializing experiences, readiness activities, health services.

**Operational characteristics** — Families' income levels, home and job location, hours of need, transportation requirements.

Hopefully, this process will yield a fairly specific profile (or profiles) of your potential consumers. For example, it might be middle to upper income working parent families seeking full-day care and socialization experiences for their preschoolers. Having your audience thus defined, your next task is to make your presence known to them.

- **Contact Referral Sources.** Where do parents turn for suggestions when they are looking for child care services? These sources of referral are the most effective points for publicizing your services. An important marketing task, therefore, is to identify the referral sources likely to be used by your potential consumers.

There seldom is a single obvious source for parents to turn to in most communities. Rather, parents utilize a wide range of formal and informal referral sources including: city health departments, welfare agencies, private social and family service organizations, libraries, churches, local employers, women's organizations, unions, licensing agencies, pediatricians, college early childhood departments, elementary schools, parenting classes, child-bearing classes, United Way agencies, local NAEYC chapters, and other child care programs.

There is no substitute for personal contact as a means of ensuring that referral sources are dutiful in publicizing your program. Jim Baxter, Worcester, Massachusetts, for example, visits the executives of the major employers in the community. He points out how many of their employees are currently benefiting from his center as well as what services his center can offer employees. If the person at the referral source has met a representative of a center face to face, the likelihood of her remembering and recommending the center is greatly increased. Once personal contact is established, it should be maintained by periodic calls, especially in the form of thanks for referrals made.

If there are no referral sources which can be readily identified by parents in a community, child care providers should seriously consider establishing some form of child care resource and referral source. Such an R and R source can simply maintain a booklet describing all forms of child care available to families in the community which is distributed widely to other referring agencies. Or centers can hire a staff or contribute staff time to answer a phone with a number which is well publicized as the one to call for child care information.

- **Secure Free Publicity.** A number of avenues are available to directors in pursuing free publicity. The most common means is the issuance of press releases. Press releases should periodically be sent to community newspapers to keep your name before the general public. Additionally, they should be sent to the newsletters of local unions, businesses, and social service organizations to more directly communicate with potential users.

A second approach is to capitalize on the visibility of your facility. Efforts should be made to make the outward appearances of your building attractive and to prominently display a sign from which passers-by can easily read the center's name, type of services offered, and phone number. Some programs also boldly display the center's name and phone number on their school buses.

Centers should be alert to the publicity potential of fundraising. In all fundraising activities, whether fairs, sales, or phone solicitations, your center should be clearly identified as the sponsor. Brochures describing your services should be distributed to participants. Representatives should be eager and able to describe your services.

- **Utilize Advertisements.** Centers have found that paid ads yield mixed results. Display ads in local newspapers, for example, often yield few results. On the other hand, centers report that a brief classified ad under the "Child Care" listing in the same paper brings satisfactory results.

Once again, the focus should be on placing the ads where potential users, not just the public at large, will see them. Effective locations for ads can include listings in the yellow pages (particularly if your listing is highlighted in a box); window displays at shopping malls (especially for drop-in and part-day services); brochures left at pediatricians' offices, handed out in child-bearing and parenting classes, or handed out door to door in a center's immediate neighborhood; and posters displayed in maternity wards, maternity and children's stores, libraries, and employee lounges in major businesses. Centers report that TV and radio ads, open houses, and flyers handed out on the street generally prove ineffective.

## Creating Interest: Communicate Your Strengths

***Guideline 3. Identify and emphasize your program's dominant features and marketable differences.***

- **Know Your Strengths.** To prompt parents who know about your program into seriously considering enrollment for their children, there must be some spark for their interest. They must perceive some unique feature which causes them initially to select your program from among the various alternatives.

To communicate its dominant features to its potential users, a program must first define for itself what these features are. What are the program's strengths? What are its major goals? What aspects of the program are unique? Why should a parent select it as the best place for his/her child?

Examples of dominant features might include curriculum characteristics such as an emphasis on *strengthening cooperative behavior* or *enacting Piagetian principles*, service characteristics such as *comprehensive health component* or *24 hour care*, or operational characteristics such as a *highly trained and skilled staff* or a *sliding scale for fees*.

- **Establish Your Image**. Having defined your major strengths, it is necessary to communicate them to potential users. The most direct approach is to make the center's dominant features a central theme in all publicity and advertising. In the long run, however, it is also vital to concentrate on establishing a public image based on these features.

Although Madison Avenue tends to act as if public image can be created overnight, a more realistic view is that . . .

*an organization is not a chameleon capable of acquiring any desired image. . . . One does not acquire an image simply through public relations planning. The image is largely a function of the actual deeds of the organization.* (Kotler)

If a child care center wants to convey an image of providing "comprehensive developmental services," for example, it must, in fact, be providing "comprehensive developmental services." If a center is unable to deliver on its promises for quality of care, no amount of public relations will establish a positive public image. On the other hand, if a program's performance is as high as its pronounced standards, there are a number of techniques available for supporting the communication of a positive image.

- **Promote Personal Recommendations.** In child care, the great majority of children are recruited by word of mouth. Potential users of services are most influenced by recommendations from their friends who use the services because the method of delivering the endorsement is personal and the source of the endorsement is known and trusted.

Given the prime importance of word of mouth, a director might do well to encourage and influence the flow of personal recommendations. The director should tell parents that their spreading the word is very beneficial to the program and is most appreciated. One center even goes so far as to offer parents who recruit another family a free week of child care.

In addition, the director should provide similar encouragement to other center representatives. Teachers, board members, volunteers, and parents of preschool alumni all come into contact with potential users in their lives outside the center. The director should identify and encourage all such potential promoters.

In encouraging all of these informal representatives of the center, the director might find it beneficial to remind them of the dominant features of the center. A one-page fact sheet listing the program's goals and strengths, services, and enrollment requirements might be distributed as a resource to those likely to spread the word.

- **Establish Your Reputation**. A center's reputation for providing quality child care can be communicated more widely if the center provides other services to families with young children. Families not currently in the market for child care have many other child-related needs. By helping meet these needs, your center can strengthen its image in the community of being a reliable and caring resource for parents and children. Examples of such services include:

**Parenting workshops**. Ongoing or one-shot workshops could be offered to parents to provide practical advice on a wide range of problems they encounter in raising children. Topics could include first aid with children, dealing with aggression, developing self-image and independence, discipline problems, sex issues, talking with children, or designing children's rooms.

**Babysitting referral**. The center could screen and train babysitters and charge them an initial fee to be listed. Parents needing babysitting would then pay an initial registration fee to be able to call in for recommendations on sitters.

**Newspaper column**. An arrangement could be made with the local newspaper whereby the center would provide a regular column on practical advice to parents on child-rearing or children's activities.

**How-to pamphlets**. A two to four page pamphlet could be designed and written by the center on how to select children's books, with selection pointers as well as an annotated list of recommended books for children at different age levels. Similar pamphlets could focus on selecting children's toys, designing children's rooms, engaging in creative play, or dealing with behavior problems. Pamphlets could be advertised in the local paper or over the radio and distributed widely through pediatricians, churches, libraries, and service clubs. Those on books and toys could be promoted most effectively prior to Christmas.

**Children's activities**. Once a week, classes for children could be offered in creative movement, gymnastics, or swimming. A children's entertainment series with puppet shows, plays, or films could be provided on Saturday mornings.

Two final pointers: First, select services which not only are needed in the community but also are challenging to your staff. These services should provide a stimulating outlet for the talents of your staff, as well as a refreshing change of pace for them. Second, be sure to get proper credit for your center. In any of these services, clearly identify your center as the sponsor, and briefly describe your services and outstanding features.

## Securing Commitments: Consider the Parents' Needs

***Guideline 4: Make doing business with you an easy and pleasant experience for parents.***

When you have succeeded in interesting parents in your center, you should be able to convert this interest into a commitment if you can meet their two primary needs at this stage of readiness. First and foremost, they will need to be assured that your center is a reliable place to leave their child. A national parent survey revealed that the most important factors for parents in selecting a child care center or nursery school are:

1. Well-trained staff;

2. Warm and loving caregivers; and

3. Clean and safe environment.

In the parents' initial contacts with the center, therefore, you should be especially careful to satisfy their concerns about the staff and the environment.

Second, you should be alert to the fact that in initiating contact with your center parents may well experience the uneasiness and uncertainty of entering a new situation. You should take steps in the early stages of contact to put the parent at ease. If you make parents anxious and frustrated in doing business with you, they may well choose not to do business with you at all.

- **Improve Phone Contact**. The manner in which a parent's initial inquiry, usually in the form of a phone call, is handled will often be a major factor in shaping his/her opinion of the center. No matter how wonderful a center is, if it creates a disinterested, disorganized, or bureaucratic impression in the initial phone call, chances are it will be eliminated from consideration by that parent. The following suggestions, along with a heavy dose of courtesy, might be helpful in overcoming early turn-off:

Be specific in describing your program. State your goals and strengths in more than stereotyped generalities. Outline how your staff is qualified to achieve your goals.

Be clear in describing the admissions process.

Let them know that you are sensitive to the specific concerns parents have about their own children.

Encourage them to visit the center. Without exerting pressure, try to set up a time for a visit.

Offer to provide them names of parents who have used the center and who can be called for reactions.

- **Facilitate Observations**. The moment of highest anxiety for parents is when they come to observe your program. Entering a room of unknown children and adults without a clear role to play can make a parent observer feel quite awkward: Should I sit or stand? Should I play with the children? Should I talk to the teachers? How and when should I leave?

Centers can help eliminate much of this anxiety with a few simple procedures:

When prospective parents schedule visits, they should be sent a description of the program as well as a list of suggestions on what they might do and look for in their observations.

When parents arrive at the center, there should be someone ready to greet them by name. The greeter should give them a tour of the facility, provide a brief description of the classroom structure for the room in which they will observe, review the pointers on observing, and answer any last-minute questions.

In bringing parents into the classroom, the greeter should introduce them to the teachers and to the children.

At some point during observations, the head teacher should come over to explain what activities are going on.

Parents could be invited to bring their child to participate in classroom activities while the parent observes. This can be reassuring to parents if the teachers are skilled at easing a child into a new situation.

Thought should also be given to the effect the environment has on parents when they first enter the center. If their immediate impression is of shabbiness or carelessness, the likelihood of their being impressed with the center's positive features will be lessened considerably.

- **Sharpen Interview Techniques**. Many parents also request an in-person interview with the director to clear up any final areas of uncertainty. Directors find that the following ideas make for the most effective interviews:

An informal format is best — opening with the parents' questions and closing with the director's explanation of enrollment procedures and operating policies.

Some directors find it beneficial to discuss parents' perceptions based on their observations. Other directors like to discuss the needs of the child and how the program would deal with these needs. It may be reassuring to discuss the background and skills of the teachers as well as to offer the teachers' resumes for review.

If finances are a problem, the director might offer to explore parents' potential eligibility for public subsidies or private scholarships. If these do not apply, the rebate under the tax credit should be explained.

The bottom line, once the parent has been moved from awareness to interest to the point of making a decision, is that this final decision will be based on the quality and appropriateness of the program in the eyes of the parent.

If a program's quality is low, parents will not decide to sign up no matter how effective its marketing is. On the other hand, if quality is high, an effective marketing strategy will provide for stable growth for the center and informed decision making by the parents.

## Helpful Resources


Kotler, P. (1975). *Marketing for Nonprofit Organizations.* Englewood Cliffs, NJ: Prentice-Hall, Inc.

Martinez, B. F., & Weiner, R. "Guide to Public Relations for Nonprofit Organizations and Public Agencies." *Grantsmanship Center News,* 1015 West Olympic Boulevard, Los Angeles, CA 90015.

O'Brien, R. (1977). *Publicity: How to Get It.* New York: Harper and Row, Publishers.

Unco. (1976). *National Child Care Consumer Study.* Washington, DC: HEW/OHD.

White, R. M., Jr. (1977). *The Entrepreneur's Manual.* Radnor, PA: Chilton Book Company.


## Credits


Ideas for this article were contributed by directors from:

Town and Country Day School, Eugene, Oregon; Kids' World, Orlando, Florida; IACC Day Care, Ithaca, New York; Family Service Center, Omaha, Nebraska; Child Development Center, San Diego, California; Wee Wisdom School, Unity Village, Missouri; Northedge School, Sudbury, Massachusetts; Day Nursery Association, Lakeland, Florida; El Ada Head Start, Boise, Idaho; Beginnings, Belmont, Massachusetts; Kendall Lab Center, Evanston, Illinois; Westmorland Day Care, Washington, DC; Community Service Center, Kansas City, Kansas; Jack and Jill Nursery, Missoula, Montana; and Paul K. Kennedy Child Care Center, Chicago, Illinois.

# Who Cares? Eight Principles for Dealing with Customers

**by William H. Franklin**

*Every workday when the doors are unlocked and the lights are turned on, employees take over the real control of this country's businesses.*

*People who are put off by the way your employees look or the way your place looks aren't coming back, because they're out of their comfort zone.*

*Your customers can buy their products and services from anyone, but they choose to do business with you.*

Recently, I was in a bookstore which is a part of a national retail book chain. I couldn't locate the book title I wanted, so I went to the "customer service" counter — at least that was what was printed on the sign hanging above the attendant's head. Scrolling through the computer catalog, he located the title. "We're out of it," the attendant said. After several seconds of ensuing silence, it became apparent to me that the attendant had concluded our brief encounter — in fact, he had left the counter to do something else. After all, I suppose, I was the one who wanted the book, not him.

Thumbing through the family mail recently, I came upon an important looking letter from a prestigious firm addressed to me — William H. Franklin. I opened and read the letter. It described a variety of financial services the firm could provide if I chose to become their client. Unfortunately, the letter began, "Dear Mr. Williams," evidence that the writer had signed the letter without reading it. I concluded that if the writer couldn't get my name right, he probably couldn't keep my account straight either. So the letter was routed to the trash can.

It should be a bit unsettling to business managers on hearing tales like these to realize that, as a practical matter, they don't run their businesses — their employees do; these examples prove it. When I buy a meal, rent a car, or search for a book, I don't deal with the company's president, or its manager, or its stockholders; I deal with an employee. And the employee determines the service level I will receive. Every workday when the doors are unlocked and the lights are turned on, employees take over the real control of this country's businesses.

But in a private enterprise economy, like ours, there are choices. And the customer, as the expression goes, is king. Customers ultimately determine which businesses will prosper and which will fail. A large part of that determination is the way they are treated. And when customers are treated badly, they usually don't get mad. They just don't come back. And their business goes to our competitor, probably permanently.

## Principle 1:
### Customers buy solutions — not products or services.

Obviously, when someone has a problem, he wants it solved. I think too many selling situations overlook this fact.

Regardless of the way you promote your business, whether through advertising or direct selling, you raise the expectations of potential customers by what you say that you or your product will do for them. The customer buys the expectation of a solved problem and the benefits of the solution. For example, I don't really buy gas as much as I buy the right to continue to drive my car — and get to where I'm going. Gas is the solution that enables me to do both. I don't really buy a suit of clothes as much as I buy an image, nor do I buy a quarter-inch drill bit as much as I buy a quarter-inch hole. A fine meal in a five-star restaurant should be an experience. I can eat at home.

Better customer service will occur when employees understand that they are in the problem-solving business. If the employee follows all the rules and the customer's problem doesn't get solved, it's a "no sale," even though money changed hands. Employees mustn't forget that their expertise is on the line when they are in front of a customer — and that's the business you're really in.

## PRINCIPLE 2:
**Ask questions.**

If customers buy solutions, you must understand the problem to be solved. The difference between selling something and taking an order for it is who does the problem research.

Asking questions minimizes the chance of making a mistake that could later result in a frustrated customer, who may or may not come back to allow you to sort it out. Asking questions is clearly an important selling technique. It demonstrates interest and concern. From the standpoint of rendering customer service, it's important because it singles the customer out to be treated in a special way. A question as mundane as "Smoking or non-smoking?" at a restaurant indicates that there is some concern for a diner's comfort during a meal.

Several years ago I was shopping for a pair of binoculars. The clerk who was waiting on me began putting every model of the binoculars in the display case on the sales counter without a word. Apparently he thought I would make my choice based on weight and color. "Look," I said, "I don't know anything about these things, tell me something about them." Well, this guy had a sales IQ in the single digits because he said, "I really don't know binoculars, I usually work in cameras." I turned to leave, but another clerk, who happened to be waiting on a customer nearby and had overhead the conversation, interrupted and said, "Excuse me, sir, how were you planning to use the binoculars?" "To watch football games," I said. "Then this pair is what you need." The sale was made —but just barely.

## PRINCIPLE 3:
**Build relationships.**

Use the customer's name where it is appropriate, and give yours too. Recently, I took my wife to an upscale restaurant to celebrate our wedding anniversary. After being seated, our waiter approached the table and said, "Mr. Franklin, welcome to 103 West . . . my name is David, I will be in charge of your service tonight, and let me also introduce you to John and Marcos who will be assisting me." Each time he approached the table, he used my name again. I've dined at many five-star restaurants all over this country, and I'm used to first-class service. But somehow the waiter's tasteful use and reuse of my name when addressing me personalized the service in a way that made us feel that we weren't just one of several tables David was assigned to serve.

How do your employees look? How do they sound on the phone? Does your correspondence read like a canned speech? — or worse still, like stilted bureaucratese? How does your place look? All of these are important elements in developing lasting relationships with customers. People who are put off by the way your employees look or the way your place looks aren't coming back, because they're out of their comfort zone.

## PRINCIPLE 4:
**If you can't solve a customer's problem, at least say what you can do.**

Don't say, "I'm sorry, we're out of that book" (in other words, you have a problem, friend). Say, "We don't have a copy in stock, but I can check our other stores for you." At least the second approach indicates the clerk doesn't have the book, but he does have the problem to solve. So the customer can now let go of the problem. Nothing is more irritating than a mindless robot who in essence says, "I'm sorry, but I can't help you . . . period."

## PRINCIPLE 5:
**If a customer must be referred to someone else, at least have the courtesy to stay with the customer until the connection with the other party is made.**

This is true whether it is on the telephone or in person. Take the responsibility to run interference through your company's bureaucracy and make sure there is a clean handoff to the next person. Too many times, customers are told they must take the initiative to wander around without help to find the right department or the right person or the right telephone number they need to call.

For example, don't say, "I'm sorry that's not my department — you'll have to call. . . ." Instead say, "Let me take you to Mrs. Harris to introduce you. . . ." Then, before leaving the person with Mrs. Harris, ask them, "Is there anything else I can help you with before I leave you?" You have done your job, and by that last question, you demonstrated that to your customer.

## PRINCIPLE 6:
**If customers are angry, there's a reason. Deal with the reason, not their anger.**

Most customers prepare themselves to receive an insensitive, bureaucratic response to their problems. Anger can often be defused with sympathy. "I don't blame you for being angry that the dress doesn't fit. . . . Let's see what I can do about it for you."

In other words, focus on discovering a solution with a customer. In the customer's mind, the two of you are on opposite sides of the problem. You must convince that customer that you have come over to the "other side."

## PRINCIPLE 7:
### The resolution of a customer complaint begins with an agreement on a course of action — not an action itself.

As I've just said, most problems arising out of botched customer treatment involve emotions. These must be dealt with first. Consider this: "Why don't you leave your car here and we'll look at it?" How much better it would be to say, "You may be right in suspecting that your front-end is out of alignment, but it could be caused by your tires. . . . Let's switch the tires to see if the car pulls in the opposite direction. . . . That won't take but a minute and is less expensive than putting the car on the alignment rack. . . . Would that be agreeable to you, Mr. Clark?"

When a customer has gotten what he didn't want (the wrong suit, the wrong rental car, no book, or an incorrectly addressed letter), it's reasonable for him to expect he is not going to get his problem resolved either. After all, the person who has goofed it up can't be relied on to straighten it out. Moreover, a wronged customer feels powerless to bring about the necessary corrective action. Getting an agreement before acting is both symbolic and practical. It is symbolic because the customer is invited to participate in identifying corrective action. It is practical because it avoids doing something — even something that would work — that the customer isn't convinced will be satisfactory.

## PRINCIPLE 8:
### Do something more than the customer expects, then be sure that the customer knows it!

Recently my wife took her car in for the third time to have the mechanic do something about its squealing brakes. Nothing could be found wrong. She refused to accept the car back. The service supervisor concluded the problem was the brake rotors. The conversation went something like this: "Mrs. Franklin, your brake rotors are thin; the manufacturer doesn't recommend turning them. We'd like to replace them and will do it for our parts cost only, if you are willing to leave your car with us tonight. Can someone pick you up and bring you back tomorrow?" They did more than expected, despite the return trips she had made to resolve the problem. And they were willing to lose money to make things right. After all, they were the brake experts, not she.

I've said on many occasions that customers have an internal accounting system. They view a purchase as a favor. After all, your customers can buy their products and services from anyone, but they choose to do business with you. Whether you conducted the business transaction correctly or incorrectly, customers now view the purchase as a favor, as a "credit," and they "debit" your side of the ledger so that you are always working your way out of a deficit condition with customers. This shop did a good job of breaking even in the only way it counts to a customer.

When you or one of your employees has fouled something up, you really owe the customer — big time. So it is essential that you not only correct a problem, but also you must be willing to lose money to set things straight. If Federal Express, for example, fails to deliver by 10:30 AM, the service is free. They didn't do what they promised: "Absolutely, Positively, Overnight." I recently took my daughter to a very nice restaurant to celebrate her thirteenth birthday. The service was slow, and the waiter had reduced my bill before he handed it to me. And he told me why it was reduced. Just like the mechanic's approach — "We'll switch your front tires to see if the car pulls then in the opposite direction, and we'll do that at no charge to you. . . . How does that sound?" It sounds like a winner talking!

*This article was adapted, with permission from the publisher, from William Franklin's book, Street Smarts: New Ideas for Small Companies (1990). To order a copy send $24.95 to the Georgia State University Business Press, College of Business Administration, Atlanta, GA 30303-3093, or call (404) 651-4253.*

# Compete or Die!

by Julie Wassom

*How do I compete with public school tuition rates? What do I do to combat the big new center down the street? What impact will changes in government funding have on my center?*

## Part I

Have you been wrestling with these questions? There's no doubt it's a jungle out there in terms of a competitive market. Yet, even in the thick of it, there are strategies and techniques that work to increase and maintain enrollment.

Having a high quality program, first-rate staff, and well-maintained building is not enough anymore. To be a winner in today's competitive child care game requires a keen awareness of what's happening in the marketplace, a proactive and positive approach to marketing and enrollment building, and a willingness to take the competitive initiative.

To build and keep your enrollment when the competition is breathing down your neck, you must do two things. First you have to be brutally honest — about your center, your services, and the current needs of your target markets. Second you must be open — to what your parents want and need, and to changing the way you market and provide your child care services.

*"But I've always done it this way, and it has worked until now,"* you say. When a particular approach becomes comfortable, it's easy to close your eyes to the changes going on around you. As your market becomes more competitive, you have a choice. You can change, or get left behind. To move forward successfully takes being honest and open.

It also takes smart moves to be a victor over, rather than a victim of, your competitive circumstances. What are those moves? They are to investigate, differentiate, and educate.

### Investigate Your Market

Knowledge is power. Who exactly is your competition? Is it public schools, home care, or the big new center down the street? Decide who are currently your three stiffest competitors. Then decide who is most likely to be the biggest threat to your enrollment one year from now. You may find that even your competition is changing with time.

Investigate each current competitor to determine what they do that is similar and different from the way you do it. Go visit your competitors with a goal in mind. That is, to find three things they do as well as you do, three things they do better, and three things they don't do as well. Maybe their building is new, but you have stronger parent involvement or better teacher tenure. Note your findings. Invite them to visit you. Remember, be open. Who knows? Maybe you'll develop a professional relationship that can serve you both well in terms of referrals of children and staff.

Investigate what is important to your parents. Do this with a brief written survey, a telephone survey, or focus groups. Ask not only about their level of satisfaction with your center, staff, and programs but about their expectations as well. Do they perceive that you will meet their changing needs better than your competitors can?

Once you have good information about your customers and your competitors, carefully analyze just how you are promoting your services to your prospects, customers, and referral sources. What image or perception are you creating in the minds of your parents and prospects? In what ways are you presenting or marketing your image? That image, or positioning, can affects parents' decisions to enroll and remain in a center.

What mix of marketing techniques are you using to attract new customers? Do you have a brochure that makes you sound unique and inviting, or does it look and read like the brochures your prospects will pick up from your competitors? Do you use newspaper ads, flyers, newsletters, or coupons to market your center? List everything you are currently using.

Are your enrollment building skills as sharp as they should be to help parents make a good buying decision and to get them to act on your recommendation? Do you follow up with inquiring prospects? Does your competition follow up?

What are you doing to keep your currently enrolled parents happy? Be honest. What are you doing to create value? Are they getting more than they expected? You want them to be more than just satisfied. You want them to be enthusiastic about your center and services. That enthusiasm will translate into loyalty and word of mouth referrals, your most cost-effective advertising.

Also investigate your industry. What are the changes taking place in child care? How does it affect you? Join your local and national child care associations. Go to the meetings, read their newsletters, get involved as a professional colleague. Read *Exchange* and attend legislative committee meetings when the topic at hand will impact your center.

The sooner you investigate your competition, the better equipped you will be to keep your school full despite their presence. And if you are proactive in this investigation, rather than reactive, you will already have the knowledge you need to make good decisions when the competition heats up.

### Differentiate Your Center from Competitors

The more you learn about your competition in comparison to your own services, the easier it will be to differentiate yourself from them. List differentiating factors between you and your competitors. For example, to a prospect, your prekindergarten program may *appear* identical to what the public school is now offering. However, your building is more suited for child care, you provide transportation, and your teachers have years of experience in early childhood education. These are not judgments. They are differences you should be promoting in your marketing efforts and discussing with your prospects and parents if you want to compete and win.

Don't forget enrollment building skills as a competitive differentiation. Telephone skills, in particular, can make a decisive impression on new parents who are your enrollment prospects. Be sure to state some differentiating factors during inquiry calls. Simply point out your differentiating features in a benefit statement, such as *"Our building is designed specifically for preschool children, so Billy will never feel out of place here at Wonderland Child Care."* Never criticize your competitors by name to a prospect or customer. I call that "slinging mud," and it will only damage your own image in the end.

Include your staff in the actions you take to differentiate yourself from your competitors. Make them aware of your parents' desires and how they can help you meet them, even in the face of stiff competition. Train them to become your partners in communicating to parents the unique features of your center that set you apart.

As you work to become a master at competitive marketing, keep your attitude up and climbing. Your level of success at increasing enrollment in a competitive environment is directly proportional to the altitude of your attitude. Think about it. If you believe your competition is out to get you, they will. But if you believe you can overcome them and still fill your school, you will. Either way, you're right!

## Part II

### Educate Your Target Audiences

Once you have done a thorough job of investigating your competition and differentiating your center and services from them, you are well positioned to educate your target audiences as to why you are the best child care choice.

Who are all those audiences? Everyone to whom you want to communicate your image. That includes prospects, customers, referral sources, colleagues, the general public, and even your competitors.

Point out your differentiating benefits in all your marketing communications. Highlight the differences in your written marketing materials. On center visits, use benefit statements such as *"Here at Little Learners, Susie will be involved in small groups, get lots of individual attention, and have a teacher whose only focus is on the children. Because we have a director to run the center, another staff member who prepares lunch and snacks, and another person responsible for center maintenance, Susie's teacher can give her the attention she needs when she needs it."* Focus on the features you have found to be most important to the parents you want to attract and retain. Deliver a consistent image in all your marketing communications efforts, including public relations, community involvement, and customer relations activities.

Make your prospects feel special during both the inquiry call and the center visit. Practice your enrollment building skills, so you can easily discuss differentiating features as benefits of enrolling in your center. Remember, parents may now be better educated and informed about child care options, but many people drowning in information are thirsty for wisdom. Be the helpful expert.

During the inquiry call, first ask, then educate. As you assess your prospects' needs, ask "What's most important to you in the care you select for your child?" Tailor your responses to address their concerns with your differentiating benefits, keeping in mind that the goal of the inquiry call is to schedule a center visit.

Point out the differences during the center visit. If you have long term teacher tenure and the new program down the block doesn't, present that feature with a benefit statement such as *"Our teachers have been here for years because they want to be. Your son's teacher has completed first aid and CPR training, and has received a master teacher certificate. This means Jimmy will be taught by someone who not only loves children but who has the training to provide him with the best learning experience possible."*

The percentage of centers accredited through NAEYC or NCCA is still relatively small. If you are among them, mention it to parents and explain its impact on the quality of care. It's education that can help parents make a good buying decision.

If you truly are a good choice for your prospect's child care needs, **ask for the enrollment**. Your willingness to ask may be the one differentiating factor between you and a tough competitor. But to a parent who can't quite decide, it may mean you get the enrollment.

One enrollment building technique that can easily distinguish you from most competition is follow-up. I call follow-up the "forgotten ingratiatory" because so few centers make any effort to recontact a parent who has inquired about enrollment. Send information of value after an inquiry call or visit. Make a follow-up call to determine the status of your prospect's decision. If your prospect has called five centers, and you are the only one who follows up, you have just set yourself apart from your competition.

With customers, those parents of children currently enrolled in your center, you have daily opportunities to subtly educate them about your competitive differences. In daily face-to-face conversations, written communications, and parent events, mention the little things that your investigation has proven make a difference. For instance, if you know an academic focus is important to your parents, run a column in each newsletter featuring a portion of your center's educational program. Encourage parent involvement through a parent organization or committee and parent education workshops. Use your parents as resources. Employ their talents to make your center a better place and to drive home your competitive differences to the whole parent group. Remember, the word-of-mouth advertising that comes from your parents is some of your most cost-effective marketing. Acknowledge their assistance and referrals in your center newsletter, on a center bulletin board, and with a personal thank you.

Another target audience to educate about your competitive advantages is your referral sources, or the group I call your "opinion influencers." These people may never actually become your customers, but they influence those who do. Amongst all the people who can be your opinion influencers, five groups are especially important to educate about your center's services.

1. Public schools
2. Pediatricians
3. Legislators and licensing personnel
4. The media
5. Corporations

It is essential that public schools develop confidence in the child care system. Educate them about the good job you are doing with preschool children and how it benefits the elementary schools to have children from your center come to them better prepared for primary learning experiences. It could be to your competitive advantage to form a positive alliance with the public schools surrounding your center.

Continue to work with pediatricians and health care providers to dispel the perception that children get sick more often in child care. Provide articles and information to the offices of pediatricians who practice near your center. Invite them to visit your center and to be a guest speaker at a parent event. Look for ways to interact as professional colleagues, not adversaries.

Inform legislators and licensing personnel about the specific benefits of your center that address needs in the marketplace and that position you as a quality child care provider. Include them on your mailing list for newsletters, invitations to events, and marketing mailers.

Develop a good relationship with the media. Learn how to provide newsworthy information to the press ("Guess Who's In the News," *Exchange*, July 1996). When your competitive message is delivered through the words of a newspaper or magazine reporter, it has the power of third party endorsement. That can make it more believable to your prospects, customers, and other opinion influencers.

Corporations are an environment where you can educate large groups of your target audiences with minimal effort. Offer to write a brief informative column for their company newsletters, or to be the speaker for their brown bag lunch events. Present your competitive benefits as information of value to their employees, not as advertising. For instance, if you have a new playground with state of the art equipment, do a talk or feature article on playground safety. In it, talk about the rules you practice on your new playground equipment, and why they are an important part of your approach to providing premium quality child care services.

Use your creativity to develop ways to show your opinion influencers what your competitive differentiation is, and how you offer value beyond traditional child care expectations. Then when they have the opportunity to make a child care referral, your center will come to mind.

There's one more group you don't want to forget to educate about your competitive differences. That is your colleagues and the other centers and child care providers around you. Part of professionalizing the child care industry is developing a cooperative versus competitive spirit amongst one another. Be open. The benefits to you can be enormous, both in image and enrollment.

If you and your competitors know the specifics of what each has to offer, you can feel much more comfortable referring a child who just won't fit in your center. When that happens with full knowledge of each other, it's a win-win situation. Everyone involved is happy, and you are much more likely to get future referrals from that parent and perhaps even the competitive director.

You can educate your competitors by working together on association committees, networking at conferences, inviting competitive staff to select workshops, and visiting each other's centers.

Being seen together in the community, such as at a monthly lunch, also communicates a good message to your public.

This kind of professional cooperation amongst you and your competitors can mean a greater awareness of differentiating features, a higher level of professionalism, greater industry cohesion, more balance, less work, and even more enrollment.

Investigate, differentiate, and educate. Remain honest in your assessments and open to change. Make these moves and you will be out ahead of your competition and well on your way to building and maintaining high enrollment.

# Community Marketing Made Easy

**by Julie Wassom**

*Now be honest. On a scale of one to ten, how would you rate your comfort level with community marketing? When I've asked directors around the country this question, most of them rank it a five or below. They know community marketing is an important part of the marketing communications mix. They agree it's a cost-effective way to develop awareness of their centers and early care and education services. They admit there are ample opportunities to get involved in the communities around their centers. Yet they just don't do it very often, if at all. Why not? Most say they can't find the time, they don't feel comfortable doing it, or they just aren't sure quite what to do or say.*

Community marketing means those activities you conduct, primarily outside your center, to help communicate your image and your marketing messages within your local community. It includes everything from being actively involved in your city's Chamber of Commerce, to co-sponsoring a community event, to participating in a local town parade. The opportunities are endless.

Think of community marketing like exercising. It takes more than knowing it is good for you or having the desire to do it. It takes commitment. The hardest part is just getting out there. Once you're doing it, it doesn't seem as foreboding and can actually be fun. And, when you're committed, the results are usually well worth the effort.

If community marketing is tough for you, then, like exercising, start with easier moves and work up to those that are more challenging. Use the following seven ideas as a foundation to help make community marketing easier for you and to create a community marketing action plan to which you're willing to commit your time and energy.

## Make Friendly Visit Calls

An easy first step into community marketing is to visit businesses near your center, introduce yourself as another professional in the community, leave a business card and small token from your center (such as a bookmark made by one of the children), and invite the business owner to your center for a visit or upcoming center event.

Think in your prospect's perspective. Think not what they can do for you, but what you can do for them. What could your direct, daily contact with large numbers of parents and their young children mean to that business? The more you think in the prospect's perspective and communicate the benefits to them of knowing you, the more well-received you'll be on community visits.

## Conduct Mutual-Benefit Activities

Once you've determined an advantage you can offer a local business near your center, approach them with a way you can both benefit. For example, perhaps you offer to give your local beauty salon copies of articles on parenting preschoolers for clientele to read while at the salon (a good idea anywhere customers must sit and wait). On each copy you attach a sticker that says: Compliments of; Name of Your Center; and your telephone number. This positions you as the helpful expert to call regarding early care and education; at the same time it provides the beautician with reading material that will be of interest to her clients and becomes a value-added service of her salon. It's mutually-beneficial community marketing.

## Exchange Services

To move that idea to another level, think about the businesses and organizations in your community for whom you could provide a service in exchange for a product or service from them that would be of value to you. Suppose the same beautician would agree to spend one afternoon a week at your center, providing haircuts for your customers and children. You would market the availability of the beautician's services, manage the sign-up list, and collect fees from parents. She would provide a discounted rate for the haircuts given in the center. It's easy business for her and a nice ancillary service for you.

You both benefit. You receive the residual benefit of referrals from the beautician talking to her other salon clients about your center and the haircutting services she provides there.

## Co-Sponsor Events

What are businesses and associations in your area with whom you could sponsor an event to benefit the community while giving you and the other businesses involved positive exposure to the marketplace?

A center in Virginia teamed up with the American Society for the Blind, a manufacturer of vision screening equipment, and a local media station to provide a weekend of free vision screening to anyone in the local community. The equipment was set up in the center and manned by society volunteers. Center staff provided drop-in child care while adults had their vision screened. The director was available to provide center tours to interested attendees. The media provided broad coverage both before and after the event.

This successful, well-attended event not only provided a useful service to participants, it gave positive exposure to each entity involved. For an expenditure of time and energy, each sponsor gained awareness and recognition that would have cost high marketing dollars to generate through traditional advertising channels. And the public-private partnership created by the joining together of for-profit and not-for-profit sponsors opened marketing opportunities for each and communicated good will and understanding to the audiences served by the event.

## Speak for an Organization

Colleges, corporations, parent organizations such as MOPS (Mothers of Preschoolers), and local PTA's are always looking for knowledgeable professionals who are willing to share their expertise on the platform. Call and offer to make a brief presentation on a topic of interest, such as dealing with separation or what to look for in choosing quality child care. Do not pitch your center in your talk, but do provide the meeting planner with an introduction that briefly tells about your center and positions you as the helpful professional expert. Be sure to have business cards and center brochures available for those audience members who want further information about your center and services.

## Write and Submit Articles

Most local newspapers and magazines are receptive to short feature articles on early care and education topics that are of interest to their readers. Many larger companies publish an in-house newsletter, and might welcome a guest column on topics that could help their parent employees balance work and family life, and be more productive on the job.

Regardless of who you write for, stay brief and on topic with the information you provide. Put your name, position, center name, and contact information at the end of each article. (Refer to "Guess Who's in the News," *Exchange*, July 1996, for techniques on taking full advantage of this method of community marketing.) As an added benefit, these articles could help generate some good publicity for your center.

## Network With Other Professionals

Though many of the professionals in your community may not ever become your customers, the majority of them fall into a target audience I call opinion influencers. They may not use your center's services, but they can influence the opinion of those who do. It is a good community marketing move to cultivate these referral sources in professional settings.

If you are not already a member of a child care industry association in your area, become one. In addition, join a business organization, such as your local Chamber of Commerce or a professional Women's network. If you have the time and interest, get involved in a civic group, especially if it draws a membership that includes parents of young children.

Take an active approach to these networking opportunities. Do more than attend meetings. Offer to hold one at your center, if local codes or company regulations allow. Get involved on a committee. Shake lots of hands. Susan Roane, author of How to Work a Room, says it well in Commandment Seven of her Ten Commandments of Connecting: "Make an EFFORT. Bring Your ENERGY. Exude ENTHUSIASM." And, remember to pass out your business cards freely. They are your most cost-efficient marketing tool.

## Removing the Roadblocks

Well-executed community marketing, layered with other methods of marketing communications, can help you generate enrollment inquiries and referrals. It will be easier to get started with successful community marketing activities if you keep these three strategies in mind.

- HAVE AGOAL. Is your intent to generate recognition of your center and its services, to keep your center's name in the minds of prospects and referral sources, or merely to introduce yourself to other professionals in the community around your center? If you know your goal for each community marketing activity, your actions will be much more focused and effective.

- SET AN APPOINTMENT WITH YOURSELF. Plan at least one community marketing activity each month. After each month's activity, plan the next one and set an appointment with yourself to make it happen. If you merely have a vague notion about what you'll do next, it's too easy for time to go by and other center happenings to take priority while community marketing slips through the cracks. Treat this like an appointment for a center visit with an inquiring prospect. Keep it or reschedule it for as soon as possible. No excuses.

- MAKE IT FUN! As I like to say, "The level of the success you reach depends as much on the altitude of your attitude as on the level of skill you possess." Think positive. Visualize community marketing as an easy, effortless experience. You'll be amazed at how what you think about, comes about.

One of the best ways to make community marketing fun is to have a marketing partner. Find a nearby, non-competitive colleague with whom you'll plan and carry out community marketing activities. Schedule a community marketing day at least once a month. Together, set your goals, plan your approach, schedule the activity, and do it together. When you have completed each community marketing outing, do something fun together to celebrate your accomplishments and to plan your next community marketing get-together. Whether it's going to lunch together, strolling through a mall, or buying each other flowers; knowing that you'll be rewarding yourselves can motivate you and your marketing partner to be more creative and accountable for community marketing.

If you practice community marketing using these seven ways to make it easier, you will not only feel more comfortable and confident with this method of marketing, you will likely see a significant increase in enrollment inquiries and referrals. Like exercising, it's a small price to pay for big rewards.

# Community Outreach

## Chapter 18

# Courting the Media with Special Events

by Karen Stephens

*"Courting the media! Are you masochistic? The press views child care as a sure scoop on sexual abuse and sick kids. The farther away they stay from us the better." This statement reflects the views of many in child care. In the wake of years of predominately "bad press," we have legitimate reasons for being leary. Many feel as if we have been publicly vilified as a scapegoat for a variety of social ills and, therefore, shun relations with the media.*

This article is going to challenge some of that defensiveness and urge you to work more with the media, not less. Here is an appeal to view the media objectively and to perceive it simply as a tool to be managed, not only for the benefit of children and families, but also for the child care profession.

Child care is on the vanguard of social change surrounding and involving the family. This can be threatening to a large percentage of the population who have never been in a child care setting as a child or have never used one for their own children. If we are to combat being the brunt of the public's suspicions and misconceptions, we have to become proactive rather than merely reactive. We must educate ourselves for utilizing the media in order to clearly communicate to the public who we are, what we do, and why.

Taking into consideration that 90% of American households own at least one television and that the typical American adult reads a newspaper on the average of 13 minutes per day, it becomes apparent that the media can be a very effective and efficient tool for reaching the public. Through the media, we can reach the diverse coalition of people from whom we need support — namely the business sector, churches, funding agencies, elected officials, policy makers, and the voting public.

Now I know that you are already finding reasons for why you can't take the time for public relations via the media. With the garbage disposal backing up into the ventilation system, the furnace going on strike, and three teachers calling in sick, where do you find the time? Maybe you're afraid the media won't listen to you; after all, you're *just a child care director*. Perhaps you're fearful that they will make you talk into a camera (while the tape is rolling). Swallow your fears and do it anyway. Developing a positive image for child care and its workers is just too critical to be put on the back burner. Children deserve and desperately need informed, caring persons to speak on behalf of their best interests. Like it or not, one of those persons is you.

## Creating Media Events

Increasingly, child care providers are gaining access by creating media events that can be covered in news segments or talk shows of local and/or national programming. Many have had success in presenting child care as an exciting, effective family support service comprised of competent, caring professionals. Their efforts have been rewarded by increased name recognition and visibility which helps in fundraising and recruitment. Their credibility has been enhanced as they encourage consumer awareness.

This article will identify the processes of creating successful media events. These include making an event newsworthy, selecting a skilled spokesperson, preparing for an interview, promoting the event, and following up on coverage.

Within the context of child care, a media event is a *happening* involving or relating to children and/or families. It is created with the intention of utilizing the media to help focus public attention on a particular topic, issue, or need. It can be large or small, but by design it is developed so that it will be perceived as newsworthy by the *powers that be* in media outlets. As the event is reported, a spokesperson will be asked for a statement or interview. When that time comes, it is up to the spokesperson to communicate how the event highlights the needs of children, families, and child care.

## Meeting Mutual Needs

Before successfully breaking into the game of *media monopoly*, you have to be aware of the media's goals as well as your own. Be confident that you are meeting on equal ground. There is no reason to be intimidated. In reality, the media needs you just as much as you need them.

One of the goals of the media is to acquire reliable, credible, informed sources who can provide them with contemporary and relevant stories. They want this in order to appear sincerely concerned about the community. More importantly, they want stories that will build ratings. The higher the ratings, the more the media can charge advertisers for advertising time or space.

Thousands of families are in the throes of lifestyle changes that necessitate child care and support services. If the media is going to be responsive to those changes, they are going to have to use you as a source. Remember, you are the expert. You have the training and daily first-hand contact with families that makes you uniquely qualified to contribute to public discussion.

## Making an Event Newsworthy

How do you package an event in order to spark the media's attention? It is a matter of providing them with an *angle*. They need some justification for presenting the event to their audience. The following examples dramatize the underlying principles.

Make a visual statement. During the Week of the Young Child, four centers of Illinois State University, Bloomington-Normal, Illinois, paraded balloon and sign-carrying children onto a campus quadrangle, each coming from the north, south, east, or west. They met in the center for a group sing along and *pep rally*. The event was designed to show that child care from all areas was coming together in a united effort for a common cause.

When a latchkey school-age child care bill was waiting for the governor's signature, child advocates arranged a massive mailing of old house keys to be sent to the governor's office. Mounds of *latchkeys* on the governor's desk spurred extensive media coverage on the issue.

Make it action packed and colorful. The launching of a hot air balloon at the Washington Monument with hundreds of children's smiling faces was an event created by Children's World in Washington, DC, to celebrate the Week of the Young Child. The event provided pizzazz to what might have first appeared as just another *national week*.

The 4 C's of Central Florida, Inc. co-sponsors a Children's Festival each year around Lake Eola in Orlando, Florida. Over 150 human service organizations set up activity booths for children and pass out printed material on their programs to parents. The festival represents a vast coalition and boasts of 8,000 visitors each year. The media's interest is further peaked by Disney World characters parading about and NASA astronauts mingling with the crowd. Throw in some music, clowns, a train, and pony rides, and you can't keep the press away.

The Massachusetts Association of Day Care Agencies sponsored a Look Up to Day Care Day. Held in Boston Commons (you remember, the setting for *Make Way for Ducklings*), children and child care workers simultaneously released hundreds of helium-filled balloons into the heavens. Music and face painting were the finishing touches to attract the media.

Karen Miller, then national education director for Children's World, appeared on a television talk show featuring creativity and imagination. With imagination of her own, she was able to turn the studio audience into the event. Illustrating that sensory experiences help to trigger creativity in children, she distributed gallons of homemade silly putty to the entire audience. The cameras couldn't pull away from the expressions of adults who were for the first time experiencing the squishy, slimy joys of silly putty! The phone lines rang off the hook with home viewers requesting the recipe!

**Highlight local responses to national issues or trends**. Many centers have taken advantage of the media's interest in child sexual abuse by presenting prevention programs on the topic for children and parents. The media has interviewed child care staff and parents and taped children as they participated.

Peg Delaney and Julie Cassady, while student teachers from the Illinois State University Home Economics Department, created an aerobics program for children. Parents and children, in leg warmers and sweatbands, participated with plenty of jump and jive. The media related the story to the national fitness craze.

**Involve a public official**. The 4 C's of Central Florida, Inc. hosts an annual child care tour. An event that started 13 years ago in an old, beat up, unairconditioned school bus has now become a luxury event in a plush chartered bus. The tour takes key officials, decision makers, and the press to where the action is — child care operating in full swing. The tour guide takes advantage of the captive audience during transport and explains child care funding, program diversity, licensing regulations, and the needs of child care.

Elinor Guggenheimer related the story of a center that invited public officials to visit and relive life as three year olds. The press relished reporting the traffic jam antics of the mayor and police commissioner as they explored the block area.

**Groups of people make news**. Conferences often gain attention because of the sheer numbers of people involved. When hosting the Midwest AEYC annual conference, Minnesota AEYC brought their theme, *Follow the Rainbow*, to life by literally painting a rainbow on the two blocks of sidewalk that connected the two conference hotels. Via the media, the whole city watched as it was created with none other than the city mayor in the lead.

**Focus on the unique**. Pat Clark, Bethesda, Maryland, was requested to provide babysitting at the hotel site for the Annual Arab Anti-Discrimination Committee Conference. Focusing on their stated commitment to human rights, Pat was able to convince the group to take a stand for quality child care and good working conditions for caregivers as basic human rights. Two hotel suites were transformed into a child care center. Children enjoyed quality care — appropriate group size and low ratios. Caregivers worked six hours paid. Reporters from Africa, Japan, France, Germany, and the United States were attracted to the unique situation and the statement that it was making.

Realizing that most people have not been inside a child care center, Marlene Stoiber, Cleveland, Ohio, took a sample to the people. Her organization set up a typical classroom in a shopping mall. The classroom was fully equipped and featured self-selected activities. The *center* enrolled children for half an hour at a time.

**Announce a new service**. Mary Lee Johns, reported that a parents' *Warmline* received positive attention. The project was a hotline for parents who were on the verge of abusing their child. Warmline also sponsored "Parent Tip of the Week" on local radio stations.

The McLean County AEYC caught the attention of the public by combining efforts with a crisis line to provide *PhoneFriend*, a hotline for latchkey children. McLean County AEYC also made the news when it coordinated efforts with a radio station and police department to provide free fingerprinting of children. Information on preventing child abduction was also distributed.

**Make it timely**. Patty Siegel, executive director of the California Child Resource and Referral Network, and Merle Lawrence, created the *Child Care Information Kit* which created quite a stir in the media. The kit itself was designed to educate policy makers, employers, and the media on the needs, supply, and policy issues surrounding child care in the San Francisco Bay area.

Its exposure and acceptance was maximized by timing its distribution with a press conference announcing that the White House Office on Private Sector Initiatives had come to town. The White House's envoy had come to convince Bay Area executives to become involved in child care for their employees. The kit was just the tool needed by employers and the media as they were trying to understand the nature of child care problems faced by parents.

## Selecting a Spokesperson

Before you contact the media about your event, select an official spokesperson. This person serves as a liaison with

### More Press Release Ideas

Ginger Deck and Richard D. Smith, in their book *Getting Sales* (Seattle: International Self-Counsel Press Ltd., 1981), present an extensive list of ideas for putting together a press release. Here are some of them:

**Send photos that can be used**. Use clear, crisp, good contrast 4"x5", 7"x9", or 8"x10" glossy finish black and white photos (unless the editor specifically requests other types of materials). Don't send a Polaroid or small color print, color slides, photocopy of a photo, or any picture that's blurred, too dark, or too light. If the picture isn't clear, don't send it.

**Attach captions carefully**. Always attach a caption to every photo you send. Don't use paper clips or staples to attach them as these will mar the photo. Use rubber cement or tape that will come off without tearing the photos, and attach the caption to the back of the photo.

**Identify the subjects clearly**. Give the name and title of every person in the photo and the order in which they are shown (e.g., left to right, clockwise from the top, etc.).

**Keep duplicate photos**. Set up a filing system for duplicates of the photos you've sent out and for other background photos on your events. That way, if a photo gets lost, you can supply another one.

**What Not to Do:**

- Don't ask why a feature, story, or photo isn't used.
- Never send a release without some type of release date on it, where the editor can see it clearly and immediately.
- Don't overuse the name of your organization in the copy. Don't use all capital letters for your business name or the name of your project.
- Don't call up editors or news directors asking if material is going to be used or asking for clippings or air times.

the media. It may be the director, a teacher, or board member of your program. Because this person will greatly affect your public image, she should be personable, enthusiastic, articulate, and well informed about your program.

The role of the spokesperson is to develop a positive working relationship with members of the media so that they will be receptive to story ideas. Assigning one person to communicate with the public also projects an organized image. Reporters won't cover an event if they have to track down three or four people in order to get the complete story.

One of the major challenges for the spokesperson is to become adept at the art of being interviewed.

## Preparing for Interviews

An interview provides you with your real chance to communicate with the public. Before embarking on this adventure, it's important to develop some savvy in regards to the interview process.

**Identify your goals**. What do you want to communicate? Speaking from experience, Pat Clark believes, "If you know what you want to say, you have at least half a chance at getting your message across in an undistorted manner."

**A positive attitude is invaluable**. "Style and flamboyance gets the media's attention," according to Phoebe Carpenter. Karen Miller calls it "enthusiasm that shows you have a life commitment to the cause."

**Be well prepared**. Sandra Mathers, reporter, says that a reporter needs an interviewee who has her facts and figures together. By being organized and concise, you help to make the reporter's job easier, and that always wins a few points. Present your statements in a clear, logical manner. Feel free to let the interviewer know the types of questions about child care that you usually encounter. Some programs develop a media kit that concisely describes their program through a brochure, fact sheets, and position statements.

**Keep your message short and sweet**. If you ramble on, your point is likely to be missed. A print reporter may be able to take the time to sift through your comments; but in a television interview, you may have only 20 to 60 seconds to respond.

**Anticipate key questions and your response**. Be aware of what the hot topics in current events are so that you may respond in an intelligent manner. Your response may involve giving facts, figures, anecdotes, or opinions.

**Tie in real life examples**. Mathers states that the media likes to dramatize issues with actual examples of persons involved. Patty Siegel fills this need by presenting the media with *consumer profiles* — examples of parents grappling with the issues of availability, affordability, and quality.

**State your ideas in a positive way**. Say "Child care can help to establish good health habits in young children," rather than "I know most people think that child care kids are sick because we don't make them wash their hands, but that just isn't so."

**Relax and act natural**. You want to appear as if you are enjoying the interview. If you appear tense, it will color the image that you project.

**Practice for television interviews**. Dress professionally and look neat. A jacket looks professional and provides a lapel for clipping a microphone. Avoid white clothing and flashy jewelry; they both reflect too much light which produces a glare and poor picture. Look at the reporter when you speak, not into the camera and not downward.

Beth Fredericks, Cambridge, Massachusetts, advises interviewees to be flexible and accommodating when dealing with reporters, their cords, lights, and semi-egotistical hurried attitudes. The temporary inconvenience to you and your program should be offset by the greater good of receiving positive media exposure.

## Promoting the Event

You've decided on the event, chosen a spokesperson, and are prepared for the interview. It is now a matter of promoting the event to the media. You have to identify your media sources so you can let them know who you are and what you are doing.

**Compiling a media list**. Most Chamber of Commerce offices maintain a list of local media which identifies their name, type of medium (print, radio, television), address, and phone number. This list can usually be purchased for a small fee.

Many lists also identify the designated *gatekeepers*. These are media contact people who have the power to assign and often edit stories. They ultimately decide what gets into the news and in what form. These are the people to whom you direct your request for coverage. Their titles vary; but they are typically called news director, assignment editor, producer, or other official sounding title. To this list add deadline dates for press releases and story ideas. If you plan an event too close to a deadline, you may not receive coverage. To the list you should also add in-house newsletters of companies and organization newsletters of major employers in your area. They are another means for reaching the public. If your Chamber of Commerce does not provide a media list, you may need to call each media organization directly to track down the needed information.

**Analyzing your media sources**. After identifying your media, analyze their publications or broadcasts. What type of stories do they run and who covers them? What type of talk shows do they air? Which columnists do they feature? What is their political leaning and the tone of their editorials? What sections of their publications would be interested in child care articles. In these times, the answer may include the financial section as well as family living and education. The answers to these questions will influence how you organize your event and present it to each media source.

**Sending press releases**. Press releases are used to alert the media to your event. There are many guides available to show you how to make one. You can also ask for a sample of the preferred format for each media source.

In general, you should answer the questions what, who, where, when, and why. Put it all in the first paragraph if possible. The media is busy and swamped with requests for coverage; if your first paragraph doesn't grab them, into the wastebasket it goes.

Type the release (double spaced) and put the name, address, and phone number of your organization in the top left-hand corner. Under that, put your spokesperson's name and phone number for further questions. In the top right-hand corner, type the release date for the information (i.e., For Immediate Release or For Release on April 12, 1999).

It is extremely important to hand deliver your release, at least when you are beginning to establish a relationship. It provides you with the opportunity to talk personally with reporters and gatekeepers. The rapport that you establish will be invaluable in requesting coverage.

**Public service announcements**. Public service announcements (PSAs) are used to inform the public about an event; they also help to remind the media that you are around. Contact your media for specific information on how to submit them and in what form. Many media outlets have a community affairs director or someone similar. If you are a non-profit agency, they may help you to write and produce PSAs.

**Personal contacts with the media**. Patty Siegel warns child care providers not to wait for the media to come to them. "You have to cultivate the media by going to them and keeping in touch." Keeping in touch may include phone calls, sending them your newsletter, or dropping a note of congratulations on a good story (even if you weren't mentioned). Some centers are trying to recruit media representatives to serve on their advisory boards.

Remember one thing about reporters, they always want to appear objective and unbiased. When approaching them for coverage, it is best if they perceive that you are promoting child care in general and not just your own personal gain. Reporters are very wary of self-interest. It is wisest to promote yourself and organization as one among many who are trying to improve the quality of services provided to children and families.

## Following Up on Coverage

After conducting an event, it is important to evaluate the level of success you experienced in *courting* the media. You should assign at least one person to review your coverage (or lack of it) in each media source. Note the strengths and weaknesses of the story. Did you get your message across? What quotes or examples were highlighted? What did the media *play up* most? The answers will help you in planning your next event. Save any print coverage for future reference.

**Sending thank-yous**. Remember that everyone needs strokes. You are likely to enjoy the spotlight of the media again if you reinforce their efforts. One way to stroke is to make phone calls and send letters. The letters should express your respect and appreciation for the time and effort expended by the reporter. Letters should go directly to the reporter who covered the event with copies being sent to her superiors (i.e., news director, managing editor, general manager). Writing a *Letter to the Editor* column shows that you felt the community was well served.

**About misrepresentation**. In the words of Phoebe Carpenter, "If you want the benefit of publicity, you have to be willing to take the risk of being misquoted." If you find that you have been misquoted or misrepresented, it is probably best to ignore it and chalk it up to experience. For future reference, determine how you could have restructured or rephrased a comment in order to project your views more clearly. Problems with inaccuracy can be the result of giving too much information in technical language in a disorganized fashion.

If you feel that a slanted view against you was blatant and intentional, you can talk to the reporter or editor in a cooperative manner. Remember, you want to salvage the relationship so you have a second and third shot of presenting your views accurately.

If you are still not satisfied, you can write a *Letter to the Editor*, and that's about it. You'll just have to pick up the pieces and go on from there.

## In Ending

Positive media coverage for child care and related services can be attained. It takes goal setting, planning, imagination, and a lot of persistent work. Fluke publicity may put us in the limelight from time to time, but an ongoing public relations campaign is required if we are to increase the image of child care. Through our combined efforts, we can make an impact on the way that we are perceived and supported.

# When Shaming Fingers Point: Dealing with Negative Publicity

by Dorothy W. Hewes

*Newspapers keep us well informed about the tragedies and traumas of daily life. And in their telling, they can help us find answers to some of the puzzles in our own professional lives. We have almost daily examples — faulty O-rings in the Challenger, withdrawal of a well-known elevision evangelist after indiscreet behavior, misappropriation of federal funds or misuse of federal influence.*

*How do administrators react when shaming fingers point in their direction? How do they respond when the focus is on some real or falsely rumored criminal, unethical, or otherwise shameful happening in the workplace for which they are responsible? We can use our newspapers to learn some valuable lessons.*

Haven't you read negative publicity — or seen it on television — and wondered how you would deal with something like that? Whether the accusation is true or false makes no difference in the way it should be handled. Strategies and mistakes of government and corporate administrators can be used as case histories from which we can learn valuable lessons about dealing with crises.

The powerful effects of adverse public relations have become obvious to big business and a field called issues management emerged. A public relations specialist, W. Howard Chase, introduced issues management in the *Public Relations Journal* in 1976 and 1977. In practice, issues management includes attorneys, economists, and social scientists. Their work connects advertising and issues, with emphasis upon the identification, monitoring, and manipulation of those trends that may develop into policies and regulations affecting the way a business or industry can function.

Directly and indirectly, issues management affects what we read and view concerning environmental problems, the importance of free enterprise, and other aspects of the creative tension between big business and the taxpaying public. It is a communications strategy with both positive and negative potential that relates to negative publicity — prevailing public opinion will affect the way news media deal with a situation. Our professional field is no exception. We must recognize that other-than-mother care still arouses complicated emotional reactions and that these can reverberate into our professional lives. In this sense, organizations like the National Association for the Education of Young Children and the Children's Defense Fund have contributions to make in the realm of issues management.

For directors of early childhood programs, informational strategies developed in issues management are helpful when it comes to handling emergency situations and adverse media reports. Two books, *Issues Management* by Heath and Nelson and *On Deadline — Managing Media Relations* by Howard and Mathews, include guidelines that can be applied to even small child care centers. Their detailed case studies show how negative publicity has been handled, and mishandled, so that we can interpret what we find in our daily news media. For instance, the change from an initial siege mentality to an issues management approach by the Nestle Corporation led to a resolution of the boycott over its infant formula marketing. A similar change might be needed by a center struggling to alter unfavorable community attitudes.

Although we might not aspire to the late Andy Warhol's statement that everybody is famous for 15 minutes, what might happen to make us notorious for a while in our own communities? Only rarely does the limelight shine on the positive aspects of our field that we would like to emphasize. The greatest fear for many of us is to be involved with an alleged sexual abuse case. Other things happen. A baby is kidnapped or a child is taken by the non-custodial parent. Playground accidents and drownings are newsworthy. Teachers celebrating Halloween might be accused of teaching Satanism. Armed intruders can force their entrance, or planes can fall from the sky. The treasurer is found to have been diverting the federal nutrition money to her cousin's restaurant. These are not fiction; they are news items from my own files. Let's brainstorm a bit more. What is your worst case scenario, the worst thing you can visualize in the way of negative publicity?

Now ask yourself another set of questions. What have you done to prepare for negative publicity? What would you do if something dreadful happened? Or, for that matter, how would you deal with something merely unfortunate? My own analysis of crisis situations — including those that I've survived during my many years with children's programs — has been fortified by what I've learned through reading issues management strategies. This cannot be a complete listing for your center. Only you can know what is best. However, here are my suggestions:

**1. Assume that at some unexpected time you or a member of your staff or some aspect of your program will be the focus of negative attention by the news media and the public.** You have taken all the precautions possible — and you not only have good insurance coverage but a previously established relationship with an attorney. You also are a member of an appropriate professional group, perhaps NAEYC plus one for your particular type of program. Furthermore, awareness of ways to develop good public relations on a long-term basis is part of your normal operating procedure. This includes your equivalent of a press kit, usually a brochure describing the center, plus whatever seems appropriate. If nothing else, this will mean that names are spelled correctly. For me, it once established that my program was not the one being investigated; it was the school across town with a similar name.

**2. Encourage some worst case thinking among staff members and others involved in governance of the program.** There is a superstitious fear about talking or thinking about disasters. (How many parents in your center have legal wills? What have you done to prepare for a major earthquake or typhoon or other natural disaster?) According to some depth psychologists, fears of unspoken or unthought fantasies can be more dreadful than anything that can really happen. As director, you can initiate this sort of thinking and bring it into the open. At that point, it is appropriate to move on to a discussion about how you will deal with such things. The possible alternatives can be discussed. Consider how you would deal with parents and children, as well as how you would manage the outside world. Consider coping mechanisms already demonstrated with problems.

**3. Determine who will meet the media people if there is a worst case situation.** Perhaps it is logical that you, as director, be the one to deal with reporters, telephone calls, television newscasters; but there may be someone who would be more effective than you. They say that men project authority and women are more trusted by the public. Take your choice, but make that decision **before** something happens. Then make sure that the designated spokesperson's number is available at any hour of the day or night. Howard and Mathews point out that planning helps organizations deal with potential first class media relations disasters with speed, professionalism, and at least the outward appearance of calm.

**4. The spokesperson should gather all of the facts quickly and tell the story as fully and as soon as possible.** Bad news does not evaporate if ignored. Making the initial contact with the media to tell them about the situation often makes for more sympathetic treatment. It allows for greater control, and usually makes the public exposure shorter. In some cases, taking the story to the press allows remedial action to be made part of the story.

A campus child care director who handled a situation in a direct and positive manner provides an example. Late one Friday afternoon, she received a telephone inquiry from a local television station asking about the role of an accused child molester during the time he had been a student volunteer in her center. Although this had been before her own employment, she was able to quickly find his records and tell the reporter that his sole responsibility was cleaning the rabbit hutch and painting some shelves — six years earlier. Note that she only released information that is legally permitted; she did not discuss the quality of his performance or personal attributes.

Since this was a major news story at the time, she realized that more questions would follow. She contacted her superior, the dean of student affairs, and she notified the campus newspaper. In addition, she wrote and duplicated a letter that would be in the mailboxes of the parents on Monday morning. Staff members received weekend telephone calls via an established telephone tree so that they could provide a unified response. As a result, what could have become a full-blown story by itself was just a sentence or two that was buried in more dramatic events. Only the campus paper dealt with it in more detail, and their angle was the security for enrolled children provided through the center's policies.

**5. If it is not possible to deal with adversive situations in a quick and tidy manner, prepare at the outset for communications that are frank and honest.** As long as public interest in your situation is sustained, all communications should continue to be directed through the designated spokesperson. Everyone else in your organization should firmly say that they are unable to comment; they should refer inquiries to your designated spokesperson. Staff and parents should not be encouraged at this point to speak casually about the situation or to make assumptions based upon partial knowledge. As director, it is essential that you model appropriate behavior.

**6. The spokesperson should have a basic understanding of what goes on in a news interview.** Particularly in television and radio newscasting, only a few seconds will be provided for your side of the story. This means that the most important points should be made at the beginning of each response. A slower delivery will help communicate your message; rapid speech makes it hard for a reporter taking notes and is particularly hard for a television audience to follow. One sentence may be all that is broadcast, so the person being interviewed should avoid being led into making any statement that reflects negatively upon the program. Sentences should be phrased positively, using words that are commonly understood by the reading or listening public. Sincerity and professionalism will help project a positive response and will deflect some criticism.

Even in a time of crisis, try to remember that public opinion of child care will be affected by what the spokesperson says and how he or she says it. Many directors have had encounters with the media in which the purposes and activities of their centers were distorted in the writing or filming. The press kit mentioned earlier can be of help here. Assume that the person doing the interview knows absolutely nothing about child development or early childhood education. Probably the readers/listeners/viewers don't know much either. Somehow the essence of your position must be expressed in the short time or space allotted.

**7. Recognize that the personal element of shame or guilt may dominate your thoughts and actions after an event that results in negative publicity.** It may involve some ethical dilemma. There may be a condition known as cognitive dissonance in which two or more sets of information just refuse to fit together, perhaps incoming material that just isn't consistent with what you already know or believe. You will feel tension, anxiety, conflict. A network of professional colleagues may provide support at this point, perhaps even more than personal friends and family, who cannot validate your work on the significant peer level that is needed. Taking steps toward repairing damage done by the crisis may be helpful to your recovery and will provide the staff and other involved persons with the leadership model they must have to carry forward after appropriate grief, remorse, or anger has been taken care of.

I deliberately used the phrase "shaming fingers" in the title of this article because I want to emphasize this personal element. In our society, the element of shame is one of those things that keeps us working on straight and narrow paths. From childhood, perfectly normal people have determined to do certain things and not to do others because of public disapproval. In some cases, the public may be pointing your way. Most of us have little sympathy with the owners of a child care center that is discovered to be the front for a porno photography ring! However, even when there has been a preventable tragedy, there must be a realistic evaluation of what happened, and the feelings of guilt must be recognized and dealt with. This may involve professional counseling for everybody involved, often available through a public agency or volunteer psychotherapists.

Preparation for an event that would generate negative public relations can be a factor in relieving the shame and guilt that result. Keep this idea in mind when you watch newscasts or read newspapers. Rehearsal through visualization of how other leaders and administrators deal with adverse situations can be helpful preparation. In addition to the obvious strategies that are used, try to figure out what characteristics are displayed by those who are coping. What do you think was going on behind the scenes? How might issues management have been applied to these events that have been brought to you by the media? How might they apply to your role as a program director? Heath and Nelson point out that a major trend in managerial philosophy has been the incorporation of data and advice from many people into the process of strategic planning. Most of us have been doing this all along. The field of issues management, with its techniques for dealing with crisis situations, can offer clues to help us learn some professional skills from the daily news.

## References

Benoit, W. L. (1994). *Accounts, Excuses, and Apologies: A Theory of Image Restoration*. Ithaca, NY: State University of New York Press.

Chase, W. H. (May 1976/October 1977). "Public Issue Management: The New Science," *Public Relations Journal* 32, 14-15, 33; 25-26.

Heath, R. L., & Nelson, R. A. (1986). *Issues Management: Corporate Public Policymaking in an Information Society*. Beverly Hills, CA: Sage.

Howard, C., & Mathews, W. (1985). *On Deadline: Managing Media Relations*. New York: Longman.

# Putting All the Players on the Same Page: Accessing Resources for the Child and Family

by Ethel Seiderman

*Child care is a natural meeting place to bring together the needs of children and families and the community resources that they may need to access. Families and staff share a mutual interest and common desire — they are bound together by a concern for the well-being of the child. In child care programs, it is possible to create an atmosphere of trust, comfort, familiarity, and a sense of belonging. This is fostered by daily contact with families and children, by the generational possibility of serving over time several children from one family, and — of uppermost importance — by the beliefs and attitudes of the director and the staff in creating a climate that encourages partnership between parents and providers. These are built on mutual strengths, equity, harmony, and respectful relationships. It is only in such a climate that parents will be forthcoming regarding their needs and interests, encouraged that these can be met through the child care environment.*

Don't assume that this will just happen. The director, with the staff, needs to take responsibility to create a tone that fosters these relationships. If parents are engaged only minimally or superficially, they will feel a lack of welcome. They will merely come and go — share little, linger momentarily, pay their fees, show up for command performances (plays and shows, graduations, occasionally parent meetings, and the mandated parent/teacher conference). They are not invested; they keep to themselves, reveal little, and could leave shortchanged — denied access to services and resources that could make an enormous difference in fostering greater success and well-being for themselves and their children.

Centers and schools can have a large impact in becoming the place where resources can be exchanged. They can carry out an often expressed yet unfulfilled belief that we are all a community of caring, that we are approachable to each other and able to transfer resources easily and without judgment. We want to avoid stereotypes that divide us, where the receiver of services feels needy and beholden while the giver feels bountiful, benevolent, and privileged. This creates the great divide where no one will come forward, and needs go unmet. Lists with resources are not enough. They will go unused by families. Staff may feel stuck and a bit righteous about those who didn't avail themselves of this "good stuff." How do we change this to the climate of openness described earlier? Let's review how this can occur by looking at three dimensions: the *school/center/family child care settings* and what they need to consider, the *parent and family* and their ability to begin to trust the environment by sharing their needs and interests, and the *systems of service and resources* that need to reflect on their practice of delivering services to families and their own assets and liabilities.

## The School/Center/Family Child Care Settings

The perceived gatekeepers must be willing to look at their practice. Is there a willingness to open the doors so that families can feel a sense of ownership and be acknowledged for having their own resources that they, too, can share? This notion of reciprocity — an exchange of the gifts each one of us has — leaves no one feeling like a taker. It requires that the leadership has a willingness to share the power. Though child care staffs often feel powerless in a field that is not properly honored for the valuable place it holds or the salaries bestowed, they must be on guard to avoid putting parents in a lesser role. This often unrecognized internal oppression creeps in in spite of our best intentions. Comments like "parent substitute" or "parent surrogate" imply that we can/do replace parents, when, in fact, we are there as supporters and guides, as well as links with resources.

Directors must be committed to being advocates and bringing services to their sites or having them conveniently available or arranging to get families to them. We need to give up the notion that "if they want them badly enough, they will get there." Often parents need to overcome insurmountable barriers — money, time, lack of comfort, fear.

Begin with a basic premise that families are responsible, that they want to be responsible, and that they will be responsive if the situation is welcoming and hospitable. Most of us in leadership are moved by compassion. We want to be of assistance, to give good care to the children, and to create opportunities for all.

To be the most effective, we also owe ourselves the chance to reflect and review our practice to see that it is in harmony with our beliefs. Who is answering the phone at the center? Who is in the office in a welcoming role? Who asks how one's day went? Who can make that call to make it easier for parents to set appointments or who can accompany them to an appointment that seems formidable? Often it is difficult enough to be fully staffed and quite a challenge to have the right people in the right job. Yet staff need the flexibility to do the work they do best on behalf of the programs and the families.

**Example —** *A child care center that had only recently begun to serve infants less than three years old was determined, with parents" agreement, to have children properly immunized. Work schedules made it impossible to access the clinic's hours, private physicians were costly for poor families, and a general apprehension seemed to prevail. The clinic reviewed its own mission — to have healthy children protected against disease — and sent a public health nurse to the center for 15-20 hours per month for several years until funding cuts occurred.*

*With parents' approval, and often with their presence, immunizations and regular well-baby check-ups occurred. The nurse would call parents with updates; she provided classes and workshops, gave infant first aid and CPR to staff and parents, and was a welcomed presence at the center. Her style, her compassion, and her nonjudgmental nature made her an invaluable resource. She acted as an advocate in other county systems for the family and eventually gave the children their health exams for kindergarten. Physicians were grateful that she was available. All agreed that placing these resources at the center created a cheering squad of service providers for the children and their families.*

Child care is the entry point for young children and their families. We can convey the impression that they are welcomed and embraced. We are there to give a hand as it is needed.

## Parents/Families — Stop and Smell the Roses

When the setting is genuine and welcomes families as stakeholders, parents step over the threshold and begin to test the waters. They recognize that this place is different, leave past perceptions behind, and begin to enjoy and take part in the community there.

Being present is often the first step in carving out a place for yourself. Other families may engage you, invite you to participate, greet you warmly, tell you about upcoming events. It is here that we share resources with each other, and it is here that friendship and support begin to occur. Being comfortable and at ease makes it easier to articulate one's particular needs or interests. Someone may know of a place to get children's clothes at a good price, another recommends a doctor, a third knows of a job opening that is a match for someone seeking employment. Often, in natural ways, resources and contacts unfold for a job, housing, tutoring, counseling, as well as exchanges for child care and a trip to the park or zoo. A sense of community grows.

**Example —** *A new parent at one child care center seemed reticent, doubtful, and suspicious; she questioned the director's intent to get her involved. She had a daughter and was caring for her ill sister's young son who had multiple problems related to having been drug exposed at conception. The director was sensitive to the push/pull going on, yet detected that this mother kept staying on the periphery and was also present a lot. When the mother began to attend events, there was a contagiousness about involvement that drew her in. She began to attend regularly, took a role of leadership on the parent committee, and developed friendships with others. As trust built, she asked for assistance with the Independent Education Plan (IEP) for her nephew, for whom she became the sole guardian at her sister's death. She enrolled in college and was employed part time. She reported she couldn't have done this unless child care and the community were present for her. She now has her master's degree in communications and has created a CD ROM about the child care center that her children attended and the parent support approach that it promotes. Although initially resistant, she was willingly drawn in.*

## Affecting Systems of Service

Having recognized that "official and unapproachable settings" have often served as an impediment to accessing services, resource centers now seem to be cropping up in neighborhoods where families live. The challenge is to go beyond consolidating the systems, which is a big step, to considering the atmosphere, the persons representing each system, and the ability of the systems to work for the common good of those seeking services. Resource centers or service systems may need to move out and link with child care sites so access is comfortable and easy.

This means giving up some turf issues about who is in charge, being able to shift times and locations of meetings, operating from an authentic people-to-people focus where resumes and degrees will be of less importance than who we are and how we relate.

Questions come up. Can the system be somewhat uncomfortable as it reflects on practice and makes change? Is it okay to let parents determine needs — to avoid trying to fix people? If families don't use resources, do we blame or judge them — or ask why and reshape delivery? Are we willing to have wider representation which includes the parent's voice?

It is a privilege to be present in a community where there is a consolidation of resources, systems, and players representing the widest range of social service providers, health providers, schools, early childhood, the disabled community, housing, religious groups, families, and more. All are willing to encounter the challenges, often struggles, to make their services and resources relevant and to share the power and leadership with each other. Listening is often the greatest hurdle. But we can learn from successes that benefits accrue when we honor our reasons for being in helping fields. Doing the work with a humane and caring perspective in a community with others enhances the overall success and goes beyond what each of us tries to do alone.

**Example** — *The director of a program with a large influx of immigrant families understood that many families were unfamiliar with our ordinary customs, experienced language barriers, and felt fear — all of which were keeping them from accessing resources. At the same time, the social services department recognized that these families were not coming forward for legitimately available resources and services. At the request of the child care center, and with the agreement of the social services department, a warm and nurturing Spanish-speaking social worker was placed at the center half time and eventually, as comfort and ease increased, she was available 20 hours a month according to families' needs. She might do translations, go on a field trip, take a family to a clinic, or be a mentor at the center working with children and their parents to promote learning.*

## Center Directors Alert

Consider these four tips for making a difference in gaining and fostering a spirit of cooperation between the community, service agencies, and your programs.

1. **Revise your own thinking about yourself.**

- We are part of the economic and human service infrastructure of our communities. The rest of the gears don't turn unless we are there — jobs, housing, resources, friends, and neighbors are attainable and sustainable if reliable, quality child care is in place.

- We usually do all our buying locally which benefits the economic health of our community. Point this out as part of telling our story.

- People can work and participate in training programs and school because we are here. We are a small business employer ourselves — hiring staff like other local businesses.

2. **Place yourself in strategic roles in the community.**

- Sit at tables as a partner with previously unfamiliar players — United Way leadership group, social service task force, agency board of directors.

- You can join the local Chamber of Commerce or Rotary Club. As a dues paying member (usually at the associate membership rate), your voice is heard in other arenas and your image changes — both for yourself and for others. Usually businesses and other community service professionals are present. You're not asking for funds or pleading the case of your families, but contributing to the community dialogue to create a better way of life and a better working environment. Inadvertently, you are becoming known, and you will find that resources come your way.

- Attend school board meetings to become known to trustees, administrative personnel, and teachers. This will ease the transition of younger children to school and create mutual benefits for the school-age child served by the center and the school. You and they can become greater allies and a mutual cheering squad for the children and families.

3. **Offer to present at social, business, and professional groups in the community.**

- They are always seeking speakers, and you have stories and information to relate.

- Invite them to the center where you host the meeting and let them see you in action.

4. **Use the media.**

- Learn who the key people are.

- Get press releases. Inform local papers and TV channels about events, achievements, and accomplishments.

- Do a public opinion column on the editorial page — take a position, highlight quality child care, or share your philosophy or values.

Community building based on caring relationships encourages optimal availability and use of resources. Accessing resources doesn't happen in a vacuum. A climate needs to be in place that sees the acquiring of resources as strength — the first step toward change and growth.

The child care environment is in a pivotal place to make this happen. The family, in recognizing that the environment is open and welcoming, will take their first steps to reveal their needs and interests. They can select the resources they need when options are made available and guidance is given.

Systems must align themselves with the people who may need their services. More than ever before, we are challenged to make resources accessible to children and their families.

# THE ART OF POWER NETWORKING

by Dwayne A. Crompton

*Years ago, as the director of an urban child care agency, I faced a troubling dilemma. My agency, KCMC Child Development Corporation in Kansas City, Missouri, was a success by anyone's standard. With limited resources, we had delivered high quality programming for almost two decades. We had earned recognition nationally as an innovative leader in early care and education. Yet, in our own hometown, we were a well-kept secret. Local leaders — including funders — didn't give us the time of day. When I shared my frustration with a friend and mentor in higher education, she quickly advised me to start networking with community leaders. "If you can gain access and tell your story," she said, "I'm sure you'll get what you want."*

How to identify and influence people who could help children and families had long been a concern of mine. How do I get to tell our story? How do I get access to civic leaders and power brokers? How do I reach people who can make a difference, politically and financially? I had pondered such questions with friends and associates for many years, and was eager to tell my story to a broader audience.

The power and wisdom of my mentor's advice began to become apparent a few months later when I was invited to speak at a roundtable forum called by the community foundation to help identify its funding priorities. A Kansas City council member with whom I had worked on youth issues invited me to the forum. I spoke earnestly about the need for early care and education and about KCMC's mission to build strong families and communities.

I later learned that it wasn't my reputation in child care alone that got me invited to the roundtable discussion. My involvement in a broad array of community organizations had attracted the attention of some key political leaders in Kansas City. Long before gaining access to power brokers and influential civic leaders, I had worked extensively with community organizations such as the NAACP, YMCA, my local neighborhood association, Big Brothers/Big Sisters, my university alumni association, and, of course, my church.

My active involvement in these organizations introduced me to dozens of community leaders working to improve housing, reduce crime, improve public education, expand youth programs and advance civil rights for minorities and women. Through my volunteer activism, I began developing visibility as a young leader interested in advancing the whole community, not just my career.

Years before my mentor's timely advice, I had begun building a community network that would later prove invaluable when the doors to wealth and influence began to open to me. By working to make my community a better place to live and raise a family, I had also built a broad network of people and organizations that could be used to advocate for children and families and publicize the work of my agency. All I needed to do was to expand and diversify my network and keep on talking.

Today, networking, unfortunately, has become another buzz word for self-promotion. For me, community networking is the formation of mutually beneficial relationships with others to build a better community. I see community networking as the relationships that you, your organization, and your staff create with other people and organizations to focus limited resources for greater improvement in the lives of children and families. When understood in this context, networking can become a powerful tool for dynamic change.

Power networking is positioning yourself and your agency to bring about dynamic change in the lives of children and families and in the way people think about and respond to early care and education. Power networking is an art.

The techniques of networking are well known. Successful people and organizations have used them for time immemorial. But to make community networking a powerful tool for change, we need to take a look before we leap. Early in the game, we need to answer some simple questions: "Why do I want to network?" "What will I, my agency, or the recipients of my agency's services get out of our networking with a particular group?" "What do I or my agency bring to the table?" "What do I have to give up to partner with this group?" "How will this partnership help early care and education?"

Power networking starts with a clear understanding of your vision, mission, and purpose, as well as a clear understanding of what you need from others. Networking also requires your understanding of how your mission fits with the agenda of other individuals, organizations, or businesses. You must also understand how you can help others achieve their goals. Power networking means giving as well as receiving. It builds goodwill for you and your agency, because it demonstrates that you care about more than just your personal success.

Power networking calls for a strong and diverse portfolio of partners that embrace individuals and organizations, parents and professionals. A diverse portfolio is especially helpful in fundraising and essential for capital campaigns. KCMC's success four years ago in raising more than $3 million to build a state-of-the-art child and family development center would not have been possible without our network of support which spanned from the home of low-income families to the board rooms of Fortune 500 companies. It took years to build this web of support, but it has paid big dividends ever since. Power networking takes time.

Power networking builds the system of community support your agency needs to meet its day-to-day goals. In the case of KCMC Child Development Corporation, our goal has always been supporting and strengthening children and families. When we saw that families were weakened by poor health care, KCMC formed partnerships with health care agencies to provide the health services that our families needed. When parents needed skilled training and education that would lead to economic self-sufficiency, we partnered with a federal job-training program. When we needed to improve the skills of our executive management team, we worked with the Ewing Marion Kauffman Foundation.

Moreover, when we realized that welfare reform was increasing the demand for quality child care, we linked KCMC's Head Start resources with community-based child care centers and licensed family child care homes to bolster the infrastructure of care. The result was a program innovation called the Head Start Community Partnership, dubbed Full Start. KCMC's Full Start program has strengthened Kansas City's child care system by bringing Head Start programming and resources to under-funded community-based child care centers in a way that is beneficial to all partners, but, most importantly, to hundreds of additional children and their families.

Power networking is the synergistic interworking of five fundamental components.

## Good Work

The first component is a well-managed program that delivers high quality services. A sure way to establish credibility is to make sure that you and your agency are doing good work. Community leaders are drawn to programs that show successful results in helping children and families. They shun those plagued by scandal, incompetence, and complaints.

## Leadership

In order for an organization to network effectively, key staff must be seen and accepted as leaders. As a leader, you must be professionally competent and well known within the profession and the general community. You must maintain and build supportive relationships with your professional colleagues, locally and nationally. Supporting each other strengthens our work. Outside your profession, you must be seen as a passionate and credible advocate for children and families. You must also be seen as knowledgeable and supportive of other organizations and professionals working to help children and families.

Once you've made connections with people who share your vision, keep them informed about your agency and about developments that affect children's lives.

Persistence is an indispensable leadership trait in power networking. Passion for improving the lives of children and families and optimism that we can meet the challenge and win are two indispensable traits in community networking.

## Communication

Your agency needs a communications plan that tells the need for high quality early care and education and how your agency is successfully meeting that need. You must convey to those outside the profession that while there are challenges in the care of children and families, there are solutions too.

In fact, I often rely on real-life anecdotes to convey my message. In talking with the general public, a balance between theory and practice, real life and ideal life, conveys that you know what you're talking about and are offering practical solutions to problems. This type of communication takes time to develop, but pays off with powerful dividends.

## Advocacy

As a leader in early care and education, part of your role is to be a visible advocate for children and families. Make sure that you are at the table — whether invited or not — when the welfare of children and families is at stake. Advocacy is the role in which you let your passion and optimism speak. A civic leader (who later spearheaded KCMC's $3 million capital campaign) said when she first met with me it was my passion for the subject of early care and education that impressed her most. When you advocate for children and families, let your zeal do the talking.

## Share the Glory

In the early years of my career, I wanted my agency to get credit for every success we were connected with. Now, I realize that public recognition for personal success isn't nearly as important as public recognition of the needs of children and families. In the end, it doesn't matter who gets public credit for a successful program innovation, a new partnership, or a new facility as long as the goal of improving early care and education is being achieved.

In using power networking, you will get the human and financial resources you need to carry out your mission, but the accolades may go to others.

An important culture debate is underway in America about children and families. As early care and education professionals, our ideas and voices must be part of the debate. To participate, we must be seen and accepted as important players in the total community. Power networking will put us in the community and get us a seat at the roundtable where we can be heard.

In the information age, society is changing at the speed of thought. I fear many worthy causes will be left behind. We must make sure that ours are not. That is why I believe community networking is crucial to the survival of early care and education in the next millennium. So let's start power networking now!

# Bringing Diversity Into Your Center

by Thomas Moore

*No matter where your child care center is located, chances are it fits the following description: If you're white, virtually everyone else in your center is white, too. If you're African-American, you have mostly an African-American clientele and staff.*

You're not alone. Most child care centers in the United States have teachers and administrators who look the same and come from similar backgrounds. Anyone who has tried it knows it's a challenge to develop a multiracial staff and attract children from all racial and religious groups.

But I believe it can be done. And it's worth the effort. With many kinds of people involved, a child care center becomes appealing to a wider range of people, leading to new marketing opportunities and greater financial stability. A diverse staff is more likely to help families of every hue feel welcome in your facility and, ultimately, choose to pay for your services. Families who are uncomfortable with diversity might latch onto a staff member with a similar background. The person who connects with those parents can ease their way into a new and ultimately rewarding setting.

Children learn more and have more fun with the opportunity to explore different cultures. Teachers and administrators do, too. Our differences can be jumping-off points for learning, growth, and development for all of us. It's harder to discuss the mountains when everyone in the group grew up at the beach. It's harder to convey the taste of tortillas if everyone was born in Maine.

A diverse child care center is the ultimate expression of the motto "Think globally, act locally." It is a vital first step to bringing people together to talk about who we are and what we can create together. It's one means for creating "a world that holds their children dear and loves them as they are" (from "A Dream for Children," a song by Drs. Jan McCarthy and Thomas Moore).

## Getting Started

Even after a center has made the choice to seek a diverse staff and clientele, it still can be difficult to *practice what you preach*.

Consider the experiences of Anne Jones, director of the Avondale Children's Center in Charlotte, North Carolina. When Jones joined Avondale three years ago, she came from a center that had been diverse for several decades, thanks to its location, scholarship monies, and other factors. At Avondale, though three out of 11 teachers are African-American and the center has made diversity a priority, all but one of the children served are white.

"It's a puzzle that bothers me, the board, and the church we're affiliated with," Jones says. "We've looked at it inside and out. We're just not getting a diverse group of applicants."

## Broadening Your Appeal

Whether you haven't consciously sought out a diverse population before, or you've been frustrated by limited success or outright failure, these strategies can help broaden your center's appeal.

**What do they see?** Remember that at all times we are either inviting people to join us or turning them away. Do prospects see a variety of faces in the pictures on your walls? What about the illustrations in books? Images can be a powerful way to communicate, "We want you here."

**Diversity goes beyond race.** A friend tells the story of her search for child care. She and her husband were touring a well-regarded secular child care center affiliated with a community college. She was impressed until she came to the classroom where children were gathered in a circle, listening to a recording.

"On Sunday, we all go to church, go to church, go to church. On Sunday, we all go the church, early in the morning," sang the voice on the recording. My friend is Jewish. The center's director seemed utterly oblivious to how that recording would be perceived by non-

Christians. My friend didn't say anything — and she never went back.

**Think diverse personalities.** Hire some teachers who are low key, some who are upbeat, some very organized, some very creative. They bring different styles and perspectives to your classrooms, meetings, and interactions with parents. They also serve as diverse role models for children. Kids who are very active, for instance, will benefit by seeing a quieter teacher.

**Cultivate hidden diversity.** Even if you have families who look alike, there can be diversity in ethnicity, faith, economic class, and interests. Consider asking parents to do short projects or games with children at the center to share the special things they know or do.

An example: one major industry in my community is banking, so children are accustomed to parents who work in an office. To show children that "the office" isn't the only place people work, one center invited a father to give a simple talk about his job with the symphony orchestra and play child-friendly tunes on his trombone.

**Small or at-home centers can be diverse, too.** What if you are a staff of one or just a few? Encourage diversity in your visuals, recordings, and volunteers. Contact a variety of organizations and religious institutions about volunteering at your center. Some major corporations give employees time off from work for volunteer pursuits.

*Dream, dream, this is my dream*
*for the children of the world.*
*Peace, joy, and happiness*
*for every boy and girl.*
*A world where they can play*
*all in their own way.*
*A world where they can laugh and cry*
*and think and wonder why.*
*A world where there is food to eat,*
*a home for everyone,*
*with health and safety a major concern*
*and schools for them to learn.*
*A world that holds their children dear*
*and loves them as they are.*
*Where children have the chance to grow*
*and reach a shining star.*

— "A Dream for Children"
by Drs. Jan McCarthy and Thomas Moore,
from the recording "Songs for the Whole Day"

## Hiring a Diverse Staff

Making the commitment to a diverse staff is easier than finding and hiring one. It's common not to know many people outside your own group. That makes it challenging to know how to find qualified teachers and assistants who are different from you. Here are some resources you may not have tapped before:

**Houses of worship or other religious institutions** can be a great place to recruit loving, consistent people who enjoy young children. Call the minister or other religious leader, or meet people on their turf by going to a service. Let them know the qualifications of the staff you seek. Word will spread of your interest, and people will appreciate that you took time to get to know their culture a little bit.

When you visit an institution that isn't part of your culture, you'll probably be uncomfortable. Go into the experience looking for things you can connect with — food, music, clothing, love of family, or anything else that's important to you. Take along a friend.

**Ask community leaders for help.** Determine who the leaders are in your target group — be it Hispanic, African-American, Jewish, or something else — and seek out their recommendations for potential staff members. In my town, for instance, I would call the Spanish storyteller at the public library to see if she knows others from her culture who enjoy working with children.

**Contact community colleges.** Talk with teachers or department heads about promising students in their early childhood programs.

**Contact high schools.** Ask about successful graduates from home economics and related classes.

**Contact senior groups.** Don't forget retired people as a rich source of either staff or volunteers. They'll bring a new dimension of experience to your program.

**Ask current staff** for ideas on finding diverse colleagues.

**Advertise** jobs in specialty newspapers that your target group reads. You might also research costs for advertising on Spanish-language or other radio stations. Though radio advertising costs might be prohibitive for your center alone, perhaps you can share costs for one ad with several other centers.

In some communities, **transportation** may be a problem. If you want a highly desirable staff member who lacks reliable transportation, look into whether government agencies provide special bus services, or help arrange a car pool.

## Retaining Diverse Staff

**Open and honest communication** between the director and staff is essential for retaining high-quality personnel. Let staff members know you are committed to supporting them in their work. Make yourself aware of diverse perspectives. Your supportive attitude will make all staff members less likely to leave for other jobs.

**Involve staff members in creating the curriculum.** Use their cultures as jumping-off points for fun themes. Avoid one-time "named" celebrations such as Black History Month, which inadvertently communicate that the topic isn't worth studying the rest of the year. Instead, do weekly themes or other small units, weaving diversity into your curriculum all year long. Be creative with holidays. On Presidents' Day, for example, you might bring in several presidents from diverse local organizations. They can tell children what they do and be honored at a party.

**Encourage the staff to get to know each other.** Have an open house a half hour before each staff meeting, with refreshments. Invite staffers to come early to relax and talk before the meeting begins.

**Consider age-level meetings for teachers.** If your center is big, consider paying for a simple dinner mid-year for teachers of twos, then threes, then fours. Teachers could talk about what's been particularly successful for them in activities and themes, and analyze what hasn't worked.

**Take your grievance policy seriously.** Your grievance policy should be discussed with staff and acted upon when necessary so teachers know it isn't there just for show. It's important that you establish yourself as someone who will listen to grievances. If you follow all the points we've discussed earlier, staff members will trust you and feel free to share information they might not otherwise.

**Remember your board.** If your center is non-profit, a diverse board can provide a plethora of ideas. It will also demonstrate to staffers that you take diversity seriously.

**Banish jokes that are demeaning (based on race, religion, or personal characteristics).** It's not political correctness. It's just courtesy.

The more you and your board know about diverse cultures, the easier it will be to retain not only diverse staff members but diverse families. Talk with your board and staff about the ideas in this article, and identify methods that would work for you.

Realize that it's okay to take it slow, a step at a time. At Anne Jones' center, for instance, the board has realized that its small size — 65 families — and fine reputation means there's always a waiting list, filled with the friends of children already at the center.

To increase diversity, the center is looking at funding possibilities so that certain slots could be reserved for minority children, possibly on scholarship. The center also plans to advertise in its local African-American newspaper.

"We want to make the effort, because our children are missing an important life experience," Jones says. "Children are very receptive to accepting people for who they are. If they grow up with people who are different from themselves, their neighborhood, or their community, they learn to make decisions about people based on qualities that matter, rather than appearances."

# The Art of Leadership
## Managing Early Childhood Organizations

# Resources for Directors

*Competent directors are lifelong learners. They learn from children, parents, staff, each other, and the wide variety of professional and business materials available. Such materials inform, stimulate, and motivate by building expertise, enhancing understanding, and providing insight into best practice. These are the raw materials for thoughts and plans and well executed programs that provide opportunities for everyone to grow and learn and prosper together.*

The current resources listed below have been chosen to provide information about a wide variety of topics and skills related to program management. Many of the authors have been writing in their particular areas of expertise for a long time; a few are rising stars.

### Leadership


Autry, J. A. (1992). *Love and Profit: The art of caring leadership*. New York: Avon Books.

Bennis, W., & Nanus, B. (1997). *Leaders: Strategies for taking charge*. New York: Harper Collins Publishers.

Bennis, W., & Townsend, R. (1995). *Reinventing leadership: Strategies to empower the organization*. New York: William Morrow & Company.

Blanchard, K., & O'Connor, M. (1997). *Managing by values*. San Francisco: Berrett-Koehler Publishers.

Caldwell, M. (2000). *The Tipping Point: How Little Things Can Make a Big Difference*. Boston: Little, Brown and Company.

Carter, M., & Curtis, D. (1998). *When Using Your Words Isn't Enough: A Handbook for Leading With a Vision*. St. Paul, MN: Redleaf Press.

Chappell, T. (1994). *The soul of a business: Managing for profit and the common good*. New York: Bantam Books.

DeMars, N. (1998). *You want me to do what? When, where, and how to draw the line at work*. New York: Simon & Schuster.

DePree, M. (1993). *Leadership jazz*. New York: Dell Publishing.

Goss, T. (1996). *The last word on power: Re-invention for leaders and anyone who must make the impossible happen*. New York: Doubleday Dell Publishing Group.

Helgesen, S. (1995). *The Female Advantage: Women's Ways of Leadership*. New York: Doubleday.

Kagan, S., & Bowman, B. (1997). *Leadership in Early Childhood Education*. Washington, DC: NAEYC.

Lee, B., & Covey, S. (1997). *The power principle: Influence with honor*. New York: Fireside.

Matusak, L. (1996). *Finding your voice: Learning to lead anywhere you want to make a difference*. San Francisco: Jossey-Bass.

Waitley, D. (1996). *Empires of the mind: Lesson to lead and succeed in a knowledge-based world*. New York: William Morrow & Company.

Zohar, D. (1997). *Rewiring the corporate brain: Using the new science to rethink how we structure and lead organizations*. San Francisco: Berrett-Koehler Publishers.

## Organizational Management

Alessandra, J. (1998). *The platinum rule: Discover the four basic business personalities*. New York: Warner Books.

Arkebauer, J. (1994). *The McGraw-Hill guide to writing a high impact business plan*. New York: McGraw-Hill.

Bell, C. (1998). *Managers as mentors: Building partnerships for learning*. San Francisco: Berrett-Koehler Publishers.

Brandt, S., & Cooper, S. (1997). *Stay out of court and in business: Every business person's guide to minimizing legal troubles*. Friday Harbor, WA: Archipelago Publishing.

Collins, J., & Porras, J. (1997). *Built to Last: Successful Habits of Visionary Companies*. New York: HarperBusiness.

Dayton, D. (1997). *The information technology audit handbook*. Englewood Cliffs, NJ: Prentice Hall.

Godwin, A., & Schrag, L. (editors). (1996). *Setting up for infant and toddler care: Guidelines for centers and family child care homes*. Washington, DC: National Association for the Education of Young Children.

Hummel, J. (1996). *Starting and running a nonprofit organization*. Minneapolis: University of Minnesota Press.

Kantor, R. (1997). *On the frontiers of management*. Boston: Harvard Business School Press.

O'Connell, B. (1993). *The Board Members Book*. New York: The Foundation Center.

Wilbur, R., Finn, S., & Freeland, G. (1994). *The complete guide to nonprofit management*. New York: John Wiley.

## Financial Management

Blum, L. (1998). *The complete guide to getting a grant*. New York: John Wiley & Sons.

Greenfield, J. (1995). *Fund-raising: Evaluating and managing the fund development process*. New York: John Wiley & Sons.

Gross, M., & Bruttomesso, R. (editors). (1995). *Financial and accounting guide*. New York: John Wiley & Sons.

Label, W. (1998). *10 minute guide to accounting for non-accountants*. New York: Macmillan General Reference.

Morgan, G. (1982). *Managing Day Care Dollars: A Financial Handbook*. Washington, DC: National Association for the Education of Young Children.

Steckel, R. (1985). *Filthy Rich & Other Nonprofit Fantasies: Changing the Way Nonprofits Do Business in the '90s*. Berkeley, CA: Ten Speed Press.

Stevenson, M. (1998). *Fundraising for early childhood programs: Getting started and getting results*. Washington, DC: National Association for the Education of Young Children.

Tracy, J. (1993). *How to read a financial report: Wringing vital signs out of the numbers. 4th Edition*. New York: John Wiley & Sons.

Tracy, J. (1996). *Budgeting a la carte: Essential tools for harried business managers*. New York: John Wiley & Sons.

## Personnel Management

Anderson, K. (1994). *Getting what you want: How to reach agreement and resolve conflict every time*. New York: Plume.

Beale, R., & Taylor, C. (1997). *Developing competencies to manage diversity*. San Francisco: Berrett-Koehler Publishers.

Blanchard, K., & Bowles, S. (1997). *Gung ho! Turn on the people in any organization*. New York: William Morrow.

Bloom, P. J. (1991). *Blueprint for Action: Achieving Center-Based Change Through Staff Development*. Washington, DC: Gryphon House Books.

Bramson, R. M. (1988). *Coping with Difficult People: In Business and in Life*. New York: Ballentine Books.

Brinkman, R., & Kirschner, R. (1994). *Dealing with people you can't stand: How to bring out the best in people at their worst*. New York: McGraw-Hill.

Butler, A. (1996). *Team think: 72 ways to make good, smart, quick decisions in any meeting*. New York: McGraw-Hill.

Carter, M., & Curtis, D. (1994). *Training Teachers: A Harvest of Theory and Practice*. St. Paul, MN: Redleaf Press.

Exchange. (2001). *Staff Challenges*. Redmond, WA: Exchange Press.

Connors, R., Smith, T., & Hickman, G. (1994). *The OZ principle: Getting results through individual and organizational accountability*. Englewood Cliffs, NJ: Prentice Hall.

Cook, M. (1997). *The complete do-it-yourself personnel department. 2nd Edition*. Englewood Cliffs, NJ: Prentice Hall.

Fitz-Enz, J. (1997). *The 8 practices of exceptional companies: How great organizations make the most of their human capital*. Kansas City, MO: American Management Association (AMACOM).

Glanz, B. (1997). *Care packages for the workplace: Little things you can do to regenerate spirit at work*. New York: McGraw-Hill.

Jones, E. (1986). *Teaching Adults: An Active Learning Approach*. Washington, DC: National Association for the Education of Young Children.

Kegan, R., & Lahey, L. (2001). *How the Way We Talk Can Change the Way We Work*. San Francisco: Jossey-Bass.

Larson, C., & Lafasto, F. (1989). *Teamwork: What must go right/what can go wrong. 30th Printing*. Thousand Oaks, CA: Sage Publications.

Lundin, W., & Lundin, K. (1995). *Working with difficult people*. Kansas City, MO: American Management Association (AMACOM).

Muldoon, B. (1997). *The heart of conflict*. New York: Perigee.

Plunkett, W. (1996). *Supervision: Diversity and teams in the workplace. 8th Edition*. Upper Saddle River, NJ: Prentice Hall.

Tertell, E., Klein, S., & Jewett, J. (editors). (1998). *When teachers reflect: Journeys toward effective, inclusive practice*. Washington, DC: National Association for the Education of Young Children.

Von Oech, R. (1983). *A Whack on the Side of the Head: How to Unlock Your Mind for Innovation*. New York: Warner Books.

Wilson, J., & George, J. (1997). *Team member's survival guide*. New York: McGraw-Hill.

## Program Development

Bloom, P. J. (1998). *A great place to work: Improving conditions for staff in young child programs. Revised edition*. Washington, DC: National Association for the Education of Young Children.

Coontz, S. (1998). *The Way We Really Are: Coming to Terms with America's Changing Families*. New York: Basic Books.

Diffy, D., & Morrison, K. (editors). (1998). *Family-friendly communication*. Washington, DC: National Association for the Education of Young Children.

Feeney, S., & Freeman, N. (1999). *Ethics and the Early Childhood Educator: Using the NAEYC Code*. Washington, DC: NAEYC.

Feinburg, S., & Mindess, M. (1994). *Eliciting children's full potential: Designing and evaluating developmentally based programs for young children*. Pacific Groves, CA: Brooks/Cole Publishing.

Frede, E. (editor). (1984). *Getting Involved: Workshops for Parents*. Ypsilanti, MI: High/Scope Press.

Gonzalez-Mena, J. (1995). *Dragon Mom: Confessions of a Child Development Expert*. Napa, CA: Rattle OK Publications.

Helburn, S., & Bergman, B. (2002). *America's Childcare Problem: The Way Out*. New York: Palgrave.

Kriegel, R., & Brandt, D. (1996). *Sacred cows make the best burgers: Developing change-ready people and organizations*. New York: Warner Books.

Lombardi, J. (2003). *Time to Care: Redesigning Child Care*. Philadelphia: Temple University Press.

Lynch, E. (1998). *Developing cross-cultural competencies: A guide to working with children and their families. 2nd Edition*. Baltimore, MD: Brookes.

Randall, K. (1997). *The 12 truths about surviving and succeeding in the office : *and some of them aren't very nice*. New York: Berkeley Books.

Steiner, G. (1997). *Strategic planning: What every manager must know*. New York: Free Press.

Stonehouse, A. (1995). *How does it feel? Child Care from a Parent's Perspective*. Redmond, WA: Exchange Press.

Swan, W. (1991). *How to do a superior performance appraisal*. New York: John Wiley & Sons.

Whitney, D., & Giovagnoli, M. (1997). *75 cage-rattling questions to change the way you work: Shake-em up questions to open meetings, ignite discussion, and spark creativity*. New York: McGraw-Hill.

## Community Relations

Berns, R. (1996). *Child, family, and community*. New York: Holt, Rhinehart, & Winston.

Boe, A. (1995). *Networking success*. Deerfield, FL: Health Communication.

Crandall, R. (editor). (1997). *10 secrets of marketing success: How to jump start your market*. New York: Neal Publishing.

Gestwicki, C. (1996). *Home, school, and community relations: A guide to working with parents. 3rd Edition.* Albany, NY: Delmar.

Kawasaki, G. (1996). *How to Drive the Competition Crazy.* New York: Hyperion.

Larkin, G. (1992). *12 simple steps to a winning marketing plan.* New York: Probus Publishing.

Michelli, D., & Straw, A. (1997). *Successful networking.* Hauppauge, NY: Barrons Educational Series.

Morrison, E. (1994). *Leadership skills: Developing volunteers for organizational success.* Tucson, AZ: Fisher Books.

Ries, A., & Trout, J. (1994). *The 22 Immutable Laws of Marketing: Violate Them at Your Own Risk.* New York: HarperBusiness.

Roane, S. (1993). *The secrets of savvy networking: How to make the best connections for business and personal success.* New York: Warner Books.

## References and Research

Heightened awareness about the importance of quality child care experiences has also raised issues about accountability in programming. Competent directors must not only be able to manage their programs well, they must also be able to understand and articulate the rationale behind program decisions and actions. Such is often the case when writing grants, engaging in strategic planning, and reporting to funding agencies. The handbooks, yearbooks, and statistical sources listed below provide a wealth of current, experientially validated information about children, families, and human resource endeavors. These resources are typically authored by leading experts in the field and structured to provide an in-depth review on a wide variety of topics.

Bornstein, M. (editor). (1995). *Handbook of parenting.* Hillsdale, NJ: Erlbaum.
  Volume One: Children and parenting
  Volume Two: Biology and ecology
  Volume Three: Status and social conditions of parenting
  Volume Four: Applied and practical parenting

Children's Defense Fund. (1997). *The state of America's children.* Washington, DC: CDF.

Cook, M. (1997). *The human resources yearbook 1997/1998.* Englewood Cliffs, NJ: Prentice Hall.

Damon, W. (editor-in-chief). (1998). *Handbook of child psychology. 5th Edition.* New York: John Wiley & Sons.
  Volume One: Theoretical models of human development.
  Volume Two: Cognition, perception, and language.
  Volume Three: Social, emotional, and personality development.
  Volume Four : Child psychology in practice.

Meisel, S., & Shonkoff, J. (editors). (1990). *Handbook of early childhood intervention.* Cambridge, MA: Cambridge University Press.

Spodek, B. (editor). (1993). *Handbook of research on the education of young children.* New York: Macmillan Publishing.

## Reflections

Life as a director can be all-absorbing. This last section of resources is provided as a reminder to take time, reflect, and even smile now and then. Making time for self eflection and self growth is a gift to your organization.

Allen, R., & Allen, D. (1997). *Winnie-the-Pooh. In which you, Pooh, and friends learn about the most important subject of all.* New York: Dutton.

Clason, G. (1997). *The richest man in Babylon.* New York: New American Library.

Covey, S. (1990). *The seven habits of highly effective people: Powerful lesson in personal change.* New York: Simon & Schuster.

Edler, R. (1995). *If I knew then what I know now.* New York: Berkeley Publishing.

Fulton, R. (1997). *Common sense leadership.* Berkeley, CA: Ten Speed Press.

Krause, D. (1997). *The way of the leader.* New York: Berkeley Publishing.

Roberts, W. (1991). *Leadership secrets of Attila the Hun.* New York: Warner Books.

## Exchange Articles on Demand

Approximately 1,800 articles from past issues of *Exchange* covering all the topics addressed in this book can be found in the Articles on Demand section of www.ChildCareExchange.com. From the Articles on Demand section, type in a key word representing a topic of interest and you will be presented with a list of articles that apply.